EXTREME
DIGITAL PHOTOGRAPHY

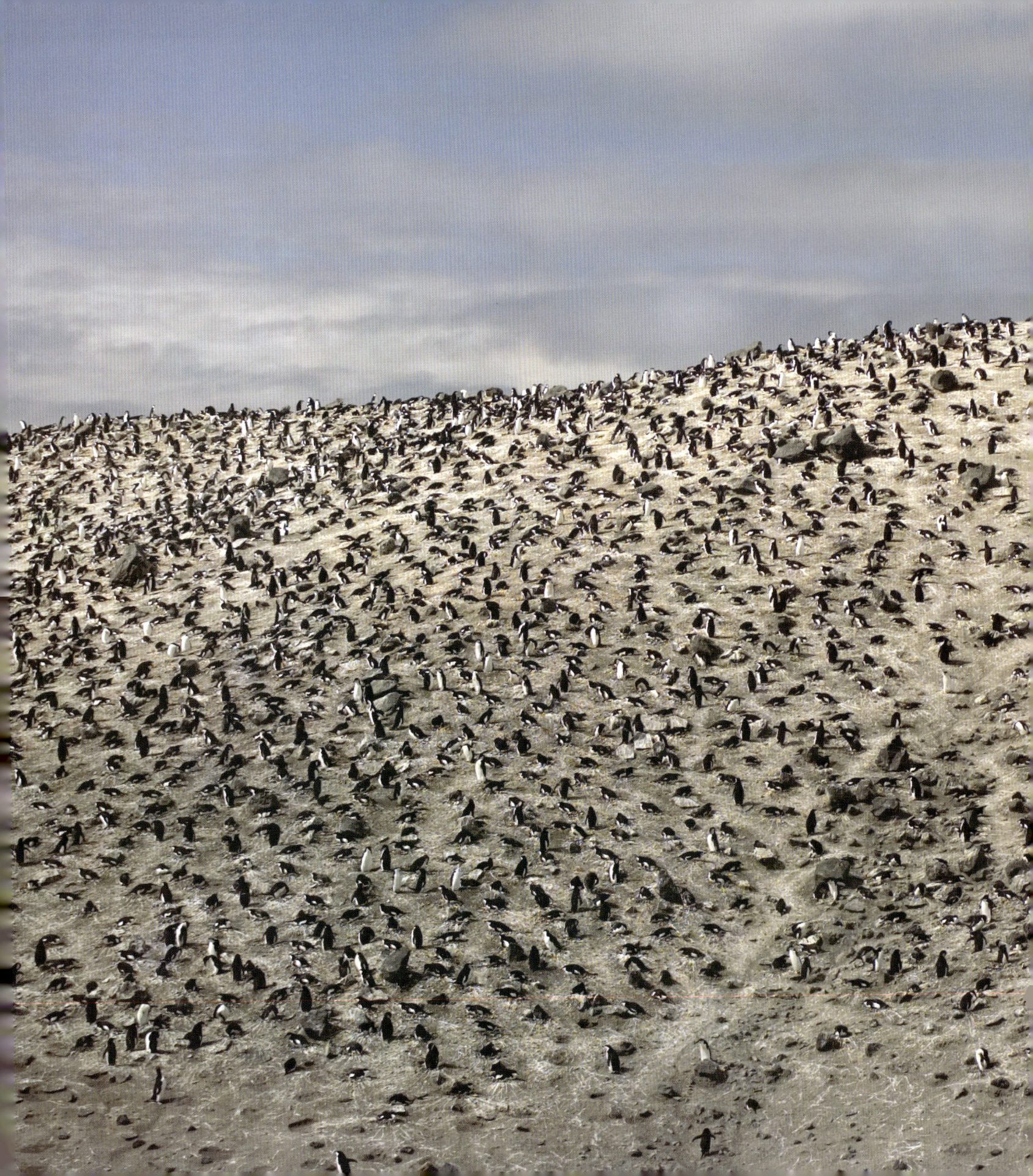

EXTREME
DIGITAL PHOTOGRAPHY

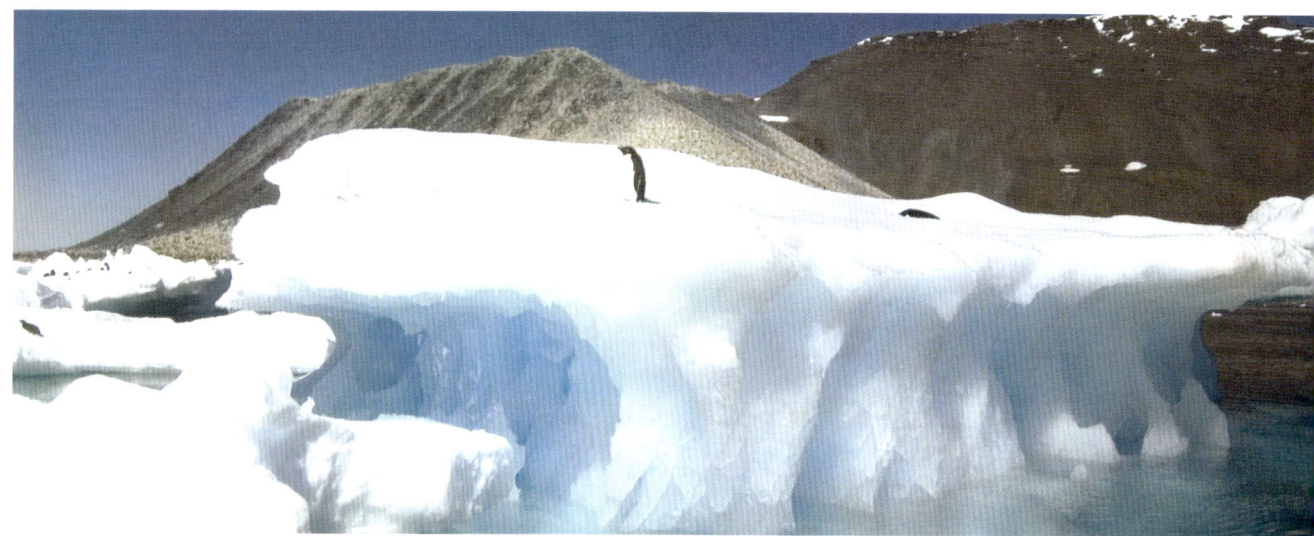

Jonathan Chester

Contributing Editor Christian Kallen

THOMSON
COURSE TECHNOLOGY
Professional ■ Trade ■ Reference

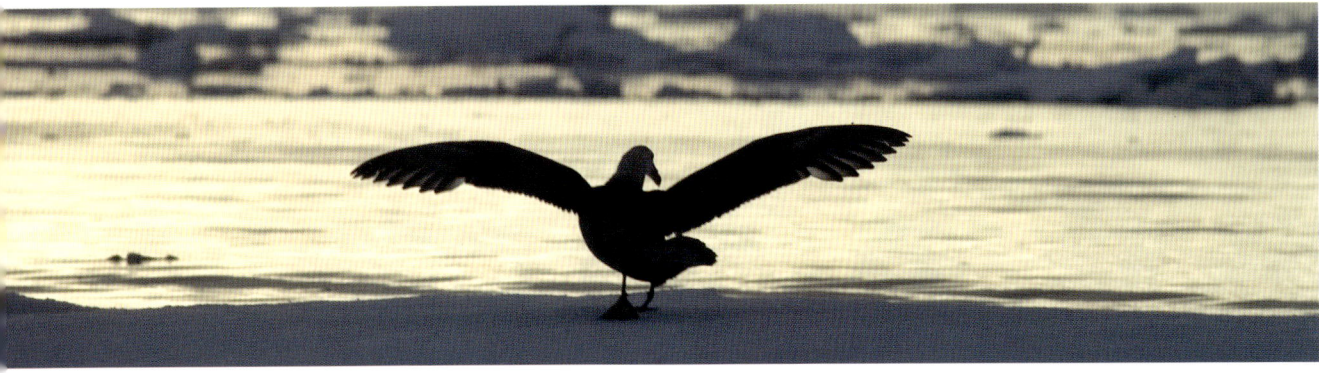

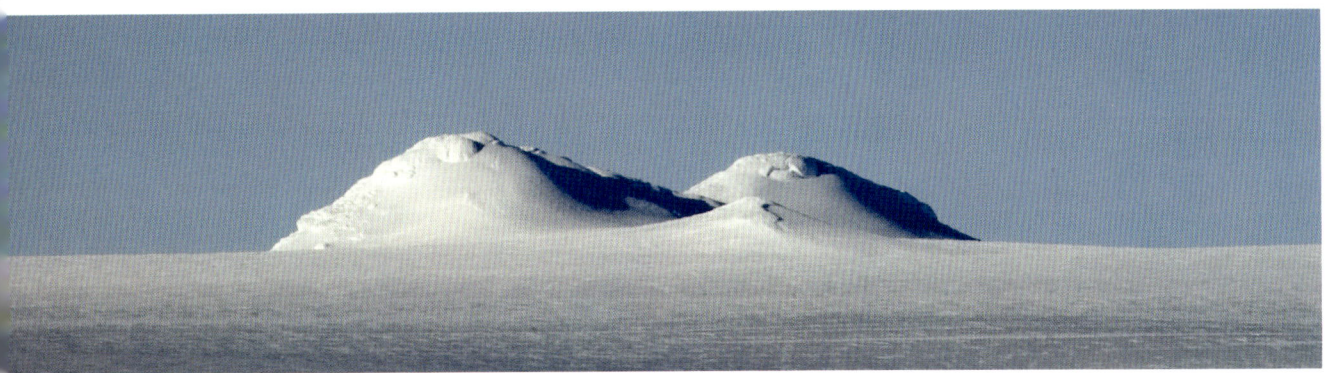

First published in the United States in 2004 by Course PTR, a division of Thomson Course Technology.

©The Ilex Press Limited 2004

All rights reserved. No part of this publication may be reproduced by any means without written permission from the publisher, except for brief passages for review purposes. Address all permission requests to the publisher.

Trademark and trademark names are used throughout this book to describe and inform you about various proprietary products. Such mention is intended to benefit the owner of the trademark and is not intended to infringe copyright nor imply any claim to the mark other than that made by its owner.

For Course PTR:
Publisher: Stacy L. Hiquet
Senior Marketing Manager: Sarah O'Donnell
Marketing Manager: Heather Hurley
Associate Marketing Managers:
    Kristin Eisenzopf, Sarah Dubois
Associate Acquisitions Editor:
    Megan Belanger
Manager of Editorial Services:
    Heather Talbot
Market Coordinator: Amanda Weaver

ISBN: 1-59200-388-5

5 4 3 2 1

Library of Congress Catalog Card number: 2004106449

Educational facilities, companies, and organizations interested in multiple copies of this book should contact the publisher for quantity discount information. Training manuals, CD-ROMs, and portions of this book are also available individually or can be tailored for specific needs.

COURSE PTR,
A Division of Thomson Course Technology
(www.courseptr.com)
25 Thomson Place
Boston, MA 02210

This book was conceived, designed, and produced by
THE ILEX PRESS LIMITED
Cambridge
England

Publisher: Alastair Campbell
Executive Publisher: Sophie Collins
Creative Director: Peter Bridgewater
Editorial Director: Steve Luck
Design Manager: Tony Seddon
Editor: Ben Renow-Clarke
Designer: Hugh Schermuly
Artwork Administrator: Joanna Clinch
Development Art Director: Graham Davis
Technical Art Editor: Nicholas Rowland

All uncredited editorial photographs
© Jonathan Chester—Extreme Images.

Printed in China

For more information on this title please visit: www.exphus.web-linked.com

CONTENTS

006 **Introduction**

EXTREME ENVIRONMENTS 12
014 **Wet Conditions** • 016 **Cold and Wind**
018 **Heat and Jungle** • 020 **Dust, Smoke, and Spindrift**
022 **High Altitude** • 024 **Latitude**

PLANNING & PREPARATION 26
028 **What Photographic Gear to Take** • 031 **Compact and Specialty Cameras** • 032 **Other Capture Means** • 034 **Digital Film Storage Cards** • 036 **Accessories** • 038 **Carrying Cases and Protection** • 040 **Power Supplies** • 042 **Hardware**
044 **Field Storage** • 045 **Software** • 046 **Communications**

EXTREME LOCATIONS 50
052 **Antarctica** • 054 **The Arctic** • 056 **Oceans**
058 **Underwater** • 060 **Rivers and Lakes** • 062 **Tropical Islands—Galápagos** • 064 **Interview: Denise Rocco-Zilber**
066 **Desert** • 068 **Mountains** • 070 **Interview: Didrik Johnck**
072 **Aerials** • 074 **Interview: Craig O'Brien**

EXTREME SUBJECTS 76
078 **Arctic Wildlife** • 080 **Antarctic Wildlife** • 082 **Interview: Alan High** • 084 **Interview: David Vaskevitch** • 086 **Extreme Critters** • 088 **Interview: Peter Gill & Margie Morrice**
090 **Interview: James Watt** • 092 **Low Light** • 094 **Interview: Peter Menzel** • 096 **War Photography** • 098 **Earthquakes and Floods** • 100 **Thunderstorms, Tornadoes, and Hurricanes**
102 **Lightning** • 104 **Wildfires and Volcanoes**

EXTREME ACTIVITIES 106
108 **Interview: Tim Wimborne** • 110 **Backpacking**
112 **Trekking** • 114 **Interview: Corey Rich** • 116 **River Rafting**
118 **Sea Kayaking** • 120 **Interview: Abner Kingman**
122 **Interview: Morton Beebe** • 124 **Surfing, Windsurfing, and Kite Boarding** • 126 **Interview: Michael Brown**
128 **Skiing and Snow Sports** • 130 **Expedition Photography**
132 **Interview: Tom and Tina Sjorgen**

EXTREME ASSIGNMENTS 134
136 **Research and Preparation** • 138 **Guides and Assistants**
140 **Clothing and Personal Considerations** • 142 **Medical and Safety Considerations** • 144 **Getting There** • 146 **Base Camp**
148 **Pre-Production Planning** • 150 **Typical Shooting Day**
154 **End-of-Day Routine** • 156 **Preparing the Daily Dispatch**
158 **Troubleshooting** • 160 **Virtual Reality** • 162 **Digital Video Multi-Tasking** • 164 **Interview: Karen Mullarkey**
166 **TerraQuest and Mungo Park** • 168 **Web Expedition Coverage—Quokka**

THE FUTURE 170
172 **Digital Capture** • 174 **Processing, Storing, and Archiving** • 176 **Delivery and Manipulation**
178 **Contributing Photographers and Experts**
180 **Books/Magazines/Websites** • 183 **Glossary**
188 **Index** • 192 **Acknowledgments**

INTRODUCTION

I have been passionate about the wild and remote parts of this planet ever since I first read *Home of the Blizzard* by the Australian Antarctic explorer, Sir Douglas Mawson. I became even more enchanted as I learned more about the subject and saw photographer Frank Hurley's now famous black-and-white prints of HMS *Endurance* trapped in the solid pack ice, of men struggling against ferocious blizzards, and of comical penguins at Commonwealth Bay.

I slowly developed a lifestyle that enabled me to experience extreme environments at first hand through sailing and climbing expeditions. For years I expressed this passion through photography, lectures, and books, but I was just following in the footsteps of so many who had forged this great tradition.

Since its invention more than 150 years ago, photography has been embraced by pioneers and explorers, with cameras now taken to the furthest reaches of the planet, and even into space. Sharing these extremes with the world has a rich tradition, from the early lantern slide shows of adventurers like Antarctic photographers Frank Hurley and Herbert Ponting, to the fine-art prints and exhibitions of Ansel Adams depicting his beloved Yosemite Valley and the California Sierra, and more recently Galen Rowell, the late master of the outdoor and adventure photography world. With adventure travel now reaching the

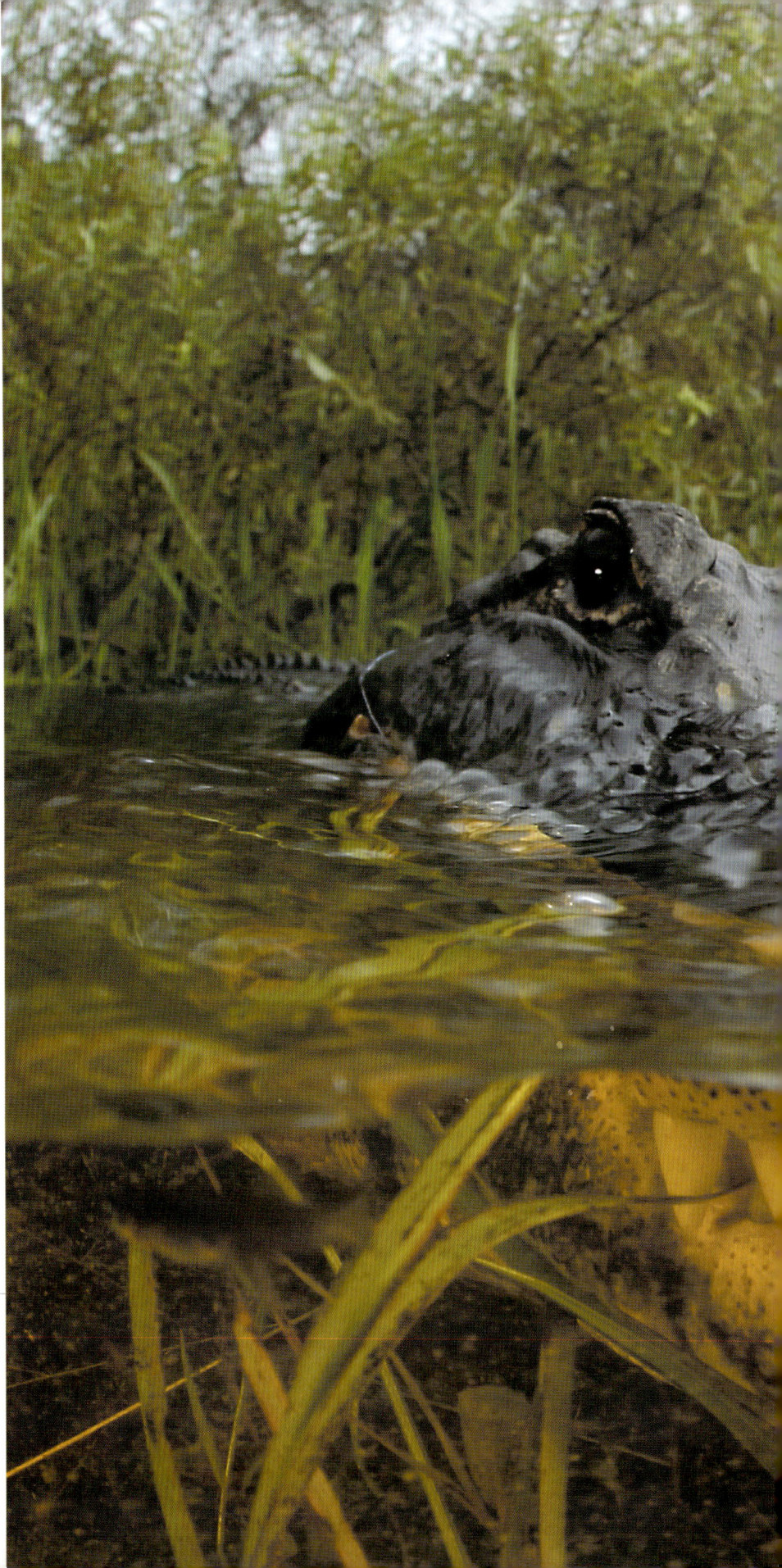

Into the Action

While a woman shines a light on an American alligator (*Alligator mississipiensis*) in Big Cypress National Park, Florida, the photographer is immersed in the action creating this split-view shot, above and below water.
© James Watt

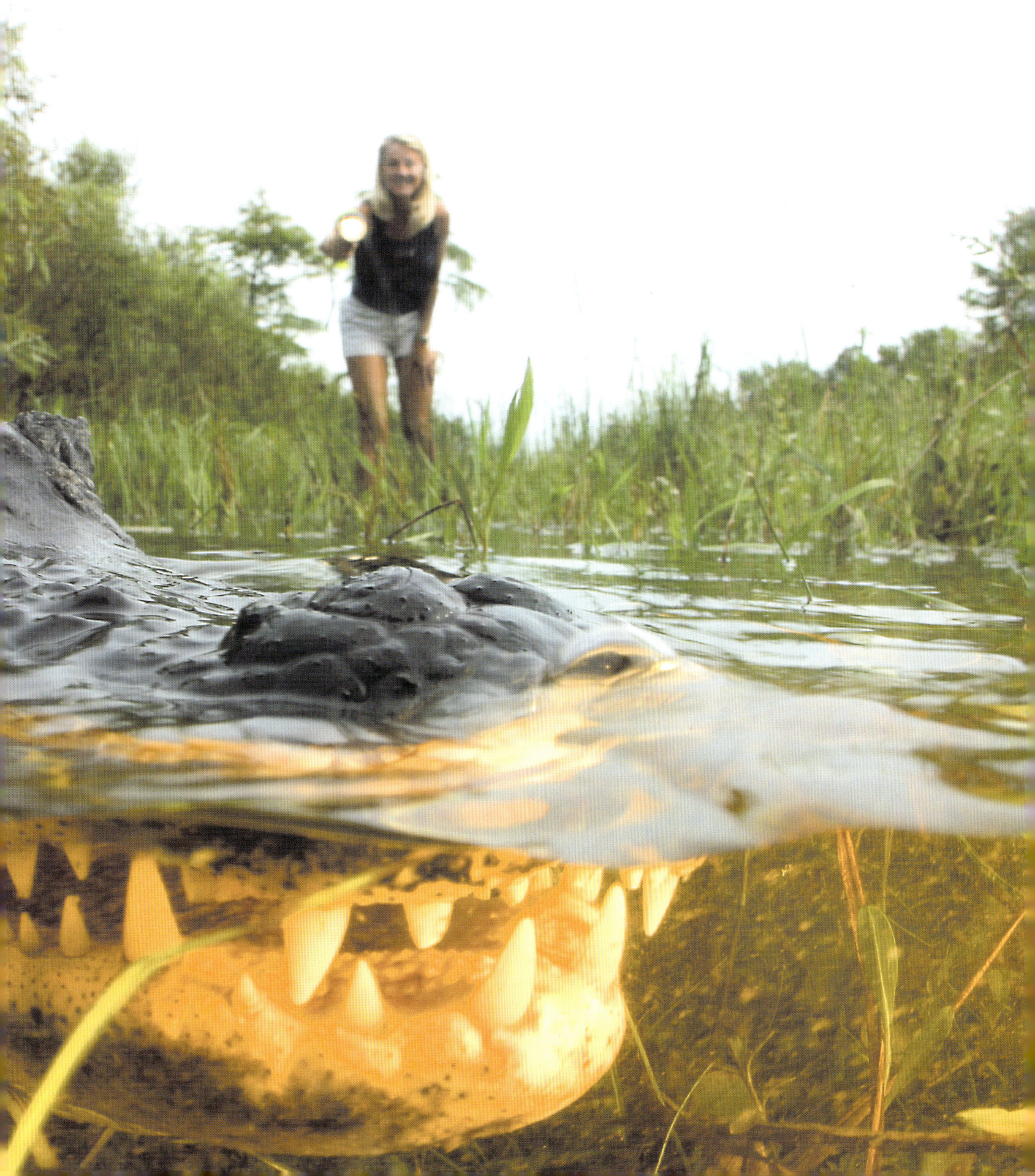

once-distant frontiers of space, and the robot vehicles *Spirit* and *Opportunity* sending us images of the surface of Mars, this tradition continues.

Until just over a decade ago, we only had film (or plates) to record still images. Now we have a new option: digital. In a relatively brief time, digital capture has evolved to the point where it is equal to film, and even surpasses it in some key ways. After 20 years of using film cameras on numerous extreme expeditions to all seven continents—especially Australia, Antarctica, the Arctic, Africa, the Himalaya, and other mountains of the world—I was ready for a new challenge. This came in the form of digital capture.

My first experience with professional digital cameras was on assignment to Antarctica in the southern summer of 1995–96 for TerraQuest's pioneering website *Virtual Antarctica*. At that time professional digital cameras like the Kodak DCS 460 were so expensive (almost $20,000) that they were primarily in the hands of studio photographers and major newspaper staff photographers. And with a capture rate of approximately 12 seconds per image, neither were they particularly useful. Freelance photojournalists could only dream of using such technology. Being Web-based, however, our virtual expedition to Antarctica was only possible if it used digital capture.

On this and subsequent assignments for TerraQuest, and later for Microsoft's online adventure travel journal *Mungo Park*, I had the opportunity to shoot digital in Antarctica, Argentina, the Galapagos, Africa, Canada, and the United States. I had to learn a whole new language and set of skills, from using Photoshop, through file

Trek to Everest Base Camp, Nepal

A trekking party crosses over a footbridge on the approach to Everest Base Camp. The mountain in the background is Ama Dablam (622,401 feet/828m), one of the most dramatic peaks in Nepal. © Didrik Johnck

Silver Surfer

A board surfer rises in surprise as a sea animal slices through a wave at Surfrider Beach in Southern California. The photograph sparked controversy over whether the creature was a shark or dolphin; the photographer and scientists agree it's a bottlenose dolphin. © Kurt Jones

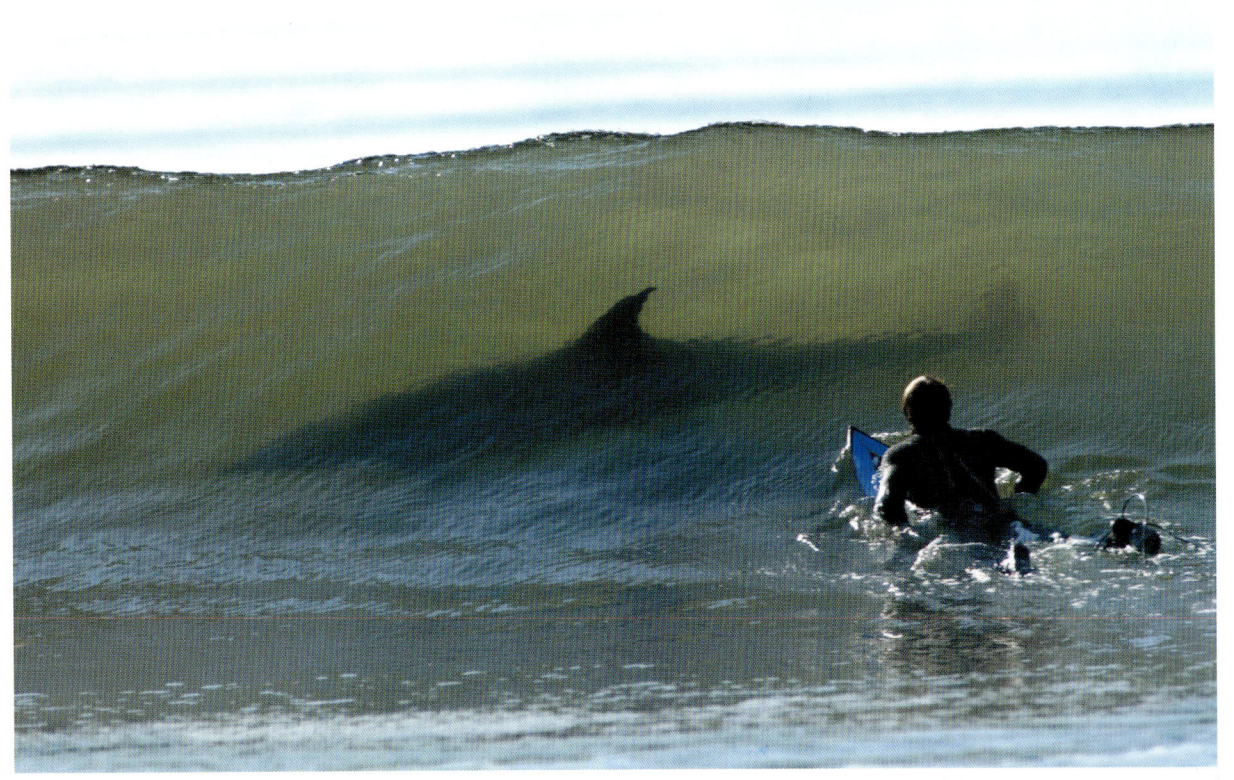

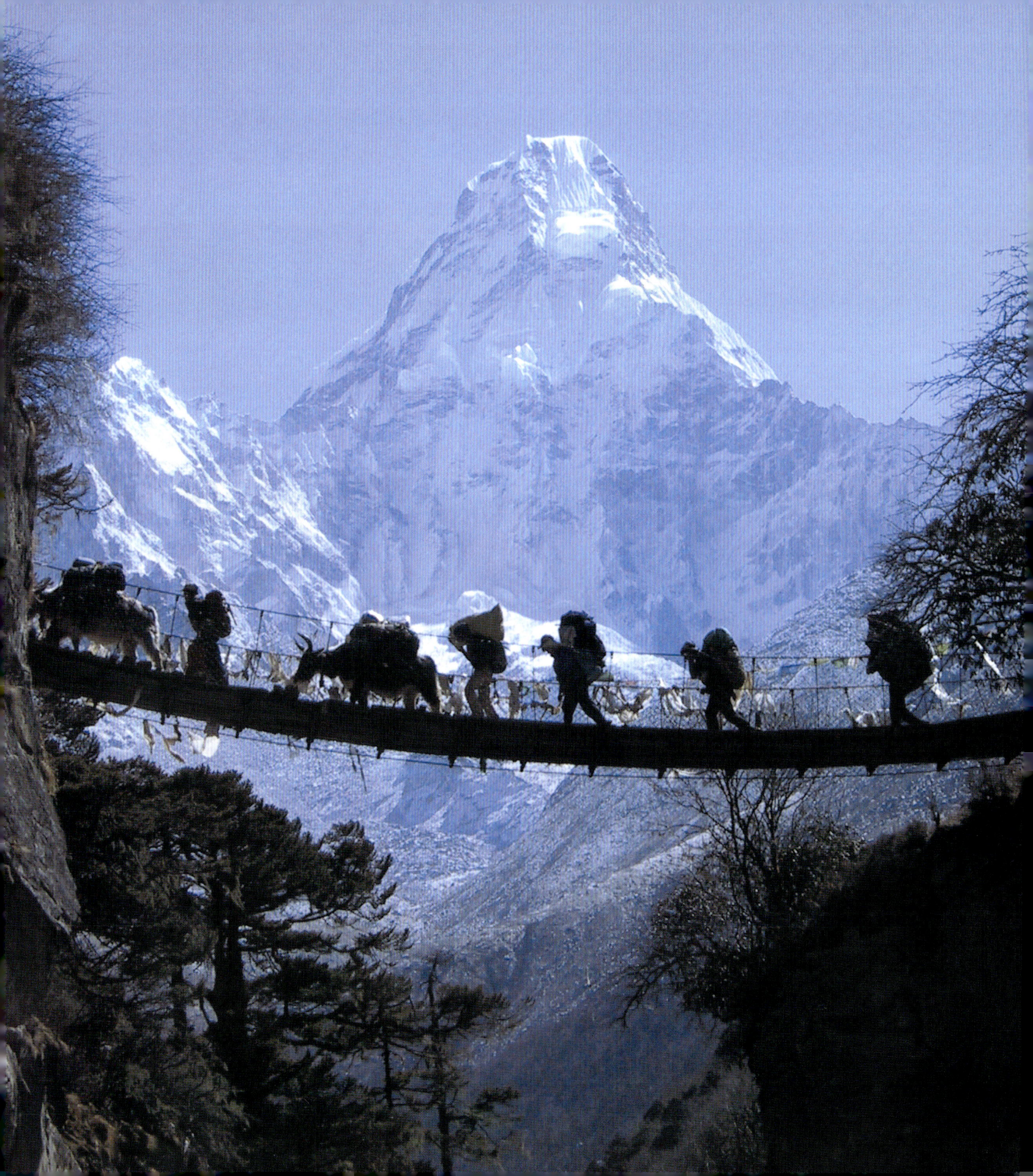

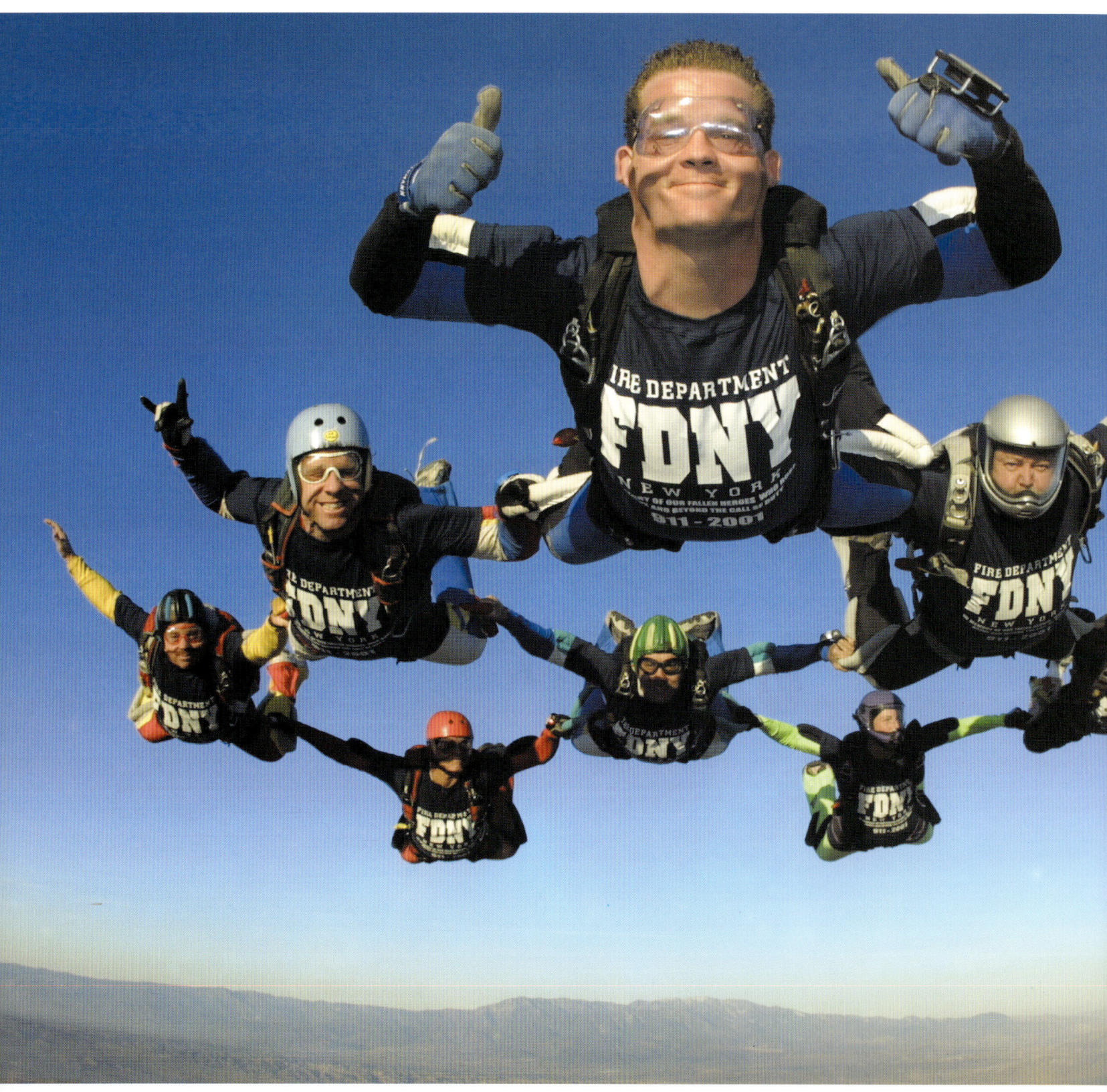

transfer, editing, and archiving programs, to satellite communications and computers. It is hard to be a digital photographer without some level of competence and interest in computers, but—like cameras—they are just tools to be understood, and I was naturally curious about all these technologies.

The next big assignment was to go to Everest Base Camp to help document the blind mountaineer Erik Weihenmayer's ascent of Mt. Everest. I was also charged with the job of getting the images back to the US for the sponsor's publicity campaign, so once again it had to be digital. High altitude, cold, and rugged conditions were a great test of digital cameras and the technology.

More recently, I led a team of nine digital photographers and filmmakers to Antarctica on a two-month assignment. None of the cameras missed a beat and we were able to document the far south in all its moods.

Through all these assignments, going digital led me to see the world in a new way. I took advantage of the digital camera's "instant feedback" from the review screen; post-processing in Photoshop allowed me essentially to do my own color processing and development in the field; having large flash memory cards meant I could take more photos, covering the subject more thoroughly, and thereby experimenting with more and different technical approaches. Like many other photographers I've talked to in researching this book, I think my own photography has improved and, perhaps at least as importantly, it has become more fun.

In 1995, I was there at the start of extreme digital capture. Today, there are digital photographers and adventurers the world over documenting extreme activities, the vagaries of nature, and wild places, from the highest Himalayan mountains to South American jungles and on to the ends of the Earth. Photographers are skydiving, climbing, and going underwater with digital cameras, pushing the limits of technology as well as themselves.

In this book, together with a survey of extreme digital photographers and examples of their images, there is a section on planning and preparation for assignments, plus a series of tips on shooting in all manner of challenging environments. This is followed by more detailed coverage of extreme subjects and activities, and finally by a few thoughts on the future of digital photography. The digital photo world is such a dynamic place today that it is hard to keep up with developments in software and hardware. This book is at best a starting point for the medium that helped create and fuel this revolution: the Web. We have included a list of useful resources and websites to enable the dedicated specialist to dig deeper and stay up to date.

Overall this book is a celebration of what has already been accomplished by photographers pushing the limits in extreme places, subjects, and activities. My hope is that you will be inspired by the work of these individuals and their projects, and find the guidance and resources to go beyond the point where people have gone before, technically and creatively, into the extreme.

Thumbs Up

A skydiving team from Fire Department New York links up in formation for the photographer, who may need to be the best flier in the air to get the shot. Shooting digital also means never having to change film at 10,000 feet (3,000m) during freefall.
© Craig O'Brien

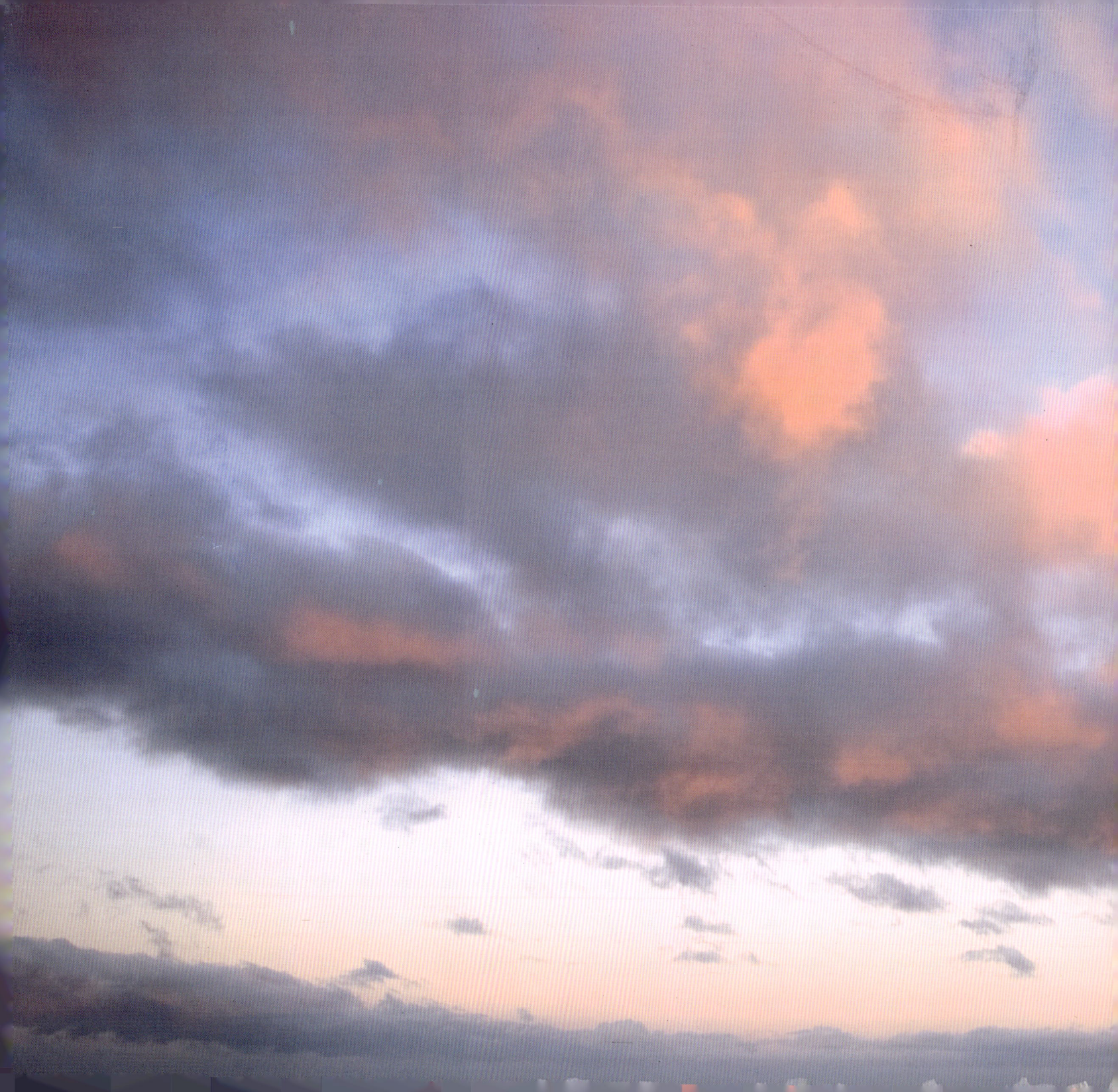

EXTREME ENVIRONMENTS

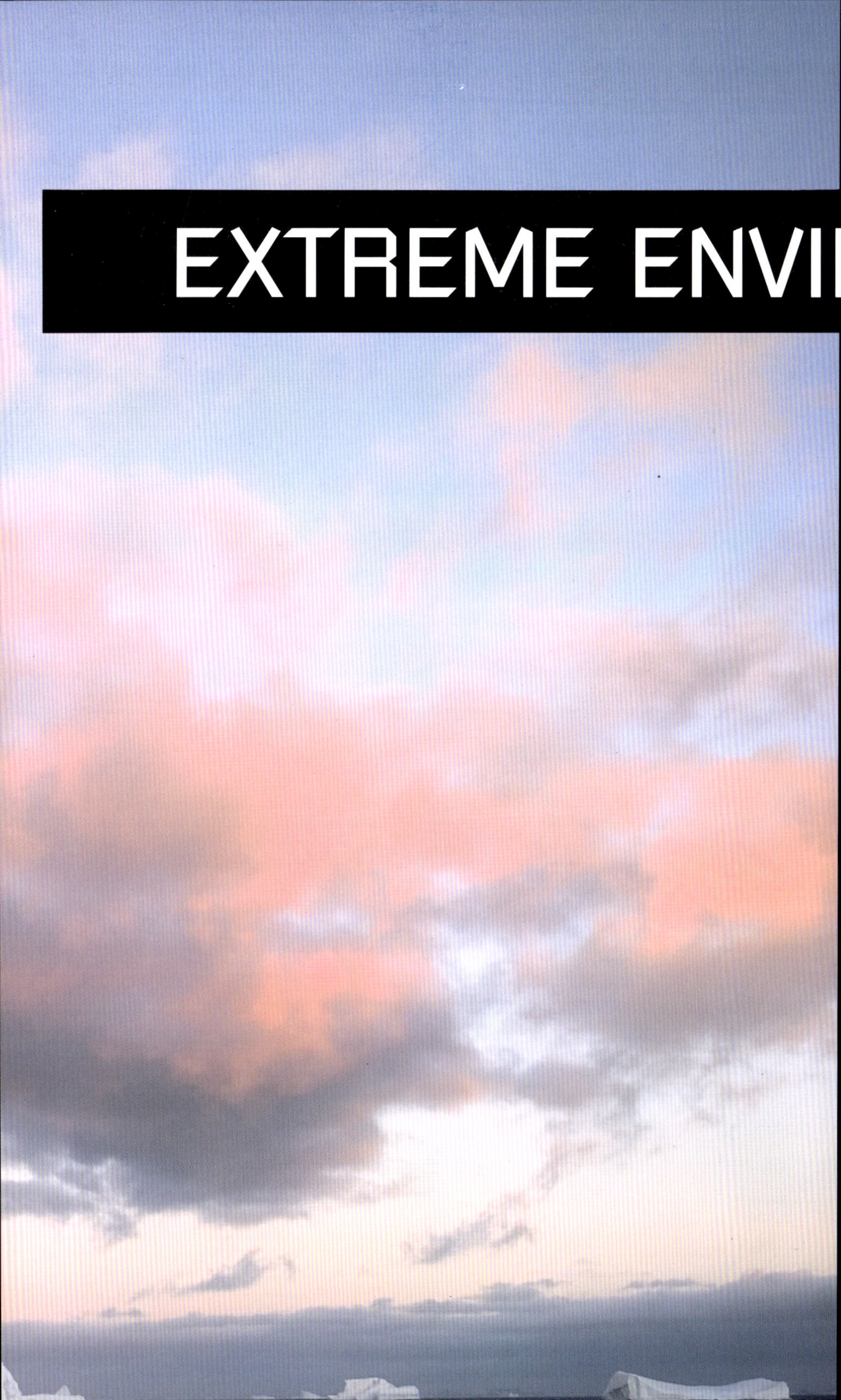

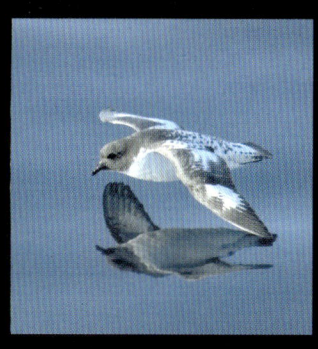

[Antarctica] is the coldest, the driest, the windiest, the iciest and (with its ice cap) averages as the highest in altitude of all the major land masses in the world. It has the least soil, the most fresh water, albeit in the form of ice, and it is surrounded by the stormiest ocean on earth.

Sanford Moss, *Natural History of the Antarctic Peninsula*

WET CONDITIONS

For months there is no rain, then there is too much. Half the world's people survive at the whim of the monsoon winds.

Steve McCurry, *Monsoon*

There are many degrees of getting wet. The monsoon rains of Asia are some of the most regular dramatic natural phenomena. The highest-recorded yearly rainfall on Earth is in the village of Cherrapunji in northeastern India, where the average for 74 years has been some 450 inches (1,143cm) per year, most of it concentrated into the six-month wet season.

Then there are all the activities on the water where spray is the usual problem, such as canoeing, sailing, and rafting; or you can completely immerse yourself by snorkeling and scuba diving. Extremely wet activities like these are some of the most challenging to document, especially when combined with cold temperatures.

Then there is plain old everyday rain, or persistent high humidity. A steady drizzle is common in maritime regions, such as the UK, Patagonia, or the Pacific Northwest of the US. Tropical rainforests and cloud forests produce a sweltering humidity that can permeate everything from clothes to cameras, whether it's technically "raining" or not. While this high annual precipitation typically leads to luxuriant vegetation and colorful creatures, such environments present unusual technical as well as aesthetic challenges for the photographer.

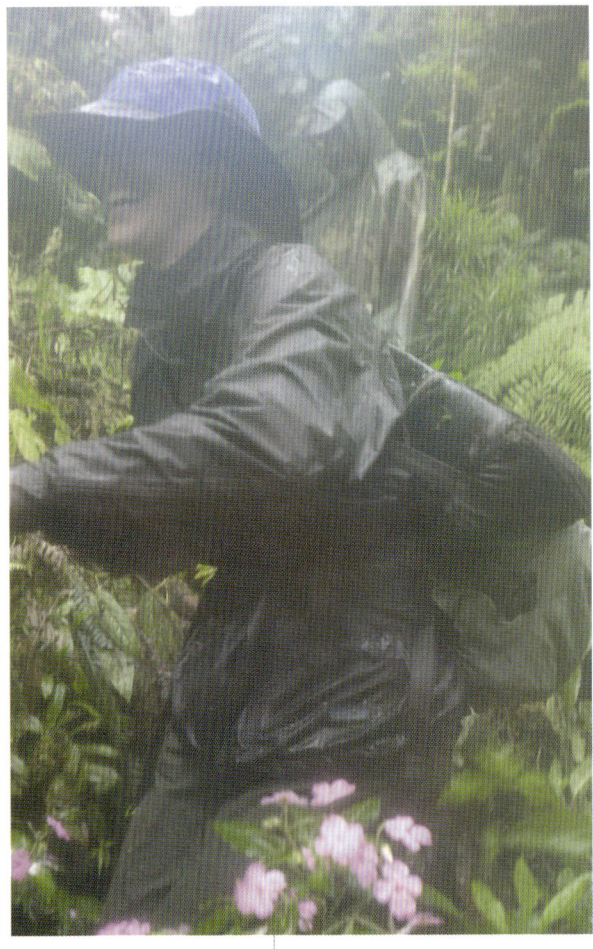

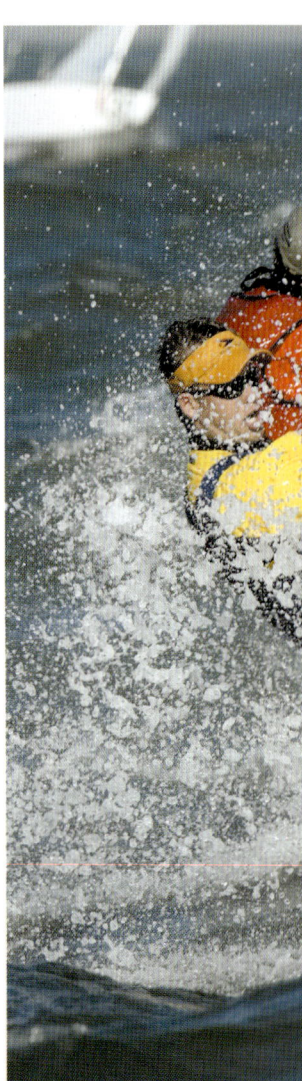

Mountains of Spray

Rafting action shots are too risky for most digital cameras without a waterproof housing. "Splashproof" models, however, are made for such conditions, where spontaneity and immediacy trump technical sophistication. © Didrik Johnck

Cloud Forest

Constant precipitation, like that which occurs in the Monteverde Cloud Forest of Costa Rica, is the enemy of camera electronics. It's best to start with the most well-sealed models available, then use waterproof camera covers—and constant vigilance. © Denise Rocco-Zilber

WET CONDITIONS 15

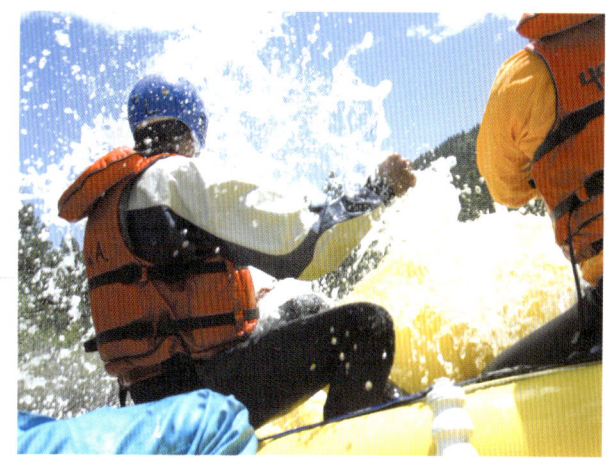

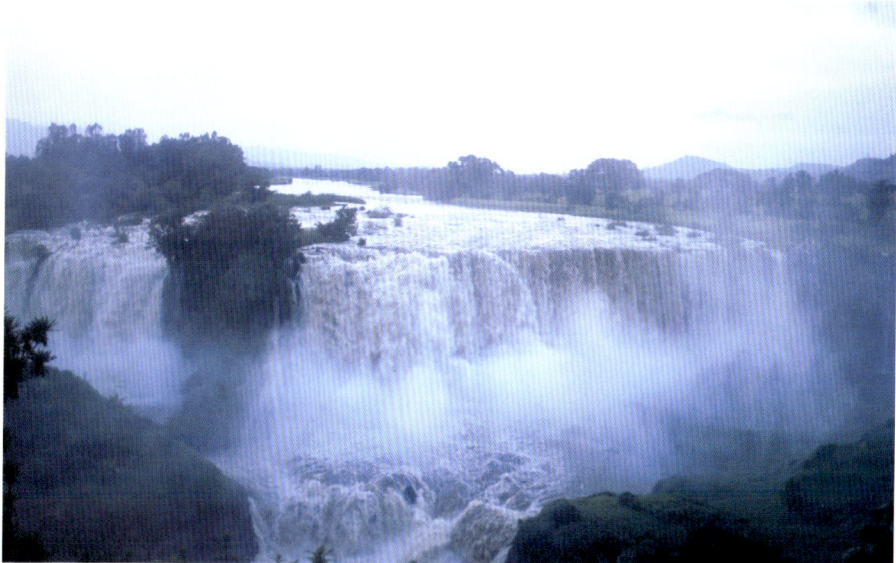

Constant Mist

Massive waterfalls like the Tissisat Falls on the Blue Nile send spray into the air so that you are constantly being showered with a fine mist. Even on a "sunny day" an umbrella becomes essential gear.

Deadly Salt Spray

Small-boat sailing can be captured with a long lens, but sea spray is your constant enemy on any boat. Frequent cleaning of the lens with a clean damp cloth helps prevent corrosion and other damage. © Abner Kingman

COLD AND WIND

The coldest temperature ever recorded on Earth was -129° F (-89° C) at Vostok, a Russian base in Antarctica, in July 1983. But extreme cold can be found on every continent, either as a function of the ebb and flow of seasons or of geographic factors such as latitude or altitude.

Cold affects both people and equipment. There is wet cold and dry cold, and most agree that wet cold is more chilling. Cold at extreme altitude is inevitable but escapable, but wind at altitude is the real killer. When the sun is shining, even if the air temperature is below freezing, it is viable to be partially exposed, but the minute the slightest breeze springs up, you have to seek shelter or add layers. High winds suck the heat out of your body and dramatically accentuate the cold, creating what's known as the "wind chill factor."

The most violent winds on land often result in twisters or tornadoes; at sea they are known as hurricanes and typhoons. Very strong winds make outdoor life difficult and affect people psychologically. Around the world there are legendary hot dry winds, associated with high fire danger as well as increased crime rates. These winds go by many different names, including the *Föhn* of the European Alps and the *Zonda* winds of Argentina. In the Rocky Mountains they are the called the *Chinook*; north of the Sahara it's the *Scirocco*, and south of the desert it's the *Harmattan*; and in Southern California it's the *Santa Anna*.

Polar regions have what are known as katabatic winds. These are caused by cold dense air flowing down off glaciers or the polar ice cap under the influence of gravity, and they can blow freezing winds for days on end. Commonwealth Bay, Antarctica, is reputedly the windiest place in the world, described by Australian explorer Douglas Mawson as "The Home of the Blizzard."

Everest Base Camp

Dry cold conditions found at Everest Base Camp are made bearable when you have the best possible clothing and camping gear. Strong wind combined with freezing cold quickly turns any photographic exercise into a finger-numbing challenge.

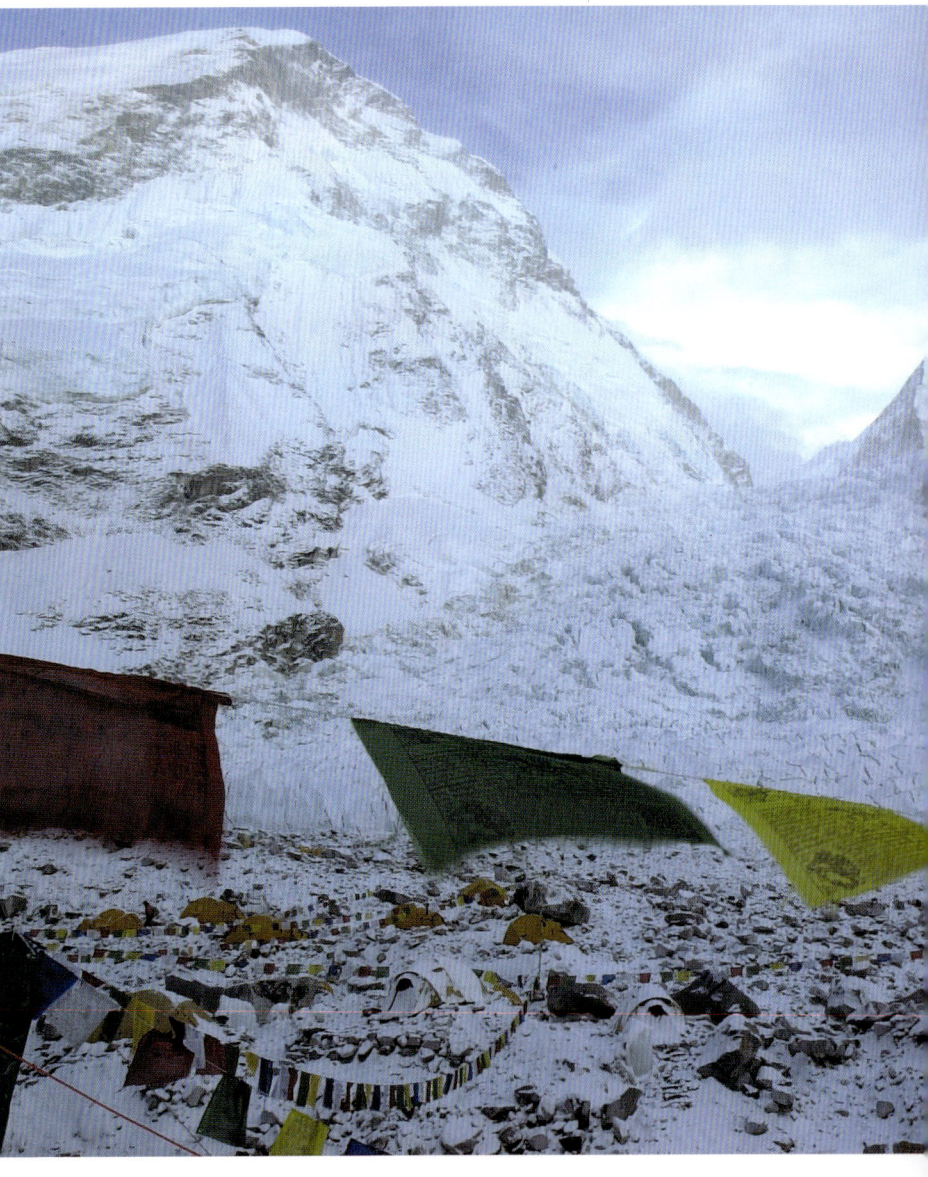

We had found an accursed county. On the fringe of an unspanned continent we dwelt where the chill breath of a vast polar wilderness, quickening to the rushing might of eternal blizzards, surged to the northern seas.

Douglas Mawson, *The Home of the Blizzard*

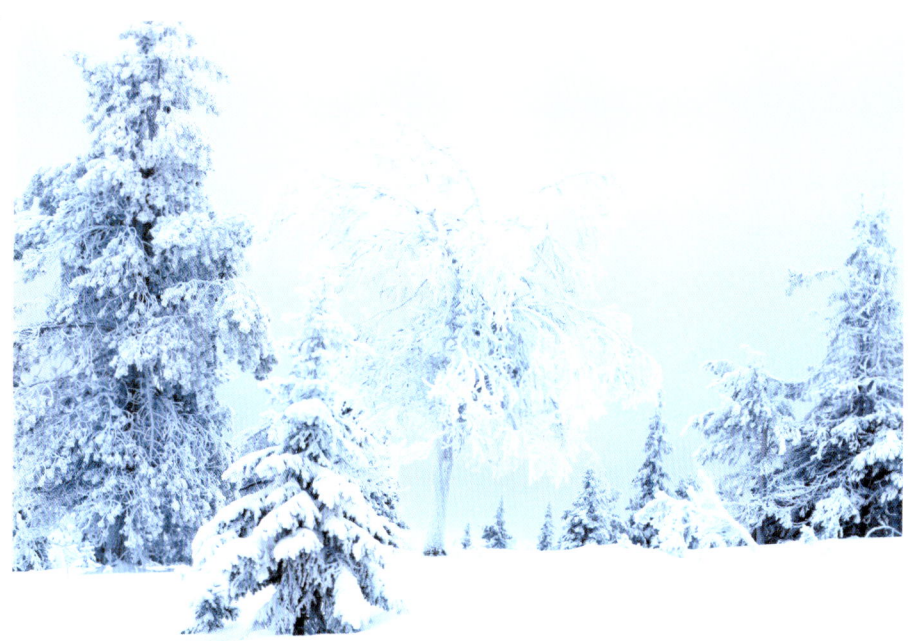

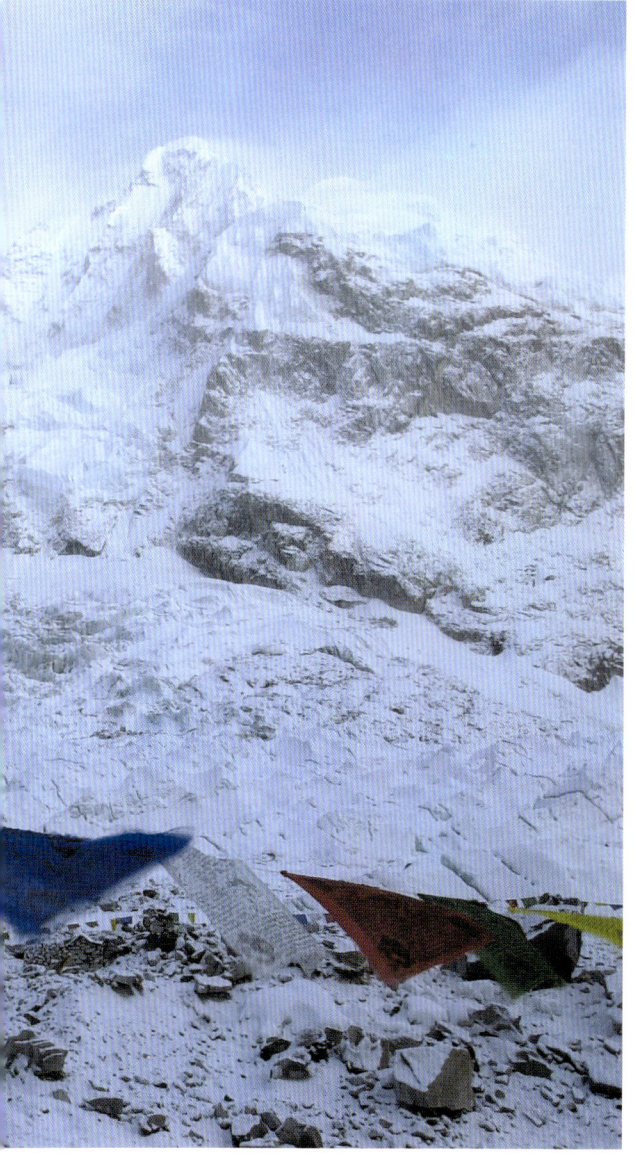

Lapland Frosting

Snowy landscape on a cloudy day in Riisitunturi National Park, Lapland, Finland. When it gets this cold, camera batteries are short-lived or won't work at all, and handling the metal casing becomes a challenge in itself. © Jean-François Maïon

Hanging Out to Dry

When you hang your washed clothes out to "freeze dry," then you know it is cold. Such temperatures were formerly anathema to photographers because film would turn brittle. © Didrik Johnck

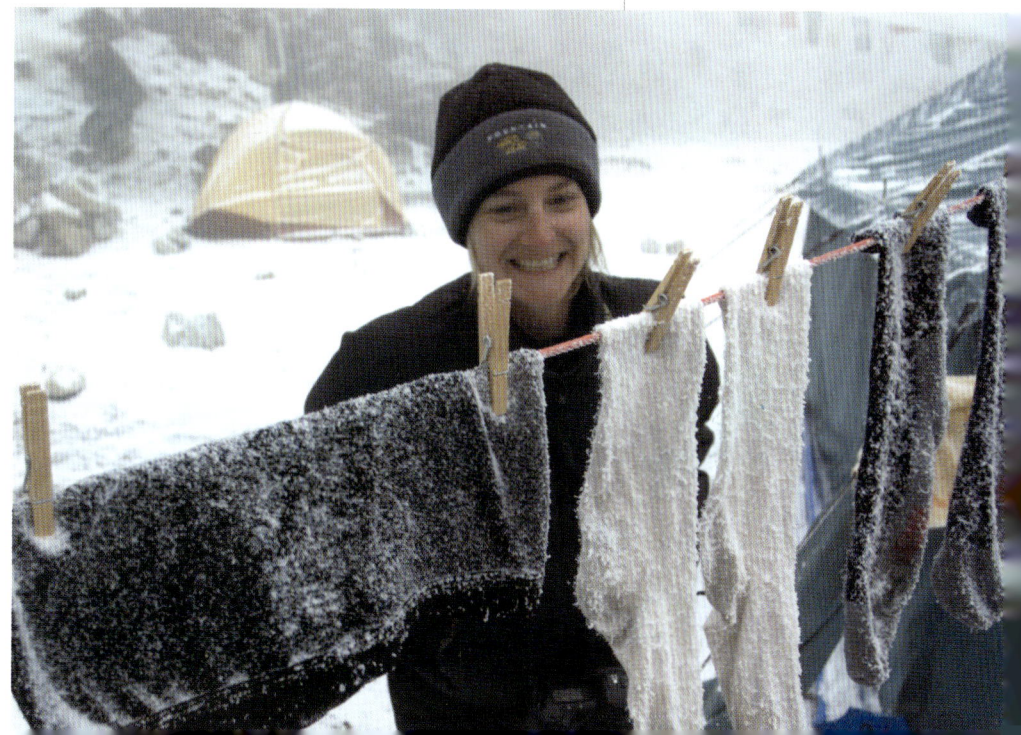

HEAT AND JUNGLE

Heat usually comes either as the dry heat of the deserts or the moist heat of the tropics. Dry heat is often associated with dust, especially if it is windy, but heat alone can be unbearable. Such dry-heat deserts predominate in the subtropical regions of the globe, where hot as it is during the day, it can be sub-freezing at night.

> *The tropical forest may be a naturalist's paradise, but for a photographer it can be a nightmare. Once you are inside it is all blood, sweat, and leeches. Whatever you take into the forest becomes part of the food chain, whether it's your equipment or yourself. I have seen leaf cutter ants eat my tent, fungi grow in my lenses, and larvae emerge from the flesh of my leg.*
>
> **Frans Lanting,** *Jungles*

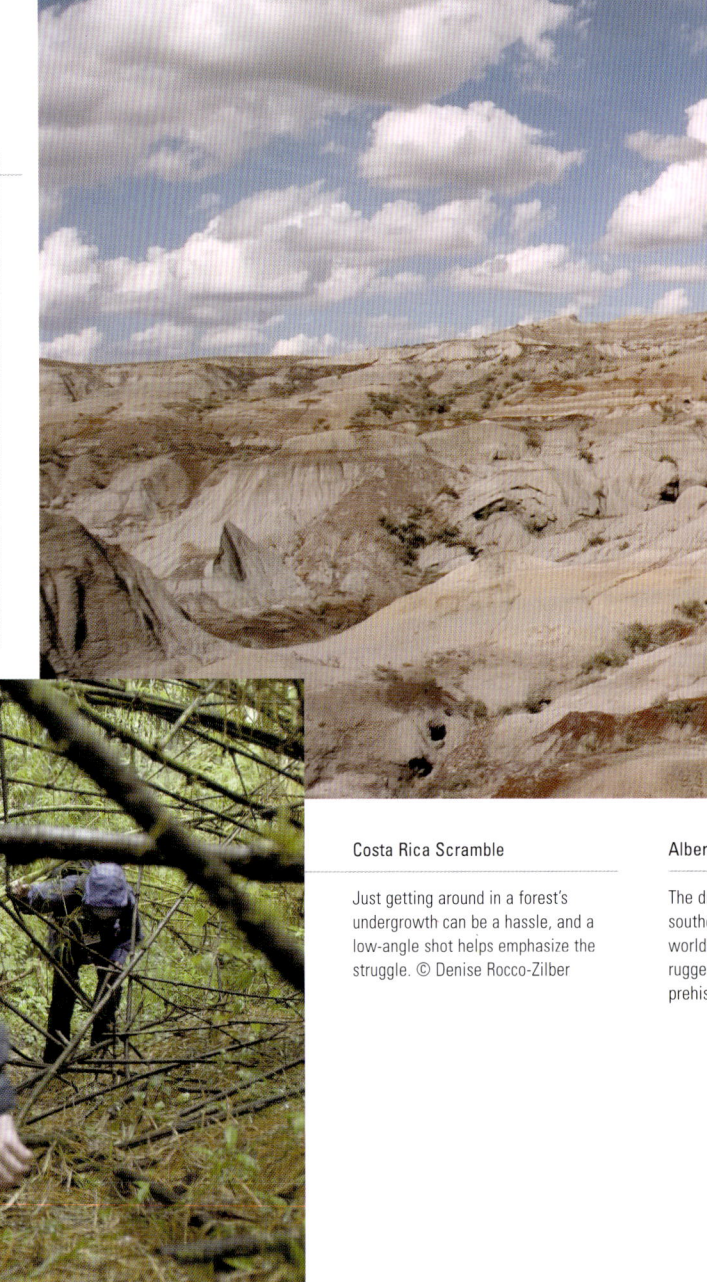

Costa Rica Scramble

Just getting around in a forest's undergrowth can be a hassle, and a low-angle shot helps emphasize the struggle. © Denise Rocco-Zilber

Alberta Badlands

The dry sandstone badlands of southeast Alberta are among the world's richest fossil sites, with rugged scenery that is almost prehistoric in nature.

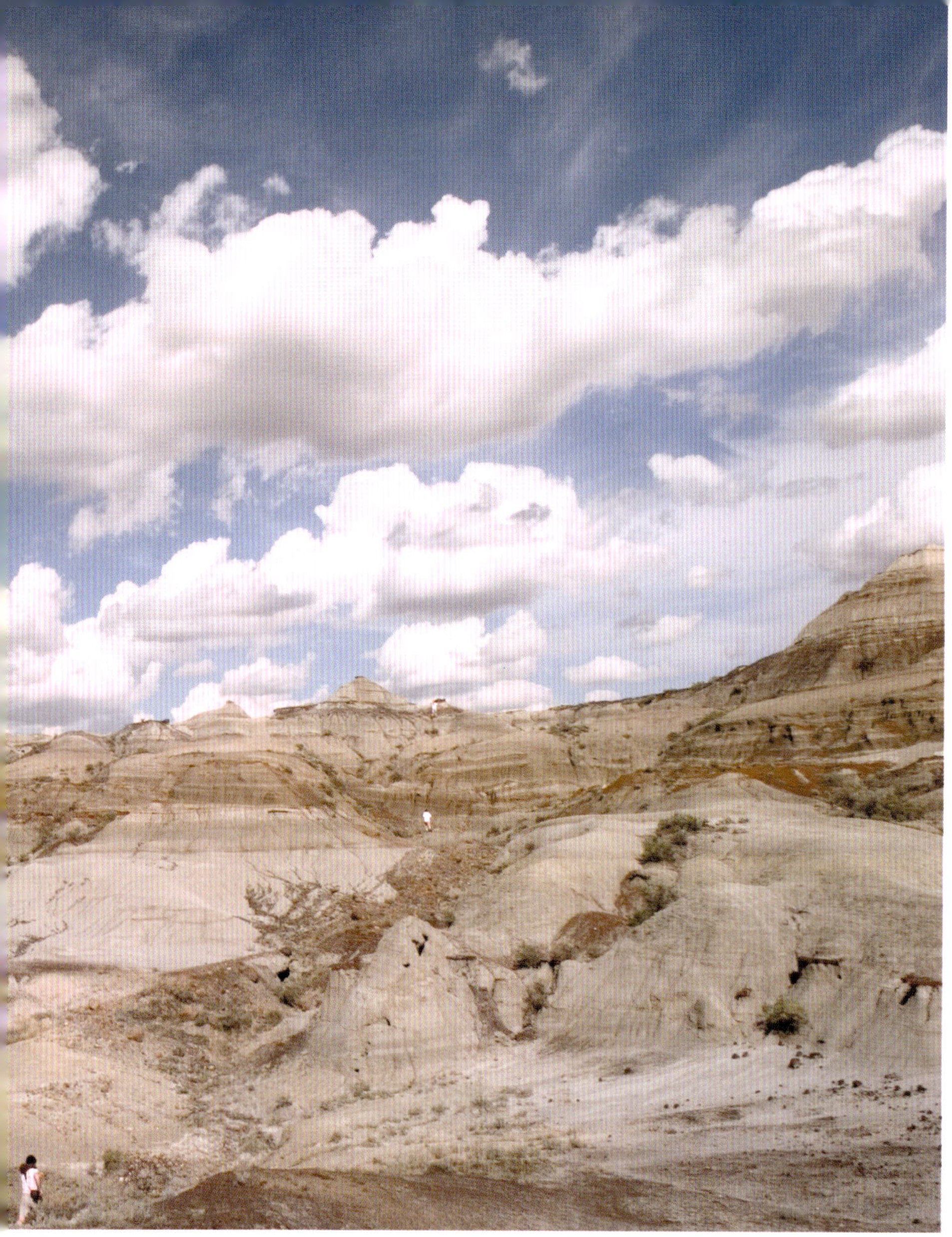

HEAT AND JUNGLE

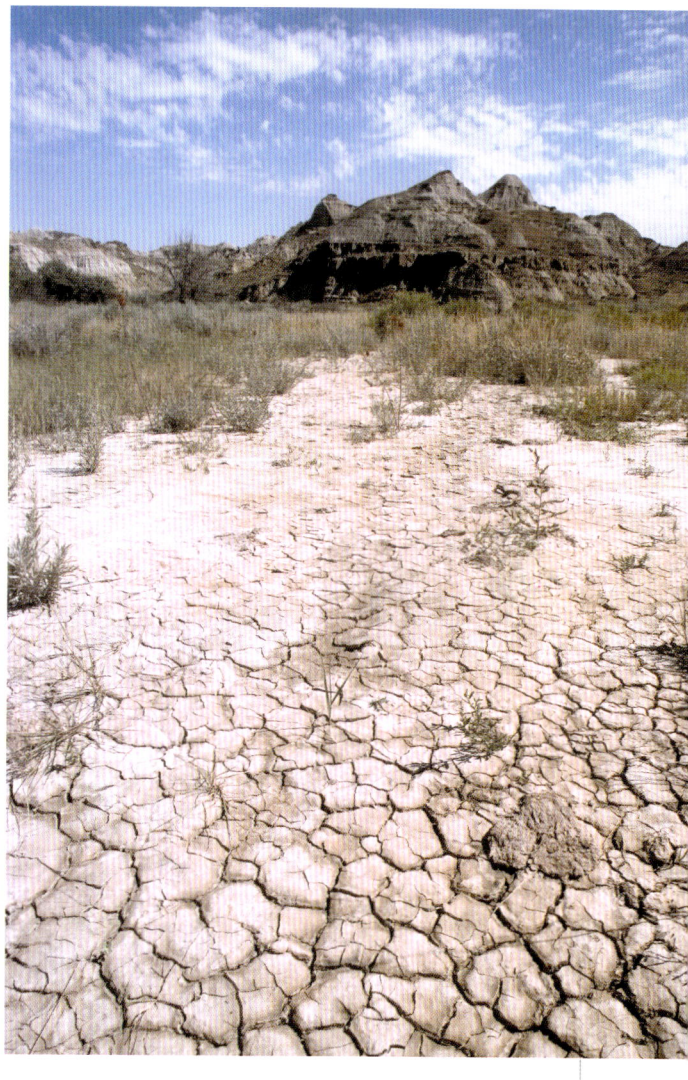

Yesterday's Mud

The dry bed of the Red Deer River Valley in Alberta, Canada, reveals shrinkage fractures in the large quantities of mud that are transported every time there is a storm.

Deserts are wonderful places to photograph landscapes and geographic features, but you have to be careful and well prepared to work in the hottest deserts. The hottest place on Earth is Death Valley in eastern central California, where a record of 134° F (56.7° C) was recorded in 1913. This is also near the lowest place in the Western Hemisphere, 240 feet (73m) below sea level—a factor contributing to the heat.

Tropical rainforests, on the other hand, create a potential nightmare for human existence, and they are not much better for electronic equipment, such as cameras and computers. High humidity promotes mold and corrosion, which are both deadly enemies of optics and electronics. The high prevalence of disease-bearing insects, predatory animals, and masses of impenetrable vegetation, mean that tropical jungles manage to combine many of the world's most extreme environmental factors into the one location. Yet the rewards—brightly-colored flower blossoms and exquisite bird plumage, luxuriant foliage, and amazingly adaptable people—are numerous for the attentive photographer.

DUST, SMOKE, AND SPINDRIFT

Dusty conditions are usually associated with hot dry desert environments, but cold deserts can have their own form of dust—"ice dust" or "spindrift," as it is known. Dust in the sky creates haze that can dramatically affect landscape shooting, for good or otherwise. At sunset and sunrise, dust and smoke can help create vibrantly colored sunsets and sunrises, but distant features are often hazy.

Dust and, especially, smoke are bad for human health, so when working around fires and in dust storms you may need to wear some form of mask or breathing apparatus. However, these conditions offer photojournalists a chance to really show their mettle: people struggling in dust storms or fighting fires can make for some extremely dramatic images.

The deforestation of major parts of the globe over the past few decades means that today you are much more likely to encounter desert and dusty conditions on your travels. Dust can affect not only what you are shooting,

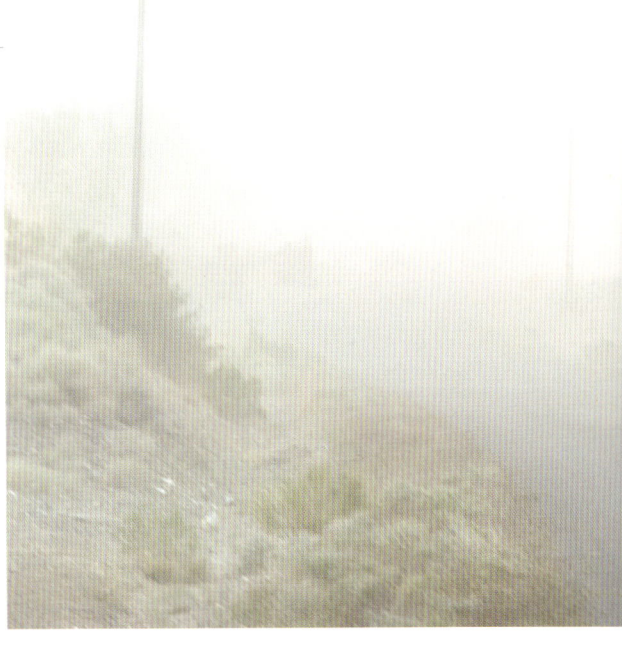

Desert Dust Storm

Difficult environmental conditions can even be found close to home, as this unusual dust storm in the Northern Nevada Desert makes travel as well as photography difficult—and underscores the importance of being prepared for anything. © Jessica Brandi Lifland

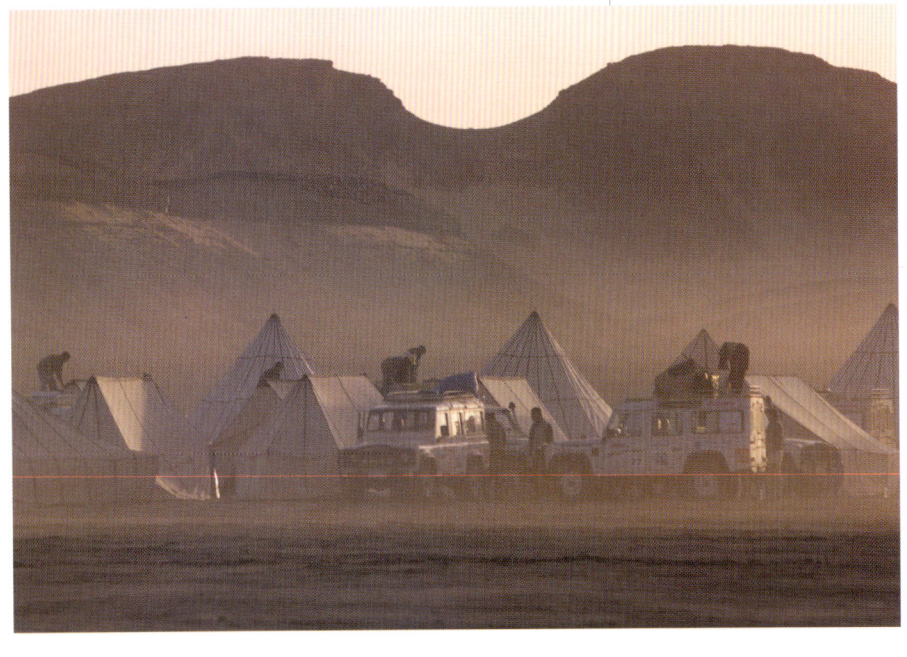

Desert Storm

Dust storms in the Sahara of southern Morocco are a nightmare for the participants and organizers of the Marathon des Sables, the "toughest race in the world"—six days, 151 miles (240km) of desert. © Corey Rich

but also your gear, especially cameras and computers. In these places, when traveling on rough dirt roads, it pays to be very careful in how you transport and store your gear. You should be prepared for dust when heading to many parts of the world.

Fine ice particles are known as spindrift to veterans of Antarctica, though this term is more typically associated with spume, the spray that is blown off the tops of waves in storms. Spindrift is a major component of the "ground blizzard," when fine ice particles are blown across the surface of the ice. This icy dust finds its way into every crevice and crack, through doors, windows, zippers, and clothing. If it melts, you have the problem of icy water to deal with, which can make you cold or damage your electrical equipment, but most often spindrift just piles up and buries you and your gear. It is easy to lose items of equipment left outdoors, or even to get lost yourself if you don't keep close to your encampment.

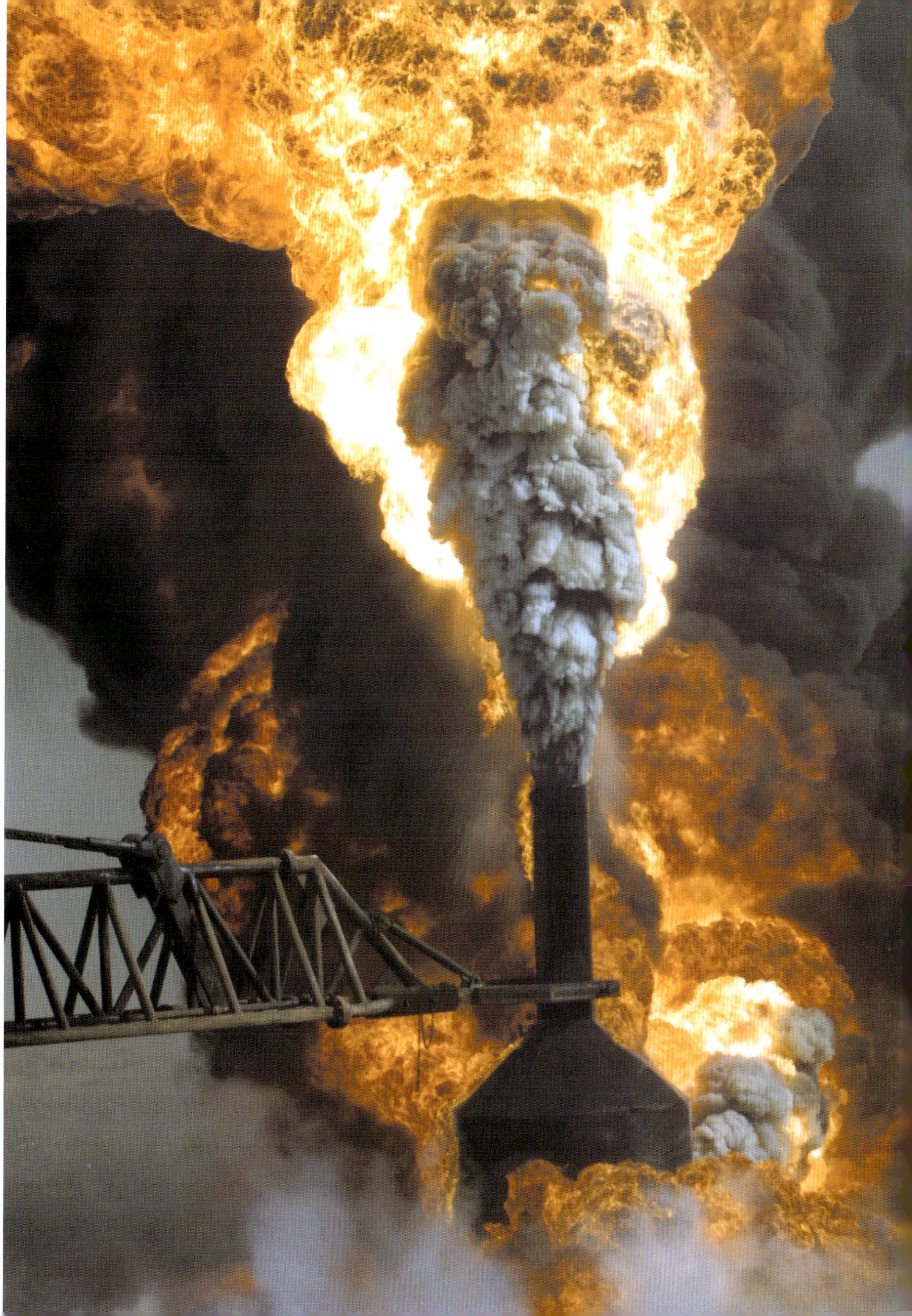

Fire in the Hole

Documenting the capping of a burning oil well in Iraq has to be one of the most environmentally challenging assignments imaginable, combining black soot, billowing smoke, and extreme heat with fast action and personal danger. © Peter Menzel

HIGH ALTITUDE

Mt. Everest, the highest peak on Earth, 29,035 feet (8,850m) above sea level, is one of the most extreme places that most people could imagine photographing. Even with the advent of commercially guided parties, only some 150 people climb Everest each year, and fewer than 2,000 people have been to the 5½-mile (9-km) high summit since it was first successfully climbed in 1953. Any photograph that results from the highest reaches of this peak, or the summit itself, is a worthy accomplishment.

There are myriad dangers, both objective and subjective, that face the photographer at such great heights. Not least of these are the punishing weather, the lack of oxygen, dehydration, and the fact that you are frequently pushing yourself to the limits of human physiology. Even with the use of supplementary oxygen, you are climbing in a state that closely resembles extreme intoxication ("hypoxia," or the lack of oxygen), and even the simplest tasks are very hard to accomplish. Taking photographs and operating complex cameras above 26,000 feet (8000m) is fraught with problems, as much due to inevitable "operator error" as to the extreme conditions.

Most people who live at or close to sea level can travel to about 10,000 feet (3,050m) by plane without suffering more than breathlessness and the occasional headache. Above this height you need to acclimatize gradually. This means that you should ascend at the rate of about 1,000 feet (305m) per day; otherwise you can be affected by one or more forms of altitude sickness. The most serious of these is cerebral edema, swelling of the brain, which can result in death in a matter of hours.

Climbing above 26,000 feet even with bottled oxygen is like running on a treadmill and breathing through a straw.

David Breashears – *Everest cameraman and Imax film producer*

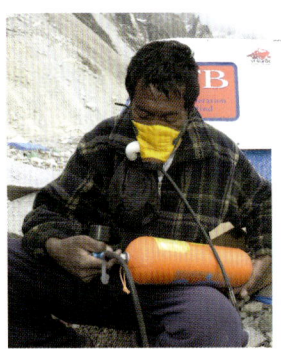

Checking the Oxygen

A high-altitude sherpa prepares for his ascent by adjusting the flow of his supplementary oxygen tank. Most mountain camps are below the 26,000-foot (8,000-m) "death zone," above which supplemental oxygen becomes advisable.

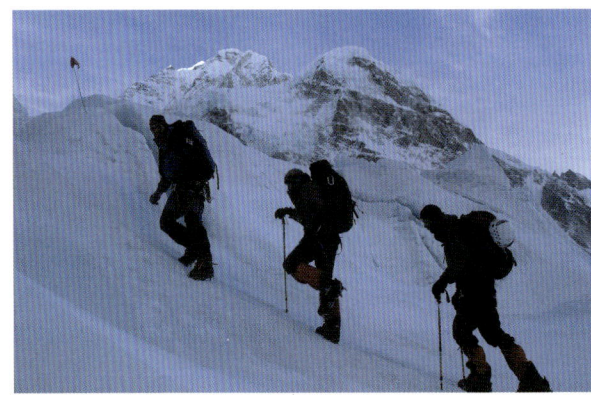

Heading Up to Mount Everest

Climbers depart for Camp 1 well before the sun hits the Khumbu Icefall, to minimize the danger of melting ice and avoid the searing heat of the reflected rays later in the day.

Prayer Flags over Pumori

The summit of Mt. Everest is not visible from Everest Base Camp, but nearby Pumori Peak (23,4435 feet/7,145m) makes a dramatic backdrop for this silhouette shot of Buddhist prayer flags.

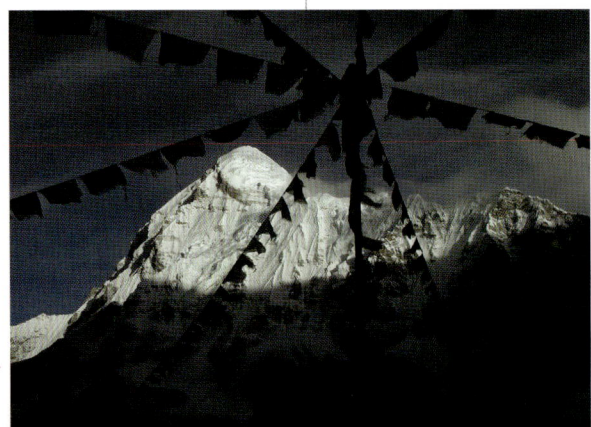

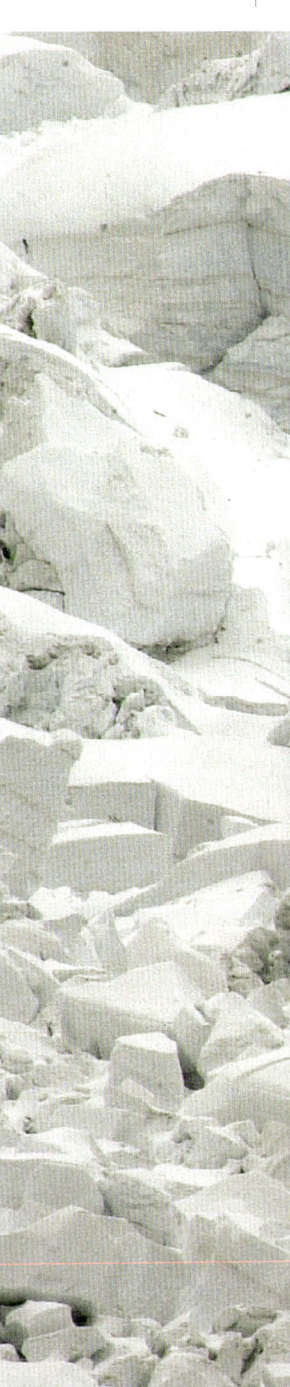

HIGH ALTITUDE 23

Deadly Jumble

The Khumbu Icefall, a deadly and ever-changing maze of seracs and crevices, is one of the most dangerous parts of the climb of the southwest ridge of Mt. Everest.

Mount Everest Sunrise

Mountaineer Mike O'Donnell soaks up the first rays of sun just below the South Summit of Mt. Everest. Colors are extremely bright and crisp at such altitude, and visibility is extreme.
© Didrik Johnck

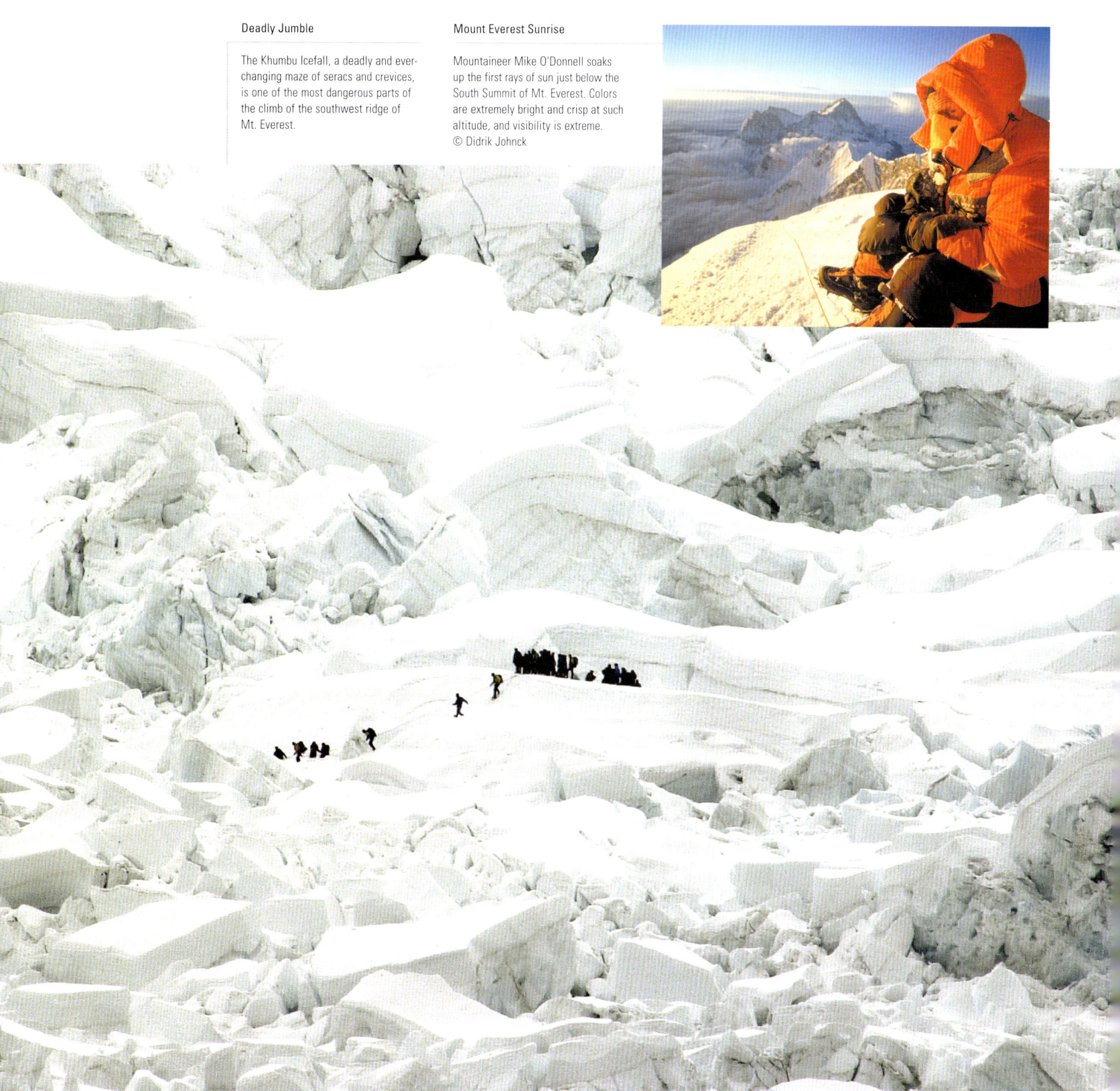

LATITUDE

Latitude and longitude are a basic navigation system that enables every position on Earth to be located. The longitudinal lines run north–south, and latitude east–west. With handheld GPS systems, anyone can determine their exact location to within a few feet.

Higher latitudes approaching the polar regions are typically more extreme in weather and geography, but latitude alone does not give the complete picture. It is latitude combined with altitude that dictates the most extreme environmental conditions, and the higher the latitude, the more dramatic the seasonal range. You can be on or near the equator (latitude 0°) in places such as Kilimanjaro in East Africa or Puncak Jaya (formerly Carstenz Pyramid) in Irian Jaya and yet be above the snowline. Also, since the Earth's axis is tilted at 23.5°, parts of the globe above the Arctic or below the Antarctic Circle are always either in complete darkness for months or have months of daylight for the winter and summer seasons respectively.

Latitude also has an impact on the effects of altitude. The Earth is not a perfect sphere—it bulges at the equator and is slightly flattened at the poles. This results in the Earth's atmosphere being less dense at high latitudes at a given altitude. Climbers on Denali (Mt. McKinley, 20,320 feet/6,197m) say that the altitude-related difficulties encountered there are equivalent to climbing a mountain several thousand feet higher in the Himalaya.

Southern Ocean sailors talk about the "Roaring Forties," the "Furious Fifties," and the "Screaming Sixties" when crossing those latitudes en route from Ushuaia, Argentina or New Zealand, referring to the power of the winds and intensity of storms that circle the bottom of the world.

The high-latitude region of the south is dramatically different from that of the north. At the North Pole there is an ocean covered with a thick layer of floating ice that moves in a giant swirling gyre as the earth spins. On the other hand the South Pole is near the center of Antarctica, the highest, driest, coldest, continent on earth. There aren't many people who have ever been to this point— you can't get more extreme than this.

> *Polar exploration is at once the cleanest and most isolated way of having a bad time which has ever been devised.*
>
> **Apsley Cherry-Garrard,** *The Worst Journey in the World*

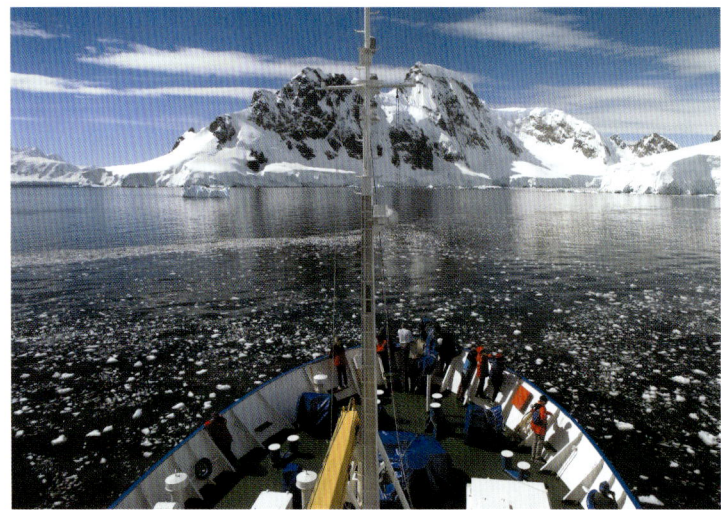

Livonia in Antarctica

Ice-strengthened ex-Soviet research ships like the RV *Livonia* make ideal expedition vessels for "high-latitude" cruising. Small and strong enough to explore open pack ice, they typically carry about 50 passengers from Argentina, Chile, Australia, or New Zealand to the Antarctic Peninsula.

Antarctic Peninsula

A mountainous spine runs the entire length of the Antarctic Peninsula, from Vinson Massif to Deception Island, with many peaks rising over 6,500 feet (2,000m). This most commonly visited part of Antarctica has very dramatic scenery, and holds many challenges.

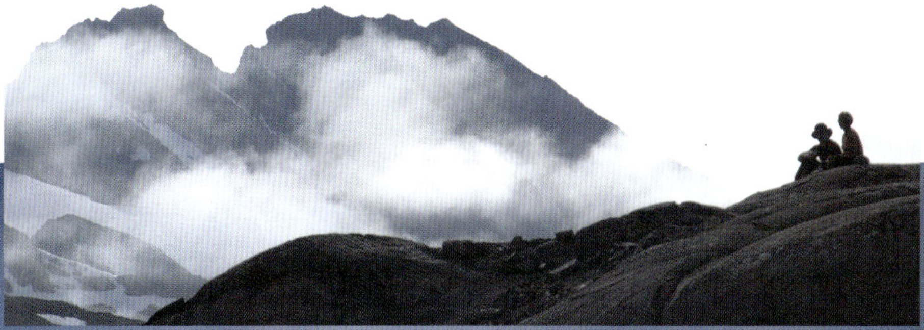

LATITUDE 25

Greenland Grandeur

The rugged west coast of Greenland attracts extreme adventurers during the summer. Fjords and mountains offer some spectacular backgrounds to sea kayakers and climbers.
© Mark Langley

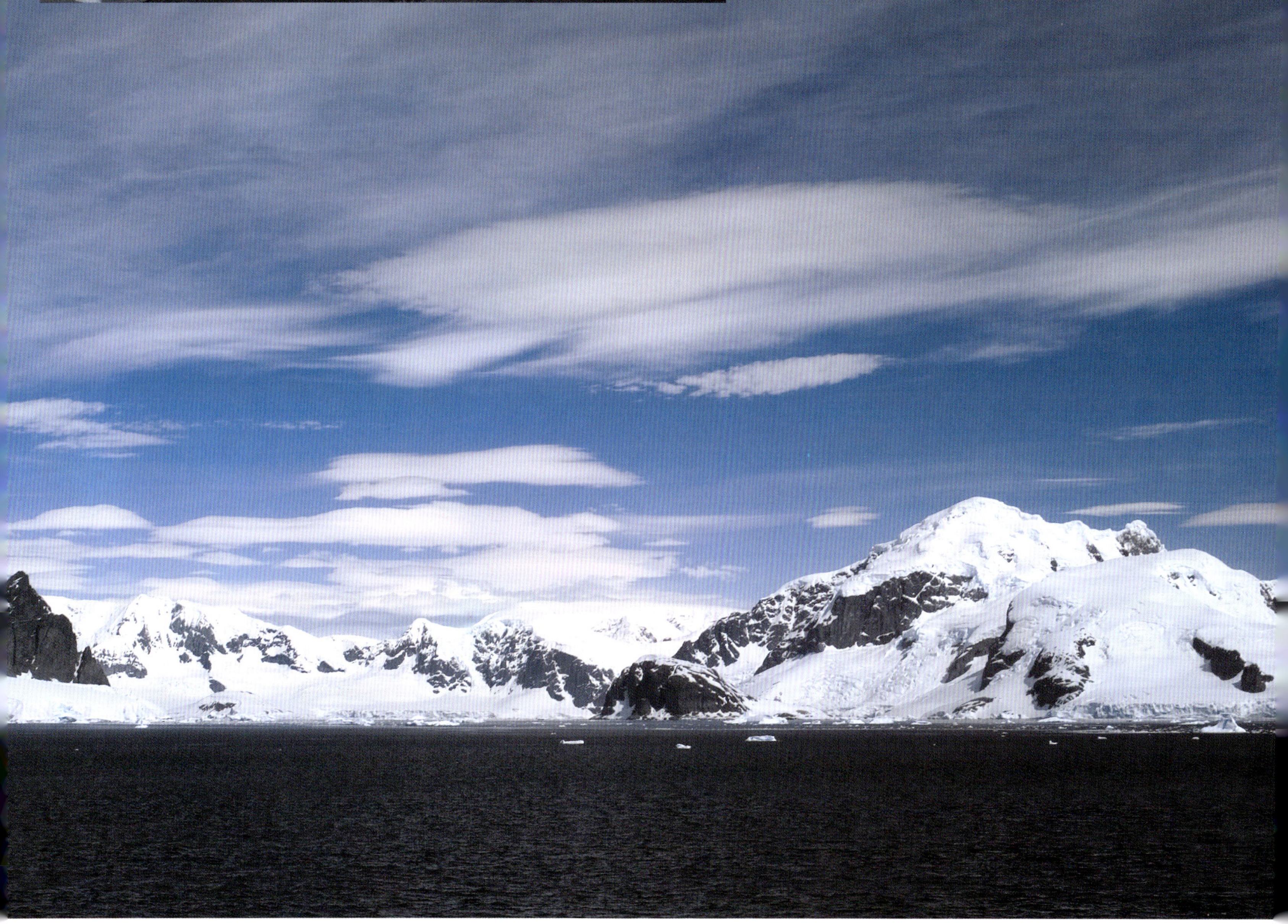

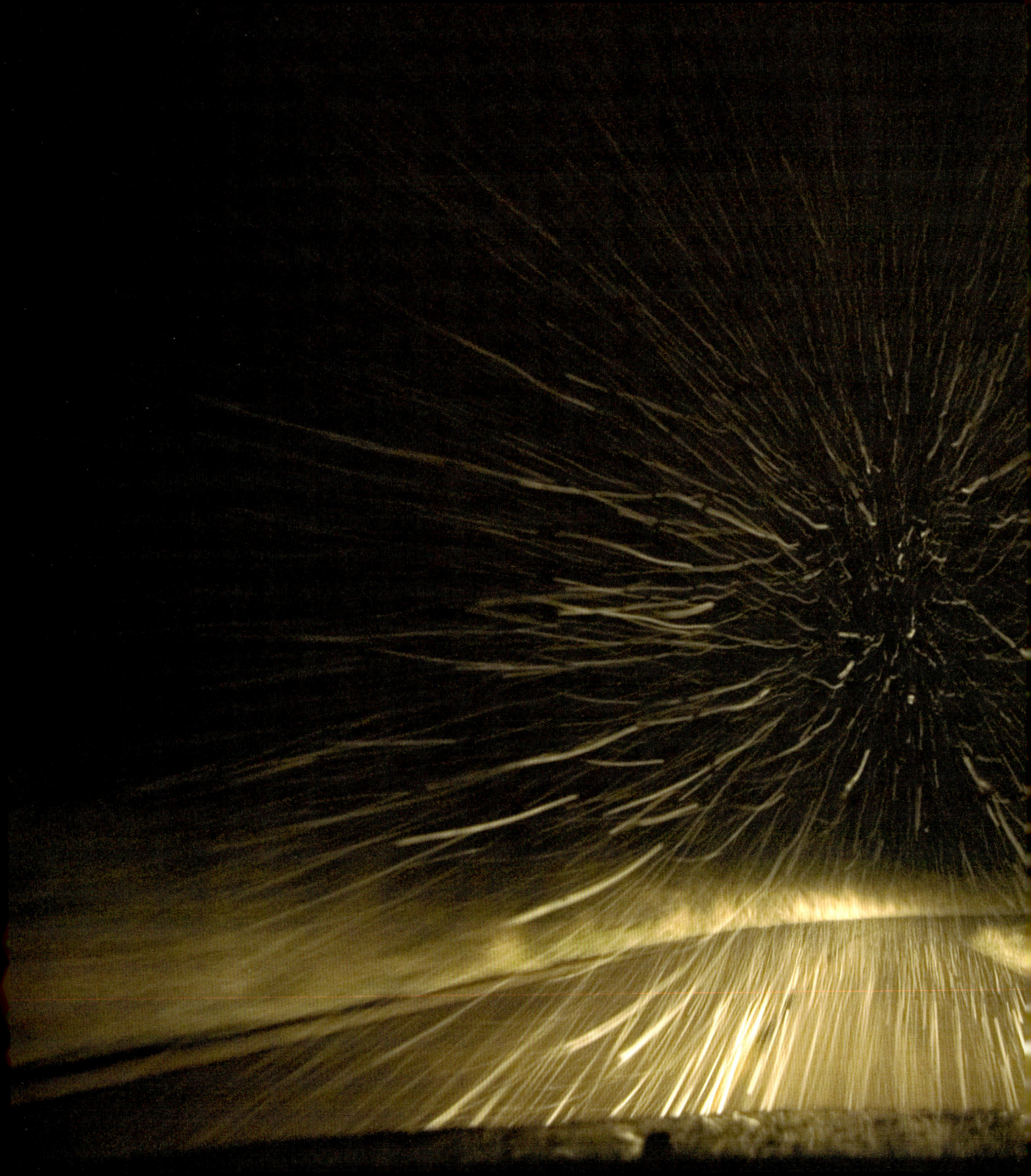

PLANNING & PREPARATION

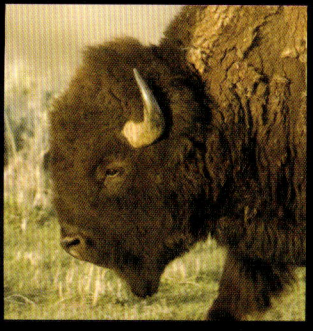

After three hectic months of preparation we met in London on the eve of our departure, for a final review of our plans. Only Jungle, who was to have spoken on the use of the radio gear and his own methods of route-finding, was absent. He rang to say that he had taken the wrong bus and was not quite certain of his whereabouts; but he had just caught sight of the North Star and expected to join us shortly.

W.E. Bowman, *The Ascent of Rum Doodle*

All images. © Jonathan Chester

WHAT PHOTOGRAPHIC GEAR TO TAKE

Photographers are by nature among the biggest gadget lovers around, but a major assignment, expedition, or journey is the worst time to be experimenting with new models of vital components, or, heaven forbid, breaking into the world of digital photography. The more you can work through the bugs in your system and get to know its foibles ahead of time, the better. This is especially true if you are taking on additional roles, such as being responsible for satellite communications, or if it is going to be a particularly taxing trip.

Whether it's a small day outing or a major expedition, you still have the same basic elements to consider. You will need one or more digital cameras and appropriate lenses, adequate storage cards and batteries (and the power source to recharge them if necessary), and probably some means of archiving or storage the digital images. Plus, of course, you need to have the means to carry and protect all these items.

Basic Camera Kit

Digital SLR camera bodies, or DSLRs, are digital cameras to which different lenses can be fitted, and which are capable of producing image files adequate for large-format color printing as well as digital reproduction (for Web use, e-mail, etc.). Since their introduction in the 1990s, they have become more affordable at a consumer level and increasingly reliable. It has now become a reasonable proposition to shoot all-digital in even the most extreme environments.

Serious shooting of extreme activities or in wild locations usually means that you want to have the most rugged and reliable equipment available. You should also incorporate some level of redundancy or backup: a second camera body and/or a compact digital camera. Despite the commitment to all-digital capture, some photographers also regard a film camera body and 50 rolls of film as a last-stand backup solution. This can save the day in case of the complete loss of some critical aspect of the digital workflow.

A second digital SLR camera body such as a high-end Canon or Nikon, however, may seem like expensive insurance, and the weight of a second body can become demanding if you are carrying it about with you all day. The decision is usually dictated by monetary cost and how important maintaining image quality is to you. As prices come down and reliability goes up, then the decision becomes a little easier.

When there is a lot of fast-breaking action, such as photographing an adventure race, you may need to have two camera bodies at the ready with lenses of different focal lengths, say a 24-mm wide-angle and an 80–200mm

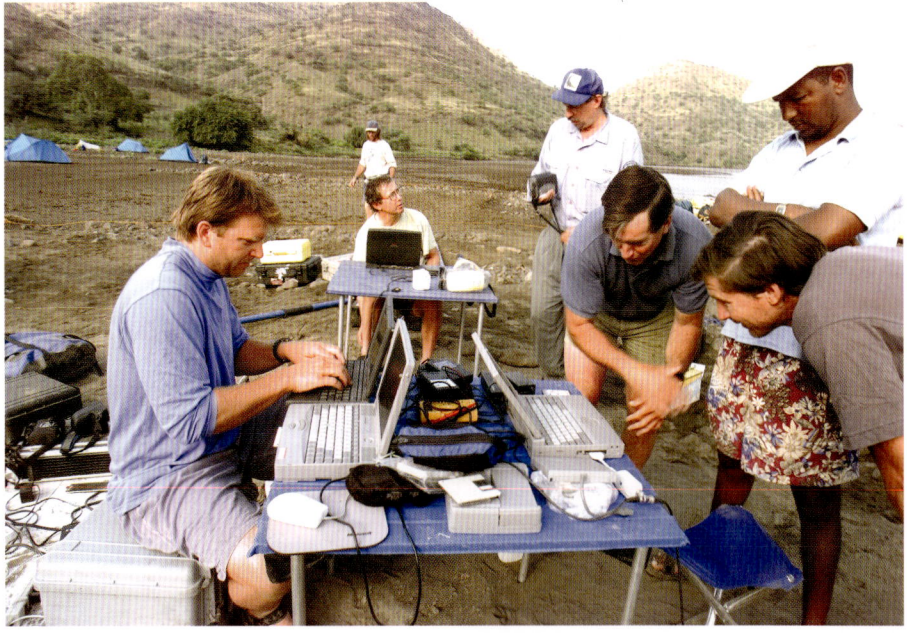

Extreme Workflow

The *Mungo Park* team working on the banks of Ethiopia's Tekeze River had to contend with digital extreme issues of power, storage, and technology.

telephoto zoom. You may also need to use high-performance cameras with a high burst rate and a large buffer. The Nikon D2H is rated at 8 frames per second for 40 frames at 4.1 megapixels for JPEG capture, which is excellent for most action and adventure journalism. A less expensive camera may have a 3 frames per second burst rate, which may be only adequate.

There is a range of DSLR brands to choose from, many from the same manufacturers that are the leaders in film cameras. Most photographers who are shifting into digital from film base their decision on which camera to go for on the type of lenses they already have—be they Canon, Nikkor, Pentax, or other familiar names. Canon currently heads the field in the range of cameras available, from top-of-the-line 11-megapixel 1DS for the pro photographer, to the relatively inexpensive EOS Digital Rebel with its still-adequate 6.3-megapixel capacity. Nikon has three current professional-level digital cameras, while both Kodak and Fuji manufacture DSLR camera bodies that use Nikkor lenses. Sigma and Pentax also make pro-level digital SLRs. The Sigma SD10 camera is significant for having the much-heralded Foveon X3 chip, which captures three times more color data than a standard CCD. The Pentax *ist DSLR camera (6.1-megapixel) is one of the smallest and lightest digital SLR cameras.

Olympus has the E1, a 5-megapixel digital camera designed from the ground up specifically for digital capture. Its 4:3 format was jointly developed with Kodak and supported by Fuji, and lets digital image capture correspond to the format of standard print sizes. (The film 3:2 ratio is only accurately represented in 4x6-inch prints.) Sony also makes high-end digital cameras, though none with interchangeable lenses. Sony's DSC F828 has an 8-megapixel sensor, which "sees" in four colors instead of the usual three. It also has an extended range in the infrared spectrum, which makes it capable of night vision. This model comes with a standard 28–280mm lens, and has Compact Flash card (CF) capability in addition to the standard Sony Memory Stick.

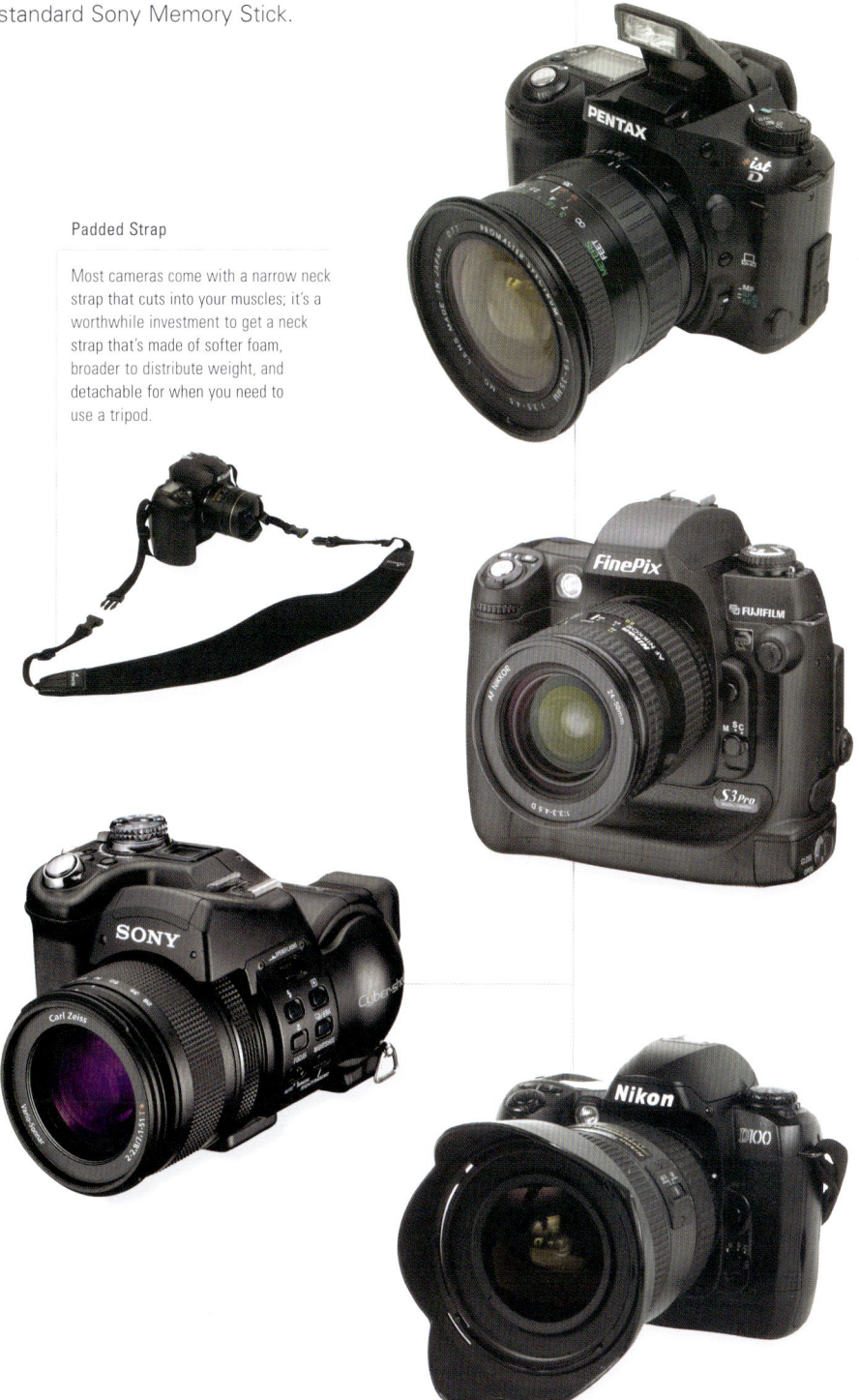

Padded Strap

Most cameras come with a narrow neck strap that cuts into your muscles; it's a worthwhile investment to get a neck strap that's made of softer foam, broader to distribute weight, and detachable for when you need to use a tripod.

Camera Choices

Most major camera manufacturers produce a range of cameras. Choose a model based on your needs, such as more megapixels for print work, or high-burst speed for sports photography.

Lenses: Fish-Eye, Wide-Angle Zoom, Telephoto, VR/IS Lenses

Most serious photographers use very wide-angle lenses in the 18–24mm range as a standard, combined with a midrange zoom such as a 35–70mm and an 80–200mm telephoto zoom. Sometimes a fixed focal-length longer lens of 300–400mm is used; very occasionally a 600mm lens is necessary for shooting wildlife or sports such as surfing, where it is not always possible to get in very close. Other specialties will require a macro, or close-up, lens which can also be a portrait lens of around 60–100mm.

Vibration Reduction (VR), as Nikon calls them, or Image Stabilization (IS) lenses to Canon users, designed to reduce camera shake when shooting handheld are now an accepted part of the photographer's kit. They are not a panacea for all situations, however. They are expensive, bulky, and only useful if you are stationary.

Most SLR cameras have a chip smaller than the area of 35mm film, but with the same 3:2 aspect ratio. The result is a 1.4–1.6 multiplier effect when using traditional 35mm lenses—great for telephoto work where a 200mm lens becomes the equivalent of up to a 320mm, less so at the wide-angle end, as an 18mm super-wide lens becomes only a 28mm wide-angle.

Some makers produce special digital lenses to match the smaller chip area. Nikon has the dedicated DX lenses, ranging from the very wide-angle 10.5mm fish-eye lens to the 17–55mm zoom. Nikon's Capture software has a filter for correcting "keystoning" or horizontal or vertical curvature to convert fish-eye images into straight-sided wide-angle ones. Canon's Digital Rebel has a dedicated 18–55mm lens, effective to a film 28–90mm lens, to overcome the limitations of the 1:6 multiplier effect.

The multiplier effect can only be overcome with an imaging chip that is the same size as 35mm film. New Canon and Kodak cameras use such a chip, so all the standard 35mm lenses maintain their designed focal lengths. The data files from these cameras are far bigger, however, requiring larger storage cards and greater computing power to efficiently handle the considerable file sizes that are generated.

Don't forget what may be the most important and least expensive "essential" in your kit. Whatever DSLR camera you use, a neoprene cushioned neck strap is vital. Look for one with quick-release buckles that you can easily remove to shorten the strap when you use the camera on a tripod (a full strap can flap about in a breeze, causing the camera to vibrate).

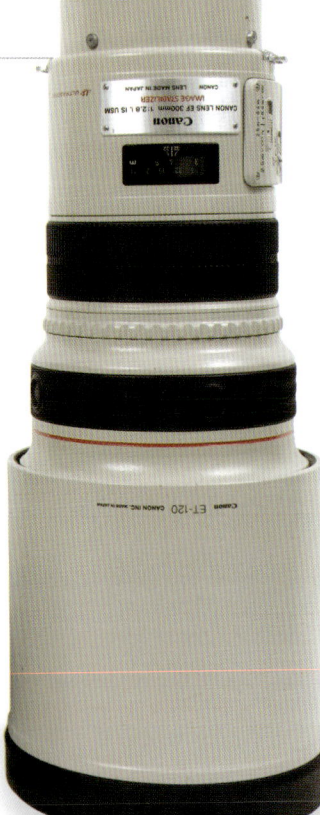

Super-Wide Angle

The digital multiplier effect—smaller chip size means relatively "larger" image capture—means the super-wide angle lens has become standard in many digital kits.

Stop that Shake

Electronically "stabilized" telephoto lenses have become popular, in part to compensate for the digital multiplier effect—a 210mm lens captures like a 340mm, making handheld shots difficult.

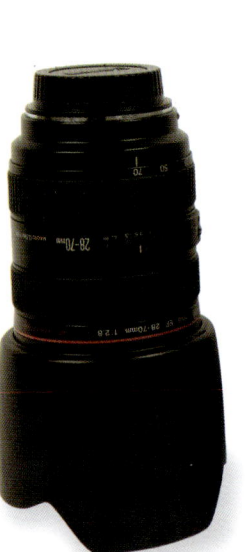
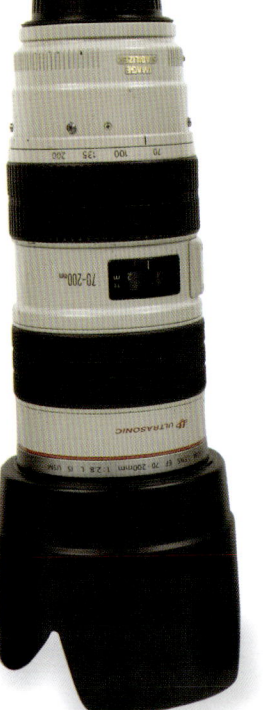

COMPACT AND SPECIALTY CAMERAS

Not that long ago, many photographers would bring along a Polaroid camera to shoot test images so that they could evaluate composition, lighting, and so on. Today, smaller point-and-shoot cameras fill this role in the serious photographer's field kit, with the added advantage that the smaller camera can also serve as a backup or as that "always available" camera for snapshots.

These cameras often have megapixel capacity equal to all but the most expensive DSLRs, and many automatic features that at first sight may appear seductive. However, professional photographers usually find these frustrating to use, especially side-by-side with a digital SLR, owing to the lag time between pushing the shutter button and the moment when the image is captured. The newer models are improving in this regard all of the time, and there are certain tricks that can help you to get around this limitation.

Choosing a point-and-shoot digital camera can prove almost as daunting as choosing a high-end camera, due in part to the large number of models that each manufacturer has developed and is constantly releasing. Finding a model with good optics is key, of course, but try out several models to find one with an interface that you find intuitive and "user-friendly." You might also find one that uses the same storage cards as your DSLR, but several high-end cameras (such as the Kodak 14n and Fuji 2) are capable of using both CF and Secure Digital (SD) or XD cards.

The Fuji FinePix 7000 is also interesting because of its compactness, yet it has 6.2-megapixel Super CCD SR technology and also has the ability to capture RAW images. The camera only accepts XD cards, however.

There are also some special models that are particularly rugged or splashproof. The Pentax Optio model 33 WR, a so-called "water-resistant" model, is marketed as being designed for rain, snow, and beach, like its popular comparable film WR series. Dedicated underwater housings for many compact models are available from Ewa-Marine and other manufacturers, especially for the Canon and Nikon Coolpix brands. But for seriously wet conditions, a full underwater digital compact camera from Sea & Sea called the AquaPix, might be the answer to your needs.

Underwater Point-and-Shoot

The AquaPix DX-3100 from Sea & Sea offers 3.14-megapixel digital image capture down to 150 feet (45m). Built-in color filters, macro, flash and flash diffuser, and even interchangeable lenses enhance its usefulness.

Waterproof Housing

Specialized waterproof housings, such as this model from Olympus for their C740 & C750 digital cameras, are made of durable polycarbonate and make digital photography when diving, snorkeling, or surfing possible. Canon offers similar housings.

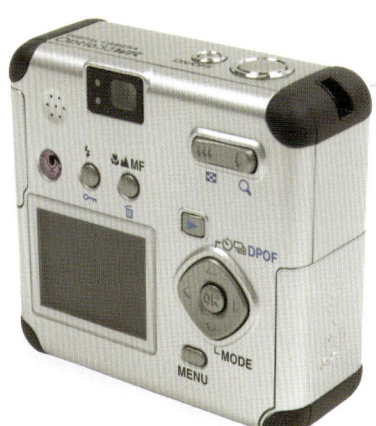

Water-Resistant

The square Pentax Optio 33WR provides 3.2-megapixel capture in wet situations, but is not meant to be taken underwater. Rafting, canoeing, or a day at the beach are better uses for this consumer camera.

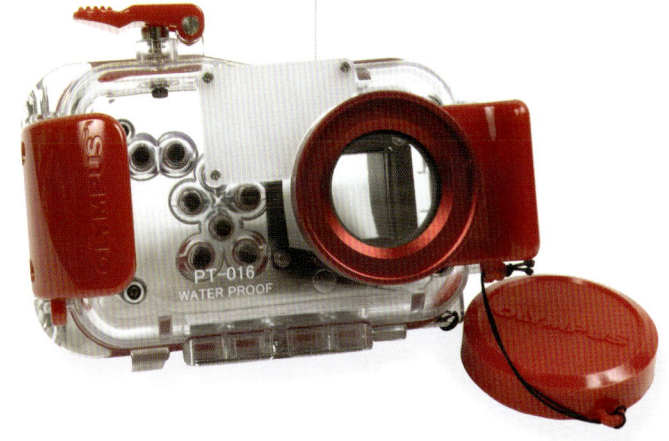

OTHER CAPTURE MEANS

Video Cameras

Many prosumer video cameras, especially those from Sony and Canon, have a still capture or "photo" mode that can acquire a still image and write it either to some form of flash memory card (such as the Sony Memory Stick) or to the mini DV tape itself. Traditionally, this has been a low-resolution VGA image (640 x 480 pixels), but Sony now makes the DCR-PC 330 Mini DV Handycam, which can capture a 3.3-megapixel still image.

Photo mode can be a very useful feature for certain extreme applications where saving weight is paramount and where video is more important than still images. A summit bid on a particularly high mountain might fall into this category, but if your goal is to capture high-quality digital photography you are far better off using a dedicated DSLR. Your control over the image is much more complete and accurate than it is by just clicking the "photo" button on a digital video camera, which will only deliver what is more accurately called a "frame grab" and not a photograph.

You can also capture frame grabs from videotape after shooting by using programs such as iMovie or Final Cut Pro on a Mac (or Windows Movie Maker or later versions of Adobe Premiere on a PC). However, since video images are captured by a different process from still images, these have to be de-interlaced.

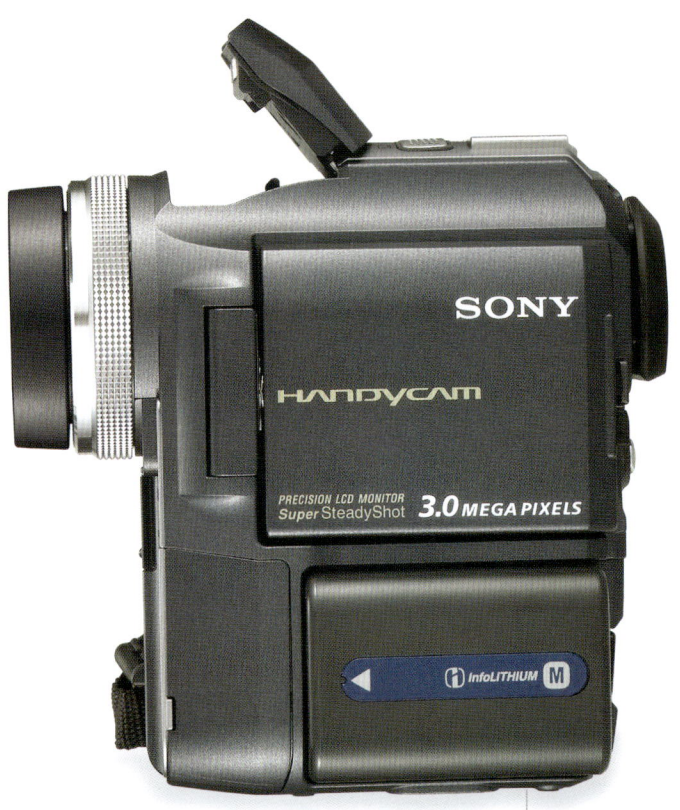

Cell Phone Cameras

Cell phones with cameras are one of the fastest-growing segments of the consumer communications world, and with improving quality they can increasingly be considered a viable proposition for certain extreme uses. Most phones currently on the market are VGA 640 x 480 pixels, which is the minimum you should look for in acquiring such a device. SVGA phones, which acquire a 600 x 800 pixel image, are also being released. Some models are now being released in Japan that can capture a 2-megapixel image.

The better models offer a variety of features, including storage for 20 images in the phone's memory, 2x digital zoom, three levels of acquisition quality, and some sort of removable storage card; either a mini SD card or a

Double Duty

New-generation digital video camcorders can double as digital still cameras. Though this feature is common on many DV camcorders, only a few—such as the Sony DCR-PC model shown here—offer adequate image quality of 3 megapixels and above.

Memory Stick Duo (which are half the length of the standard Sony Memory Stick). Acquiring at the highest resolution is always the best policy, but sending VGA images from phone-to-phone is the most efficient means with current technology.

VGA is fine for wallet-size prints and ideal for satellite phone transmission and displaying on the Web. These images are typically 30 to 70KB in size; sending the highest resolution will take between 10 and 30 seconds via one of the data networks.

Where there is adequate coverage, carrying a cell phone in the hills or backcountry can also be a worthwhile strategy in case of emergency. Some networks have wider coverage than others. Tri-mode CMDA phones that have digital and analog modes have the most reliable coverage in the US. Much of the rest of the world works on what is called Global System Mobile (GSM), but even here there are three different flavors. In Europe Tri-band GSM phones are the best for globetrotting, but they often do not have good coverage in the US outside of the major metropolitan areas.

PDA Cameras

A few Personal Digital Assistants (PDAs) have built-in cameras, while many more now accept small cameras via SD or other flash card slots. Palm, Handspring, and Microsoft PDAs all offer these cameras, the Ipaq from Hewlett-Packard has several such units. The resolution of these plug-in cameras rarely exceeds 1.2 megapixels, comparable to the current range of cell phone cameras. Both of these technologies amount to little more than novelties for the time being, inappropriate to the needs of professional photographers, but perhaps useful for guerrilla-style adventure travel on the Web.

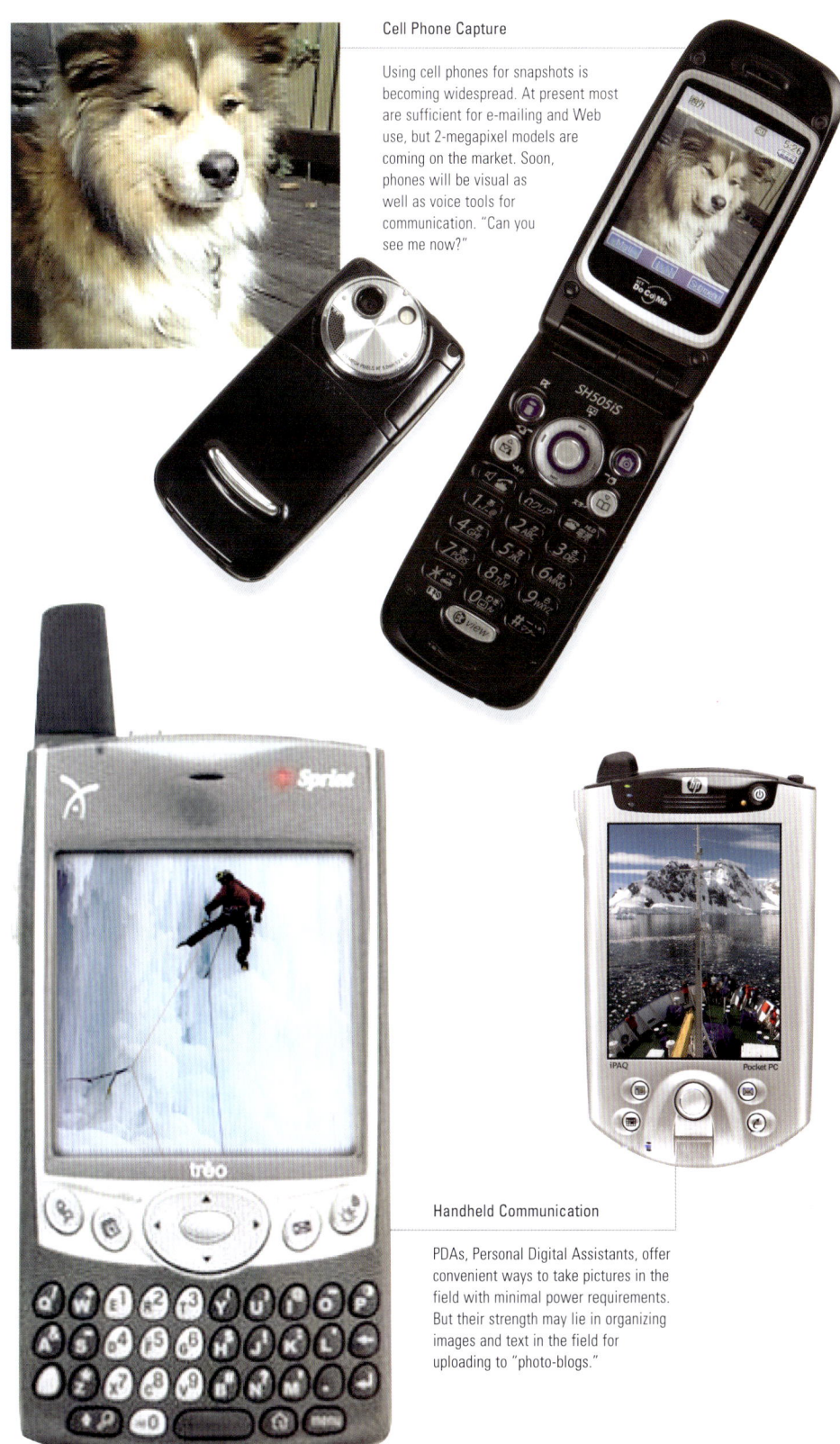

Cell Phone Capture

Using cell phones for snapshots is becoming widespread. At present most are sufficient for e-mailing and Web use, but 2-megapixel models are coming on the market. Soon, phones will be visual as well as voice tools for communication. "Can you see me now?"

Handheld Communication

PDAs, Personal Digital Assistants, offer convenient ways to take pictures in the field with minimal power requirements. But their strength may lie in organizing images and text in the field for uploading to "photo-blogs."

DIGITAL FILM STORAGE CARDS

The major difference in film storage between film and digital cameras is obvious: digital cameras don't use film, but instead store the image as computer-readable files on a compact data-storage medium. While there are many different styles of data storage cards (sometimes misleadingly called "digital film") currently on the market, and new ones are still being created, the leading professional cameras and many compact models use what are called Compact Flash or CF cards. These use solid-state or "flash memory" to store the zeros and ones that are the nub of digital photo information.

Other notable flash memory storage media include SmartMedia (SM) cards, Secure Digital (SD) cards, and the Sony Memory Sticks. SM cards are smaller and lighter than CF cards and are found in many consumer digital cameras. SD cards are tipped to become the next generation of storage used by professional digital SLR cameras. Some professional cameras, such as the Fuji Finepix 2, already accept these cards. SD cards have a small switch on the side that enables the card to be locked so that they cannot be erased. Sony Memory Sticks are incorporated in much Sony imaging equipment, including digital video as well as still-photo consumer cameras.

CF cards are the most common type used by pro digital photographers. Currently, there are two thicknesses of CF cards—Type I is 3.3mm thick and Type II is 5mm. Most CF-capable cameras accept both. CF cards range in capacity from 8MB up to 6GB. They continue to drop in price and their capacity still seems to be increasing.

Digital storage cards have a number of variables, not just in their overall capacity. The critical dimension for many action and adventure photographers is the speed at which the data can be written to the card. This is usually at write speeds of up to 10MB per second; faster write speeds are better for capturing bursts when shooting in continuous mode, up to 8 frames per second in the Nikon D2H, though more usually around 3 frames per second in most cameras. Some cards are now also performance-rated to a wider range of temperatures, such as SanDisk's Extreme cards, which can operate from –13 to +185° F (–25 to +85° C).

As cameras are able to capture larger and larger image files, so the demand for storage increases. However, many photographers prefer not to use the largest card available in case they lose all their work for that day or session; they regard swapping flash cards in the same way as changing rolls of film (though far less frequently). But changing cards regularly leaves part of the camera open to potential invasion of dust and moisture. There are some situations where it is more effective to use the

Memory Card Formats

A confusing array of flash cards competes to capture the digital market. Most common are, left to right, Secure Digital (SD), Smart Media (SM), and Compact Flash (CF) cards. The second row includes the Mini-SD, the XD, and the Memory Stick (MS) from Sony.

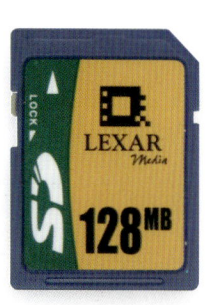
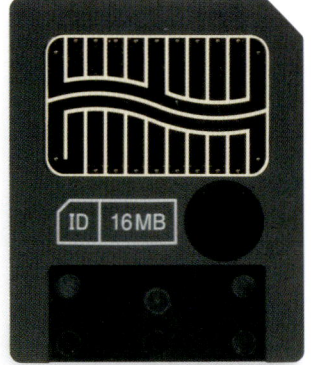
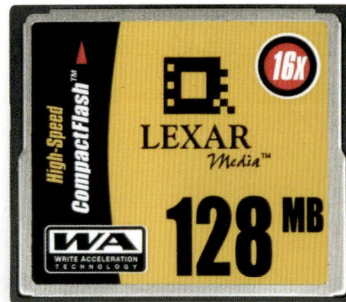
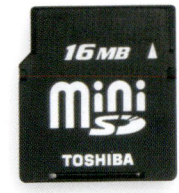
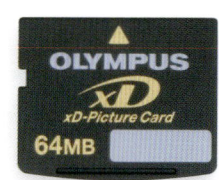
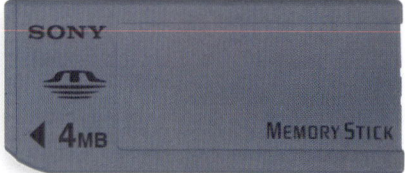

DIGITAL FILM STORAGE CARDS

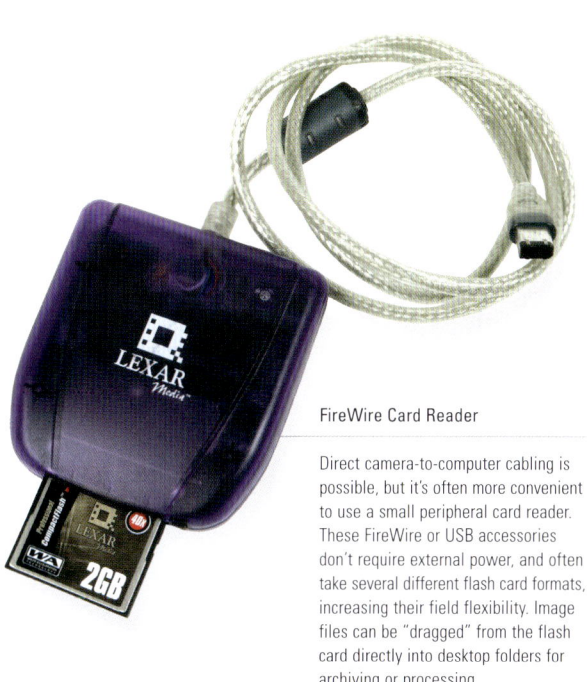

FireWire Card Reader

Direct camera-to-computer cabling is possible, but it's often more convenient to use a small peripheral card reader. These FireWire or USB accessories don't require external power, and often take several different flash card formats, increasing their field flexibility. Image files can be "dragged" from the flash card directly into desktop folders for archiving or processing.

hold larger amounts of data for large-megapixel cameras, but with the development of higher-capacity CF cards they are less popular.

Card Storage and Protection

Whatever form your memory card takes, securely storing and carrying them is a high priority. Lowepro, Tenba, and others make zippered wallet-like cases, and there are also a number of waterproof hard metal or plastic cases, some even designed to float.

There is always the possibility of losing or damaging cards, and occasionally cards become corrupted. There are a number of programs, such as SanDisk's Rescue-PRO, that can be used to try to rescue data from cards that have become corrupted. And there is now a memory card cleaning kit made by Norazza that cleans and polishes the card connectors on the camera.

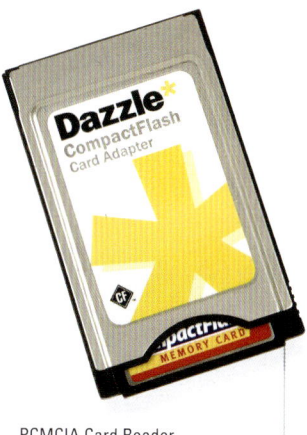

PCMCIA Card Reader

For laptop users it's often most convenient to use a PCMCIA card reader that accepts Compact Flash, Smart Media, or other memory card formats. These devices are rugged and cable-free, and hence invaluable for field use.

largest-capacity card possible, for instance in an underwater housing where you would otherwise have to surface to change cards.

Many digital cameras cannot use the large 2GB and 4GB compact flash cards. The problem is in the way that the file structure works. Cards of 1GB or less size use the older FAT structure, but larger sizes require FAT32. The FAT32 file type is currently supported only by the Canon EOS-1Ds, Canon EOS 10D, Canon EOS Digital Rebel, Kodak DCS Pro 14n, Kodak DCS Pro Back, Nikon D100, and Nikon D2H cameras.

Microdrives are tiny spinning hard disks with the same dimensions as CF cards, though again not all cameras that can use CF cards will accept Microdrives. Their main drawback is that they are relatively fragile because they have moving parts, so are not generally recommended for extreme field use. These were first made by IBM in a strategic business alliance with Hitachi. Mircodrives used to be important because they could

Organize Your Memory

Though digital memory cards can hold hundreds of images, keeping them in order can be a headache. Many digital photographers use card storage folders to keep multiple cards securely arranged so that they can easily grab a clean card when needed.

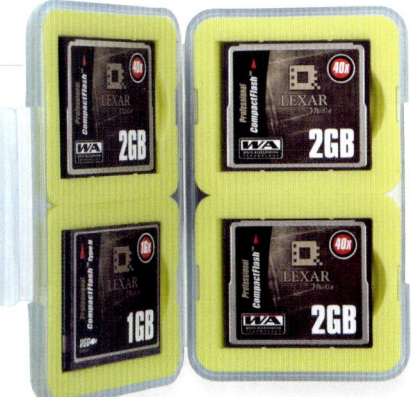

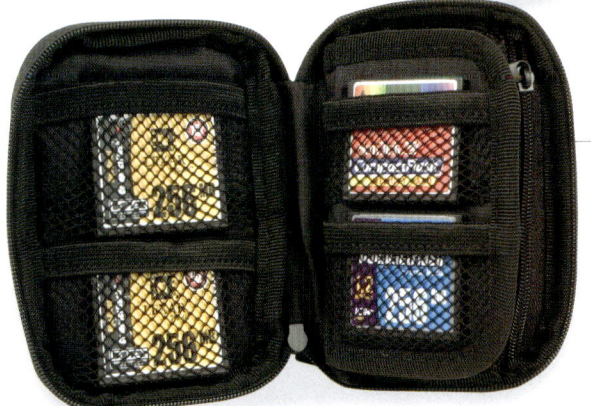

Flash Card Wallet

Card holders such as the "memory card wallets" from Lowepro let you keep cards handy so that you are never without additional storage on assignment. On short trips, such memory card wallets can become your entire archive system.

ACCESSORIES

There are items that will always be useful, and there are those that you need only at the end of the day, or only occasionally. Ultimately, the duration and seriousness of the undertaking will dictate many of your needs.

Flash

Most entry-level DSLR cameras have a built-in pop-up flash—useful as fill light, but limited by not having a very wide angle of illumination, or adequate power to illuminate further than 16½ feet (5m) or so. It may not work with bulky or faster wide-angle lenses that block the flash's light path. Most DSLRs (and compact digital cameras) have a hotshoe mount, even those with pop-up flash, so an external flash is the first accessory. For digital work the Nikon Speedlight SB800 flash is highly regarded, as is the Metz flash system. Some photographers find a digital flash meter such as the Gossen Digi Flash worth carrying for tricky lighting setups.

Camera Cleaning and Maintenance

Always carry a blower brush and microfiber cleaning cloth, but keep the rest of the kit at base camp. A special pen (even a clean pencil eraser) for keeping electrical contacts clean can rescue a dicey battery connection. As a contingency, you might want a CCD cleaning kit at base camp, as the CCD or CMOS imaging chip itself can get dust on it. Special pens and blowers are available but, as any speck will usually only show up in the sky of a shot, cleaning up the image in Photoshop is preferable to taking a chance on the delicate imaging chip.

Filters

Apart from an ultraviolet, or other protective filter, most serious digital photographers will have a polarizer to fit all lenses, and sometimes a set of neutral-density graduated filters as well, for dealing with scenery where there are large contrast ranges.

A Gray or White Card

For a custom white balance, carry a neutral gray or white card to assure accurate color tones.

Light Modifiers, Reflectors

A small collapsible reflector, with gold or silver on one side and white on the other side, comes in useful for either portrait or macro shooting.

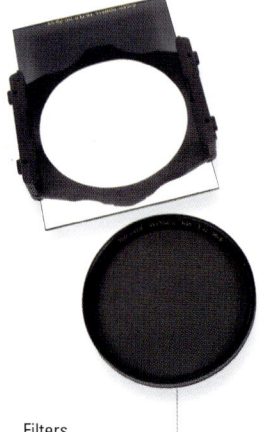

Filters

The Cokin filter system is a special effects modular series that lets users slip filters into a square holder, thus avoiding the requirement of duplicate filters for different sized lenses.

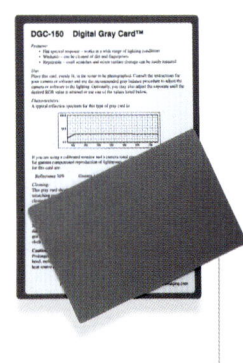

Gray Card

For correct exposure, use a gray card to take an "average" exposure reading. The 18 percent gray tone card is available in camera stores. It is also an extremely useful tool for setting a custom white balance.

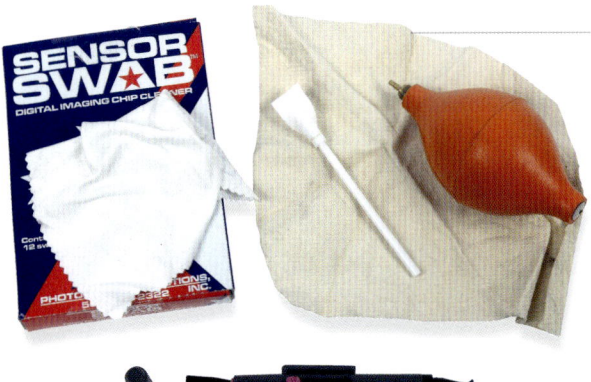

Keep It Clean

Keeping your camera dust-free is especially important in digital photography, where dust specks on the imaging chip can affect hundreds of shots. Special brushes and blowers are necessary to clean this highly delicate component.

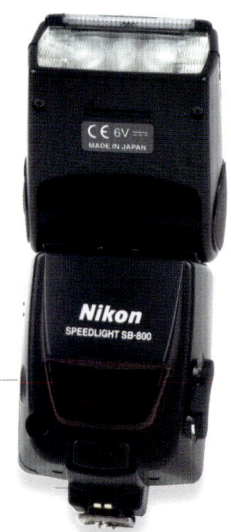

Flash Accessory

The built-in flash on most cameras needs to be supplemented with a standard automatic flash. Digital cameras have their own requirements for flash attachments, however, so test your camera's response.

Remote Triggers

Electronic or manual cable release is advisable for long lens and low-light shooting, but for more specialized work, a programmable digital wireless transceiver is best.

Tripods, Monopods

Supporting the camera is as essential for digital as it is for film. VR or IS lenses (*see page 30*) lessen the need for a tripod, but there are always times when there is no substitute for rigid support.

There are two main styles of heads: ball and pan tilt. Ball heads are faster to use, but those that support very long lenses are heavy. For static subjects, the Arca Swiss B1 is the most widely used ball head, but if saving weight is a priority, try the Linhof Profi II. For wildlife shooters the gimbaled-type design, such as the Wimberley Head where the camera can be panned and tilted effortlessly, is preferred. Serious photographers mix and match tripod legs and heads to suit the circumstances.

The choice in tripod legs is between metal and carbon fiber. The leading manufacturers, Gitzo and Bogen, make metal and carbon-fiber models. Extreme long-lens photogaphers favor lightweight carbon-fiber tripods, but they are very expensive and more fragile than metal ones. Carbon fiber is more comfortable to use in cold conditions because it does not conduct the heat. Three-section legs are sturdier than four-section models, but when collapsed the three-section is of course more bulky.

Monopods are best when you can't use a tripod. They are easy to transport and unobtrusive—great for stalking wildlife. These too come in both metal and carbon fiber. You often need a small ball head on a monopod to enable you to tilt the camera from vertical to horizontal. When the monopod is attached to a lens collar, this is not necessary.

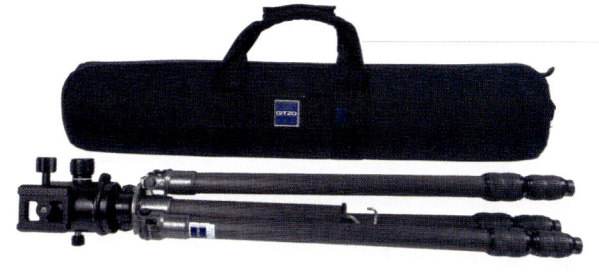

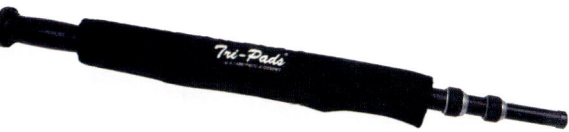

A mini lightweight tripod such as an Utrapod or an Ultraclamp is ideal where weight-saving is a premium and you are only using a compact camera. The clamp can be used to attach a DSLR to an ice-axe head.

A quick-release system for DSLR cameras and tripods is used by many pros. Really Right Stuff makes the leading camera plates and clamps that enable you to rapidly mount and dismount the camera on a support.

Panorama, QTVR Heads

For shooting panoramas or 360° landscape images, there are specalized tripod heads available that help you properly compose the overlapping series of images so that they can be seamlessly stitched together on the computer. Manfrotto (a subsidiary of Bogen), Kaidan, and Peace River Studios are the leading manufacturers, each with different models. This is a real specialty skill at the high end, but anyone can achieve remarkably good results with these dedicated heads and careful use of a regular tripod. Adding a leveling head between your tripod and panorama head helps speed the setup of a panoramic sequence.

Keep It Steady

A stable platform for photographs of action or in low light is crucial for sharp focus. Today's tripods and monopods are lightweight, portable, and strong, often being made of carbon-fiber material.

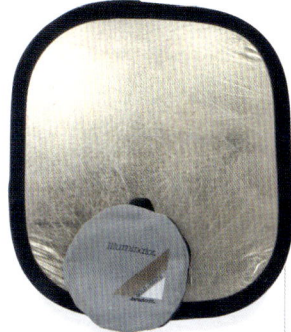

Reflected Light

Bringing along a collapsible reflector can help add professional-style lighting effects to a field shoot, with little added weight or bulk.

Remote Triggers

Using a remote to trigger your camera or flash has several advantages, ranging from synchronous firing to hands-free shutter release, which keeps camera vibration to a minimum. The old cable release (right) has now been replaced by more sophisticated electronic models (left).

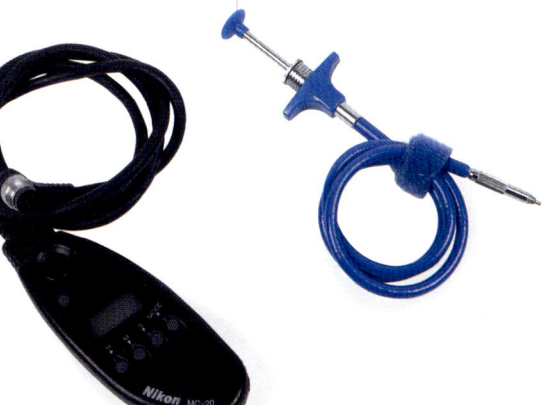

CARRYING CASES AND PROTECTION

When initially traveling to the location and then during the assignment, your primary aim is to protect your gear. Weight, bulk, and the level of protection are important but, on the actual shoot, weight and ease of access become critical: lens pouches and SLR camera cases made of neoprene are a good first line of protection, inside any other bag or case combinations.

Traveling

For transporting your photographic equipment, hard plastic, dustproof, waterproof cases are mandatory. The leading brand, Pelican, makes cases of all shapes and sizes, the larger ones with wheels and handles. Some smaller models incorporate a matching soft case inside, which doubles as a separate camera bag once you are on the job. The drawback to the larger cases is weight, which is mostly a problem when traveling by plane. I often carry a full-size Lowepro camera backpack inside a rolling Pelican case, but it is all too easy to go over the airline weight limit using this combination.

Now that it is more difficult to have locked cases when traveling by plane, thick plastic cable ties are an ideal way to keep cases sealed from quick hands during transit. Ask to be present when your bags are inspected and add these ties immediately after, under the watchful gaze of the baggage inspector. To minimize the likelihood of being ripped off, never advertise the fact that you are carrying expensive equipment. I often ship Pelican cases inside cheap, tatty-looking duffel bags.

Pelican cases are made of a durable "Ultra High Impact structural copolymer" material and are virtually watertight—you could use one for flotation if your boat goes down—and most models have a pressure-relief valve to equalize atmospheric pressure before you open the case. Seahorse manufactures similar cases in bright colors for cameras and computers.

Zero Halliburton, amongst others, makes aluminum cases, but be wary of metal cases as they are prone to corrosion. All feature gasketed closures to protect your camera from dust and moisture, scored foam inserts that you cut or shape to secure your gear in transit, and eggshell padding on the lid. Go for padded dividers for these hard cases rather than foam, because the latter tends to break down, and thin partitions disintegrate after a few trips.

For air travel, use a backpack or rolling camera case that can be hand-carried on the plane; one that also has a compartment for a laptop is the best way to transport all the basics that you

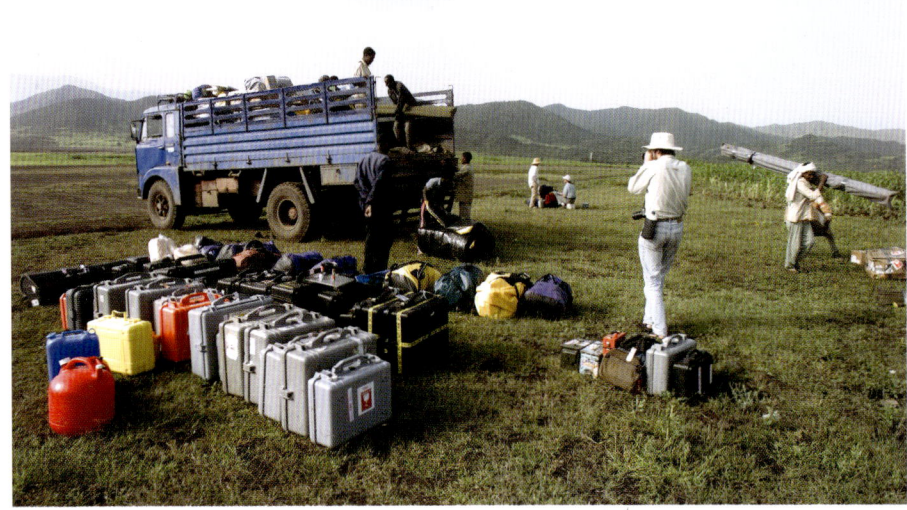

On Location in Ethiopia

At the road head for an expedition to make the first descent of the Tekeze River we had to make up porter loads of luggage for the next stage of the journey. The combined gear for an eight-person film crew, a Web-reporting team of five, and support staff added up to a full truck load of rafts, dry bags, and Pelican cases.

CARRYING CASES AND PROTECTION 39

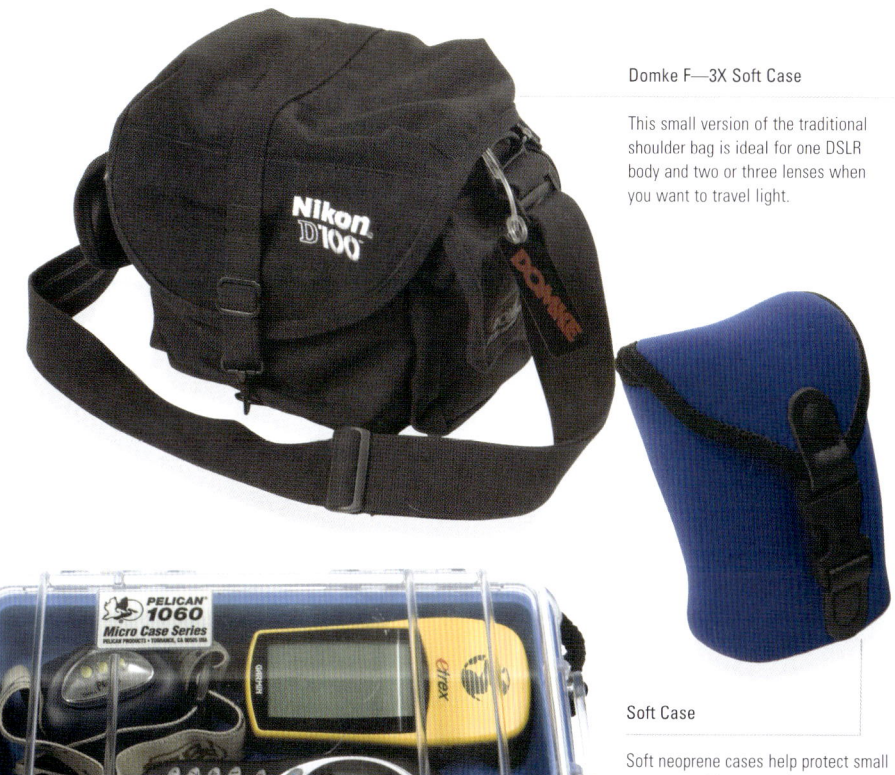

Domke F—3X Soft Case

This small version of the traditional shoulder bag is ideal for one DSLR body and two or three lenses when you want to travel light.

Soft Case

Soft neoprene cases help protect small cameras and lenses, and can be worn on a belt or attached to a larger bag for ease-of-access.

See-Through Storage

The Pelican 1060 is one of a series of durable, watertight cases—"dustproof, crushproof, and submersible"—that keep gear dry and secure, while simultaneously allowing quick recognition of container contents.

Lowepro Pelican

The combination of a waterproof Pelican case and a removable Lowepro interior soft case is a winning one for expeditions where dust, water, or rugged means of travel are involved.

Pelican Micro Case

These lightweight, totally waterproof small cases are ideal for protecting fragile electronics and small digital cameras in wet and dusty conditions.

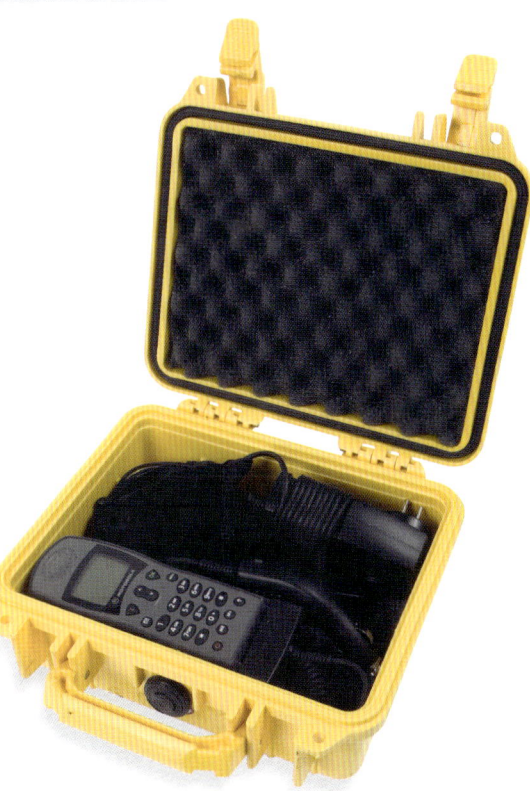

need for digital photography. This way, if your checked luggage gets lost, you still get to work. Recent allowances permit photographers to hand-carry two camera bags on flights, in recognition of their value to our profession.

For security's sake, a series of digital photographs of each bag or case, open and closed, can be useful to show to lost-luggage offices and police to help speed the recovery of stray items, or at the very least make insurance claims less of a headache. Certainly carry an inventory, including serial numbers of all your equipment, with your passport and other valuable paperwork.

Working

As protecting your gear goes hand-in-hand with ease of access, a soft case with a padded shoulder strap, or a backpack shoulder harness, is usually the preferred means of carrying your camera. Lowepro, Domke, Tamrac, and Tenba are the leading brands, all designed with multiple pockets and compartments. Lowepro is often the professional's favorite—their All Weather (AW) models have sprayproof covers that are deployed from a hidden pouch to envelop the bag. Another Lowepro line, DryZone fully waterproof backpacks, makes an excellent option for water-based extreme digital photographers.

A padded soft case that can be carried on your belt is the best way to carry smaller compact cameras. This keeps your second camera out of the way, but handy.

Kayakers have a special range of dedicated dry bags that attach to the deck of their boats; water sports photographers can use these as well. A dry bag inside a regular backpack is yet another method or protecting gear in very wet conditions, and waterproof camera housings of flexible or stiff plastic are available from Ewa-Marine for a wide variety of camera bodies.

POWER SUPPLIES

Batteries

Batteries are one of the biggest bugbears of shooting digitally in remote locations. Spare internal camera batteries are a must on every day's shoot. You want to have several backup batteries for a full day's work—say three or four, depending on their age and condition and how much you will be shooting.

Where conserving power is a priority, don't use the camera's LCD to preview images: nothing uses up power as fast as the preview or review mode. Keep batteries warm inside your coat or with a chemical hot pack when you're not using them, to extend their life in cold conditions. Cold and heavy use will tax even the best supply of dedicated batteries.

Being able to recharge batteries each evening is ideal for extended periods of intensive shooting, but not always possible. On a summit bid on Everest, for example, where saving weight is paramount, other strategies have to be employed, which may mean limiting the number of photographs you take, and making each one count. Where weight is less of a consideration than reliable power, say on an extended river trip, an external camera battery pack, such as the Quantum Turbo or UnderDog flash battery pack, is a good idea.

A plentiful supply of lithium AA batteries for cameras and flashes is a cheap power backup. They are expensive compared to regular alkaline AAs, but lightweight and do not lose their power in the cold. For some cameras, such as the Nikon D100, you can buy an additional battery holder that enables the camera to be powered by six lithium AA batteries—a huge advantage for very remote work where even a solar recharger is not an option.

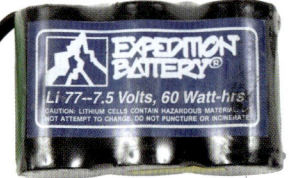

Expedition Battery

Though not rechargeable, Automated Media Systems' rugged power supplies offer lithium-based power for computer, video, and film equipment in harsh, remote conditions. This 3-cell model puts out 7.5v for 60 watt hours, and weighs 12 ounces (340g).

Generators

A small generator is the standard way of powering base-camp communications, battery charging, and handling other media needs. This means finding the right fuel and transporting it—both tasks can be difficult in the Third World. Small Honda generators in conjunction with a sealed car battery are a good system. The generators can be used to directly run appliances that require 120/240 mains power and, because they also have a 12v DC outlet, to run computers and charge camera batteries. With the generator running, you can also simultaneously recharge a 12v sealed lead-acid battery in order to power devices that need to run for long periods, without having to keep a noisy, thirsty generator going all the time. The Honda EU1000 (29 pounds/13kg) produces 1000 watts, and the EU2000 (46.3 pounds/21kg) 2000 watts—more than adequate for most expedition needs.

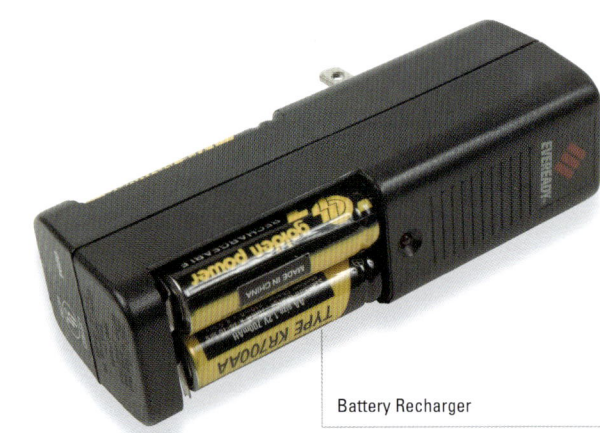

Battery Recharger

Most electronic equipment can be powered with rechargeable AA batteries, so having a reliable recharger and a good number of spare batteries is essential.

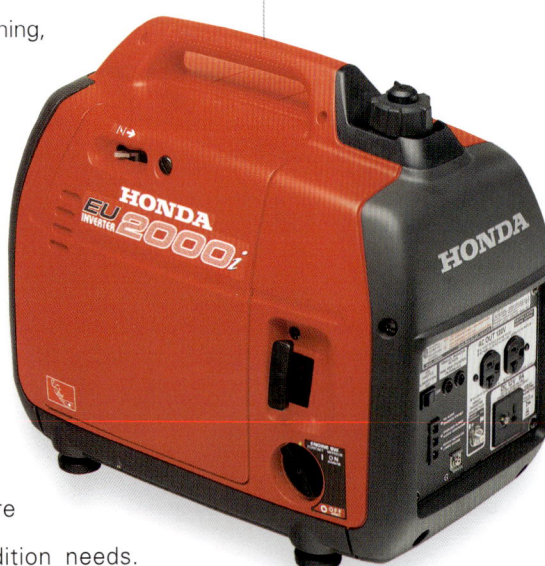

Gas Generator

Something has to recharge the rechargeables, and a gas-powered generator at base camp is invaluable. The Honda EU2000 promises low fuel use, reduced noise, and stable output in a generator weighing less than 50 pounds (23kg).

Both have AC and DC outlets and are relatively economical and quiet. Depending on the load, they can run for 4–15 hours per tank of petrol.

At altitude, generators need special air-intake jets to perform properly. Use a relatively long extension cord to help isolate the noisy generator from the rest of the camp. Make sure you filter the fuel through a chamois if there is any doubt as to its cleanliness; many a generator has failed due to dirty fuel.

Solar Panels

Solar panels can be a viable means of powering a mobile or base-camp communications setup, providing you have enough sunlight and enough panels. There are lots of details that need to be worked through to get this equation right, and getting advice and equipment from specialized suppliers, such as Stuart Cody's Automated Media Systems or ExplorersWeb, is advisable. Automated Media Systems specializes in photovoltaic solar electric systems, useful for recharging and powering equipment in isolated environments. Their models range in size from backpack kits all the way up to permanent base-camp modules, utilizing 10–30-watt solar panels sized from 17.5 x 10.5 inches (44 x 27cm) and weighing as little as 2.6 pounds (1.2kg) per panel.

If recharging is going to be out of the question, then SO2 lithium-powered Expedition Batteries can provide eight times the energy of standard NiCads. Relatively light and compact, although they cannot be recharged or recycled, Expedition Batteries are a solution of last resort, but a solution nonetheless.

It is always a good idea to have a backup battery with you, even if you are running solar panels. The panels can be used to charge a sealed lead-acid car battery.

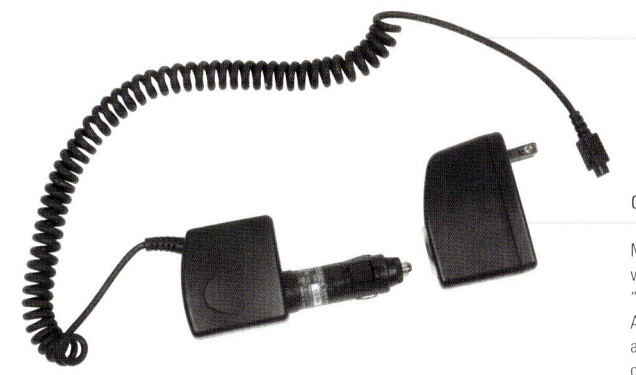

Recharging a battery with a portable wind turbine is also a possibility in some locations. This is an evolving field, and keeping in contact with the suppliers listed above will keep you up to date.

Other valuable accessories in the power department are lots of spare cables and distribution boards, and several different-sized portable inverters that convert 12v to 110 or 240v AC, depending on the appliances you are using. Silicon rubber-coated cables stay flexible in the cold. A combined voltage regulator/circuit breaker is essential to avoid power spikes that can result in blowing up computers and other sensitive equipment. Remember that a reliable power source is one of the key components of successful digital photography.

Outlet Adapters

Many digital cameras can be recharged with 12-volt adapters that plug into car "cigarette lighters" and similar outlets. Always take the AC charger as well, and a multitude of inverter/power options is good insurance.

Solar Panels

At Everest Base Camp the geodesic design of North Face tents is put to good use as support for an array of solar panels. Available sunlight enters into any equation about their usefulness, as does their weight (30 pounds/14kg for a 20-watt panel) and the mobility of the expedition.

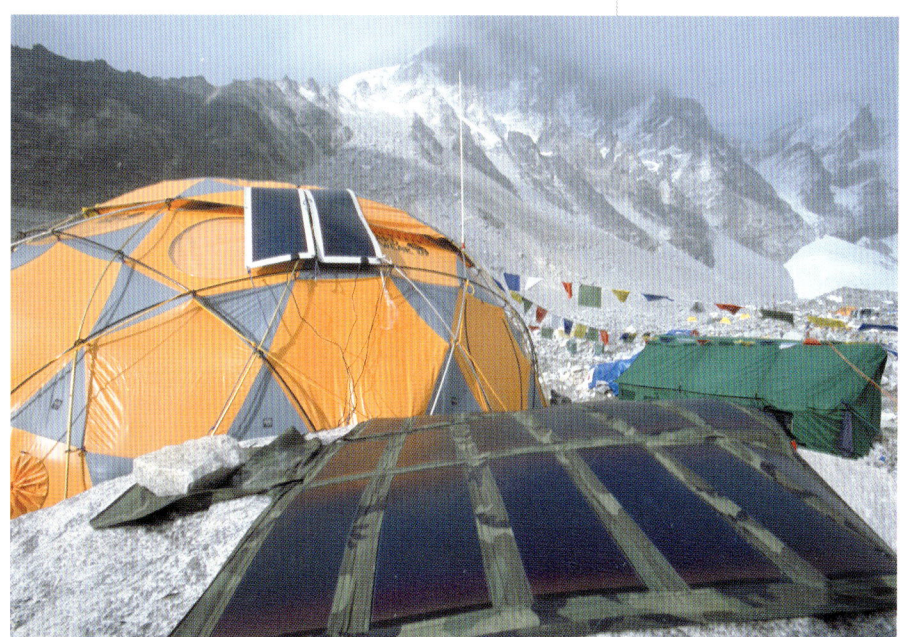

HARDWARE

Having two ways of doing everything on an important expedition or major assignment is more than just prudent, it is vital. Redundancy should be the motto of any extreme photographer. This includes data processing and storage.

Field Computers

Any serious digital photographer will have a powerful home computer system, and regular backups of image data on CDs, remote hard drives, ZIP disks, and so on. Computers that go on the road must be rugged and powerful, and backing up data regularly should become a habit.

For most fieldwork, a fast, reliable laptop is essential. Having plenty of RAM for processing the images is helpful, as is a relatively large internal hard drive. Being able to burn backup CDs is extremely valuable, as is of course some means of downloading your camera's flash memory into your computer, either through a dedicated USB card reader or PCMCIA adapter. Some laptops even have built-in flash card slots—the Apple PowerBooks take a CF card, whilst many Sony Vaio models have Memory Stick (MS) slots.

Many photographers and imaging specialists are strong advocates of the Mac system, and in most environmental conditions Apple PowerBooks and even iBooks work as well as PCs. But for very extreme situations there are more options with PCs, and some models running Windows OS are built to withstand enormous punishment. The expedition standard in this niche is the proven Panasonic Toughbook series.

The Toughbook 29 has a touch screen, which can be very handy for some operations where you are wearing gloves, and the screen is designed to be readable out of doors. The backlit keyboard is very useful when working at night or in the dim light of a tent. The computer is extremely well built and splashproof.

Other brands of laptops built to military specifications include the Terralogic Toughnote series and GoBook MAX from Itronix. These are typically more expensive than consumer laptops, as they are built with cast aluminum chassis, waterproofing, protective rubber port plugs, easily removable hard drives, and other features. If the expected conditions are going to be extreme, then for peace of mind it is cheap insurance to have the most rugged system available. That said, many of the embedded reporters in the recent Iraq war simply used IBM ThinkPads or Fujitsu LifeBooks enclosed in plastic when out in the field.

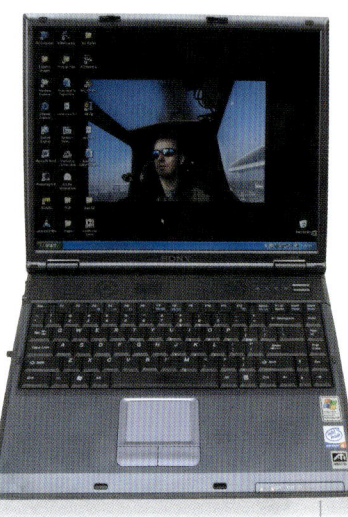

Sony Vaio

Sony manufactures a media-savvy computer line called the Vaio, which offers ascending levels of hardware and software capabilities. Their laptops are generally reliable PCs, though for truly extreme conditions more rugged solutions are advised.

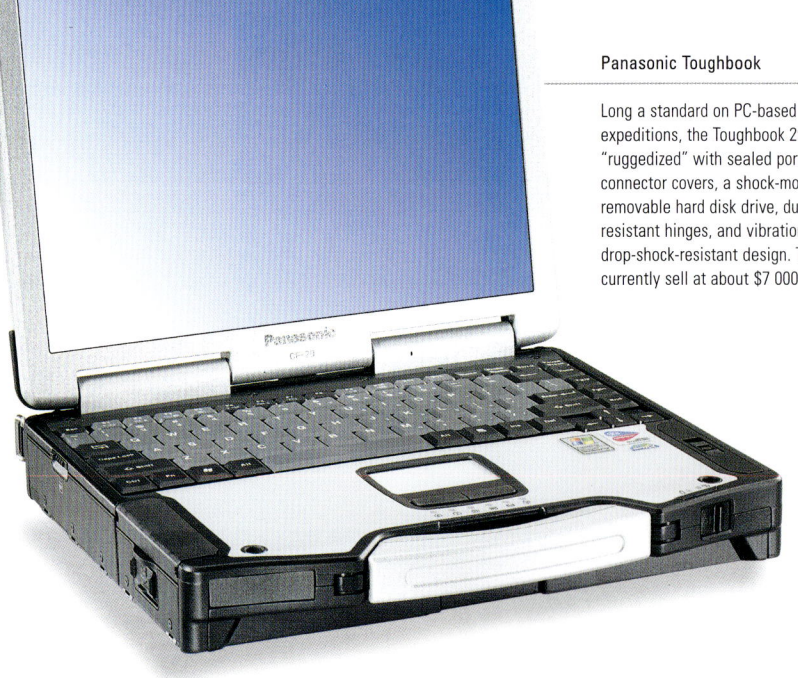

Panasonic Toughbook

Long a standard on PC-based expeditions, the Toughbook 29 is "ruggedized" with sealed port and connector covers, a shock-mounted removable hard disk drive, dust-resistant hinges, and vibration and drop-shock-resistant design. They currently sell at about $7 000.

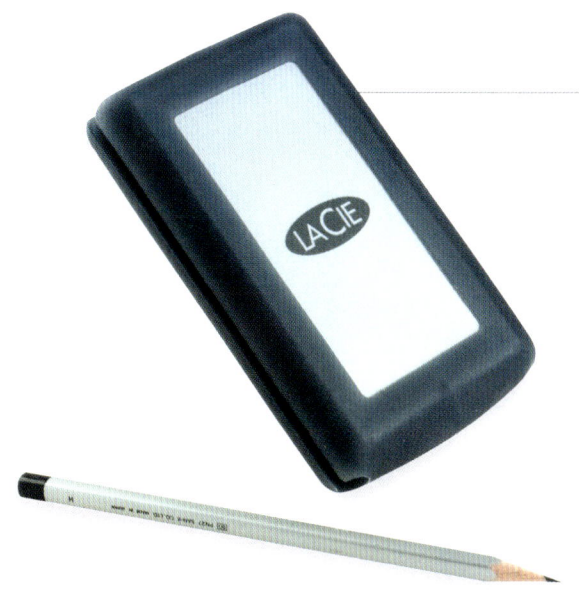

LaCie Pocket Drive

Portable storage devices such as the LaCie Pocket Drive can hold up to 80GB in a compact handheld unit. USB 2.0 and IEEE 1394 inputs make it easy to hot-swap from different computers, download media archives and therefore free up disk space.

are becoming increasingly common. If your laptop doesn't have a floppy (A:) drive, then bring along an external USB one just in case.

PDAs are fast becoming part of the working photo-journalist's kit and may be the only computer available on an extreme assignment or expedition. Some of these can be used for editing and transmitting to a satellite or cell phone via Bluetooth or IR. The HP iPAQ running Microsoft Windows Mobile 2003, for example, is ideal for keeping blogs updated during a lightweight expedition.

Other Hardware
Backup Drives

No matter what system you take, it is always advisable to have a backup. As swapping a hard drive ranges from straightforward (as on the Toughbook) to difficult (on most consumer models), it is best to have a separate support computer if at all possible. At the very least, a spare hard drive fully loaded with all the software needed, or backup software on CDs, prevents loss of crucial programs in the field. Repair utilities such as DiskWarrior (for Macs) and Norton Utilities (for PCs) can help you debug your system and even rebuild the computer's entire hard drive.

In many parts of the world, particularly Asia and South America, "cyber cafés" are a viable backup means of transmitting images and e-mails for an assignment. Typically these use older PC machines that only accept floppy disks, but CD drives

iBook with CD Burner

Apple's 12-inch iBook offers moderate performance with rugged aluminum alloy casing, free of protruding doors, latches, or levers. Video and audio are on board and a wireless card can be added. Larger models add FireWire, DVI, and other features. Take an external floppy drive in extreme locations, in case you find that you need to transfer files at a cyber café that only has an ancient PC.

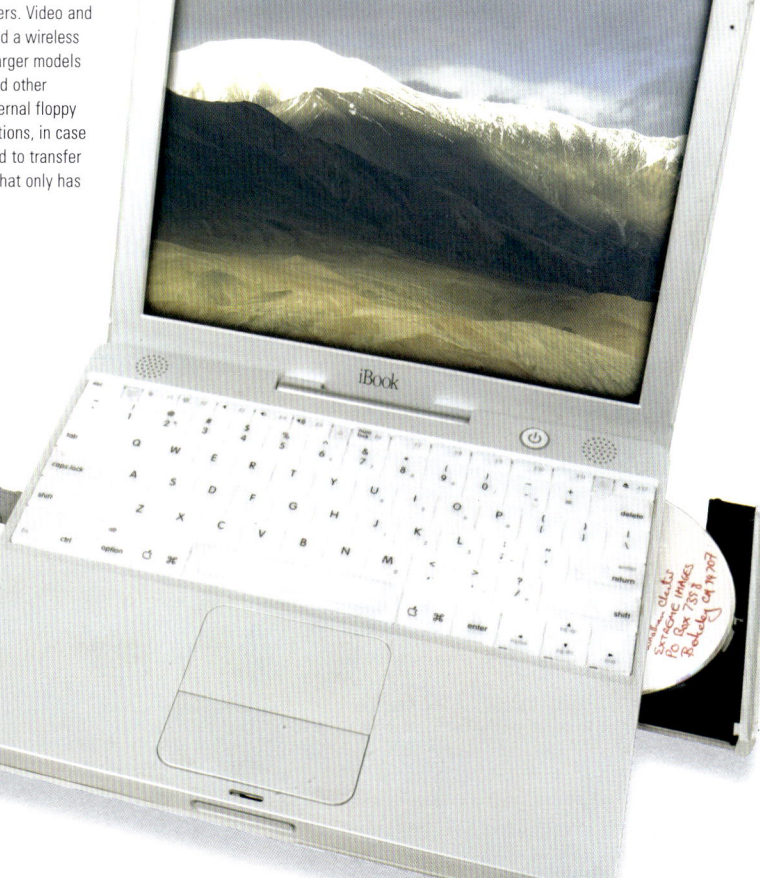

FIELD STORAGE

Carrying a large number of flash memory cards is one way of handling the issue of storage, but after a day of shooting with a camera that captures images at 11 megapixels or more, it becomes impractical. There are now a number of dedicated portable devices that can download a digital storage card to a small hard drive, and some that will even burn directly to a CD-RW. One of the best devices seems to be the SmartDisk FlashTrax, which will download images from a flash memory card to either a 40 or 80GB USB 2.0 hard drive, and allows image review on the LCD screen. (The former leader in this field, the Digital Wallet from Minds@Work, has unfortunately gone out of business.)

Long-Term Storage

Storage of digital media on the road is a necessary chore, but with the right equipment it can be relatively straightforward. No storage medium is permanent, but backing up to good-quality CD-ROMs and DVDs is for the moment the best method. CD-RWs are not recommended as they are much less stable than CD-Rs.

External hard drives are today's preference for backing up in the field. These drives are becoming increasingly affordable, and will connect to your computer either through USB 2.0 or IEEE 1394 (FireWire) cabling. They do often require a separate power supply, however, which may not always be available.

The ability to burn any flash memory card direct to CD-R is now also possible using the Apacer Disc Steno CP200. Its multi-session mode enables you to burn multiple cards to a single CD, and another function enables you to burn 1GB cards and above to multiple CDs.

Power Adapters

When working away from a reliable power supply during an assignment, a spare computer battery is always useful. Laptops should have transformers capable of charging from a 12v power supply; always take the AC charger as well, for when you are able to jack into mains power en route. This can also be used with an inverter off 12 volts, if your 12v charger stops working. Make sure that you check all voltages for compatibility before plugging anything in. Many Asian and European countries have 240v circuits, and most laptops will work fine on those circuits. When traveling, always be sure to bring a complete supply of adapter plugs.

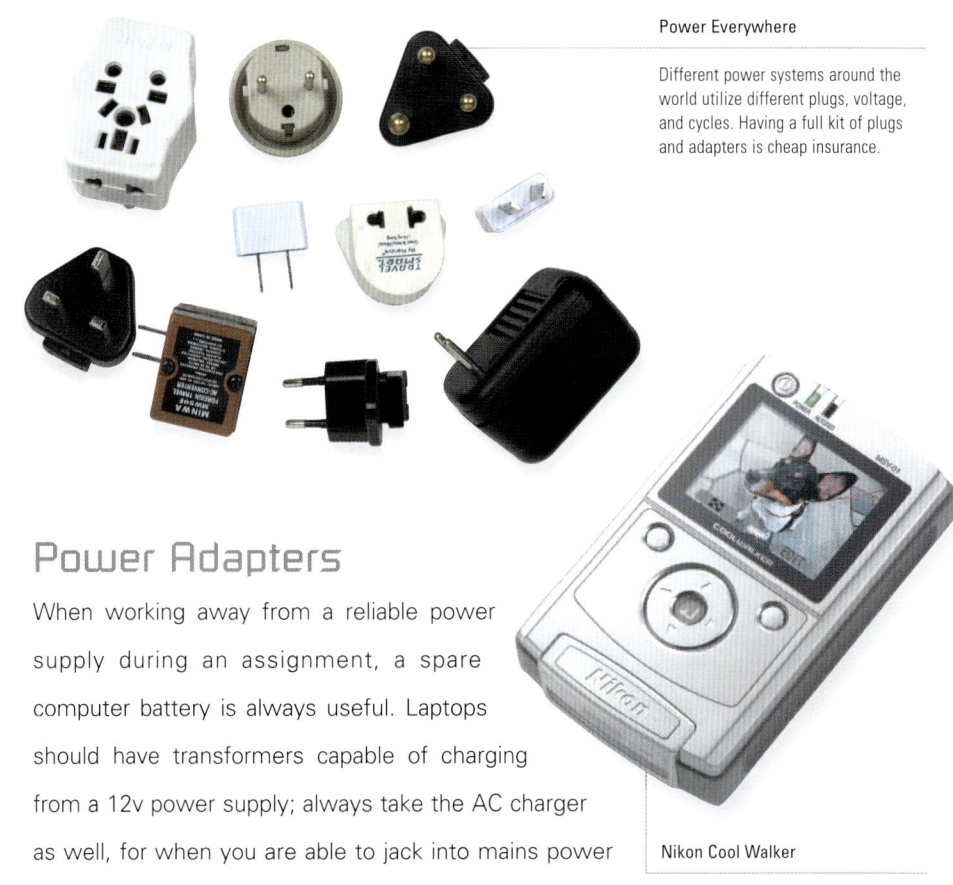

Power Everywhere

Different power systems around the world utilize different plugs, voltage, and cycles. Having a full kit of plugs and adapters is cheap insurance.

Nikon Cool Walker

This could serve as a portable backup for photographers. It includes a 2.5-inch LCD display, a 30GB hard-drive, a USB 2.0 interface, and a CF card slot. It supports JPG, RAW, TIFF, and QuickTime files for playback and review. A rechargeable Li-ion battery and charger are included.

Disk Steno

The Apacer Disc Steno is a portable, battery-operated, multi-session CD recorder that's useful for transferring image files or other data from flash memory cards to CD-R or CD-RW discs without a computer.

SOFTWARE

Any digital photographer traveling with a computer will want software to handle all the steps of digital workflow, from capture to viewing, editing, cataloging, captioning, manipulation, burning, compression, perhaps even networking and transmission. Then there are the software programs for troubleshooting the cards and computers themselves.

DSLR camera manufacturers have proprietary programs, such as Nikon View, Canon RemoteCapture, and Kodak Photo Desk, for ingesting images, and there are several good third-party programs: Capture One is cross-platform for Canon and Nikon prosumer cameras. Photo Mechanic from Camera Bits enables you to batch rename files as you import them and simultaneously make a copy on the hard drive and an external drive. Others are ACDSee, MacBibble, DigitalPro, iView MediaPro, and new ones are being introduced all the time.

Adobe Photoshop, the industry standard image-manipulation program, can be used to import RAW images. Its lighter version, Photoshop Elements, has sufficient power and features to do most of the work needed in the field. Photoshop is built for either Mac or PC operating systems, though on the PC, more affordable programs like Ulead PhotoImpact and Microsoft's Picture It! have their following.

In regard to sending and storing your images, on the Mac Fetch and Transmit are two reliable FTP programs, and Stuffit is the standard for reducing and expanding files. Roxio Toast is the premier burning software, though using OS X on the Mac you can burn from the desktop. For the PC, Ipswitch WS_FTP Pro is hands-down the choice file-transfer program. WinZip can be useful for bundling a dispatch image set into a single folder, but image-compression programs as such do not save much space when applied to a JPEG, which is already a compressed image format.

Dedicated expedition blogging software is also available. ExplorersWeb's PC-based Contact 3.0 enables you to take a picture, write a dispatch, and upload both directly to a website in a matter of seconds. WebExpeditions.net has a similar service, X-Journal Remote.

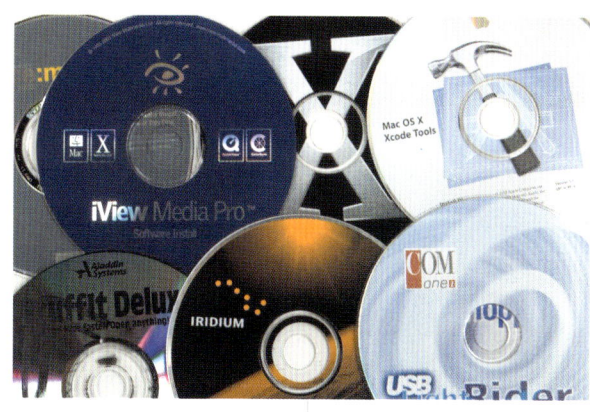

Backup Software

Don't forget to carry installation software (including the operating system) with you, especially if you will be out in the field for any length of time. Programs do fail and computers do crash, and rebuilding your workspace may become necessary.

Picture It!

Consumer-level photo management software, such as Microsoft's Picture It!, builds on user familiarity with the Windows interface while providing simple tools for image manipulation.

Digital Light Box

Image browsing and archiving programs, such as Photo Mechanic, rely on the familiar "light box" metaphor for viewing and organizing images. Photo Mechanic is used in both PC and Mac environments, and has proven extremely useful in workflow solutions for large, multi-photographer projects.

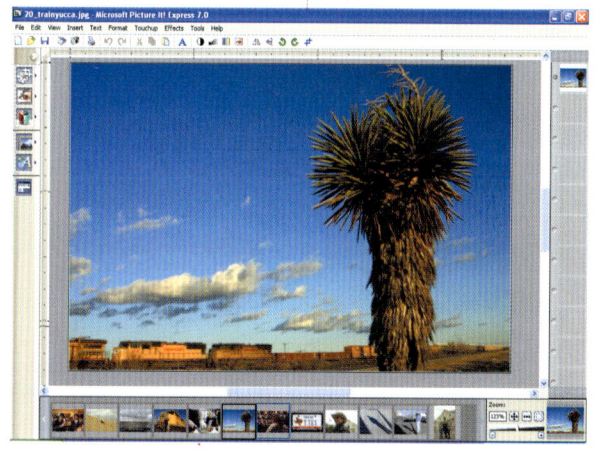

COMMUNICATIONS

When you are in the field for an extended period, you often want to communicate with your home, your office, or a client. Today, this can be accomplished with just a cell phone from a surprising number of locations, especially using the GSM system so widespread in much of the world. If, however, you want to send e-mails, high-quality images, video, or broadcast-level audio, you need a more sophisticated communication system. This means using one of several satellite networks in orbit around the Earth.

There are two main systems, Inmarsat and Iridium; between them they cover much of the globe and offer communications solutions that can serve almost any purpose. Inmarsat has a set of four geo-stationary satellites that orbit 21,750 miles (35,600km) above the equator, while Iridium relies on a network of 66 satellites that circle the globe in LEO, or Low Earth Orbit. For those who say "It's not rocket science," digital explorers are fond of saying that it is.

Inmarsat

Inmarsat (International Maritime Satellite) has been the prime system of remote communication for many years. Its four high-altitude satellites cover most of the globe except for the very extreme (polar) latitudes. Their satellites support two main phone systems, for voice and data traffic. These are the mini-M phone, which has relatively poor voice quality and low-speed data (and has largely been supplanted by the Iridium system), and the M4/GAN (Global Area Network) system, which is a voice and data system, and can transmit data at ISDN speed (64Kbps). It makes use of so-called spot-beam technology. There is also the Inmarsat C store-and-forward system, but this does not support voice traffic and is mainly used by yachts for sending position reports and e-mail.

There are five different manufacturers of the Mobile Satcom Units (MSU), the most popular models being the Nera World Communicator and the Thrane & Thrane Capsat. These MSUs are expensive (roughly $9,000 to $10,000) and relatively heavy (in the region of 8–11 pounds/ 4–5kg), so they are best suited for vehicle and base-camp settings.

You need an ISDN connector to use the M4 sat-phone with a computer. The USB Light Rider 128K from COM One is small and easy-to-use, but works best with a PC. Connecting to a Mac is possible, but it is more difficult.

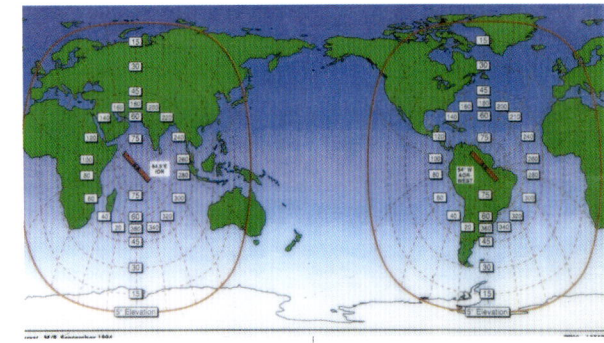

GAN Footprint

The area of coverage from the two Global Area Network satellites, in geostationary earth orbit. The satellites shown are for the Inmarsat M4 System, and utilize spot-beam technology to concentrate service in high usage areas on land.

Light Rider

The USB Light Rider 128K from COM One allows connection to the Internet at the high speed of 128Kbps. Using the Ethernet port, the Light Rider passes signals to an M4 satellite phone, allowing data transfer via "direct-dial" to the home server.

Regional Bgan

Compact, inexpensive, and effective, the Regional Bgan unit is poised to become the international standard for digital satellite communications. A satellite IP modem, it has USB, Ethernet, and Bluetooth interfaces, connects at ISDN speed, and weighs just 3.3 pounds (1.5kg).

Earth to Orbit

The M4 communications setup in action. From the base camp in Chiapas, Mexico, a field producer sets up the Thurya M4 satphone, preparing to point its fold-out antenna toward the satellite location. A laptop can then use the satphone's data port to make connection with a home server.

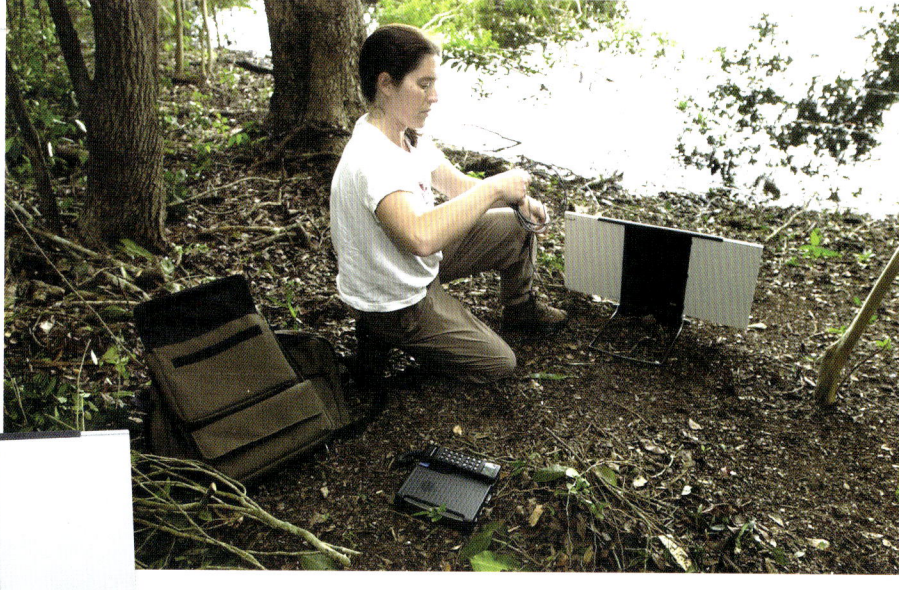

The most recent advance in satellite phone technology of note, is the Inmarsat Regional Bgan IP modem. This is a very lightweight (3 pounds/1.4kg) and high transmission speed (144Kbps) data-only laptop-sized device that makes use of the existing Thuraya satellite system to provide coverage to 99 countries. At around $1,500, this is a very affordable system for data communication, as long as you are located in the area that it covers—primarily in Europe and Asia. The Regional Bgan modem was used extensively by journalists and photographers in the 2003 Iraq war, and it is ideal for a base-camp situation.

You can connect a computer or a PDA to this modem by using a USB, Bluetooth, or Ethernet port, and the high-speed data link allows for Web surfing, e-mail, and FTP transmission. The lack of a voice connection is mitigated by the use of instant messaging systems, or by the use of a backup Iridium phone. This system is an always-on connection where you pay according to the megabytes that are transferred.

Still, sending high-resolution photos back to magazines for print reproduction can be expensive, as satellite communication costs add up fast. Transmission costs can range from $1.50 per minute for a simple Iridium phone call to $18 per minute for data over the Inmarsat ISDN speed M4/GAN. A one-megabyte file costs around $50 to transmit. There are, however, monthly pay plans that include equipment purchase or rental and the airtime. All of the Inmarsat phones can be used with or without a SIM card to help manage billing when there are multiple users. It often makes more sense to rent the more expensive satellite phones, unless you are going to be using them regularly or for a long period of time.

In some countries, such as Pakistan and Nepal, you need a permit to operate a satellite phone. If you are on a high-profile expedition doing webcasting, this is a necessary burden; your visibility means that government security officials will be watching sooner or later. Better to get the liaison officer on your side from the outset than have to explain what you're doing in a sensitive border region with high-tech communications equipment during the expedition.

Iridium

The Iridium satellite system has become one of the mainstays of remote expedition communications. It is based around a constellation of 66 Low Earth Orbit (LEO) satellites that rapidly circle the planet, "handing off" the signal on any given call from one satellite to the next as it comes within range.

The phone has to be used out in the open, as you need to see both horizons so that the call gets handed off efficiently or it will get dropped. Therefore it has limitations in mountainous areas, but because the satellites are just 485 miles (780km) high, there is less delay (latency) in the signal than there is with the Inmarsat system (where the satellites are over 133,800 feet higher). At sea there is seldom any such problem, especially if you are using an external fixed-mast antenna, which enables you to make calls inside shelter away from the weather. The Motorola 9505 handset is relatively rugged and compact and costs around $1,300. It is also the only system that can be used for data and voice transmission in the Antarctic and the Arctic, and proved effective enough to provide Will Cross with coverage throughout his 630-mile (1,015-km) ski to the South Pole early in 2003. The phone can be recharged from a 12v source as well as a solar panel; spare batteries are also available. Using the optional data kit, the phone can be used to send and receive e-mail and low-resolution photos at 2.4Kbps using the Windows platform. It can also receive text (Short Message Service, or SMS) messages from the Web or another phone, and there is an optional voicemail service. There is also a very compact Iridium pager, the 9501 model.

There are other systems that target a specific region. The Thuraya satellite sits in a geo-stationary orbit over the Middle East and has coverage that extends from Europe and North Africa to the Himalaya, and is the foundation of the Bgan system (*see page 47*). Globestar covers the US, Europe, North Asia, and South America. Asia Cellular Satellite (ACeS) has one satellite that covers most of Asia, and has the lightest phone that can be used on the GSM network with one antenna; shifting to a larger antenna enables it to reach the satellite for global communications. Clearly not all satellite systems are equal in terms of their coverage and their features.

Two-Way Communications

Communication between individuals and teams in remote locations is another challenge to consider. One team may be out in the field, on a summit ascent for instance, while a support team may be holding down at base camp. Here, two-way radios are the most appropriate, and there are no transmission charges. For very short distances (about 2 miles/3km) the Family Radio Service (FRS) handhelds are an option. Inexpensive models or kids' "walkie-talkies" use only one channel, but more expensive models use up to 14 channels for more sophisticated purposes. While FRS units are relatively inexpensive and don't

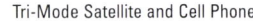

Tri-Mode Satellite and Cell Phone

The Globalstar 1600 offers voice and data communications worldwide through three separate technologies, including Qualcomm's Code Division Multiple Access digital technology and North American analog for cellular service, and Globalstar for satellite service.

Safe and Secure

Keeping your satphone in a Pelican case protects it from moisture, dirt, and falls. This kit from Remote Satellite Systems includes the Motorola 9505 satphone with built-in modem, charger, batteries, cigarette-lighter adapter, and case.

require a license, they seldom have the range that the manufacturers claim. Some more expensive FRS models have GPS built in, such as the Garmin Rino 120, which retails for about $250.

For more reliable and longer distance, but still line-of-sight communications (up to 10 miles/16km under ideal conditions, or 25 miles/40km with a fixed-mount antenna), handheld Very High Frequency (VHF) radios are ideal, with models starting at around $100. For communicating over long distances with ships and other emergency services in places such as Antarctica, a compact High Frequency (HF) radio is another option. HF waves can bounce off the atmosphere and reach ranges of 1,860 miles (3,000km), making them far more valuable for big expeditions. They are more expensive, however, and can be affected by weather conditions, time of day, and other limiting factors.

Tracking

If you are out in truly remote conditions, some means of tracking your location can be quite important. GPS (Global Positioning System) units have become quite common over the past few years, and can help you locate your position to within a few yards. However, this information is only useful for you; if your team has lost track of you, then they won't know where you are unless you have an emergency beacon of some sort.

For very lightweight expeditions, especially in the ocean and polar regions, the main emergency and tracking system is the 1000g Argos TAT 3. This was first developed for tracking migrating wildlife by satellite. Two satellites pick up signals two to seven times an hour, and these can then be transmitted to a home base via a simple e-mail message. Using a system of 16 pre-arranged codes, teams can communicate basic information about health and safety with a minimum of weight and fuss. These compact rugged units will work down to −40° F (−40° C), and have a battery that will last for 60 days (even longer if they are only switched on in the evening). The more compact Adventure Beacon weighs only 21 ounces (600g) and has 10 message positions. These and many other such "survival kit" items can be rented from ExplorersWeb.

The Emergency Personal Locator Beacon (PLB) has replaced the EPIRB (Emergency Position Indicating Radio Beacon) as the new standard emergency signaling device. When you activate a PLB, it sends your signal to one of seven satellites that are continually circling the globe. This signal is then relayed to a ground station so that search and rescue personnel can be notified. In less than an hour, aid can be on its way to you. After several passes, the satellite pinpoints the PLB's location to within a 2.5-mile (4-km) radius. When interfaced with a GPS receiver, your precise position is sent immediately.

The GyPSI 406 Personal Locator Beacon from ACR weighs just 17 ounces (480g). These beacons have to be registered with a government authority so that when they are activated, the rescuers know who they are looking for.

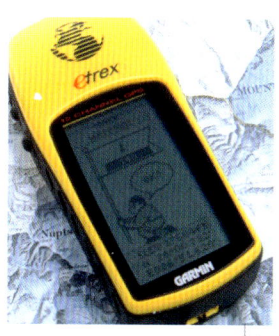

GPS Locator

GPS connects with 28 satellites, to zero in by triangulation on any location with an accuracy of 50 feet (15m). This model can be plugged into the companion GyPSI 460 PLB, invaluable for emergency use.

Erik Phone Home

Mountaineer Erik Weihenmayer, the first blind man to climb Everest, places a triumphant call home using a Nera WorldPhone Mini-M, useful for international dial-up, fax, and data networks at 2.4Kbps (data) – 4.8Kbps (voice). © Didrik Johnck

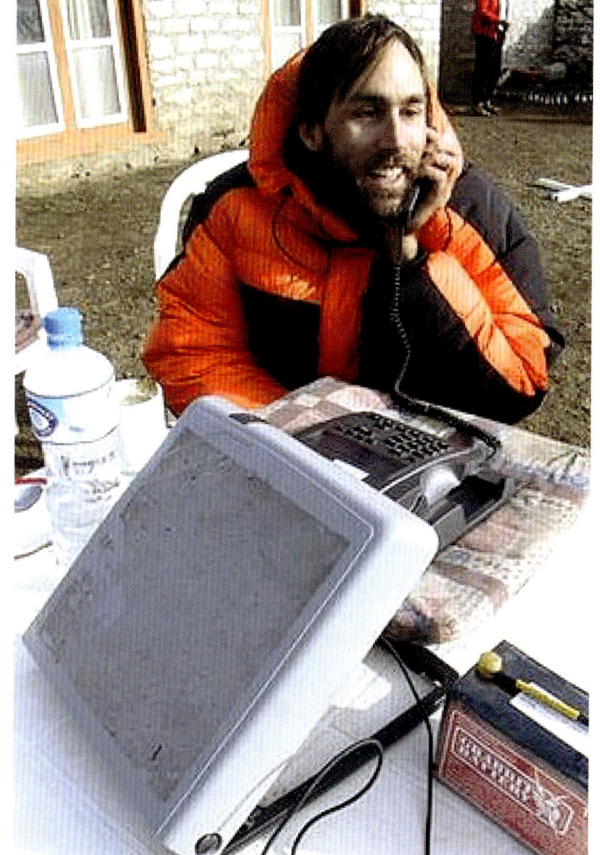

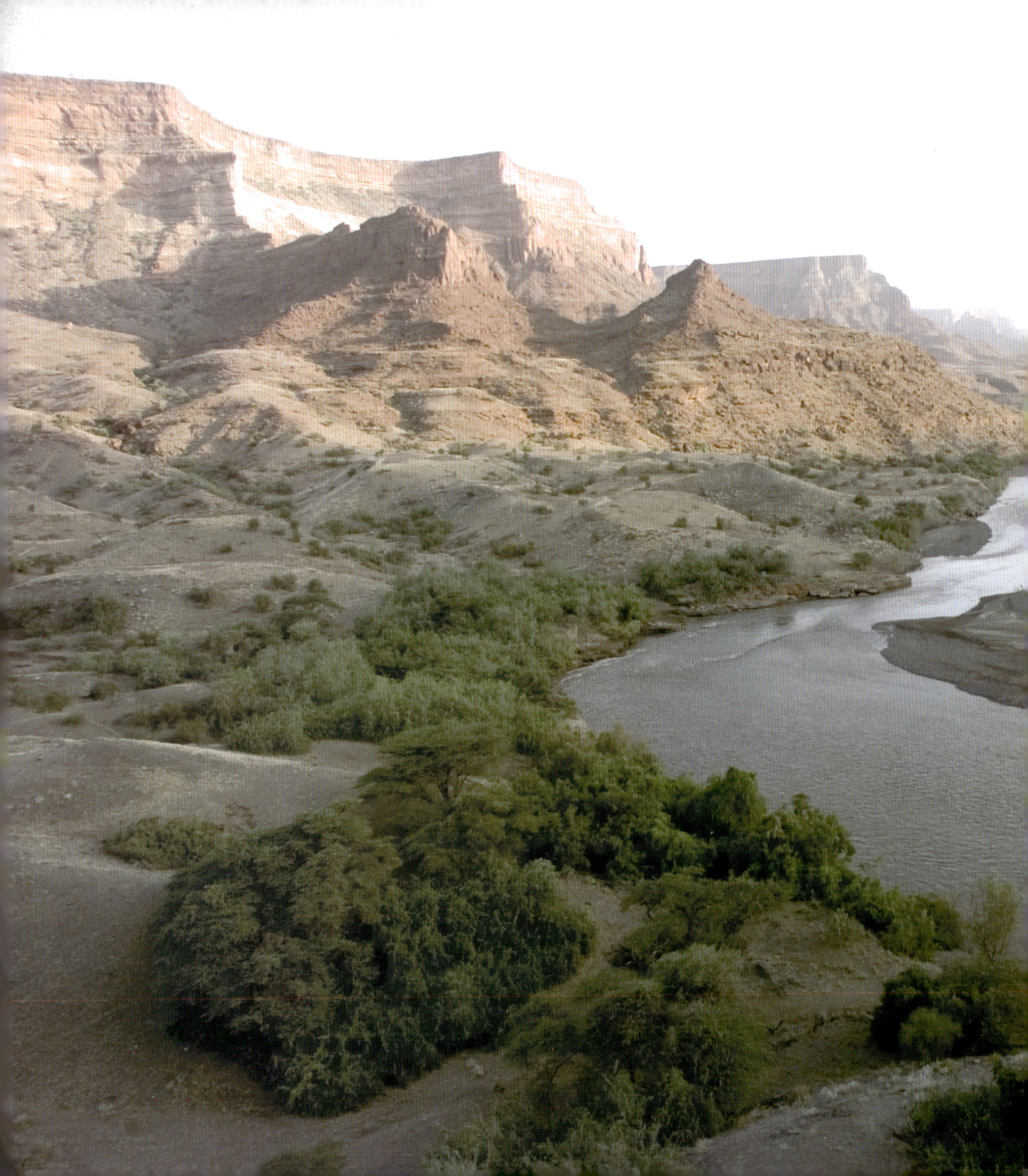

EXTREME LOCATIONS

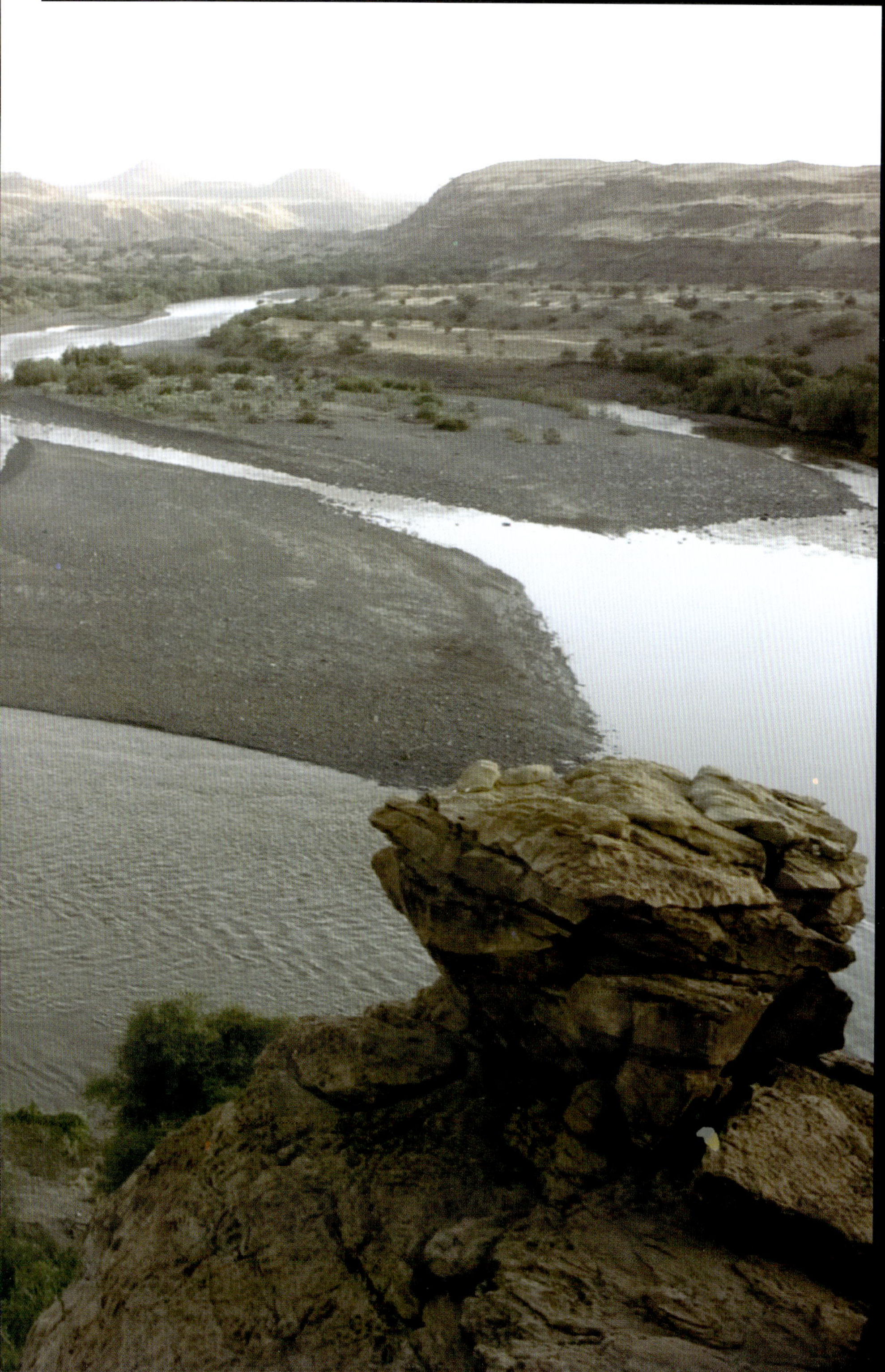

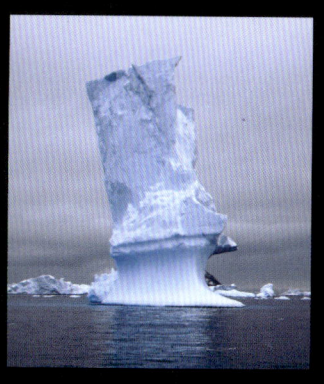

Dusty crepuscular rays splash light on a landscape that looks older than history, a river that seems to have gulped time. ... In the Ethiopian language, Amharic, a river is called wenz, and our maps show three different Tekeze wenzes, all converging in the next hundred miles.

Richard Bangs, *The Lost River*

All images: © Jonathan Chester

ANTARCTICA

Cold, high winds, sea spray, blowing snow, and ankle-deep, very rank penguin guano… These challenges apart, shooting conditions in the far south vary dramatically depending on when you go and where. Antarctica is one and a half times the size of continental US (just a bit larger than Australia), so at any time of the year weather conditions depend very much on your location.

Whatever the month, or the location, however, you are going to be quite remote from civilization. You have to look after your gear and yourself better than usual for there are no repair shops or supply stores. Extra care when cleaning lenses and cameras at the end of each day to remove salt and moisture can pay dividends. To beat the cold (at the South Pole itself, even in summer, it can be –30° C (–22° F) and down to –70° C (–94° F) in winter) you'll need plenty of hats, gloves, and mittens, a down jacket, and very good waterproofs. Calf-length Wellington boots large enough to take several pairs of socks are the best footwear for shore excursions of several hours. When getting to and from shore by Zodiac, store your gear in a large dry bag or Pelican case, although this can mean missing out on some shots. This is where the all-weather point-and-shoot digital camera (Pentax Optio WR-style) comes into its own. You can risk the elements if you are careful and use a regular DSLR with a top-of-the-line waterproof case such as the Aquatech Sports shield. Once ashore, unless it's snowing or raining (which it can do in the summer as a result of global warming), most digital cameras will function quite happily if handled sensibly.

Most adventure travelers to Antarctica go in summer (November through March) aboard expedition cruise ships that typically take from 50 to 400 passengers. A hardy few sail on smaller chartered yachts. Their digital photography regime is much more exacting. Being ship-based means you have power and warmth at the end of your shooting day, so while the location and weather can be extreme, the personal comfort level is usually quite high. It also enables you to run a laptop and archive and review your material on a regular basis. (Be very careful about the voltages of the outlets on these ships as they invariably carry 240 AC; if you do not have the correct settings, plugs, or a transformer, you can easily blow up some vital component.)

Remaining on board may prevent you getting close to your subject, but when the weather is really wild, shooting from the bridge, or braced in a corner on the upper deck, is very comforting. The option of shooting from low down from the rear deck or high up from the crow's nest can add to the variety of your shots. Vibration from the engines and the ship crashing in the waves make it pointless to try tripod shots, but if you are using a very heavy lens, shooting wildlife with a monopod seated in a flagpole holder at your waist can ease the strain.

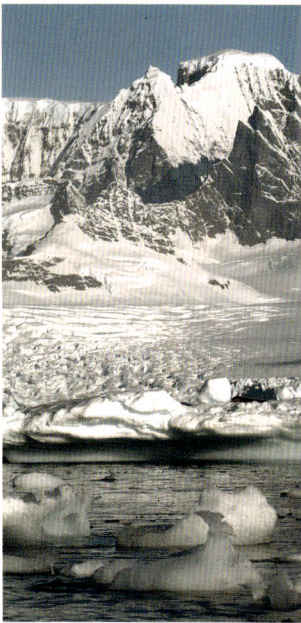

Cruising on the Peninsula

For big subjects, like icebergs, being on a cruise ship is less of a problem, but when you want a more intimate perspective, the Zodiacs come into their own. These sturdy inflatable craft are ideal for getting into position for the best shots of wildlife and ice formations. Including another Zodiac in the shot helps give a sense of scale to the surrounding landscape. The digital multiplier effect of most DSLR chips can be an advantage when shooting pictures from a ship, giving your telephoto lenses extra range.

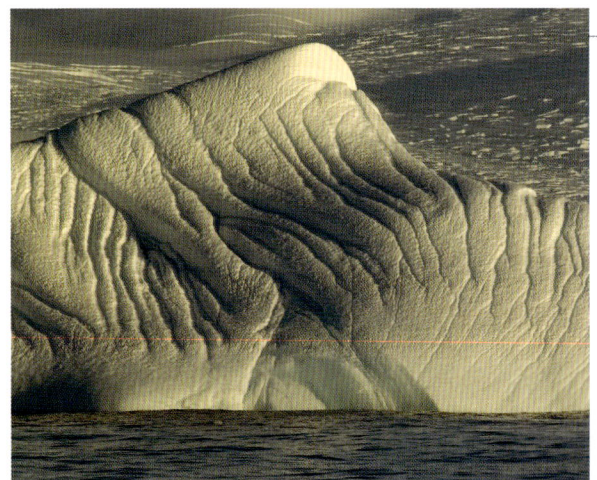

Ice Sculpture

Ice has a multitude of forms, each presenting opportunities for interesting shots, and the Antarctic weather can be so variable that you can return to the same place many times and feel as if it is a brand-new visit. A dusting of snow, a shroud of fog, blazing sunshine, or a sunset with light reflecting off the underside of clouds onto the ice-strewn sea, turns the world into a kaleidoscope of colors. At times like this you will appreciate the extra batteries and cards you have lugged around. In this image, the golden light of the lengthy polar dusk reveals intricate patterns that were carved when the iceberg was underwater.

ANTARCTICA 53

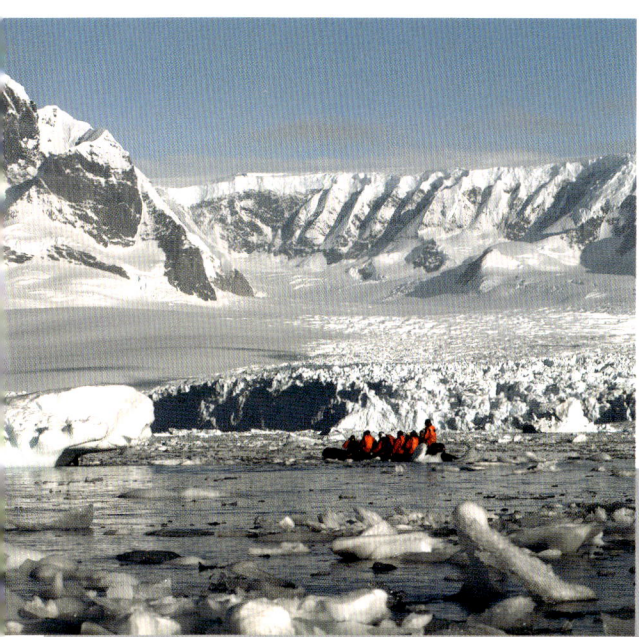

As a photographic subject, Antarctica is stunning. There are times when it is wild, or sullen and overcast, and very occasionally indescribably beautiful. The wildlife is a whole subject itself (*see pages 80–81*), but the landforms, or more accurately the icescapes, can be spectacular.

For most people the biggest problem with a photographic trip to the Antarctic is that it is totally addictive. You will just want to keep going back time and time again. I am up to my 15th season—and counting.

Tunnel Iceberg

Antarctica is a photographer's paradise. Massive tabular icebergs hundreds of miles across are impossible to convey in scale, though framing a person or boat in the shot can sometimes help. At the micro level, tiny fragments of sea ice (brash), or even ice crystals under a macro lens, yield fascinating images.

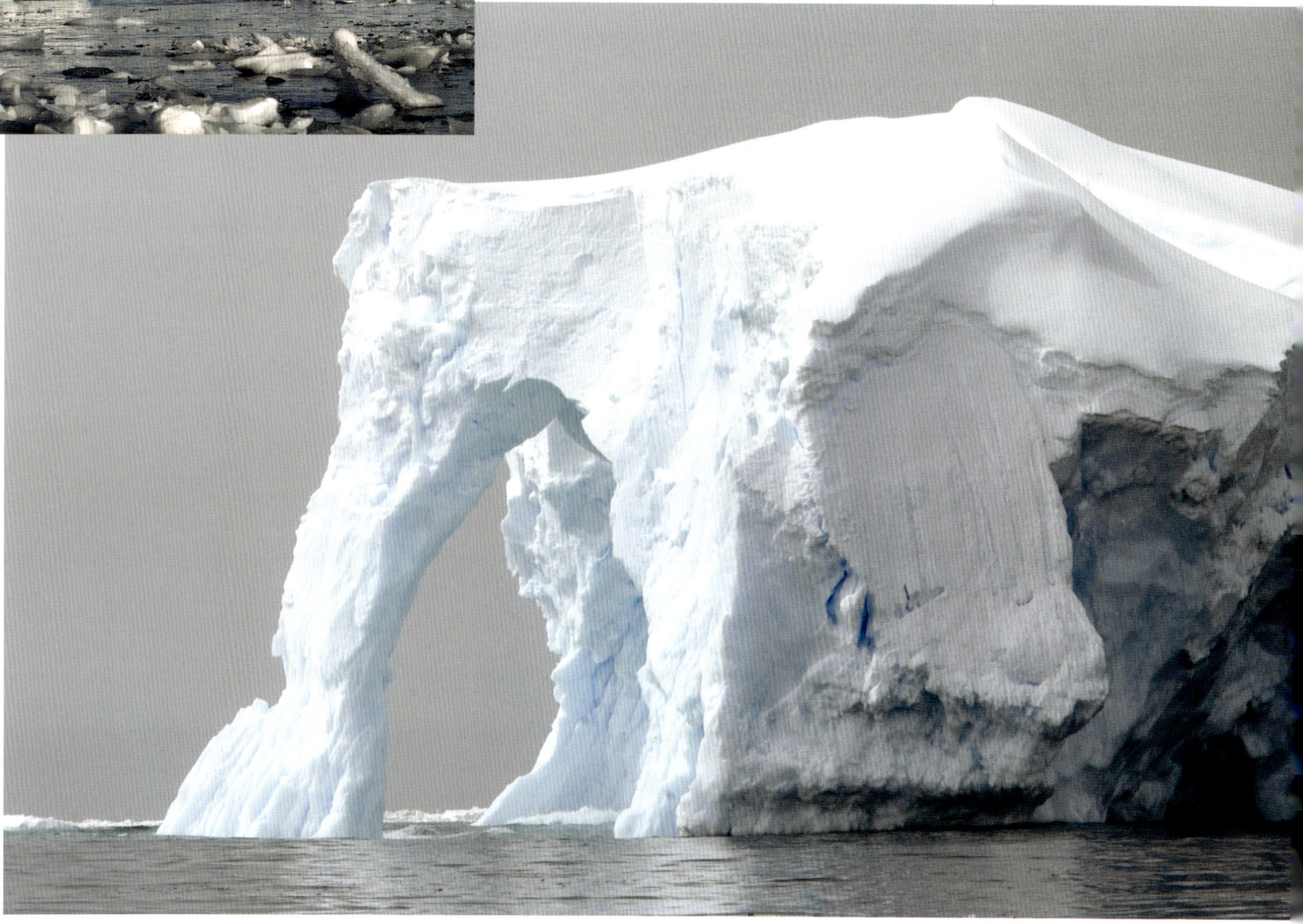

THE ARCTIC

The geography of the Arctic is vastly different from that of the Antarctic. The North Pole is in the middle of an enormous frozen ocean, larger than the US and surrounded by the subarctic regions of Alaska, Canada, Greenland, Iceland, Scandiniavia, Siberia, and the Russian Far East. Parts of this broader region are rich in natural and mineral resources, which have pushed economic development to extreme latitudes.

> *The snow was incredibly heavy going today, heavier than it has ever been before, though the surface was hard and firm. The wind packed snow is no better than sand. We had to pull against the wind too...*
>
> **Fridtjof Nansen,** *The First Crossing of Greenland*

One of the biggest economic drivers in the region is tourism and, for the photographer, there are numerous tours to key destinations. Northeast Greenland is the world's largest national park. Churchill in Canada is famous as the "polar-bear capital of the world" and is one of the most accessible places to see the "Northern Lights," the Aurora Borealis, and beluga whales. Cunningham Inlet on Somerset Island is another hotspot for Arctic wildlife, including polar bears, seals, and arctic foxes (*see pages 78–79*). The Arctic is relatively easy to reach, with a great

The Endeavour

The ice-strengthened expedition ship *Endeavour* approaches a waterfall spilling off the Northeastland Ice Cap. This ice cap forms a continuous wall of ice that stretches for over 100 miles (160km). In summer, when the sun never sets, meltwater channels form icy waterfalls where they spill from the ice cliffs to the sea. © Ralph Lee Hopkins

East Greenland

In summer many parts of the Arctic are a playground for adventurous mountaineers and sea kayakers. North East Greenland National Park is the largest national park in the world, an area larger than France and Britain put together. Countless fjords and U-shaped valleys cut from glaciers dot the coastline in eastern Greenland in late August. In this image of mountains around the Tasilaq fjord, underexposure by one f-stop and the use of a UV filter preserved shadow details while cutting out the haze. © Mark Langley

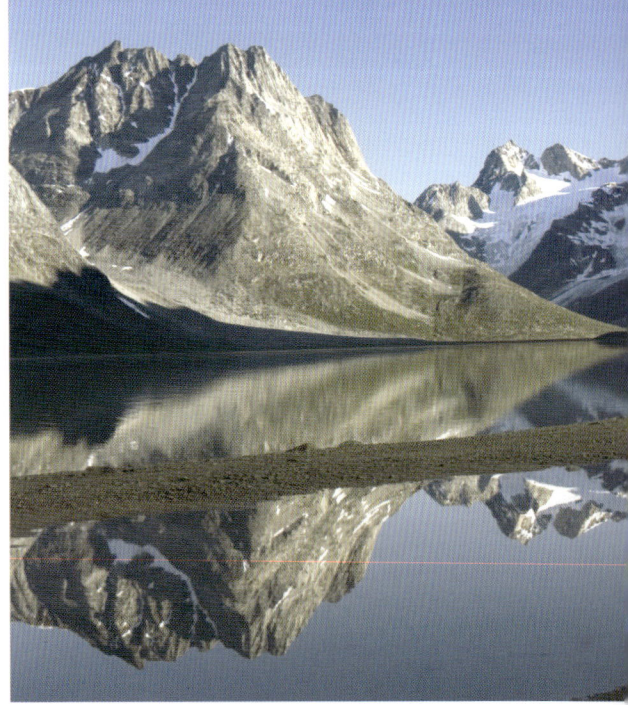

variety of subject matter, from landscapes and culture to wildlife, as well as photogenic extreme activities: dog sledging, sea kayaking, and cruising iceberg-choked fjords. Hard-core geographic expeditions trek across the moving ice from the northern tip of Elsemere Island to the North Pole, a journey that is without a doubt one of the most challenging extreme adventures possible.

The Arctic has its share of mountains, but overall the altitude is not very high. This factor and the moderating influence of the Arctic Ocean result in far milder weather conditions than an equivalent latitude in the south. Global warming is also affecting the weather and sea-ice extent.

Traveling to the Arctic is fairly simple. Settlements around the Arctic rim are accessible via scheduled or charter flights, and there are even roads like the Dalton Highway (Haul Road) from Fairbanks to Prudhoe Bay. The North Pole can now be reached by a fit person with relative ease and comfort. You can also photograph in the Arctic in the winter, which is far less feasible in Antarctica. A tent village, Camp Borneo, is put in each winter on the 6½-foot (2-m) thick floating ice 60 miles (97km) from the Pole, and there is a permanent settlement at Longyearbyn.

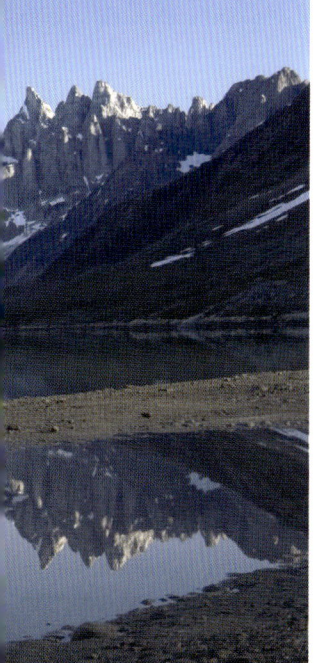

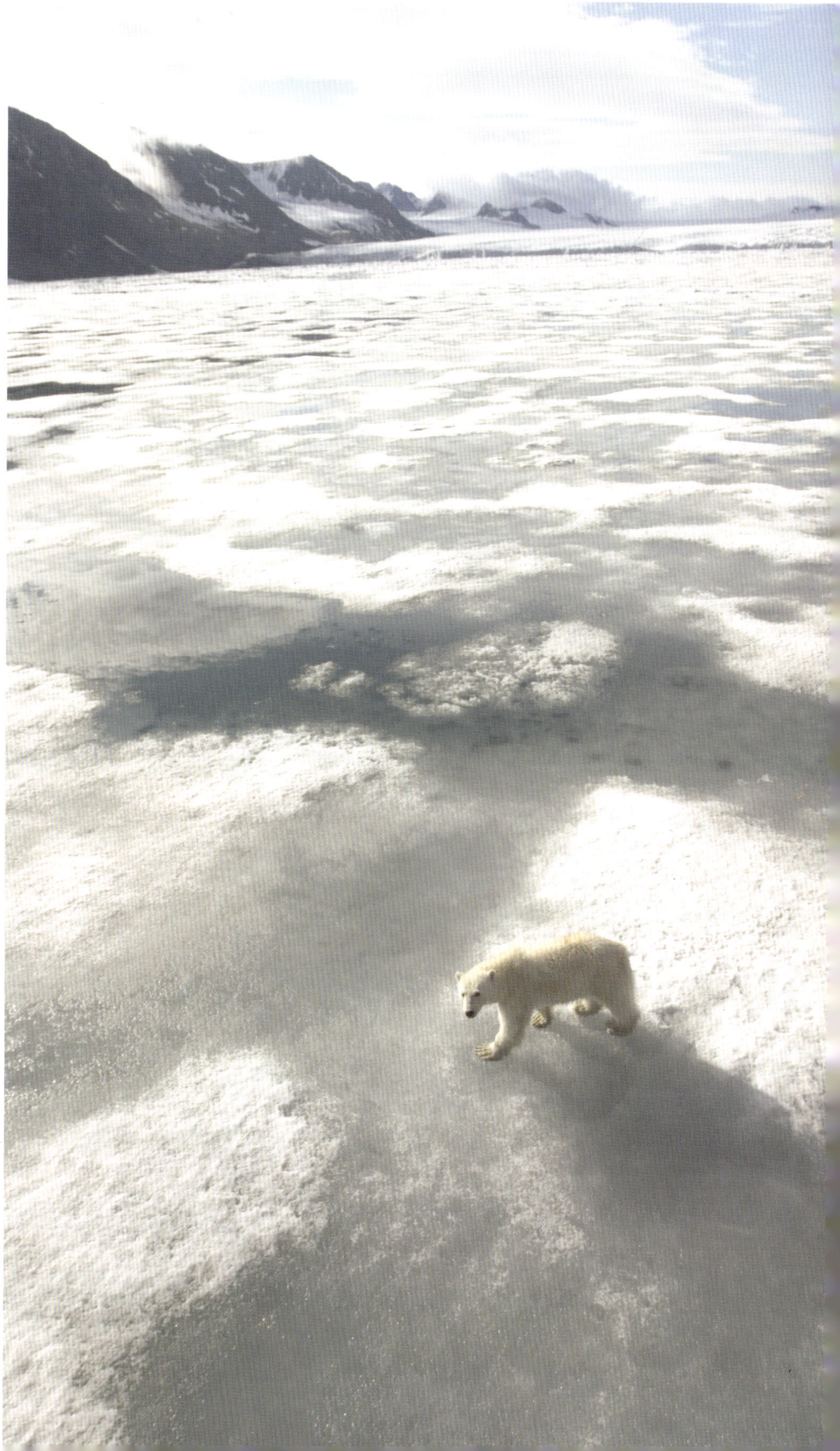

Roaming the Fast Ice

While the polar bear is the signature species of the High Arctic, it was once hunted widely, and around Svalbard today polar bears are uncommon. Photographing in Hornsund Fjord Spitsbergen, from the deck of a cruise ship, is the safest means of getting close to these top predators.
© Ralph Lee Hopkins

OCEANS

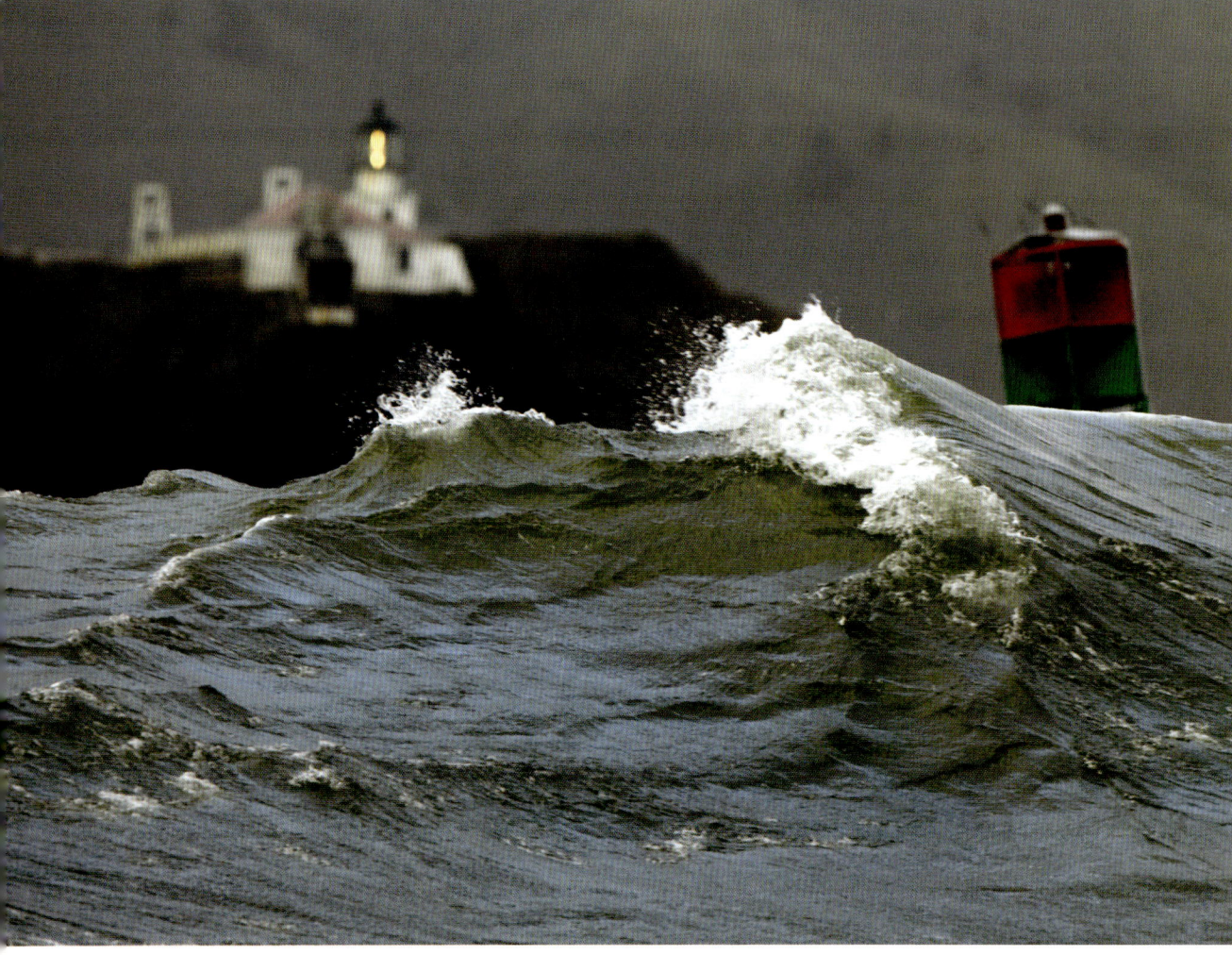

Pt. Bonita Lighthouse, San Francisco

On a yacht in heavy seas you will want to wear a proper sailing safety harness or jacket clipped on to a safety line to guard against being swept overboard. This way you can concentrate on shooting with more confidence. You often also need to shoot one-handed, leaving the other to keep your balance.
© Abner Kingman

It pays to have you and your gear well insured for shooting on the high seas, which must be the most challenging extreme digital photography going. Digital technology is more sensitive to water and salt than film cameras, so well-sealed bodies and lenses and the best protective covers are your starting point. Better preparation and maintenance are also needed, particularly on a long voyage, but backups also play an important role. If the cameras rarely get out of their cases, you will not get good coverage, so you need to take some risks.

The same basic principles apply whether you are on a yacht or an expedition cruise ship. When there is any rough water or bad weather imminent, you need to be able to safely stow your gear and know that it will survive the worst rock and roll. Constant vibration from the engines, or the vessel pounding through heavy seas, can loosen screws and throw unsecured items about.

If you know that you are in for a rough passage or a bad storm, then a few minutes' preparation in packing things away properly can avoid a broken lens, or damaged camera or computer. The lowest point in the cabin is the best place for heavy cases and bags, but in heavy weather things will still take off, so wedge everything in as tightly as possible and use locking closets. You can rig up a workstation on a ship with octopus straps and non-slip mesh matting that will survive even the roughest treatment. Whether you can still work in these conditions is another matter altogether.

On board ships, wide and medium zoom lenses work well to compose shots. Interiors of cabins on ships and yachts can be notoriously cramped, so try the shots with a very wide-angle lens, perhaps even a fish-eye, to capture all of the subject. Check the LCD screen (if using one) to make sure you like the effect. Tilting up or down from the horizontal can dramatically affect the look of the shot.

Getting the scale of the ship or yacht in its environment is best accomplished away from the boat. If the weather is calm, then it is safest to do this in a small dinghy or powered Zodiac.

When the deck is awash with water, you will want a fully waterproof housing or camera, or a Ewa-marine bag, or at the very least an Aquatech spray cover. If your camera does get wet with salt water, take immediate action—don't wait until the end of the day. Wipe off water from the exterior, then check to see if any moisture has made it inside. Remove the batteries immediately and use fresh water or alcohol to clean the exterior and interior (if you have seen any water inside) of salt residue. Then sit the camera securely under a hot light for an hour or so to try and dry it out. Placing the camera in a sealed plastic bag with some fully charged silica gel will also help to resuscitate a wet camera or lens.

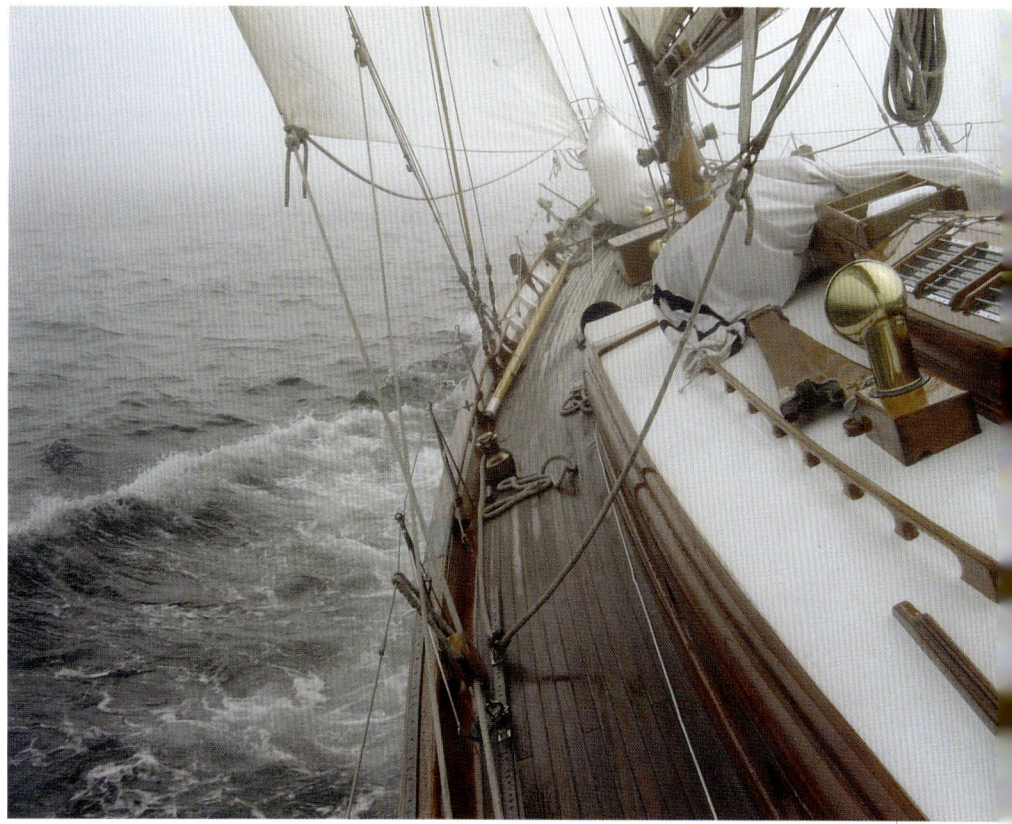

Flukes at Sunset

When out on deck shooting, most of the time you can use a digital camera without any housing, but if there is spray in the air or it is raining or snowing, you need to take precautions to keep out moisture. Sailing affords the opportunity to see and photograph wildlife and scenery unavailable to the land-lubber. Keep your eyes open for opportunities, and anticipate your shot.

Classic Ketch

Ocean passages aboard a yacht such as the *Ticonderoga* can be extremely demanding on digital camera gear. From salt spray and fog above decks to high humidity below, good camera protection and maintenance are a must. © Michael Brown

UNDERWATER

Three-quarters of the planet is covered by ocean, yet all but a fraction is beyond our normal reach. Most of us only personally experience sealife through snorkeling, though there is nothing like a ride in a submarine (*see pages 122–123*). For the adventurous there is scuba diving, which has grown into a mainstream recreational activity in the 50 years since Jacques Cousteau developed the aqualung (and gave it the acronym SCUBA, for Self-Contained Underwater Breathing Apparatus). Scuba divers bring us the most intimate images of life underwater, as they literally swim with the creatures of this submarine world. Their photos are hard-won, as underwater photography is one of the more expensive and technically exacting specialties. Cousteau himself first explored this art form, and his books and television documentaries helped to open up the underwater world to everyone.

Dedicated, fully waterproof point-and-shoot digital cameras, such as the AquaPix DX-3100 from Sea & Sea, do exist, but the underwater world is still waiting for a digital Nikonos-style camera—a fully functional camera built specifically for underwater use. At the moment, most serious underwater digital shooters use a DSLR inside a dedicated housing, such as those from Ewa-Marine or Sea & Sea. These place Canon, Nikon, or other professional cameras inside housings with full controls and one or even two flash mounts on extended arms.

Whether shooting film or digital, camera housings need to be very carefully maintained to prevent flooding. They all have one or more "O"-rings that make the seal, and the deeper they go, the more pressure there is, and the better the seal needs to be. If the O-rings are maintained, and the case remains watertight, cleaning is largely a matter of hosing off the housing with fresh water, to keep salt from building up, especially on moving parts and lens plates. Using flash underwater is crucial,

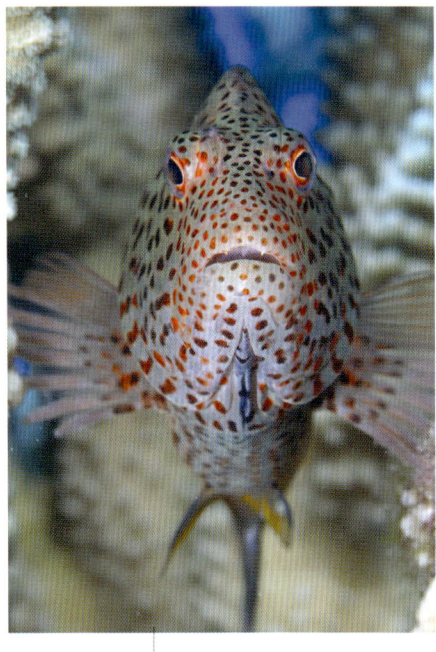

Hawkfish in Coral, Hawaii

Point-and-shoot cameras in fairly inexpensive housings can be used on or near the surface by snorkelers and casual scuba divers. You can pick up a disposable point-and-shoot for under $20, but you get what you pay for. Shots taken while snorkeling tend to give a "bird's eye view" of sea life, as it is difficult to get down to any depth and stay long enough for more face-to-face shots. © James Watt

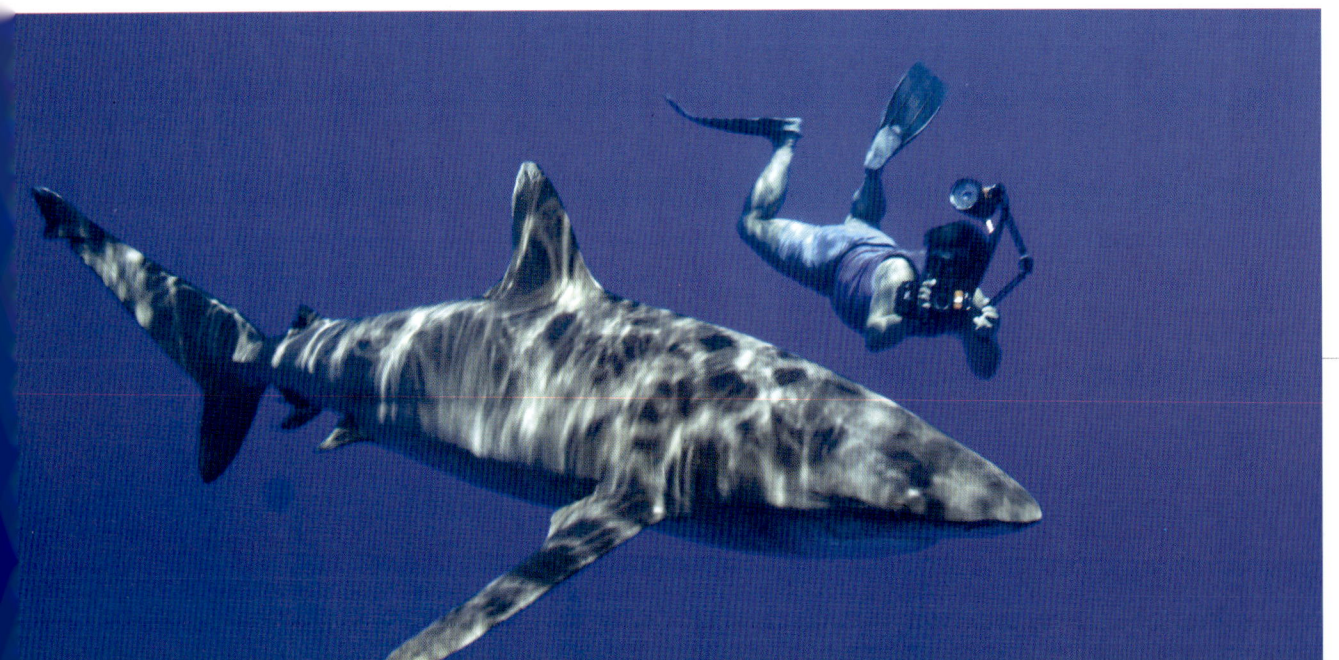

Oceanic White Tip Shark, Hawaii

To be a successful underwater shooter you need to be a competent diver, and be able to manage buoyancy control with ease. You also need to be able to move freely and be relaxed underwater so as not to disturb the very creatures you wish to photograph.© James Watt

because when shooting deeper than a few feet, all shots seem to have been taken through a blue filter, which is pretty much what happens. Water absorbs the warmer colors, the reds and yellows, so everything appears blue-green. Our eyes compensate, but the chip does not lie.

Point-and-shoot or onboard camera flashes seldom have enough power to light the scene properly, and the back scatter from the flash can create a snowstorm effect. You need to use one or more flashes, or "strobes," as the diving fraternity calls them, to bring out the natural colors. Most professional underwater housings have extended flash arms for one or two strobes.

The most compelling images are taken with flash and super wide-angle lens, with the subject very close in the foreground, or macro shots of creatures. Exposures underwater can be tricky, especially when balancing ambient light with the strobe effect, but digital gives you a little more exposure latitude than film, and the advantage of being able to check your results in the LCD screen. A big plus with shooting digital underwater is that you are not restricted to 36 shots, unlike those using film. With some of the very large storage cards now being produced, divers usually run out of air before they manage to fill up a card.

Since you must load your camera into its housing before you descend, you are limited to whatever lens you put on the camera. One solution is to take multiple cameras, each with a different lens.

Gradually more and more shooters are taking digital cameras underwater as they become cheaper and better than film cameras and more DSLR housings come on the market. Underwater photography will never be cheap, or easy, but digital cameras have created a new niche in the extremes of the underwater world.

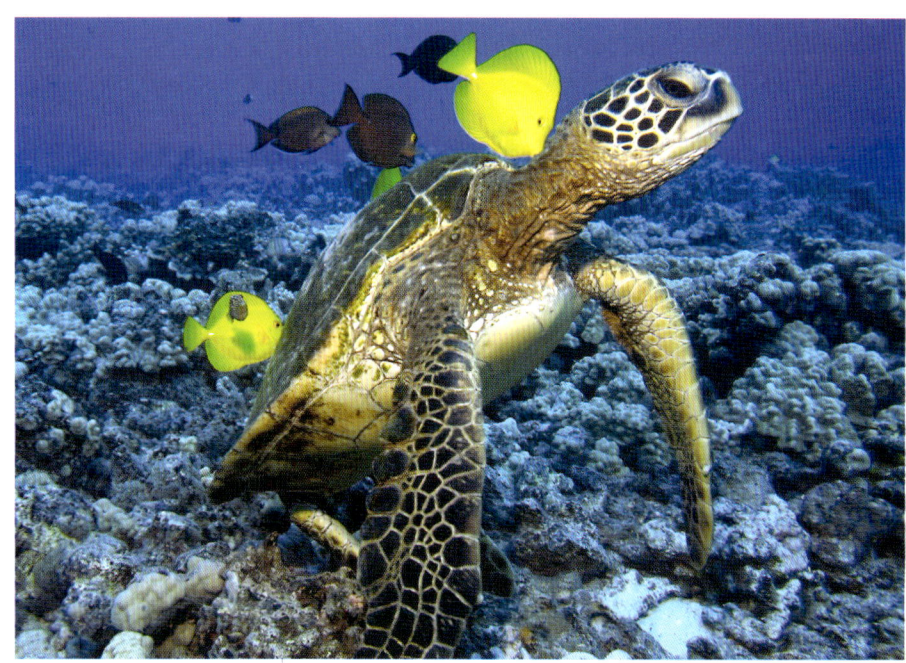

Green Sea Turtle

The endangered green sea turtle is attended by reef fish in waters off Hawaii. Research shows that sea turtles have extremely long lifespans, and migrate enormous distances every year. © James Watt

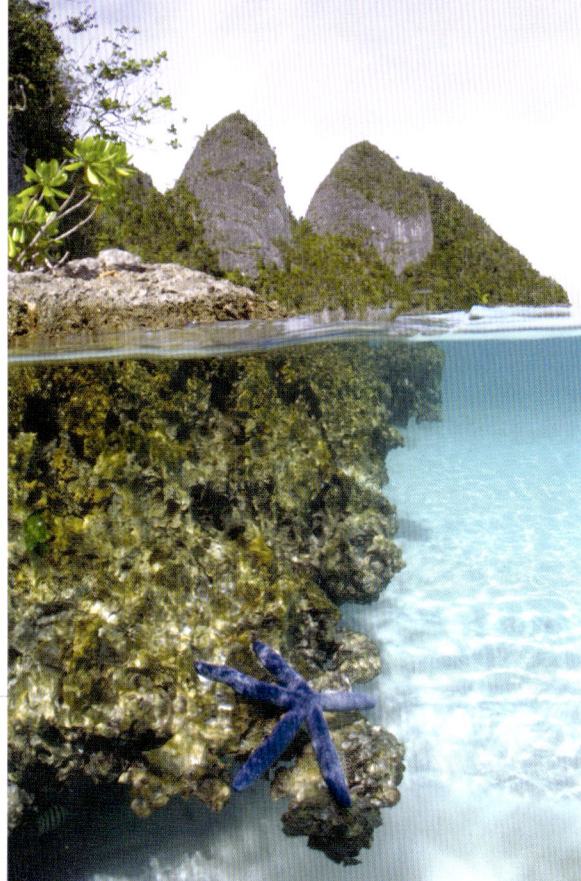

Starfish, Irian Jaya

The clarity of the water is everything in underwater photography. Even apparently crystal-clear water has particulate matter floating in it, which catches the light from strobes and can ruin an otherwise interesting shot. You need to be as close to your subject as possible. © James Watt

RIVERS AND LAKES

Water is one of the most dramatic elements in photography. Think of the simple elegance of Ansel Adams' aspen, reflected in the cold waters of an alpine lake; of the power any waterfall adds to a landscape; or of the grace of a kayaker slicing through rapids.

Water not only inspires the photographic spirit, but also challenges the equipment. Today's professional digital cameras are fairly robust and well protected against the elements, but special considerations always need to be taken around water. At the very least, you should have a clean towel on hand to dry the camera if it gets wet from fog, spray, or rain. However, fresh water as found in these situations is far less corrosive than salt water from the oceans or shores, and a simple yet thorough drying of a damp camera is probably as technical as your repairs need be (see the sections on Oceans and River Rafting, pages 56 and 116).

Ewa and Pelican both make an inexpensive yet effective raincover, essentially a clear plastic "rain hat" that protects your camera, but allows you to manipulate the controls with your hands inside the cover. You may need several lenses to fully capture the environment, from fisheye for dramatic settings to telephotos for more detailed compositions. A large-capacity padded shoulder bag or a photographer's backpack is good for carrying all this glass. Lowepro have a range of bags, many featuring an "AW" hood that unzips to drape the entire bag in a rain cover. A tripod is also essential: for time exposures and low-light conditions a monopod or clamp just won't do.

Rivers, lakes, and waterfalls provide a landscape of contrast, between the generally smooth texture of the water and the more detailed, dimensional quality of the land. Emphasizing this contrast is one key to taking a good picture, such as by composing the image in terms of long verticals (the river or lake surface) with the horizontals (geology, vegetation, and signs of humanity).

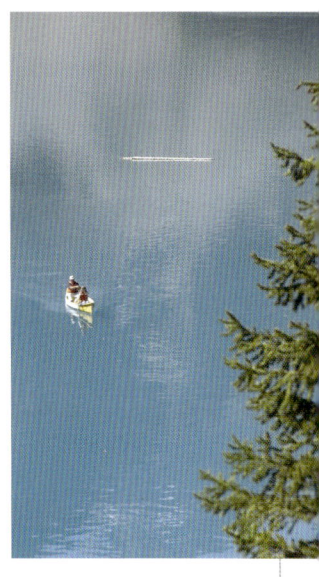

Moraine Lake

These paddlers seemed to wander aimlessly for 30 minutes, but persistence, the mid-morning mist, and the beauty of glacier-fed Moraine Lake made this photo. Manual focus was needed to keep the autofocus from "hunting" when most of the field of view is water. © Mark Langley

Athabasca Falls, Jasper National Park

This shot required use of a circular polarizer to increase color saturation and spot metering off the light-colored rocks on the right to keep the water from overwhelming the camera's exposure meter. A tripod and slow shutter speeds can be used to "soften" the water and convey the motion and power of the falls. © Mark Langley

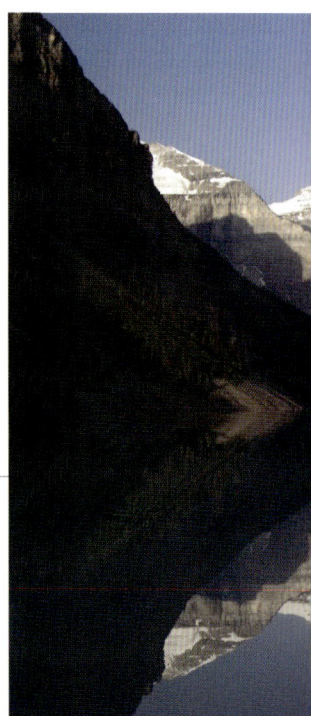

Mirror Lake

Lake Louise is one of the most photogenic lakes in the New World, its peaceful surface reflecting the dramatic mountains of Alberta's Banff National Park. The early morning is ideal for still waters, lack of boaters, and agreeable sunlight. In contrast to the photo above, where reflections were minimized, this photo uses them as a key compositional element. © Mark Langley

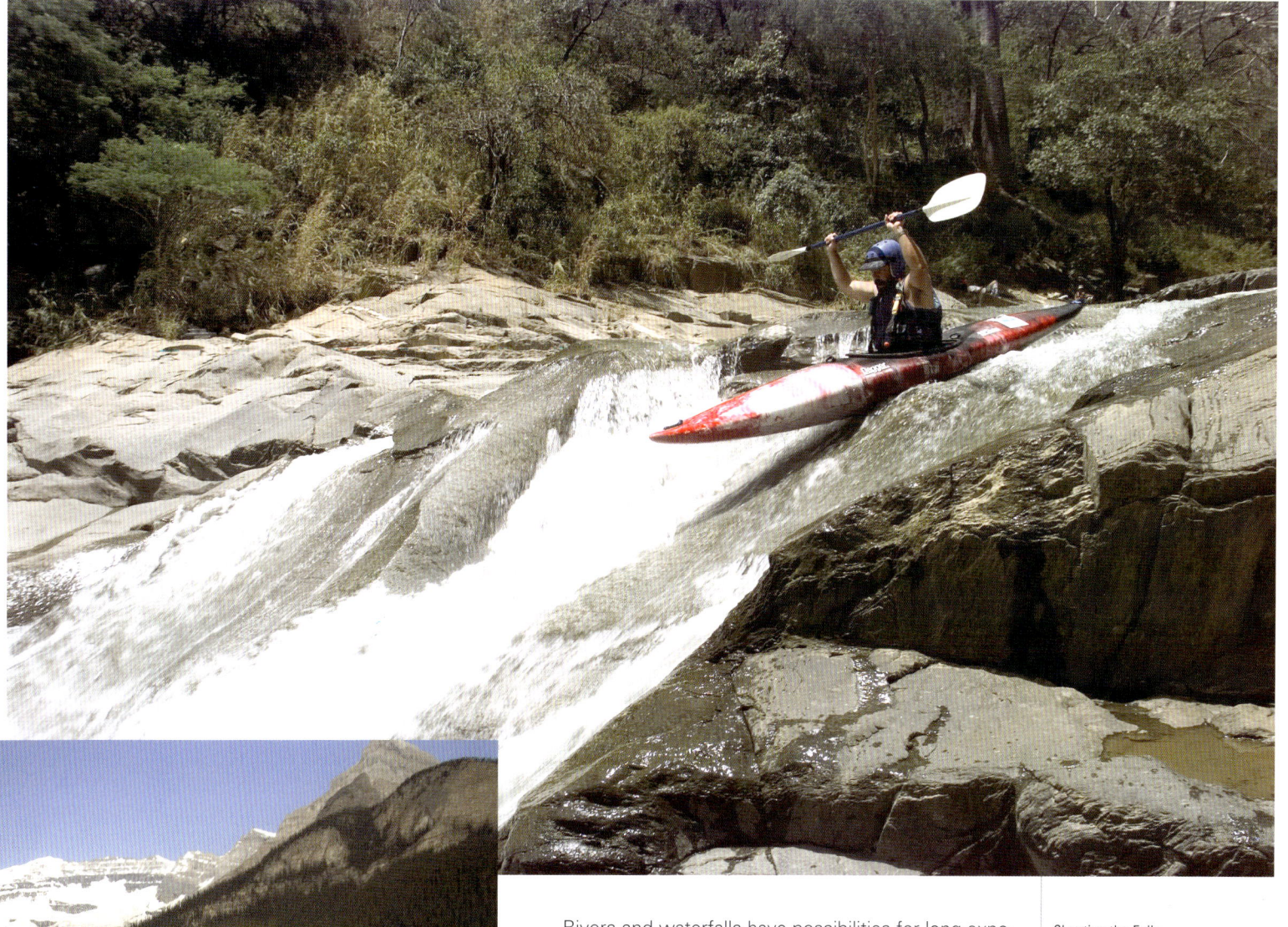

Rivers and waterfalls have possibilities for long-exposure images. Flowing water shows a different quality over an 8-second exposure than over 1/500, or even 1/8. Its current lines are softer and more evident, and a river's course is a misty yet powerful muscle snaking through the frame. The world is thus transformed by photography, showing something we otherwise could never have seen.

Be aware, however, that long exposures on imaging chips produce digital noise, just as high ISO speeds do. There are some things for which film may still be the better medium—so far.

Shooting the Falls

On a side tributary of the Tekeze River in Ethiopia, we got to try our hand at kayaking over a small drop. Crocodiles dissuaded us from testing our paddling skills in the main river.

TROPICAL ISLANDS—GALÁPAGOS

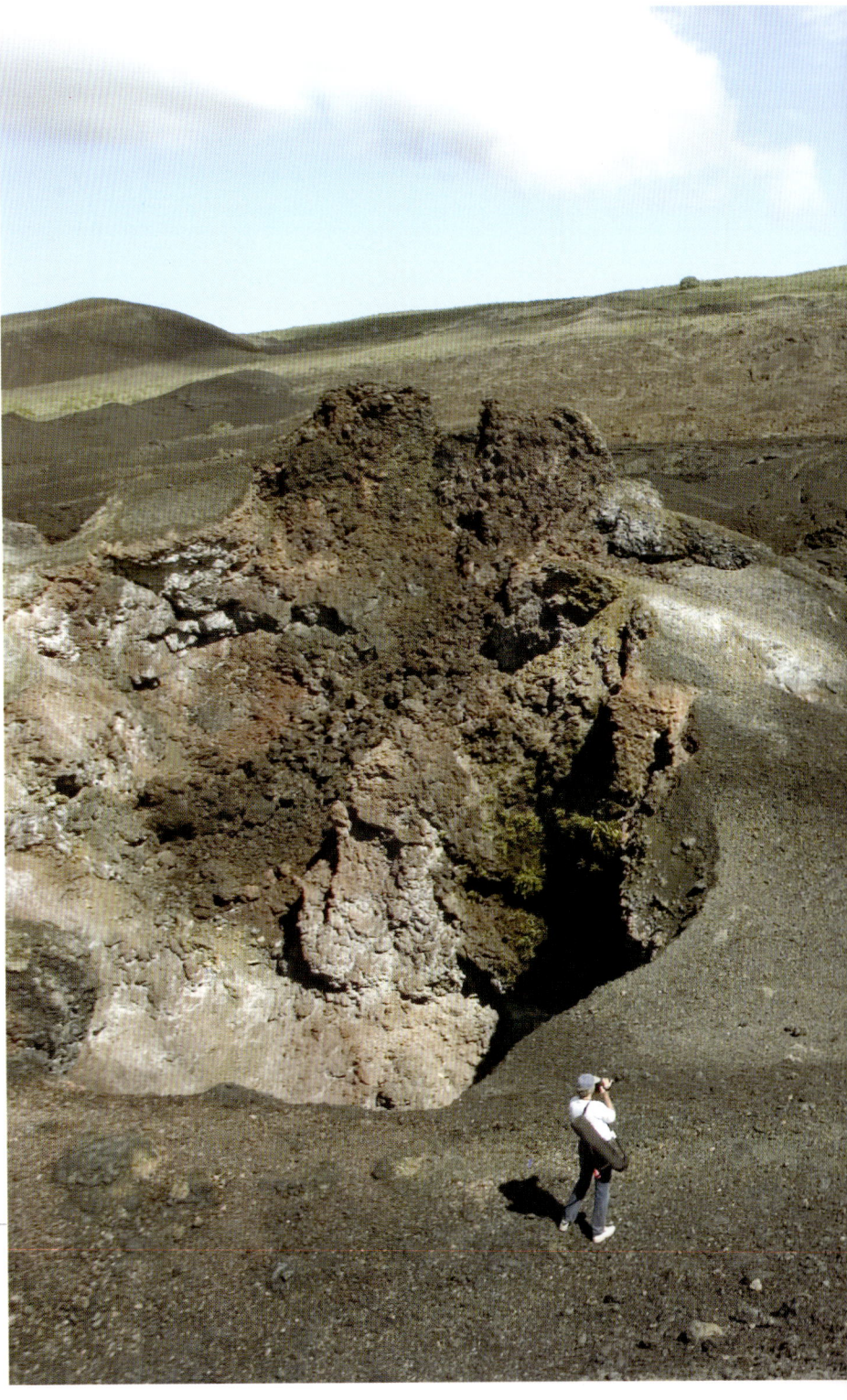

The Galápagos Islands, 600 miles (965km) off the coast of Ecuador, are one of the ultimate natural-history field trips. Many unique species have never learned to fear humans, so you can get close-up images with ease. It's also a great location to have an underwater digital camera rig for the array of tropical fish, even hammerhead sharks.

Yachts and small motor boats cruise around the islands for 11 months of the year. These trips are not cheap (usually about $5,000), but the usual end-of-day digital bugbears—power and a secure dry work area—are not an issue.

Even though it is a popular tourist destination, Galápagos National Park is well managed and feels relatively uncrowded. A serious limit for photographers, however, is that when onshore you are not allowed to wander freely from the main settlements before dawn or after dusk unless accompanied by a guide.

Shooting on land can often mean hiking for several hours at a stretch in the heat, so take a hat and sunscreen and drink plenty of liquid. Have a good camera backpack for that extra camera body, long lenses, and a tripod.

Overall, the Galápagos is a great digital photo vacation and one with plenty of easily accessible and unusual subjects. On top of this you can go at almost any time of the year. It's one of the Top Ten most spectacular wildlife photo destinations in the world.

Fauna, Galápagos

Hiking onshore brings you close to blue-footed boobies, iguanas, giant tortoises—and volcanoes. Much of the best wildlife photography is to be found at the shoreline. Patience and some knowledge of the species will always improve your success rate.

TROPICAL ISLANDS—GALÁPAGOS 63

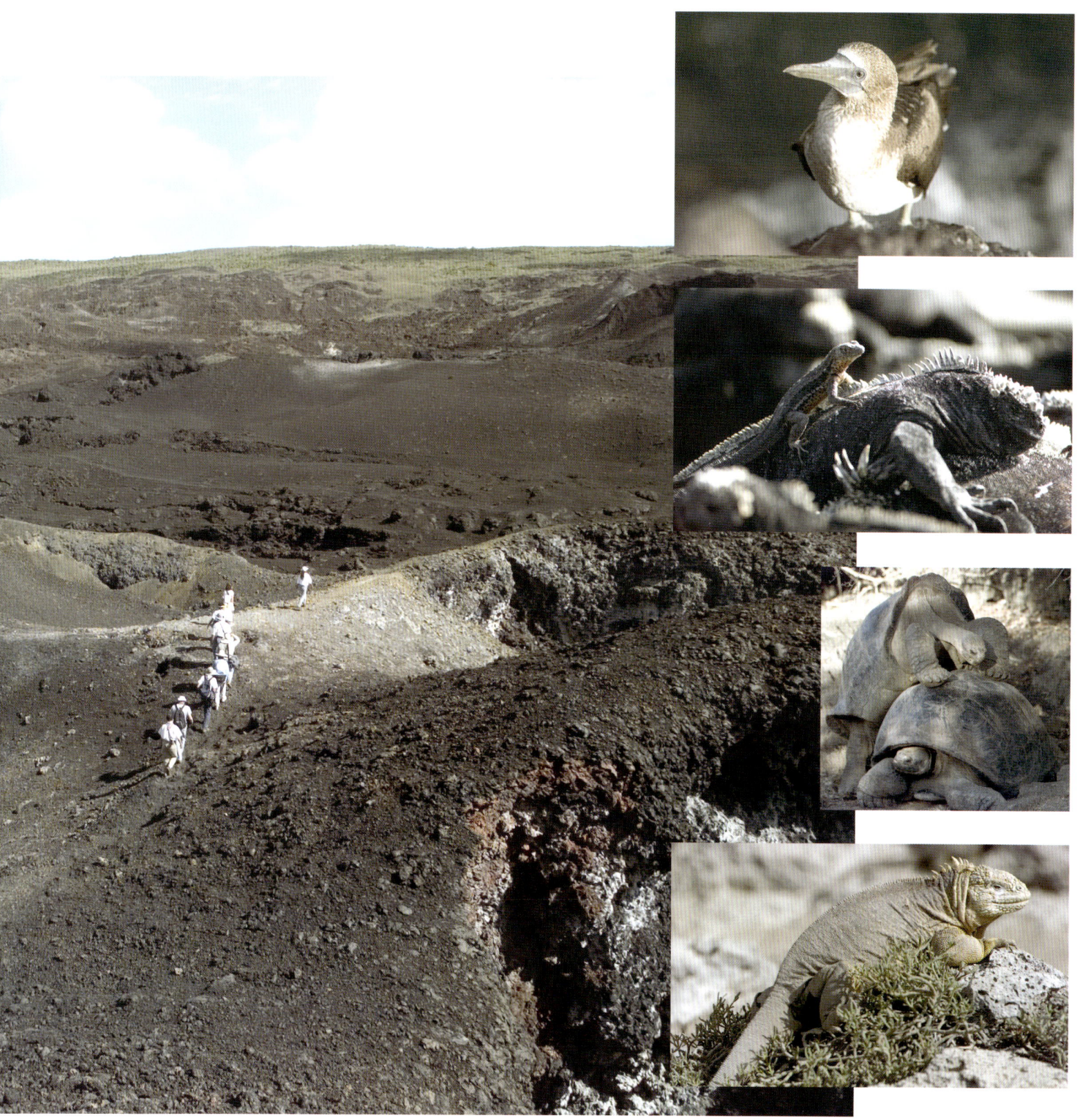

TROPICAL RAINFOREST—DENISE ROCCO-ZILBER

Working digital photographers are as immersed in the projects themselves as they are in the photography. It takes research, preparation, production, and hard work to make a story come alive through pictures. Denise Rocco-Zilber has been doing these projects for over a decade, from her time with Rick Smolen's Passage to Vietnam, through her assignments at TerraQuest and Mungo Park, up through her role as senior producer with One World Journeys. Two projects at OWJ, in Costa Rica and Mexico, took her into the hot, wet, muddy, difficult environment of tropical rainforests.

The One World Journey project in Mexico was to help build research scientists a home base in Calakmul Biosphere Reserve, Yucatan, to track jaguars in their habitat. The humidity must have been 105—it was just soaking, not raining but really hot, really wet jungle. One day in particular I remember for two reasons—we tracked down a wild jaguar, and my batteries wouldn't work.

We were running with all our gear through the jungle for eight hours; it was horrific. I was wearing jeans, which I shouldn't have been because they're too heavy. I had two heavy cameras—the Nikon D1—I had lenses, I had a tripod, I had six batteries with me because we had no idea how long we'd be gone. But at the end of the day, we found the tracks and caught up with the cat. We were standing right under the tree the jaguar had climbed, and maybe it was the humidity, but I wasn't getting any power to my camera. I kept taking the batteries out, wiping them off, cleaning off the connectors, and putting them back in, changing batteries ... Considering I had a jaguar in a tree above me, I was freaking out because my camera wasn't working! Finally it powered on and I got the shot.

I anticipated that we'd need to keep things dry, because when we went to the Yucatan to talk with the scientists they were saying they had trouble with the

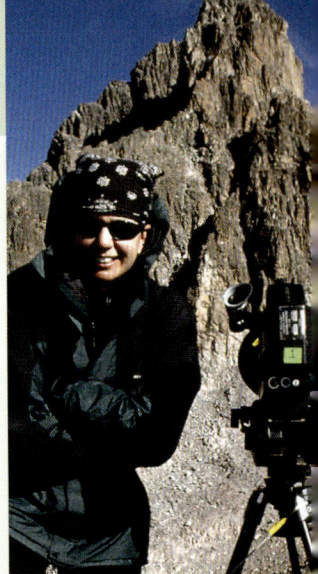

Mt. Kenya

Denise Rocco-Zilber on assignment on Mt Kenya, one of Africa's highest peaks. © Denise Rocco-Zilber

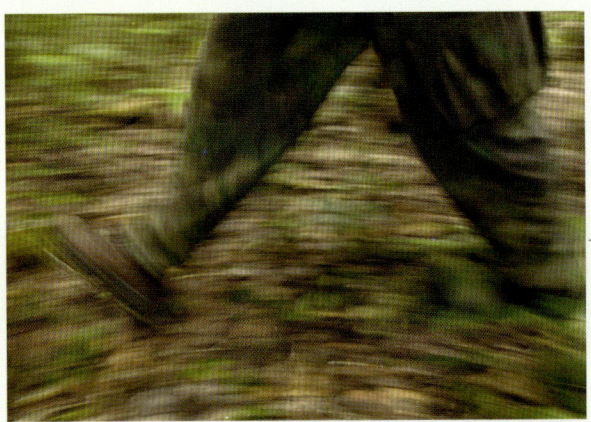

Jungle Trek

Photographing jungle animals means being ready to go at a moment's notice, dashing off into the jungle in pursuit of photographic prey. Using slow shutter speeds to communicate speed is a reliable trick, whether shooting film or digital. © Denise Rocco-Zilber

Captured Subject

Researchers use drugged dart guns to sedate the jungle cats for study and electronic tagging. The jaguar has been identified as a five-year-old female weighing approximately 77 pounds (35kg). © Denise Rocco-Zilber

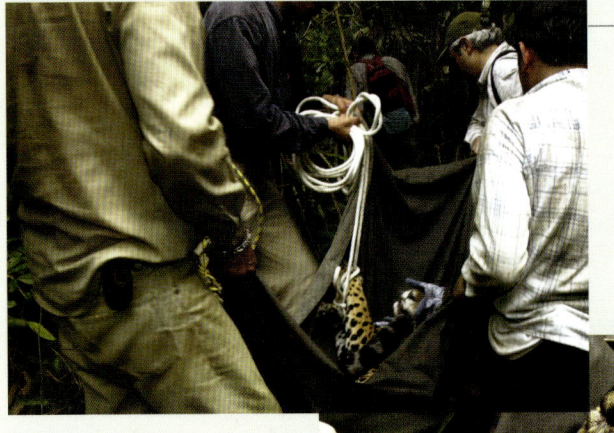

Taking Measure

By measuring her teeth and checking their coloration, it is determined that this jaguar is about five years old. This collar is for restraint should the cat wake up, not a radio collar for tracking. © Denise Rocco-Zilber

humidity. They had this lamp idea for a drying system, using just a flood lamp (not a heat lamp) to create enough heat to dry things out. So at night I'd stick the camera in a dry bag with boxes of silica, under a flood lamp, then tent a towel over the camera and the lenses in the bag with the silica, and let the bag heat up half an hour or so. I never had the camera fail.

I think every digital photographer has one particular problem shooting outdoors: if it's harsh or bright light, you can't see the LCD. I take my coat most of the time, or a chamois towel if I want to see if I'm getting the shot, to hood over myself so that I can see. It's kind of ironic, it's almost like the old 4x5s, the old practices!

In the Monteverde Cloud Forest, in Costa Rica, we spent two weeks with scientists in the area, who were studying climate change. Each scientist had their specialty —plants, orchids, weather, frogs—and we visited them and talked about the results of their studies, and what they're learning about our world and climate change.

The advantage in Monteverde was we weren't camping, we had a place with electricity to go back to every night. But the conditions were probably the harshest that I've ever had to deal with, even more so than the Yucatan. There was far more rain, thick, thick jungle, and sometimes knee- to thigh-high mud that we had to walk through. So the wetness, the mud, and the cold got to be a lot to deal with. It was harder on me than on the camera! Regarding the cameras, although I had a couple of bodies, I had the one Nikon D1 body I was really attached to—it had all my settings and everything, so day after day I kept abusing that one same body, and it still performed. I can't believe that camera held up.

I had never done any wildlife night photography, but using the digital camera out in the field, using strobe, I

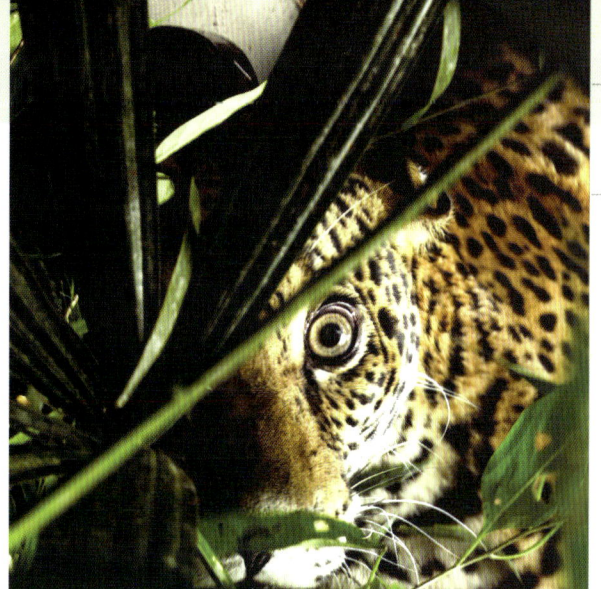

Spots of the Cat

A sedated jaguar fixes the camera with a stare as she begins to awaken. The jaguar's rosettes or spots are as unique as a fingerprint from animal to animal, and researchers closely monitor their subjects to evaluate the health of the ecosystem. © Denise Rocco-Zilber

was absolutely amazed by the quality we got. There's nothing more thrilling than when someone asks, "Did you get it?" and you can see it right there in the LCD.

In my work I have to say that not only the immediacy of digital is such a thrill, but being able to make that connection with people, and showing them the images when you're doing it—it's always so great to connect with them through the pictures.

Cat up a Tree

When the jaguar was finally trapped up a tree by the chasing hounds, after a six-hour chase, Denise found her batteries wouldn't give juice to her digital camera due to the humidity. Finally contact was made, and using a tripod to steady the 300mm lens, this intimate shot of a jungle cat at bay resulted. © Denise Rocco-Zilber

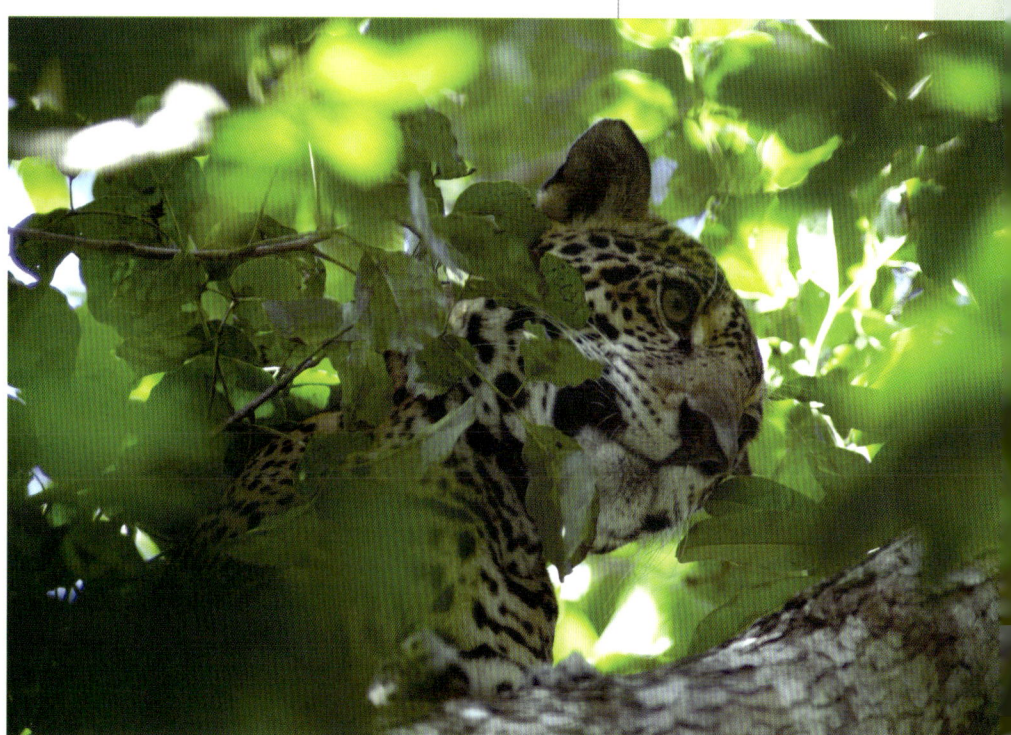

DESERT

Few places cause such anguish among professional photographers as deserts. Heat, wind, and especially sand create conditions that are physically demanding, professionally challenging—and hell on equipment.

Although today's cameras are rugged examples of modern technology, they use moving parts in the lens barrels and rely on an especially delicate component, the CCD or CMOS imaging chip—all highly vulnerable to sand. Film photographers will know that a bit of dust or sand inside the mechanism can scratch a whole roll of film, or become lodged in the advance mechanism permanently and ruin an entire shoot. So it is with digital—dust on the imaging chip can create an unvarying spot on the image itself. This spot is usually too small to perceive on the LCD preview screen, and only shows up when processing and cataloging the images following a day's shoot, and sometimes not even then.

Pulitzer Prize-winning desert photographer Jack Dykinga takes the simplest approach to this problem: "My first defense is to bring two of everything: cameras, digital-spot light-meters, lenses, tripods. Repair equipment like duct tape, jeweler's screwdrivers, lens wrenches, and lens cleaning kits are essential. 'Canned air' is good for blowing off accumulated dust and sand."

But two of everything is only part of the solution. The only way sand gets into digital equipment is when changing lenses. Peter Menzel's solution is never to change lenses. "One thing I learned is you don't want to change lenses with digital. If you get some sort of dust inside your camera, every one of your pictures is going to have a big piece of dust on the image. You can only see it when there's a sky or something, but it's a hassle.

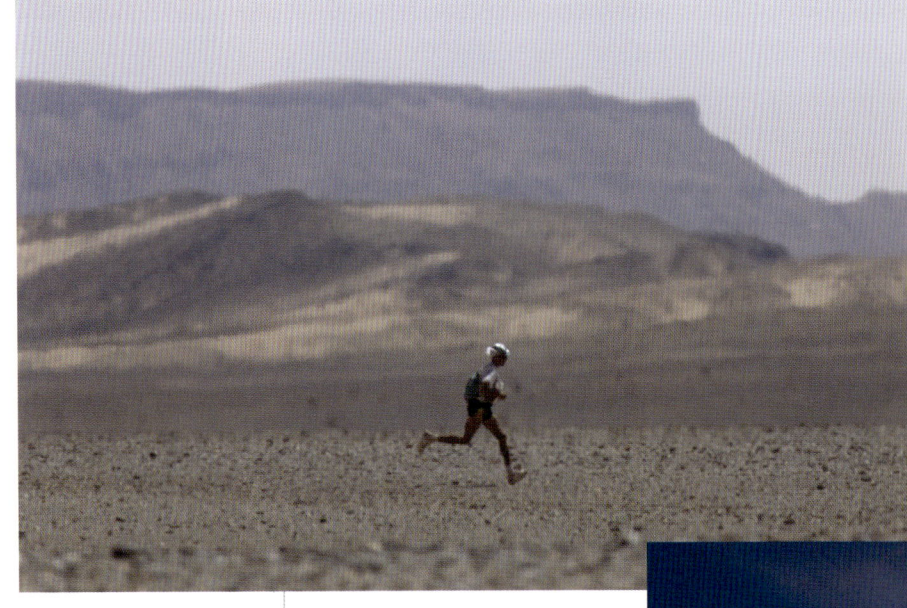

Desert Dash
A competitor in the Marathon des Sables races across the inhuman landscape of Morocco during the 1999 competition, covered digitally by Quokka Sports of San Francisco. © Corey Rich

Wide-Angle World
Alberta's badlands around Drumheller are a prime area for finding dinosaur bones. Natural processes have exposed a rich cache of fossils and even complete dinosaur skeletons. Using a wide-angle lens (18mm or less for most digital cameras) helps communicate the scale of the landscape.

That's why I've got three bodies now, each with a different lens, dangling around my neck at all times, and never change lenses. Then they can get all dirty and screwed up on the outside, but nothing's going to damage your image quality as long as the lens is clean."

If you do extensive work in extreme environments such as deserts, you need to know how to perform basic camera maintenance, including imaging chip-cleaning in the field. Before you leave, go to a reputable camera store and ask to see a chip-cleaning demonstration, using an antistatic brush or "sensor swab." This is still evolving technology and the results are not guaranteed, so you may have to repair your image in Photoshop. Best bet is to have your camera and lenses professionally cleaned following a trip. This may cost several hundred dollars, but can extend the life of your equipment enormously and save your professional work and reputation.

Preventing sand from reaching your equipment is probably the wisest precaution. When the camera is out and shooting, it may be unavoidable, though keeping a fanny pack or other soft case at hand can cut down on sand risk. But take extra measures to prevent infiltration when it's packed. Hard-shell Pelican cases offer almost inviolable security. Zippered camera cases or "dry bags" are simply not to be trusted.

For the most part, while it's sand that affects the equipment; it's the heat that's so tough on the shooter. Dehydration is a real medical risk in a desert, as is extended exposure to the sun. Camera batteries, mechanisms, and software are mostly impervious to these factors: people are not. Wearing sunglasses, large-brimmed hats, and neck scarves or bandannas are necessary parts of the desert photographer's wardrobe.

Sandy Swoop

Composing a tight geometric shape can give aesthetic strength to a landscape shot. The simplicity of a desert dune can create sensuous, flowing lines. Sand is one of the main enemies of anything mechanical, so keeping your gear in dustproof cases whenever possible makes good sense. © Corey Rich

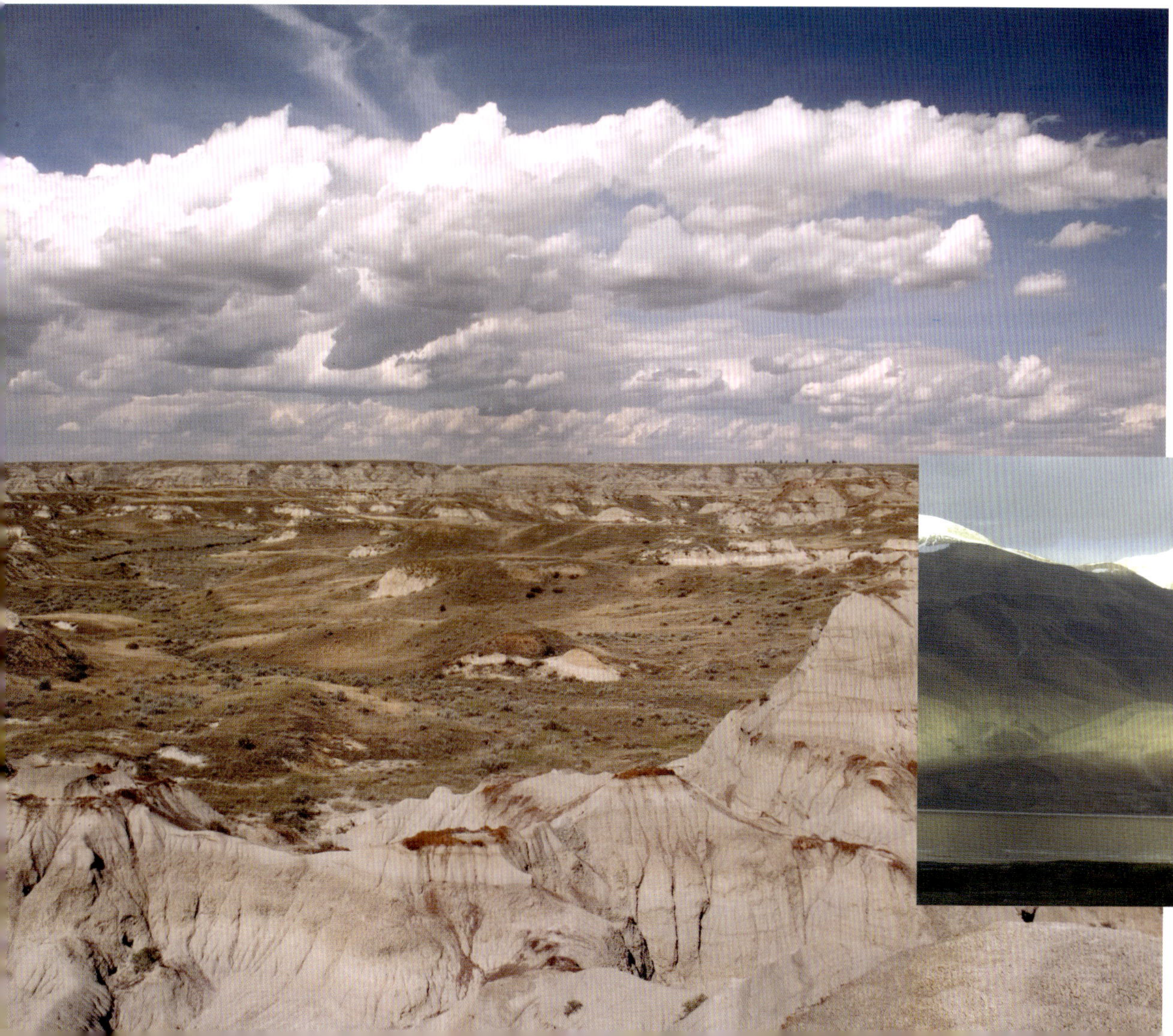

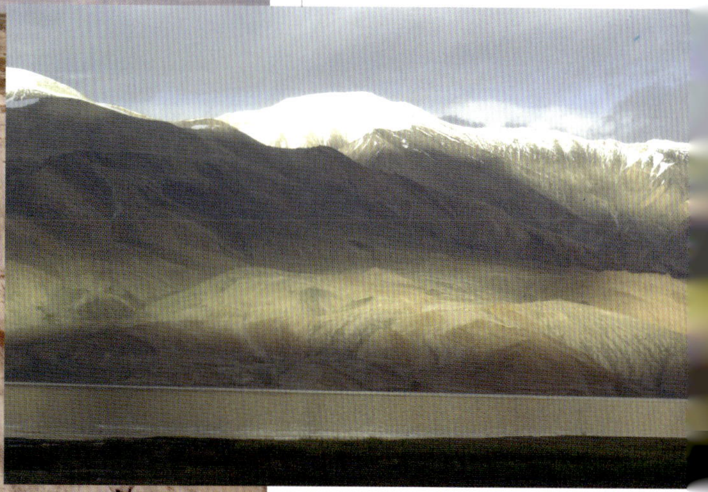

Bands of Light

Distance and drama of the Tibetan border region are conveyed by this horizontal composition of land, water, mountain, and ice beneath an evening sky. The high desert of Rupshu in India's eastern Ladakh holds Tso Mori or "Mountain Lake" and the 350-year-old Karzok monastery.

MOUNTAINS

Mountains are places of great beauty, spiritual connection, physical challenge, and sometimes human drama. These facets can be expressed in good photography, be it film or digital. Mountain environments also have a dynamic quality that is more difficult to capture, from avalanches that last just a few dramatic seconds, to slow-moving glaciers. Still photography is able to freeze motion, not show it; but there are dynamic elements at play where it pays to watch the weather and light in your quest for great composition and color. Swirling clouds, rising mist, a dusting of snow, and the transient effect of alpenglow can transform a mountain scene into the sort of powerful image produced by internationally renowned nature photographer Galen Rowell.

Part of the challenge is to impart some sense of scale. With wide-angle and medium focal-length telephoto zoom lenses, you can compose more powerful compositions in the camera than with fixed focal-length lenses.

Laptops and external hard drives can be susceptible to altitude problems. The differential in air pressure between the interior of the sealed hard drive and the altitude can rupture the hard drive case or otherwise prevent it from working. Most are manufactured for use below 9,000 feet (2,750m), but problems can occur at much lower altitudes. Solutions to this hard-drive problem include using the SmartDisk Flashtrax for memory storage up to 80GB, or saving everything directly to CD via a battery-operated CF card-to-CD-R writer like the Disc Steno (*see page 44*), though you are not able to review the images.

Shooting digitally in mountains, you have the usual weight, power, and storage constraints. A lightweight DSLR like the Nikon D100 or the Canon D10 is ideal for climbing or backpacking with. Storage problems can be minimized by shooting with the highest-capacity memory cards possible using the lesser resolution of JPEGs, rather than RAW files, and camera power can be conserved by not using either the LCD screen or the autofocus.

In very remote areas you are more likely to set up a base camp. The most famous base camp is on the Nepal side of Mt. Everest at 17,600 feet (5,370m). Digital shooters going above Everest Base Camp into the "death zone" have the greatest challenge of all, but many have now proven that digital is up to the challenge of working reliably at the top of the world.

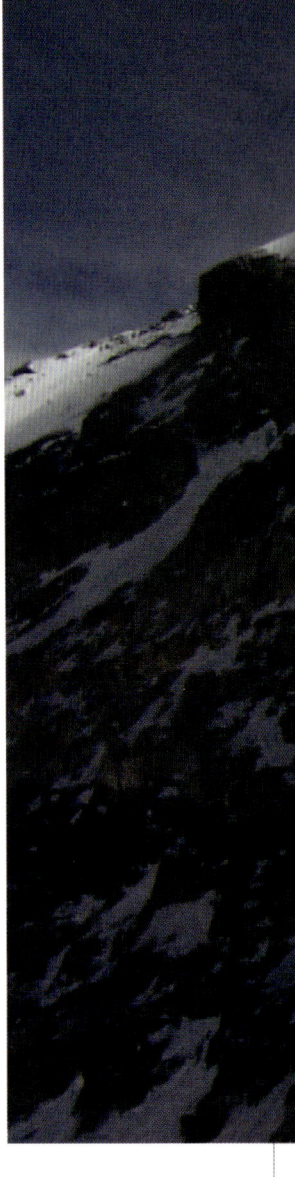

Everest Summit Approach

Climbers working their way along the South East Ridge toward the Hillary Step on the upper slopes of Mt. Everest. This shot is a frame-grab from the HD video *Farther than the Eye Can See*. Each frame is 5MB in size.
© Michael Brown

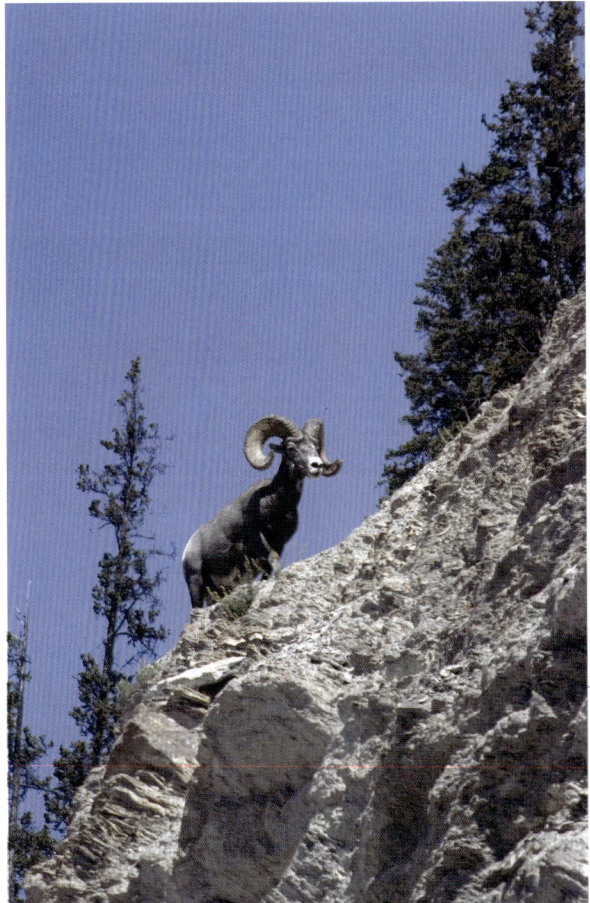

Bighorn Sheep

Timing is everything. This magnificent animal was just yards from a main road, and he contrasted very nicely against a deep blue sky. These animals frequent the mineral licks near Sunwapta Gorge, Icefields Parkway, between Jasper and Lake Louise in Alberta, Canada.
© Mark Langley

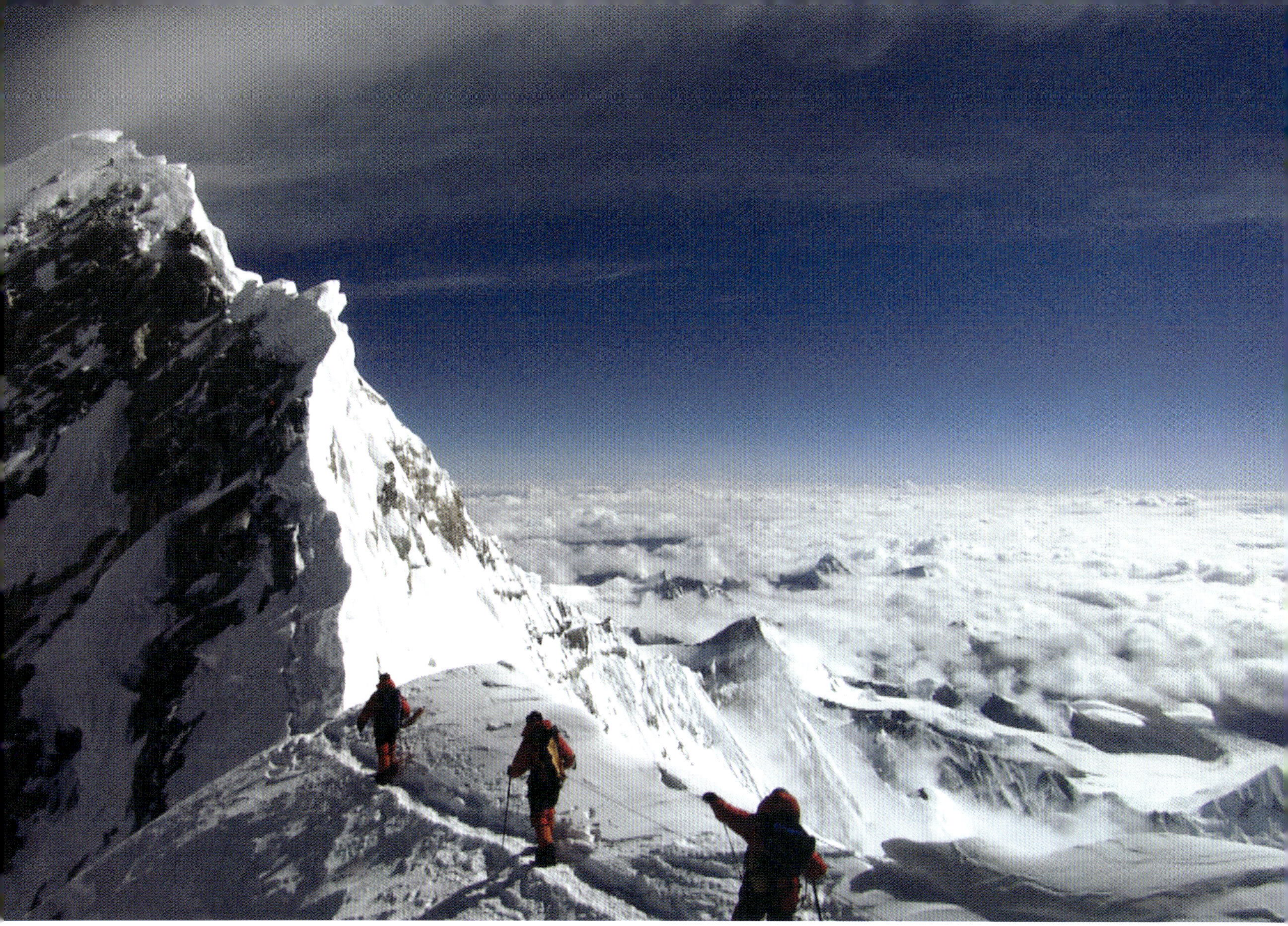

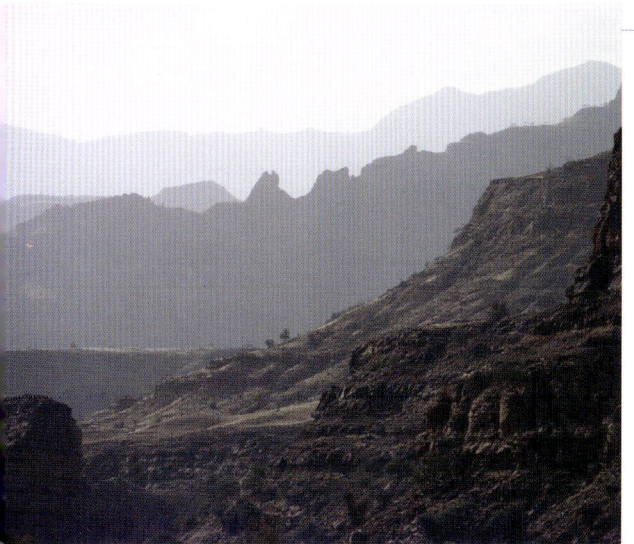

Simien Mountains

Ras Dashen, the highest mountain in Ethiopia (15,157 feet/4,620m), as seen from the Tekeze River. The hazy skies and evening light add a sense of depth to receding lines of rugged ridges.

Canadian Escarpment

Dark rock and shaded trees against a snow-capped peak at high noon made this exposure challenging. Use of a circular polarizer and underexposing by one f-stop preserved the detail without washing out the highlights.
© Mark Langley

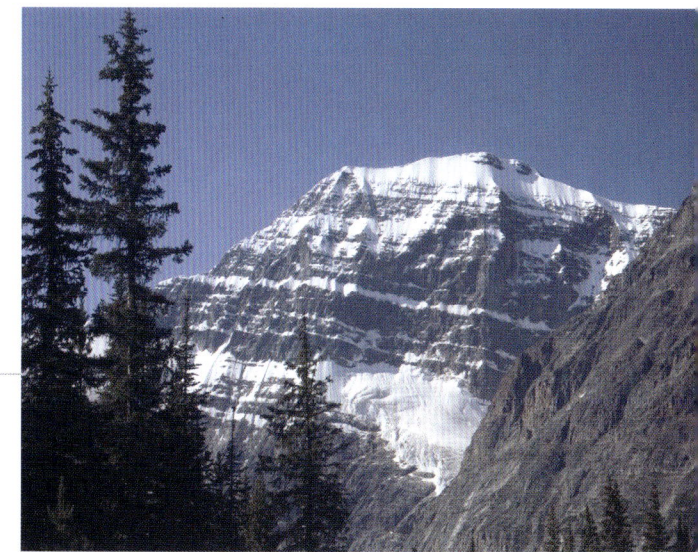

INTO THE DEATH ZONE—DIDRIK JOHNCK

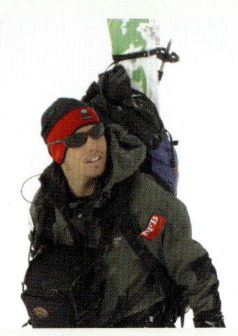

Not every photographer gets his work on the cover of Time magazine, but then not every photographer reaches the top of Everest. Didrik Johnck was still in his twenties when he joined blind climber Eric Weihenmayer on his successful "seven summits" climb of Everest in 2001. Didrik has been engaged in adventure and photography for years and has shot climbing, skiing, and snowboarding all over the world. He made the switch to digital with his 2002 climb of Mt. Elbrus.

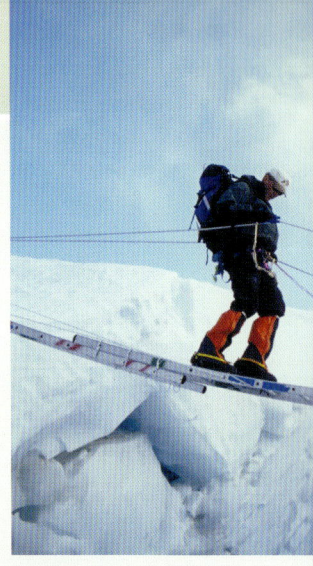

During April and May 2001 I worked from between base camp at 17,500 feet (5,370m) to the summit of Everest, 29,035 feet (8,800m). There are four camps on Everest, and I was constantly going between all four. We reached the summit on May 24; Eric was the first blind man to get there.

I used a Canon G3 compact digital, and the Canon EOS 1N film camera; today I'd take the Canon 10D, no question about it, and probably a G5 backup. It's small, lightweight, uses Compact Flash memory, and the same batteries as the 10D. There's definitely something to be said for the fact that cameras are getting smaller, lighter, just to shave down all the weight on a big climb like that.

The longest I ever spent up there was about a week, and even in the extreme cold, shooting 200 images a day, I could get at least a day out of each battery, depending on how much flash I was using. I wouldn't do any editing in camera—only if I ran out of space on my last CF card. Right now I use a 1-gig and a 2-gig card, and I've found I have a hard time filling up a 1-gig card in a day. That's 148 RAW images on a 1-gig card, 6.3-megapixel files.

At altitude, sometimes you're dumbed down a little bit. So you have to rely on certain auto settings—I leave the white balance on Auto, but I still shoot in the manual mode, to adjust both speed and exposure for each shot.

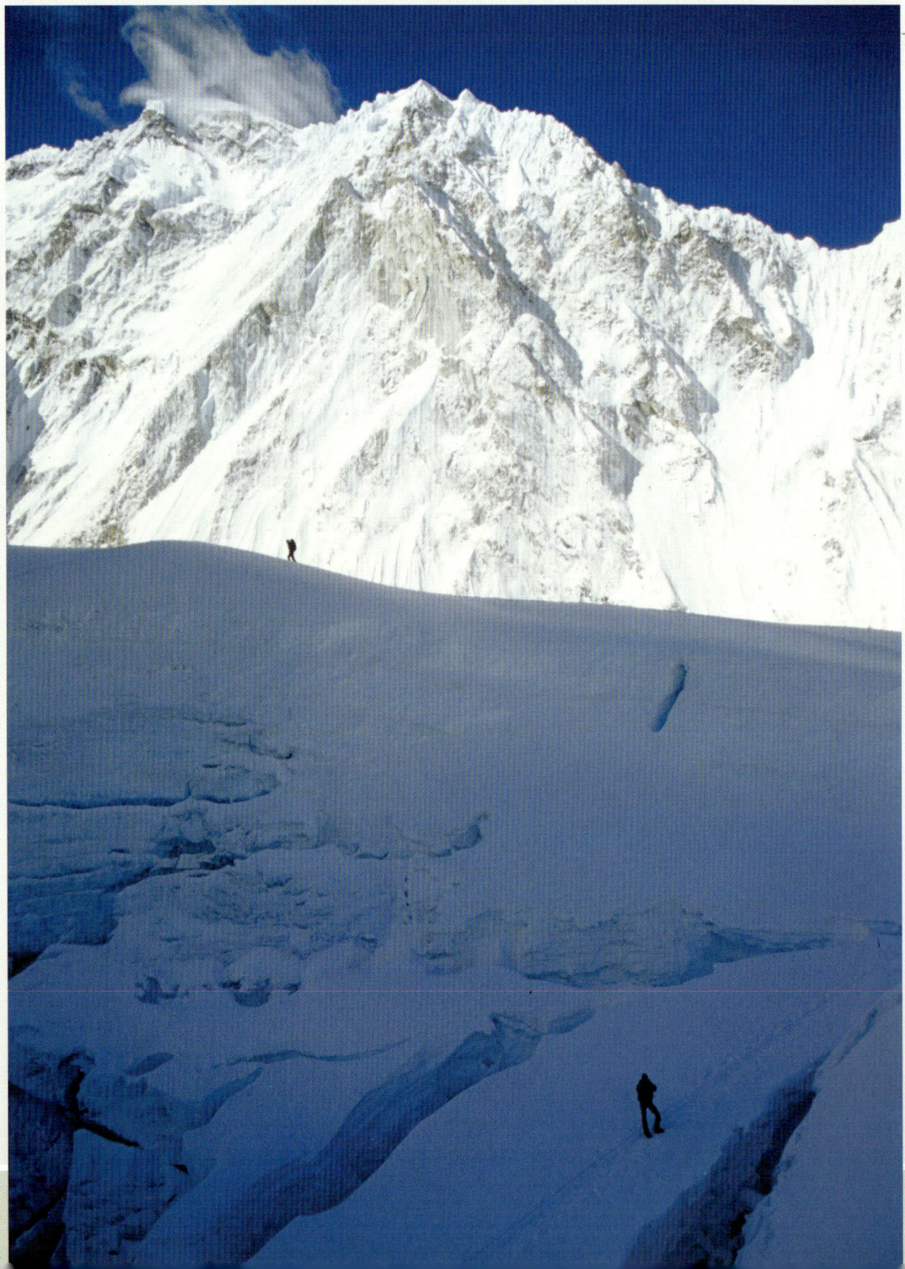

DIDRIK JOHNCK

Crevasse Crossing

The drama of mountaineering is often as difficult to capture as it is to endure. The photographer "crawled on my belly up to the edge of the crevasse… made sure the camera strap was secured around my wrist and placed camera into the crevasse, and angled the lens towards the climber."
© Didrik Johnck

Card Game at 26,000 Feet

Something as prosaic as a card game can become remarkable if the game is played on Everest, at the edge of the mountaineer's "death zone", and one of the players is blind—Erik Weihenmayer, center, on his successful summit attempt. © Didrik Johnck

Khumbu Icefall

"One of the toughest situations to shoot is where you have bright sunlight and dark shadows in the scene. In this instance having a digital camera enabled me to shoot four to five frames before I got the exposure I wanted. With film I would have shot a whole roll on this scene." © Didrik Johnck

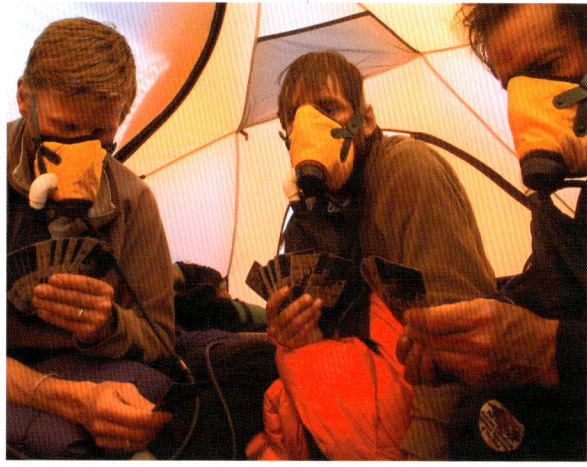

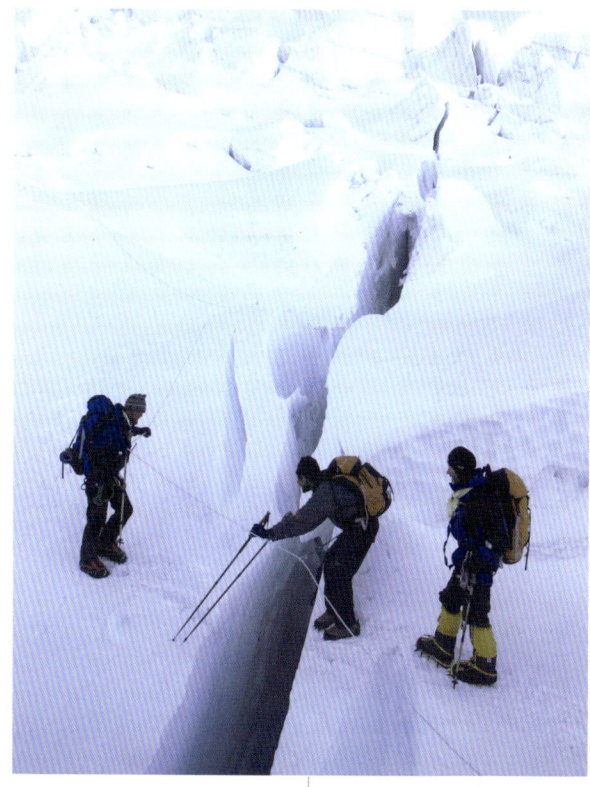

Feeling His Way

Erik Weihenmayer uses trekking poles to check his next step approaching a crevasse on Everest, while his team mates verbally coach him on. This shot was chosen to appear in *Life* Magazine's Year in Pictures. Photographed with a Nikon D1, ISO 200, 1/160 sec at f6.7. © Didrik Johnck

Sundown on Chomolungma

The massive southeast face of Everest (Chomolungma to the Tibetans) catches the last daylight in this evening shot. "I fought the ice forming on the LCD by continuously wiping it with my sleeve." Taken with a Canon 10D, 1/45 sec at f11. © Didrik Johnck

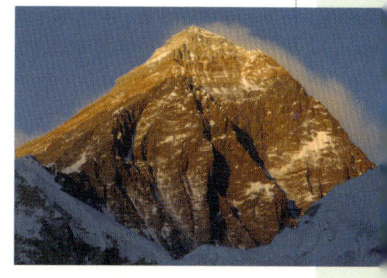

Once you're familiar with the system, and see the little green arrow on the side of the viewfinder, you know what to do to get the right exposure in conditions like snow.

It's interesting, though, with a film camera you have to over expose in snow conditions one to two stops, but the D60 that I used on Elbrus was only about half a stop off. You could make up the differences in post-processing, but I'd rather be out there taking pictures than sitting in front of a computer. And with the power issues on an expedition, you want to keep editing time to a minimum.

I've learned to check the 1- or 2-second preview just to double-check the image is being recorded and the exposure is right. But you've got to be careful—if you have the brightness of the LCD too bright, you can underexpose your images, or too low and you'll overexpose to compensate. You have to do some testing to make sure your preview image reflects your result.

I use polarizing filters and some others in a soft-padded filter pouch. I have graduated neutral-density filters, the Kokin system—I use them only infrequently, but when you need them they're worth their weight. I have both the hard-edge and the soft-edge filters, ranging from 1/3 to a full stop. For power, I use those disposal Expedition Batteries by Stuart Cody, who makes them out of his garage—those will be used in conjunction with the camera battery charger, to power the charger so that I can charge up the camera's batteries.

I've dropped flash cards in the snow; the camera gets dropped in snow and it works, it gets dunked in water and it works—they're making the cameras pretty reliable. I think the whole thing with digital is that I shot both film and digital for almost five years because I was afraid to switch over, but finally I was convinced that digital gear is just as reliable as film under pretty tough conditions.

AERIALS

Getting an aerial perspective on the world is ideally suited to digital capture techniques and equipment. With the right gear and plenty of power, you can shoot for long periods without having to rewind or reload. Several fast identical cameras with big buffers, sharp fast lenses, and plenty of large, fast-writing cards are just the starting point. You may even want a Kenyon Gyro Stabilizer if you have to shoot at slow speeds, or in low light.

The basic techniques of good aerial photography are the same whether shooting digital or film. And you need good weather conditions—when flying and shooting, ensure you have full knowledge of the weather you are likely to encounter: safety is your utmost priority. To charter an aircraft, decide on a light plane or helicopter for the job, then find the right pilot and model of plane. Discuss your needs and planned series of shots thoroughly before you take off. Sketches of the shot you are after can help the pilot understand how to get you into position.

Any aircraft encounters turbulence and has a lot of vibration (helicopters especially) so don't rest your arms and camera on any part of the aircraft. You typically need

Mixmaster belong Jesus Christ.

The Pidgin English term for helicopter as spoken in Papua New Guinea

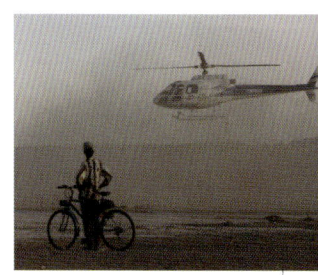

Whirlybird Whirlwind

Helicopters are one of the most useful means of getting airborne to shoot landscapes and to follow long-distance races, though they are not without their hazards. Beware of the blowing wind and dust at take off and landing.
© Corey Rich

Aerial Action

Alinghi, the Swiss winner of the 2003 America's Cup in New Zealand, is pursued by a fleet of spectator boats in the Moet Cup Race held in San Francisco in 2003. This action can best be shot from a helicopter.
© Abner Kingman

Glaciers of Greenland

Low haze, clean aircraft cabin windows, smooth air, a cloudless sky, and a generous pilot all played a role in capturing the rugged beauty of this Greenland glacier valley. Shooting through Plexiglas is difficult, not only because of light and color effects, but because autofocus often "sees" the window, not the landscape.
© Mark Langley

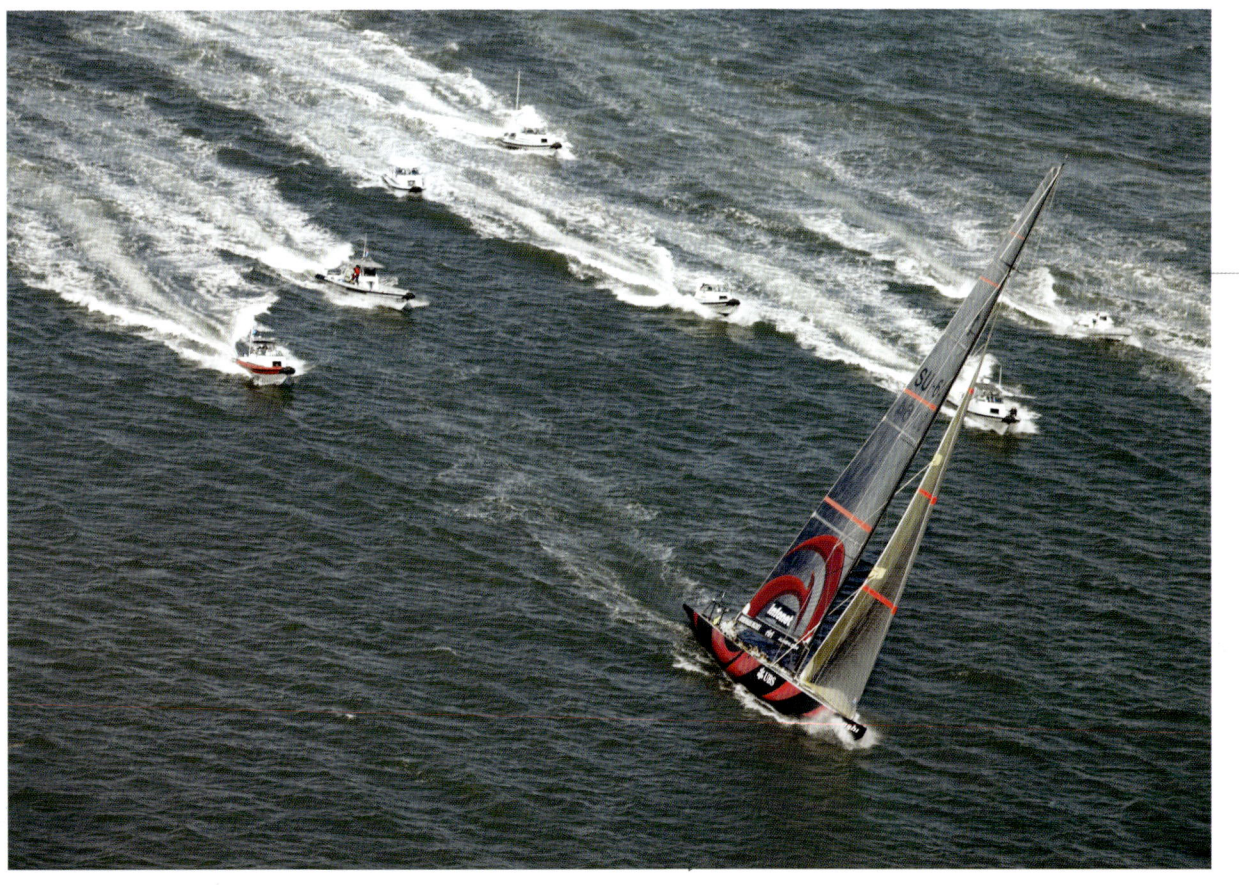

to shoot at speeds triple or four times the focal length of the lens to keep everything sharp, so for a 100mm lens you would want to have minimum of 1/250th (but preferably 1/500th) of a second shutter speed. Zoom lenses help you frame your subject more precisely. Some aerial shooters recommend taping the focus ring to ensure that it does not vibrate out of focus.

Shooting from hot air or helium balloons, or kites, or model aircraft is a whole other specialty.

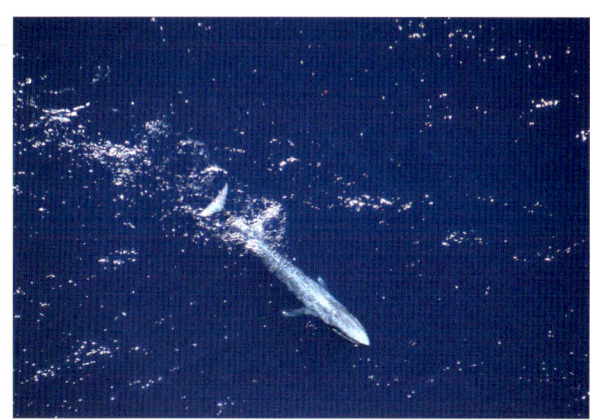

Blue Whale Below

Getting an aerial view from a light plane with a digital camera has revolutionized the possibilities in scientific research, as this picture of pygmy blue whales testifies. Unless you want low-level shots, a light single-engine plane with a high wing, such as a Cessna, may be your best proposition. For certain shots, having your camera wired to a GPS can help locate the images accurately with coordinates imported into each frame's metadata. The Nikon D1X has a serial port RS323C connector that can be linked to a Garmin GPS.© Peter Gill and Margie Morrice

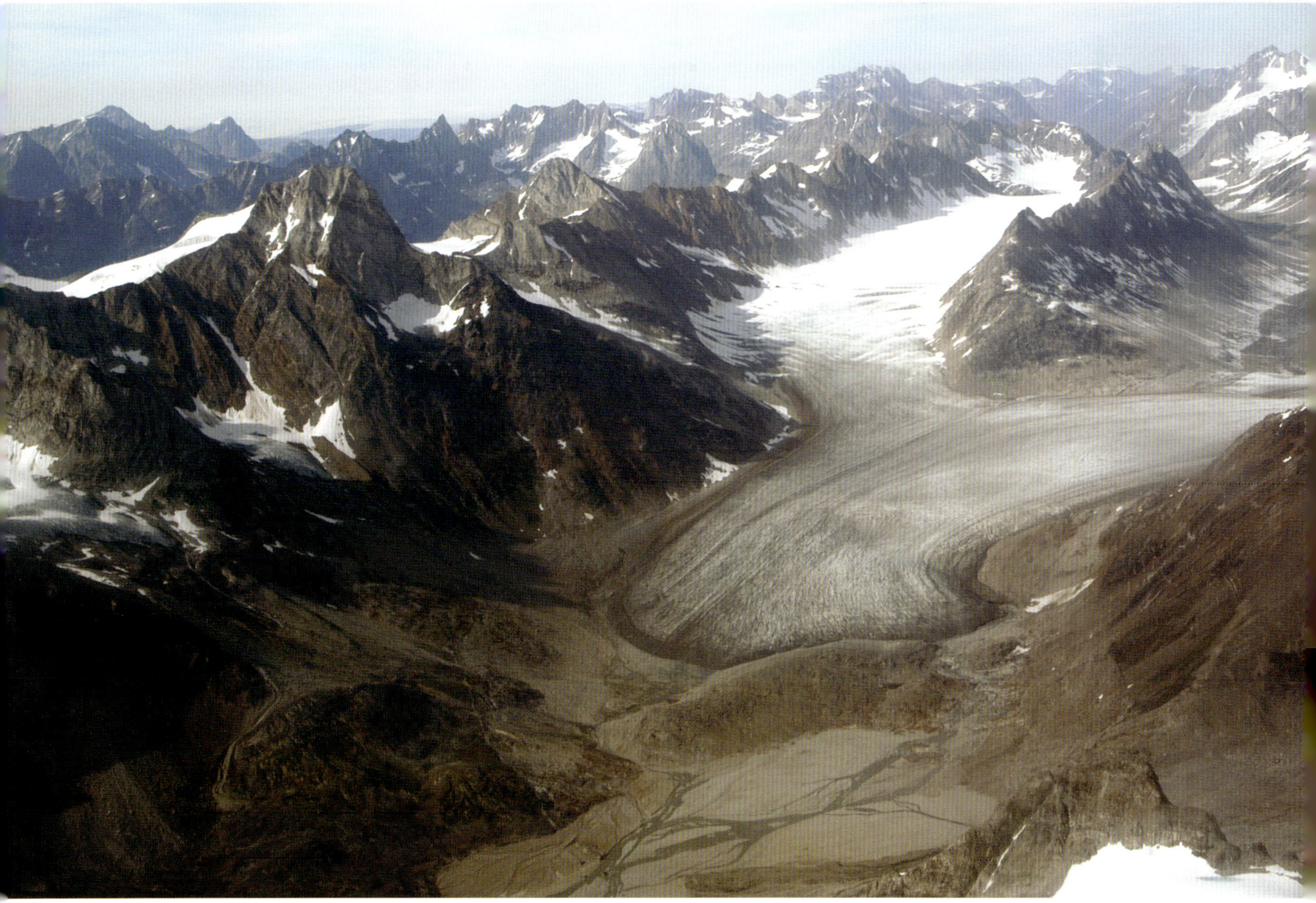

EXTREME AIR—CRAIG O'BRIEN

Throwing yourself out of an airplane more than two miles above the Earth is hard enough, but try taking pictures on the way down—that's extreme. Craig O'Brien has managed to make it all seem, if not easy, at least "doable" on more than 8,000 jumps in the past dozen years. Widely acknowledged as one of the world's leading skydive photographers, and for three years running a half of the tandem world champion skysurfing team (with his wife, Tanya), Craig has found that doing commercial skydiving photography has finally become more lucrative than his "day job" as a union electrician—thanks to digital.

I actually started shooting digital in the fall of 2001, after being one of these guys who kept saying, "I'm not going to go digital, film is where it's at; I love the film look, I'm never going to change." Then Canon came out with a reasonably priced digital camera, the D30, and I started looking at that and said, "Wow, that's pretty cool, that's actually really nice." I started thinking that for what I do, it's got to be the way to go. As it's turned out, it really is.

As soon as I saw that I could jump out of an airplane, photograph my subject, land, download these pictures onto my computer, and print out a photograph before these people even have a chance to get their parachutes packed for their next jump, I had an immediate sale. For skydiving and most sports, it's all about the excitement and the adrenalin. If you can show these people a picture of themselves while they're still high on an adrenalin rush, they can't get in their pockets fast enough.

Most of the time the photographer has to be the best flier. To get the shot, most skydivers travel all around the sky, and you need to have the ability to move along with them, and maintain the framing you want, the sunlight you want, the angle you want, and so forth.

I set up my camera based on what I'm shooting. Obviously if I'm shooting an individual I'm going to be much closer; if I'm shooting a large formation I know I'm going to be further away. Even if I'm going to shoot a

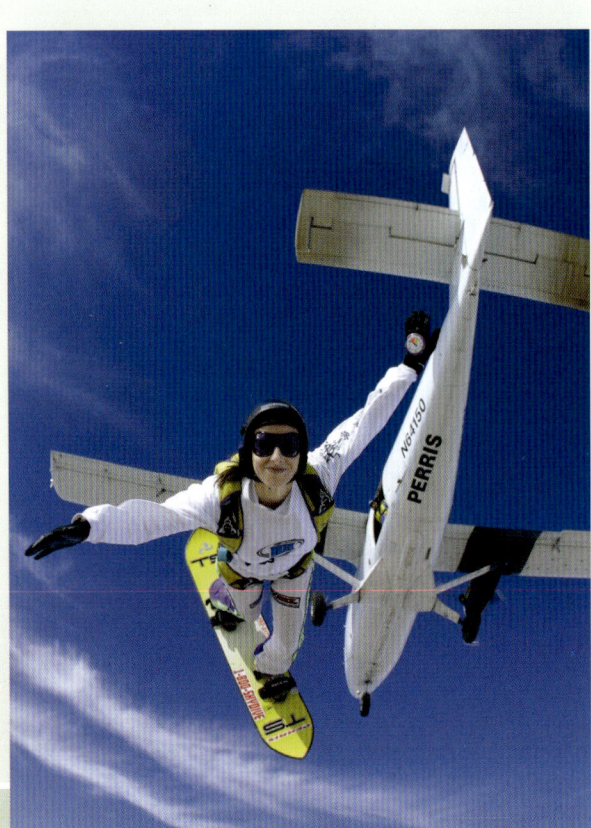

How Cool is This?
World champion skysurfer Tanya Garcia-O'Brien catches air in a big way, exiting the Twin Otter jump plane high over Perris, California. © Craig O'Brien

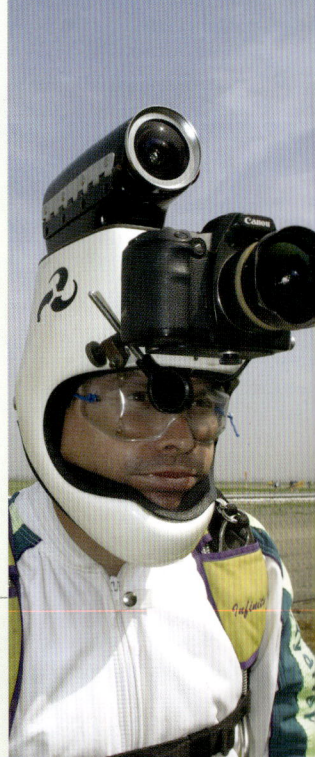

Camera Man
Craig O'Brien shows off his helmet-mounted cameras. A single-chip Sony digital video camera is on top, with a Canon D60 digital still at the front. Note the ring sight over the eye, giving a reference to center of the frame. © Koji Mizoi

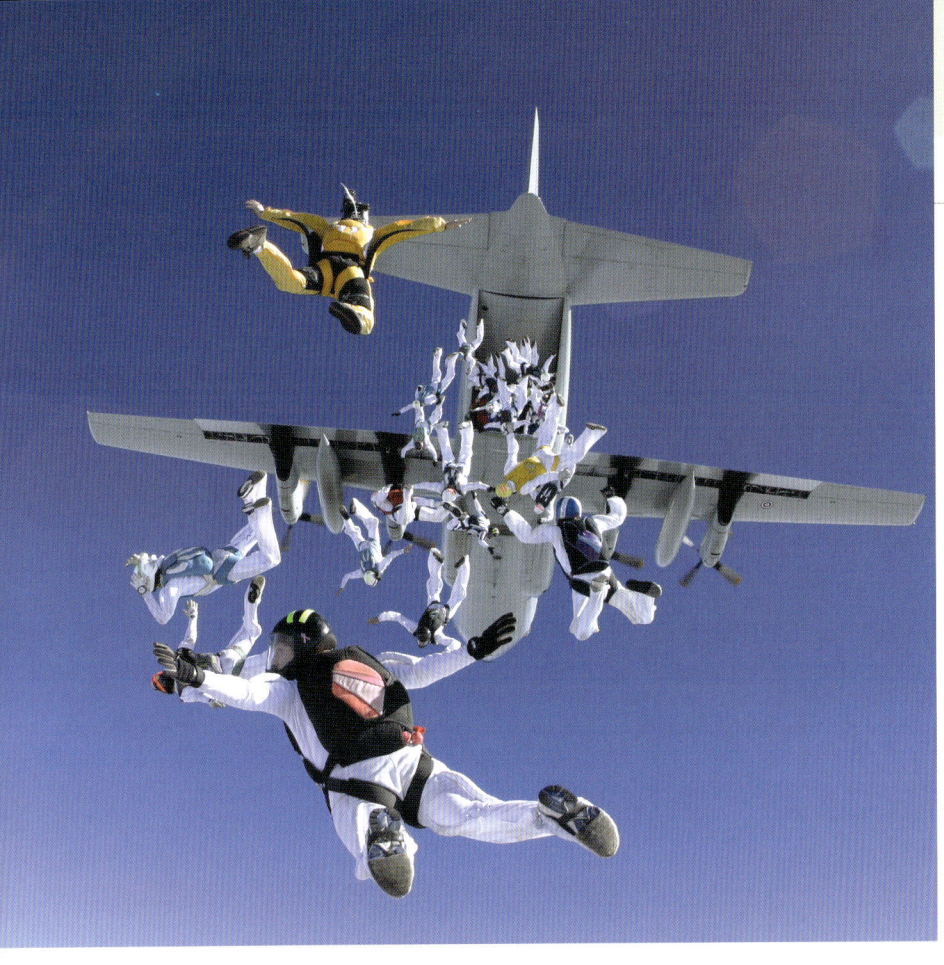

Strange Cargo

One of 14 planes discharges its cargo—20-plus skydivers falling toward a world-record formation of 357 jumpers—over Thailand early in 2004. Using a wide-angle lens helps keep all of the jumpers in view, but being close to the action is crucial. © Craig O'Brien

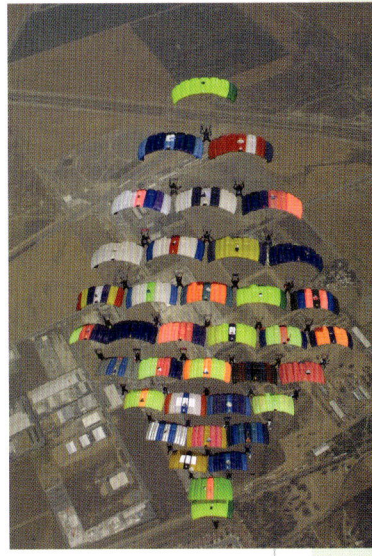

Aerial Ballet

A trial formation of 37 parachutes holds its shape in the skies above Perris, California, a high desert town known for auto races, sport biking, and skydiving. © Craig O'Brien

Wheels in the Sky

One of only three shots capturing all 357 jumpers linked, to set the world record for the largest freefall formation. Buffer issues prevented the photographer from catching more shots of the formation, which held for just six seconds. © Craig O'Brien

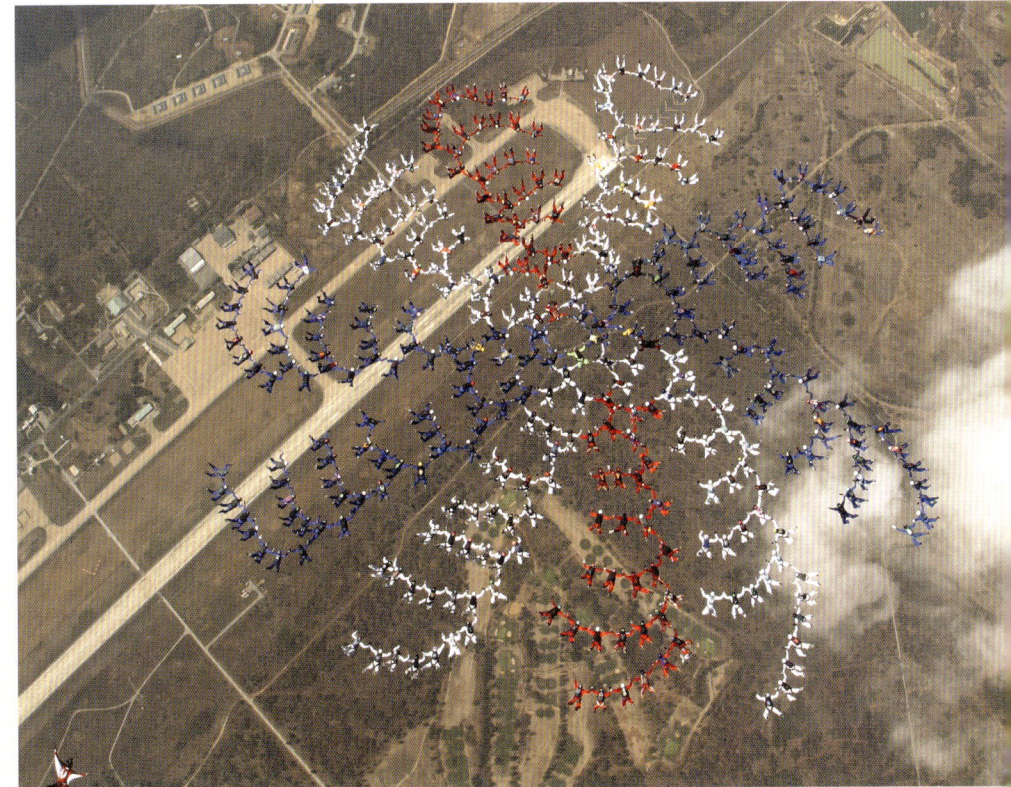

group of people, but there's one person that I might want to focus on in that group, I'm going to be closer to them and they're going to be featured in those shots, but I'm going to set my camera up for the proximity in which I'm going to fly to my subject.

With skydiving photography or videography, you don't have the ability to look through the viewfinder. These cameras are strapped to a helmet, and you basically have to learn your proximity just by experience, and based on the equipment you're using. Most of the time you're shooting with a lens that's more on the wide range, since it's a little easier for framing and focus. Depth of field—that's your biggest friend; if you don't understand how depth of field works, you don't stand a chance. Basically you're making your setup before you leave the airplane, and if you don't understand your setup, the chances of you consistently getting good photographs are slim.

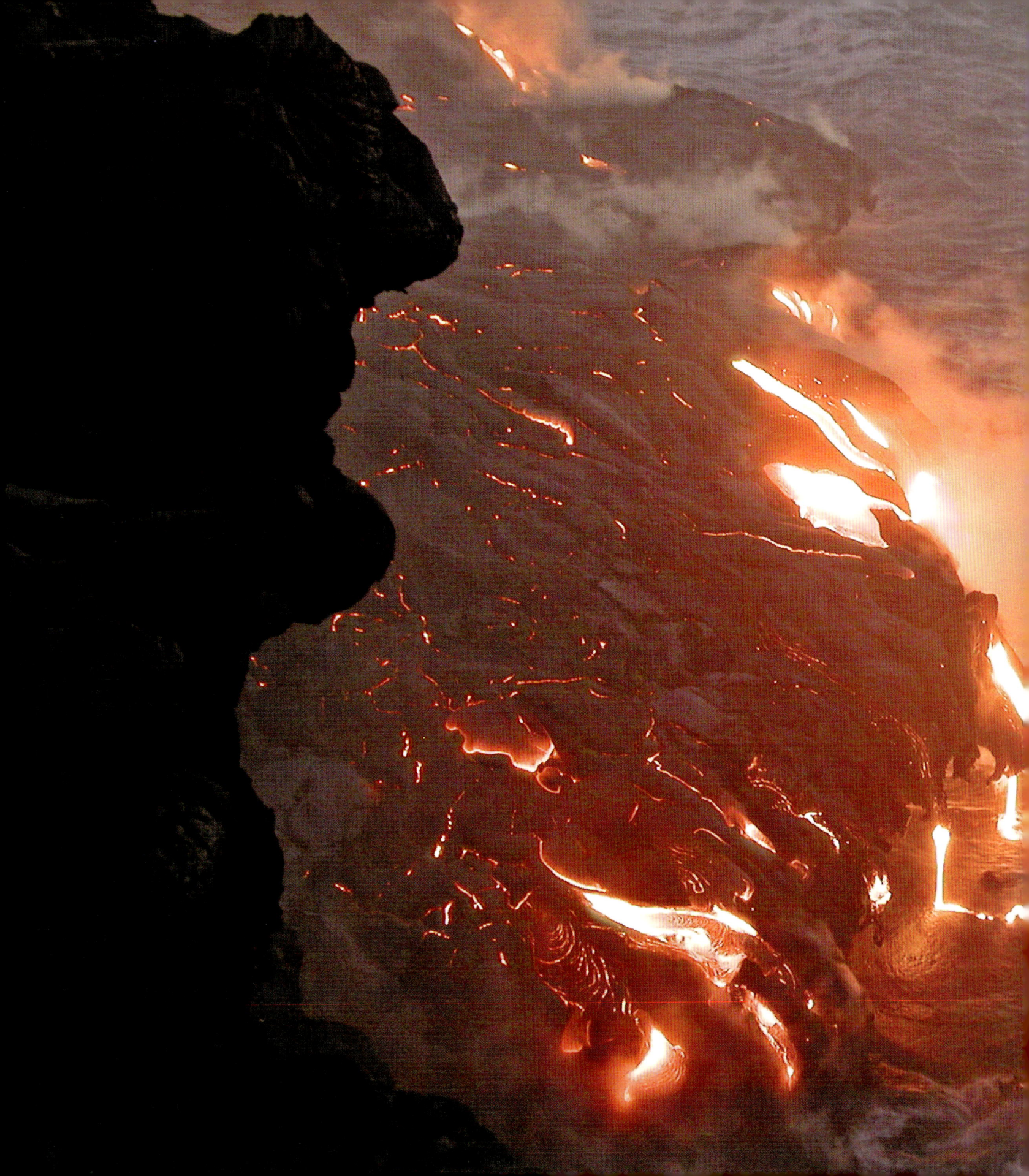

EXTREME SUBJECTS

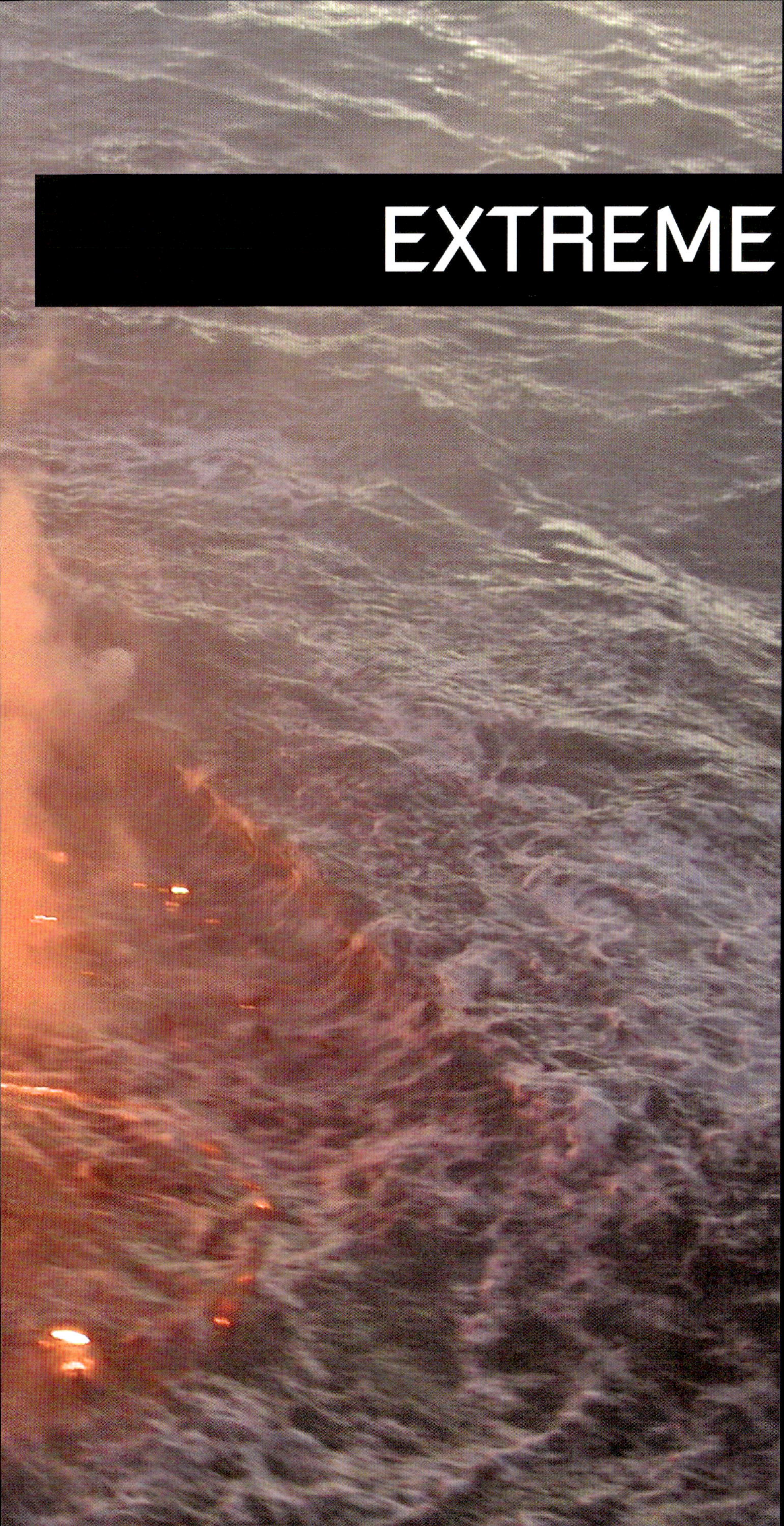

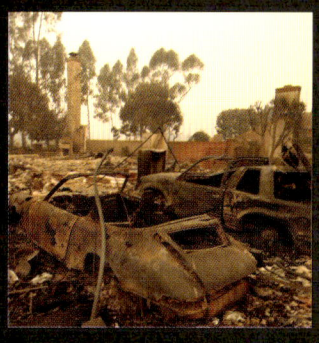

Pictures of famines and war have to be uncompromising. You can't pull punches when you're trying to show people what's going on. I don't want to make generic images that just show that something's happening out there.
James Nachtwey

Main: Don Swanson USGS

Top: © Robert Eplett / OES / CA

ARCTIC WILDLIFE

Polar bears, walrus, reindeer, Arctic foxes, and more than 130 bird species including kittiwakes, Arctic terns, little auks, and guillemots: all this in the Arctic island nation of Svalbard. Iceland is famous for its puffin colonies; Greenland has its musk ox; the Canadian Arctic has belugas, narwhals, and harp seals, while Alaska's 19 million-acre (8.6 million-hectare) Arctic National Wildlife Refuge (ANWR) has herds of caribou, migrating birds, wolves, wolverines, and three species of bear (polar, grizzly, and black).

Arctic wildlife has had to contend with traditional Inuit hunters and more recently European explorers; now it's tourists and environmental threats, not least global warming. This is having a significant effect on sea ice formation and temperatures, which in turn affects the habitats and productivity of the oceans and the wildlife.

The polar bear is the top Arctic predator and one of the most sought-after photo subjects—though it is very dangerous to be in the vicinity of one without a reliable means of defense (or escape). Bears are big business in Churchill, Manitoba. Several outfits run photo tours using "Tundra Buggies" as shooting platforms and as a means to get you where the bears congregate. Photographing from these vehicles is an advantage for digital users since power is available for all workflow needs and there is no limit on weight. You don't need super-long lenses, though telephotos are always helpful for intimate shots.

There are key places where you can shoot wildlife from land-based camps (*see pages 54–55*). They use Inuit guides, and travel is by snowmobile or four-wheel vehicles, so weight is less of an issue, but you need to conserve power and cope with the cold if you are living in a tent. Joining an expedition cruise ship is a more

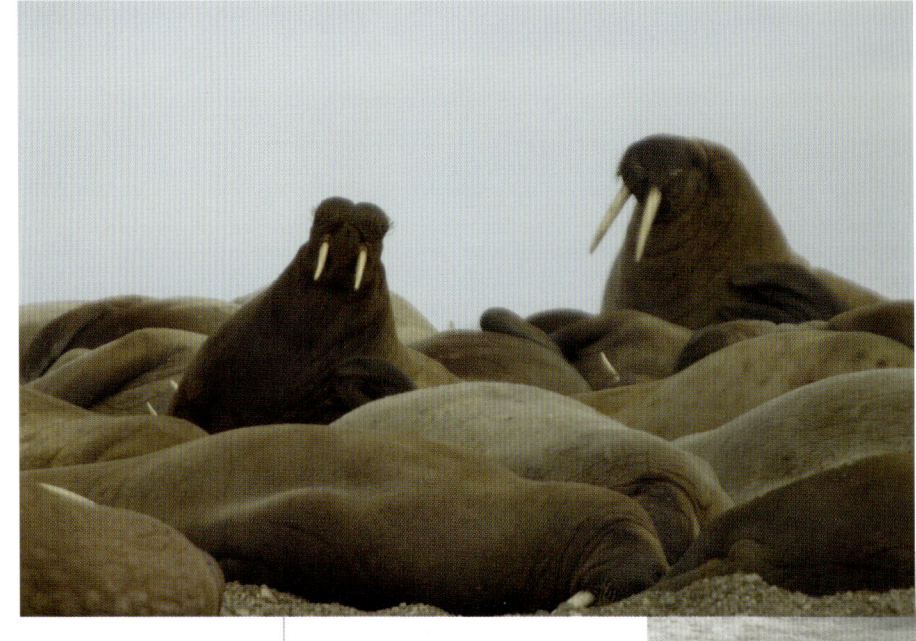

Walrus Hordes

Walrus on shore, Northeastland, Svalbard. Although almost wiped out by hunting, the walrus of Svalbard have been protected for decades. When hauled out on shore, they can be slowly approached from a safe distance for great photo opportunities, though a telephoto lens is still advisable. © Ralph Lee Hopkins

Arctic Fox

The small compact arctic fox is found throughout the north in arctic and alpine tundra. They occur in two color varieties—white, and this so-called "blue" form—and with their heavy coat are well adapted to arctic conditions. They are relatively easy to photograph with a longer telephoto lens as they are somewhat curious. © Mark Langley

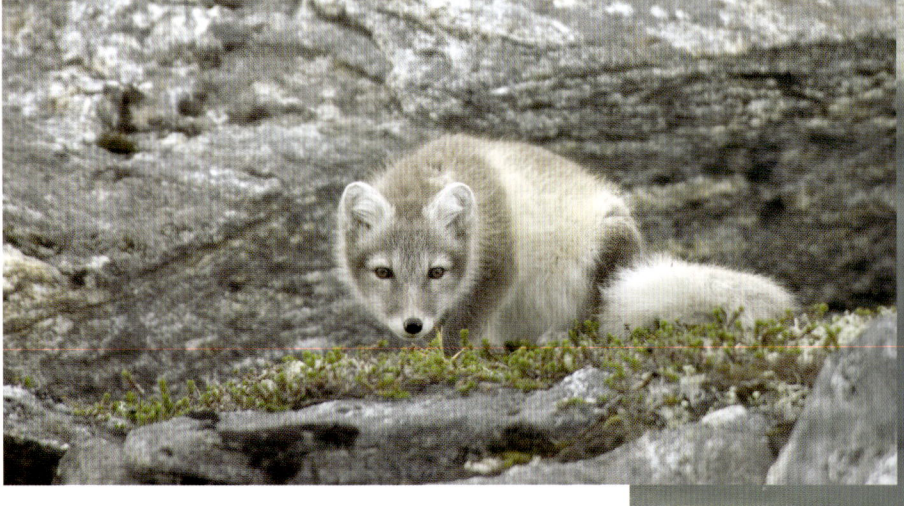

comfortable option. Ralph Lee Hopkins, wildlife photo instructor with Lindblad Expeditions, made the transition to shooting digital back in 1993. "I like the instant feedback of digital. Digital also takes away all the hassle of traveling with film. I use a G4 laptop and 1-gig cards with my Canon 10D. Being able to look at the histogram with the 2-second review and see you are getting the maximum out of the images is much better than film."

Shooting wildlife in the Arctic necessitates certain technical adjustments. Hopkins claims he carries less gear and fewer filters with digital equipment. "I only need a polarizer and neutral density. Any other adjustments I can make when I import the RAW files in Photoshop."

Arctic Terns

Arctic terns adorn an ice floe in Hinlopen Strait, photographed from a Zodiac. Arctic terns are the champion fliers of the bird world—they breed and raise their young in the Arctic, then fly south—all the way south, to Antarctica, for the winter.
© Ralph Lee Hopkins

Polar Bear

A polar bear walks on fast ice in Hornsund fjord, Spitsbergen, Svalbard. Polar bears in Svalbard have been protected from hunting since the early 1970s. They are always seeking their next meal, but younger bears often waste time and energy to approach an expedition ship. Polar bears are best (safely) photographed from ships or Zodiacs, not on shore!
© Ralph Lee Hopkins

ANTARCTIC WILDLIFE

Certain special places on the margins of Antarctica are a natural living zoo. A visit to these locations at the height of the breeding season is a window into what much of the world was probably like before the ravages of humans. The biological rhythm of this vast land is tied to the seasons more profoundly than anywhere else.

Crossing the Southern Ocean or Drake's Passage en route to the Antarctic Peninsula, you encounter magnificent sea birds, notably albatross (wandering, black-browed, and light-mantled sooty species). Good shots require a long lens, say a 200 or 300mm, and patience, but if they follow the ship you can blaze away for hours with a digital SLR. A fast shutter speed and fast-writing cards, plus a big buffer, help with this sort of subject.

On these crossings you never know when you will see other interesting subjects, so it pays to always have a long lens on your camera and have it easily accessible. The cruise ships mostly have open bridges, so you can watch with a degree of comfort and still be ready to leap into action if something interesting is spotted. Whales are sometimes seen, but not until you get closer to the coast will you be likely to encounter pods of feeding minke whales, humpbacks, or orcas—the "killer whales."

When conditions are right, being able to get into a Zodiac and cruise among them can result in exciting whale encounters. Having a humpback spy-hop right alongside is a thrilling experience. Here you need a very fast response and a very wide-angle lens to catch the moment.

Southern Elephant Seals

While molting in the austral (southern) summer, these cumbersome elephant seals lie cheek by jowl in stinking wallows at select points on the Antarctic continent. Here at Hanna Point on Livingston Island, which is part of the South Shetland Islands, they present an easy target for digital shooters wanting to capture their social behavior.

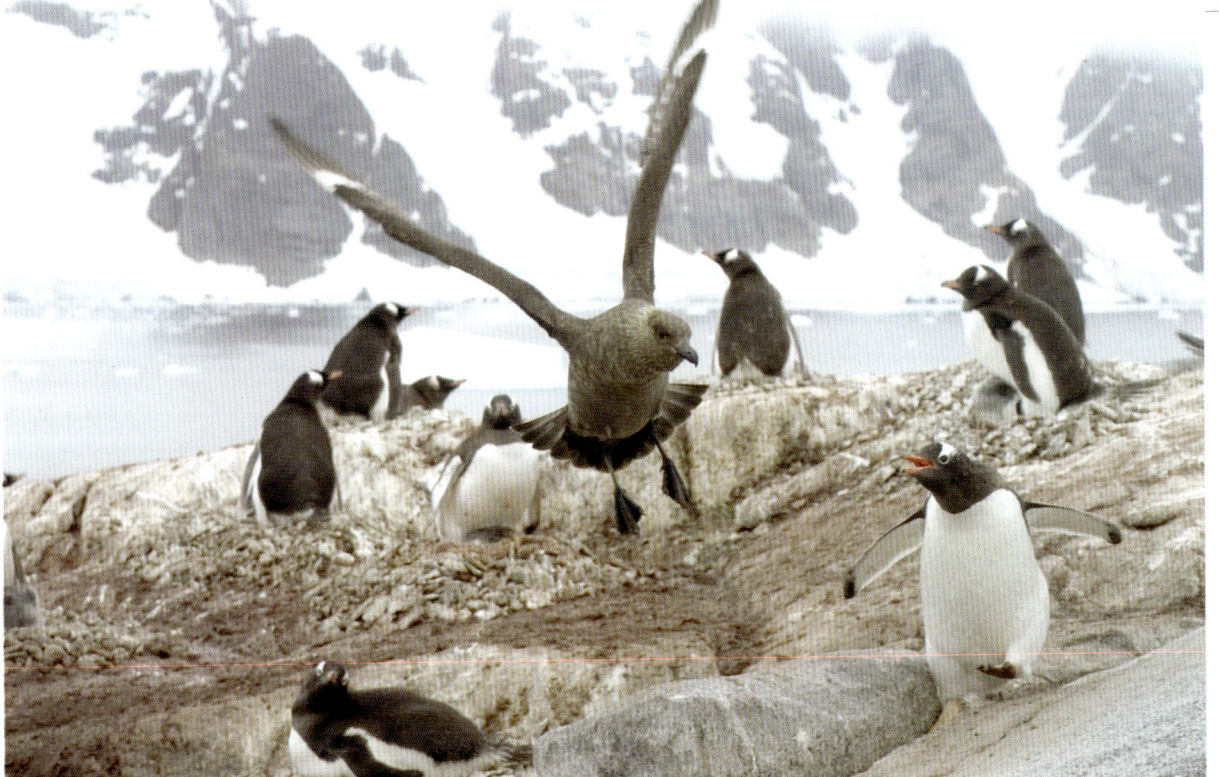

Defending the Nest

Marauding skuas work in pairs, swooping down to steal eggs or separate chicks from the safety of their parents, but the penguins staunchly defend their nests when breeding. Apart from these aerial threats, Antarctic penguin species have no predators on land and can be easily approached and photographed.

Whale Ho!

Minke whales are seldom easily photographed in Antarctica. They usually slice through the ocean alongside a ship, heading off at a fast tack, and you're lucky to get more than a few frames. Here in Andvord Bay on the Antarctic Peninsula we were treated to several hours with a pod of minkes leisurely circling our ship.

While I know of no instance where a big whale has touched a Zodiac full of people, the same cannot be said for the notorious orcas. Once we were photographing a whale pod that was time and again rushing at our tiny boat and brushing alongside. In one sweep, a wave of water was sent crashing into the boat and all over an open camera bag, drowning a high-end video camera.

Another species that deserves respect and caution is the leopard seal, the main predator of penguins. One once bit and punctured one of the pontoons of a Zodiac. We managed to beat a hasty retreat to the ship for repairs, since the Zodiac's many watertight compartments make this stable craft virtually unsinkable.

Most wildlife, however, is very benign. Penguins are the signature species of Antarctica, although only four of the 17 species breed in this biological region. Three of them, the Adelies, chinstraps, and gentoos, breed in summer, while the largest and most magnificent, the emperor penguin, breeds in winter in only a few colonies close to the continent on the fast ice. It is very difficult and expensive to see an emperor colony first hand; you either have to take a helicopter-equipped icebreaker cruise with Quark Expeditions, or fly into the Dawson-Lambton Glacier on the coast of the Weddell Sea with Adventure Network International (ANI). For the rest of us, it is more than enough to be satisfied with the delights of the wildlife experiences that can be encountered on the Antarctic Peninsula.

Whatever your motives for heading to Antarctica, it is not uncommon for travelers to come home enchanted with the wildlife, especially the penguins. Even non-photographers take hundreds of images, and most become interested in bird-watching. The subjects are special and the settings invariably dramatic.

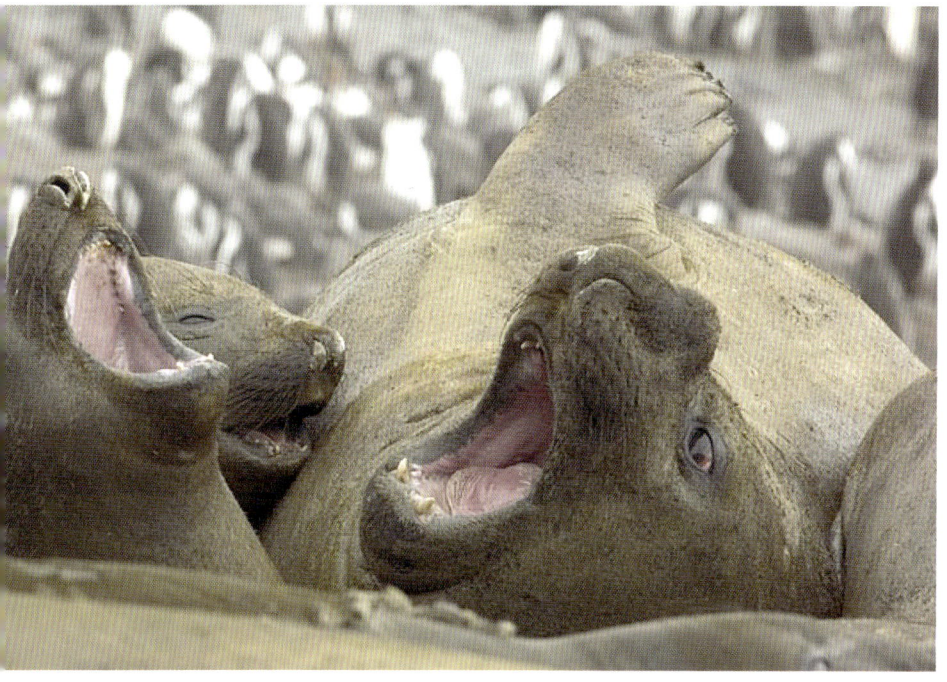

Domino Theory

Adelie penguins, the archetypal Antarctic penguin species, display characteristic flock behavior when entering or leaving the sea. They rush in or out as a group to minimize the chance of any one individual being taken by a predator. You can wait 10 or 15 minutes to get this shot, so it's best to have your camera set on burst mode and a high shutter speed, as it all happens very quickly.

AURORA—ALAN HIGH

Shooting amazing auroral displays, the Northern or Southern Lights, is one of the biggest technical challenges for digital capture. It is no less of a challenge for Canadian photographer Alan High, being out in the freezing-cold polar night for hours on end, pushing the limits of the technology. Ironically, it was the many years he spent as a paramedic that led Alan into the field of firefighting photography—about as different from photographing the Northern Lights as one can get.

Digital capture is better than film because CCDs don't suffer reciprocity failure like film. Different film stocks handle low light/long exposures uniquely, each with its own characteristics (good and bad). CCDs are very much "what you see is what you get." Digital will register/record lower light levels, fainter auroral details. I have captured aurora digitally that wouldn't even register on film.

There are reasons I don't shoot most of my auroras on the D1X: batteries, batteries, and batteries. The EN4s are bad enough when it's warm; useless in the cold. If the D1X was the only way I could shoot auroras, an external battery pack inside my jacket, like a Digital Camera Battery pack, would make sense. The sensors generate a fair bit of noise artifact, and the longer the exposure time and the higher the ISO setting, the worse it gets.

There are ways around the noise. You can shoot a dark frame during the session, then use that information to subtract the hot pixels (in Photoshop). The dark frame must be made at the same time as the capture, as the amount and location of hot pixels will change depending on ambient temperature, how long the sensor has been powered up, and exposure time. Newer cameras (Canon in particular) have a built-in noise reduction feature which essentially creates an "in camera" dark frame after your exposure and removes the hot pixel data. This prolongs the processing time when shooting, though—you might end up missing something. Post-capture noise reduction software works well, but takes a fair bit of time, as it needs to be calibrated for file sizes/formats, ISO, etc.

The sensor conversion factor is another deterrent to shooting auroras digitally. This, luckily, is becoming a moot point as manufacturers make real wide-angle lenses for digital cameras (the Nikon 10.5mm f2.8 full-frame fish-eye is one). I shoot really wide, and need all the light-gathering ability from a lens I can muster. Lenses with a maximum aperture of f2.8 are the bare minimum for this type of work.

Some general advice on shooting auroras: keep the ISO and the exposure times as short as possible —there's less noise artifact

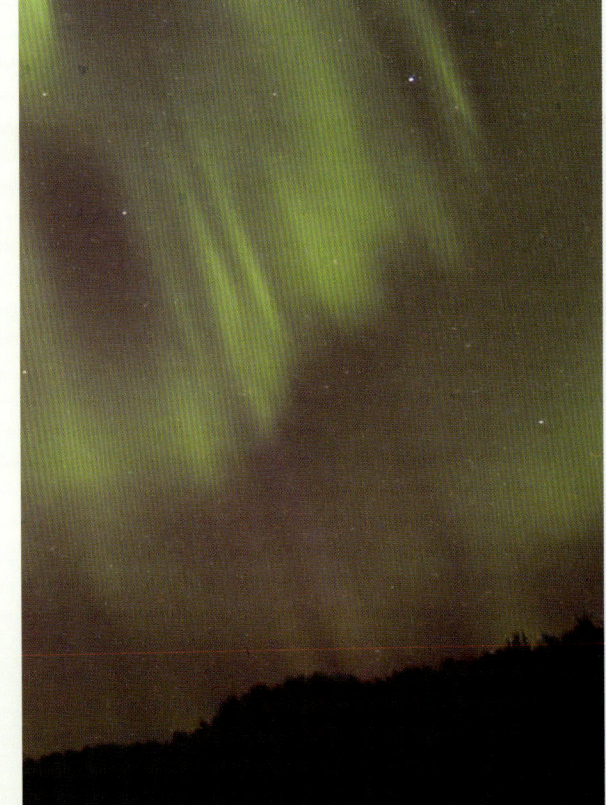

Nocturnal Display

Aurora Borealis, like all night phenomena, requires time exposure, leading to potential "noise" on the imaging chip—but sometimes a rewarding experiment to conduct. "This was a rather faint display that I would not have bothered with shooting film, but it registered on digital." Exposure times were around 30 seconds, ISO 1600, f2.8. © Alan High

from the sensor. Based on an ISO of 800, exposure times range from 2–5 seconds on more active displays, to 30 seconds on more diffuse stationary curtains. Keep notes (or EXIF data) on what is working for you. Like all digital capture, expose for the highlights. One can always suck detail out of the darkness, but you can't put pixel data back where none exists.

In-camera histograms may be of little value. The highlight areas that burn out are often small sections of the aurora, and small sections of the overall frame—in other words, a small percentage of the entire pixel data and histogram display. I use the "highlight warning" feature on my D1X to tell me when I've gone over the edge on highlight details; out-of-range areas flash white/black.

If you want to learn more about the aurora, check out the Space Environment Center on the Web for the latest "space weather" (www.sec.noaa.gov.)

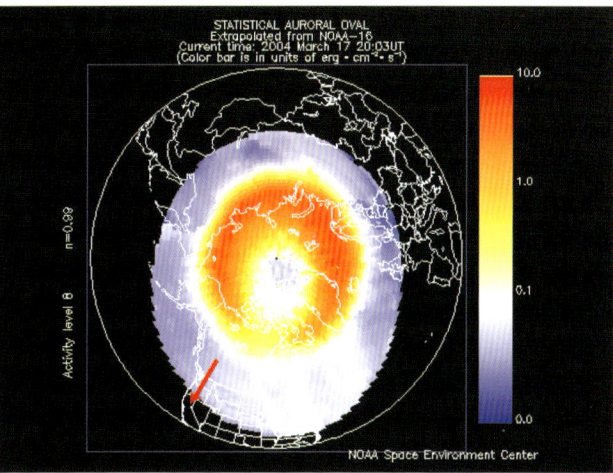

Light Print
The Space Environment Center in Boulder, Colorado, is an excellent resource to use, both for aurora forecasts and general knowledge. This screen shot shows the position and intensity of the auroral oval over the pole—the redder and larger, the better.

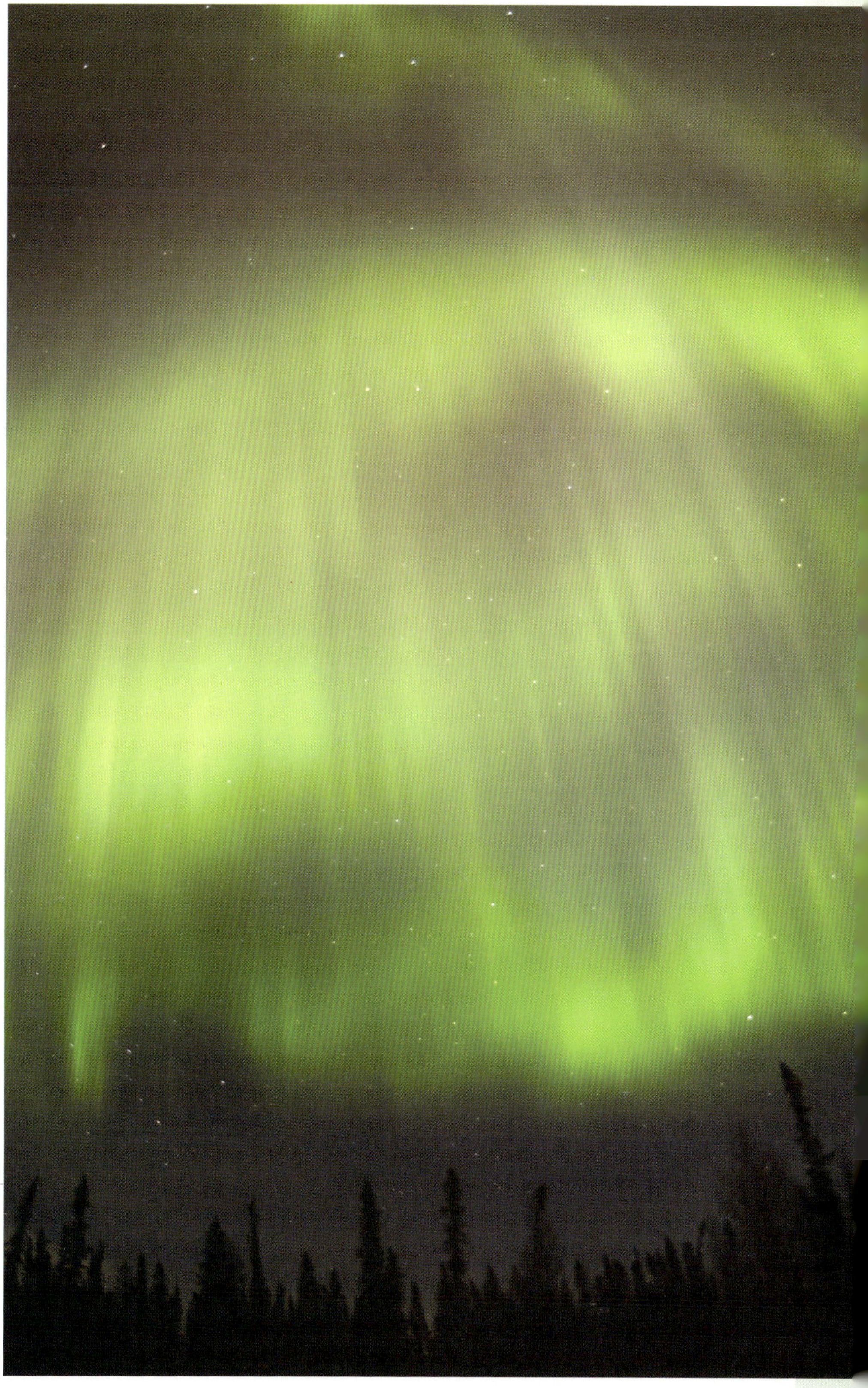

Cascade of Ions
"This was one of my first attempts at shooting auroras digitally. For my first exposure I used the same times as I would have for film (given the intensity of the display at the time) and quickly learned that digital capture doesn't need nearly as much exposure."
800 ISO, 10 seconds, f2.8, 14mm.
© Alan High

WILDLIFE—DAVID VASKEVITCH

Digital photography is the province of both geeks and photographers, and has the effect of turning one into the other. David Vaskevitch is a good example: he's Senior Vice President and Chief Technical Officer at Microsoft. A casual photographer in the years of film, he found himself pitching the idea that computing would become more central to people's lives through music and photography. After making this argument time and again, he returned to photography—using digital this time. And, possibly due to his friendship with US wildlife photographer Art Wolfe, he found himself drawn to that genre of photography.

I use a Nikon D1X, top of the line, and particularly on a serious trip I'll always have two camera bodies, in fact I'll always have two of everything. Typically I'll have a 500 or 600mm lens and a doubler. I'm a long-lens enthusiast. If you give me a choice between longer and wider, I'll always take longer.

But I also love macrophotography. I have a 105mm macro lens. It's just incredibly sharp, so I have all these amazing pictures of flowers or lizards and insects that you can't get if you don't have a macro. I sometimes use it for portrait photography; it has a really shallow depth of field, and you see the people, not the surrounding details.

I'm a big believer in image-stabilized lenses. Nikon has only recently gotten into what they call Vibration Reduction. My new favorite lens is their 80–200 VR silent wave lens. Even when you put the doubler on it, it's still lighter, smaller, and focuses faster than the 80–400 lens. And you still get a better image, even with the doubler on, because the glass is so much better.

Africa's got to be the Mecca for people who shoot wildlife. I took a 500mm lens and a doubler, and a Bogen super-clamp, which clamps onto the roll-bar on the safari

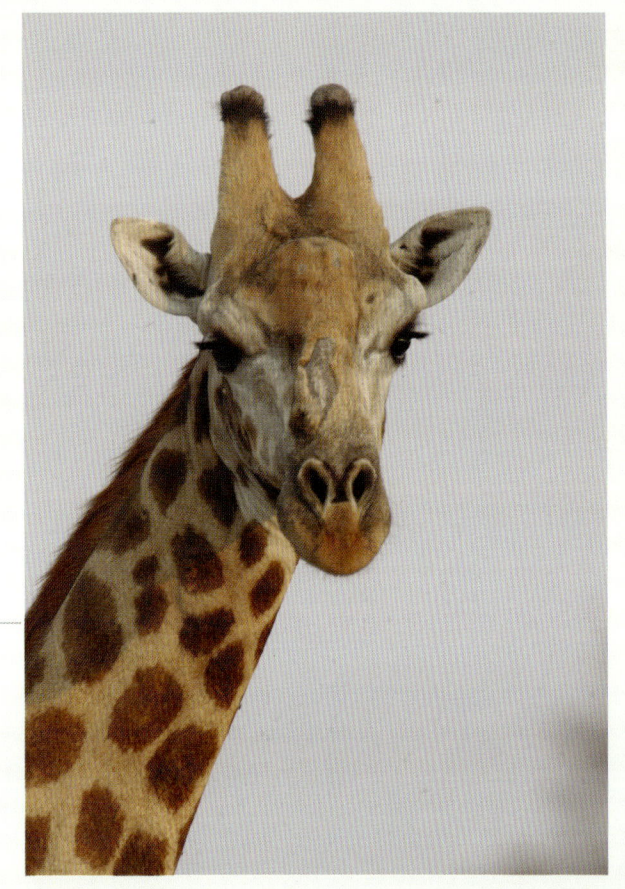

Giraffe Portrait

Giraffes are found in open forest, grazing on the high leaves of trees. Though they can run quite fast, they don't usually regard humans as predators and can be good photo subjects. Shot at Vumbura Game Camp, Botswana, with a 500mm lens with a X2 adapter; 1/125 sec, f13, ISO 400.
© David Vaskevitch

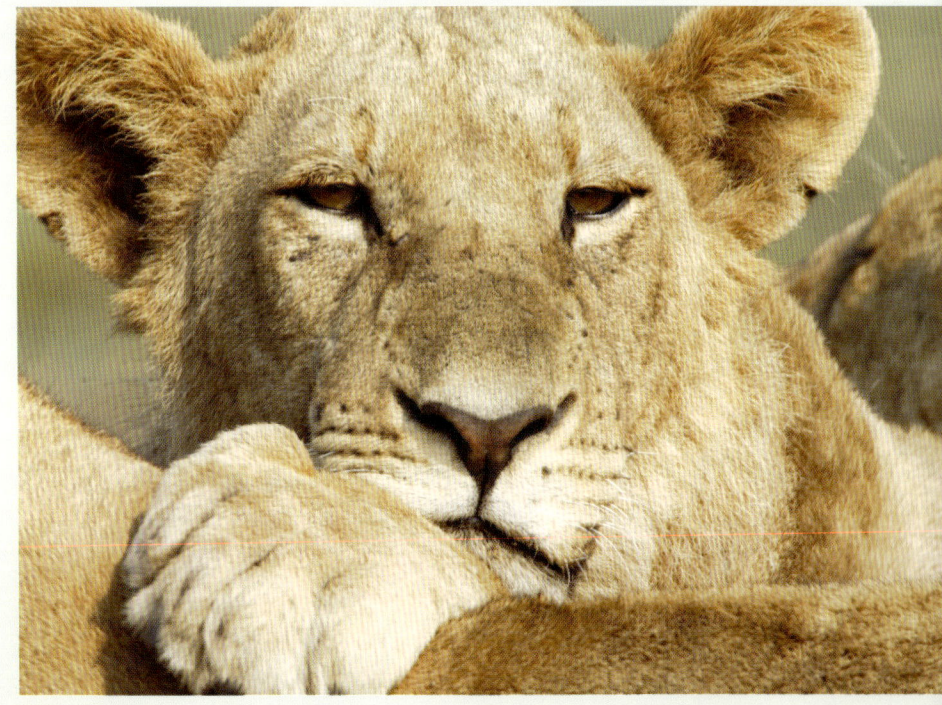

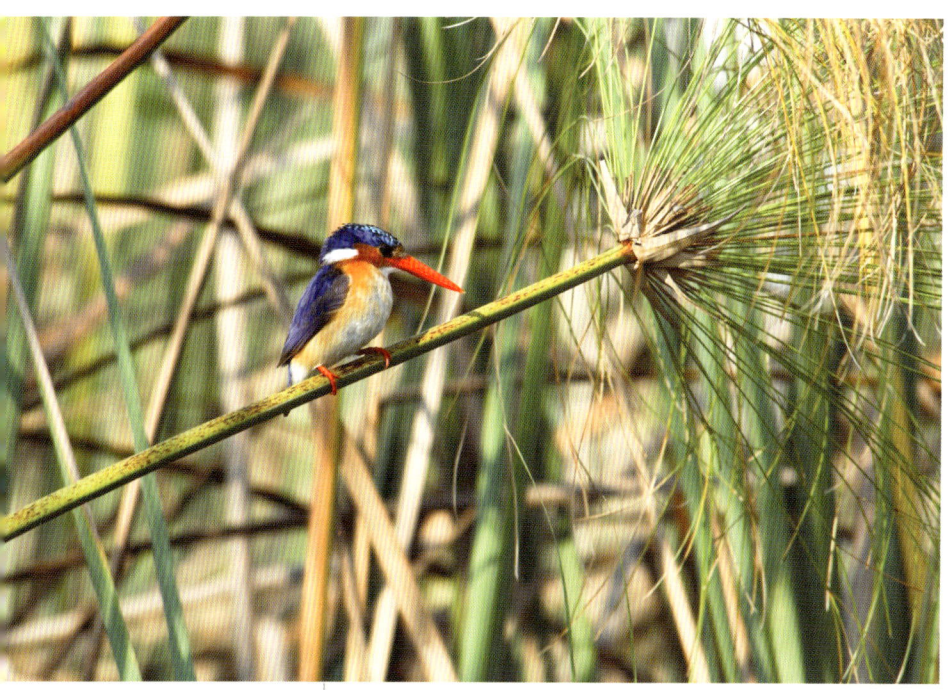

Malechite Kingfisher

Birders enjoy the variety of winged wildlife found in Africa, such as this colorful kingfisher at Xigera Game Camp, Botswana. A narrow depth of field helps isolate the bird from the confusion of the background reeds. Shot with a 80–400mm zoom lens at 400mm, 1/400 sec, f8, ISO 400.
© David Vaskevitch

Drowsy Lion

Lions can be approached in game drive vehicles, usually open-topped Land Rovers. They travel in packs and are relatively docile if well-fed and kept at a safe distance. Vumbura Game Camp, Botswana, 500mm lens with a X2 adapter; at 1/80 sec, f13, ISO 400.
© David Vaskevitch

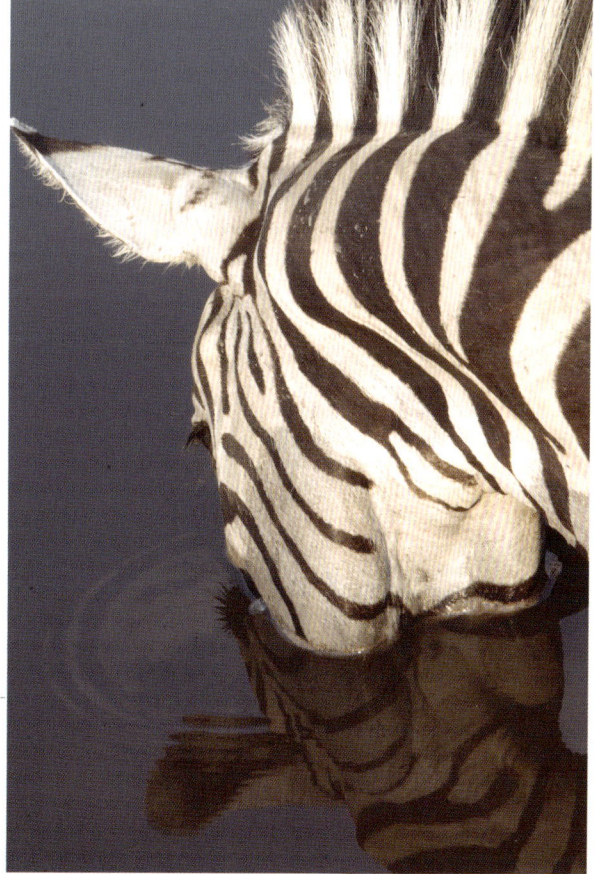

Zebra Reflections

The play of forest light on a zebra makes them relatively camouflaged in shadow, but there's no mistaking the distinct patterns of the plains zebra, here at Kings Pool Game Camp, Botswana. 105mm lens, 1/80 sec @ f20, ISO 400 © David Vaskevitch

vehicle. When you set this thing up it looks like you've mounted a machine gun. You'd pull up and see something in the distance, maybe an eagle, and nobody else would be taking pictures, but I could get a full-frame shot.

One night we saw a leopard. The SB28DX flash is like a professional flash—it's got lenses in it and it really shoots the light a hell of a long distance. So with the 500mm lens and the flash, I was able to get pictures of the leopard even though he was 50 yards away.

I'll typically carry two chargers, mostly because I'm always afraid one will break. If you're on a trip and your charger breaks, you might as well not have a camera. I also carry an inverter. If you have an inverter and a car battery with a cigarette lighter, you have the ability to charge your batteries. Now when I was in Zambia there was no electricity, but there were cars. So at night I'd plug the inverter into the cigarette lighter—you don't even need to have the engine running—and charge up the batteries. It takes about 90 minutes to charge a battery off an inverter, less off direct current.

It's a lot easier doing a big trip where you're taking tons of pictures using digital rather than film. Let me give you an example. When Art Wolfe went on a safari, he took 1,200 rolls of film. So that's a logistical problem all by itself. He really had to think through how to transport the 1,200 rolls of film in both directions, then he spent a lot of time worrying about what would happen if he lost some of it.

The other thing is, he didn't get to see a single one of his pictures until he returned. Now that's just one of the things people get used to with film photography, but once you realize there's an alternative, you never go back to shooting 1,200 rolls of film and not getting to see a single picture until you get home. Once you switch to digital it's very hard to switch back.

EXTREME CRITTERS

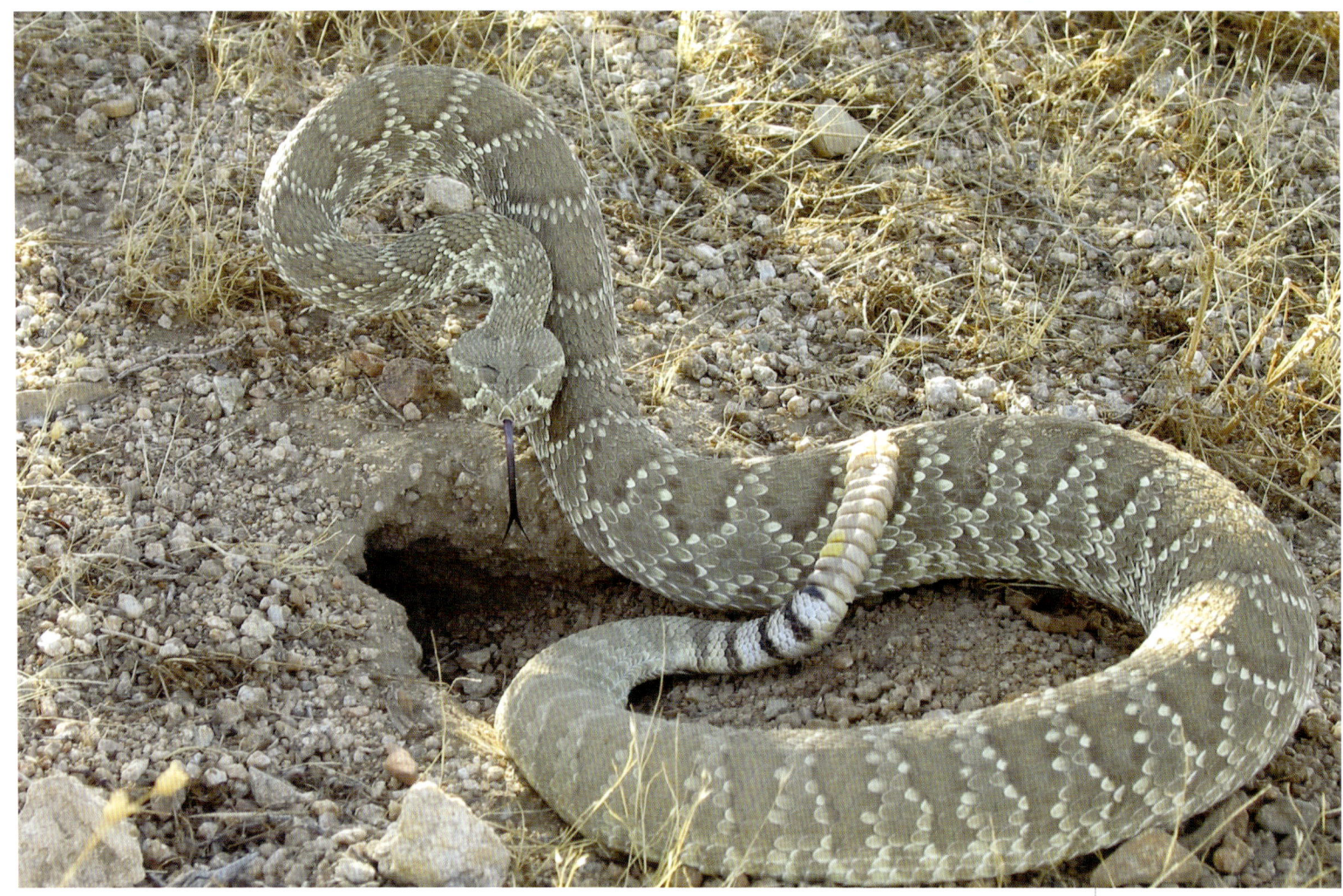

What could be more extreme than having your subject attempt to strike you and inject a lethal toxin? To American Mike Cardwell and Australian Rory McGuiness, venomous subjects are all part of a day's shooting.

Photographers deploy certain tricks in making images of captive deadly reptiles. One is to cool them down in a freezer before putting them in a natural setting, then snap away. Snakes are cold-blooded, so their metabolism slows way down and they become relatively harmless when cold. But in a hot environment they can warm up rapidly, making this precaution of limited value. The principle can be extended to the wild: you can take photographs of reptiles at first light before it gets too warm; photographing in the shade will also help.

Rory McGuiness is one of the most sought-after wildlife cameramen in the world for shooting dangerous subjects. While Rory's experience is mostly with film cameras, his advice applies to all forms of still shooting. "Never work alone. Better still, have an experienced snake or reptile handler so you can concentrate on your

Back Off!

The Mohave rattlesnake (*Crotalus scutulatus*) may be the most dangerous venomous snake in the Sonoran Desert. Quick to go on the defensive, it has very toxic venom that has caused human fatalities, depending on many factors, including the amount of venom injected and the health and size of the victim. A person bitten by a Mohave rattlesnake should seek medical attention immediately.
© Mike Cardwell

shooting. Wearing the correct clothing is another important precaution. Good boots and protective gaiters and heavy pants are a start. My formula with wildlife is to have a good look at the animal and have a good think about how they react and how they act, behave, and respond to things—given that you always have some unpredictability—then slowly work with those responses."

Photographing snake-strike behavior is very difficult with a still camera, whether film or digital, because it all happens so fast. Instead, high-definition (HD) video may be the ideal medium to capture this very rapid action, since HD video is 25 frames per second, versus a maximum of 8 frames per second with the Canon 1D Mk II. Then stills of the peak action can be pulled from the tape to produce print-worthy images.

Mike Cardwell's introduction to digital was shooting images of the Mohave rattlesnake, the most toxic rattlesnake in North America, with a Canon G2. "I just started shooting digitally in the last year. Right now I'm experimenting on high-value subjects, shooting both film and digitally, but clearly the versatility of digital makes it very attractive."

Mike quickly made the transition to a DSLR. "Right now I'm using the Canon D10. So far I use it on the lowest ISO, which is 100 for that camera. It's always the goal to get a picture at the highest resolution and the best saturation. The high-end cameras, at least in my experience, often have many features that I'm not going to use. I typically like to shoot in manual mode, with electric mirror lock-up and a few other things; but the advantage of the higher-end pro camera bodies is that they are typically better sealed against dust and humidity. Trying to do location photography in rainforest or deserts can bring down a camera over two or three weeks."

Lens selection can also affect the look of an image, which can be particularly significant when the subject matter is dangerous, if not deadly. "Probably the most common lens I use now is a 180mm macro Canon lens; when I used a manual focus lens it was a 200mm macro," Mike Cardwell adds. "Those lenses are very convenient, but they can often give pretty ordinary-looking results. To the extent that you get very close with a wide-angle lens, you increase your depth of field and thus show just a little more background. The perspective is a little unusual, and hopefully catches the eye of the reader and hopefully the eye of the editor who's buying the images."

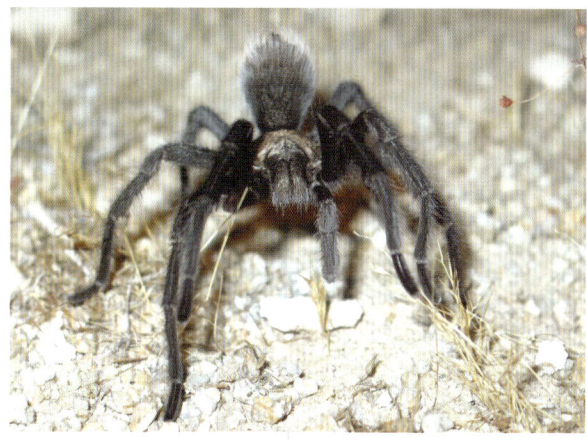

Tarantula

The male Mohave Desert tarantula (*Aphonopelma iodium*) looks more fearsome than he is, and though his bite can be painful, it is never fatal. This fellow was wandering about in the fall, looking for a mate. © Mike Cardwell

Mohave Mealtime

A good time to photograph extreme critters is when they are otherwise engaged, as with this Mohave rattlesnake eating a pocket mouse. As with other photographs on this spread, the camera—a Canon G2—is less important than being in the right place at the right time. © Mike Cardwell

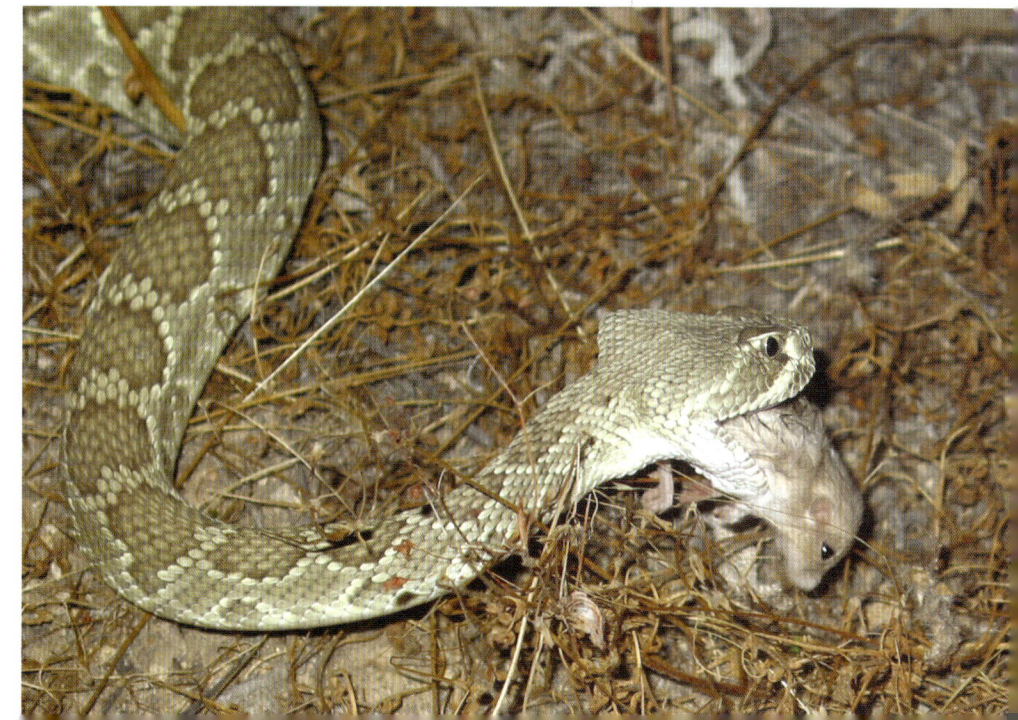

SCIENTIFIC RESEARCH—PETER GILL AND MARGIE MORRICE

It might be said that today's digital camera is a computer with a lens. The sophistication of photographic metering systems and automatic focus, which evolved out of film cameras, met with digital optics and chip technology to produce the modern DSLR, which is (let's face it) smarter than most photographers. As such, the use of digital photography in scientific research is to be expected—the Hubble space telescope is an extreme example, and the remarkable history of its deep-space investigations has literally expanded our understanding of the universe and the laws of science.

Closer to home, field researchers Peter Gill and Margie Morrice found that even consumer-level digital cameras can be used for scientific research. Both members of the Whale Ecology Group (Southern Ocean) at Deakin University, they study the ecology of blue whales along the coast of Victoria and South Australia. Their first digital was a Nikon D100. They now rely on digital cameras to capture images of whale behavior, feeding patterns, and even individuals for an identification database.

Their work focuses on a population of pygmy blue whales, slightly misleadingly named as they are about 80 feet (24m) long—just 16 feet (5m) smaller than the "true" blue whale. An upwelling of deep-ocean waters covering over 40,000 square kilometres from South Australia through to Bass Strait, called the Bonney Upwelling, provides an unusual opportunity for research. Here, the krill that the whales feed on are mostly surface-swarming,

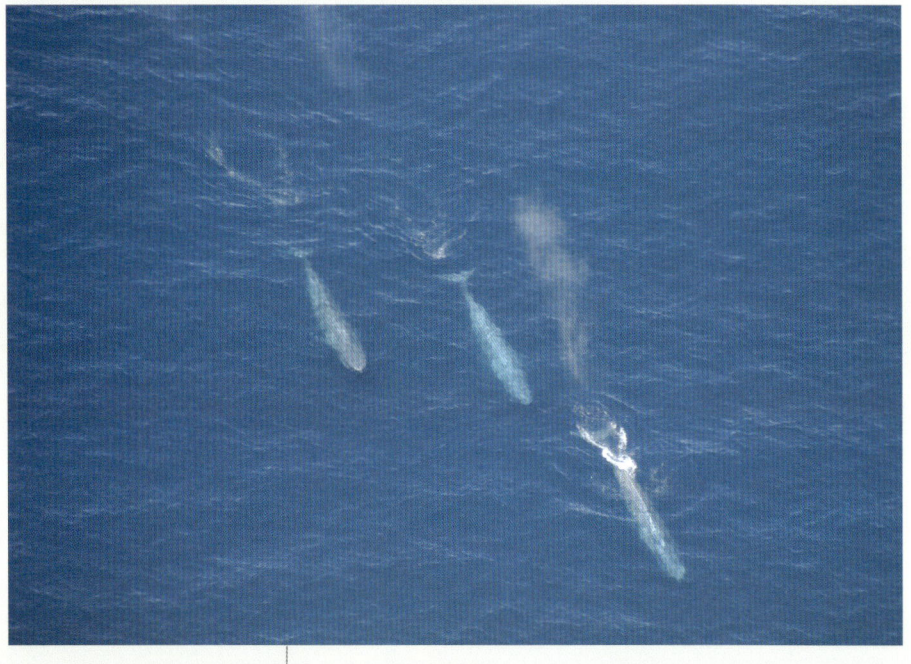

Blue Formation

Three adult blue whales swim off the coast of Victoria. Blue whales are sometimes seen in threes, moving rapidly and jostling each other in what is believed to be breeding behavior. They are more often found alone or in pairs, as their food source (krill) usually forms scattered patches best exploited by smaller groups. © Peter Gill & Margie Morrice

Roll Over

A blue whale rolls onto its right side to feed on a small krill swarm. Its throat pleats are beginning to expand to accommodate a huge mouthful of water and krill. When it rolls upright, seawater drains out through its filtering baleen, leaving the krill behind for it to swallow before the hunt for more resumes. © Peter Gill & Margie Morrice

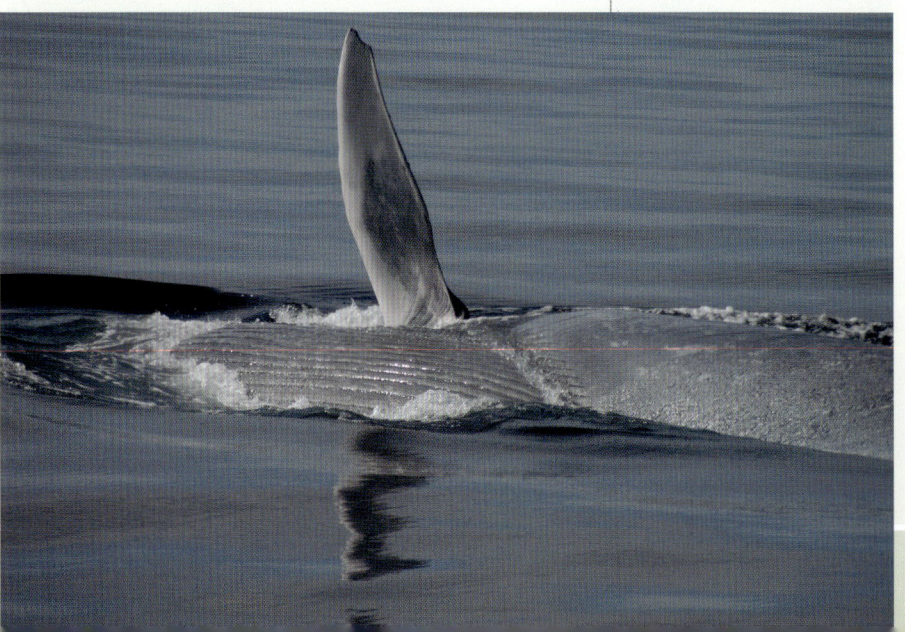

giving the researchers a great opportunity to watch the blue whales feeding. In most other parts of the world, they have to dive under the water to feed on the krill.

Getting close to the monstrous animals is not easy. Part of the work has to be undertaken from boats, using at present just the standard 28–200mm f4.5 zoom. So taking photographs from the air has become one of their key tools. From a high-wing, twin-engine plane they watch the whales in their feeding patterns and try to gauge population and other data. "We're pretty strict about staying above 1,500 feet, that's the height that we're trying to encourage other people to fly at," Peter noted. "They're a bit twitchy even at that height; they'll sometimes stop what they're doing and dive, and we try our best to minimize that."

The advantages of digital make their efforts more rewarding. "We're able to sit down that night and see the images we shot that day. Normally you wait a week or two to get your Provia back, and you lose track. It's really good to see them almost in real-time."

Sometimes, blue whale behavior is extraordinary, even beyond the boundaries of science. Watching them slap and roll over each other, Peter Gill says, "The scale and the power when you see them turn it on is awesome." Using digital photography to record data employed in scientific research is an appropriate and productive application of technology, but some of the wonders of the natural world are best appreciated by the human heart.

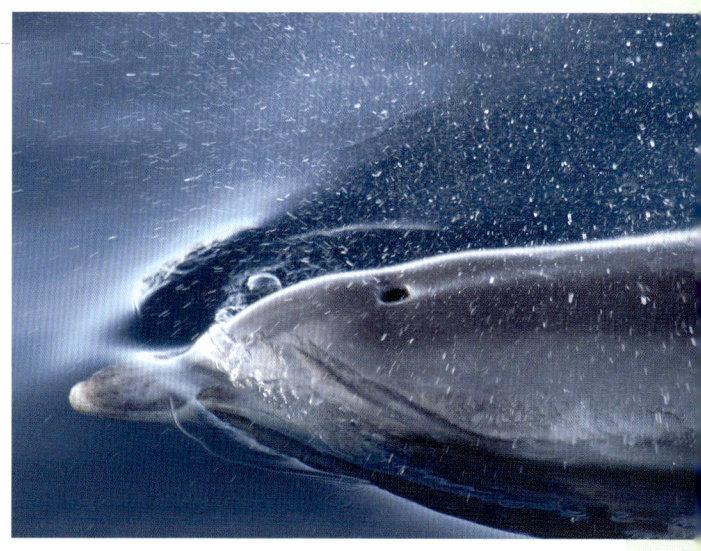

Breathe Deep

A bottlenose dolphin's blowhole is open at the moment of inhalation, after blowing out explosively. Dolphins manage to time their breathing for the split second they are at the surface. Their habit of bow-riding with boats makes them easy to photograph at close range. © Peter Gill & Margie Morrice

Dinner Dive

A blue whale cuts a swathe through a large surface swarm of pinkish krill. Its throat has expanded and is full of water and krill, and it has shut its mouth to stop the krill escaping. The throat can probably hold 50 ton(ne)s or more of water, necessary when the whales' requirement may be 3–4 ton(ne)s of food each day. © Peter Gill & Margie Morrice

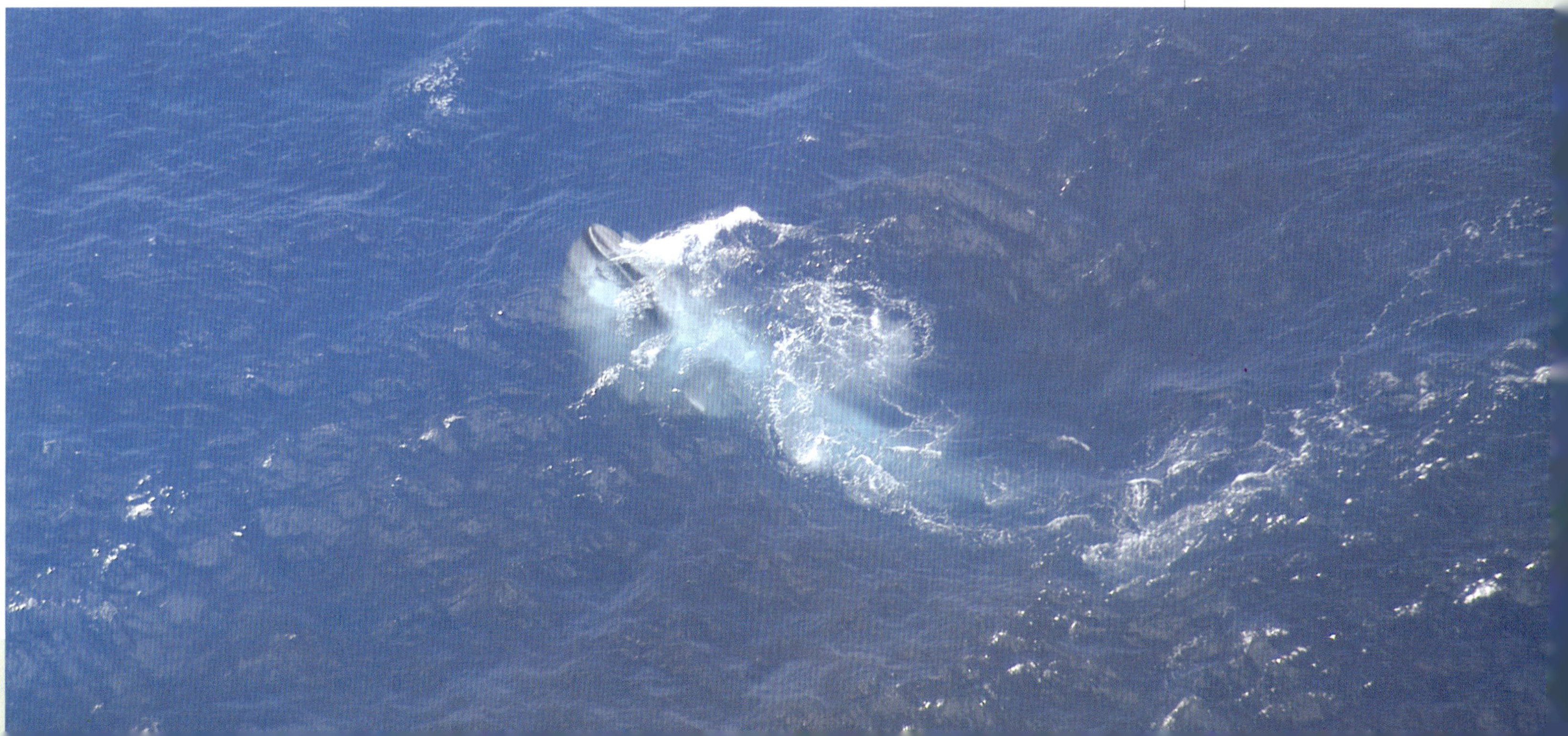

UNDERWATER PHOTOGRAPHY—JAMES WATT

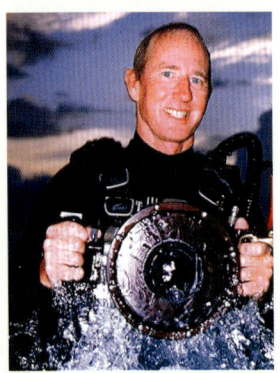

Considering that underwater photography is only a couple of generations old, it's come a long way. Today the world beneath the sea's surface is revealing beauty and diversity beyond imagining, and the art of photography is a key reason for this. James Watt is one of a handful who is exposing its wonders with digital cameras. He's been diving since 1965, and photographing underwater for over half that time. He now lives in Hawaii, running Ocean Stock for his own and other marine imagery.

The hardest part of an underwater shoot is the marine life itself, finding it and making good compositions—plus, of course, you only have so much time down there.

Since you can usually take only one housing down with you, you have to pre-select what lens you're going to use. I take two completely separate digital rigs down when I can, a full-frame fish-eye for the wide view, and a macro for the close view.

A lot of people use the Nikon or Olympus series point-and-shoots, and they get good results with them, but my basic underwater kit is a Canon D60 with a Sea & Sea underwater housing. The ability to review photos in the field is important, but to do this underwater is absolutely crucial. With this housing I can review while I'm still underwater. I use a 100mm macro and a 50mm macro, and sometimes I even use a diopter for a super-macro. And of course a twin-light setup, Ikelite 125 digital strobes. Above water I use a Canon 1D for fast action. I look forward to the Mark 2 for its frame rate—9 frames a second? I'm drooling over that one.

The most memorable thing that I have done was to swim with dolphins in the Bahamas for four straight hours without having to return to the boat to change film. I was

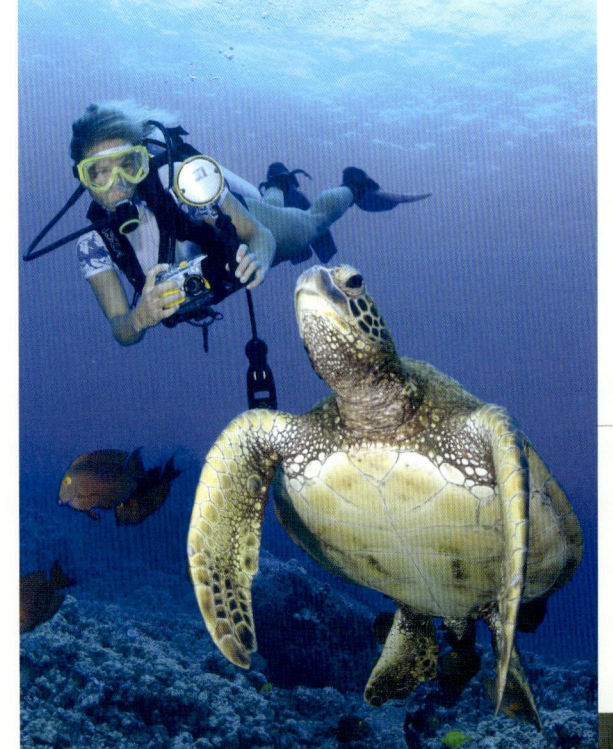

Harlequin Shrimp, Hawaii

Colorful sea creatures put your photographic skills to the test. The biggest problem is getting used to the narrow depth of field of macro, focusing on the critical part of the subject. This photo was taken with a 100mm macro lens and two strobes. © James Watt

Shell Games

A female photographer goes after a green sea turtle in Hawaii in the hope of a good shot—and becomes one herself. This shows the benefit of a good model with solid diving skills. The lens used for this photo was a 15mm wide-angle and two strobes. © James Watt

Fish in Focus

The rock-mover wrasse, seen here in Hawaii, is a constantly moving subject, and it may take a number of frames to get the right composition. The fish is separated from its background by narrow depth of field from the mid-range 50mm macro lens and fast shutter speed. © James Watt

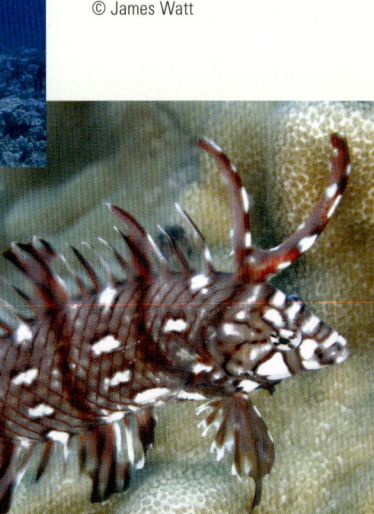

snorkeling and shot just a little over 500 frames, using a 2GB microdrive in my Canon. If I had needed to go back to the boat and switch film after 36 shots, I probably wouldn't have been able to stay with them. Sometimes you can't just put on another tank and find the same shot again. With digital you can concentrate on behavior, getting some really intimate shots, without worrying every second about your capacity.

Until recently I did not shoot RAW underwater, but now that Photoshop CS is out, I converted totally to RAW: it makes it a dream. Then I use iView Media Pro to sort the images out and start dumping stuff. On my last Indonesia trip, I shot 14,000 images, but only pulled out about 600 selects. I have a G4 laptop, but I don't edit images in the field, even though the image quality's pretty good, but not compared to an Apple Cinema display. You can't make real crucial color changes or anything.

White Tip Shark, Hawaii

"This species is very aggressive and can come from any direction. When shooting them, I always have another diver with me so that we can cover each other. An extreme wide-angle lens is mandatory." © James Watt

Great Hammerhead

This species of shark is rare in the Bahamas; the image took a solid week of diving to get a close portrait, as hammerheads are quite shy of divers. It was a matter of waiting hours for the right moment. A zoom wide-angle lens was used for flexibility. © James Watt

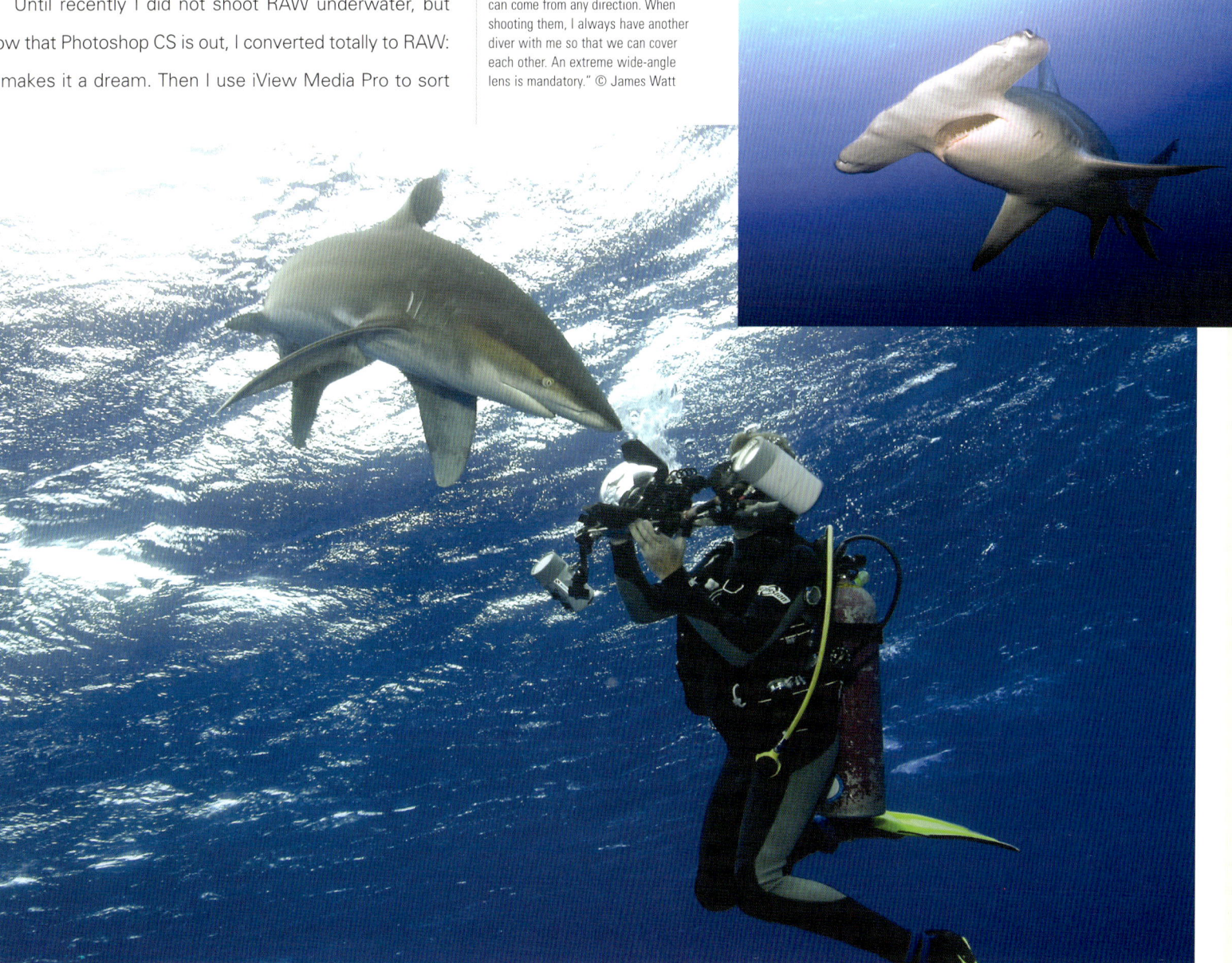

LOW LIGHT

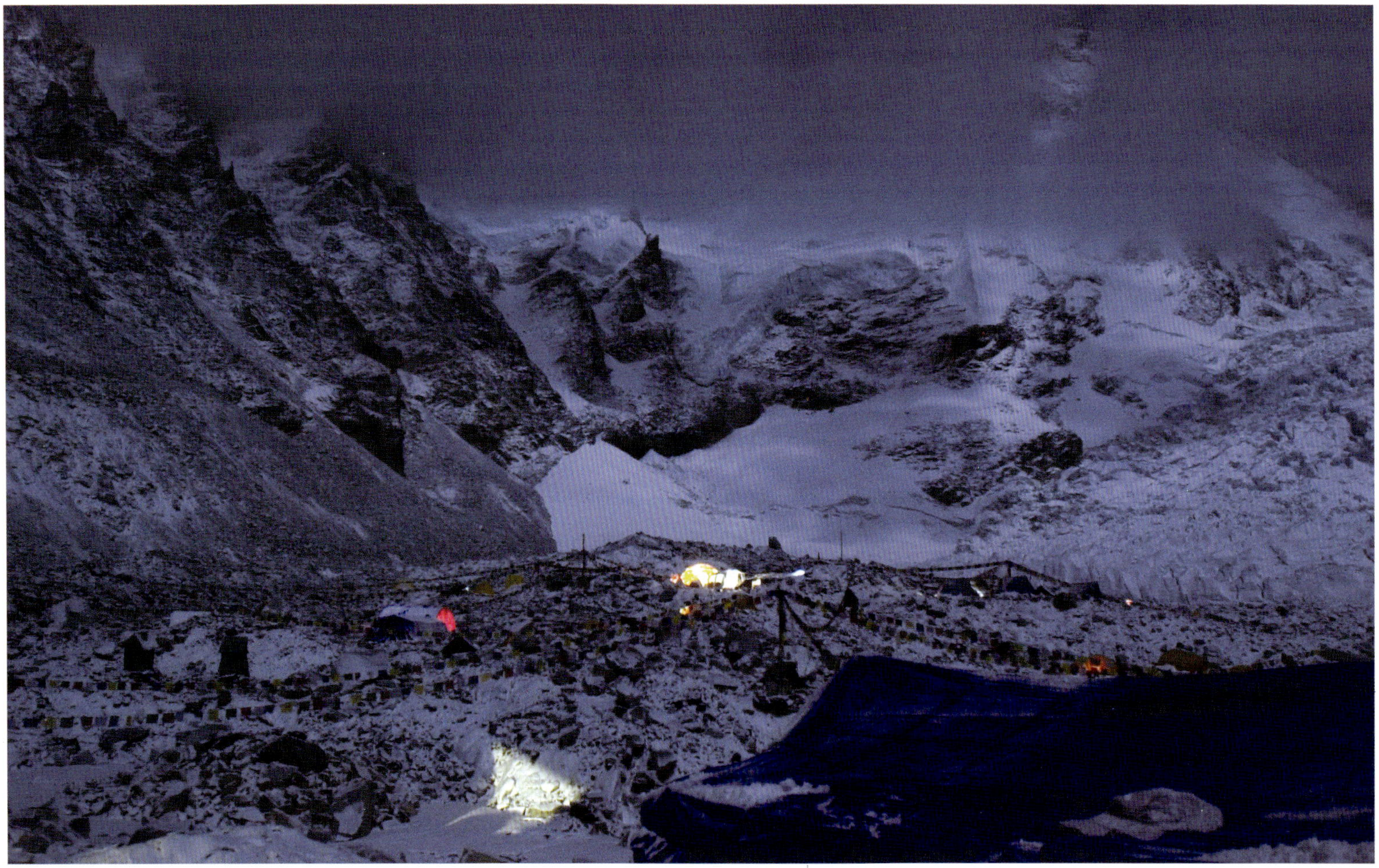

Everest Base Camp

Sub-zero nighttime temperatures at Everest Base Camp help minimize the noise buildup in this long (20 seconds) exposure of the mountains after dark. Moonlight illuminates the surrounding peaks with an eerie blue glow. A solid tripod is essential in these instances to eliminate camera shake.

All-Night Vigil

Gas lanterns create a vibrant oasis of colored light at the *puja* for Nepal's most famous Sherpa, Babu Chiri, who died when he fall into a crevasse. Keeping the exposure to just 4 seconds helps to hold detail in the camp scene.

There are many instances when you want to capture images in very low light or at night. The most challenging night shots for any medium are the Aurora Australis (in the Southern Hemisphere) and the Aurora Borealis (in the Northern); they are like slow shimmering curtains of light.

With film, the drawbacks to night shots are graininess and reciprocity failure, the variation or shifts in color inherent in a long exposure. Digital capture has similar problems, namely digital grain or "noise." Noise is the undesirable interference that usually affects the whole image, giving a similar appearance to film grain. It is mostly a function of the ISO (most pronounced above ISO 800), the length of the exposure, the ambient temperature and humidity, and how long you have been shooting. The chip itself heats up in a long shooting session.

But noise can also be a function of JPEG compression producing blocky edges and flat areas at higher compression ratios. It is most noticeable in areas of flat color and in deep shadows, so is pronounced in night shots where there is typically a lot of black in the image. The spacing of the pixels on the sensor affects the amount of noise: the larger the pixels and the more space between them, the less they are susceptible to noise. Consequently DSLRs with their larger chips display less noise at higher ISO than compact cameras with their smaller sensors.

Regardless of the capture medium or camera, to shoot at night or in low light you need a solid tripod and head or other support, and a remote trigger to avoid motion blur—a cable, electronic shutter release, or even the camera's self-timer. The most sophisticated remote triggers are wireless devices such as the Pocket Wizard, which can also be used for firing flashes or strobes. If using a compact camera, turn off the auto flash unless there is a foreground subject that you wish to light.

With today's digital SLRs there is no reason not to make low-light or night images. The results can match film, and the technology and software can only get better.

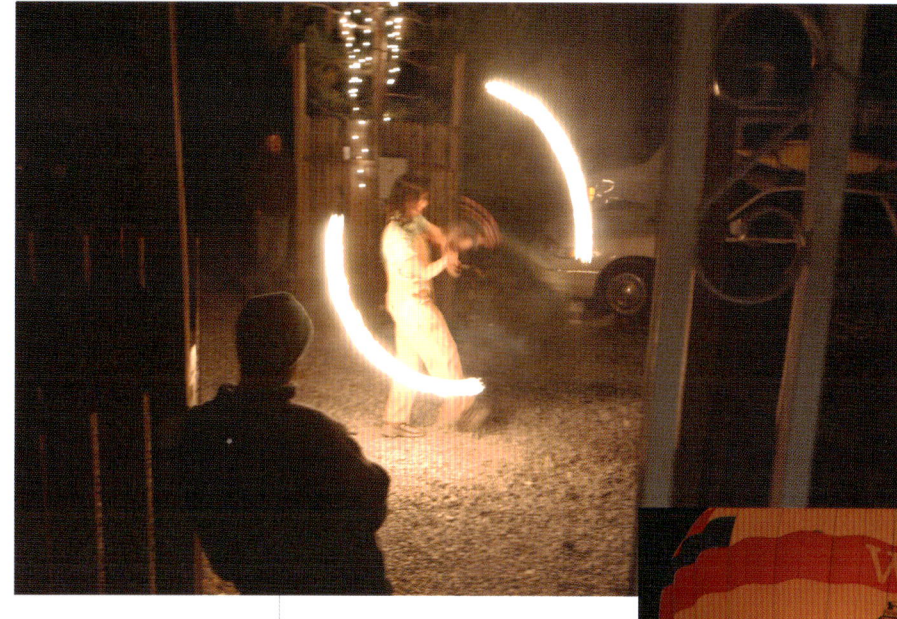

Twirling *Poi*

To capture night action, a photographer uses slow shutter speeds to make up for the lack of light. Spot meter on the subject, in this case the person twirling the *poi* (flaming batons on a rope), as opposed to matrix metering. Then either set up on a tripod or a steady surface, or at the very least brace against the nearest tree, pole, wall, and so on. Another trick is to shoot in bursts: the middle frame has the best chance of being sharp.
© Jessica Brandi Lifland

Ballooning at Night

Capturing the enchanting atmosphere at the "Balloon Glow" of the Albuquerque Balloon Festival on a DSLR requires careful choice of the ISO to minimize noise and to capture the scene before balloon movement becomes noticeable. The event begins at dusk, under rapidly changing light conditions, and toward the end of the show, balloons disappear into the night between illuminating "bursts" of the propane tanks. © Mark Langley

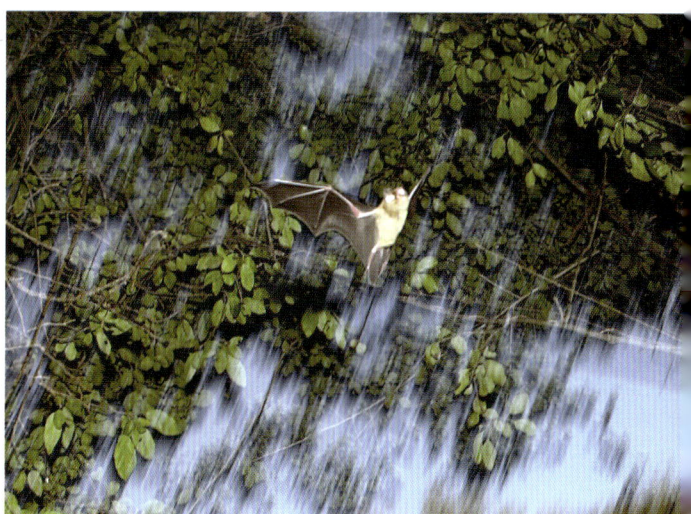

Bat Strobe

A flying bat swarm in low-light conditions, such as dusk in the Yucatan forest, creates a challenge for any photographer. Obviously a strobe is used to "freeze" the bats in mid-flight, but panning to follow an individual also helps stop the action, though it results in a blurred background.
© Denise Rocco-Zilber

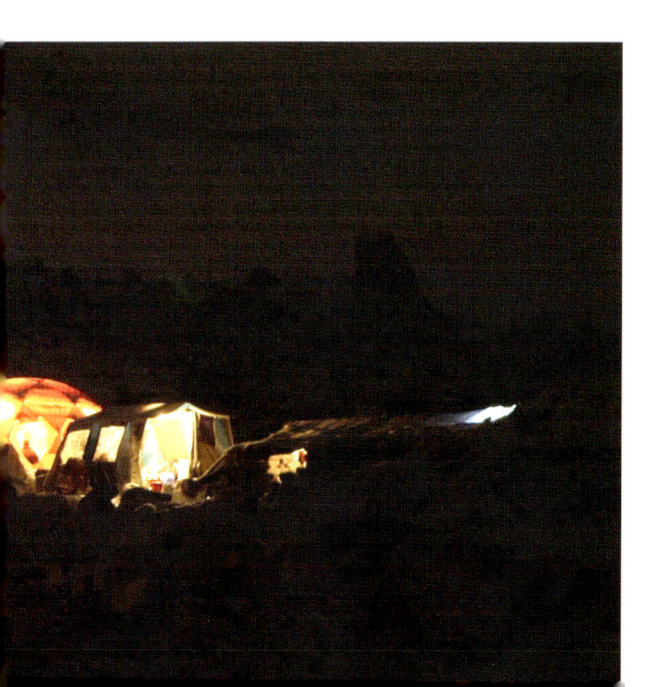

PHOTOJOURNALISM—PETER MENZEL

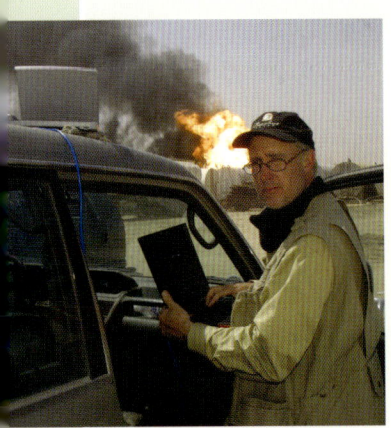

In this age of instant news, carried via satellite to websites and 24-hour cable news networks, the role of the photojournalist has become increasingly important. The pressure is enormous for the field photographer to be where the action is, to capture telling imagery, and to deliver it as quickly as possible, and it takes a uniquely talented individual to fulfill this role. One such individual is Peter Menzel, a photographer for Life, Time, German GEO, Paris Match, Forbes, and almost every other major periodical, as well as author or coauthor of several powerful books of photography.

Two or three years ago I bought the Canon D30; I stopped using Polaroids, so I would use the D30 as light checks when working with complicated light—usually just looking at the LCD and sometimes downloading it onto a laptop. So I got used to it that way. Then, when Iraq came along, I was forced to do everything digitally, so I borrowed a D60 with the D30 as a backup and everything worked fine. Digital is getting so good so fast, and I'm perfectly satisfied with it being as good as 35mm, at least for a double-page spread. I've made the switch and it saves me a lot of hassle.

The first time I was in Iraq (in 1991) I did all-film; when I went to Iraq (in 2003) I did all-digital. I had a Macintosh, but before I went, people were telling me the PC laptops were holding up better under stress, and had fewer problems with things crashing, so I bought an IBM ThinkPad and used that to download. So that was another thing I had to learn in a hurry, learning to use the PC instead of the Mac. Then I had to buy the digital modem, the satellite modem to send stuff back, because I didn't know if I was going to be in a place where I could transmit back to Time magazine.

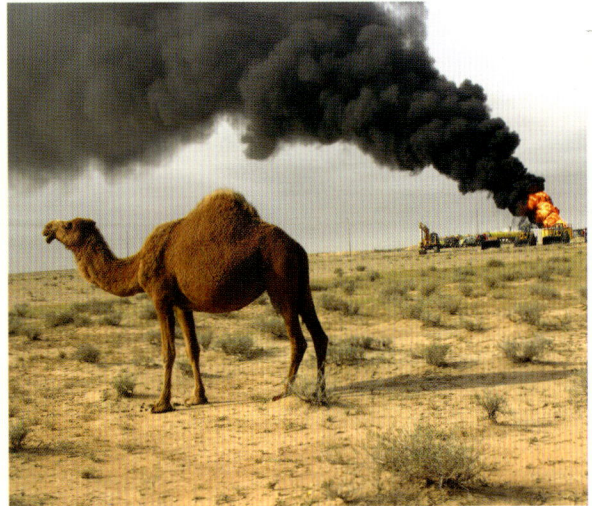

Camels in Hell

Bedouins graze hundreds of their Bactrian camels in the desert around Iraq's Rumeilah oil fields. These desert dwellers, juxtaposed with the blazing oil well fires, highlight the contrasts that photographers face in covering such assignments. © Peter Menzel

Prayer Call

The fire fighters from the Kuwaiti Oil Company, called into Iraq at the Rumeilah oil field to quell the oil well fires, do a double prayer at noon so that they do not have to stop later in the day, in case they are at a critical phase of the capping process. © Peter Menzel

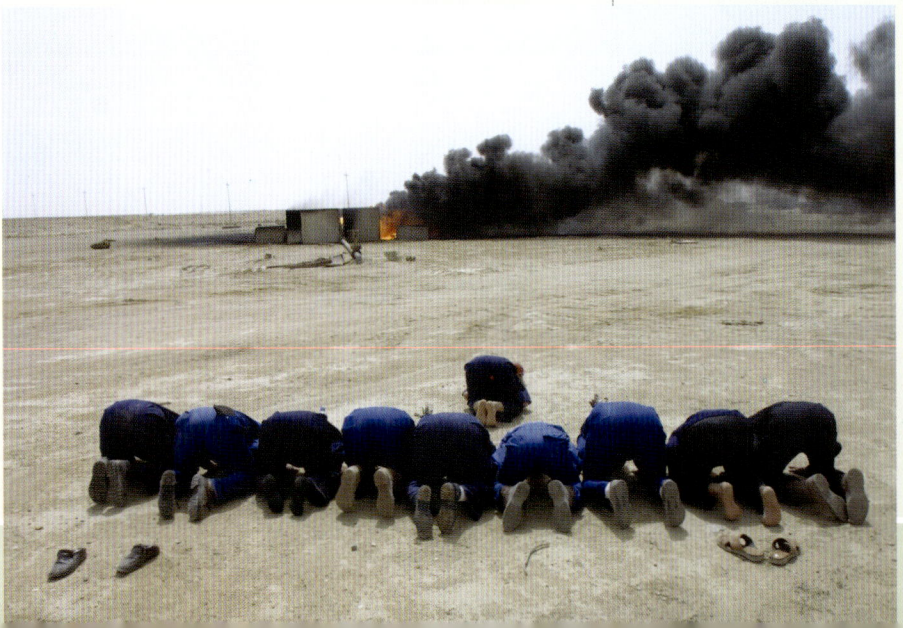

I thought shooting with digital was not a steep learning curve at all, as far as what you're doing in the camera. But if you shoot RAW, you've got another conversion factor to deal with; a full gigabyte of RAW files takes maybe an hour and a half or two hours to download and convert to JPEG, and then you've got to edit those. My analysis later, in looking at the picture, is that the big JPEGs are good enough for a double-page. I never had an editor express concern about JPEGs or RAW; they said: "it's your call, it's your library of pictures you're shooting."

Shooting digitally and selling that as stock is getting easier and easier. Most of the time now it's all done through our Web and FTP sites.

Dealing with people, it's great to have digital for interpersonal relationships. I shoot maybe 90 percent of my stuff in foreign countries, and although I know some languages, having a digital is like a Polaroid: you call people over and show them what they look like, and they go, "Oh, that's really great!" Even if you don't speak the same language, you can get some kind of bonding.

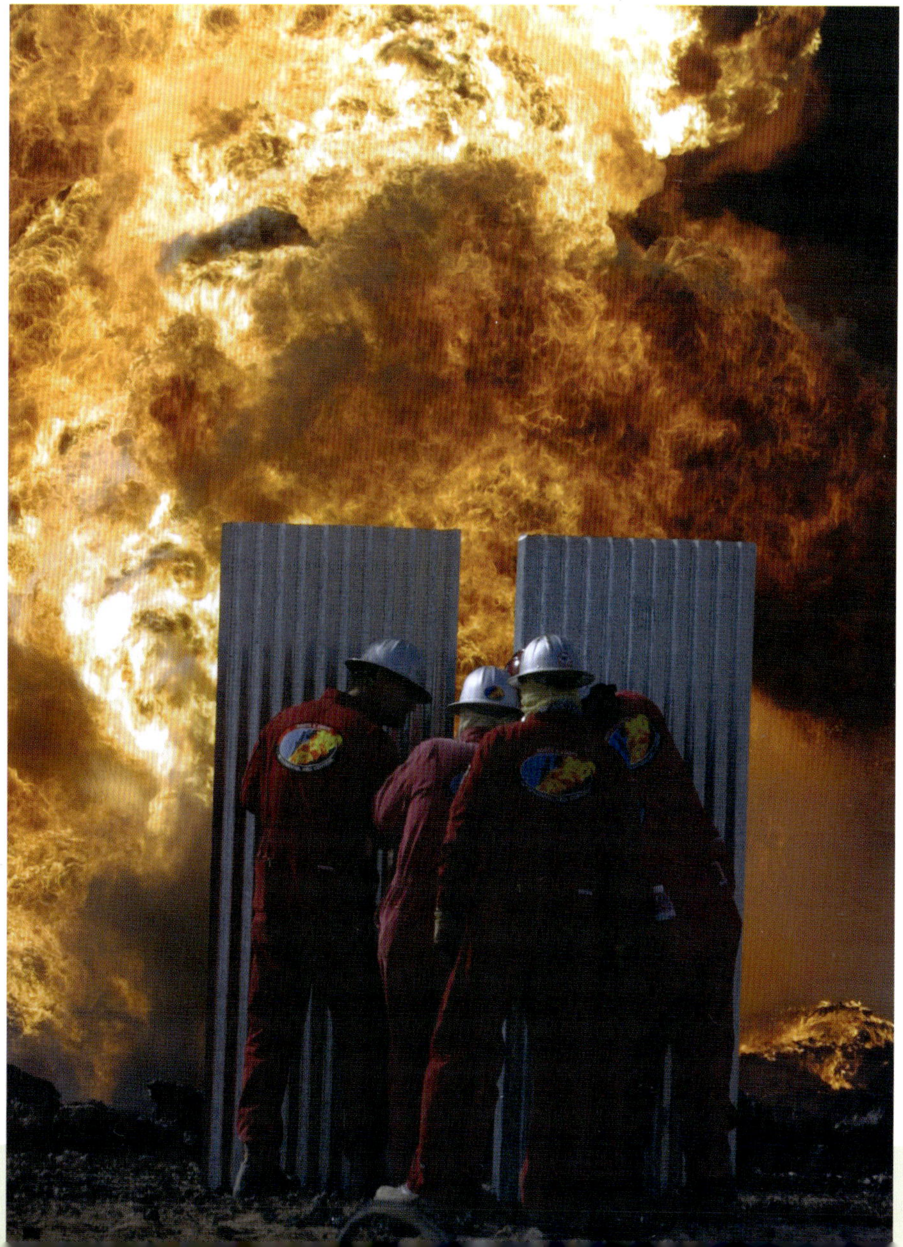

Fire Shields

Corrugated roofing iron shields protect workers of Boots and Coots (a division of the American Halliburton company) from the most intense heat. "You can shield yourself with just about anything to stop that heat flow. Even a corrugated metal roof panel with wooden handles... If your body starts burning, you know your cameras are too hot, too." © Peter Menzel

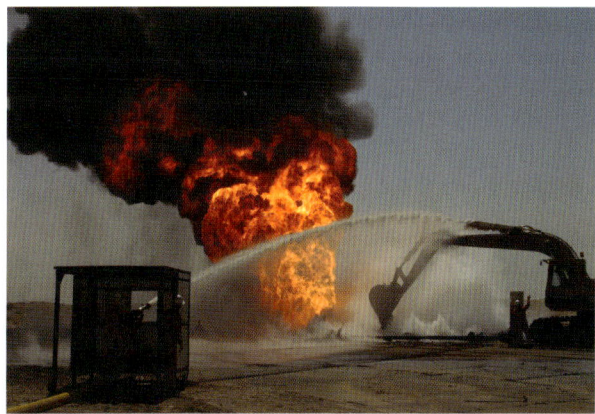

Controlling the Uncontrollable

The juxtaposition of technology run amok with the human scale puts things into perspective. Shooting in conditions such as this requires large flash cards for hundreds of shots, as things change so quickly and telling images may not last long. © Peter Menzel

Casualty of War

A shore bird suffers through an oil spill during the fallout from the Iraq war. Often the detail is the most telling image of large-scale conflict.
© Peter Menzel

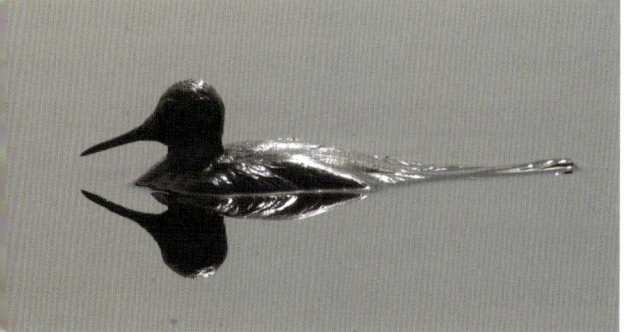

WAR PHOTOGRAPHY

There is no more extreme situation for the photographer than to be in the middle of a war. It can be termed a human-caused disaster, a rolling series of tragedies and horrors, and even a "perfect storm" in its impact on human life and spirit. Since the Civil War photography of Mathew Brady, through the World War II and Korean images of Robert Capa, to today's graphic point-of-view in the work of Chris Morris and others, war is the ultimate test for a photographer's ability to wrest a telling image out of chaos and personal risk.

The recent Iraq war was the first "digital war" from the photographer's standpoint. Some photographers, especially those associated with accredited news agencies, were offered the incentive to travel with the troops themselves, as so-called "embedded" journalists.

Peter Menzel, a freelancer, has his own take on their role. "Being with a group of military guys in overwhelming force in a foreign land as they swept up from Kuwait virtually unopposed by any military resistance was really exciting for most of them, especially the TV guys, who could at least show motion. For still photographers it was obviously less interesting... They were not free agents."

Close Focus

Iraqi Republican Guards surround a damaged US tank in Baghdad. Being on the scene is perhaps the most important aspect of a war photographer's task. The old film photographer's adage was "f8 and be there," but today it may be more important to have autofocus on and plenty of flash cards. © Sungsu Cho, Polaris Images

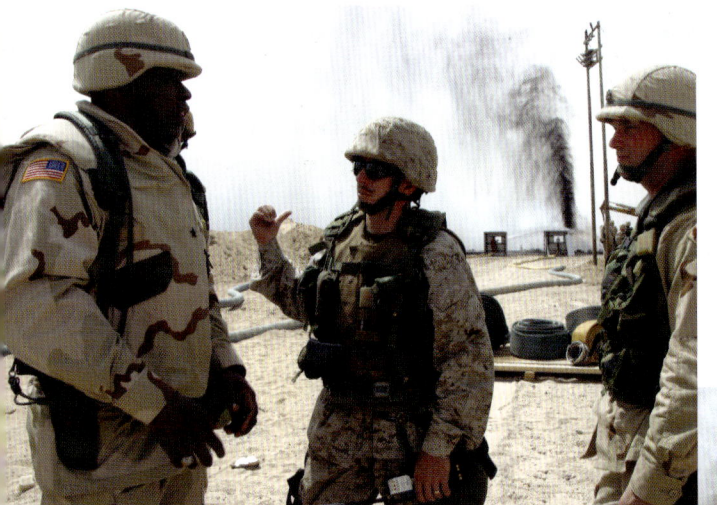

Gusher Guard

US soldiers and contractors evaluate their course of action in dealing with a rogue oil gusher at the outset of the second Gulf War. Photographer Peter Menzel had a previous relationship with the personnel in this field of operations, and parlayed those contacts into a freelance assignment when he refused to become "embedded." © Peter Menzel

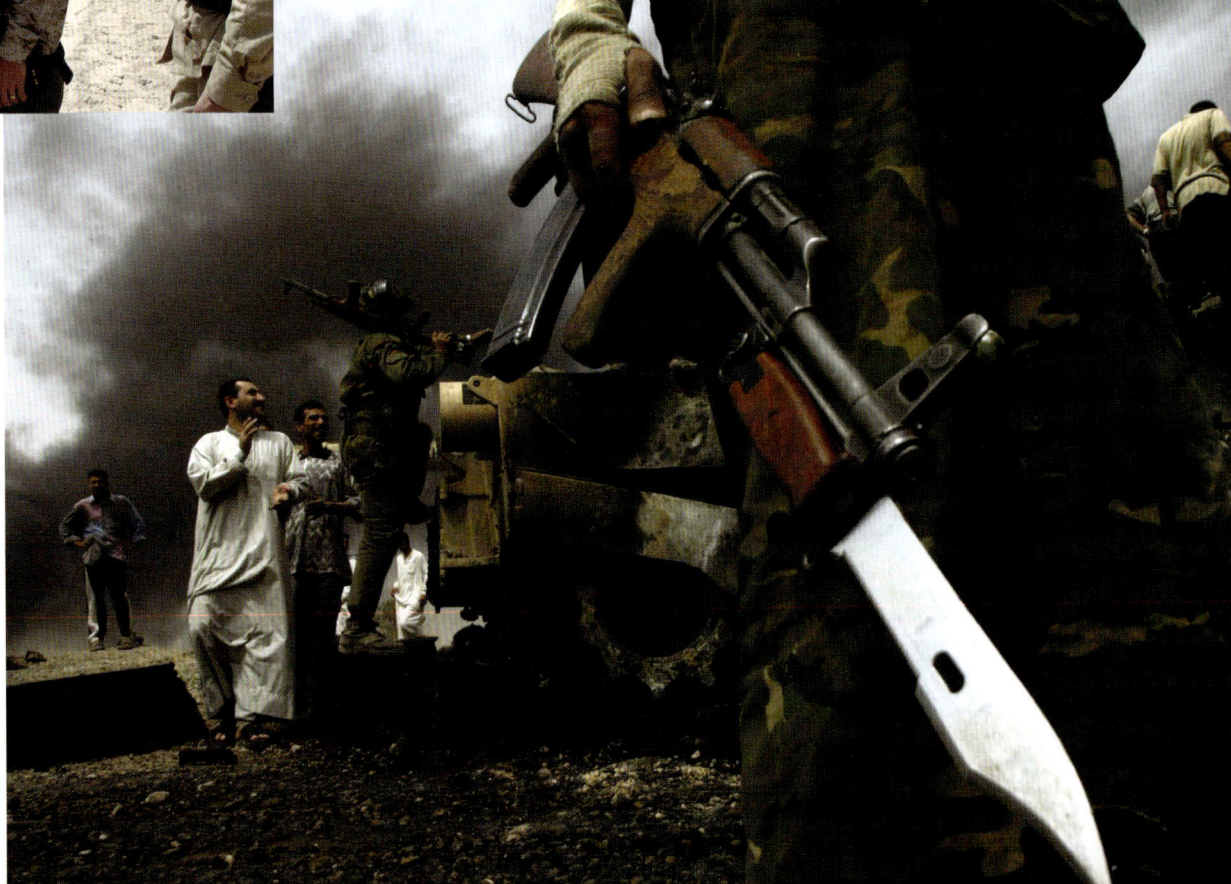

Whether they were embedded or not, field photographers had to upload their images via satellite to their editors. Of great use was the Inmarsat Regional Bgan, or R-Bgan, system—a dedicated satellite IP modem that weighs less than 4 pounds (1.8kg) and transmits at speeds of up to 144Kbps via Inmarsat's European satellite. This limits it at present to coverage from England to India, a region that encompasses 99 countries (among them many of the hot-spots in the current geopolitical map). The R-Bgan is comparatively simple to set up, connecting to PC laptops via USB, Ethernet, or Bluetooth, and runs on long-lasting lithium batteries.

A capable wartime photographer must have detachment to match his or her passions, quick reflexes, and a full command of technical toolkit. The range of work photographers do in wartime and other extreme situations ranges from the compelling eyewitness visuals of James Nachtwey at the fall of the World Trade Center, to Christopher Morris' action shots of Croation fighters under attack on the urban frontlines of Vukovar, and Kate Brooks portrait of a US soldier cradling an injured Iraqi civilian. What is most striking about these images is the absence of politics and the presence of humanity.

Face to Face

The realities of war are always personal. Whether it's negotiating with a security guard for access to a scene, or facing battle, the people on the front lines provide the strongest images. © Peter Menzel

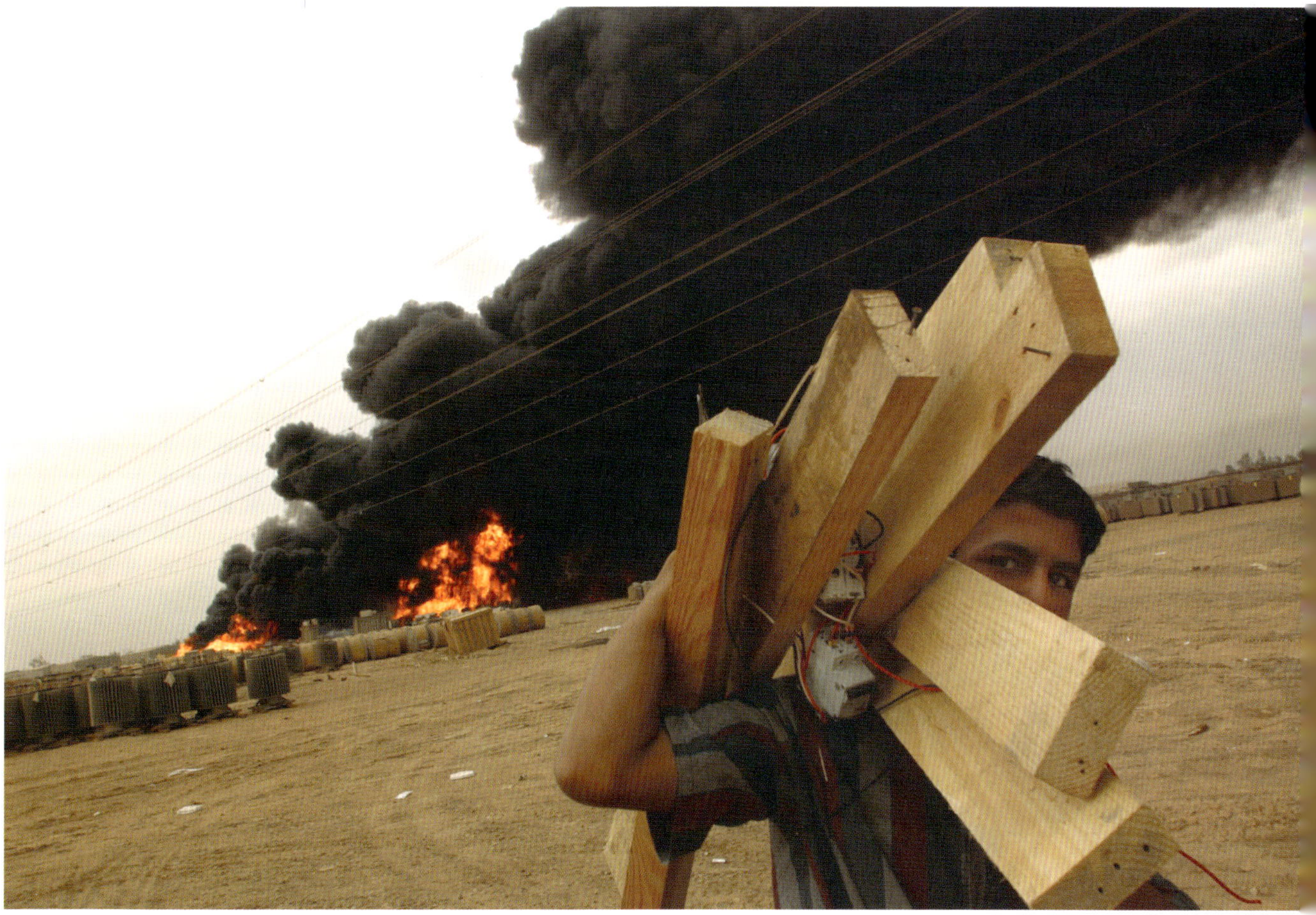

Looter's Swag

Looters take wood and building materials, then set fire to what's left. After five days of countrywide looting, the US military was ordered to intervene and stop it. Too late: almost everything that could be stolen already had been. © Timothy Fadek, Polaris Images

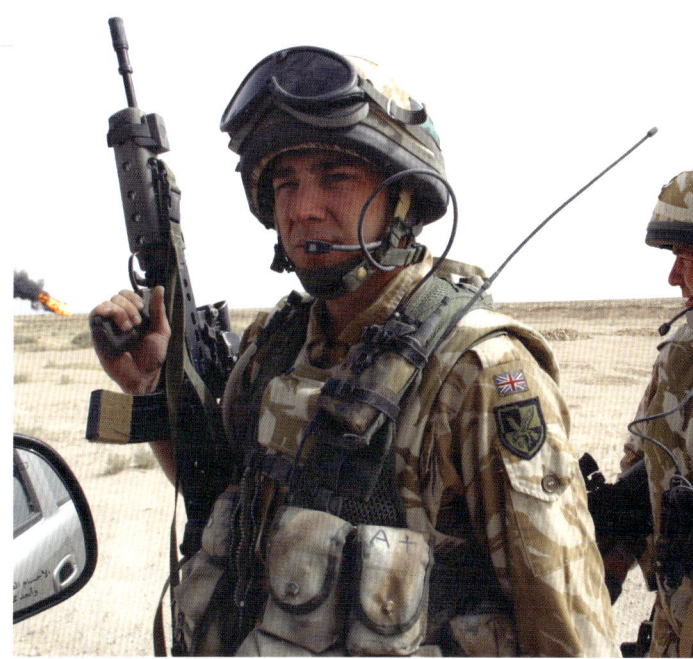

EARTHQUAKES AND FLOODS

The biggest challenge in photographing disasters is not becoming a casualty yourself. Notwithstanding trying to keep yourself physically safe, the ethics surrounding documenting the misfortune of others represent a very fine line. Telling a good story in photos about a flood or fire means more than just showing raging water or flames. It's about people's lives, tragedy, and the heroism that natural disasters inevitably bring to an individual or a community. Having a simple and very reliable pair of high-performance DSLR bodies, fast lenses, fully charged batteries, and big memory cards is essential.

While on average floods cause more deaths each year than any other natural disaster, large earthquakes are one of the most extreme examples of the vagaries of nature. Earthquakes have a rating system known as the Richter scale. Unforgettable images of the top-deck Oakland Bay Bridge collapsing onto the bottom deck were flashed around the world following the 7.1 Loma Prieta Earthquake of 1989. The Great San Francisco Earthquake of 1906 is estimated to have rated 7.8, and to have killed up to 10,000 people, but most of the damage was done by the fire that raged uncontrolled for three days.

Earthquakes are very brief, but the degree of devastation depends on whether they occur in a built-up area or in relatively uninhabited terrain. Earthquakes that occur under the sea result in tidal waves, or tsunamis, which can cause disaster on the other side of the world for coastal communities. Earthquakes are most common

Grim Detail

Rescuers work on recovering two bodies covered in debris after the collapse of a two-story building in Paso Robles, Calif., Monday, Dec. 22, 2003. The 6.5 quake struck at 11:15 am, when most people were at work.
© Joe Johnston / The Tribune

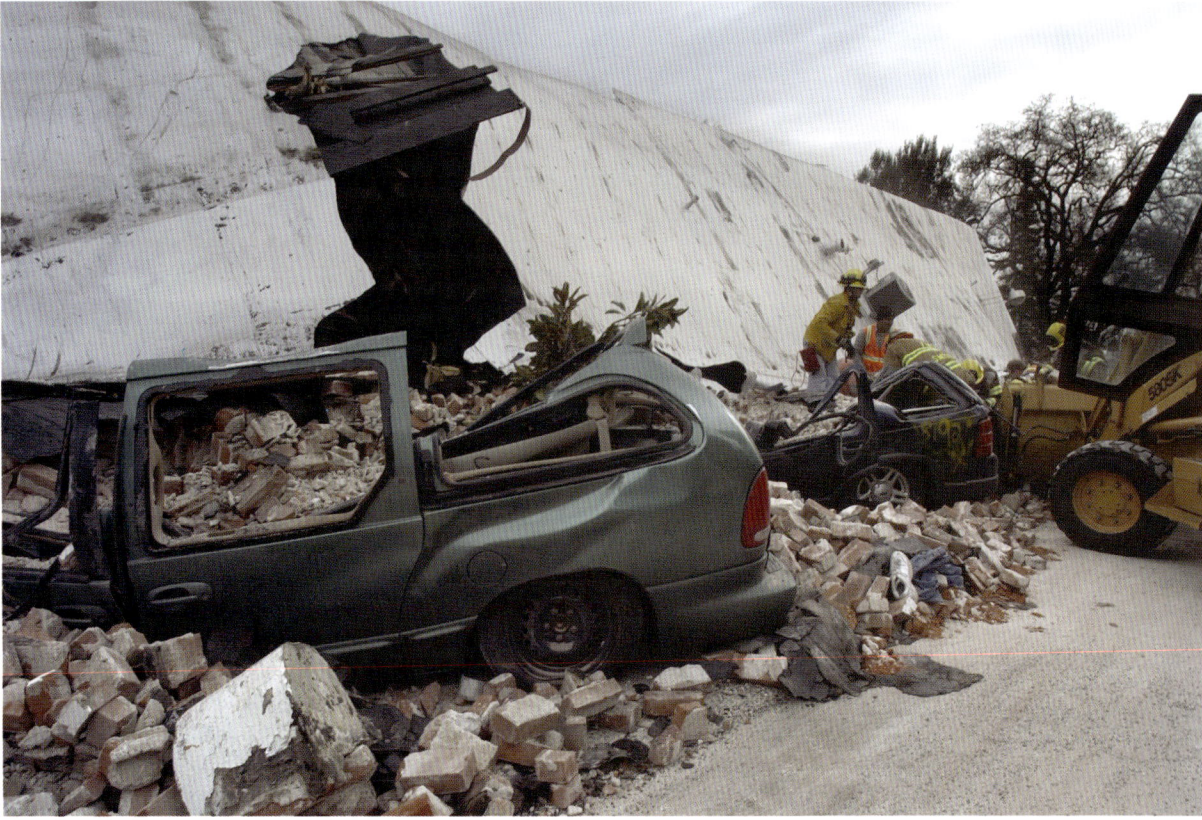

God's Eye View

The collapsed wall of the Acorn Building on the day of the San Simeon earthquake in Paso Robles, California. Flying over a disaster site is one way to get an overview of the scale of destruction. © Jayson Mellom / The Tribune

around the globe where the tectonic plates are colliding. The west coast of the US is one such region, where the likelihood of such an event occurring along key fault lines is quite significant. My own home is only a few hundred yards from the Hayward Fault, which US Geological Survey (USGS) scientists estimate has a 70 percent probability of a magnitude 6.7 or greater Bay Area earthquake between 2000 and 2030.

It is extremely unlikely that you will ever catch an earthquake as it happens, even on video, let alone on a still camera, so you are mostly going to be photographing the aftermath. But aftershocks, which can occur days or sometimes even weeks after the event, can still be deadly serious, especially if there are damaged structures remaining from the original quake. Fire is another big concern following an earthquake, so you need to be prepared to cope with fire as well as all the dangers of severe property damage, such as dangerous buildings and devastated infrastructure.

Floods are usually a more long-lasting form of disaster. The worst in US history, the hurricane-induced Galveston Flood of 1900, took at least 6,000 lives. The worst in the modern world was on the Yangtze River in China in 1931, resulting in the cumulative deaths of three million people from flooding and starvation. Floods are often best depicted from the air. Getting to the heart of a flooded area can itself be the challenge. Trying to work with the emergency services is the best way to smooth the path to getting access, and it pays to have contacts in these organizations to help you get to the right place and take the best pictures. While floods are usually the result of very high rainfall often associated with storms, the actual flooding can occur a long way from the source of the excess water. Flash floods are common in desert areas and can be very dangerous if you are in deep canyons, even though there may be no rain in sight.

Flood Alley

A resident maneuvers his boat down a back alley during a flood situation. One thing to keep in mind when photographing a flood is to park on high ground, then proceed by foot until a boat is available. © Jessica Brandi Lifland / Evansville Courier & Press

THUNDERSTORMS, TORNADOES, AND HURRICANES

Experiencing extreme weather for science, and more recently as a hobby, has developed a cult following in certain parts of the world, especially since the Hollywood movie *Twister* came out in 1996. There is the element of danger and the thrill of the hunt, and some individuals actually make a living from extreme-weather imagery.

Visually speaking, thunderstorms are some of the most amazing weather formations that exist, especially at sunset. Most thunderstorms build up during the day in areas of very moist air. Severe thunderstorms, especially long-lived ones with a persistent rotating updraft called "super cells," generate one or more of the following: tornadoes, winds over 58 mph (93kmph), and hail 0.75 inches (1.9cm) in diameter. Storms of this severity number some 10 percent of the 100,000 thunderstorms recorded each year in the US.

Big thunderstorms can stay on the ground for half an hour or more and cut a swath several miles wide. You want to be at least 5 miles (8km) from a big storm for safety. Shooting storms with a telephoto zoom lens is therefore recommended to give yourself plenty of distance. Frame grabs from video appear on many

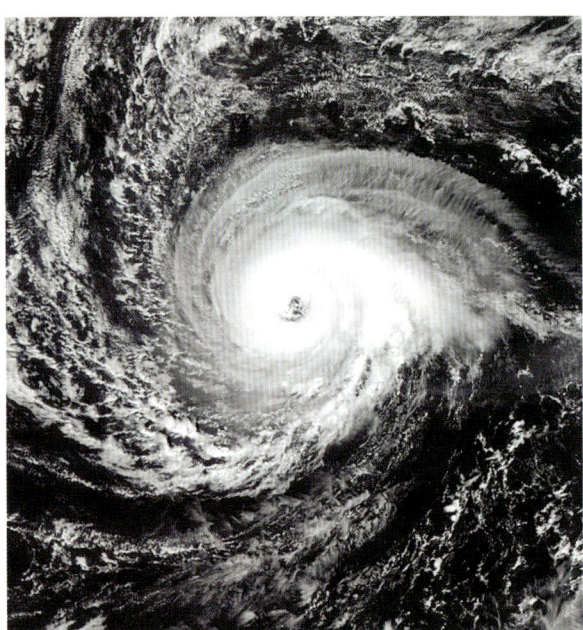

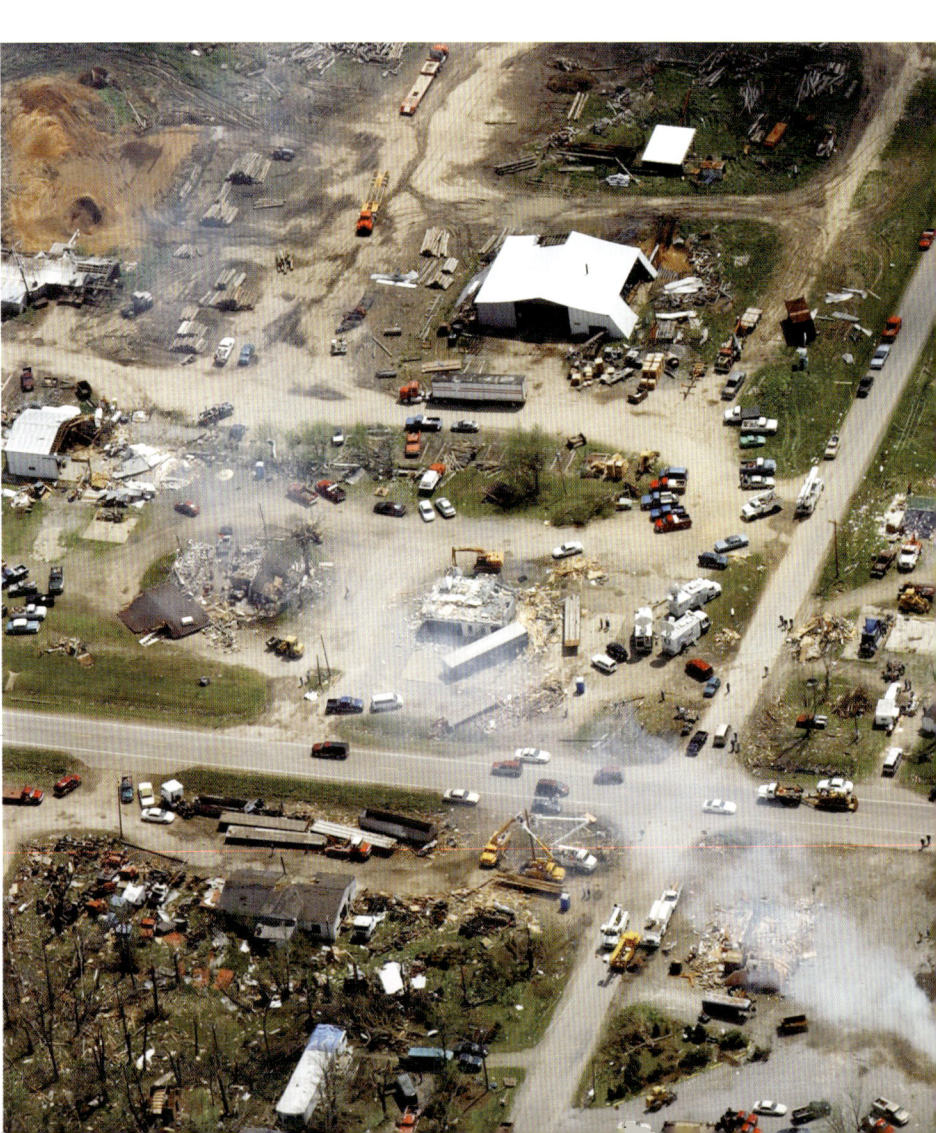

Hurricane Formation

Hurricane Kate churns in the Atlantic Ocean in its early stages as a small but well-organized storm. Much can be learned about disasters from satellite imagery, useful for tracking forecasting and scientific research. The leading resource is NASA's Earth Observatory (http://earthobservatory.nasa.gov). © Jacques Descloitres, MODIS Rapid Response Team, Terra satellite

Tornado Damage

An aerial view of the town of Sims, Illinois, taken from a single-engine plane. It is essential that communication between the pilot and the photographer is strong, so talking before take-off is a good idea. It also takes a strong stomach as the plane needs to bank sharply so that the camera angle can be close to flush with the ground. © Jessica Brandi Lifland / Evansville Courier & Press

websites that document tornadoes. The holy grail of this sort of coverage is to have a camera rolling in a storm-proof box as it gets sucked up into the vortex; recovery is an altogether more challenging proposition. If shooting digital stills of tornadoes, then having a DSLR capable of a high burst rate and fast writing buffer is essential.

Tornadoes are mostly found in the so-called "Tornado Alley" parts of the southern Great Plains and east-central US states, centered on Oklahoma and Texas. If you are close enough for a great wide-angle shot, you should perhaps be seeking shelter yourself. But there is one even more deadly form of extreme weather—the hurricane. Hurricanes move over a period of days, and their paths can be tracked with satellite photos and radar, so settlements in their path often get some warning. In the US, hurricanes are most common in the southeast, with the highest incidence along the coast of Florida, Georgia, and the Carolinas. Winds in a hurricane can be over 150 mph (240kmph), but the biggest danger comes from the coastal storm surge, which can reach over 20 feet (6m).

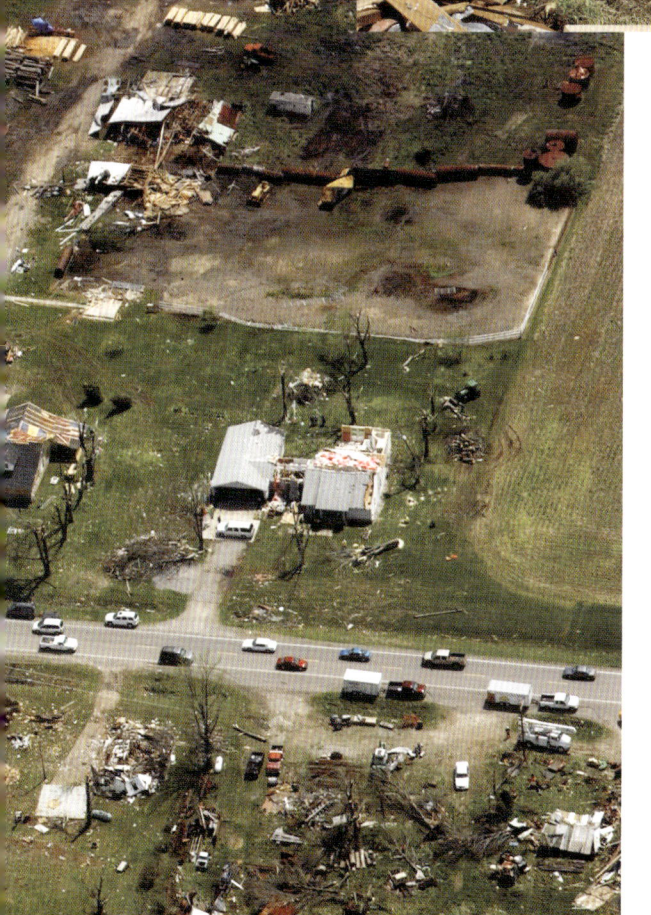

Tornado Center

A woman victim digs through piles of her things in the wake of a tornado that tore through Providence, Kentucky. In photographing victims of natural disaster, a photographer must be sensitive to the people and the trauma they have just been through. One suggestion: use natural light, as flash photography can unravel already stressed-out nerves. © Jessica Brandi Lifland / Evansville Courier & Press

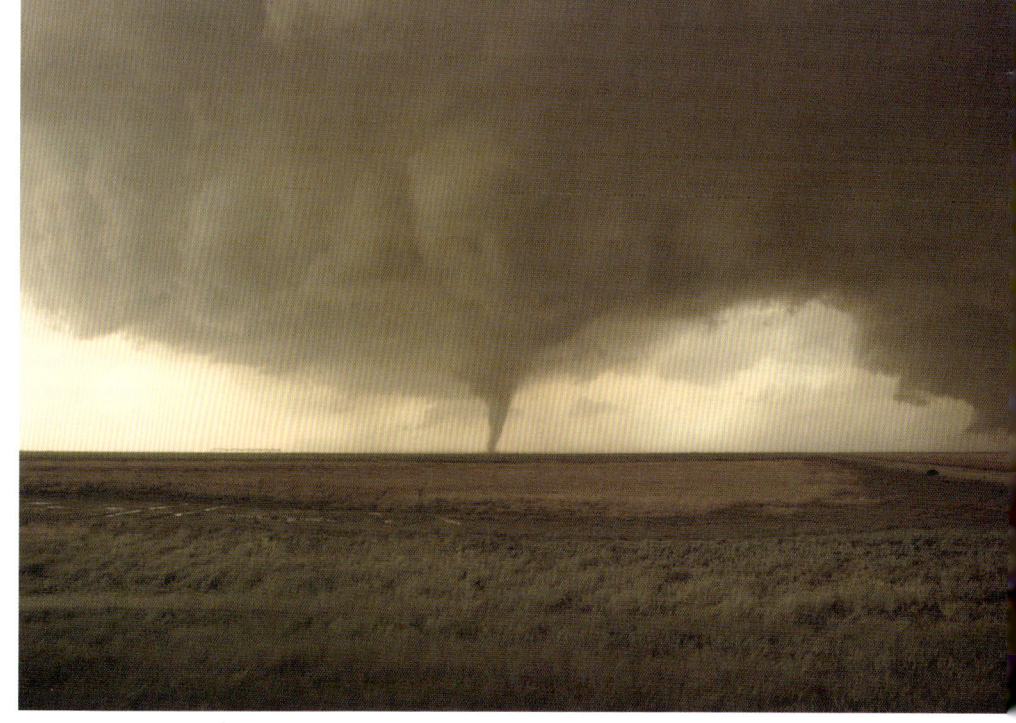

Funnel Cloud

The classic funnel-shaped cloud of a tornado touches down in the distance in this atmospheric shot. Action movies, storm chasers, the Weather Channel, and *The Wizard of Oz* have made tornadoes familiar to modern audiences, but their destructive power cannot be taken for granted. © Kyle Gerstner

LIGHTNING

Lightning is one of the most dangerous natural phenomena to photograph. While images of lightning can be dramatic as well as visually beautiful, perhaps the first point of sensible photography is to recognize the safety measures that you should take. If you are watching a storm approach, you can estimate how far away it is by counting the seconds between the lightning flash and the thunder—it's approximately 5 seconds for each mile (1.6km). But sometimes lightning can strike 5 miles (8km) or more away from a storm, so don't feel that you are immune from the lightning if the storm is 10 or even 20 seconds away from you.

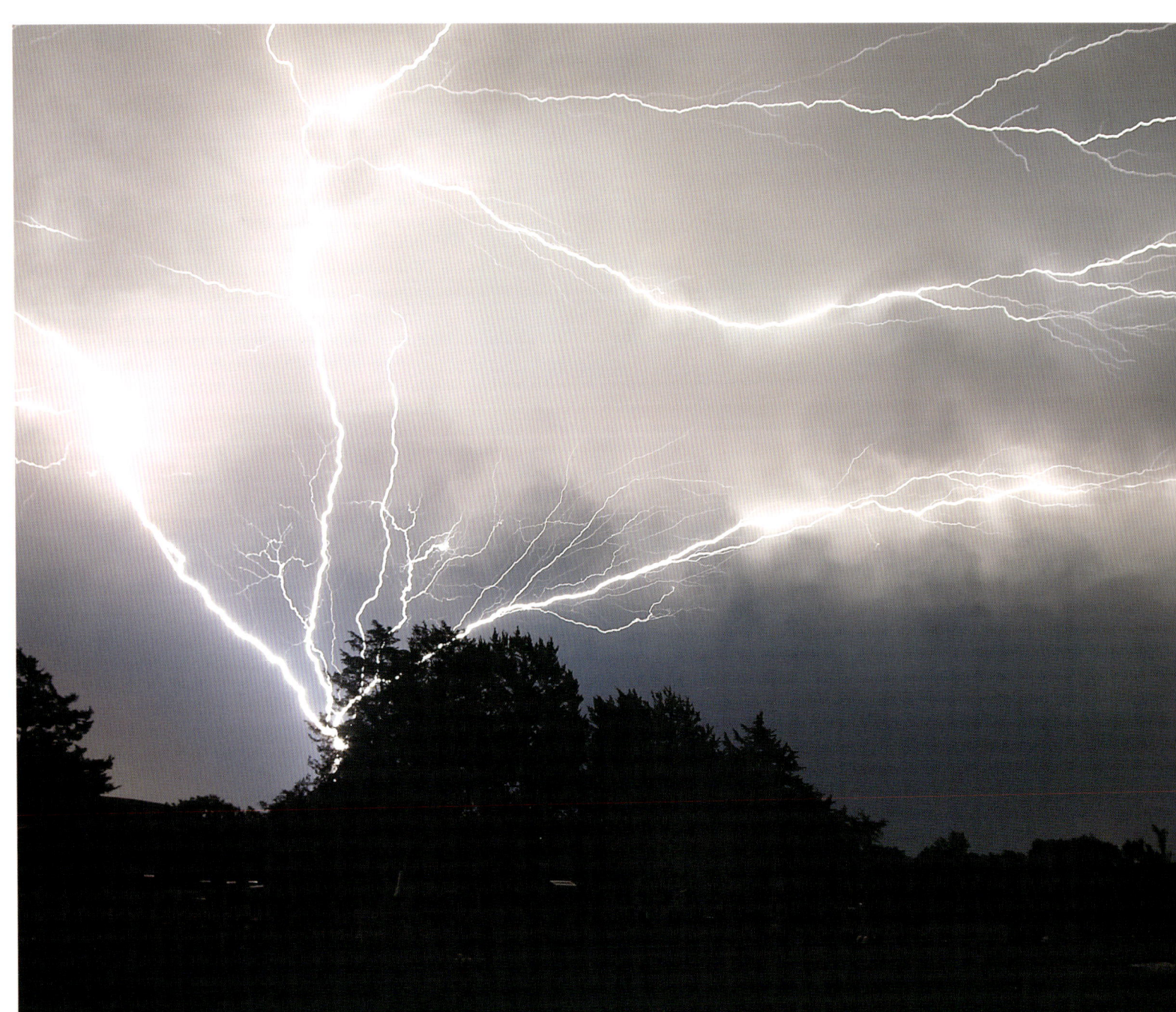

During the day, lightning is very difficult to capture effectively. Human reflexes are simply not fast enough to capture the flash by pushing the shutter when you see a bolt, and where they will strike is almost impossible to predict. If the storm is very active and the sky is dark enough (or you use ND filters), you can get shots of lightning in daylight, but they are seldom as dramatic as night shots. Lightning is also much easier to shoot at night because it in fact makes its own exposure. The darker the night, the longer the exposure you can make, and the more chance you have of capturing a bolt.

You need a DSLR capable of a time exposure with the camera set on T or B (bulb). Using an electronic or cable release, keep your ISO setting as low as possible and choose a middle aperture, f8 with the autofocus off, focus on infinity. Station the camera on a stable tripod and aim it at the storm. Then keep the shutter open for one or more strikes of lightning. For exposures longer than half a second, if it is available, have the noise-reduction program activated to further eliminate camera movement. However, the long exposures needed for a lightning series may lead to a buildup of digital noise. Sometimes in an active storm you may be able to get a number of bolts in the one frame without too much buildup, as the exposure time need not be too long.

In photographing lightning, digital has the advantage that you can review your work as you go and adjust your length of exposure accordingly. The intensity of the storm, your distance from it, and the amount of dust or smog in the air will affect the exposure, so you may need to open up a stop for best results. You can also shoot at sunset and sunrise by metering the available light on the horizon and closing down a stop. The best shots are those where the lightning is balanced with the ambient light.

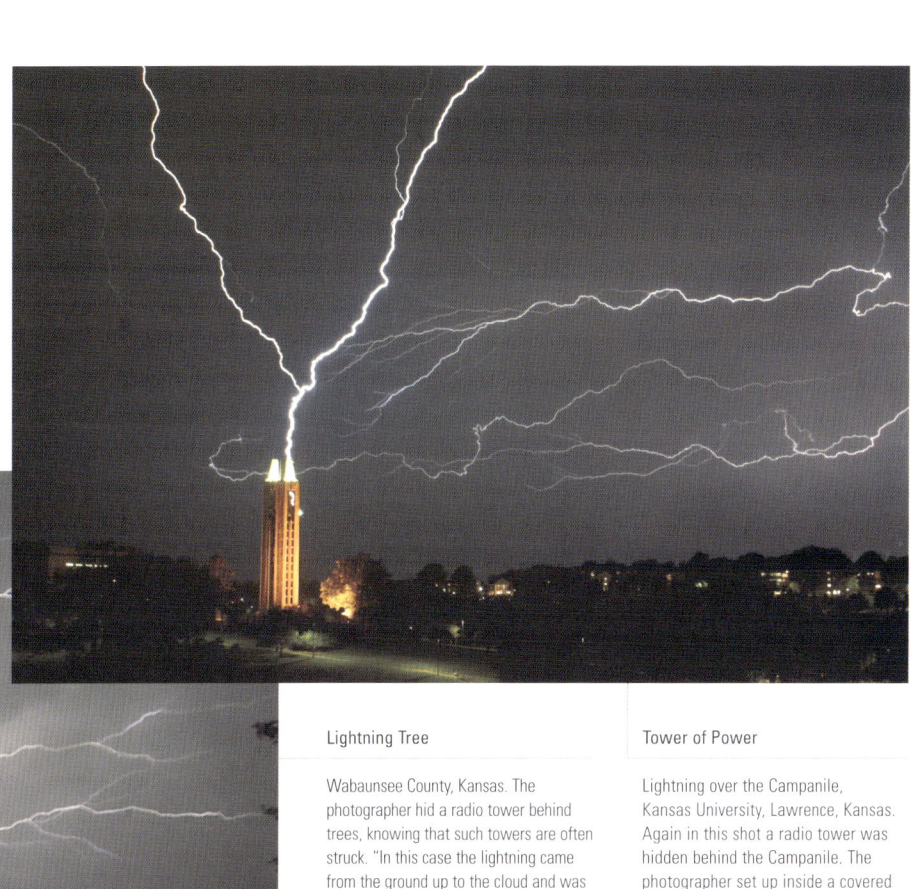

Lightning Tree

Wabaunsee County, Kansas. The photographer hid a radio tower behind trees, knowing that such towers are often struck. "In this case the lightning came from the ground up to the cloud and was the first time I've witnessed that. I shot from my car with a tripod set up in the driver's seat." Taken with a Canon D60 with 17–35mm, exposure 18 seconds at f4.5, ISO 100. © Kyle Gerstner

Tower of Power

Lightning over the Campanile, Kansas University, Lawrence, Kansas. Again in this shot a radio tower was hidden behind the Campanile. The photographer set up inside a covered parking garage for some degree of safety. The camera was a D60 17–35mm lens, exposure 3.2 seconds at f5.6, ISO 100. © Kyle Gerstner

If you are caught in the proximity of a thunderstorm, be attuned to the signs of an imminent strike: you may feel a tingling through your body, and your hair may stand up from static electricity. Crouch down, but remain on your feet. Wait for lightning to strike before standing back up.

If you persist in taking photographs, stand well away from any metal (especially camera tripods) and avoid finding shelter under trees or at the tops of hills. If you shoot from within a few feet of a car, you can retreat to this at the first hint of static electricity, and with a wireless remote keep triggering the camera from within it. If you are indoors, stay away from windows, doors, and switch off all appliances (or, better still, unplug them).

WILDFIRES AND VOLCANOES

Wildfires or bush fires are among the most treacherous natural disasters you can attempt to document. An intense fire can reach temperatures of 2,000° F (1,093° C). Driven by powerful self-generated winds, these fire storms torch everything in their path. Photographing wildfire is like being in a war zone. There is so much happening so fast that, from a technical standpoint, you want as many media cards as you can lay your hands on, as you probably won't have much time to select when it is all happening.

Being right on the fire line is where you get the most compelling action photographs, but this is also the place most fraught with danger. A sudden wind shift, smoke, or a falling tree can cut off your escape route, or worse.

Tim Wimborne, veteran of Canberra bush fires, has some hard-won tips. "First of all, preparation: I always have a little kit in my car, with things I might need if I'm out there—eye drops, aspirin—it's useful for more than just fires. And water, when you're shooting fires it's invariably going to be a hot day. In Australia, I have a Nomax suit (the material that firemen wear). It doesn't burn, it smolders. I also have boots just in case, which are handy in case you walk through a burn site and hit a pit of coals." Other photographers recommend a helmet with a protective shroud that prevents burning ash and embers from getting down your neck and clothing. "A good thing for a photographer is to have a good pair of goggles that fits tight to your eyes with a rubber seal—not a big one, the small ones, so you can still see through the viewfinder."

The last-resort lifesaving device that wildfire professionals carry is a fire shelter. This tentlike wrap made of fire-resistant aluminum-foil and fiberglass cloth enables you to crawl inside if you are trapped and overrun by a fire.

> *Fires are hard, because you get right in there to make shots, and the one you want is everyone running away. So have your car pointed away from the fire, and have the engine running if the fire's close—cars don't start well if it's smoky.*
>
> **Tim Wimborne**

The heat of fire is unlikely to damage the camera or flash cards, but smoke and ash fill the air in a serious fire setting and all your images can take on a nuclear winter look. Shooting RAW will enable you to refine the look of your images later, though in peak action you may need to shoot JPEGs to speed up capture and writing. Canadian photographer Alan High says, "Turn your camera lens mount down when changing lenses so you at least have gravity on your side for the big chunks."

Another popular disaster subject with an extreme dimension is volcanic eruption. Volcanoes can be explosive and potentially disastrous—witness the eruption of Mt. St. Helens in the Pacific Northwest of the US in 1980. Avoid being downwind and in river valleys downstream of an erupting volcano. Ensuing landslides and mud flows are typically more devastating than the eruption itself. Like wildfires, ash and smoke from volcanoes are an ongoing frustration for digital photographers who have to change lenses in dusty environments. There are often also toxic gases to contend with, from which there is little safety except distance.

The best time to shoot volcanic activity is at dusk, or in the night, when the glowing magma stands out. For normal lava-flow access, good boots and sun protection and plenty of water to prevent dehydration are advisable.

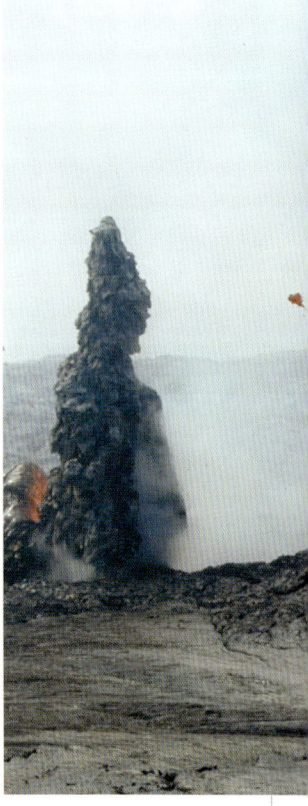

Molten Fountain, Kilauea, Hawaii

Erupting lava is caught as it burbles up from a lava tube. Photographing volcanoes is a dangerous trade: Reid Blackburn of *National Geographic* was killed when Mt. St. Helens erupted on May 18, 1980. Donald Swanson, Hawaiian Volcano Observatory, USGS

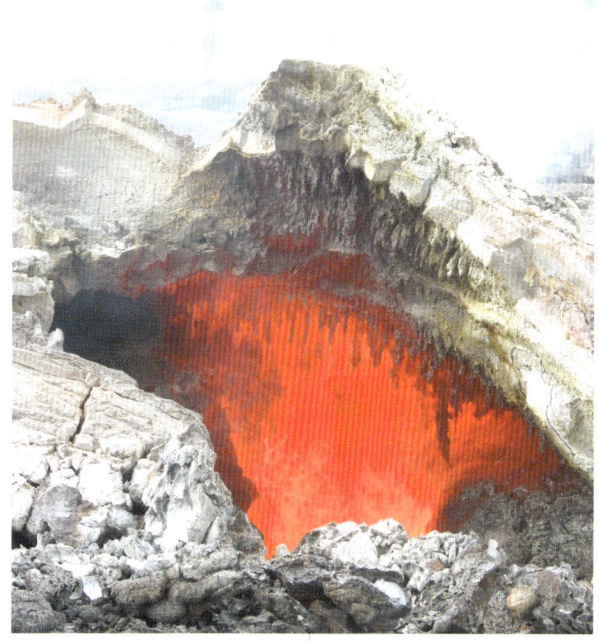

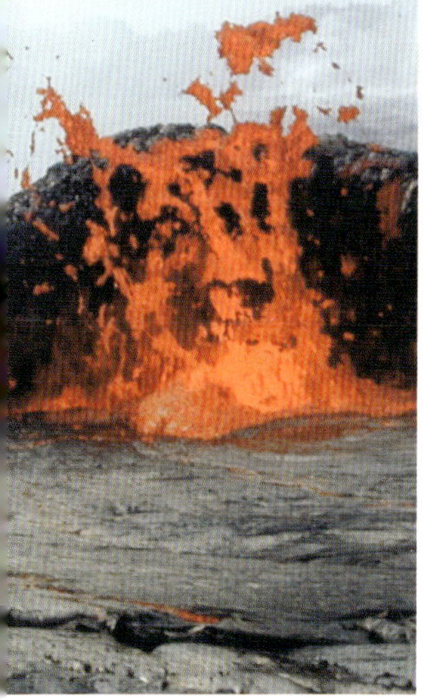

Lava Dome

Two volcanologists, their images distorted by the heat, gather data while magma glows through the bulge of a lava tube at Kilauea Volcano, Hawaii. Image taken on November 16, 2001, at 10.41 in the morning. The camera was a Canon Powershot G2, 1/125, f4.0, ISO Auto. Richard Hoblitt, Hawaiian Volcano Observatory, USGS

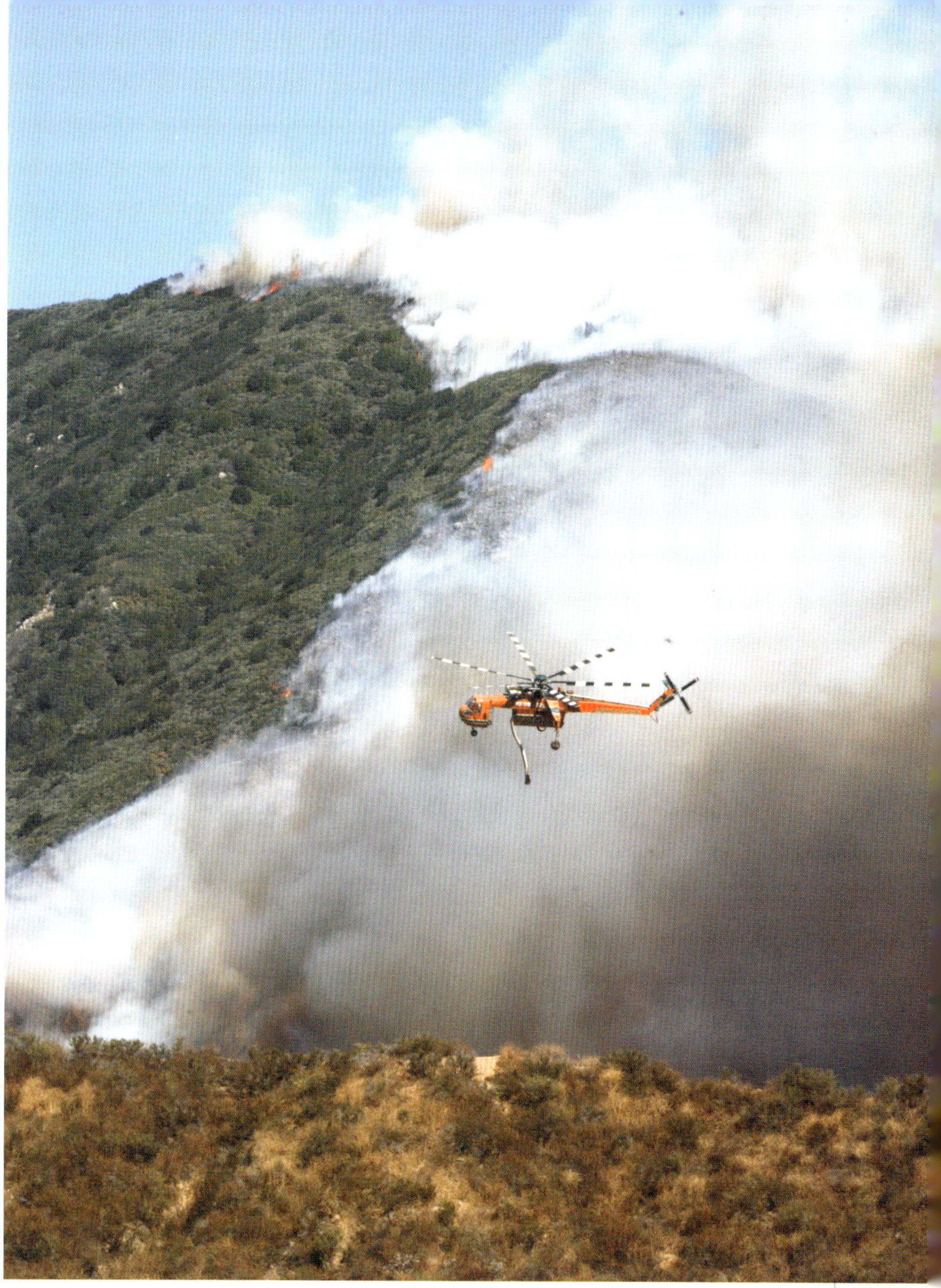

Wall of Smoke

Even massive aerial-water bombing by plane and helicopter could not diminish the disastrous Southern California wildfires of 2003. Not all the action in firefighting is on the ground: sometimes it's in the air, and flying over the scene can give a better perspective, and clearer pictures. © Robert Eplett / California Office of Emergency Services

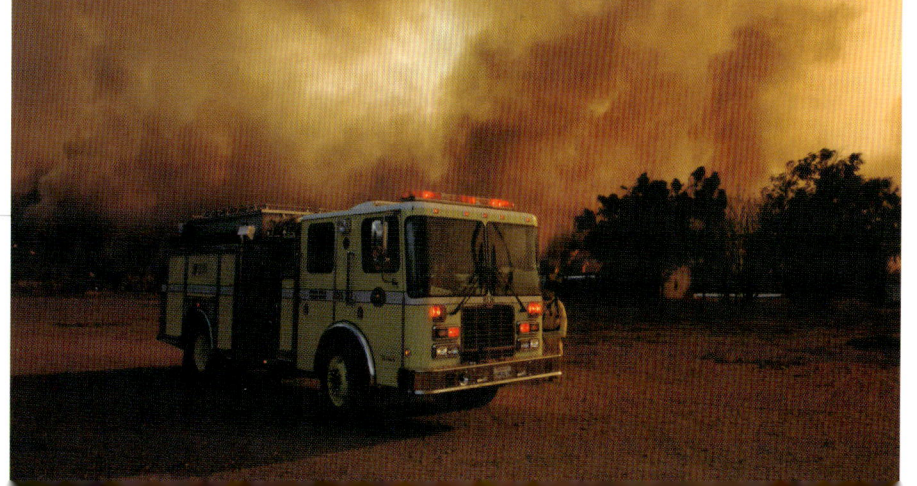

Truck under Trial

A community fire truck meets its match as a Southern California wildfire invades the neighborhood during the summer fire season. © Robert Eplett / California Office of Emergency Services

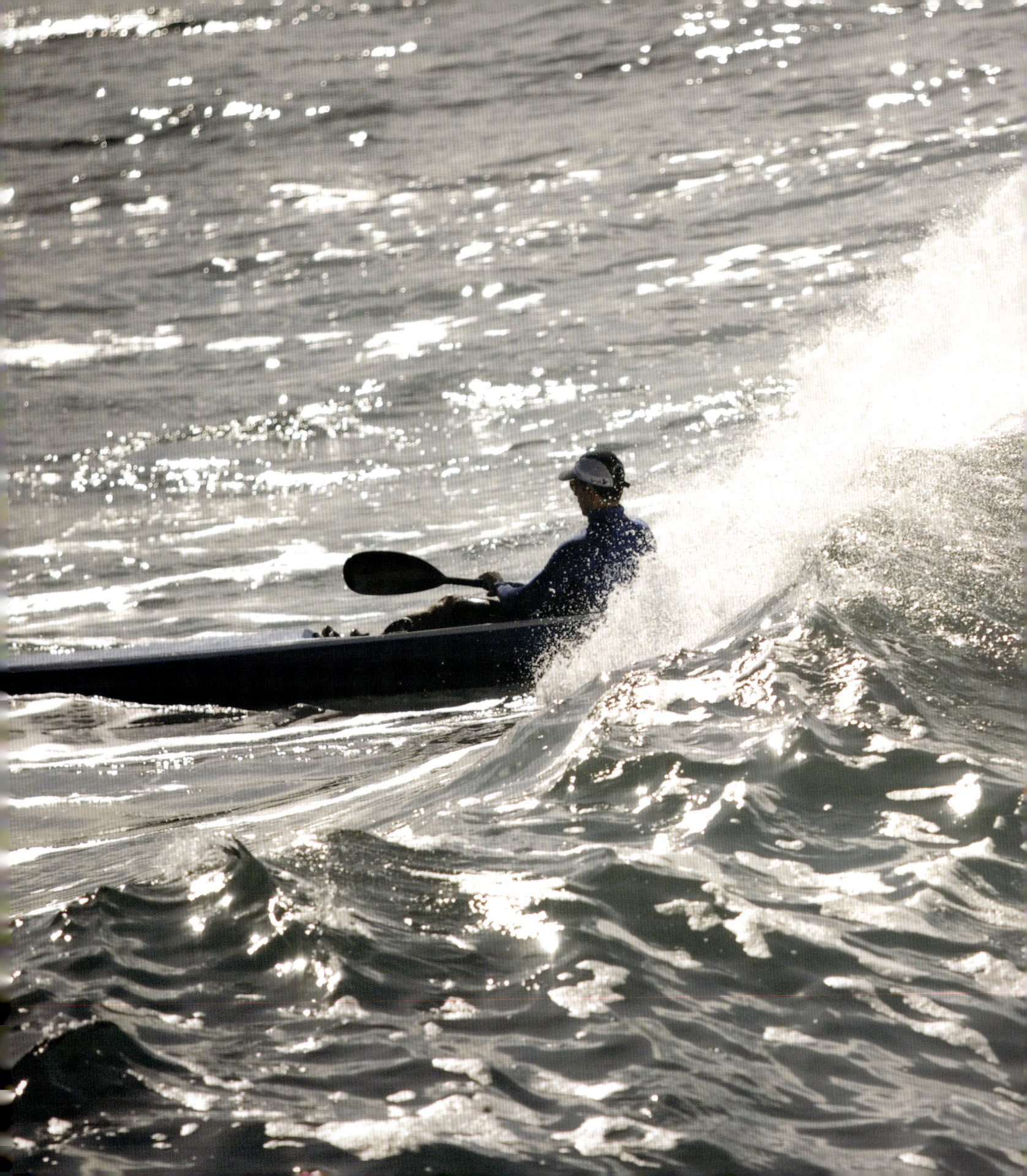

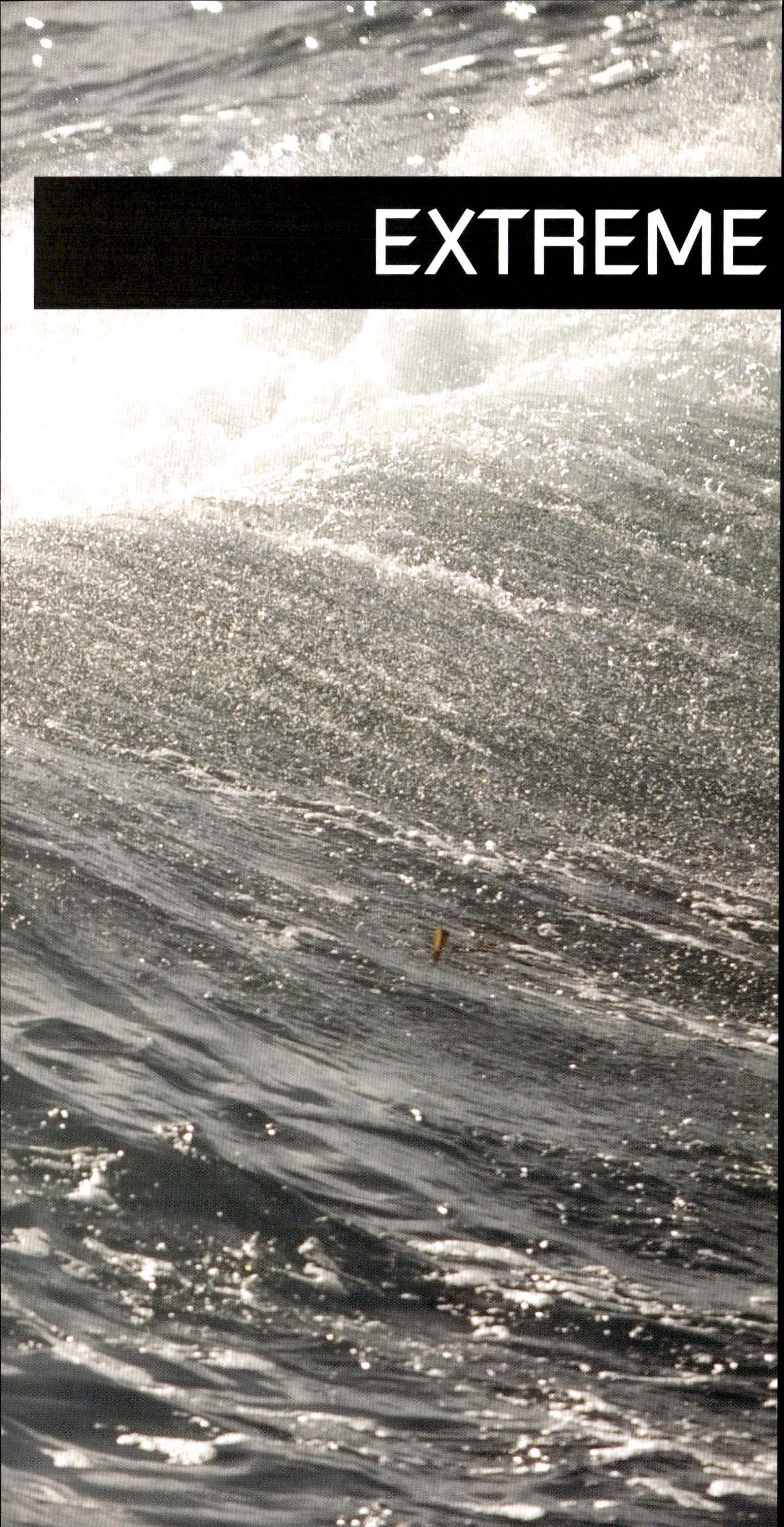

EXTREME ACTIVITIES

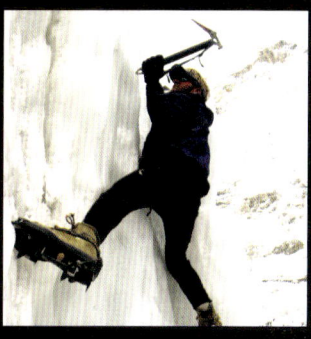

People cheer us on and that really helps in our darkest hours. We in turn inspire them, at our end sharing our shortcomings or success against the odds. In that effect we are the modern gladiators. Except this game is based on personal growth and human discovery.

**Tom & Tina Sjorgen,
ExplorersWeb.com**

Main: © Martin Sunderberg
Top: © Jonathan Chester

ADVENTURE RACING — TIM WIMBORNE

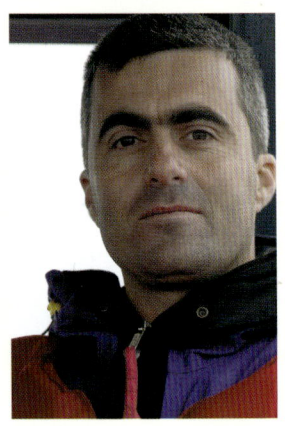

Adventure racing didn't exist until a little over a decade ago. The first widely recognized event was the Raid Gauloises, in New Zealand in 1989—400 miles (645km) of mountaineering, horseback riding, kayaking, canoeing, and rafting, held almost non-stop over a two-week period. Photographers who cover adventure racing must be polymaths of technique, skilled in shooting action, ambience, landscapes, portraits, and sports in equal measure. One such shooter is Tim Wimborne, an Australian who has covered adventure races in Argentina, Switzerland, New Zealand, and the Appalachians.

I use a Nikon D1-X, I've got two—and all the paraphernalia that goes with them. I've got a 16mm, a 17–35mm, 35–70mm, 60mm macro, 80–200mm, 300mm f2.8, and 1.4 tele-extender. I always have two bodies out of the bag, one with a long lens, the other a medium-wide lens. You shoot them coming on with a long lens, then when they get next to you, you shoot them wide with whatever's around them.

When I cover races, I'm doing different things. A few months ago I was doing the Appalachian Extreme, and I was watching one team only—and while that made planning simpler, it didn't make the actual photography any easier. At the world championship in Switzerland a couple years ago, I think I had 14 teams on my shoot list. Having a great assistant makes a world of difference.

Shots of teams at transition points are boring. A team on a glacier with a great view behind them, slugging it out up some ice slope—compared to some guys changing wet suits at a transition point, with a bunch of cars behind them. Guess which shot you see on the posters.

I've never had any really bad problems with getting dust in the camera. When I change lenses I always hold the camera with the mount facing down, and have the lens off for the smallest time possible. I know what lens I'm going to put on next, so I'm not wasting time rummaging through my bag.

Of course you've got to be in great shape. You're following around some of the fittest athletes on the planet, and you're doing it full-time, non-stop, day after day. If you aren't in shape yourself, you'll get exhausted by the third day and your work will suffer.

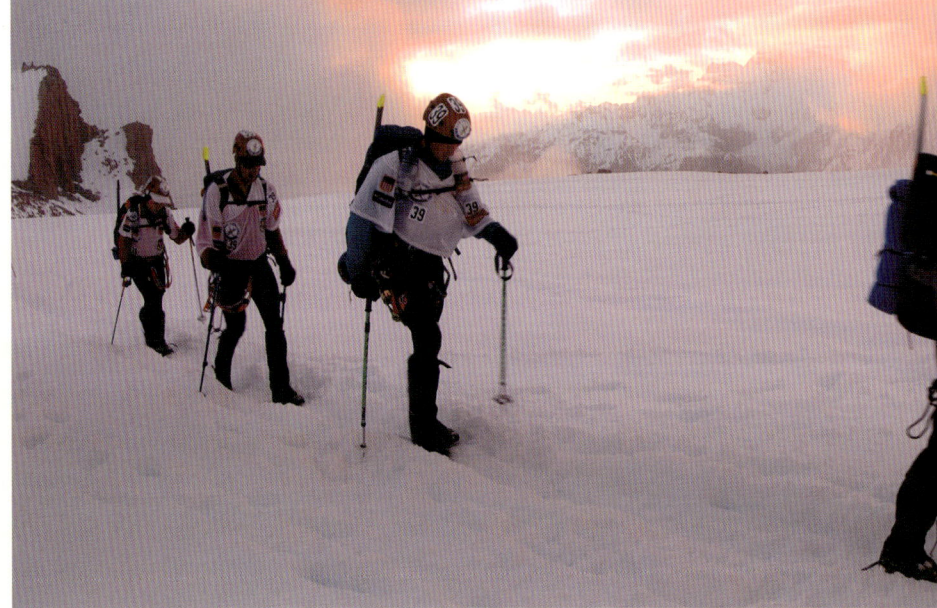

High Pass Crossing

Adventure racing means covering teams through a wide variety of terrain as well as over long distances. At the 2001 Eco-Challenge, held in New Zealand, that variety included glacier crossings during the trekking leg. Here, Team America's Air Force competes on the ice below Liebig Col, near Mt. Cook. © Tim Wimborne

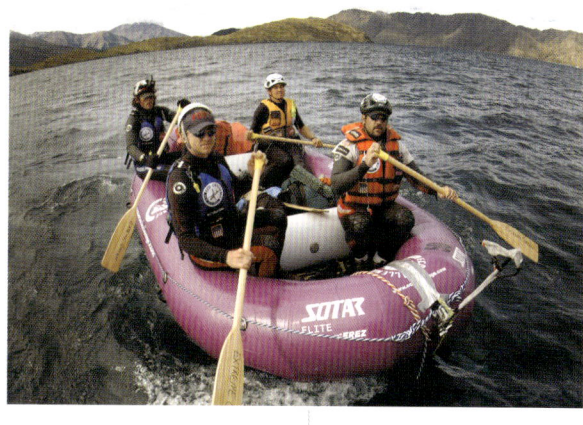

Raft Portage

The rafting leg of the 2001 Eco-Challenge passed down the Matukituki River valley toward the end of the 10-day adventure race. At this point the Philippines team portages over a hillside to get a better position. © Tim Wimborne

Team Paddlers

A super-wide-angle lens captures members of Team Go (USA) on the waters of Lake Wanaka, as the final teams inch their way closer to the finish line. © Tim Wimborne

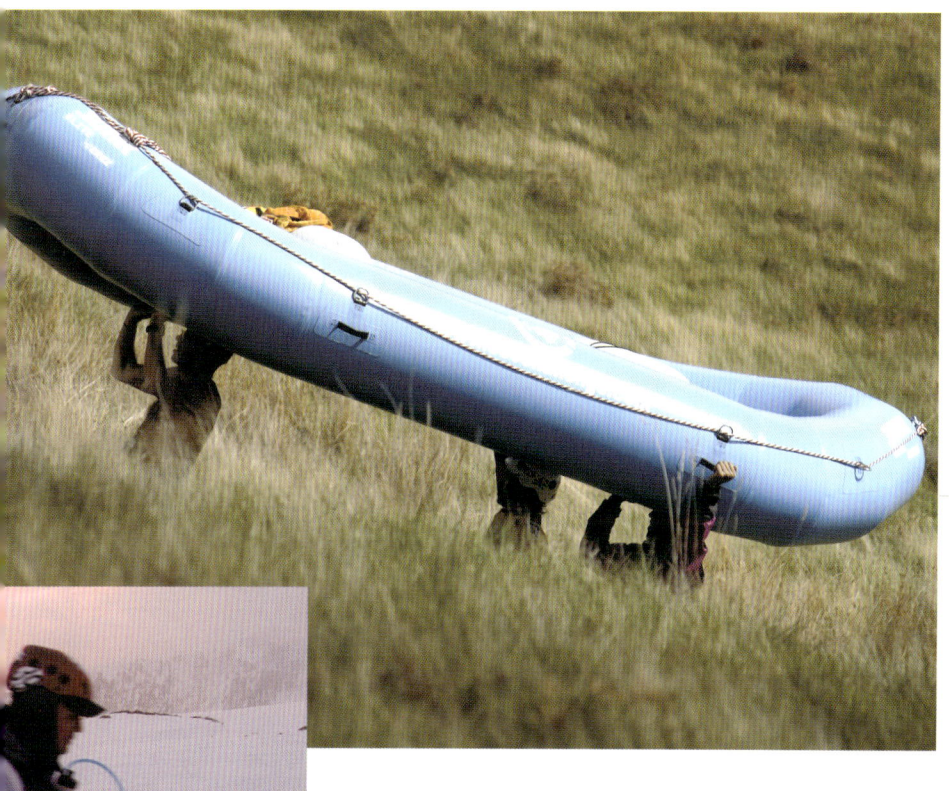

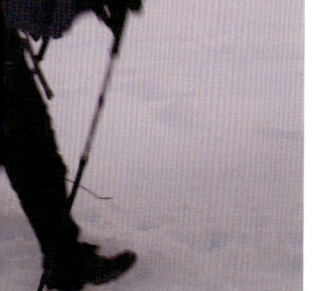

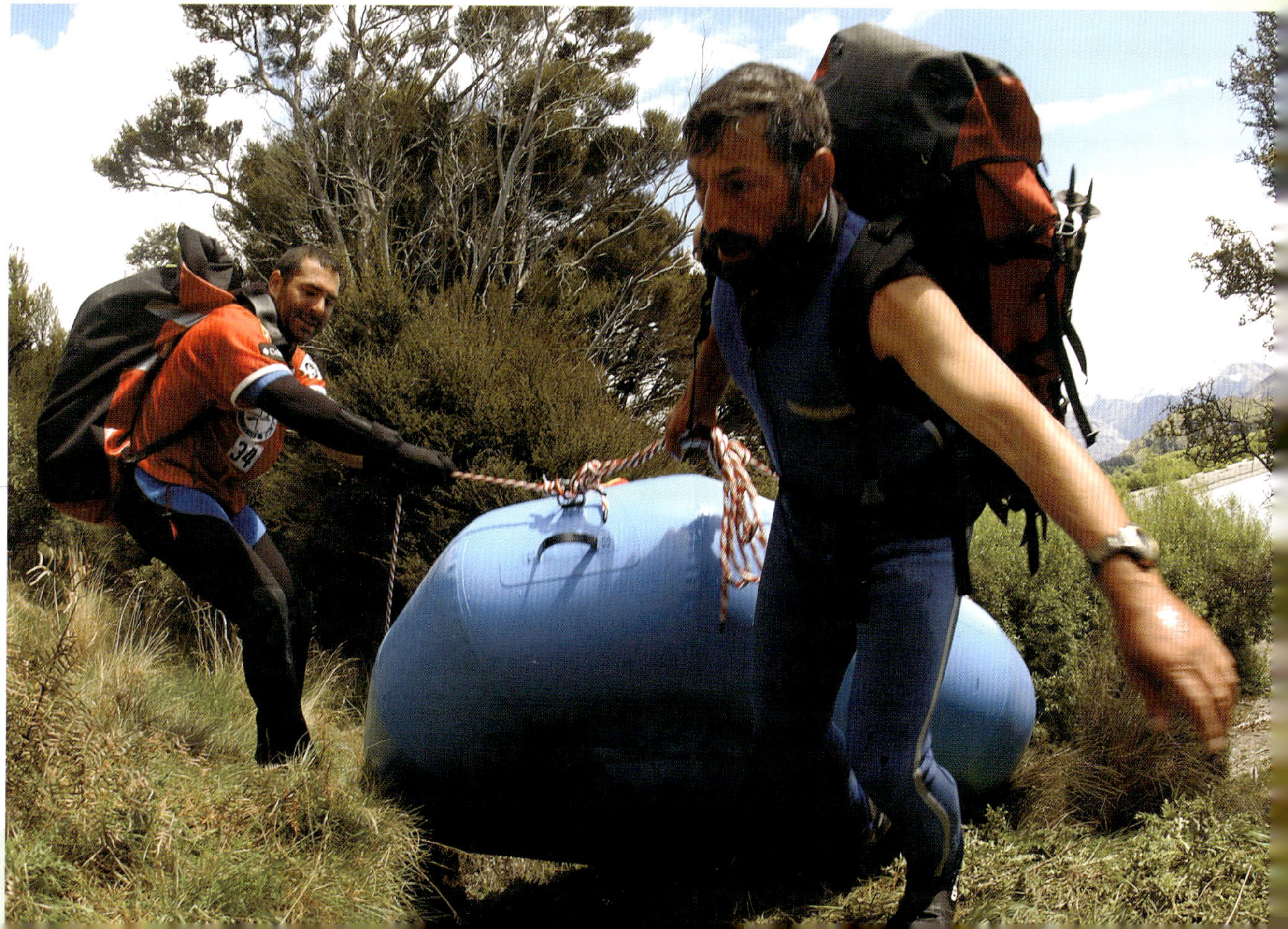

Rafting Uphill

Team 34 (Turkey) struggles to complete their portage during the rafting leg of the 2001 Eco-Challenge in New Zealand. © Tim Wimborne

BACKPACKING

Venturing into the backcountry carrying all your needs on your back for an extended period is a dream for many, but a reality for very few. Weight is always a big issue when backpacking, so lugging even a few ounces of camera gear makes it even more daunting. But serious backpacking photographers have been doing this for years.

Now you can backpack with digital cameras and a small extra kit to take care of battery and storage issues with confidence. The secret to this form of shooting is keeping it simple. Being able to power your gear with lightweight lithium or rechargeable AA batteries will make life a lot easier on an extended trip. When going all-digital, the choice of camera naturally has great importance. With cameras like the Nikon D70 or Canon EOS Digital Rebel, which are both very economical on power, you can go for a long time with just a few extra camera batteries, never having to recharge.

Next to power, storage is the biggest consideration. The most compact (and most expensive) storage is the original flash media card the image is written to, whatever the form (SM, CF, MS, or other). If you can shoot lower-resolution images for the less critical shots and save storage for the subjects that you really care about, you may be able to get by with just flash cards on a backpacking trip, if you bring plenty of them along. True, this only gives you one copy of the image (at least until you get home), which is what we were used to with film, but nowadays we feel the need to back everything up. If it's not possible or economical to carry as many cards as you might want for a long shooting trip (high-capacity cards are expensive), you need to have some way of offloading the images in the field.

A compact hard drive device like a Smartdisk Flashtrax is one way of downloading flash memory cards, providing you are not spending time at high altitude. Like all computer gear, this device is sensitive to heat and cold, being rated from 41° F to 131° F (5° C to 55° C). It also sucks power, even when it is not being used. A fully charged battery lasts for about 1.5–3 hours of downloading, and the more you use the LCD screen for review, the faster it drains.

If you choose to, you can recharge your cameras and storage devices on the trail, with either an external lithium battery supply, like those available from Automated Medial Systems or Human Edge Technology, or a small solar system, like the Brunton Solar Roll. But all this adds weight and expense. If you are carrying this gear on your back, you may think twice about whether it is really necessary, especially for a shorter trip.

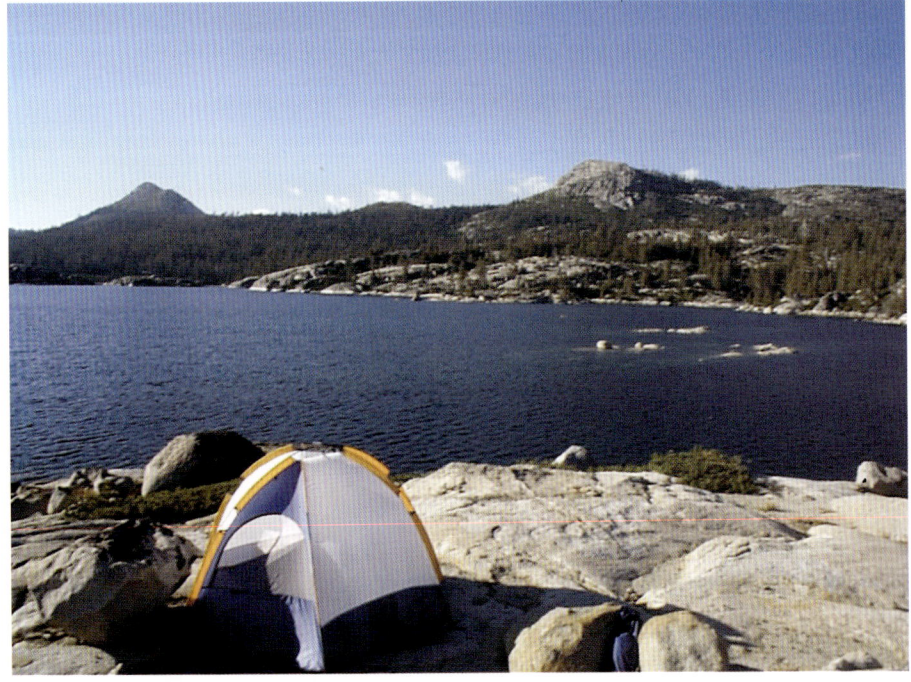

Room with a View

Extreme assignments have their advantages; foremost among them are remote and photogenic locations. Digital technology adds another dimension to self-reliance, already so important in backpacking.
© Kim Johnson Morris

BACKPACKING

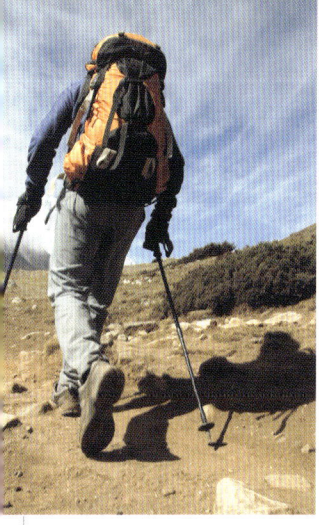

Ansel of Arabia

Hiking in the desert is scenic (use your polarizing filter), but persistent sand and wind makes it an inherently risky environment for equipment. Make sure that any gear that's not in use is securely stowed. © Russell Sparkman / One World Journeys

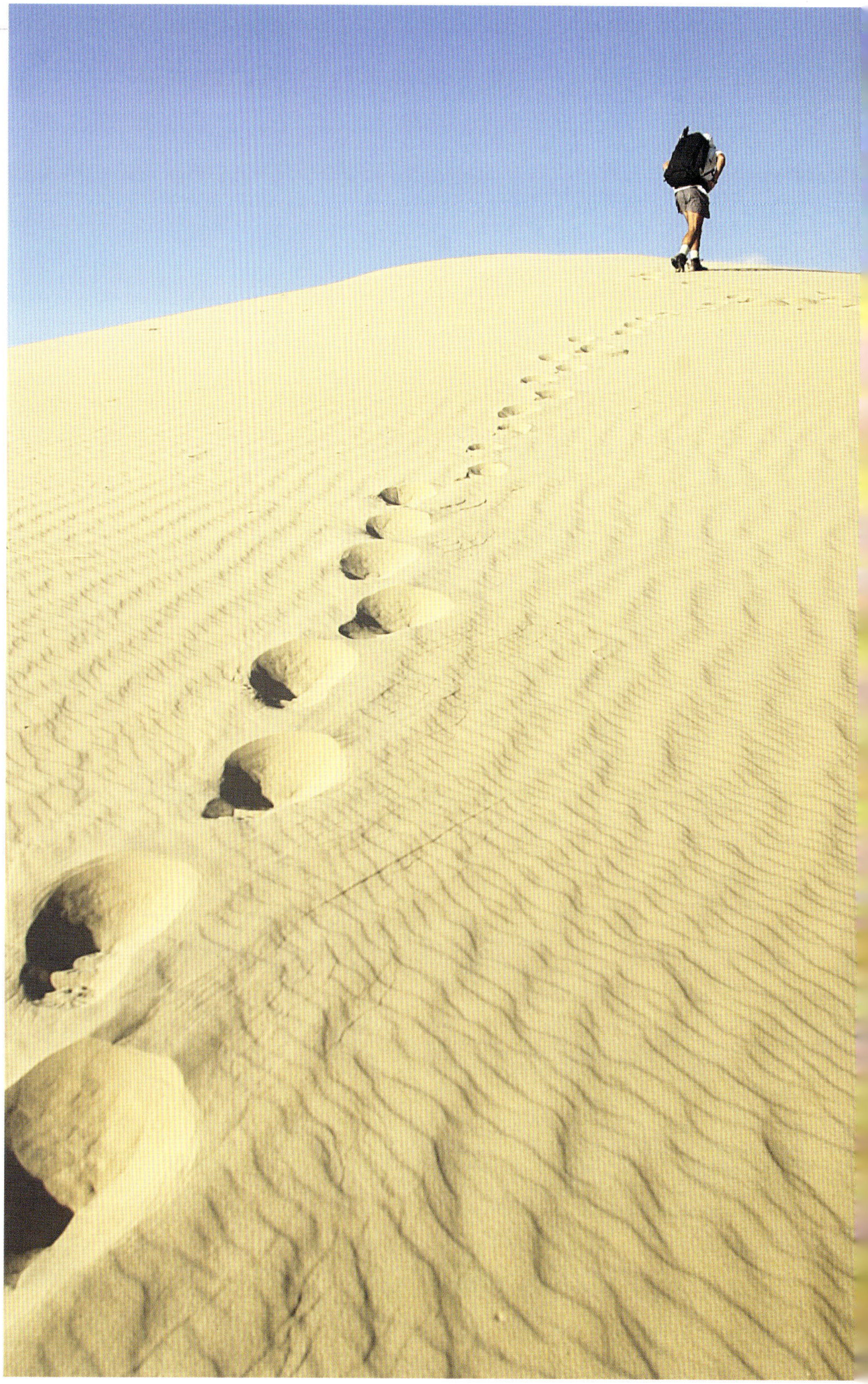

Trekking Poles

Covering long distances over varied topography is often made easier by trekking poles, but using two of them makes it harder to get your camera in position. Solution: use one, which can double as a monopod for photographic work. © Didrik Johnck

Rock and Ice

Ice is a difficult terrain, both for walking and shooting. Overexposure is a common trick to compensate for automatic exposure, but many digital photographers have found that the wide latitude of RAW files minimizes the need for spot-on exposure. © Mark Langley

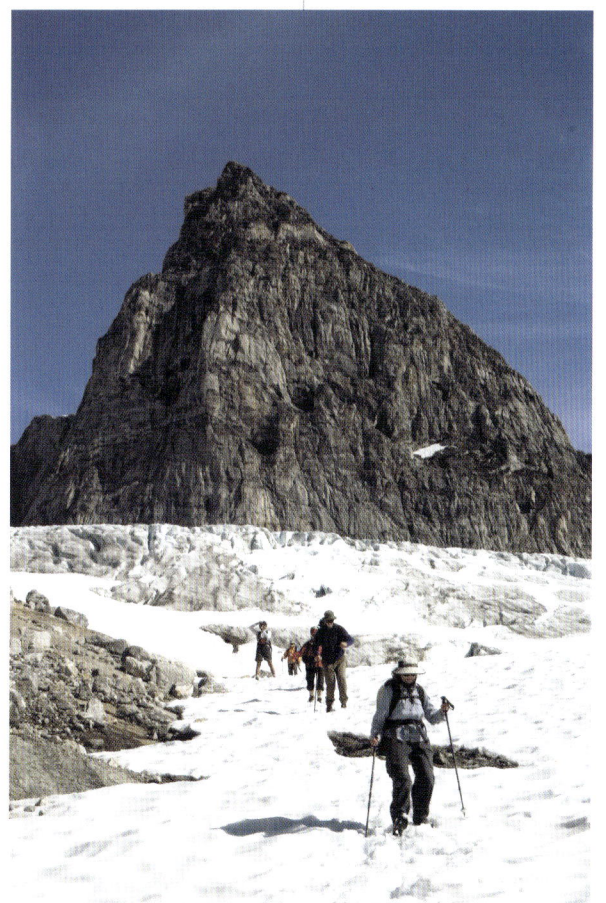

TREKKING

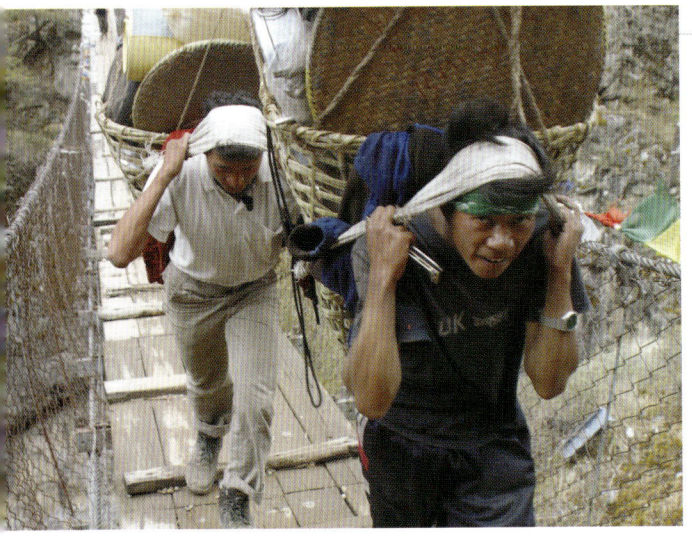

Porters on Trek

Long-distance travel in the Himalaya, en route to Everest Base Camp, necessitates having porters to carry expedition gear. They carry these massive loads with the weight borne around their foreheads by the "tumpline". In a place where no cars exist, these porters get food, building materials, and everything else from one place to another for the locals as well. They are always happy to pose for a photo. © Didrik Johnck

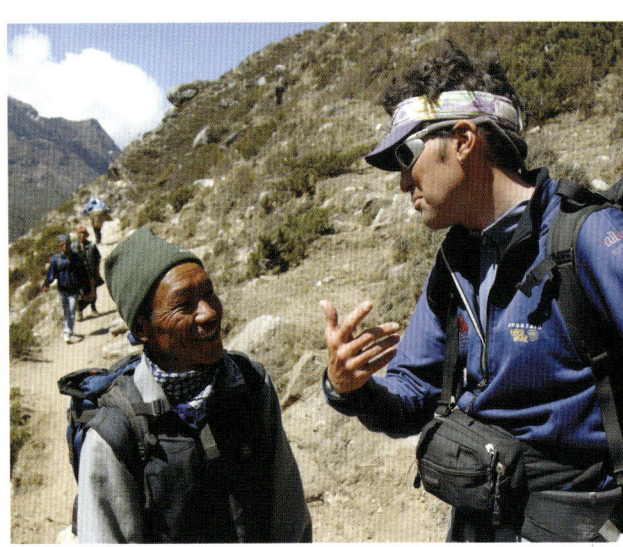

Trekker and Guide

The lengthy trek to Base Camp allows time for acclimatization to the high altitude of the Himalaya, and time for cultural interaction. Here-three-time Everest summitteer Luis Benitez chats with a Sherpa cook named Tenzing. After visiting the Nepal Khumbu region so many times, you become good friends with the locals. ©Didrik Johnck

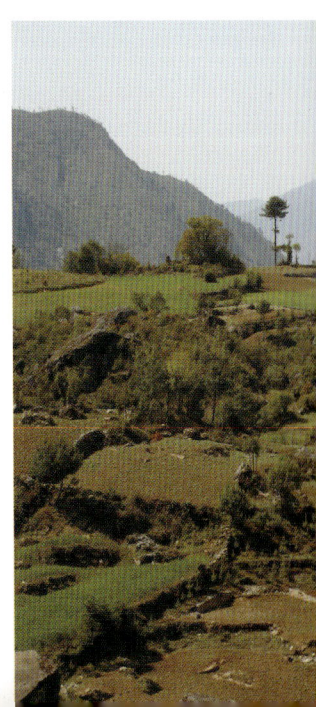

Trekking as a form of adventure travel originated in the Himalaya, but has also been adopted for journeys in other mountain areas of the world, especially the Andes. It does not involve technical mountaineering, but it may mean going to higher altitudes than you would ordinarily. Trekking is not necessarily a wilderness experience. Many popular trekking trails are also ancient trading routes that carry a constant flow of local people and porters, plus mules or yaks bearing supplies.

Many of the techniques of digital shooting and workflow incorporate all that applies to backpacking, with a few major exceptions. Weight is not as much of a consideration as it is in backpacking, but you may well be away from a reliable power grid for much longer. Increasingly, remote villages in the Himalaya have some form of distributed power, so there may be times when you can recharge your devices at inns and teahouses, but this should never be relied upon. Don't forget your primary power connectors for cameras and computers, though you may also be needing 12v connectors.

Regarding storage, while dedicated portable hard-drive media-card transfer units like the Flashtrax are ideal for many styles of remote shooting, these are rated to less than 10,000 feet (3,050m). Many consumer laptops and hard drives will keep on chugging even as high as 17,000 feet (5,185m), but if you are putting all your images on one device, you don't want to risk it crashing. Once again, base your workflow around redundancy.

"Ruggedized" laptops are available, with hard drives that are specially sealed for altitude, such as one of the Panasonic Toughbook series, although these can be heavy—the Toughbook 48 weighs in at over 7 pounds (3.2kg). One alternative is a device that can burn CDs directly from media cards, such as the Disc Steno CP200 by Apacer ($300). If power is not an issue, these have the advantage of letting you burn multiple copies of your image files and so reuse cards with confidence.

Sensitivity to the physical and cultural environment, no matter where you are trekking, should be a priority. Then you will return with great images and memories.

TREKKING 113

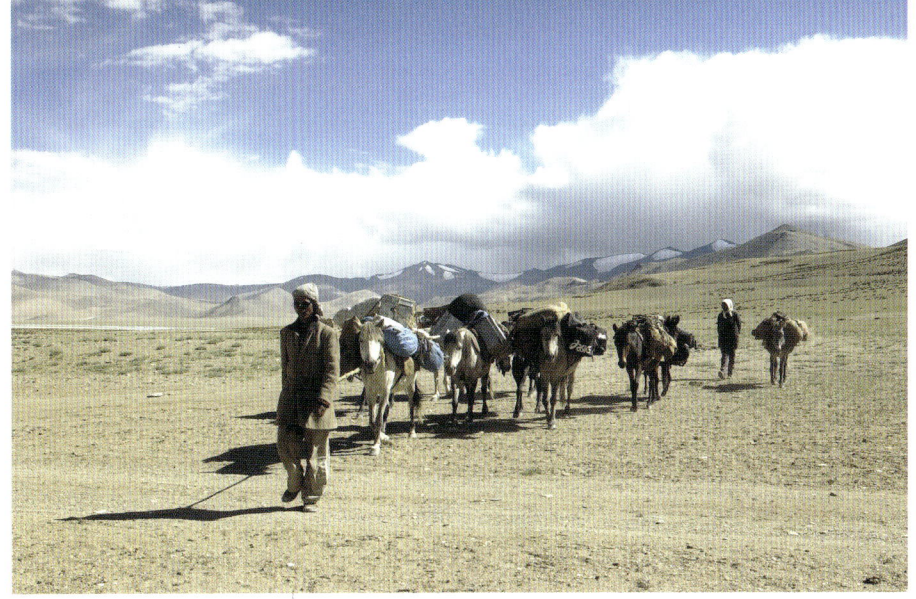

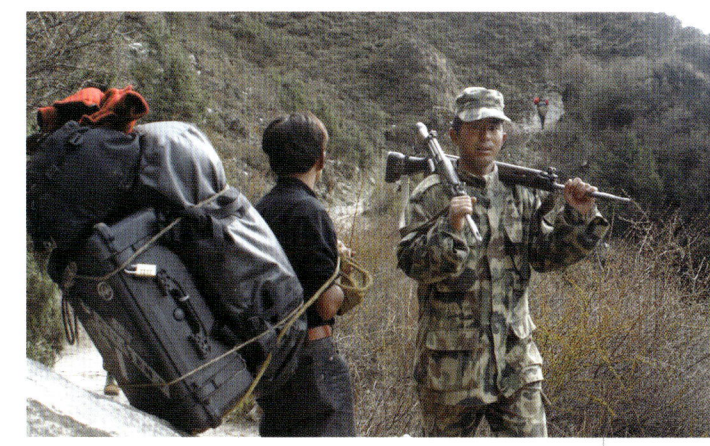

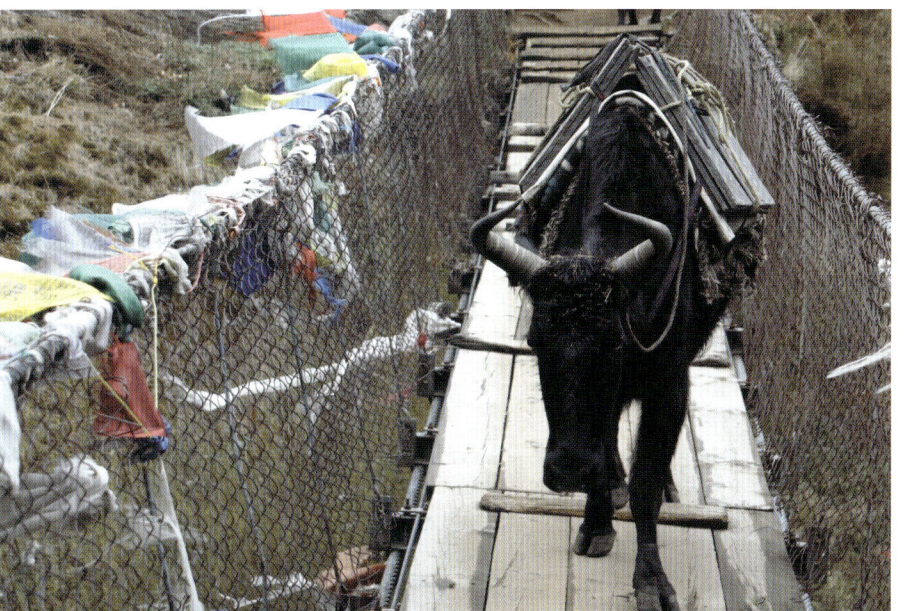

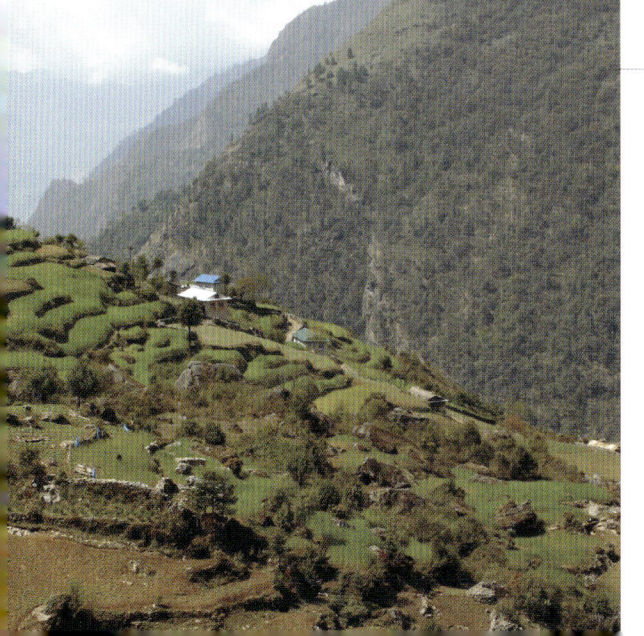

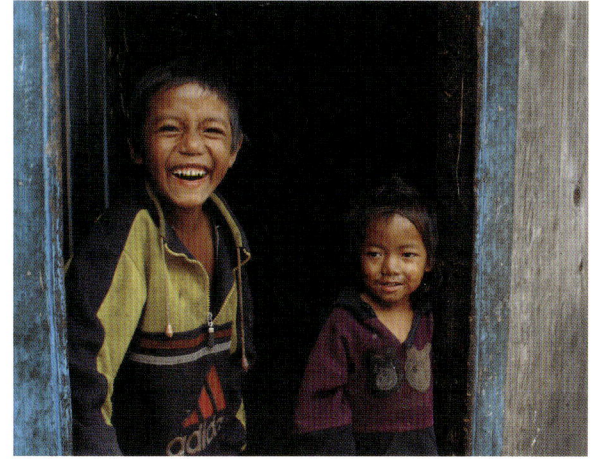

Pony Caravan

The high desert country of Ladakh straddles the often-contentious India/Pakistan border area, with much of the landscape ranging above 20,000 feet (6,100m). Visitors should be prepared for travel by any means necessary.

Wire Suspension Bridge

Travel in the mountainous regions of Nepal has been made safer and easier with the introduction of numerous wire suspension bridges. These replaced rickety wooden bridges that used to get washed away every monsoon when the streams become raging floods.
© Didrik Johnck

Soldier on Patrol

Nepal, once an idyllic mountain kingdom, has become ever more tense as Maoist rebels have attempted to overturn the feudal monarchy and take an ever larger role in local affairs. Today the army patrols the mountain areas on regular basis. They are quite amenable to being photographed. In this case my Nepali porter rests his load while waiting for the army patrol to pass. © Didrik Johnck

Nepali Children

Keeping such infectious smiles from being merely "Kodak moments" often involves contextualizing the scene, with details of living conditions. This pair were watching trekkers pass by. I put my hand out in a "High-5" gesture; the boy here recognized it at once and slapped my hand. Since my camera was ready to go, a quickly composed shot caught their energy. © Didrik Johnck

Terraced Hillsides

Trekking is not a "wilderness" experience. Most treks pass through landscapes long since settled, where small agricultural communities make use of every inch of arable land. Although you can't tell from this photo, there are huge mountains looming all around. It's easy to get caught up in the obvious. I like the way the green terraced fields were compressed into the landscape with my telephoto lens.
© Didrik Johnck

EXPEDITION PHOTGRAPHER—COREY RICH

Extreme photographers must, by definition, be willing to undertake extreme activities. Corey Rich, photographer for Backpacker, Sports Illustrated, *the (now defunct) website* Quokka Sports, *and many other publications, is one such photographer. He's covered expeditions in the jungles of New Guinea, the sands of the Sahara, the steep snowy slopes of the Rockies, and on the faces of some of the biggest walls in technical climbing.*

I'm trying to simplify everything that I do. I notice year by year that the more I shoot, the simpler everything gets. When I'm shooting with a film camera, I'm often shooting with one camera body and two lenses, an EOS 3 (which is a very light professional camera); it takes either CR-11 or CR-22 batteries, they're tiny and really lightweight. I think I can shoot close to 35 rolls of film on a single battery when it's cold out, closer to 60 when it's warm. So I can carry five extra batteries for a month and I'll never make it through the batteries.

But the instant you need live coverage, you've got to shoot digital. I think that's the example of everything we did with Quokka Sports. Even though we were ahead of our time in shooting with digital—in many cases the image quality was horrible, the cameras were really difficult to deal with—what we could do was get the images up online in a timely manner.

I use two Canon D60s, shooting Fine JPEG, one with a 70-200mm zoom, one with a 16–35mm, because changing lenses is so risky. I'm definitely a fan of big cards, I hate changing out the cards; I'll shoot either on a 1GB or a 512MB. The D60 is a big improvement over the D1X, it's a professional camera minus a data back.

When I'm taking photographs in an adventure environment, during the day I'm not only trying to make interesting photographs, working with the light, working

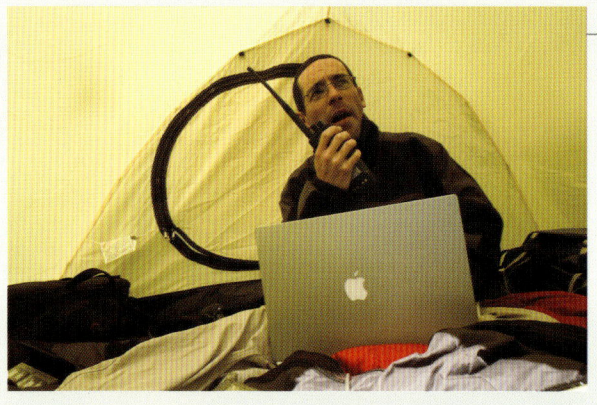

with the subject, and working really hard physically; when the day ends for the team, the real catch—and this is the hardest part of digital—is that you're not done. There's still two and a half hours or three hours of moving files onto the hard drive of your laptop, backing them up on a FireWire drive, processing, and all that.

I have a G4 laptop and I'll import the image into Camera Bits Photo Mechanic and simultaneously save it to the hard drive and an external FireWire drive—you can name the files at the same time. Those are the coolest features that Photo Mechanic has going, it's such a gigantic saver in terms of time.

When you're on your own, that's when it comes down to being familiar with your equipment. Certainly on the climbing front, if I know I'm going to be hanging off the side of a rock, sleeping on a porta-ledge, and managing assets on a laptop—keeping it simple is the absolute key,

Tent Office

Laptops and two-way radios are becoming as common as down bags on climbing expeditions. For the working digital photographer, both are necessary—to keep your images off loaded and archived, and to stay in touch with your team mates for planning the next day's shoot.
© Corey Rich

Flying the Flag

The Marathon des Sables is a six-day, 150-mile (243-km) endurance race across the Sahara Desert in Morocco, normally taking place at the end of March or beginning of April. It attracts colorful as well as patriotic participants from around Europe and Africa, and was covered in a digital website in 1999 by Quokka Sports.
© Corey Rich

especially when shooting digitally. I would probably in that case streamline my operation to one camera, two lenses, and bring an iBook rather than a G4 laptop.

The year that I was in Morocco, we never got hit by a single real sandstorm. We occasionally had some high winds, and I would put the camera away, in a fanny pack or an Orion bag, to cut down on the majority of the sand getting in. I have definitely had problems with film cameras in sand; I have scratches across everything, even when I've made my best efforts to keep my camera out of the sand. With digital, of course, the biggest issue is dirty CCDs—you'll end up with a speck of dust on 700 images in the same spot.

I should also point out that with everything I do, domestically or internationally, I bring duplicates. Whether it's with me or sitting in the car, I always have an extra body, I always have an extra 70–200mm, an extra 16–35mm, an extra 14mm, even an extra 300mm f2.8.

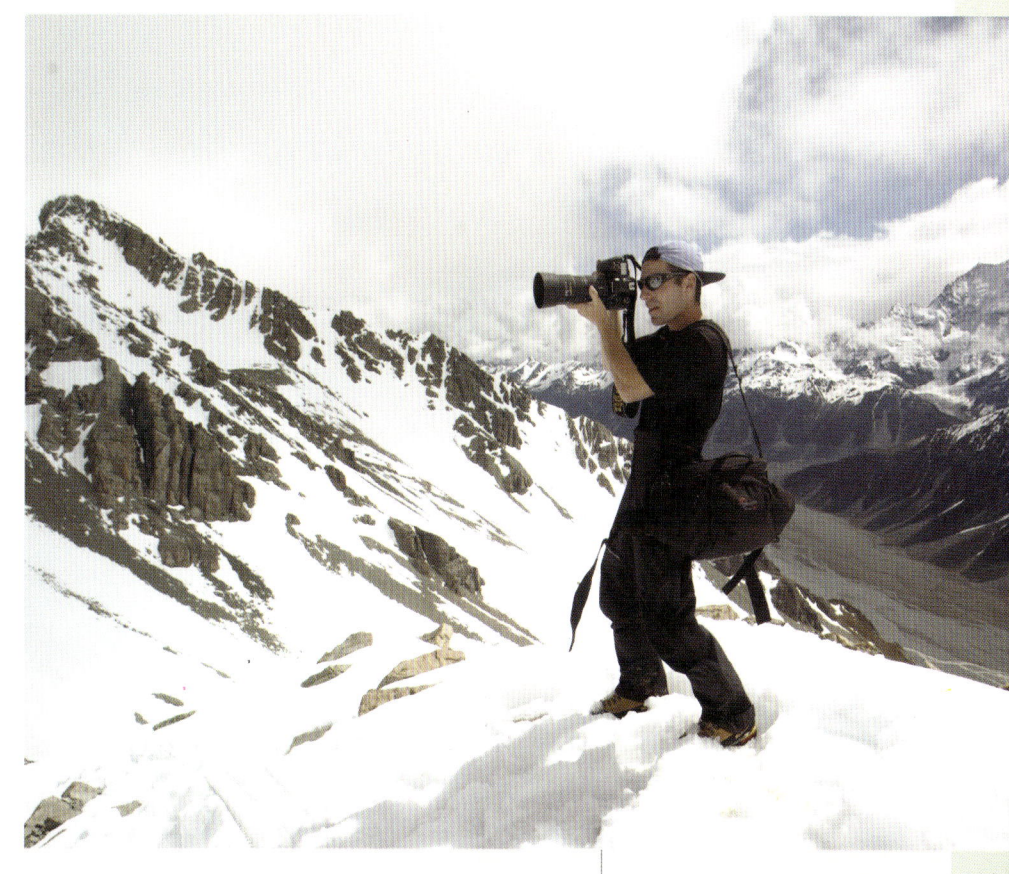

Corey Rich on Assignment

Shooting the Eco-Challenge New Zealand on the flanks of Mt. Cook, for Discovery Channel in 2001. Like Quokka Sports, Discovery's coverage was Web-centric and demanded the quick turnaround and delivery of digital photography. © Corey Rich

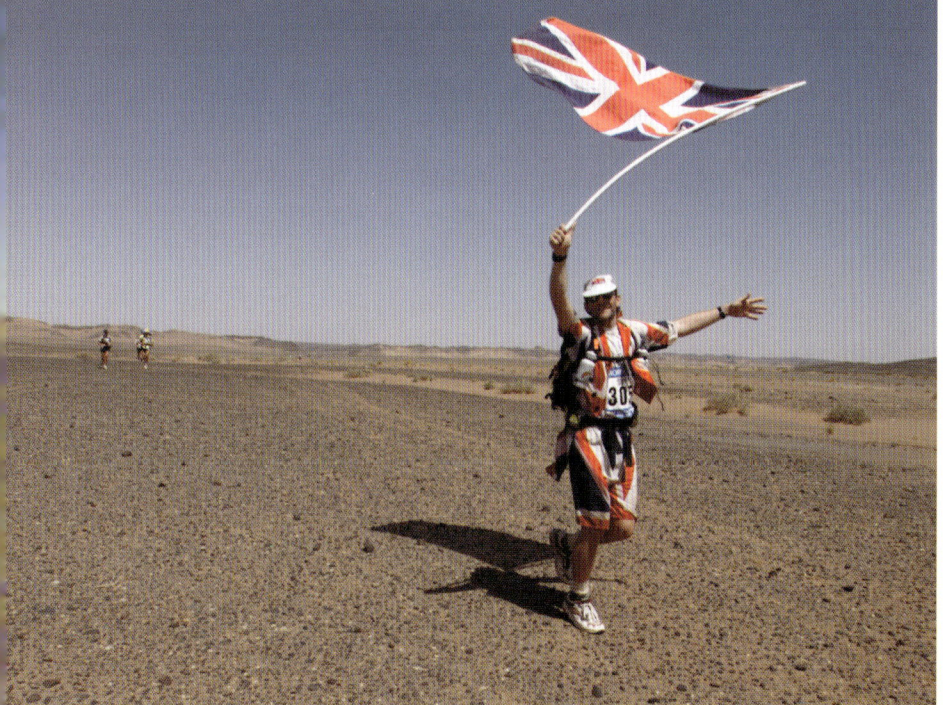

Footsore

One of the most compelling images of Quokka's Marathon des Sables coverage was this detail shot of racers' feet at the end of a long hot day on the sands. Shooting digital or film, the goal of an assignment photographer is the same: show the story. © Corey Rich

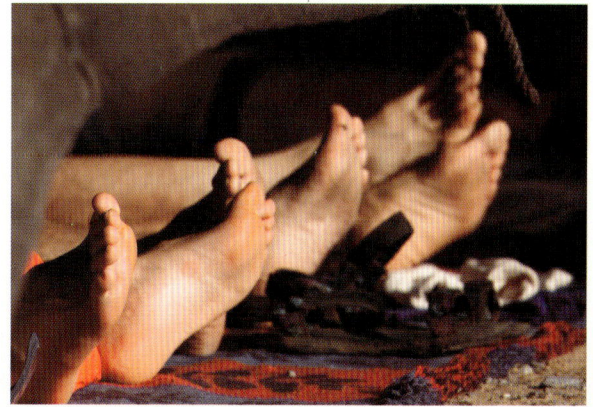

RIVER RAFTING

Few sports are as dynamic and implicitly "adventurous" as river running, with its crashing waves, rocky drops, and powerful currents. Capturing the adrenalin on film is a bit trickier than it looks, though, especially if you're after point-of-view shots. Adding digital to the mix makes it at once easier and more difficult, depending on the duration of your rafting trip and the power constraints.

You will need both ends of the lens spectrum: wide-angle for inside-the-boat shots of the guide pulling on the oars, over-the-bow shots into the waves, and shots of your fellow passengers. From shore, a long lens is crucial for getting up close and personal with the boat in the waves.

It is possible to do a river trip without a waterproof camera; be sure to stow your camera in a dry bag or waterproof case while riding through big rapids, or run the risk of losing it all if and when you get thrown from the boat. The new generation of Pelican cases, small enough for easy storage, yet waterproof and easy to use, has largely supplanted the waterproof ammo can that was once standard issue. Bring your own short strap and carabiner for attaching your case to the raft or its frame.

Getting off a shot from the boat as it is completely immersed in rapids is another matter. Waterproof camera cases from Ewa-Marine or AquaTech are useful for the

Downstream Drifters

River running is an ideal sport for outdoor photographers, involving action, scenery, and colorful personalities. The full range of lenses and other field equipment will come in handy, but traveling light is necessary on a rafting expedition. © Mark Langley

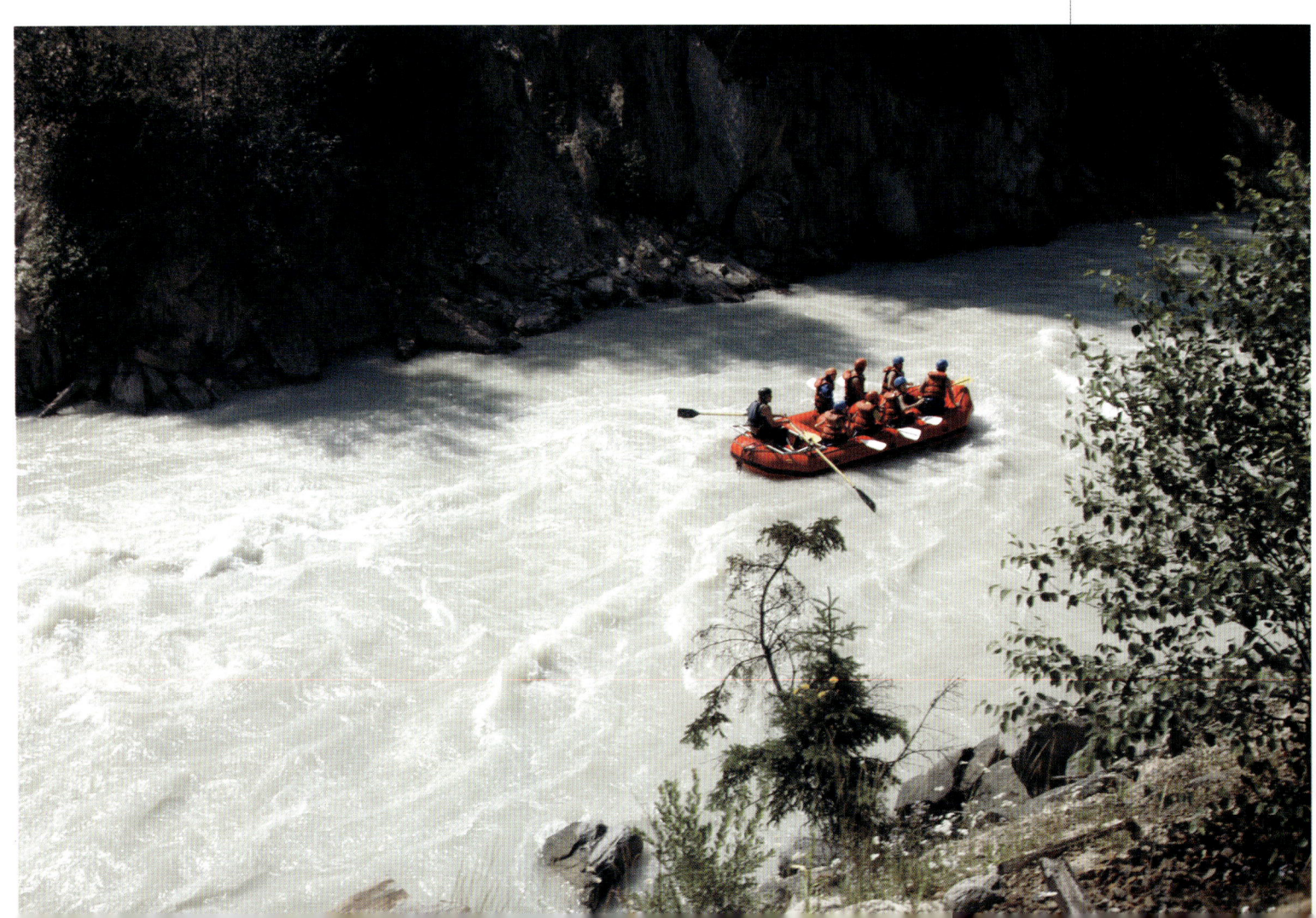

RIVER RAFTING

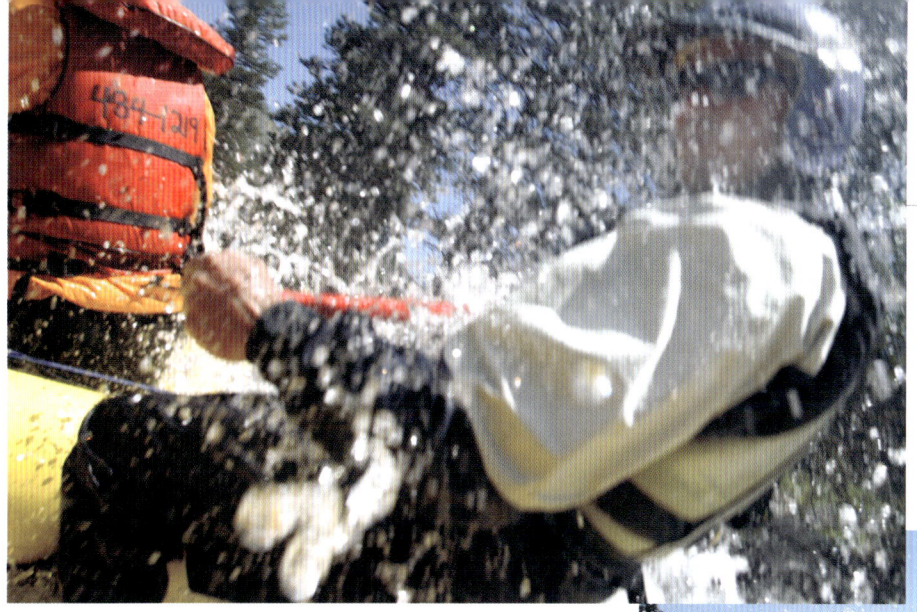

Splash Job
A rafter turns away from a wall of water on the Cache La Poudre river in Texas. Obviously waterproofing your camera is a good idea, preferably in a custom case. © Didrik Johnck

Backseat Shooter
Often the most comfortable person in a river raft, and thus most capable of getting good action shots, is the guide, but they need to control the raft. Here young friends from Los Altos, California, get hit by a wave while entering a rapid along the South Fork of the American River, California. © Jessica Brandi Lifland

serious photographer, but it's quite difficult to get a shot from a boat as it plummets through a set of rapids. From-the-shore shots are both much easier to get and in many cases more expressive than shots taken from inside boats. Try to pick your location to allow for multiple opportunities. Shooting in bursts is also a good idea, as things move so fast that it's impossible to anticipate the single best moment in a run.

On film, whitewater behaves like snow, and it is usually necessary to overexpose a couple of stops; with digital, shoot a few test images of the drop to gauge any compensation you need to make.

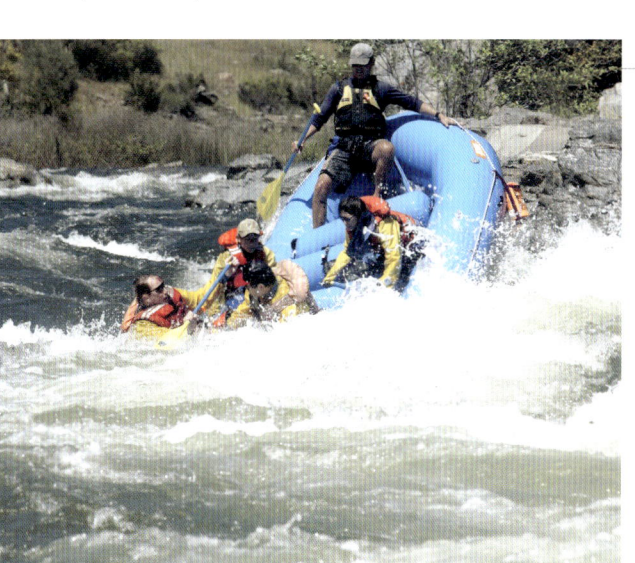

Satan's Cesspool
A paddleboat drops into a hole on the South Fork of the American River, a popular one-day run near Sacramento. Setting up to photograph from shore is half the battle; knowing when to click the shutter—or using a high burst rate—is the other half. © Jessica Brandi Lifland

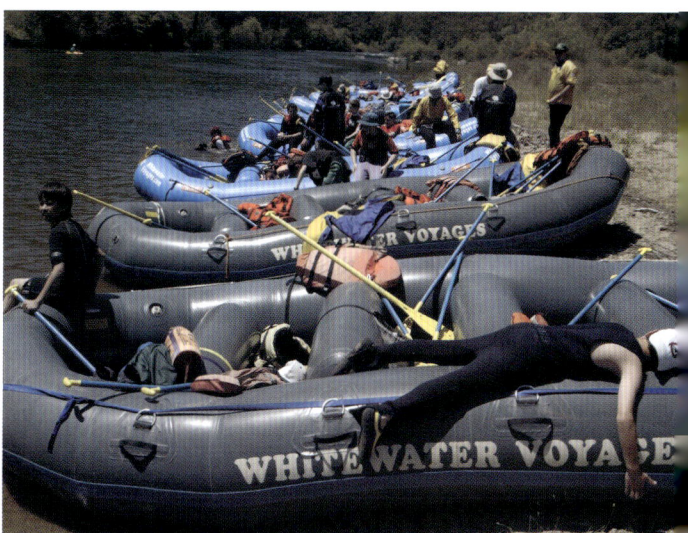

Lunch Break
Among rafting's attractions is its visual vocabulary, of quiet moments and boats at rest as well as the splash and flash of whitewater action. © Jessica Brandi Lifland

SEA KAYAKING

Sea kayaking offers exceptional opportunities to get close to the shorelife of lakes, sheltered seas, inland waterways, and even flat-water rivers. But taking photographs can be tough. Kayaks are self-propelled vessels, and it takes both hands to control the double-bladed paddle. Tandem kayaks provide one solution.

If you're just starting out, a light water-resistant digital point-and-shoot, such as the Pentax Optio 33 WR (3.2–megapixel, 37–104mm effective zoom), is a good bet. Other similarly sized cameras from Olympus, Canon, and Kodak frequently have waterproof housings (available for around $200). But waterproofing is by no means essential. Smaller digital cameras can be tucked inside lifejackets while paddling or in spray, and allow you to get unusual angles, close to the water's surface or an arm's length away from the boat; and the "instant feedback" of image preview lets you see what you're doing right, or wrong. It's true, a small water-resistant camera allows you to shoot with a bit more nonchalance and creativity, but many sea kayakers eschew waterproof cameras in favor of the greater flexibility and power of a DSLR with inter-changeable lenses. Waterproof "dry bags" for cameras are available from many manufacturers, such as Sagebrush Dry Goods, for as little as $80. The general rule of thumb is to keep your camera in its dry bag while you're paddling (especially in surf, windy or open-channel crossings), between your legs and under the spray skirt.

Using a lens hood wherever possible keeps spots of water off your glass, protects the lens surface from impact, and helps prevents lens flare, which is even more of a problem around water than in normal photography. To stabilize your shooting, obviously a tripod is not possible,

Golden Gate Glow

Open-sea kayakers on a calm day venture out beyond the Golden Gate Bridge into Pacific waters. Sit-on-top kayaks are easy to paddle, but don't provide much security for photographic equipment. © Martin Sundberg

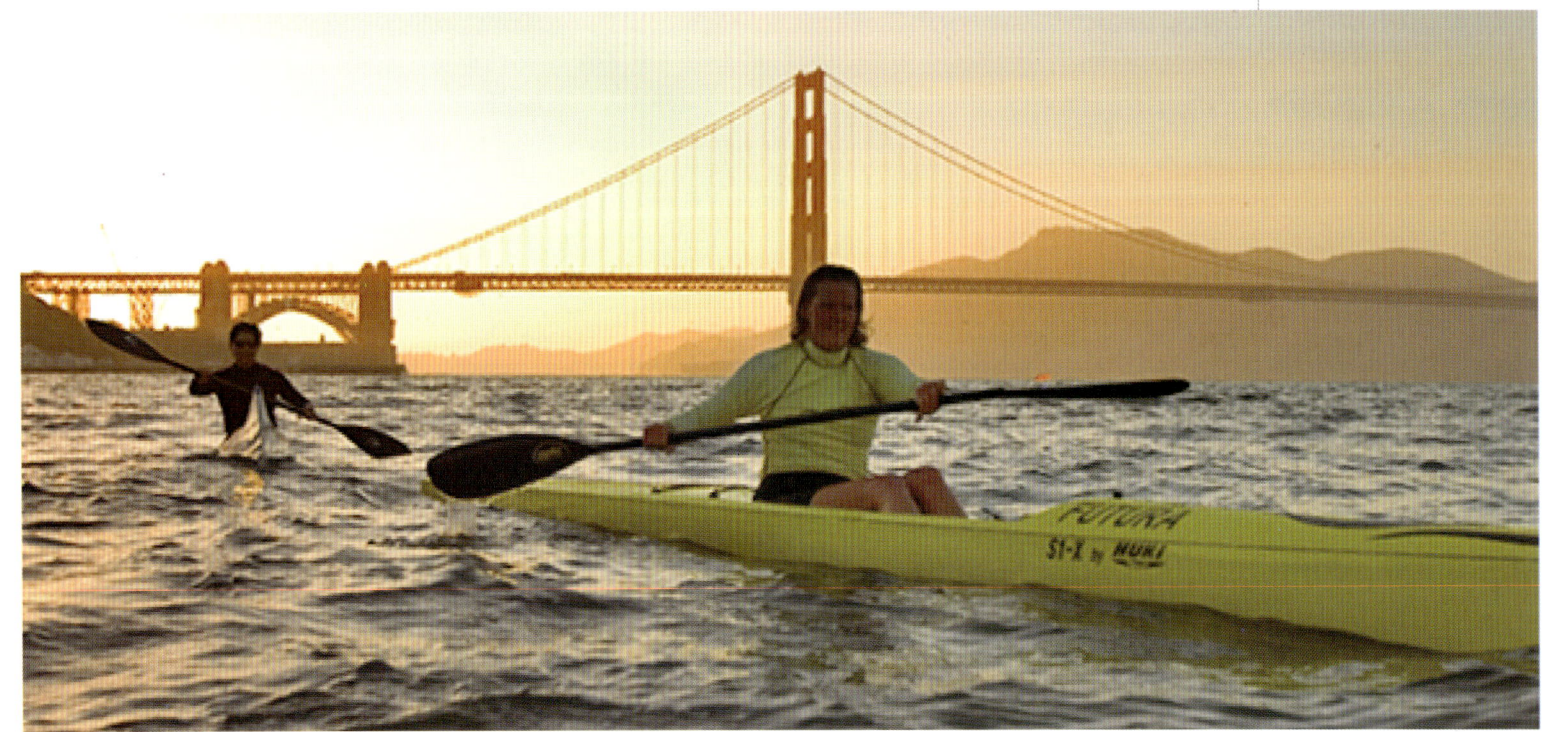

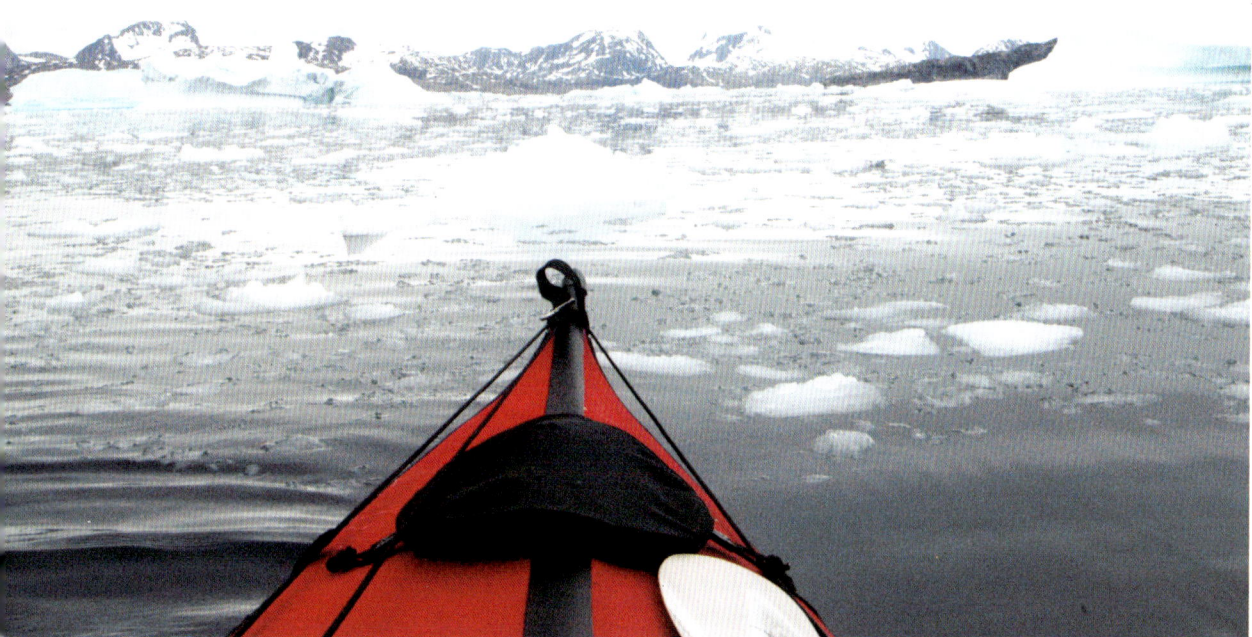

Greenland Ahoy!

The remote shores of eastern Greenland emerge from the fog beyond the ice-choked waters of the fjords. Paddling in such inclement weather puts waterproofing skills to the test. © Mark Langley

Making Camp

A quick scramble up a rugged hillside to photograph the landing doesn't leave much time for removal of water spots on filters or adjustments to limit the reflections off the water. As a result such photographs are often "immediate," but technically disappointing. © Mark Langley

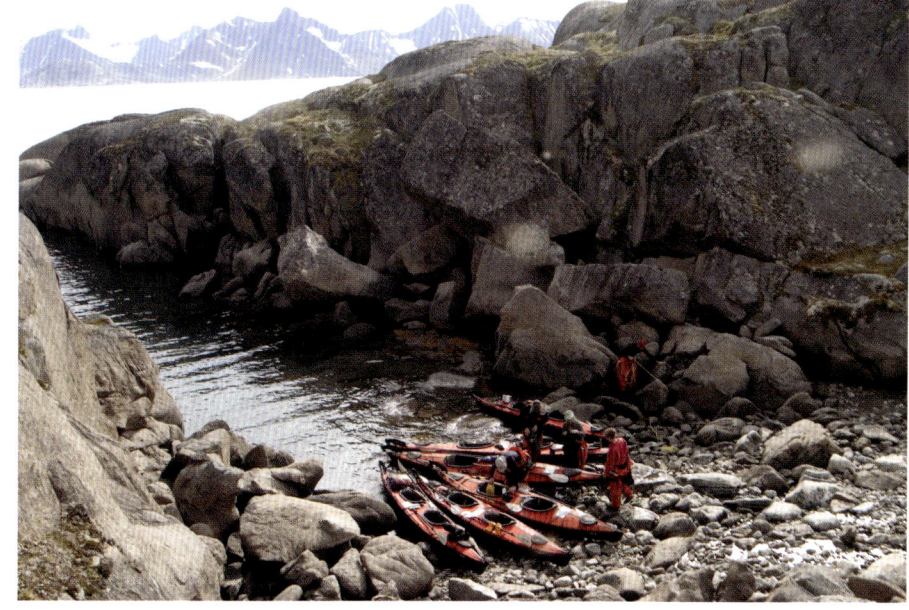

but another brace is nearby: just lean your elbows on the boat when you take pictures and the results will be sharper and the available shutter speeds broader.

You'll find that shoreline wildlife is more prevalent than you might have thought, so a good telephoto lens comes in handy. Naturally, a stabilized lens is valuable given the inevitable motion of the water; the Canon 75–300mm f4–5.6 IS sells for under $500, so you don't have to break the budget (and its digital equivalence of 120–480mm should give all the close-up power you need). At present the only comparable VR (Vibration Reduction) lens for Nikon is the Nikon VR Zoom 80–400mm f4.5–5.6, which costs about three times as much.

Speaking of lenses, changing lenses while in the kayak can be a challenge. It's best not to have to, as you never know when, for instance, a whale might surface nearby for a closer look and swamp your boat. Of course you can anticipate (that magic word for photographers) your needs, or keep one flexible telephoto on camera throughout the day. Packing two DSLRs, each with a different lens, can make it awfully crowded between your legs in a tight kayak. Instead, try a point-and-shoot for wide-angle shots, kept dry in your lifejacket, while keeping the SLR with the long zoom within reach in the dry bag.

SAILING—ABNER KINGMAN

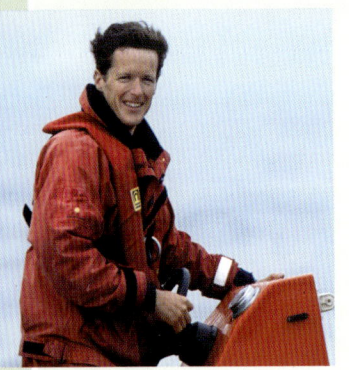

Wind, salt water, unsteady surfaces, sudden movement, and the possibility of immersion: shooting on a sailboat sounds like every photographer's nightmare. But when it all "clicks," the results can be dramatic—big billowing sails against choppy seascapes, primary colors, and weather-toughened athletes. Abner Kingman is one of a handful of digital photographers who has made sailing photography a specialty. With a background in marine biology and journalism, he is well suited to documenting the drama of competition on the water.

Telephoto Action

Like many action sports, sailing photography often requires long lenses to bring the viewer into the moment. Wind, water, billowing sails, and other textures compete for the eye's attention, making composition doubly important. The Swiss yacht *Alinghi*, the winner of the America's Cup, races here in the Moët Cup on San Francisco Bay. © Abner Kingman

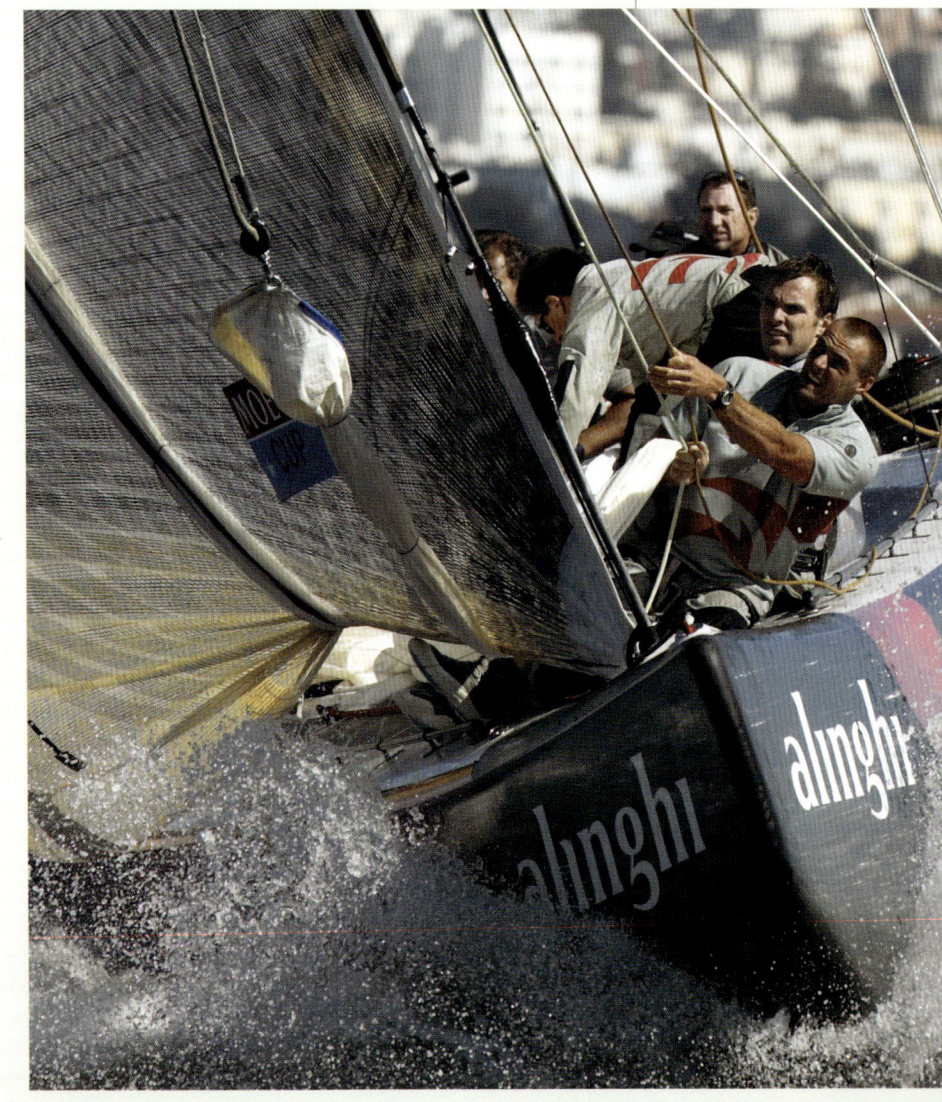

What makes for good race photography is tight shots. The challenge in a race is to get close without disturbing the race. Some guys get by using press boats or borrowing boats, but I want to be where I want to be, not where a group of photographers wants to be by consensus. Having my own boat is pretty important for the way I work.

In races, most shots are from a distance. I often use a 300mm 2.8 on one camera, and a 70-200 2.8 on another. Having two bodies means I can switch between lenses without exposing the inside of the camera to spray. When I'm close to, or better yet, on board the sailboat, I shoot with wide angle lenses. Sometimes I use an Aquatech sport shield to protect the camera from spray. If I'm down next to, or in, the water, I use a waterproof housing.

One advantage of digital is that I am now shooting at ISO 100, whereas before I was shooting at 40 with Velvia. At the processing stage, I get all the saturation I used to get with Velvia, but I get an extra couple of f-stops. I try to shoot for 1,000/sec, so now I can shoot f5.6 or f8, whereas before I was at f4. I try to shoot as low as 1/500th, but I like to keep it up to 1,000/sec. I don't like shooting anything above 100 ISO, to avoid noise. The only time I use a higher ISO is in dim light, dusk, or dawn.

Convenience is another big advantage that digital photography has over film. I can now send images to more than one client at a time, whereas with film I had to wait and get the film back before I could send it out to somebody else. And 36 images on a roll is a serious limitation with film. Using a two-gig card shooting RAW on the Canon 1DS, I get 167 images.

Another thing is that I'm not opening the back of the camera all of the time. In an environment like sailing, with a lot of spray, I used to get rust all over the inside of the camera back. Now, I'm much more careful opening up the slot for the flash card, and I only have to change it a couple of times a day.

The Image Stabilizer lenses have little use on the water, where I'm shooting from a moving platform and the subject is moving, but I do use IS in a couple of situations. There are two modes on the IS lenses; the first stabilizes both the horizontal and the vertical axes, and the second stabilizes only the vertical. So with the vertical stabilizer on, you can pan horizontally, and get much sharper pans.

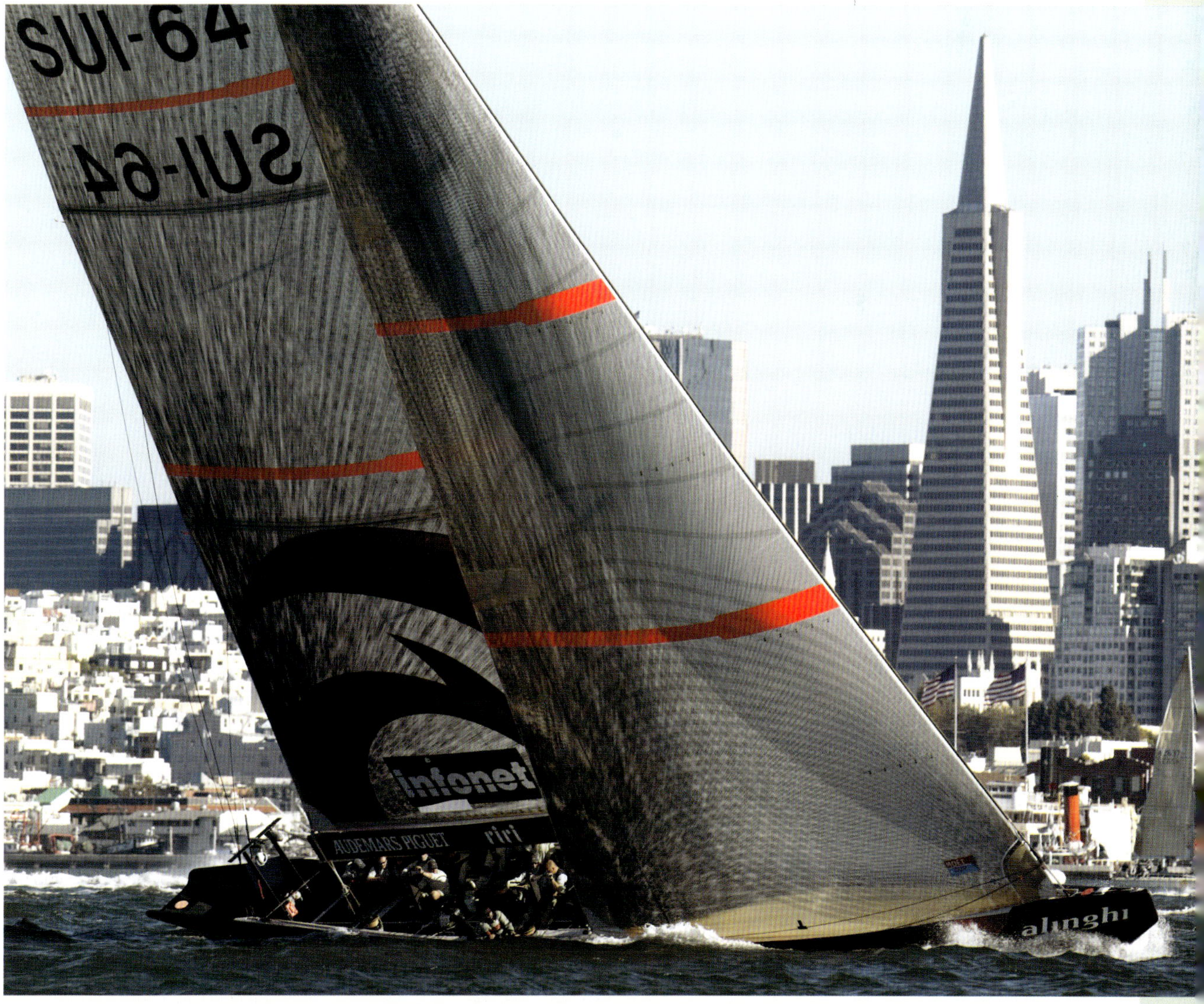

Action in Angles

Sailboats often pitch at a dramatic angle to get the most force from wind, and this angle can communicate both speed and action in a still shot, especially when contrasted with a vertical line. © Abner Kingman

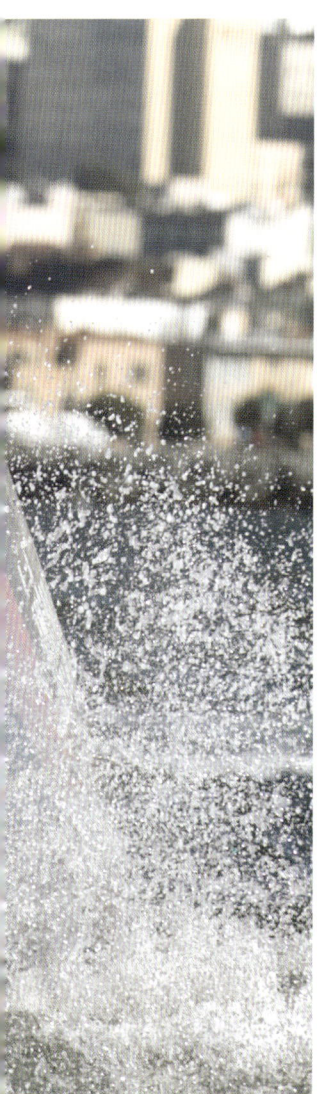

SUBMERSIBLES—MORTON BEEBE

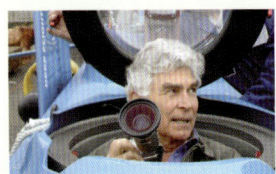

Shooting underwater if you're scuba diving or snorkeling is one thing, but from the cramped cockpit of a personal submarine it's quite another. Few people have much experience at this sort of work, but if you're Mort Beebe, you don't let that stand in your way.

Descending to the ocean depths has been in Morton Beebe's family for generations. Mort is a relative of deep-sea explorer William Beebe, who set the dive record at 3,028 feet (9,235m) with Otis Barton in 1930. Mort began his own sub-aqua career in the Bahamas in 2003, just before his 70th birthday. He combined his training sessions toward becoming a licensed sub-sea aviator with his experience as a Navy photographer in Antarctica.

The vehicle for this sub-sea career is the Deep Flight Aviator, a dry submersible capable of carrying two people to a depth of 1,500 feet (458m). "Getting into the Aviator I guess is similar to a NASCAR race car," said Beebe. "It's so tight you need two people to help you in and out. Once inside, it's too tight to carry much gear."

It's his extreme submarine photography that interests us. "I shot with a Sony DCS F-717 Cybershot Pro with a wide-angle adapter. It's 5 megapixels and I shot RAW files. I like being able to swivel the lens separately from the camera body, so I could compose with the LCD screen in a very crammed space. I had to tape the lens to prevent the focus from shifting. Shooting through the Perspex bubble is not ideal. We did not have any lights, so everything was very blue when we got down to 300 feet.

"I also shot some video whilst I was down there. I had to have the camera that I wasn't using at the time wedged between my legs, and it was hard swapping from one to the other. It was very hot and humid in there. With all the moisture and tropical heat, there was so much rust that when I got back from the Bahamas I had to have my video camera serviced."

The Aviator has airbags and neutral buoyancy. With the turbines, cruise speed is up to 10 knots. Each pressurized pod holds an aviator, and the dual controls enable either person to control the electrically powered thrusters. "I was sitting in the rear. When Graham (Hawkes, the inventor) asked me to take over the controls, it was a bit of a juggling act with all the cameras. You have foot pedals, a joystick, and a throttle. With my flying experience it did not take me long to get the hang of it."

Beebe took along his Friday Films associate, Tim Kelley, who shot underwater video with a Sony DCR-VX1000 and stills of the aviator swimming alongside with scuba gear. (See an edited video clip on Tim's website at http://fridaysfilms.com/deepaviator.html.)

"There is a lot of excitement about this craft. It could open up a whole new way to explore the undersea world. I'd love to be able to continue this work. I like exploring, whether it's the undersea world or the digital world."

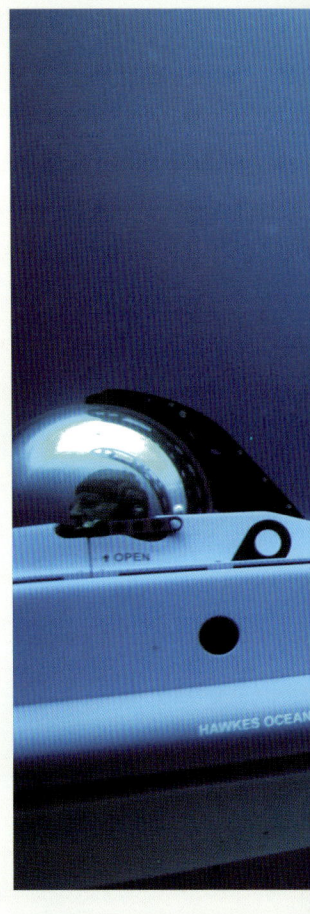

Cockpit View

The view from the rear cockpit of the Aviator. Passengers sit in recumbent position similar to a reclining bike, strap in a five-point harness like a race-car driver, and use controls similar to those found on an aircraft. Only the view is one of a kind.
® Morton Beebe

This is a beautiful blue ocean planet… You don't have to be a scuba diver to appreciate the beauty and excitement of actually flying underwater… To break through to that true freedom you have to have wings.

Graham Hawkes

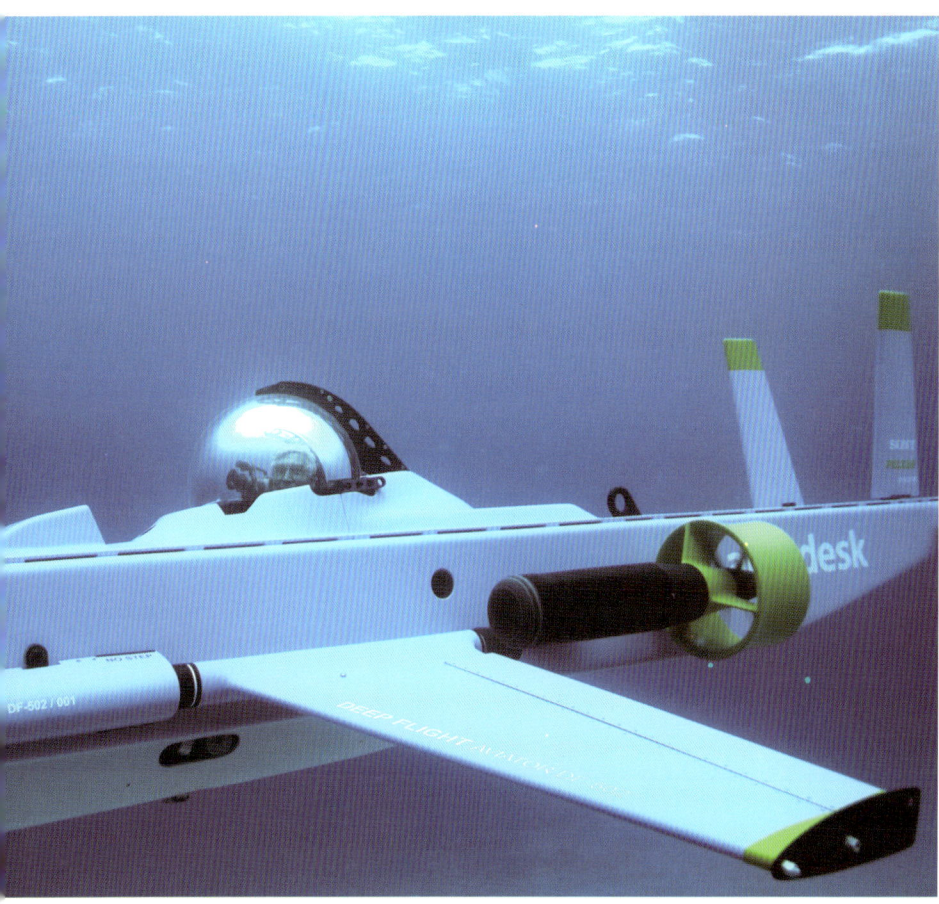

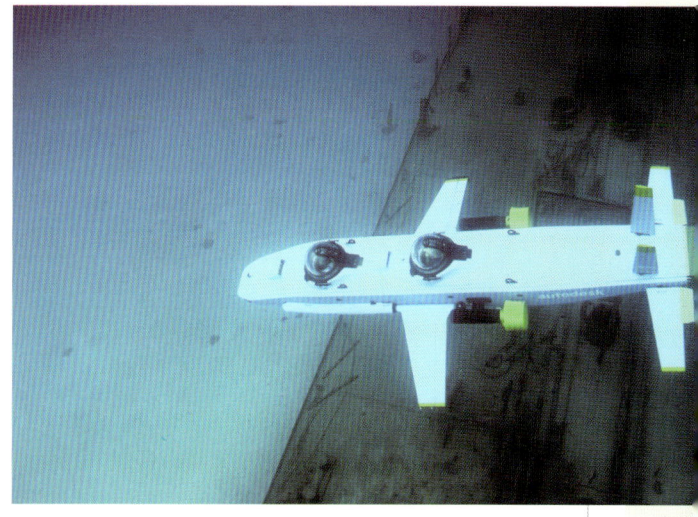

Free Flight

"A torpedo with wings" is one description of the Deep Flight Aviator, a submersible craft that can descend to 1,500 feet (458m) below the surface. Two people can "fly" the craft, each sitting in their own dry bubble.
© Jay Wade

Underwater Recce

The Aviator soars over the submerged deck of a battleship, off the coast of New Providence Island, the Bahamas, where Deep Flight Submersibles has run a "flight school." © Jay Wade

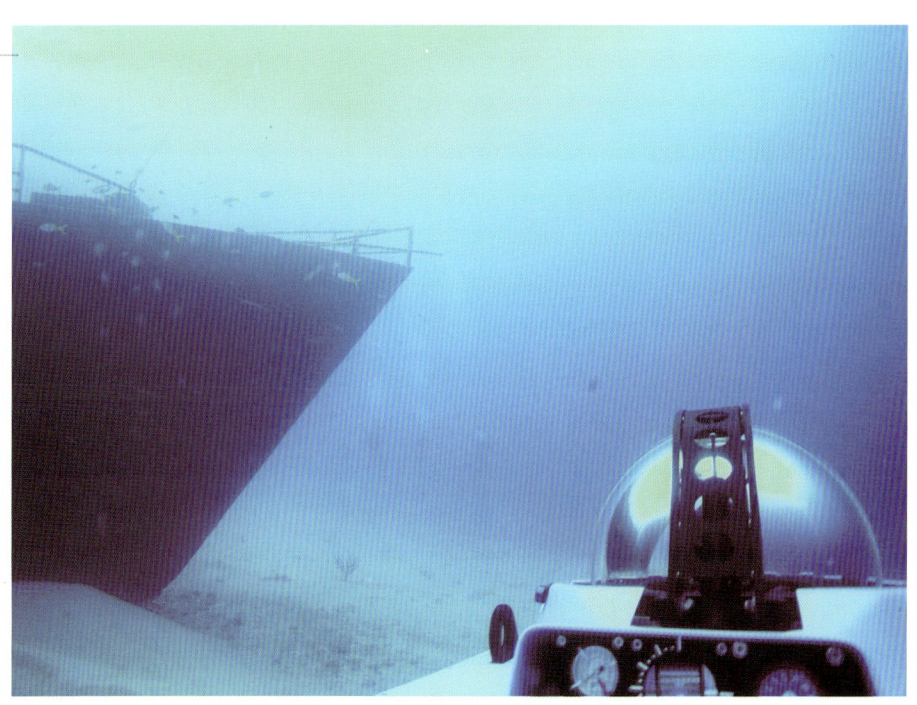

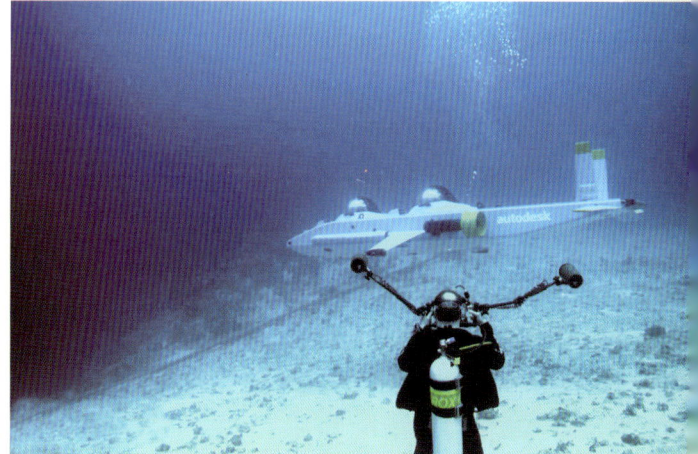

Underwater Photographer

A scuba diver shoots the Deep Flight Aviator on one of its training flights. Sunlight penetration rapidly falls off underwater, making flash mounts on extended arms absolutely essential for submarine photography. © Jay Wade

SURFING, WINDSURFING, AND KITE BOARDING

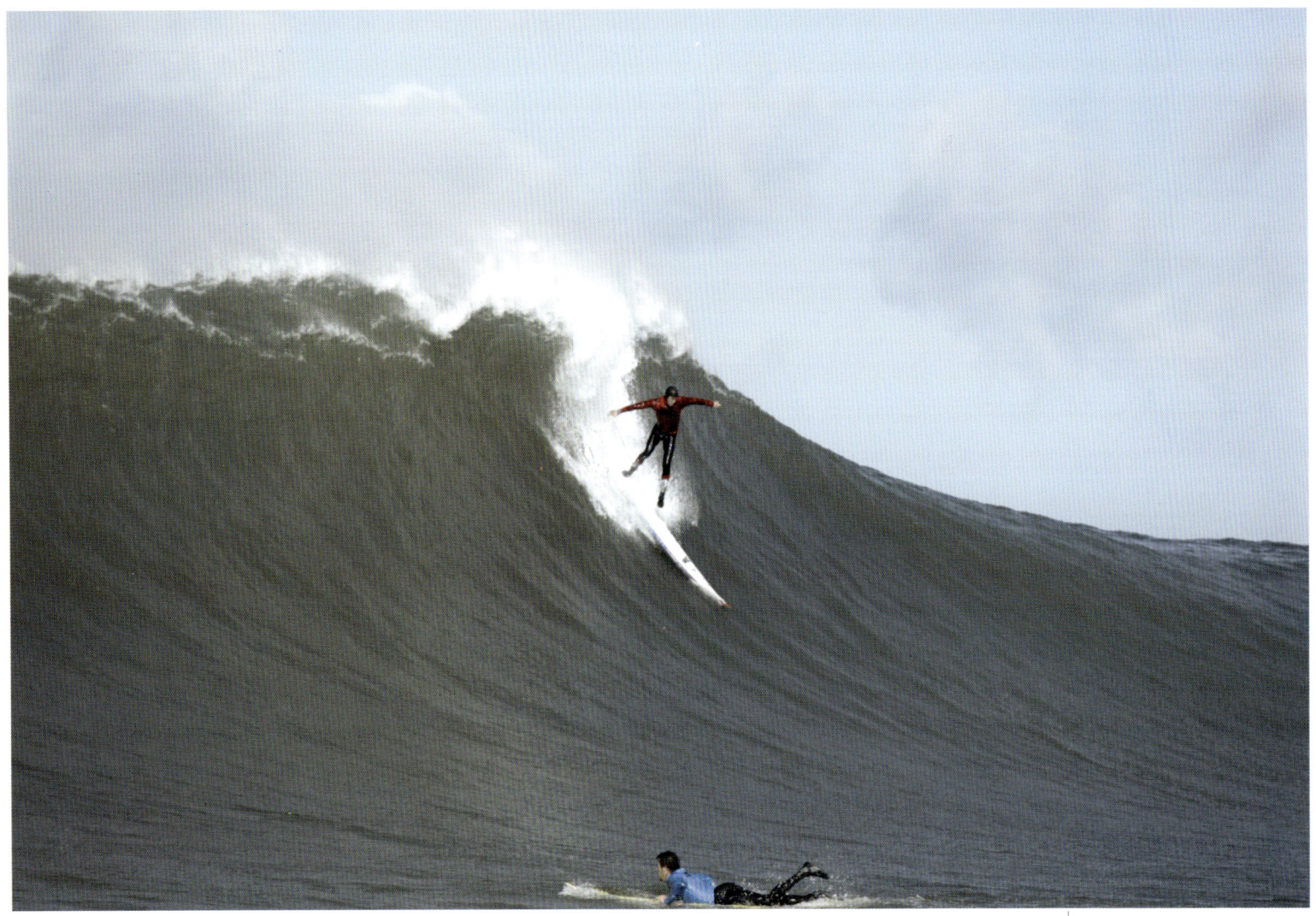

Mavericks

When the surf is up at Mavericks, an offshore big-wave break near Half Moon Bay in Northern California, word spreads quickly. Photographers often use personal watercraft such as a Polaris Virage to shoot from the water; this image was taken with a Canon EOS 1D and a 70–200mm Canon lens. © Aric Crabbe

Wind-and-wave-powered water sports—surfing, windsurfing, and kite boarding—combine fast action with demanding shooting conditions. There are three main ways of getting good shots: from a high vantage point onshore, from a boat, or, the most challenging of all, from the water itself. A helicopter is also an option, though this is usually too costly. If you are really inventive you can also jury-rig a camera in a housing on a surf board or windsurfer mast or boom.

Kite boarding is the fastest-growing of the three sports, but surfing has a global following and a circuit of competitions, publications, and promotions. Pierre Tostee is just one professional who has made the switch to all-digital capture using the Canon EOS 1Ds and EOS D10.

To shoot surfing, the best times of day are dawn and dusk, with low sun as front lighting. Shooting from the shore, you need a very good tripod and a long, long lens. A 600mm, 400mm or 300mm lens with super-fast autofocus and a camera capable of a high burst rate are the standard kit (and many photographers add 1.4X and 2X converters). Top-of-the-line DSLRs from Canon, the 1D Mark II, and Nikon, the D2H, both fit the bill. There is little point in using a lower-end camera, as the burst speed and buffer capacity will not be sufficient to capture the action. Eight frames per second is considered the benchmark for this type of work.

Shooting from a boat is more of a challenge. Here the shorter lenses, including everything from 15mm wide-angle to a telephoto in the 80–200mm range, are more useful. Fast lenses and fast shutter speeds are needed to deal with the rocking boat and provide enough depth of field. Pelican cases and AquaTech camera shields are also advisable for transporting and shielding your gear as much as possible.

Shooting from in the water is by far the most challenging task. Water-sports specialist Abner Kingman wears a full wet suit and a lifejacket so that he floats higher in the water, making it is easier to capture the action; swim fins and a water-sports helmet complete his outfit. His camera is in a full underwater housing and occasionally he uses a waterproof strobe. The whole rig is tethered to his wrist with a Velcro band and a leash, like those used by surfers to stay connected to their boards.

"You need to be working as a team with a kite boarder, windsurfer, or surfer to get the best shots," says Abner. "You need to get the person to steer straight at you, or jump over you to get really good shots."

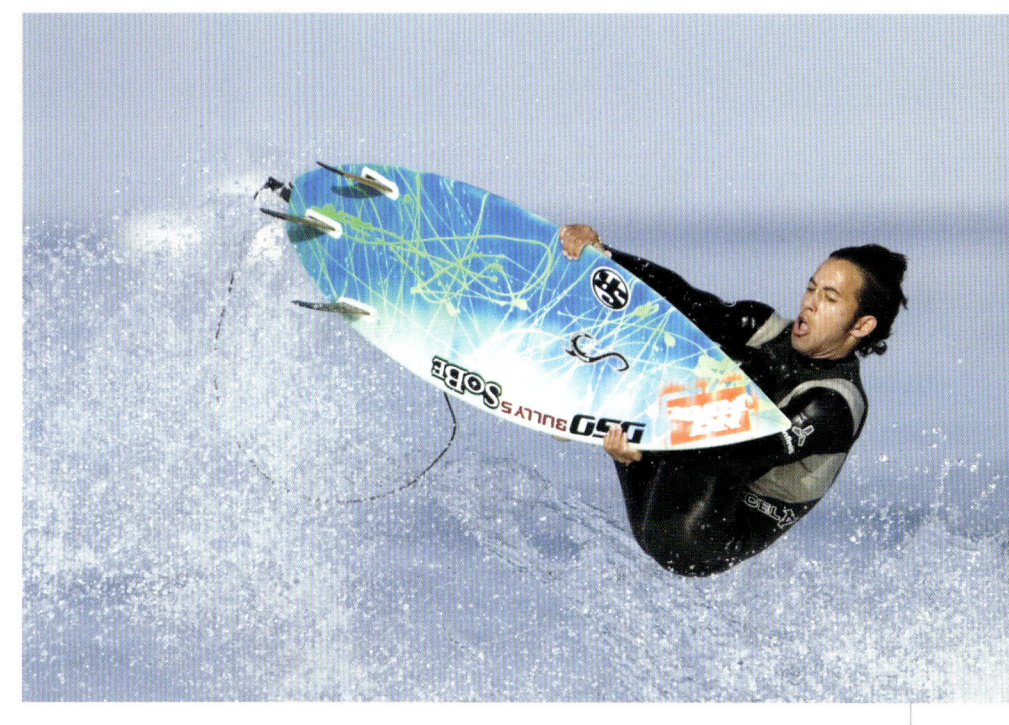

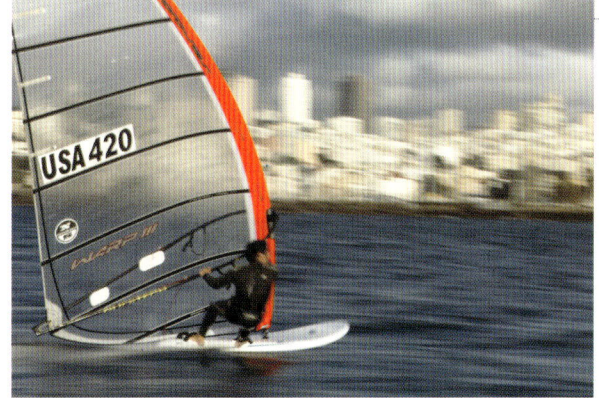

Full Tilt

A VR lens helped get this panning shot from my moving Titan chase boat, which was tracking the speeding windsurfer on San Francisco Bay. A good assistant who can also drive the boat is essential for the best results when shooting on the water. © Abner Kingman

Hotdogger

Julian Ganguli catches air at Salt Creek, near Dana Point in Southern California, in this shot captured with a Canon 1D in RAW mode. Action is stopped at 1/1250 sec, and the generous f6.3 aperture helps keep the action in focus. © Kurt Jones

Broken Dreams

Sometimes surfing isn't quite as fun as it looks. Toby Ogden contemplates his broken board at an Oceanside competition, perhaps just glad that the accident doesn't involve any health insurance. © Kurt Jones

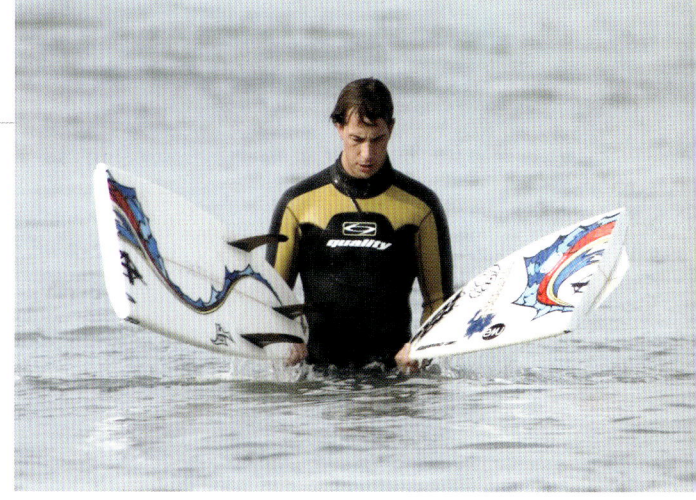

VIDEO PROFILE—MICHAEL BROWN

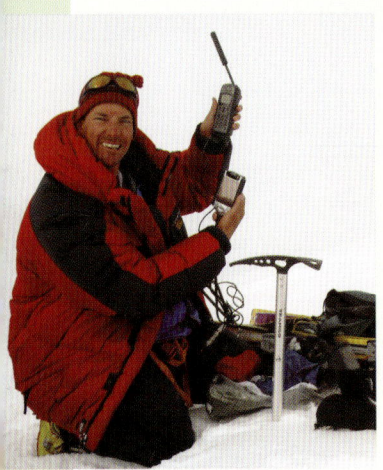

The art of extreme documentary filmmaking dates back to Robert Flaherty and his 1921 Nanook of the North. *Today, the technology of choice is digital video, as filmmakers climb the highest peaks, and plumb the deepest depths, in search of a good true story. Michael Brown comes from a family of such filmmakers; his father Roger made the classic* Ski the Outer Limits *(1968); one brother (Gordon) is a death-defying kayaker and climber, while another (Nicholas) does reality TV. But Michael Brown is perhaps best known as "the extreme blogger" for his video reportage from the summits of Everest, Elbrus, and other adventure destinations.*

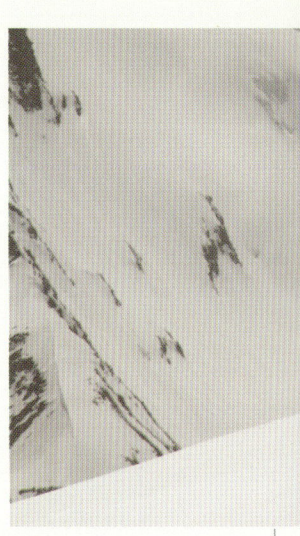

Action Photographer

Skiing off Mt. Elbrus, Europe's highest point, on a 2001 expedition. Michael Brown's family traditions of action sports and filmmaking put him at ease in extreme situations and assignments.
© Didrik Johnck

We just got back from the South Pole, for *National Geographic*. In Antarctica we were shooting with the new Panasonic AJSDX 900, a 24-p camera—it's pretty phenomenal. It has a great way of processing images, there's more detail in shadows, and because it's 24-progressive scan, and it also has this sort of flicker, to me it looks a lot like 16mm film. It has a richer feel to it than the standard 29.97 frames-per-second video.

I've climbed Everest three times—all three times I've had at least a digital video camera, if not a digital still as well. In 2000 for Quokka Sports we used a Sony Vaio notebook all the way to Camp Three, just under 24,000 feet, but [no computers] would work above that. The digital cameras had no problem, right up to the top.

Up on Everest, charging batteries above Base Camp was nearly impossible. Even in Base Camp it was difficult, because generators are annoying to other expeditions. Solar panels work great, but with the laptops and all the stuff that ends up at Base Camp, there's not really that much power floating around. Above Base Camp we really didn't use the onboard batteries; we would use Stuart Cody's Expedition Batteries all the way to the summit. Those are fantastic; they're such a great technology, it's too bad they're not rechargeable! I would keep one battery for maybe three days, and I only used two or three on the whole trip. We were above Base Camp a week or more, 10 days at the longest. We'd go up to Camp Two to do our acclimatization.

ExplorersWeb featured an article that called me "the extreme blogger," but at the time we didn't really think of it as blogging; to us it was just doing simple dispatches, and then those dispatches became blogs. We sent the blog from Base Camp while we were climbing up Everest, in May 2001. We just used a satellite phone and made a con-

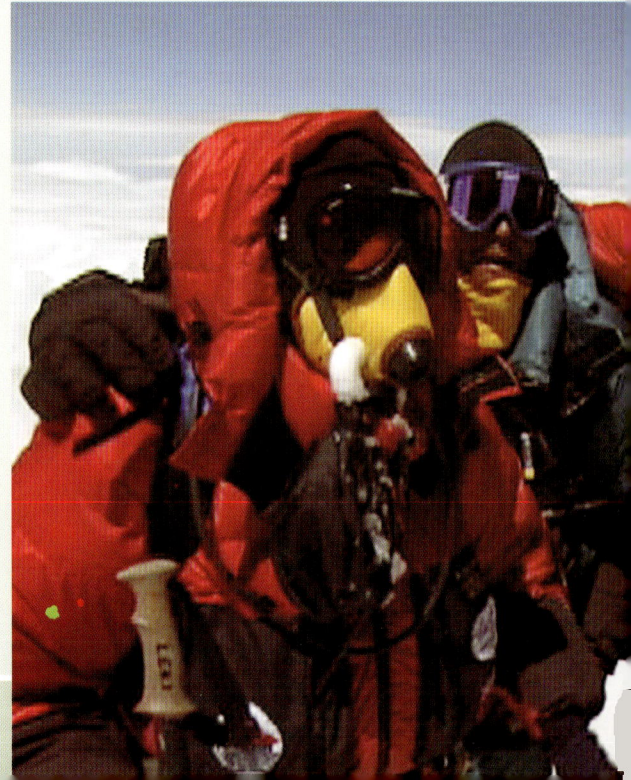

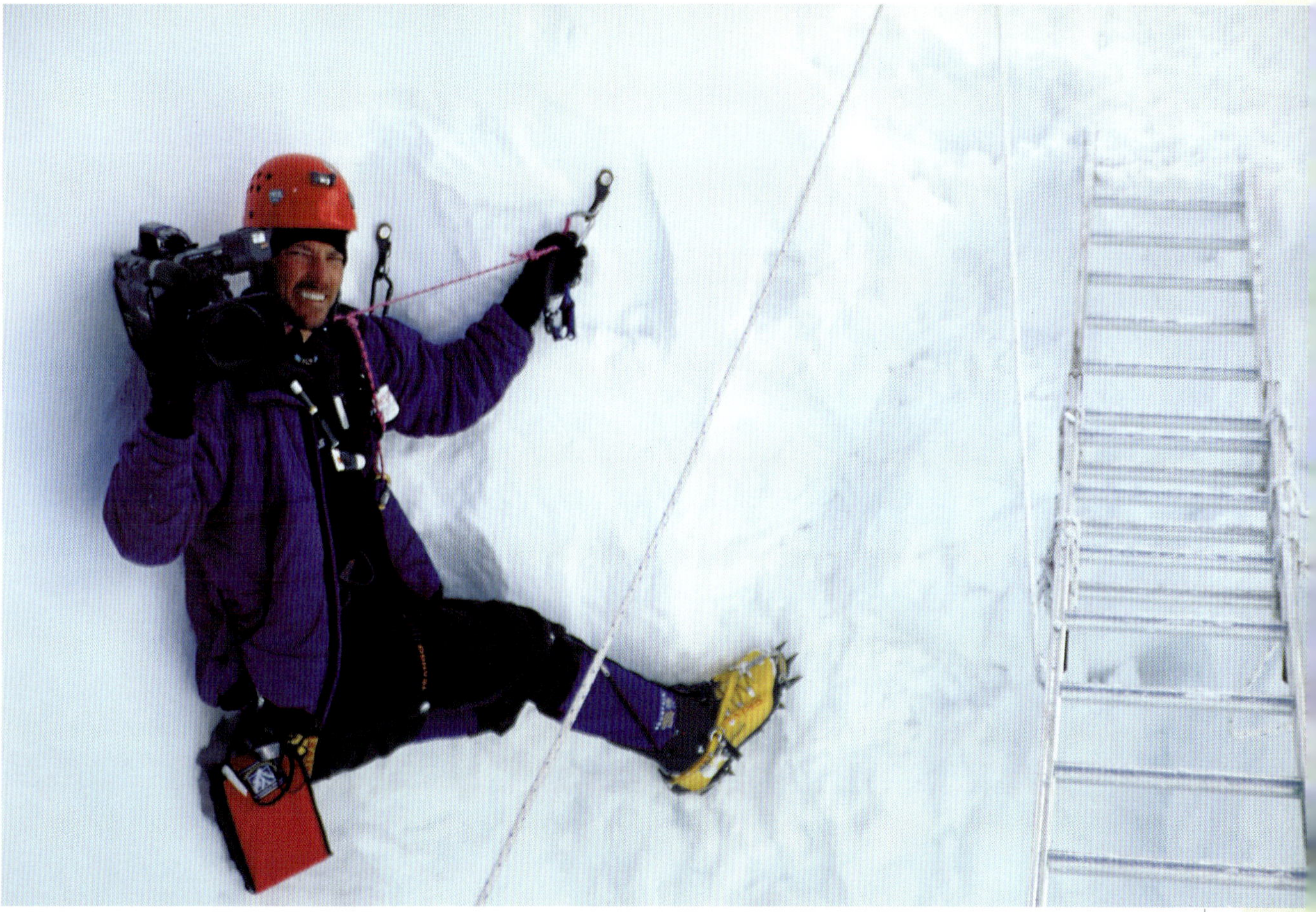

Summit Scrum

Successful climbers embrace on the summit of Mt. Everest, at the climax of Erik Weihenmayer's ascent. This shot is a frame-grab from the HD video *Farther than the Eye Can See*, which produces five-megabyte image files for stills. © Michael Brown

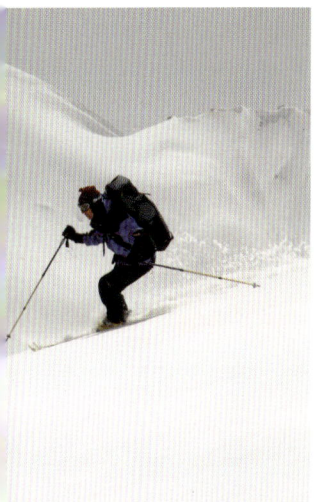

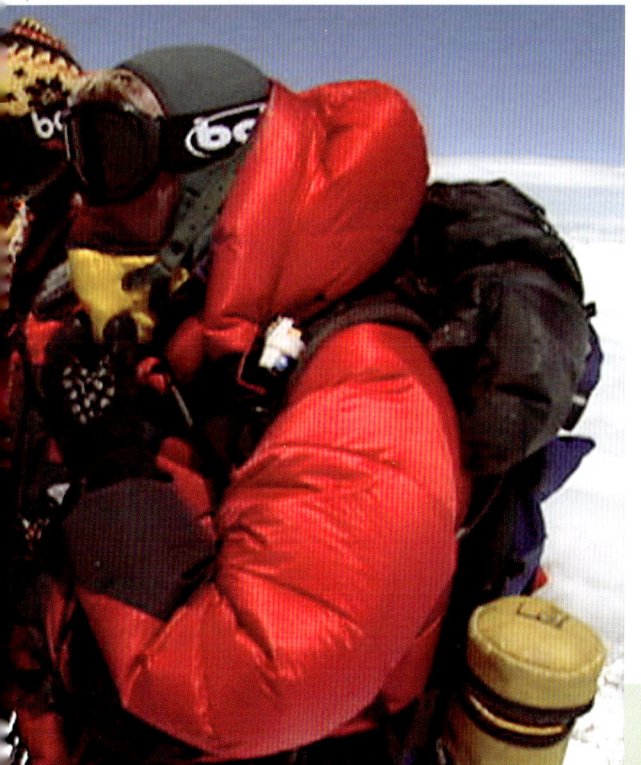

nection with my website and then went to town on it, because we were desperate to get as much of the information as possible to our families.

I've got an expansion for my HP iPAQ that accepts the Sony Memory Stick. I download the image into my PDA and resize it—Palbum is the software I use. The Contact software is pretty user-friendly; you click on the Still Image or Video Component, browse through the PDA to find the clip or image you want to use. Then below that it has a little space to write a dispatch, and at the top there's a space to write a title or date. Then just make a call to the server, using a satellite phone or cell phone, or even a high-speed Internet line, and hit Send. A couple minutes later it hangs up, and it's live on the Web.

Cameraman on Belay

Michael Brown filming with a Sony 700 HD camera in the Khumbu Icefall. Feeling absolutely comfortable in dangerous situations makes capturing images and action that much easier.
© Didrik Johnck

SKIING AND SNOW SPORTS

Skiing and snowboarding present a combination of challenges for the photographer—physically demanding sports, in cold weather, in difficult if not inhospitable terrain, under lighting conditions that can range from the subdued to the intense. Plus, these are fast-paced action sports, whose primary appeal is subjective: the thrill of speed and near-misses with danger.

Photographers who undertake the challenges of snow sports should themselves be fit and skilled in skiing or snowboarding, for several good reasons. First, they need to understand the specific techniques of the sport, so they can best represent its excitement in images. Second, they need to anticipate an athlete's moves and most photogenic moments, and set up accordingly.

Finally, the physical demands of mountain sports—the altitude, the aerobic activity, and the performance skills—can be debilitating for a novice.

From a technical point of view, digital photographers point out that their cameras may not need the same compensation for snow photography that film cameras do. Light meters often overcompensate for bright snowy scenes by recommending underexposure, so photographers learn to overexpose (counter-intuitively) by one or two full stops to get proper skin tones. Digital cameras, or their light meters, seem on the whole to have reduced this flaw. "It's interesting, though, with a film camera you have to overexpose in snow conditions one to two stops, but the D60 was only about half a stop off," noted mountain photographer Didrik Johnck. "I suppose you could make up the differences in post-processing, but I'd much rather be out there taking pictures than sitting in front of a computer."

There's another kind of exposure when shooting snow sports: exposure to the elements. "When it's snowing, everything is more difficult," says Corey Rich, a frequent contributor to *Sports Illustrated*. "For instance, I never bring lens hoods when it's dry out, I'll just hold my hand out to prevent flare. However, any time I'm in weather, the lens hoods are so valuable. They keep the front of your lens clear of dust or water residue.

"Shooting film, I always bring a motor drive, because things are moving so fast," continues Rich. "If I shoot digitally, I need to pick my moments when shooting skiing, because I don't have a fast motor-driven camera. Really, there's only one—or maybe two—really fast, high-end digital bodies out there, the D2H and the 1DS."

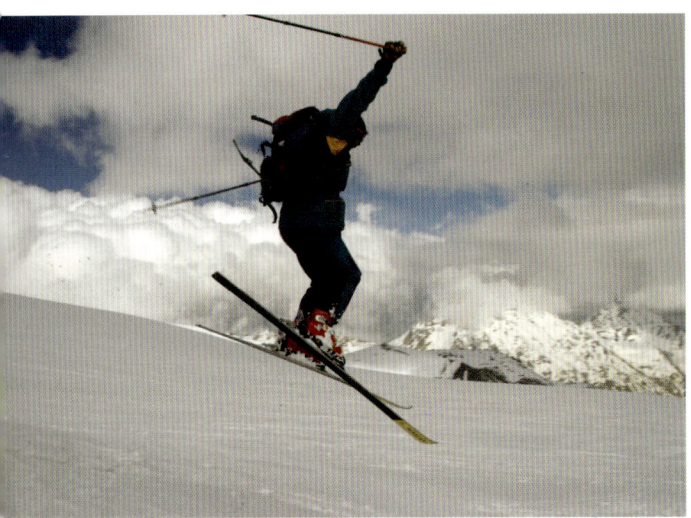

Catching Air

Knowing the sport can help you find the right location to set up for a dramatic shot. Says photographer Johnck, "It's better to be competent at a sport, so the people you're working with aren't bummed out, and you know where the best angles are going to be. You know what all your options are."
© Didrik Johnck

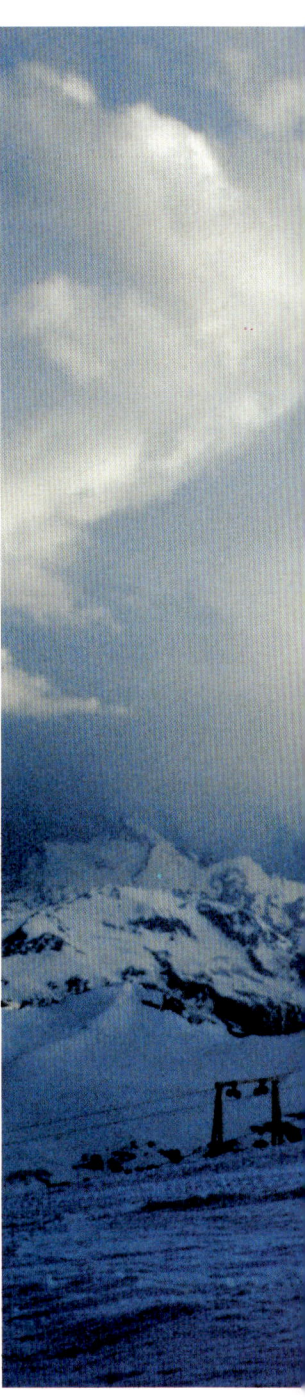

SKIING AND SNOW SPORTS | 129

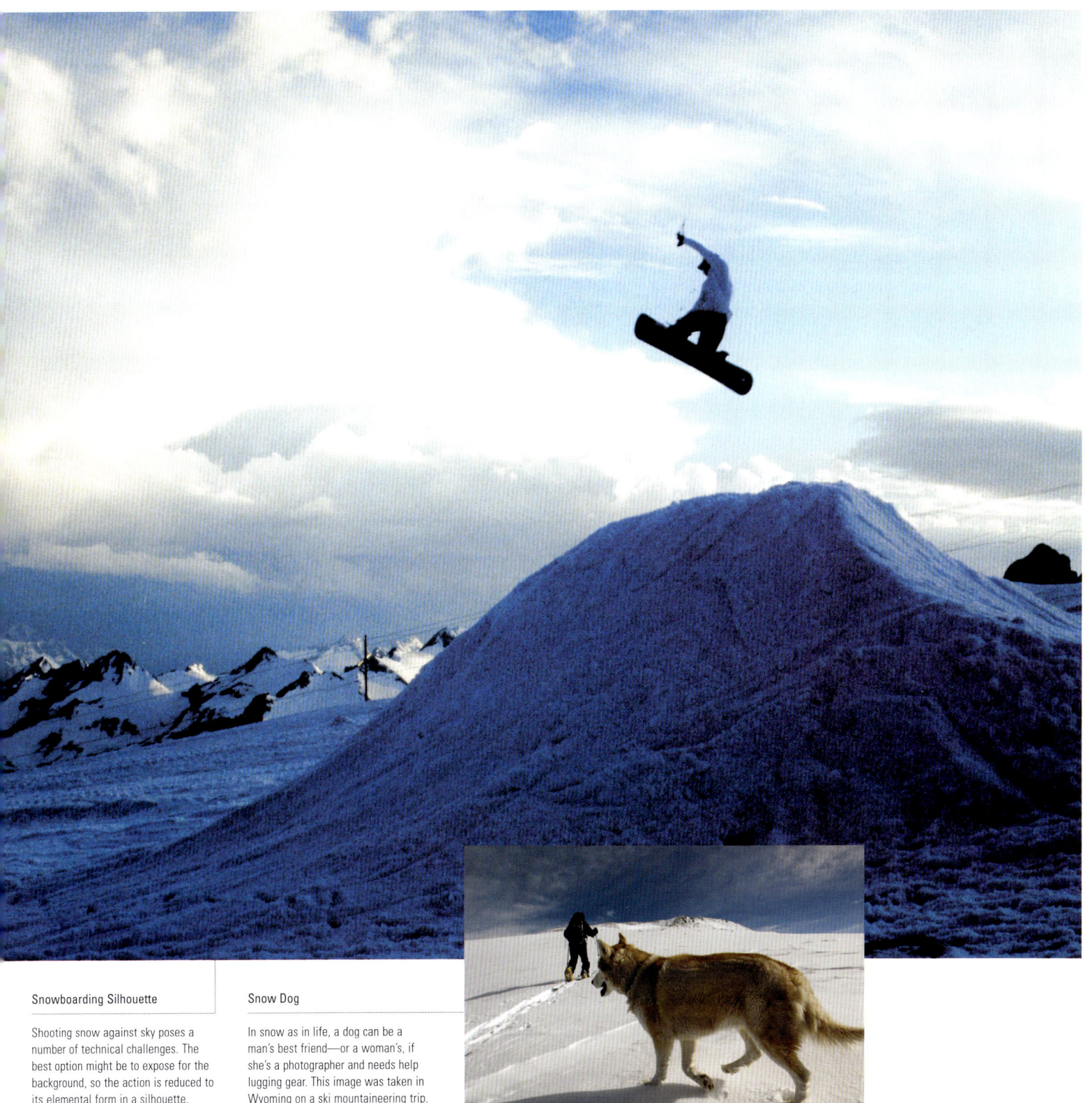

Snowboarding Silhouette

Shooting snow against sky poses a number of technical challenges. The best option might be to expose for the background, so the action is reduced to its elemental form in a silhouette.
© Didrik Johnck

Snow Dog

In snow as in life, a dog can be a man's best friend—or a woman's, if she's a photographer and needs help lugging gear. This image was taken in Wyoming on a ski mountaineering trip.
© Martin Sundberg

EXPEDITION PHOTOGRAPHY

When you are part of a full-blown expedition that may last for a month or more, you usually have an objective or goal that dictates all other considerations: you might be sledging across some ice cap or even to one of the Poles, or climbing a remote mountain peak. In these instances photography or media coverage will play only a minor part in the day's effort. Capturing images is for use after the fact—books, magazine articles, slide shows. In such circumstances shooting digitally may be more trouble than it's worth, according to Corey Rich.

"With the extreme assignment, I still think film is the most logical option. When you're in a remote place, power is the biggest issue, power and weight. Carrying 100 rolls of film is much easier than carrying a solar panel to charge batteries, and a laptop and some sort of device for downloading the data. And oftentimes, on many of the expedition-type trips that I'm involved with, the issue is that we're never in one place long enough to set up a solar panel. Battery power quickly becomes an issue with any of the high-end digital cameras these days."

Rich cites a recent trip he made to Carstenz Pyramid, in Irian Jaya (16,021 feet / 4,884m). "I was going on a trip with Stephen Koch, who's trying to snowboard the Seven Summits (see http:/www.stephenkoch.com). This was his sixth peak in the line-up. It's really remote, sort of an expedition of its own getting to the peak—you're going through jungle terrain, crossing rivers, getting in boats... So the reality was we would be gone for a month, there would be extreme temperature changes, and we were carrying everything we needed. So that was a great example of keeping it as simple as possible, and eliminating a laptop or storage device helped make it possible."

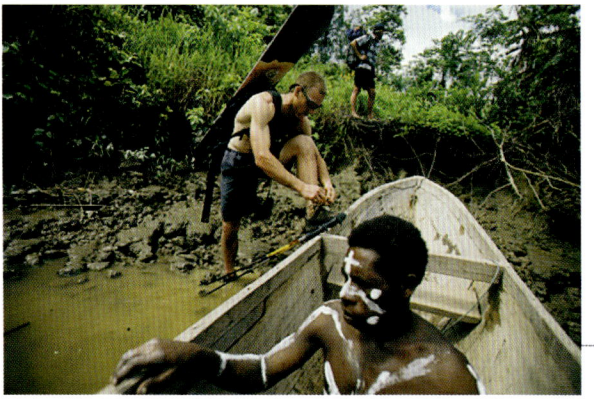

Although Rich prefers to capture on film on these big trips or assignments for advertising agencies, like many professional photographers, once he gets home his original images are scanned, to be delivered to clients digitally. Today, all photography becomes digital.

Many high-powered polar and mountaineering expeditions these days send reports or blogs to websites on a daily basis, often via satellite telephones, to keep in touch with sponsors, supporters, and friends. Media-savvy outdoor photographers and videographers use blogging to keep their work before their clients and friends (see Michael Brown's www.seracadventure-films.com). These reports all demand some level of digital shooting. But as images for the Web have to be very small files, most consumer cameras can acquire more than adequate file size, putting expedition blogging within the reach of almost anyone.

If the expedition is operating from a fixed base camp, weight and power are not as much of a consideration. Up to and including a base camp, all the suggestions and advice for digital shooting for trekking apply (*see page 112*). On the climb itself, the same considerations apply as for backpacking (*see page 110*), only much more so.

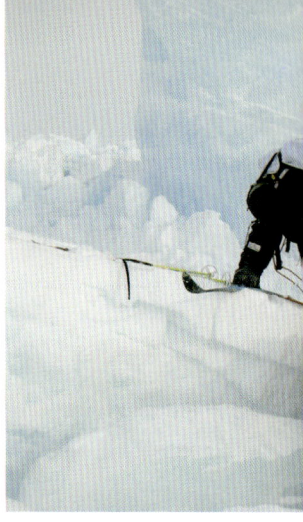

Tropical Snowborder

Snowboarder Steve Koch on the lengthy approach to Carstenz Pyramid, high above the jungles of Irian Jaya (western New Guinea). The remote location of the mountain called for a month-long expedition through various environments, and for the relatively low demands of film over digital.
© Corey Rich

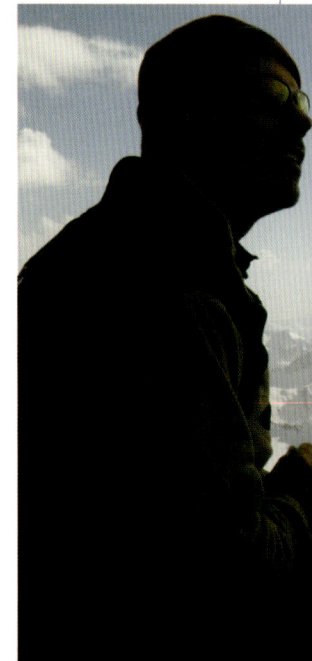

Remote Transmission

Michael Brown using an iPAQ and Iridium phone to connect to the Web from high on Mt. Elbrus, Russia.
© Didrik Johnck

EXPEDITION PHOTOGRAPHY

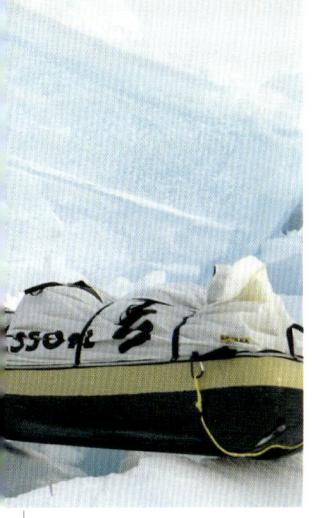

Snow Bridge

On expeditions, the ability to find solutions is paramount. Using an equipment sled to make a stepping-stone across a crevasse is one example; the same thinking needs to apply to finding technical or photographic solutions as well.
© ExplorersWeb

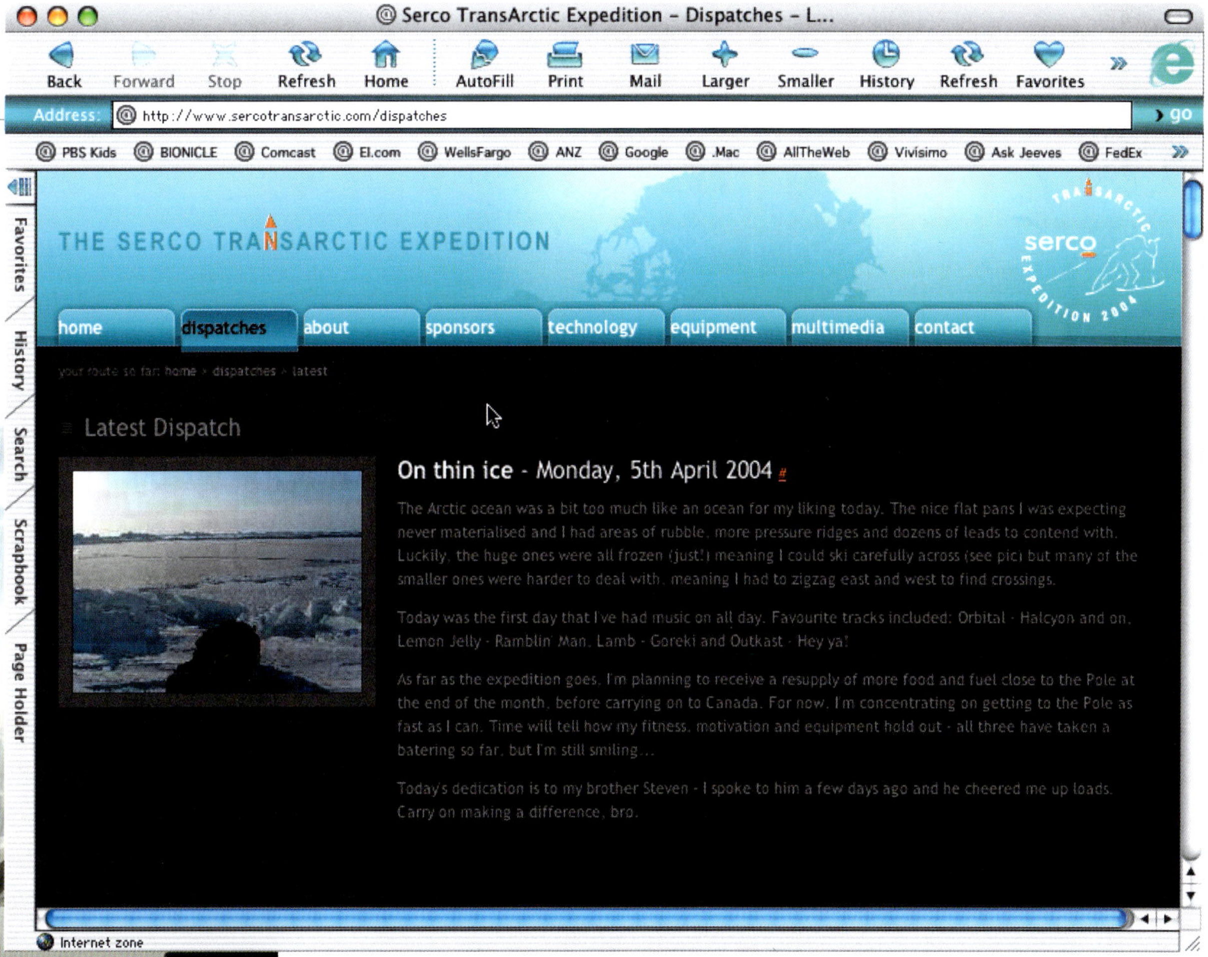

Expedition Blog

Web logs of even the most extreme expeditions can present a cool interface with pleasing graphics, if the design parameters are set prior to departure. In this case, Ben Saunders' solo expedition to the North Pole was kept updated using Contact Software from ExplorersWeb. (www.sercotransarctic.com)

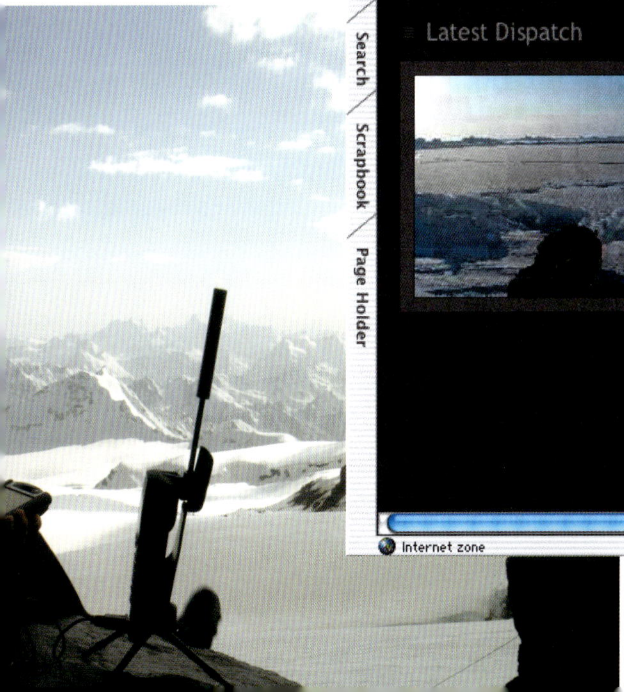

If the expedition is traveling from point to point, say over an ice cap, then saving weight is everything. In such cases (going light, yet still wanting to upload on a regular basis), all that is needed is a small digital camera such as a Sony Cyber-shot, an HP iPAQ PDA, a satellite phone, and the proprietary software. On trips of this kind, cold, condensation, and power conservation are the bugbears.

In mounting one of these ventures you can take advantage of a number of resources, such as www.webexpeditions.com, or www.explorersweb.com and their offshoot site www.humanedgetech.com. These offer everything from reams of advice, to hosting expedition blogs, and specialized software (such as Contact 3.0) for uploading text, images, and even video. They also sell or rent the latest technology to outfit a media-conscious expedition and put them online.

Some sites have also become a clearing house for expedition news and information, with deep editorial resources. Tom and Tina Sjogren have been pioneering digital technology in extreme locations for a decade (http://www.mounteverest.net/eie/EIE.html; *see page 132 for their story*). Other early expedition portals were www.mountainzone.com and www.everestnews.com.

With proper concern for safety and the expedition's success, you can use the Internet and digital photography to bring your extreme adventures to a global audience.

POLAR EXPLORATION—TOM AND TINA SJORGEN

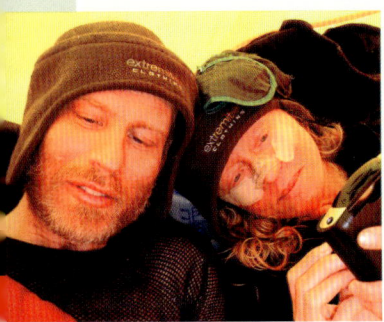

"To us, cutting edge technology is a thrilling adventure." So Tom Sjorgen states the case that he and his wife Tina make for their powerful and compelling obsession, ExplorersWeb. The Manhattan-based company supplies software, hardware, and Web space to adventurers going to the extremes—the poles, the mountain peaks, the deepest seas—and telling their stories on the Web. While they include mountain climbing and ocean exploration among their interests, their polar expeditions (to both the North and South Poles) have sparked their most creative digital innovations.

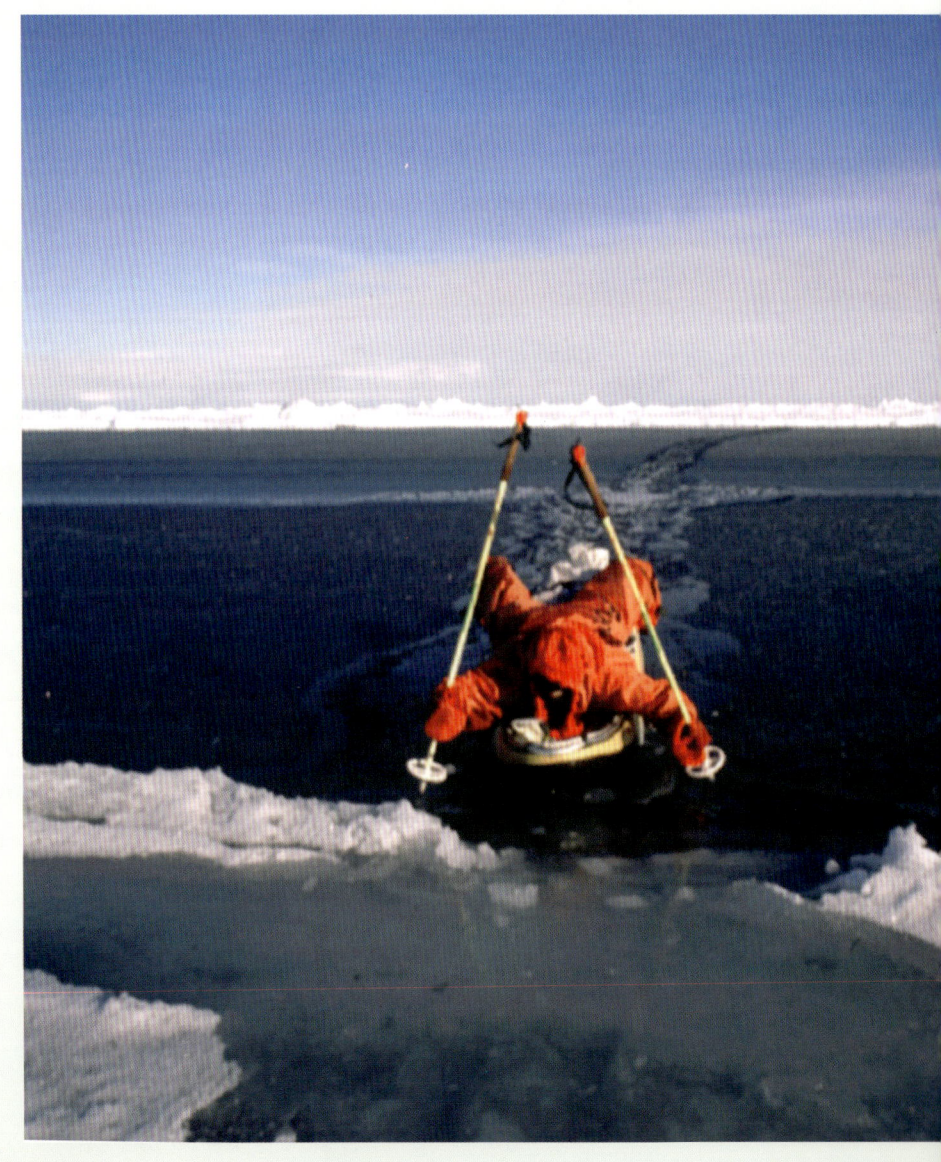

We had to develop technology ourselves to cover our Everest and polar expeditions. Tina and I had another business in Sweden, not at all related to adventuring, but we decided to do something we really liked doing. So we started ExplorersWeb and all this just happened.

Essentially we created the Contact software and ExplorersWeb because we wanted to lose the webmaster. This came about on the Everest expedition in 1999—we were going on the summit push on a Friday, and the webmaster decided that he needed to go on vacation with his family. We wanted people to be able to go directly to the Internet, and to communicate immediately what was happening.

When we went to Antarctica, we still wanted to show what it was really like on an Antarctic expedition. Iridium wasn't up at that point, so we used a system called Orbcom—a text-messaging system that could only send 108 characters at once. So we used a really small digital picture, only 3 or 4K, and we divided it into 20 pieces, and sent 20 separate messages that were put together back home at the server.

That was cool, and then we started to get interested in bringing down the weight. For the North Pole we wanted no ground support and we knew we needed to

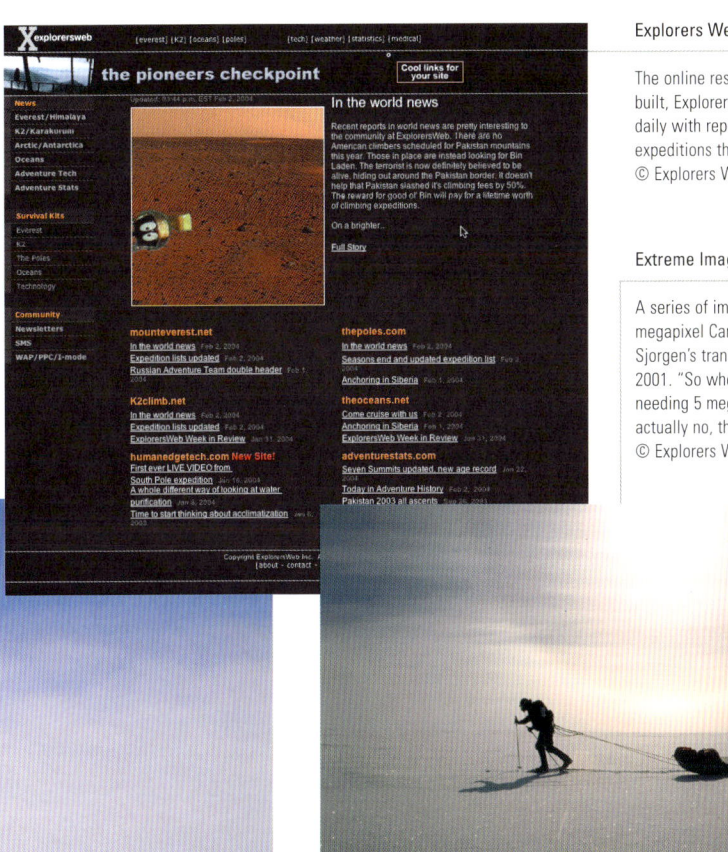

Explorers Web

The online resource the Sjorgens have built, ExplorersWeb.com, is updated daily with reports from the many expeditions their services support.
© Explorers Web

Extreme Images

A series of images taken with a 2.1 megapixel Canon Powershot on the Sjorgen's trans-Antarctic crossing, 2001. "So when people talk about needing 5 megapixels or whatever, actually no, that's not important."
© Explorers Web

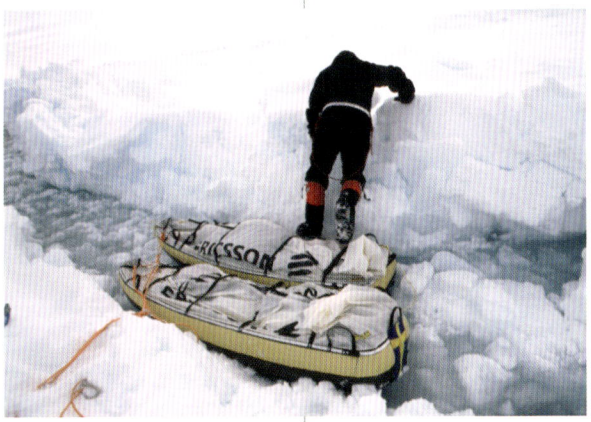

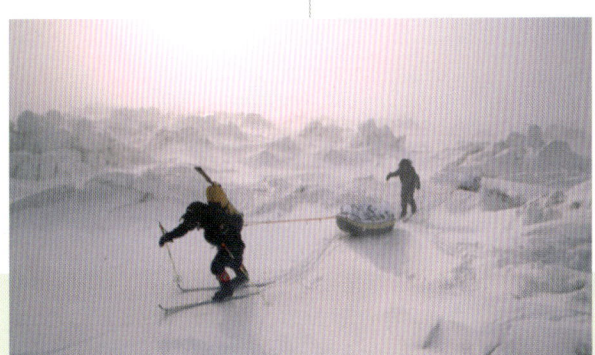

do some really serious stuff to bring the weight down. So we set a goal for ourselves to have less than 1 kilo total weight for satellite communication, digital camera, and computer together.

We're using more and more only the pictures from the digital camera—the first camera we had in Antarctica was the small Canon, the Powershot. We used the Canon Powershot for a couple of expeditions, but the power system is terrible.

The reasons that we now use the Sony Cyber-shot (our kit includes the DSC-P31/P72) is because of the power system, number one; and number two is that it can take MPEG videos. We don't have any programs that can do video editing on our PDAs at the moment, so the MPEG format is pretty good—you can upload it easily, and can click from any browser and it works. When you shoot video you can set it for e-mail format, the lowest resolution, and it's pretty good. If we could find other ways in the future, we would probably go for other compression techniques that would be more effective, but MPEG today is pretty useful.

Sony also seems to have a very good image-stabilizing system, because with a camera very often it's better to have a good image-stabilizing system than a lot of pixels—that's our view anyway. There might be other cameras out there that are really better. But I think the small digital cameras now are absolutely awesome, I'm shocked by how good they are.

The people that we support with the camera, most of the time they are not top-notch photographers. They're explorers, or adventurers; what we do is make it possible for them to take photographs all the time and present them on a daily basis up on the Internet, but also bring them back home afterward.

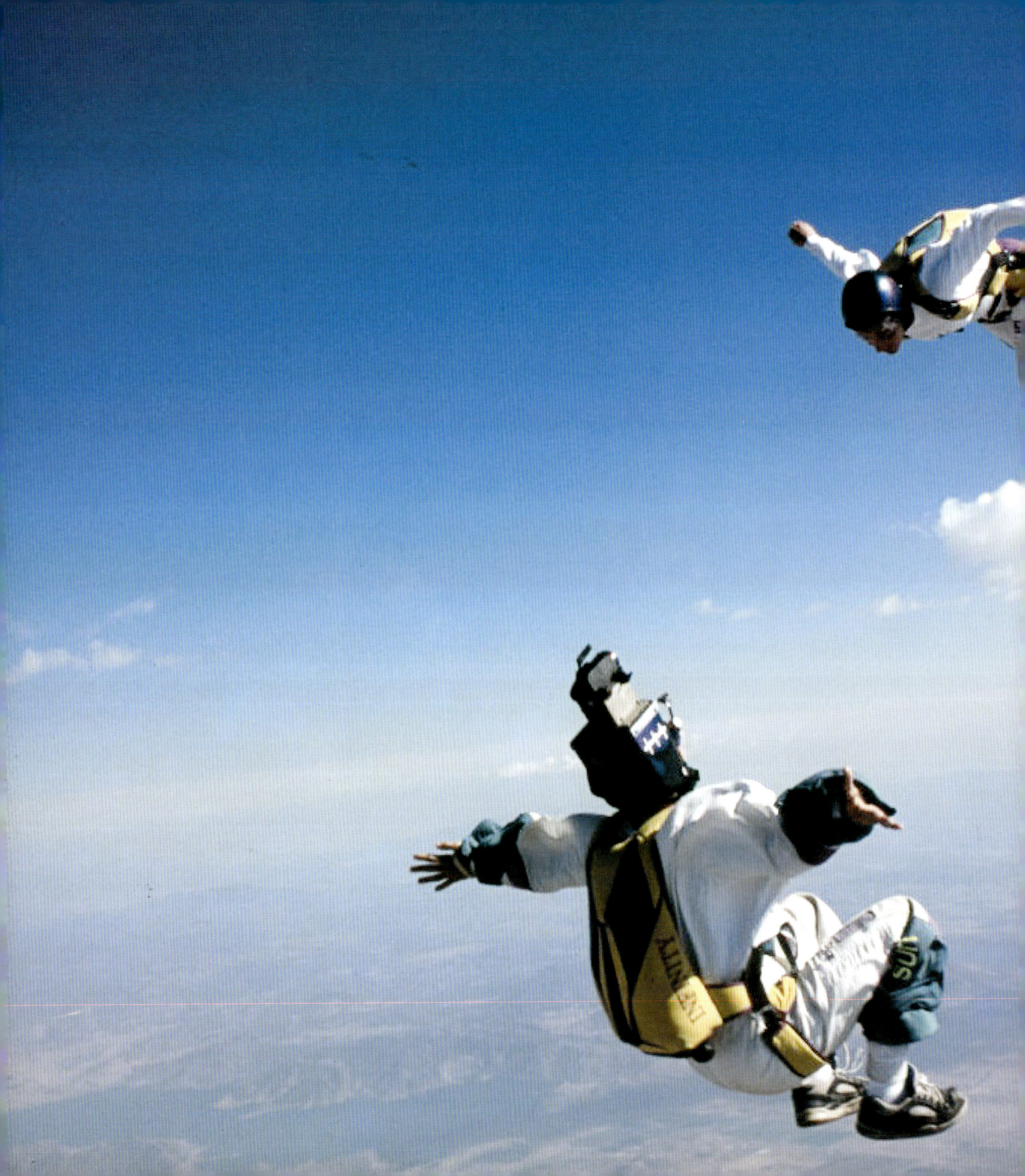

EXTREME ASSIGNMENTS

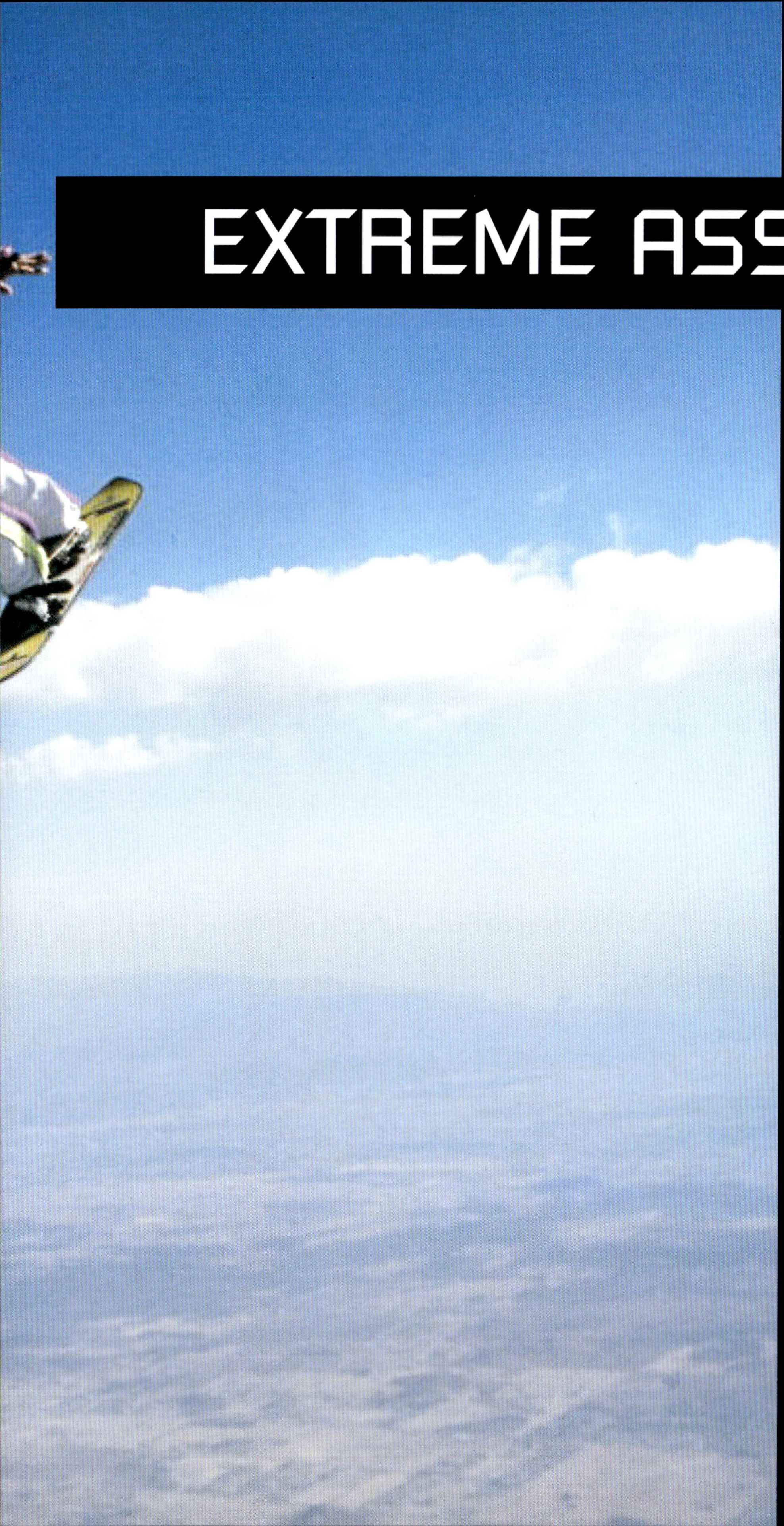

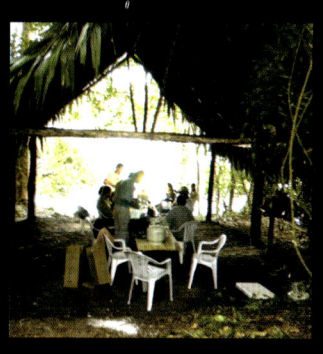

The thought process of photography is not obvious or wholly intuitive. Over and over again, many of the best and brightest minds of each generation have floundered at the simple act of taking a meaningful photograph.... It's all in our heads but not in all our heads.

Galen Rowell,

Galen Rowell's Vision

Main: © Craig O'Brien
Top: © Denise Rocco-Zilber

RESEARCH AND PREPARATION

If you want good photographs of anything, it helps to know your subject. If landscape photography is your thing, then the more you also know about the geography of a place, the better you will be able to capture the classic shot of a location and to recognize when you see something unusual. If your subject is extreme wildlife (a major predator, for example), then knowing the ecology, behavior, and diurnal rhythms of the species will help you identify the best time and place to get the images you are after (and avoid getting eaten or trampled).

Having good reference material with you is often a help, such as a guidebook or wildlife checklist. There are often times when traveling to an assignment or location when you will have an hour to kill and you can get better acquainted with your subject. Having good maps or charts can also be a big help, not just to avoid getting lost, but perhaps to find your subject more easily. These days you can get CD-ROMs (or DVDs) of all sorts of reference material, maps, and even nautical charts, which you can either load onto your laptop or carry with you if you don't want to fill up your hard drive with large files. Your GPS can also be connected to the laptop so that it can display and track your position. Soon digital cameras will doubtless have GPS built in, and images will have their precise location included in the metadata.

Hiring a knowledgeable local guide, biologist, or assistant can also be a good investment. They can watch your back in dangerous circumstances, take you to out-of-the-way-spots, and of course help lug your gear, set up camp, and do other essential chores. If they live in the area, they are already several leagues ahead of you in many respects, and their help will become invaluable.

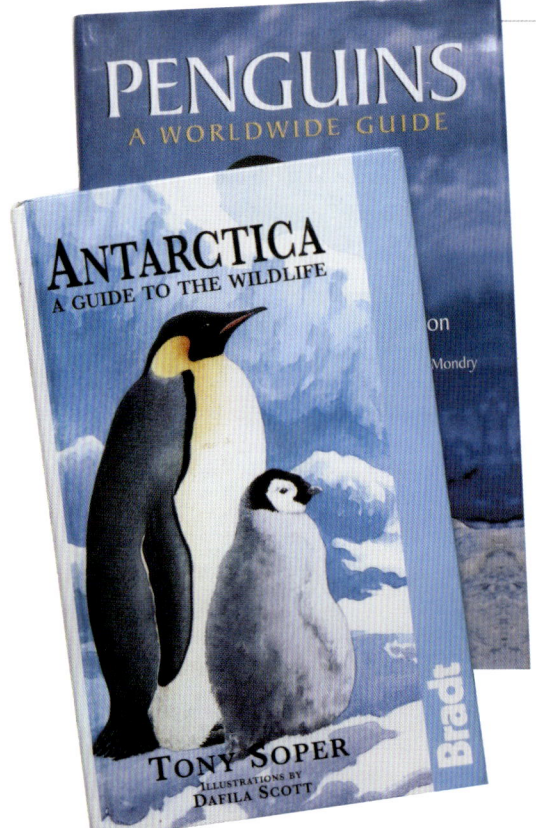

Guide Books

If you know your subject well before setting out, then you are more likely to get great photographs efficiently on location. Whether it is learning about the behavior of the wildlife, weather patterns, or when and where the sun rises and sets, this information is usually available from good reference and guide books.

Maps

The more remote the assignment, or the more foreign the destination is to you, the better it is to have a complete range of maps and charts to work out your route and know the terrain once you are there. The magic of reading good maps forms an art in itself—take the time to perfect this skill.

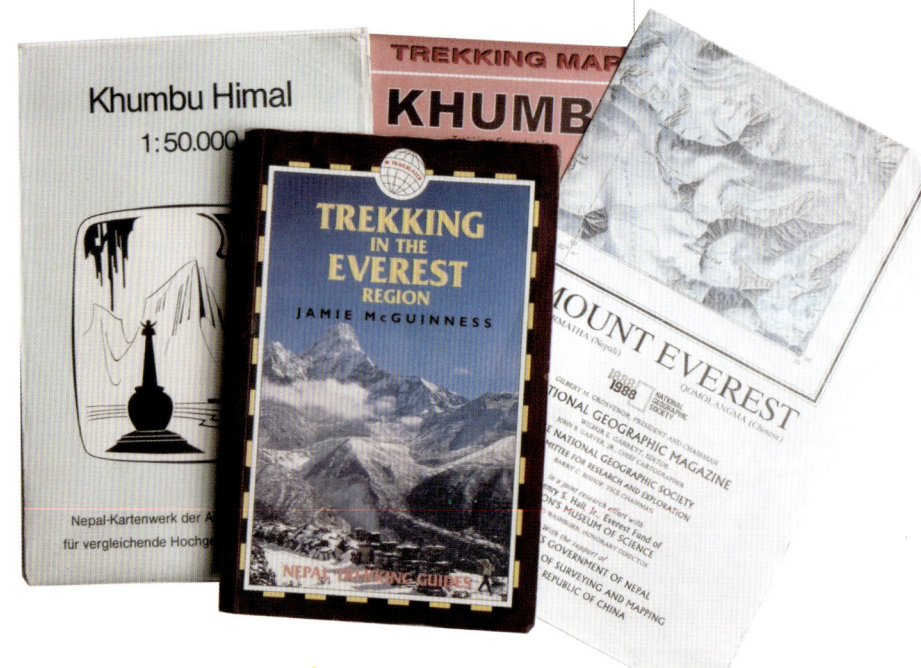

RESEARCH AND PREPARATION

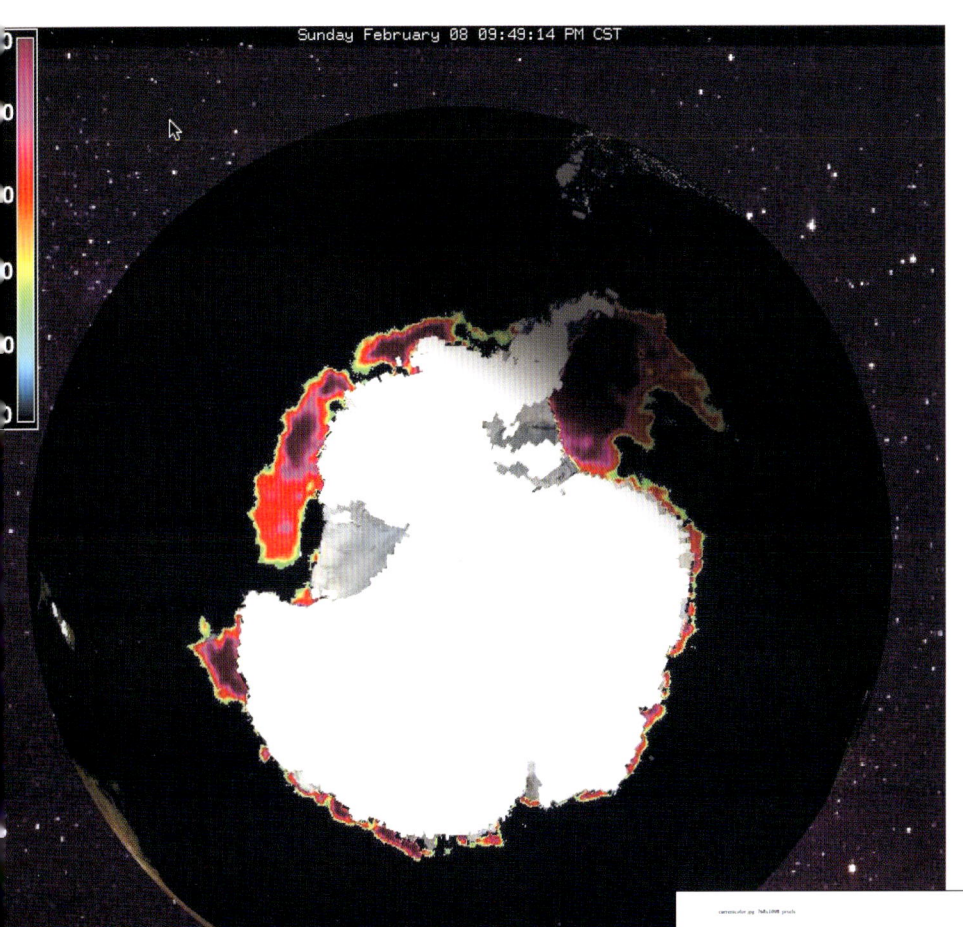

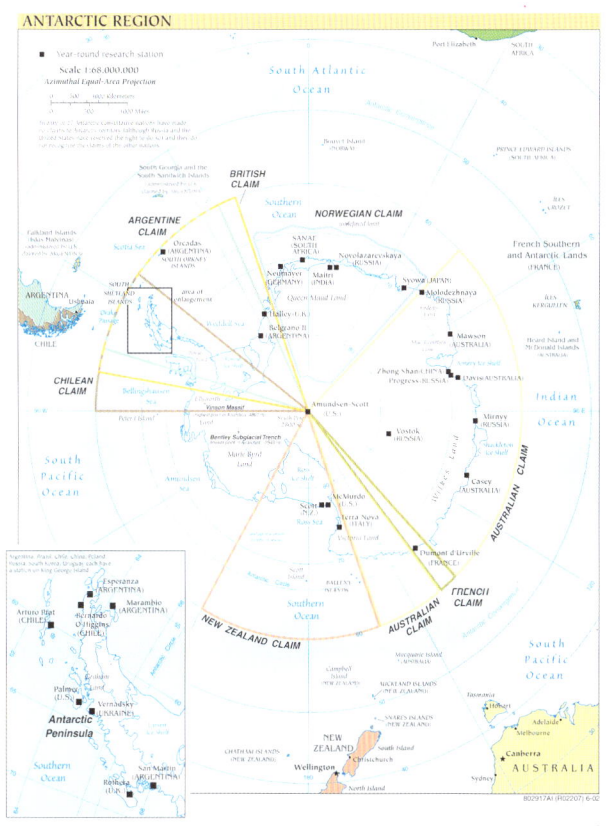

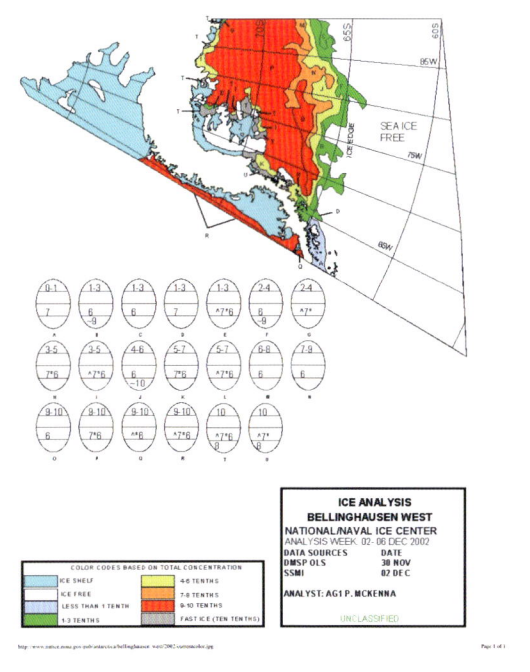

Satellite Images

Satellite imaging has revolutionized mapping, weather forecasting, and other areas of scientific research. Aerial images like these that show ice coverage of a whole continent are invaluable in giving you literally "the big picture" of a place. *The Cryosphere Today,* University of Illinois, Polar Research Group

Ice Charts

Being able to utilise a Web connection via satellite while on assignment or expedition in remote places can enable you to download detailed daily weather or ice information, like this, for the Antarctic Peninsula. Such regular updates are useful in planning your daily program and for operating safely in extreme environments. National Ice Center, www.natice.noa.gov.

Web Resources

All manner of information can be found online about a country, subject, or region. A Web search can help you quickly get the background of your assignment or project's destination. The CIA *World Factbook* (http://www.cia.gov/cia/publications/factbook) is an excellent starting place for broad country-by-country information with regional maps, basic facts, and statistics.

GUIDES AND ASSISTANTS

A good professional photographic assistant can read your mind, juggling lens and camera needs when there is a lot of action, and can even act as a "second unit" to capture video, if you are doing a Web project.

Then there is the whole question of the post-processing, the hours of work after a day's shoot. Many of these processes can be handed on to a sharp and enthusiastic assistant, especially one who has worked with you before and knows your ways. Many photographic clubs or other professional associations have listings of photographers' assistants, and tracking down a good one is a find indeed.

Base-Camp Geek

A techno-wizard who can also take pictures is the ideal combination for a field assistant. Being able to share the load with a second-unit cameraman or videographer and post-production assistant is vital on a big assignment, especially if you have to post to the Web or to clients on a regular basis.

Testing, Testing

You can never test your field communications setup too many times. Typically it's prudent to have a complete backup of all components as well, in case of equipment failure or, in the case of international travel, lost or delayed baggage.

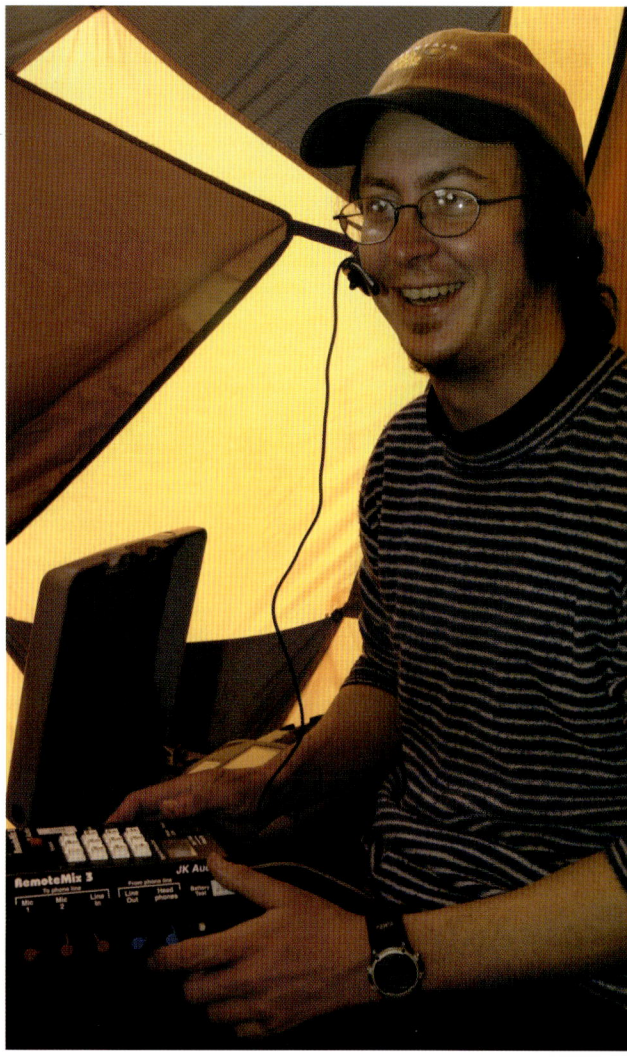

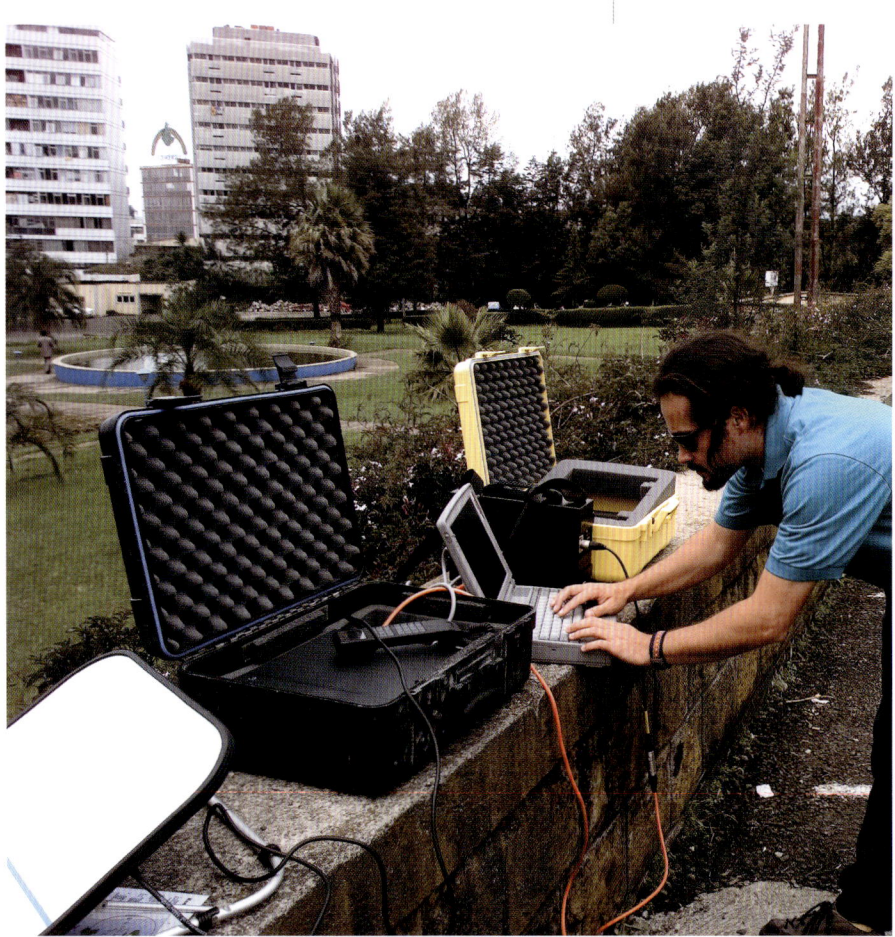

Sometimes you can get an assistant who will join you on a trip just for expenses, if there is not the budget for a second salary. I took one such person to Everest Base Camp. This is good insurance if you have tight deadlines and there is an element of risk. It is not uncommon to get altitude sickness or twist an ankle on the trek, and having someone to look out for you, carry the load, or even do the shooting if necessary can be a very prudent move.

GUIDES AND ASSISTANTS

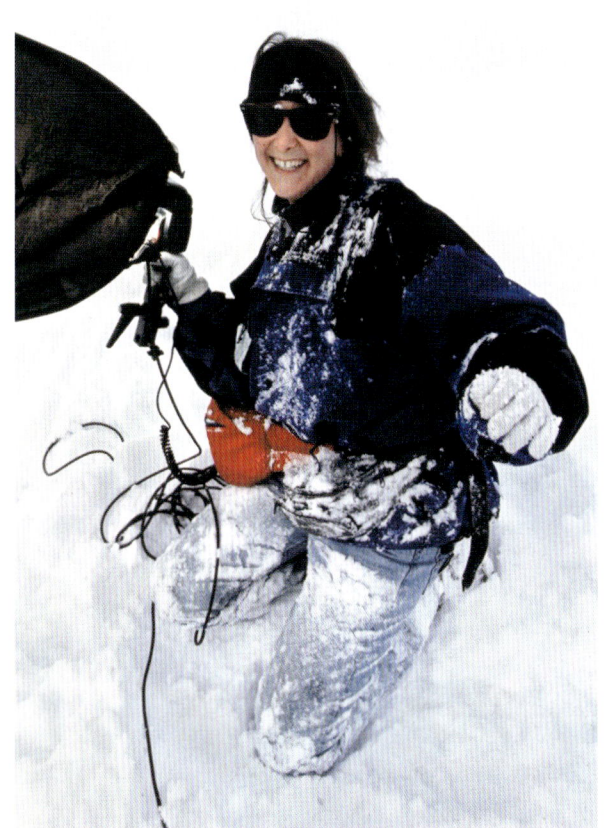

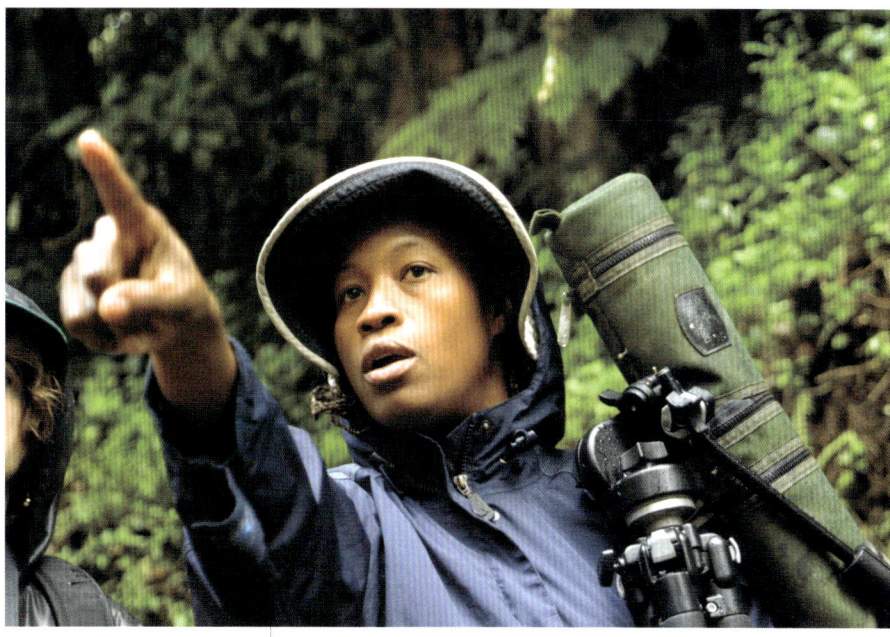

Wildlife Guide

A local naturalist or guide is invaluable on assignments for spotting and identifying animal life that a shooter might otherwise miss. Here, a Costa Rican guide points out a trogon on a birding trip. © Christian Kallen

Field Assistant

The value of helping out, from an assistant's point of view, is experience. You are exposed to situations in which you learn skills and techniques that may prove useful in your own photographic career, and you concern yourself with the details, allowing the photographer to focus on image making. © John Storey

Sirdar Speaking

The head Sherpa guide on a climbing team in Nepal is called the "sirdar." He is in charge of all the other guides and the logistics for the team while it is in the country. Veteran sirdar Pasang Kamai was instrumental in getting Erik Weihenmayer of the National Federation for the Blind Expedition to the summit of Everest.

Men go out into the void spaces of the world for various reasons. Some are actuated simply by a love of adventure, some have the keen thirst for scientific knowledge, and others again are drawn away from the trodden path by the 'lure of little voices,' the mysterious fascination of the unknown.

Sir Ernest Shackleton

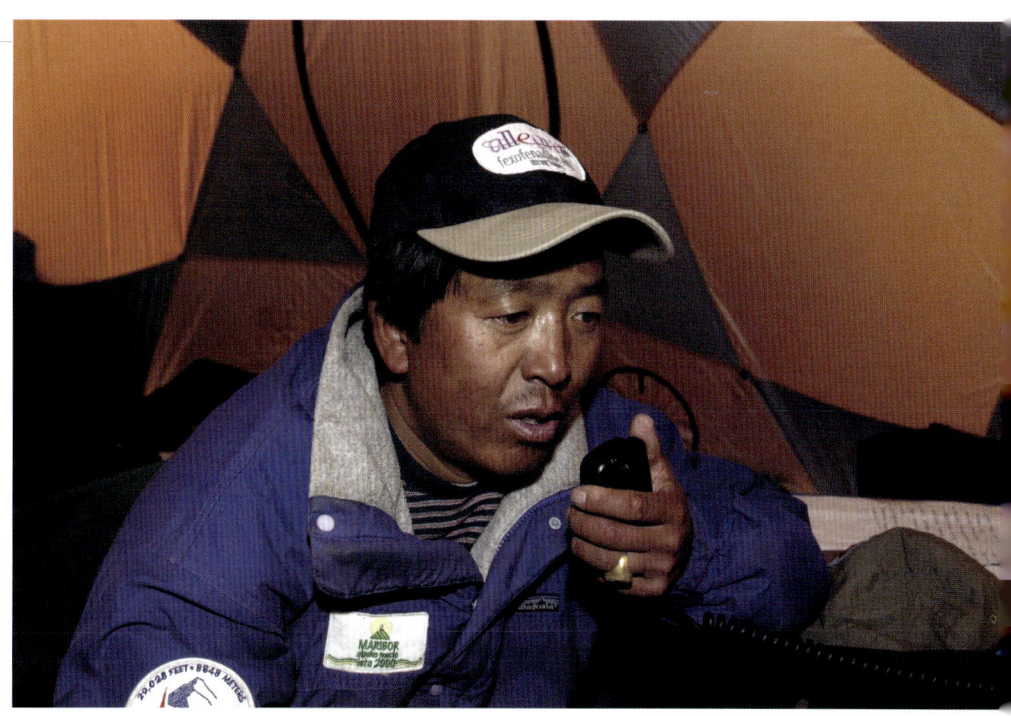

CLOTHING AND PERSONAL CONSIDERATIONS

There's an old saying that "There is no such thing as bad weather, it's only being poorly dressed." Of course the conventions of attire vary; every culture that survives in an extreme environment has a clothing formula that has evolved over the centuries, be it the penis gourd for the Dani of West Papua or the sealskin anorak used by the Inuit of the Arctic. With the application of high technology to clothing and camping gear, however, we can now be much warmer, or cooler, and generally much better clothed than was possible just a decade ago.

The development of synthetic fabrics, from a polar fleece for warmth to semi-permeable membranes such as Gore-Tex for wet weather and polypropylene wicking garments, has led to a revolution in outdoor clothing. Aside from clothing, inventive designs have created such innovations as the Camelbak hydration system and made trekking poles and waist packs an essential part of every well-heeled trekker's outfit.

The main principles for staying warm have not changed over time. These are layering, staying dry, and being windproof. Layering, or being able to adjust your clothing easily to respond to changes in your own body temperature, is an important piece of the puzzle. Your hands, head, and feet radiate the most heat, so keeping your extremities well insulated with a hat, gloves, and good footwear is the most basic consideration.

Once you begin working hard, even in sub-zero temperatures, you may begin to sweat. Removing layers one-by-one helps prevent you from overheating. This is not just a matter of comfort; if you lose moisture through sweating, you are in danger of becoming dehydrated, which can cascade into serious health problems.

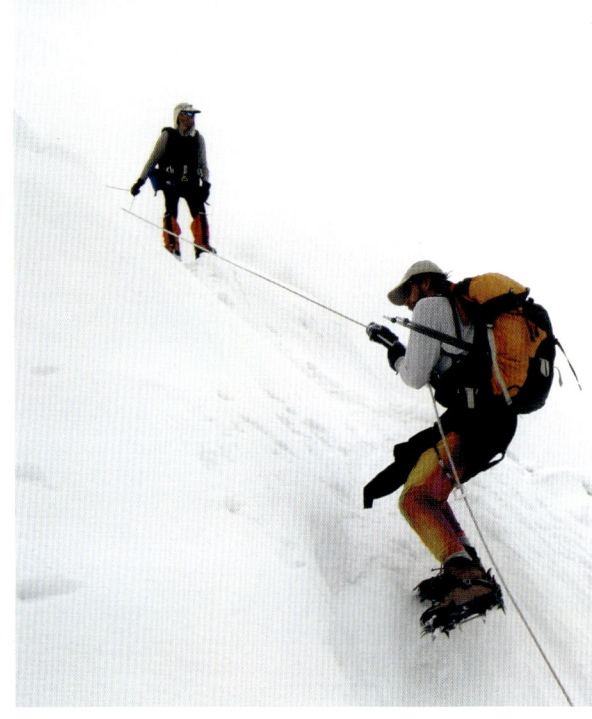

A breathable windproof outer layer for your upper body is the best first level of protection. You should always think about carrying a lightweight Gore-Tex jacket in your backpack or in your camera bags if the weather is dodgy, no matter what the temperature. A fleece hat and finger gloves are the next basic part of my kit, which I ensure is always with me in cold weather.

If you are dealing with really serious cold, you will probably be wearing three or four layers of clothing on most parts of your body. First, an underlayer of a wicking fabric like polypropylene to transport moisture away from your skin (if it collects there, then you become cold and clammy). Next, a middle layer of lightweight insulating fleece, followed by a top layer of down, and perhaps even a one-piece wind suit of Gore-Tex to keep you covered in almost any condition.

Hot and Cold

Being on a high mountain or ice field, you can be sweltering in bright sunshine one minute and freezing the next. To stay comfortable you need to be able to adjust your clothing very easily. Having full-length zippers in the legs of overpants enables you to quickly strip down to your long underwear, as Erik Weihenmayer has done during this pitch on Everest.

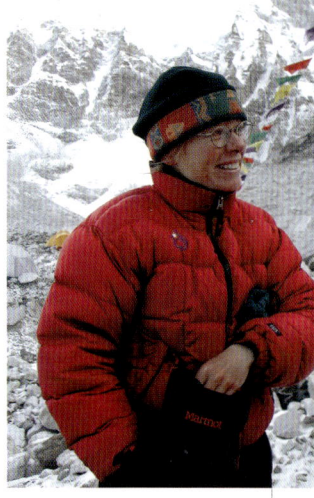

Down Jackets

Windproof jackets or parkas and warm headgear are essential to stay comfortable at high altitudes or latitudes. Pound for pound, fine goose-feather down is still the best insulation for sleeping bags and clothing in dry cold extreme environments.

For serious cold, sometimes the two top layers are combined into a one-piece Gore-Tex-covered down suit. It makes you look like the proverbial Michelin man, but it may keep you alive.

If you are forced to stand still to capture a shot, or are otherwise unable to exercise, then you will become colder than if you can move around. In these cases, even warmer clothing, (especially footwear,) will be necessary.

As well as maintaining your working temperature, there are safety considerations with your equipment. To hang in a precarious location you may need a basic climbing harness and belay equipment. A mechanical ascender, or Jumar, on a static line is a very good safety consideration. It can be locked in place and you can suspend not only yourself, but also your heavy camera gear, from the line, relieving yourself of their weight.

If you are in snowy country and you are not a very competent skier, then you may find that snowshoes are easier to use when you are actually shooting. A small plastic sled or a kid's toboggan can also be useful for moving your camera gear around when you are in deep snow. If it is very icy, then crampons are a wise addition to your gear. On inexperienced feet, full 12-point ice-climbing crampons can be a little dangerous, so consider using what are known as instep crampons.

Things are considerably simpler in hot or warm weather. But since you'll be exposed, it's possible to lose a great deal of body liquid without being aware of it; so make sure you stay hydrated. Don't forget the importance of sunscreen to protect you from UV radiation, no matter what the temperature, and especially at altitude or high latitudes. Not only is the atmosphere thinner, but the notorious hole in the ozone layer is not just a myth—it's a health risk for the extreme traveler.

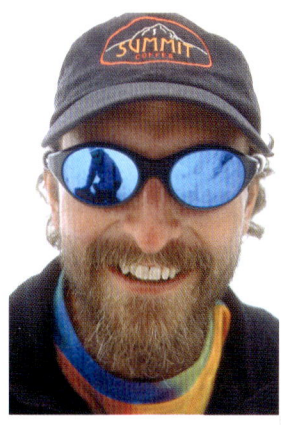

Glacier Glasses

Intense reflections from snow and ice can quickly blind you, unless you have very good eye protection and wear a shading hat. Glacier glasses have very dark lenses and UV filters, as well as side flaps or a wrap-around design to minimize light damage to your eyes.

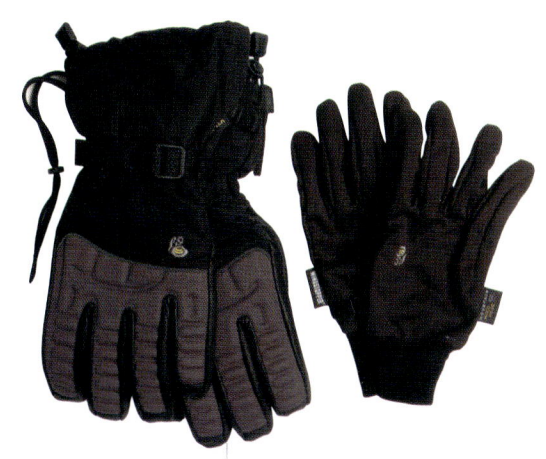

Gloves and Mittens

Mittens are warmer than gloves, but less useful for cold-weather photography when you need to alter lenses and dials. Better to have two or three layers on your hands, from light polypro gloves to heavy mittens, so that you never expose your skin to the elements.

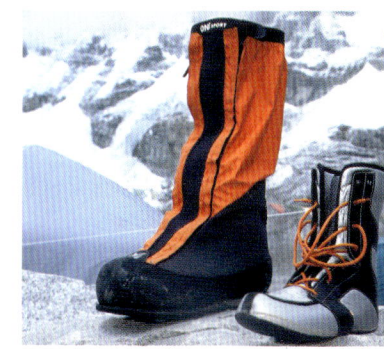

Vector Watch

Modern outdoor watches can be more like information modules, with many models having altimeters, barometers, a thermometer, and a compass (as well as the time). Some now also have built-in GPS capabilities.

Double Boots

Frostbite is always a potential problem when standing around for long periods of time in extreme cold. Rigid synthetic double boots are the best answer to staying warm, especially when you need the security of crampons.

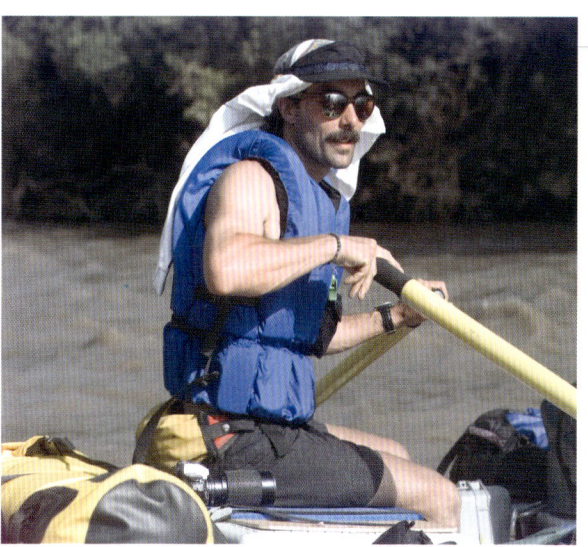

River Guide

For staying cool on a summer river trip, it's best to adopt "Lawrence of Arabia"-style headgear, sunscreen, and dark glasses. Of course a lifejacket is mandatory safety attire.

MEDICAL AND SAFETY CONSIDERATIONS

Prevention

Before going on a big trip or assignment, it pays to have a thorough medical and dental checkup. Having a toothache or worse while on the road or in the mountains is an almost unforgivable disruption because it is often preventable. If you are going to altitude, it is even more critical to have a clean bill of health, because treatment and evacuation are often difficult—sometimes impossible.

Just because you have been to altitude before does not mean you are immune to problems. Even if you are healthy, proper acclimatization is essential. If you fly to altitude, factor in a rest day or two before you begin your work or hiking to any higher altitudes. It is often best to hike to your high-altitude destination rather than fly in, if you can afford the time.

Regardless of altitude, jet lag can make you feel drowsy when you first arrive at your destination. Allowing a period of recuperation is advisable. If time is short, try to stay awake as long as possible to get your body adjusted to the new regime.

For many extreme destinations it is mandatory to have a range of vaccinations for diseases such as yellow fever; it is also wise to have preventative shots for conditions such as hepatitis. And taking anti-malarial medication is extremely prudent when going to many parts of Africa and Asia. Be sure you are getting the right sort of medication for wherever you are going, as there are strains of resistant mosquitoes. Seek the advice of a travel specialist group or the World Health Organization.

Poor public sanitation and hygiene in many countries are among the biggest causes of medical problems on the road. Becoming fastidious about washing with soap and hot water before eating can help reduce the chances of getting sick. Where running water is not available, using an alcohol-based antibacterial hand wash such as Purcell makes good sense. Drinking contaminated water is one of the biggest causes of diarrhea and parasitic infections such as giardia. Carrying your own water-purification chemicals such as iodine, and/or a filter pump, is advisable in many remote areas and foreign countries.

Support

Your level of medical safety preparation will depend on the size of the team and the degree of remoteness of your destination. In a larger team, you will need a group medical kit as well as a personal one, with a wider range of drugs and trauma-related items. Having an emergency medical technician (EMT) or doctor as part of the team may also be advisable, especially on a big expedition. A specialist like this will need a more extensive range of

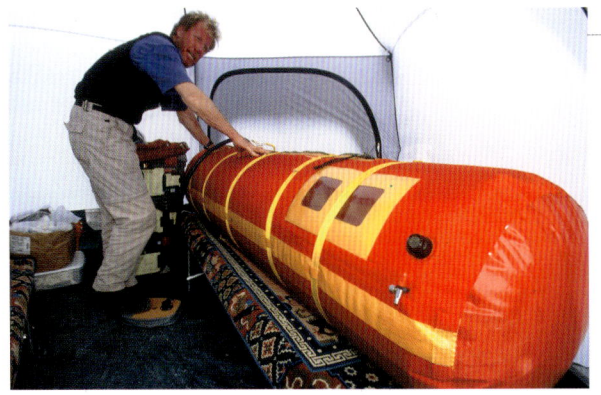

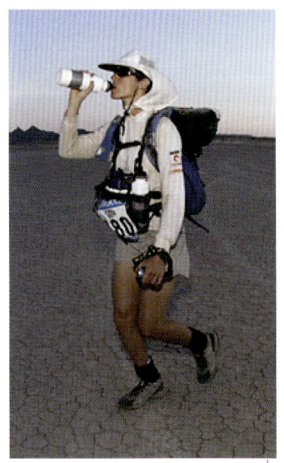

Gamow Bag

Named after its inventor, Dr. Igor Gamow, this inflatable pressure bag capable of holding a person has been successful in treating people suffering from severe altitude sickness. The effective altitude can be reduced some 5,000 feet (1,500m). Most big expeditions will have this type of bag as part of their emergency kit.

Staying Hydrated

Dehydration can be one of the biggest problems in hot dry climates for athletes and expeditioners. Carrying water bottles and portable hydration systems has helped to minimize the problem. © Corey Rich

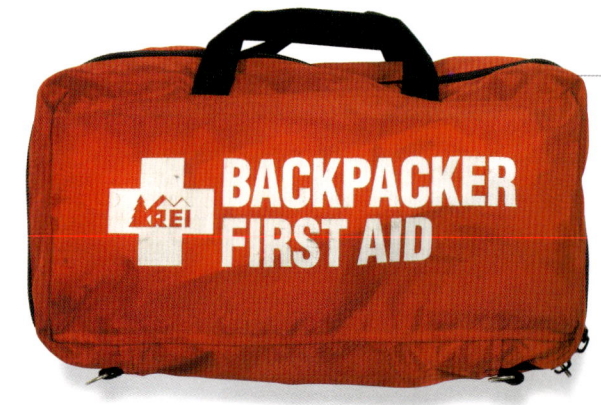

MEDICAL AND SAFETY CONSIDERATIONS 143

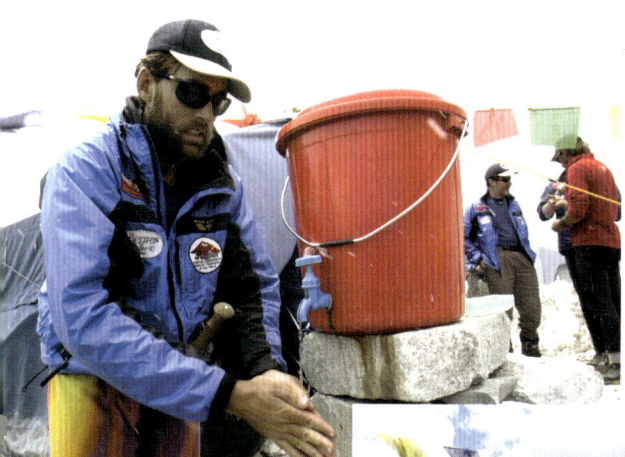

Wash Up!
Basic hygiene precautions, like washing your hands with antibacterial solutions before eating, are necessary in most Third World regions, but especially so on trekking or other expeditions.

Supplementary O₂
Cylinders of pressurized oxygen are now standard on ascents of very high mountains when above 26,400 feet (8,000m) in the so-called "death zone." Each full bottle, mask, and valve weighs around 8 pounds (3.6kg).

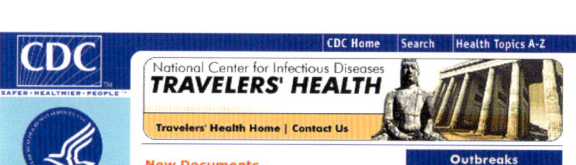

CDC Website
The Center for Disease Control runs its own Travelers' Health website (http://www.cdc.gov/travel/) with invaluable, up-to-date information and advice on health precautions, disease prevention, and vaccines (both suggested and required), organized by region, for the prospective traveler.

First Aid Kit
A simple first aid kit should be a part of every travel or assignment kit. It's best to supplement the contents with additional medications and preventative lotions, depending on where you're headed. Mosquito repellant, sunscreen, lip balm, and antiseptic hand cleaner are all necessary additions.

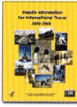

drugs and supplies to do his or her job properly, so packing and logistics become even more of a headache. Bringing professional-level supplies is easier when you have motorized or water-borne transport, but even so there has to be a limit on what can be taken along.

Rescue

In spite of all precautions, there are times when you have to get yourself, or your patient, to a medical facility as fast as possible. Having an evacuation plan in mind before getting to a remote setting is advisable. In some places, like the mountains of Nepal, it is possible to get lifted out by helicopter in an emergency, so having a reliable means of communicating with your agent or the rescue authorities is essential. This is where radios or Iridium satellite phones become a vital part of any safety plan.

When someone needs to be evacuated it is usually a job for outside professionals—the police or fire department, coast guard, or a local dedicated wilderness rescue outfit. Stabilizing the patient as much as possible before they are shifted is the priority. International evacuation can be very expensive, so having insurance to cover such contingencies is prudent.

Insurance

Joining a club or organization such as the American Alpine Club or British Mountaineering Council will often give you automatic coverage or good rates on personal injury and/or evacuation insurance, travel, and baggage, for a range of activities that most insurers would not touch. Having separate worldwide coverage on camera gear is often a wise investment. Remember to fully inventory your camera (and other) equipment, with receipts and serial numbers, to facilitate quick processing of any claim.

GETTING THERE

Going to extremes usually, if not always, means travel. Whether you're on assignment or pursuing your own stock photography, reaching a remote site can mean dealing with travel agents, airlines, customs, passport agencies, international visas, as well as in-country services. All of these take planning and paperwork at the very least, and in some cases considerable cash outlay. Budgeting your time and resources is an essential part of pre-trip planning.

Lining up international transportation used to mean consulting a travel agent or specialist. Now, in the age of the Internet, everyone is a travel specialist, or sees himself or herself as one. Beware: although anyone can log on to Travelocity, Expedia, or Cheaptickets.com to look up and buy airline tickets, some of the technicalities of routing to remote destinations are convoluted and arcane. Make sure you explore your routing thoroughly, leave plenty of time for plane changes and transfers (especially in unknown airports), and read the fine print when you book your ticket. Some do not allow changes in departure (or return) without considerable penalty fees.

This means that consulting a travel agent may still be the best course of action. If you are going to an area serviced by a reputable adventure travel outfitter, you might contact them for suggestions and even ticketing assistance, but be prepared to pay a small "research fee" for their efforts. This can be money well spent if you get what you need—valuable information and services, leading to your safe arrival in a remote destination.

The first item on your travel checklist should always be your passport. It should be up-to-date and valid for at least three months (and sometimes longer) beyond your travel date. Getting a renewal or a new passport can take between two weeks and a month. "Express passport" agencies can expedite this process, but this can double or triple the cost of a passport (currently $80 for a new US passport, $55 for a renewal).

While travel in certain areas of the world, particularly the European Community, is easier now than it has been in the past, many countries still require visas for entry, which must be applied for and approved in advance. This

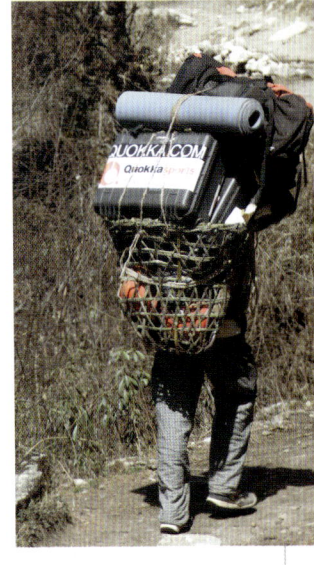

Porter Power

While trekkers prefer to carry their personal day gear, including cameras and lenses, it's worth the day rate (about $3) to hire a Nepalese porter to shoulder hard-shell Pelican cases as well as backpacks, sleeping pads, and other camp gear. © Didrik Johnck

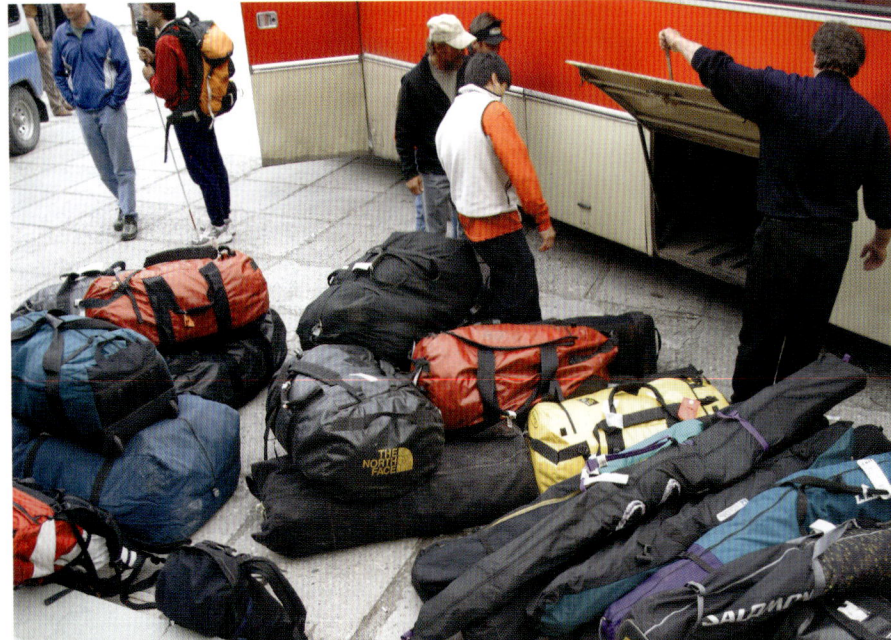

Duffle Shuffle

Gear, gear, and more gear. The amount of gear that goes into even a modest two-week expedition can be daunting. Experienced travelers like to use special tape or line to mark their bags, and always carry a list of equipment with serial numbers, in case a customs agent starts asking questions.
© Didrik Johnck

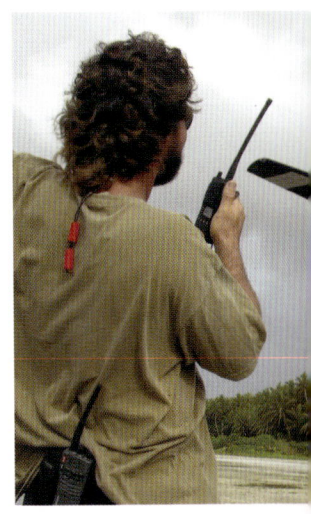

GETTING THERE 145

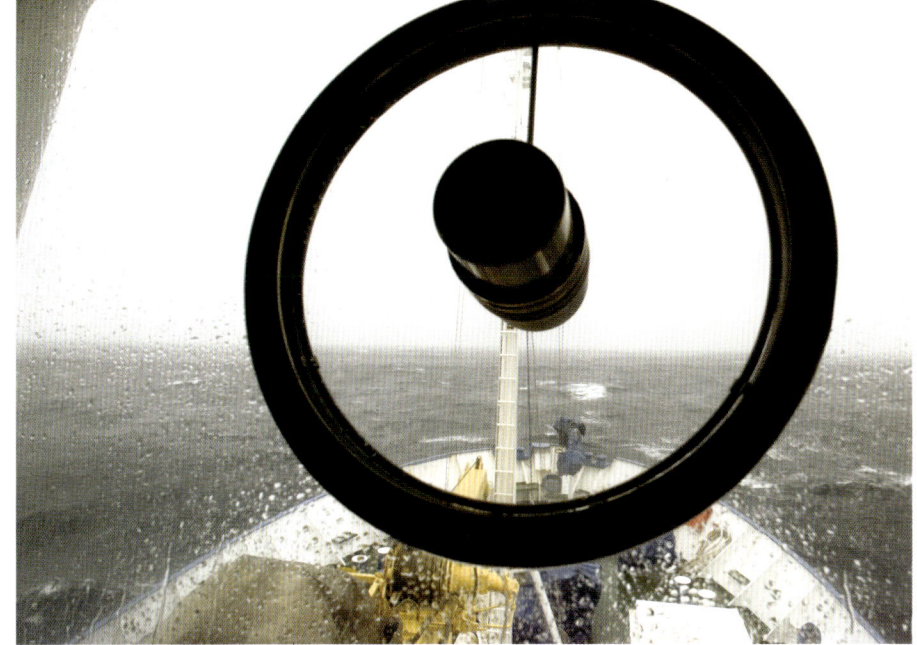

Crossing Drake's Passage

The body of ocean between South America and Antarctica is variously know as Drake's Lake or Drake's Shake, depending on your luck with the weather. Despite its fierce reputation, it is rarely stormy when most expedition cruise ships make the crossing to Antarctica.

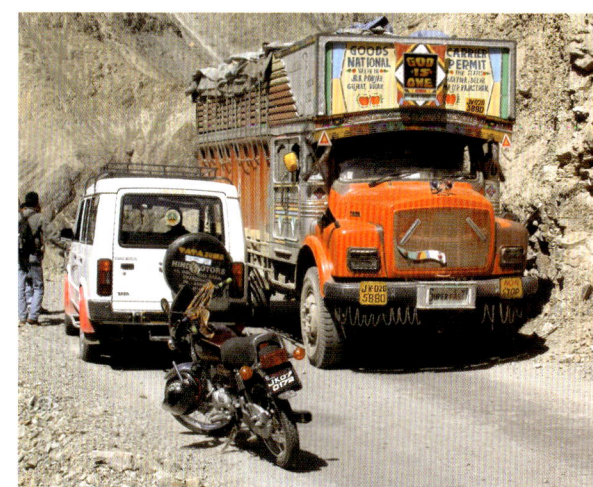

Tight Squeeze

High mountain roads in the Indian Himalaya can be very exciting, and sometimes quite dangerous. It's often a tight squeeze between trucks and other vehicles, and sometimes it's necessary to dismount to check clearance, as on this highway between Manali and Leh.

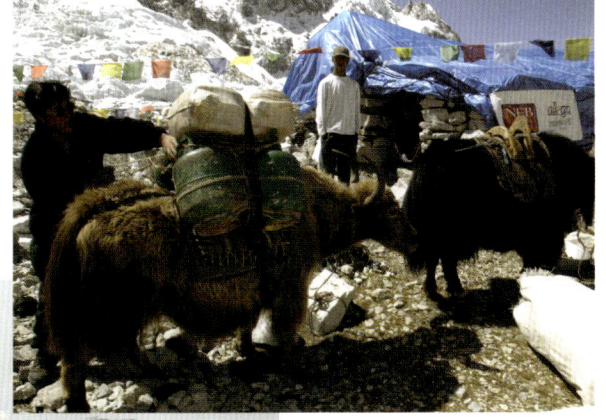

Yak Pack

At high altitude in Nepal the preferred beast of burden is the yak or the "squat woolly," a distant relative of the American bison. These tough but even-tempered creatures are all but impervious to bad weather, and can carry 40–80 pounds (18–36kg) each. Pack your gear well, however, for it's a bumpy ride.

Control Tower

Access to remote islands is sometimes only possible by boat, but occasionally there are primitive airstrips carved out of the landscape, as on this island in Palau in the western Pacific. © Russell Sparkman

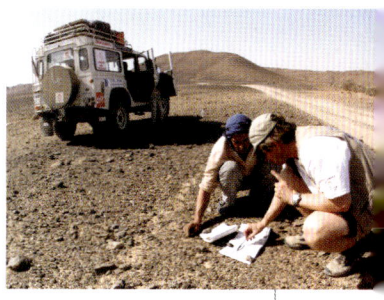

Map Check

With few distinct landmarks and poor local maps, navigating the Sahara desert of southern Morocco can be tricky. Situations like these cry out for modern GPS equipment. © Corey Rich

may be a complicated or a simple process, depending on the country you'll be visiting. Travel Document Systems, with offices in Washington, DC, and San Francisco (http://www.traveldocs.com), has visa information for US tourist, business, and diplomatic travelers to most of the world's countries.

Many countries also require international certificates of health, such as for yellow fever vaccination, if coming from an infected area (usually in the tropics). It makes no sense to have your cameras in hand, bags packed, assignment confirmed, and ticket ready, only to be turned away at the border due to the lack of a piece of paper.

Customs on entering a foreign country is another important issue. You will doubtless be carrying valuable equipment—digital camera and lenses at the very least, plus computer or digital storage device, possibly even a satellite phone or other high-tech equipment. It's important that you have photocopied inventories of all this equipment with their serial numbers—not only so that you can prove that they are yours, but so that you leave the country with the same equipment you entered with. Any permits or licenses should also be carried and photocopied, to prove your right to use the equipment.

BASE CAMP

Base camp can be anything from a hotel room to a motor home, a ship to a tent, or even an ice cave. It's a place you return to at the end of your shooting day to rest and do the back-end work, the processing and archiving that are so crucial to an extreme digital photographer's workload. Here it is (hopefully) more sheltered and wired into some sort of power system—be it generator, solar, or on a local grid.

The scale of your operation will dictate how much comfort you can afford to indulge in. If you have long hours of computer work downloading and archiving at the end of the day, then you need to have a certain level of facilities and equipment to be efficient. A table and chair inside a reasonable-sized domed tent can be a very desirable setup; even Pelican cases for your laptop and a self-inflating Therm-a-Rest to sit on can become a makeshift workstation. A tent will also give you a glare-free environment to enable you to see LCD computer screens better, and some protection from dust and insects.

If you're part of a large field team, having a comfortable communal living space where you can work, away from those trying to rest or sleep, is a very good investment. Larger geodesic dome tents, inspired by the late Buckminster Fuller, like the North Face 2 Meter Dome (capable of sleeping up to eight people), or the Mountain Hardwear Space Station (capacity 15 people), or even the smaller Satellite (capacity four), are all ideal communications tents, depending on the size of your team. Any of these is perfect for expeditions that are going to be in one spot for any length of time, and where the conditions are extreme. These tents are the norm at Everest Base Camp during the climbing season.

Lightweight tables and chairs are now part of every big expedition's kit. The vinyl Camp Time Roll-A-Table is perfect, made from vinyl-covered segmented slats, as in a roll-top desk; the matching stools provide acceptable and lightweight seating. But if you are doing serious computing at high altitude, then comfortable armchairs are well worth the weight and expense. At Everest Base Camp we had inflatable armchairs, and the computers were used to play DVD action movies every few nights, much to the delight of the Sherpas. The really serious action on Everest happens above Base Camp, so every attempt is made at this place to make it relaxing and fun.

Once the sun goes down, it can get cold extremely quickly at altitude, but often there is still a lot of work to be done. LPG (liquid propane gas) or pressure lanterns and heaters provide the necessary standard of living. Twelve-volt fluorescent lamps provide adequate light inside a tent, and LED head torches are now the way to light your operation economically when everybody else needs to get some rest.

Setting up the power supply at base camp is largely a matter of making sure the generator is far enough away from the living quarters that sleep and conversation are not disturbed. If you're using solar power, choose your campsite so that the panels attain maximum direct sunlight for as long as possible—often a difficult choice in mountainous terrain. Likewise, having direct line-of-sight to an Inmarsat or other communications satellite is a necessity if you're uploading material. While the geostationary satellites are situated over the equator and therefore directly overhead in the tropics, they can be quite low on the horizon at higher latitudes.

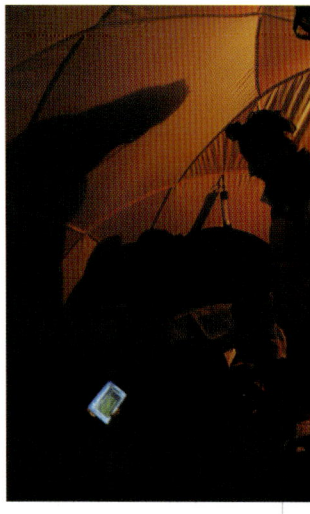

Base Camp Dome

Large domed tents are ideal for communal work and relaxation space on expeditions and big assignments. They afford good shelter and some warmth, no matter what the outside conditions. © Greg Thomas

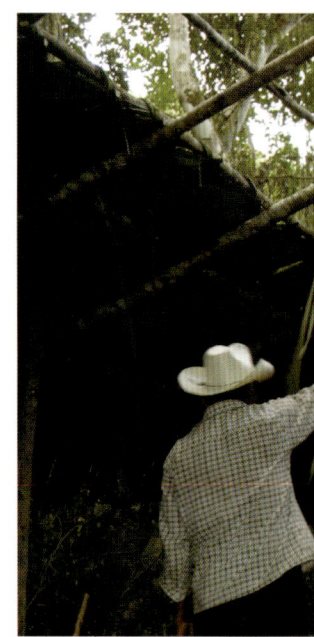

BASE CAMP 147

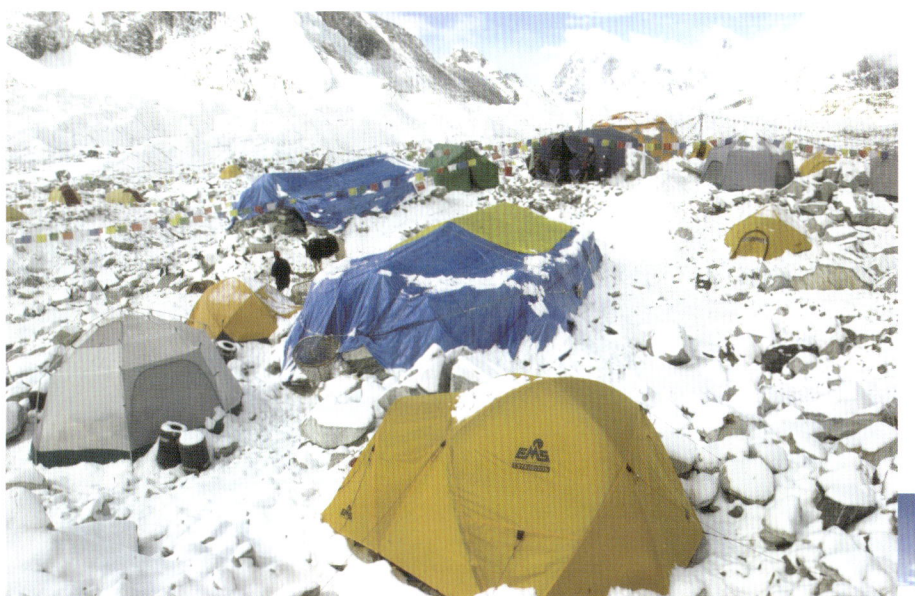

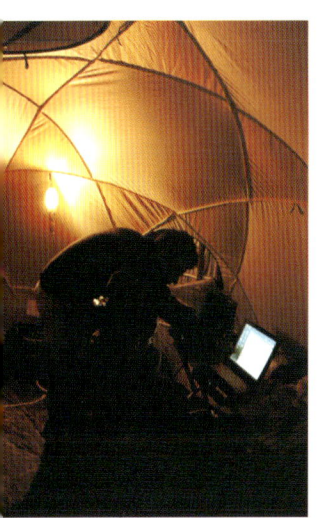

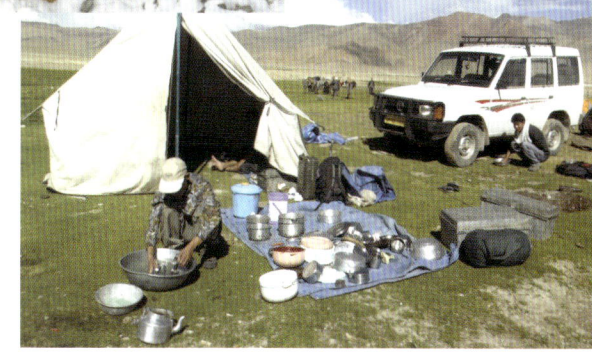

Ladakhi Car Camping

Having a vehicle as one of your modes of travel can make base camp a good deal more luxurious. It also has the added advantage of being a ready means of recharging your kit.

Jungle House

In just four days, a team of eight men constructed this working eco-camp for 23 researchers. The construction team used only materials from the forest and built structures to blend in with the jungle. © Denise Rocco-Zilber

Morning Snow

An overnight dusting of snow can give the Everest Base Camp a fresh look that makes an interesting setting for the early-bird photographer. The sun will soon melt this white mantle off, returning the camp to drab gray moraine scenery.

Open Air Cubicles

Expedition members do their daily work—writing in journals, processing photos, and so on—on laptops set up each night by the riverside. River trips and other traveling expeditions need to be adept at setting up mobile base camps for such digital activities, once unusual but now the norm.

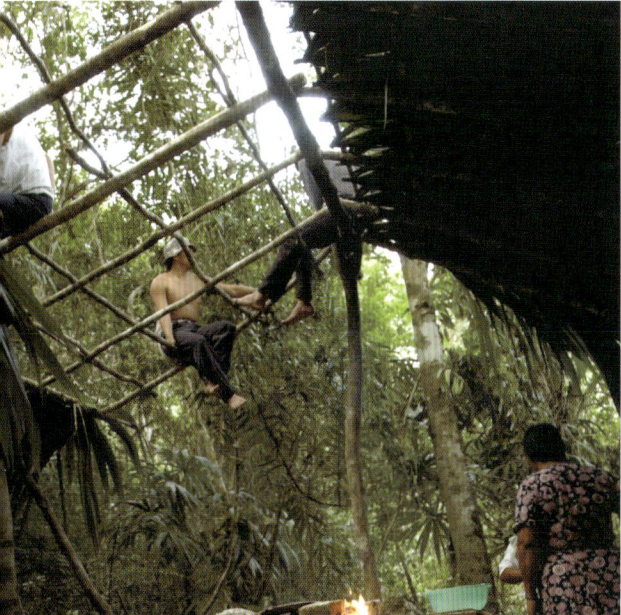

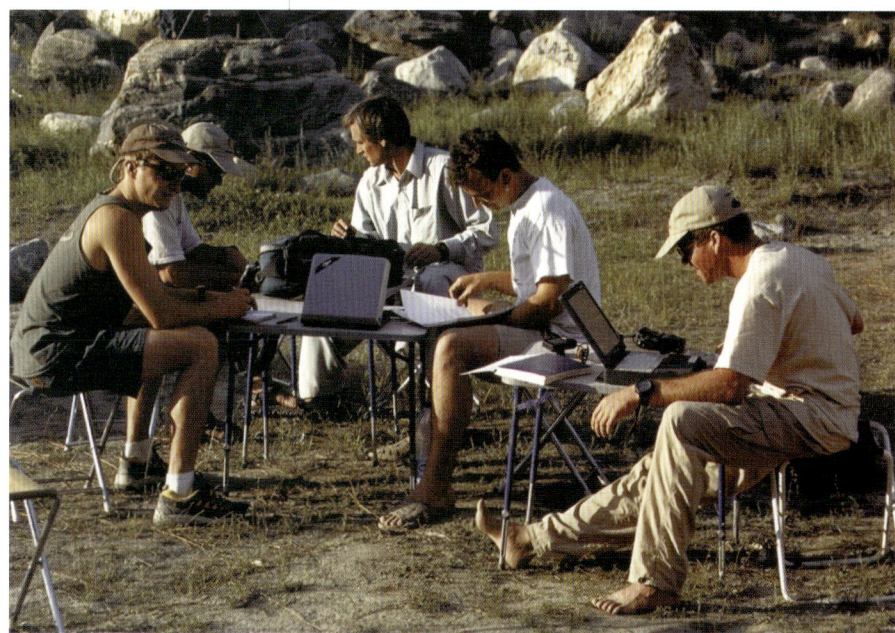

PRE-PRODUCTION PLANNING

Planning for your digital assignment is a multi-dimensional task reflecting the multi-faceted nature of digital photography. Attention must be paid not just to equipment (cameras, lenses, and so on), but to issues of power (battery or available current), storage (flash memory, short-term storage, and archiving), as well as the editorial process (review, selection, resizing, and captioning). Finally there are the inevitable "break points" that must be solved through creative troubleshooting.

Make a list: the first step in pre-production is your equipment list. Depending on the location and conditions of your assignment, you may want to include or exclude certain items—say, waterproof housing for wet conditions. A macro lens may be almost always useful, but the exception may be the team sports event you're asked to cover. If you anticipate being away from standard sources of power for any length of time, a way to recharge camera batteries is not just a good idea, but a necessity.

Start off by making a list of all your equipment needs, from the most obvious to the most minute. Note that this is a list of equipment *needs*, not possessions. If you don't have something you need in order to make this assignment work, research and order it immediately. Last-minute overnight shipping costs add up, fast. Experienced digital pros keep this list in several places, laminated, impervious to humidity, Arctic freeze, or wine spills.

Remember that computers have their own essential equipment—batteries, storage devices, dedicated cables, and so on. Software is another dimension that has to be included in your "packing list"—photo-manipulation software (usually a recent release of Adobe Photoshop), a photo-archiving program such as Photo Mechanic, and reliable Internet browsing and FTP programs. Include on this list everything that goes toward making your assignment work.

Your list will also come in handy as an "inventory" for official purposes—including customs (if you are traveling across international borders), insurance (if you lose anything), and airlines (to document "lost luggage"). Peter Menzel suggests taking photographs of your luggage, both open and closed, to show insurance and airline personnel if your luggage is delayed, to help document your loss and make the bags easier to locate.

Test everything: the most important part of pre-production is testing. Hook up everything several days before you leave, if possible. Make sure all the camera cards are good, the autofocus lenses functioning, the flash unit tested. Be sure your computer has up-to-date

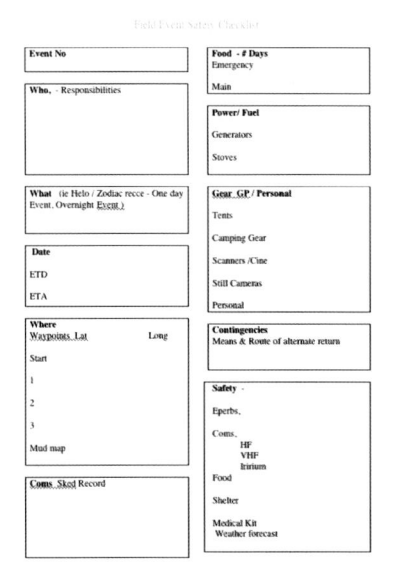

Emergency List						
	A	B	C	D	E	F
1	MIN QTY REQUIRED	2 MEN	3 MEN	4 MEN	5 MEN	6 MEN
2	ITEM					
3	Sleeping bag	2	3	4	5	6
4	Sleeping mat	2	3	4	5	6
5	HF radio	1	1	1	1	1
6	Iridium phone	1	1	1	1	1
7	Spare phone batt	1	1	1	1	1
8	Climb Harness	2	3	4	5	6
9	Prussick loops	2 sets	3 sets	4 sets	5 sets	6 sets
10	Jumars	2 sets	3 sets	4 sets	5 sets	6 sets
11	Climbing ropes	1	1	2	2	2
12	Ice axe	2	3	4	5	6
13	First aid kit	1	1	1	1	1
14	Tent	1	1	2	2	2
15	Tent poles	1	1	2	2	2
16	Tent pegs	15	15	30	30	30
17	Fuel stove	1	1	1	2	2
18	Stove fuel	6 litres	6 litres	8 litres	10 litres	12 litres
19	Matches	2 boxes	2 boxes	2 boxes	2 boxes	2 boxes
20	Pot set	1	1	1	2	2
21	Water bottle	2	3	4	5	6
22	Strobe	1	1	1	1	1
23	Compass	1	1	1	1	1
24	GPS	1	1	1	1	1
25	Food for 6 days:					
26	Muesli bar	24	36	48	60	72
27	ETA nut/fruit mixes (serve = approx 250gm pkt)	12	18	24	30	36
28	Chocolate bar	24	36	48	60	72
29	Instant noodles	8	12	16	20	24
30	Meat HungerBuster	6	6	12	12	12

Make a List

For a big project in a remote location like Antarctica, the Arctic or the Himalaya, you often need to consider the prospect of being self-sufficient for days or even weeks in the event that bad weather or some emergency. Pre-planning all needs, from equipment to food to communications gear, is absolutely essential.

Event Planning

On a recent assignment we had up to four photo teams in the field at any one time, either on land or ice, in a boat or in a helicopter. To make sure that we always knew who was where and that everyone had the right gear, communication, and emergency supplies, we developed a checklist of information that had to be filled out before any team left the base.

software loaded and working, and that the transfer process from camera to computer is flawless, both technically and intuitive to your personal work process.

Create a demonstration "dispatch" from beginning to completion. Go outside and take at least an hour of photographs, in a variety of conditions (with flash and without, long-distance and portrait, etc.). Then upload them to your computer, make your selections, edit and resize, and prepare a "test bundle" for transmission. This is most easily done as a folder on your computer, either in a directory dedicated to this assignment or on your computer's desktop. Each dispatch folder should have its own dated name (e.g., Antarctica_110204_d2), so that you can refer to its contents and sort it for archiving.

For extreme digital assignments, an FTP (File Transfer Protocol) site is far more reliable and effective than sending attachments to an e-mail address. Many ISPs put size limits on e-mail attachments, and the node-to-node nature of the Internet means that there may be a considerable delay between sending and receiving an e-mail. Far better to have a folder on a public or private FTP site (ask your ISP how to set one up) that you can log into directly, and then transfer files in and out of.

Before traveling away from home, investigate local ISPs or dial-up numbers. Calling international long-distance just to check your e-mail is unnecessary and expensive; America Online has many international numbers around the world, and it's almost worth having an AOL account for this reason.

If using a satellite phone, set it up, get a lock on a satellite, make the digital connection with your computer, connect to an FTP site, and upload a set of images and text files. Then go to the FTP site on your computer, pull down the files that you uploaded, and check them all.

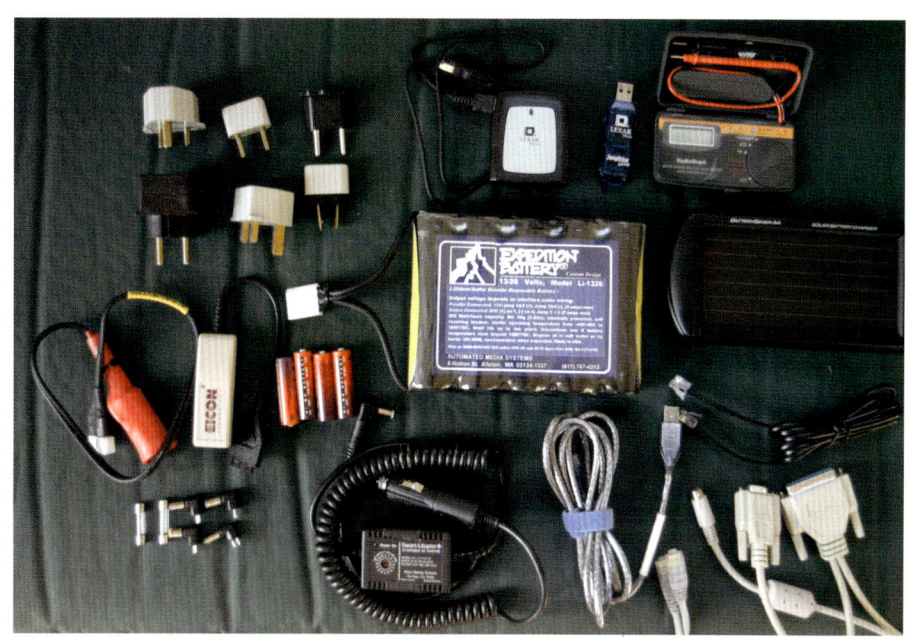

Power Supplies

You can never be too careful about having the right power sources and multiple backup options for extreme digital photography when heading off to remote places. Spare data cables, connectors, and power plugs for all voltages and standards help minimize the chance of being caught without the right solution. © Didrik Johnck

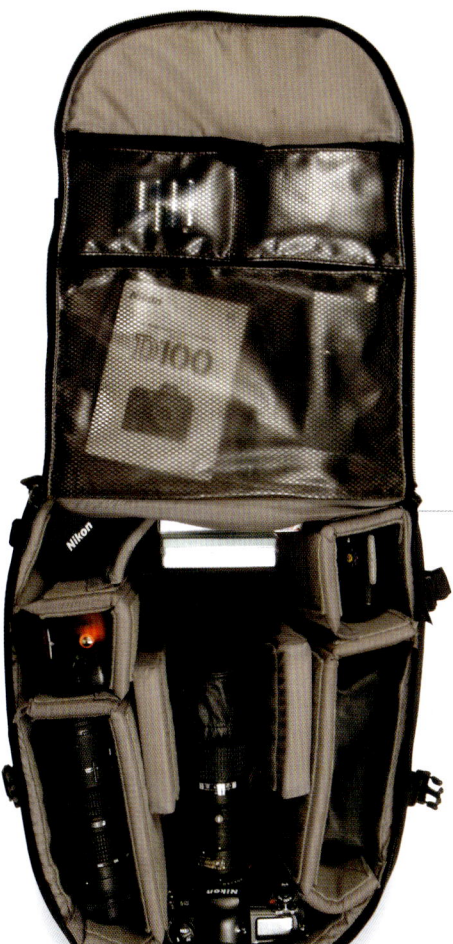

Open Luggage

In the event of items going astray in transit, be sure to have digital images (or, better still, prints of your luggage in both open and closed states) to show to baggage agents. This simple precaution can facilitate more rapid recovery, if possible, or help expedite insurance claims, if not.

TYPICAL SHOOTING DAY

If you've made it through the airline security, customs, and various overland means of transport to your shooting assignment, congratulations. The hard part is now behind you: only the work remains.

The two critical issues on any digital photo assignment, extreme or otherwise, are always the same: power and storage. Digital photography demands both in order to succeed, and if either is absent—if your batteries run low or your image storage cards fill up—your work is brought to a standstill. There is no way to underestimate the importance of power and storage in your work. All of us make the mistake of trying to "get by" with less than full batteries or a partially full flash card, and it only leads to regret and embarrassment.

The typical shooting day thus begins with a final check of battery power and storage capacity. You should have charged all your batteries the night before, so that they are ready to go in the morning. Double-checking the camera's battery read-out is only approximate, as most cameras display a "full battery" icon even when the charge is partially used. Make sure that whatever battery charging device you use displays a solid light (or whatever signal it gives indicating a fully-charged battery)—this is more reliable. Of course you'll want to bring at least one spare battery (or battery set, if your camera uses AAs), if not three or four. These, too, should be fully charged.

Likewise, your flash cards should be formatted and free of images. You should have downloaded and cleaned your cards the night before, so that you begin the day with a clean slate. You should be familiar with the image capacity of your flash card and recognize when it's clean and ready for a full day's shooting by the camera's read-out. (Digital cameras usually display how many images are left on the card, not how many have been taken.) Most photographers use more than one card in a day—many of today's digital cameras can easily fill up a 256MB or even 512MB flash card in half a day, so make sure you have spare cards, just as you do spare batteries.

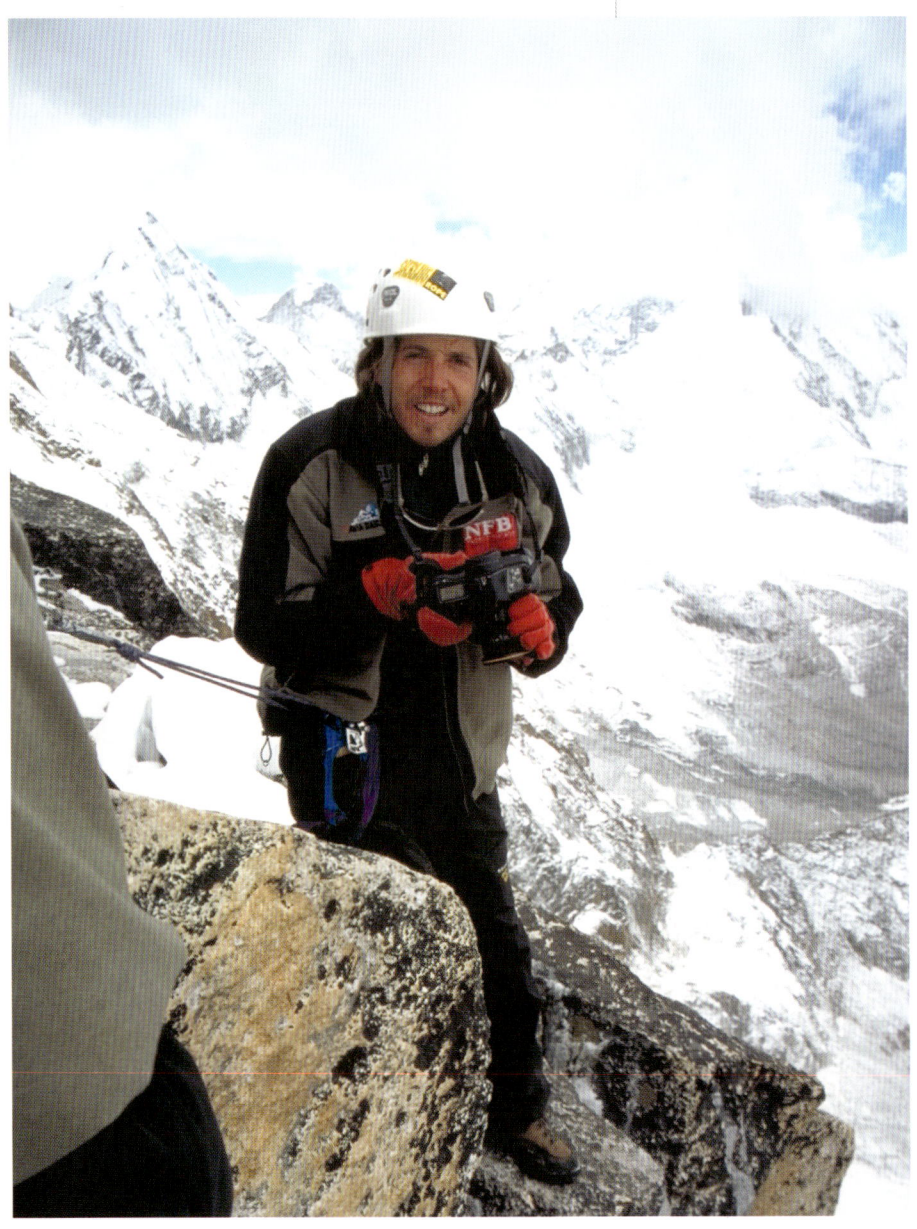

High Perch, Ama Dablam, Nepal

Didrik Johnck secures himself to a rock at about 20,000 feet (6,100m) and prepares to photograph team members as they ascend. "I had specifically requested to go up first, so I could get some shots of everyone else coming up. I built an anchor into the rock and attached myself to it, so I could hang over the ledge." © Didrik Johnck

TYPICAL SHOOTING DAY

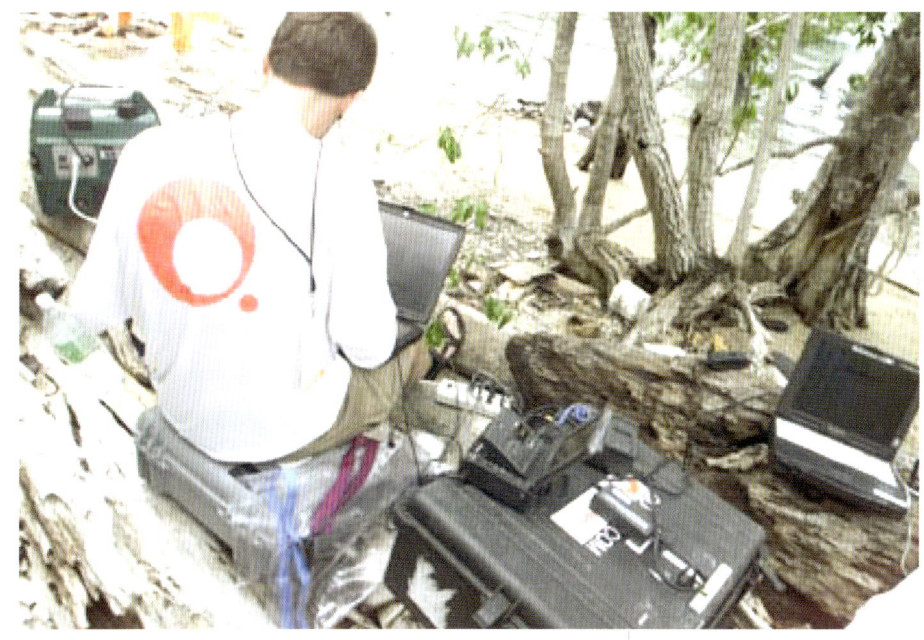

Most photographers work with more than one camera at all times. If you can afford it and are serious about your work, two or even three camera bodies are called for. This is not just to have a spare, but because many shooting situations call for a quick change from telephoto to wide-angle. It's quicker and easier to grab a second camera than change lenses, especially in athletic events (such as adventure racing) where time is at a premium.

At the very least, consider a down-scale model as your second camera—a small digital point-and-shoot, of which there is no shortage of models. Many of these are rugged, dependable, and robust cameras, such as the Nikon Coolpix series, the Canon Powershot, or the Sony Cyber-shots. They have megapixel resolution equal to many digital SLRs, though they may lack professional control features. It's handy if these "second cameras" use the same memory card as your primary camera, so that you always have multiple backups. Remember, redundancy is the key to efficient productivity: if your primary device fails, you should always have a backup.

Sometimes a flash memory card will be faulty and will not write the image. Simply ejecting and reseating it can help, particularly if there's some dust or moisture in the contacts. Although it's rare, flash cards do stop working.

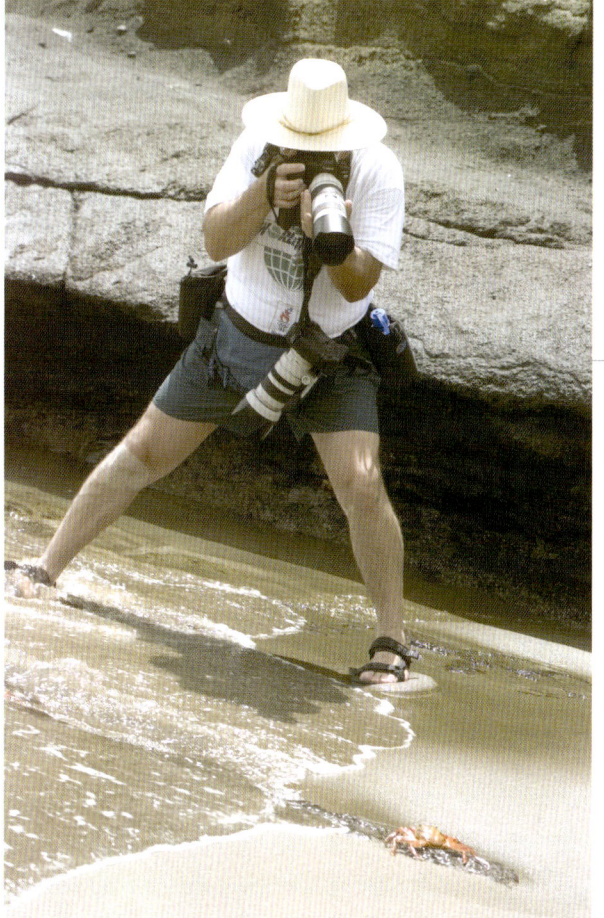

On the Beach

When covering an adventure race or any assignment where there is a daily program of uploads, you need to make use of any down time to clean flash cards, charge batteries, edit and write captions, and otherwise stay ahead of your deadlines. Whether at lunchtime on the beach or as soon as you get into camp, there is always a job to do.
© Rob Myers

Galápagos Crab

Many serious photographers find shooting with two identical camera bodies and different focal-length lenses preferable to having to constantly swap lenses on one body. As well as being faster to switch from one camera to the next, there is much less likelihood of getting dust or spray on the image sensor when you are not constantly exposing the inside of the camera body.

Waiting for the Light

At high altitudes like Everest Base Camp you can get bitterly cold standing around for hours on end taking images. I found it best to wear the same one-piece down-filled suit that climbers wear higher on the mountain. Thin finger gloves inside heavier ski gloves or mittens can give you the dexterity you need to operate a camera, without skin touching metal.

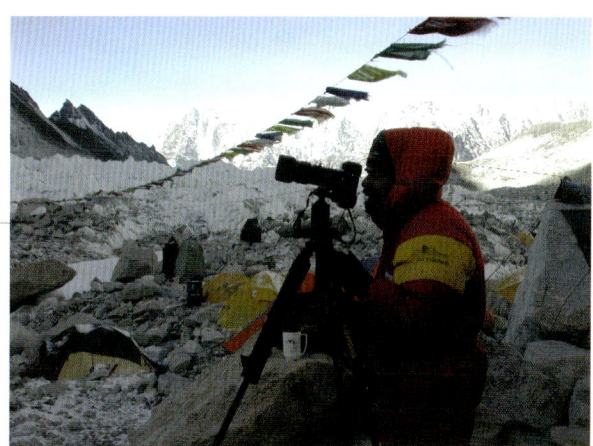

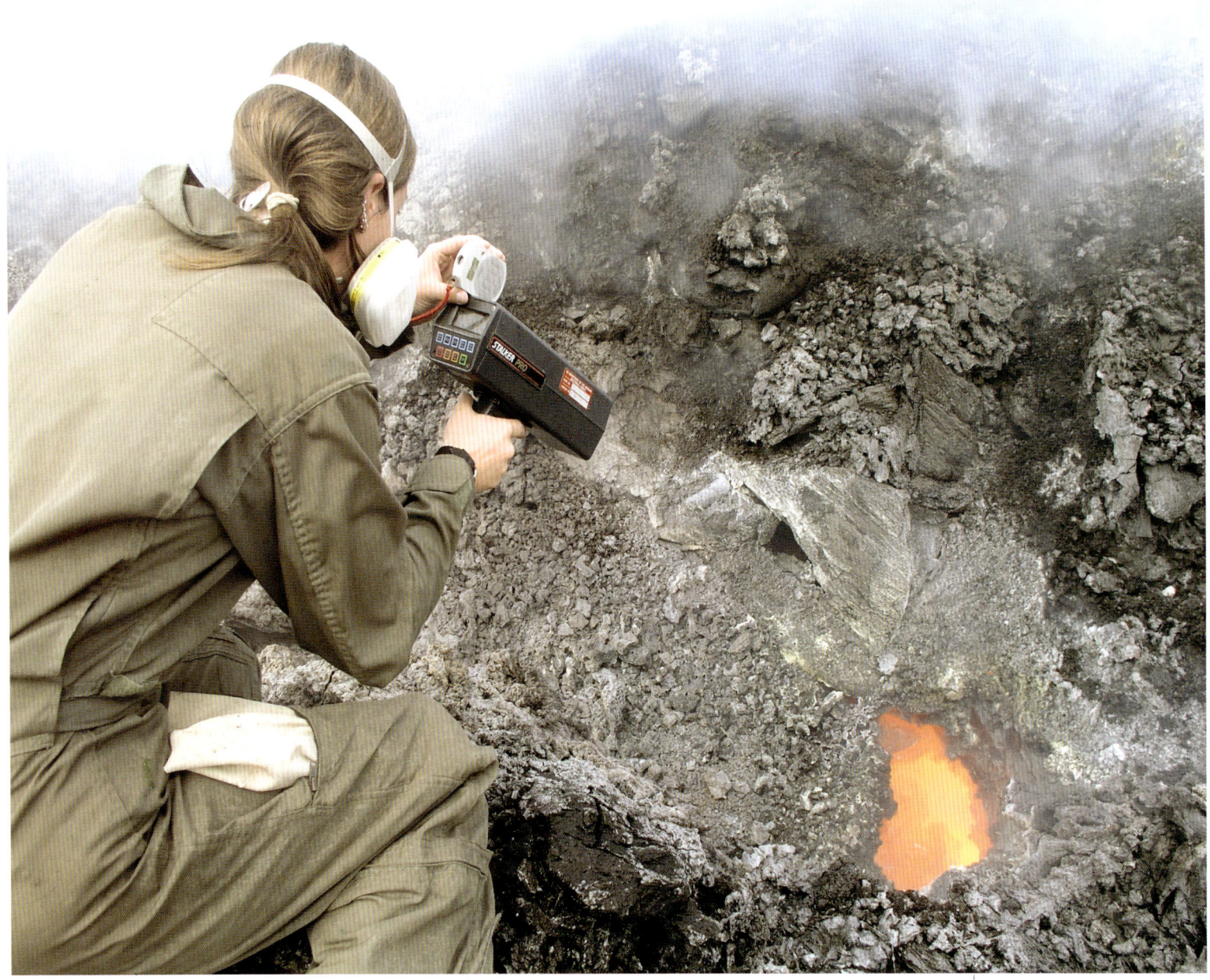

Hot Lava

A researcher uses a radar gun to measure the velocity of lava flowing in an underground lava tube at Kilauea Volcano, Hawaii. Being so close to dangerous and unpredictable heat sources means that you need to protect your body as well as your camera, using fire-retardant clothes and breathing masks to prevent poisoning.
© Don Swanson, US Geological Survey

Remember that Murphy's Law is your constant companion in extreme environments—if something can go wrong, it will. Always carry spares.

Your camera bag should be pre-packed with all your necessary lenses, filters, flash attachments, cable or electronic releases, as well as spare batteries and flash cards, so that you don't have to hunt for them first thing in the morning. Whether you're headed for the summit of Mt. Everest, the burning oil fields of Kuwait, or an early bird-watching walk, you'll be getting up hours before daylight, so have everything prepared the night before.

As you shoot, periodically keep an eye on your viewing screen to check images. You don't have to review every shot (and, if battery life is a concern, you don't want to), but when you encounter new lighting situations it's a good idea to make sure you or your camera is reading it correctly. White balance is one setting that you may need to adjust—auto white balance is usually pretty accurate in today's cameras, but you'll get better results if you adjust the camera's white balance to specific lighting situations, such as direct sunlight, cloudy, tungsten, or fluorescent light. Don't forget to change this setting as lighting conditions alter, using a neutral-density gray card if you have one, or a white surface.

Another reason to check the preview screen is to make sure that your camera is functioning properly. Flash photography is notoriously unreliable with digital cameras, whether it's on-board flash or a hotshoe attachment. For some reason the flash often isn't synched with the "shutter release" or image capture. Even if this checks out in tests, it may not always work, every time. Keep an eye on your flash-captured images.

However, remember that using the viewing screen eats up batteries. Don't use the viewing screen for framing, focusing, composition, and the like, or you'll be out of power before noon. If your camera defaults to preview mode, as many consumer digital cameras do, drill down into the menu system and turn it off, then adjust "review" (for screening the shot you've just taken) to the minimum, or off altogether.

When you check the preview screen, bear in mind that the image displayed is not necessarily an accurate representation of the image's color values or light balance. Check the histogram if you have any doubts, to make sure all light values are being represented in the photo. This is very important when you are in either full sunlight or near-darkness, when the preview screen's brightness setting may not render the actual image captured.

Whenever you need to change lenses, keep the time that the camera is open to the elements to an absolute minimum. Always have the "new" lens in hand (the one you want to attach) before you unscrew the "old" lens. Point the camera down, to prevent dust or moisture from getting into the camera body (and possibly damaging or getting dust on the image-capture chip); you may even want to bury the camera inside your coat if it's windy or dusty. As soon as the lenses are exchanged, screw the mount protector onto the old one and put it inside your camera bag or a pocket, where it's safe and available.

Changing the flash storage card is less dicey; these cards are tough and, aside from the IBM Microdrives, contain no moving parts. Make sure the card you're putting in your camera is clean of images, and file the old full card where you know it will be downloaded at the end of the day. Many photographers use card wallets with sleeves for a number of memory cards, and suggest organizing them in some visual way—clean cards upright and face out, say, and used cards upside down or facing in.

Mud Slogging

Reaching some of the best locations on the Galápagos can involve getting very messy indeed. When the deep sticky mud makes it hard even to walk, protecting your camera gear requires added concentration.

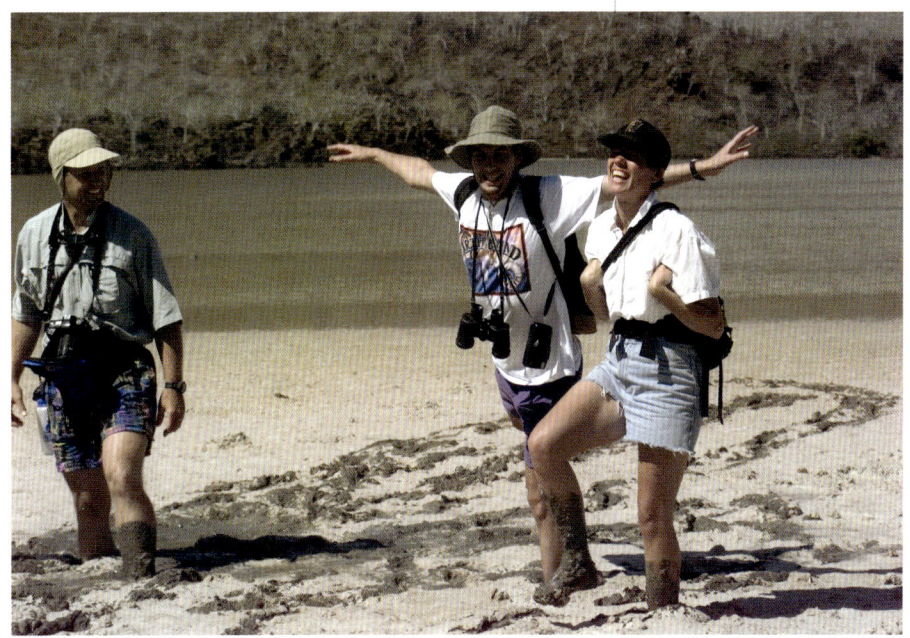

END-OF-DAY ROUTINE

The two critical issues that drive your daily workflow remain the same at the end of the day—power and storage. Now is the time to ensure that your batteries are recharged, and your camera's image files downloaded, organized, and archived. It's also important to get your gear cleaned up, including camera bags and other accessories, as well as the camera and lens. This means keeping your hotel room, campsite, or tent organized. About this, all that I can say is: Good luck.

First, start recharging all your batteries, in both (or all) cameras and flash, and line up your memory cards for processing. If you need to fire up a generator to get power, do so when you are setting up your end-of-day work routine, so that you can charge up and run your computer as you work. This is when a digital photographer finds out that the job is more than full-time.

Another key factor is maintenance. After cleaning your equipment as best you can, watch the images as you edit for dust or other impurities that may show up on the picture. Dust on an imaging chip is most visible in the sky

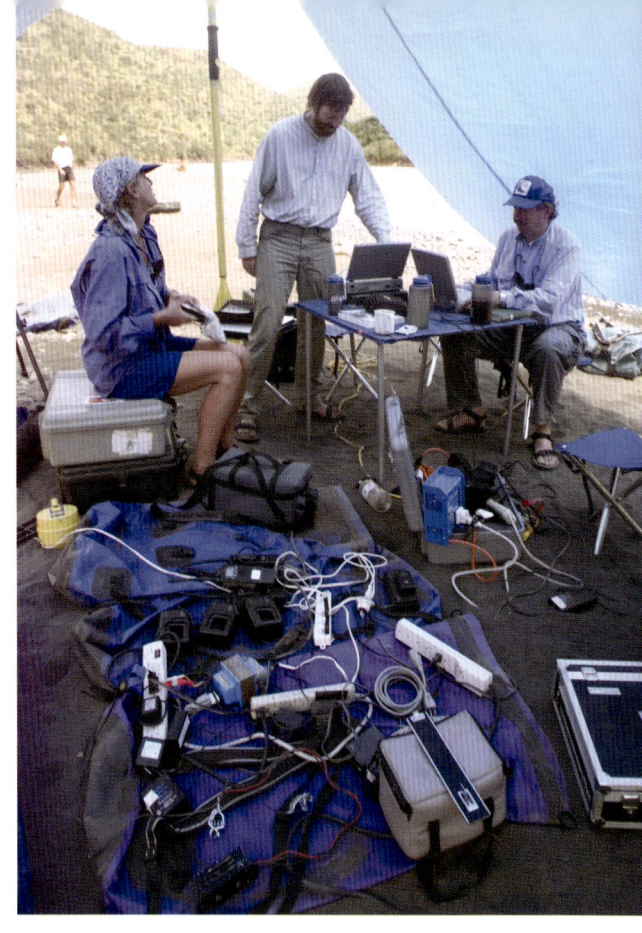

Tents on the Tekeze

Heat, dust, and insects were the major curses for the high-tech workflow on the first descent of Ethiopia's Tekeze River. Erecting a tent fly at the end of each day gave us some shade, but when high winds kicked up we had to pack all the gear away in Pelican cases, or dust got into everything. Batteries were charged from a small Honda generator that we kept well away from camp to minimize the noise.

Technical View

One of the many different ways of looking at images in Breeze Browser is the "Main View," which steps through large images with their histogram displayed to assess exposure and other shooting data. Other options include displaying a sharpened image, flashing highlights, black and white image, and focus point overlay.

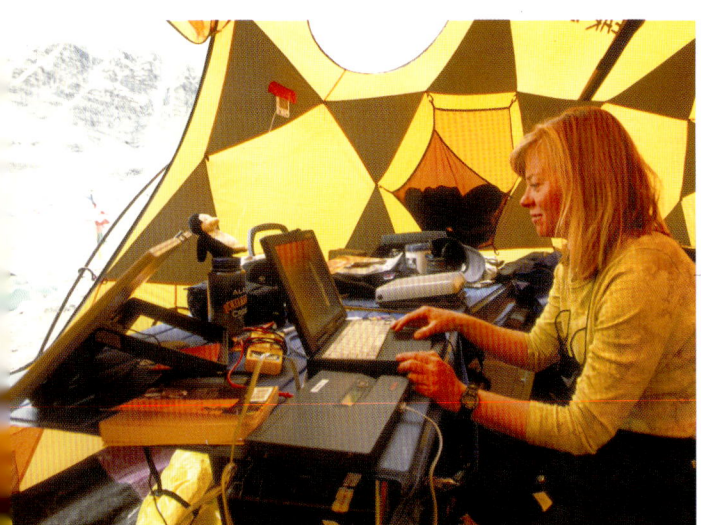

Room with a View

Being able to set up satellite phones and computers and leave them in place means you can work around the clock if necessary to meet deadlines—usually dictated by the rhythm of time zones on the other side of the world. At Everest Base Camp, we used Mountain Hardware's Space Station, which can accommodate 15, or the North Face 2 Meter Dome, which will accommodate eight.

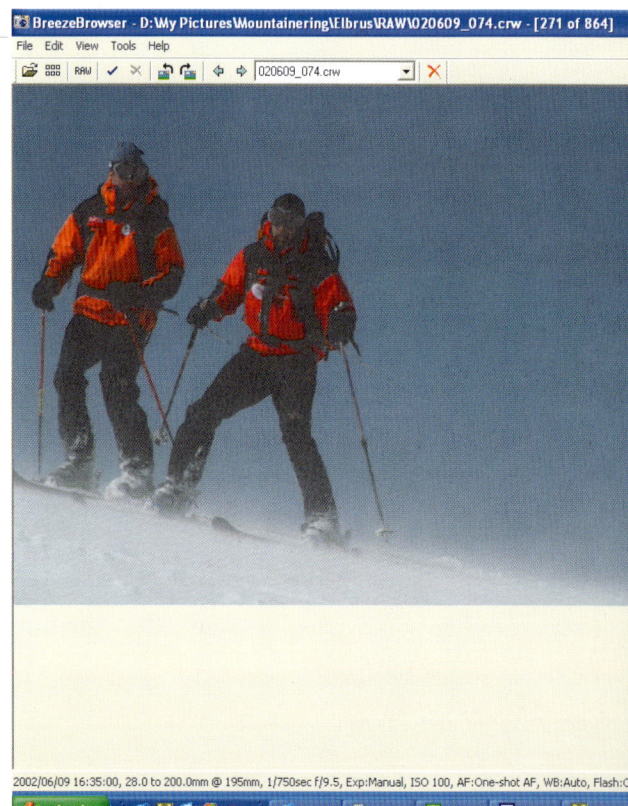

END-OF-DAY ROUTINE

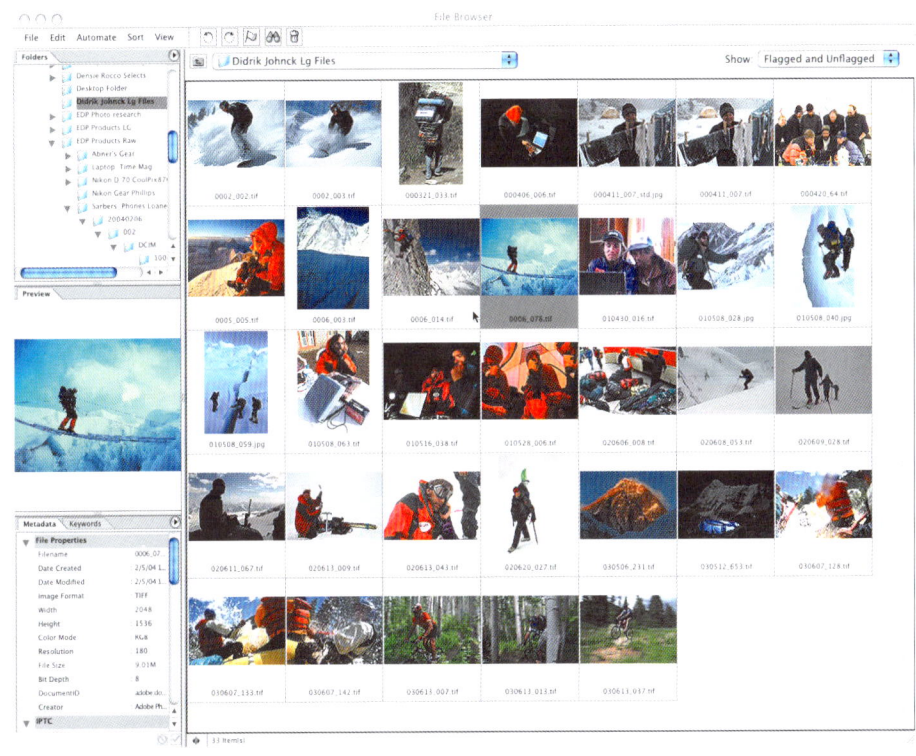

Desktop Light Box

Most third-party image browser programs—such as Photo Mechanic, iView Media Pro, ACDSee, C1 (Capture One), and BreezeBrowser—enable you to batch process and manipulate images, work with the RAW format, create proof pages and contact sheets, and create Web image galleries or slide shows.

same USB device. Or it may be a PCMCIA-compatible card reader that hosts the memory card and turns it into an accessory drive from your computer's interface. This is seen as an "E:" drive (for instance, on a PC), or as a desktop folder (on a Mac). Sony Memory Stick users may appreciate the Sony Vaio computers that come with Memory Stick slots built-in.

You can now "see" the files; in this case literally—there are several photo-management programs that view the files as thumbnails, enabling you to do a quick edit before downloading the images to hard storage. Whether or not you want to do this edit prior to downloading is a matter of personal preference. If, as a slide photographer, you threw away a fair proportion of your shots, then you'll probably do the same here; if you kept all (or nearly all) of your slides, again you'll probably follow old work habits and keep all (or nearly all) the digital images. The important thing is to download them, to archive them in a fashion that allows you to access them efficiently, and to clean your camera's memory cards. Today's shoot is over; prepare for tomorrow's as you go.

So: your cards are cleaned, your images are backed up onto at least one storage device, and your batteries are charging up. If you're on a daily deadline, however (for instance, for news media or a website), then you're not done yet. You still need to make your photo selection, resize, caption, and upload your images.

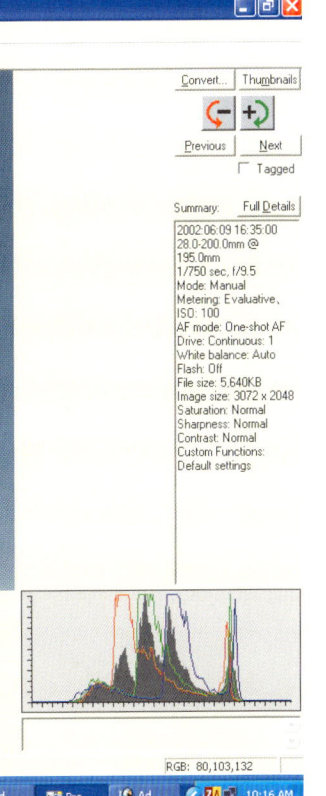

portion of a shot—you won't see it on your preview screen or in thumbnails; it only shows up on the larger views (or prints). This means that checking the sensor for spots is something that you should do at the end of the day, when reviewing your images.

Downloading Images

There are usually two ways of getting images off a digital camera. One is by the dedicated cable (usually USB) that comes with the camera. This allows you to plug your camera into your laptop so that you can access the installed memory card from the computer.

The other method is to take the memory card out of the camera and load it into the computer through a card-reader device. This can include a dedicated flash card reader, such as those from Belkin or Microtek that read several different types of memory cards through the

PREPARING THE DAILY DISPATCH

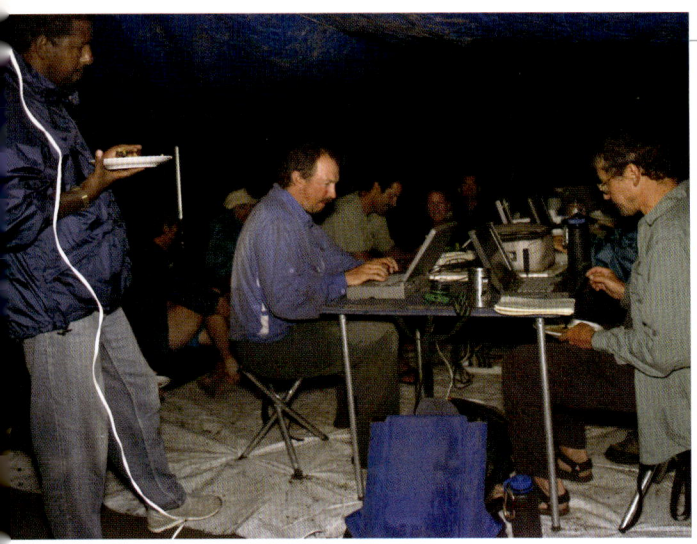

Homework

After a day's rafting there were still many hours of writing and image editing ahead. We typically used headlamps to work at night, but if the generator was running we used a fluorescent light, though a dense cloud of insects usually negated this advantage.

Teahouse Tech Team

"After downloading the digital images from the day's shooting, I shared them with one of the porters. Although the porter could not speak one word of English, and my Nepali was no better, he thoroughly enjoyed seeing all the pictures of that day." © Didrik Johnck

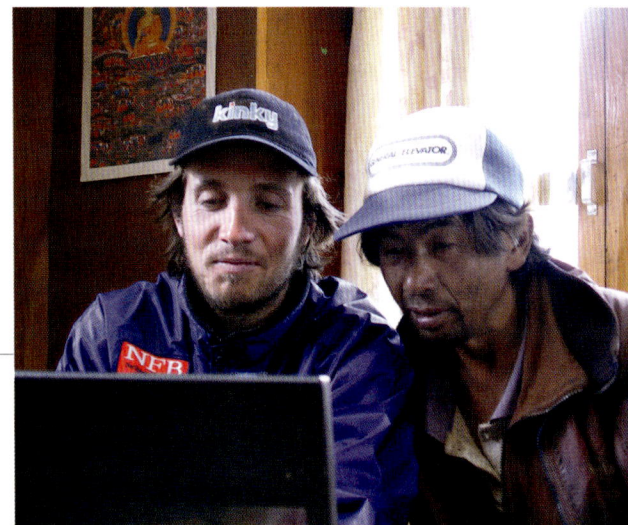

We'll leave it to other works to describe how to make the best of your images through Photoshop techniques, such as by using levels, color management, and unsharp mask. At the very least you should be familiar with these controls, and try to send your producer the best images you can. However, for Web assignments in particular, the standards of quality are muted: displaying an image at 72 dpi that's 280 pixels wide doesn't require the same attention to detail as preparing a 300 dpi image for a double-page in a four-color magazine. On a tight time budget with daily media requirements, recognize that you may only have so much time for image enhancement.

Since today's cameras take multi-megapixel images of sizes of 2560x1920 pixels and beyond, reducing this image to the size requirements of your assignment should be an automated process. For Slate.com's online travel series *Well-Traveled* (which helped earn its publisher a National Magazine Award), the specs were for images of 640x480 pixels, high-quality JPEG. Final published size was only 375x250, further reducing the scale, about 15 percent of the original size. To fulfill requirements such as this, you can build a macro or series of automated commands in Photoshop called an "action" or "droplet" that will go through a series of steps to convert your full-size image into a final JPEG for transmission. Be attentive to this process, and check the results frequently until you're confident it's working well.

One essential step in this automated (or manual and repetitive) process is to give the resulting image a new name, using a "save as" command rather than a "save." This further ensures that your working image is not accidentally downsized before you are finished with it.

When you have finished with your selection, image enhancement, and resizing, you can apply finishing touches to your daily upload. Finalize the captions—these may be included in the metadata with the image, or appended as a text file that refers to the images by file name (many editorial producers prefer this method, as it more easily allows for copy-editing and fact checking). The edited images are now ready for transferring via FTP.

Capture One Interface

Shooting in RAW image mode has the advantage that you can make adjustments in white balance and exposure at the point of ingesting the images. This can end up being tedious and time-consuming, but powerful programs like Phase One's C1 help the workflow go more smoothly.

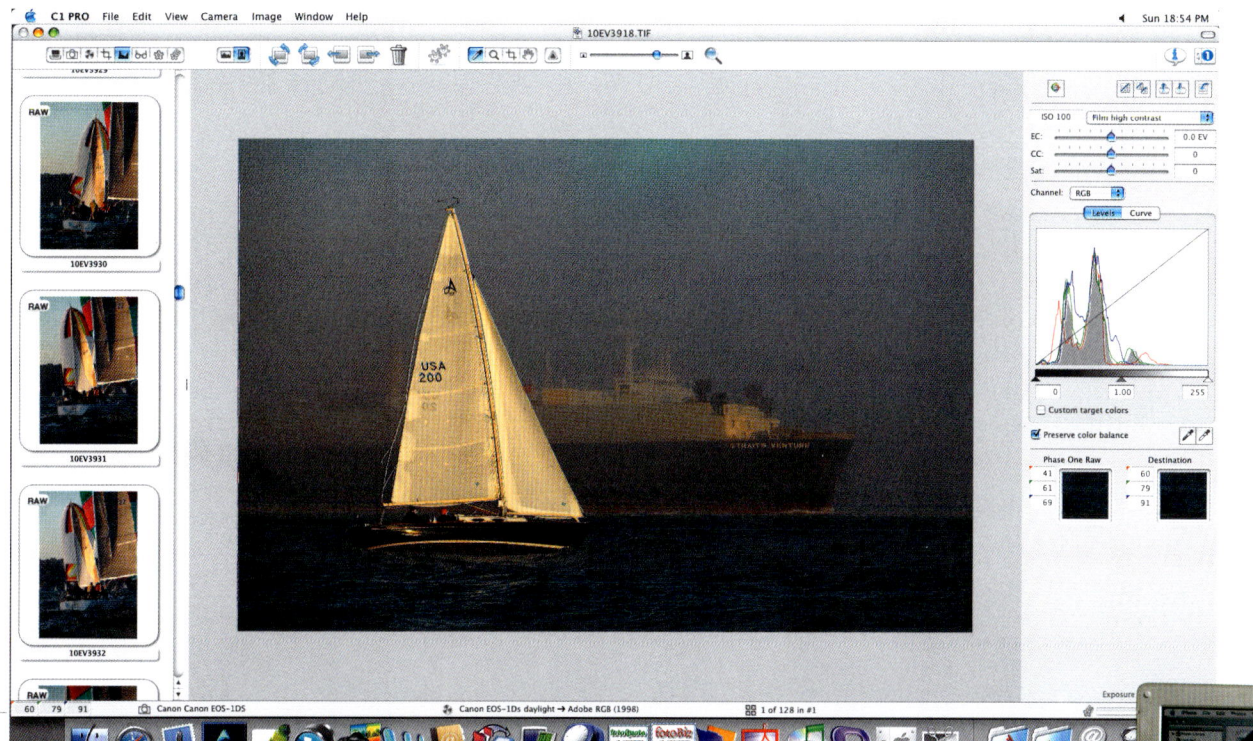

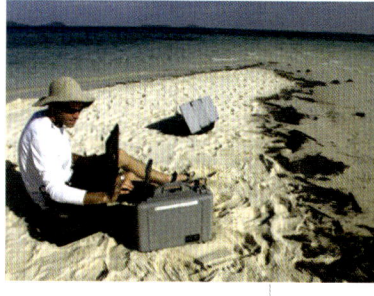

Beach Transmission

Videographer and producer Rob Myers makes the afternoon satellite transmission via a high-speed Inmarsat M4 from a Borneo "beach-front office" on the 2000 Eco-Challenge. © Rob Myers

Archiving

One more essential component of your daily process remains: the task of archiving. With digital photography, gone are the boxes of slides, slide sheets in binders, file drawers of first, seconds, and thirds. Instead you are dealing with file management, organizing your photo capture in daily increments and backing up every day to at least one, if not two, means of long-term storage.

The first storage medium is the computer itself, or a portable media storage device such as the Digital Wallet or the Flashtrax (*see page 44*). This should contain all of your RAW files or the equivalent original source images in full JPEG or TIFF format. But as these fixed storage devices fill up, it becomes important to create a second portable storage medium. Writeable CDs or DVDs are becoming the media of choice for this. Another smart choice is a stand-alone backup hard drive, connected to your computer via USB. These come in multi-gigabyte sizes, and can be an economical way to add storage space to your computer with fairly little hassle.

Burn your source images to these disks as early as possible in your daily workflow, to reduce the chance of losing a day's worth of work due to a power surge, computer crash, or "operator error." Many pros use the photo-management program Photo Mechanic; it makes all of these archiving steps easy, even allowing simultaneous writing to two different media—a computer hard-drive as well as a remote USB hard drive or a CD burner.

Another step that should be integrated to your workflow comes at the end of the evening cycle: back up your day's submission to storage media as well.

iPhoto on iBook

Apple's introductory image program iPhoto is a useful tool with a wide range of capabilities, from ingesting, organizing, captioning, and editing, to creating Web pages, e-mails, and making prints. Adobe Photoshop Album has comparable capabilities for PC-based digital photographers getting started in the world of workflow.

TROUBLESHOOTING

As you work, you will doubtless develop your own workflow solutions. The important thing is to be systematic and efficient, and leave nothing to chance. If there's an opening for things to go wrong, they will. Knowing how to fix things that might go wrong is valuable, but having the open-mindedness to improvise and figure out how to mend them once they do go awry is more valuable still.

Flash Cards Don't Work

The flash cards in your camera sometimes won't store an image, and it may take you some time to find this out. Check the review screen or image count regularly to make sure your card is filling up, and if it's not, find out why. Chances are the card is simply not seated firmly in the card slot. Take it out and replace it, pressing down firmly to make sure it's snug. If it still doesn't work, replace the card with a fresh one—it's rare, but possible, that flash cards simply stop working. That's why you bring spares.

Spots on Image

The most delicate part of the digital camera is the image sensor—the CMOS or CCD chip that receives the light through the lens and converts it into a series of digital signals. Unlike film, which presents a new image surface with every picture taken, the image sensor remains the same for every photograph. This means that when you change lenses, the image sensor is exposed to the elements. Dust is attracted to these chips, especially the CCD, and even the minutest particle can add a smudge or spot to your image.

As noted earlier, dust on an imaging chip is most visible in the sky portion of a shot, and only shows up at large resolution (or, more irritatingly, on stitched panoramas, where it can appear 18–24 times in a 360-degree view!). If you find a spot and you must fix it in the field, do so carefully. You need to lock up the camera's mirror screen and blow the delicate sensor's surface with dry compressed air, or gently daub it with a special anti-static brush, made for this purpose. This is a touchy operation, because the sensor is extremely sensitive.

If it can't be cleaned (grease from smoky fires is almost impossible to remove), you'll have to send it to the manufacturer for professional cleaning and, possibly, purchase a new one. Use the Clone tool in Photoshop to clean up the spot where it's evident, and hope you can get through the assignment without further damage.

Computer Can't Read Data

This problem can bring your project to a halt—and there are any number of reasons why it happens. The chances are good that it's not a permanent problem, however.

First, if the computer can't read a flash card, perhaps the card reader you're using—a USB or PCMCIA connection—could be bad. Try another computer to see if the

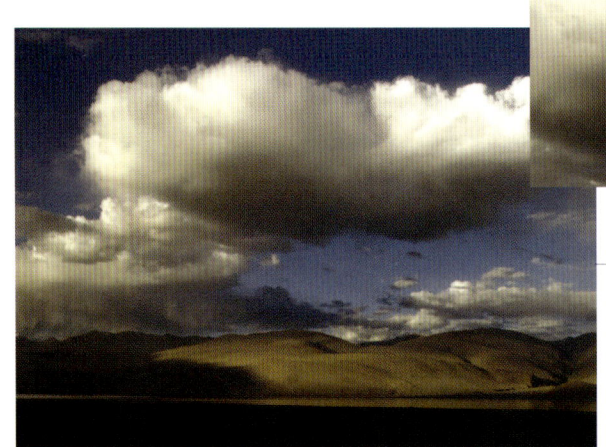

Dust Flaw

Cleaning a dirty CCD is not always possible or successful in the field. Images can often show spots that are most apparent and annoying in lighter-colored areas like snow or sky (as in the cloud in the smaller image). A few minutes with the Healing Brush tool in Photoshop CS can remove dust and other glaring imperfections.

Defragmenting

Regular maintenance on computer hard drives is advisable. Defragmenting is the process that reassembles files and data into contiguous areas, thus speeding up disk access. It should be performed every few months in most cases, and more often with heavy use.

card reader works on that one. If it does, your USB port may be bad; if it doesn't, the card reader is bad.

If you've followed the rule of redundancy, you have another means of reading flash cards. If the card reader is bad, leave the flash memory in the camera and get out the dedicated cable that came with your DSLR to connect directly to the computer; this should allow you to read the images directly from the camera to your computer. If it is a bad USB port, the cable won't do you any good; see if you can borrow another computer to download the images from the card, burn them to a CD, and upload them from the CD on your own computer.

Photoshop or other software may become corrupted; having all your key programs on installation CDs should be an essential part of your planning.

The worst-case scenario is of course that your computer has a hard-drive failure. This can (and does) happen on extreme assignments, and it's demoralizing at the very least. One cause may be that at altitude the hard drive can rupture (as the atmospheric pressure is substantially lower than the hard drive's). Other problems, including shipping abuse, can damage computers and prevent their use. The only real solution is to have a back-up computer and hope it doesn't suffer the same fate.

Computer is Sluggish or Crashes

Any computer's RAM can become filled up with temporary files, and the likelihood of this will increase the longer an editing session goes on. If you've been working on a large number of images, find a stopping place (save everything of course), and reboot. If the problem persists, you should have a utility program on your computer or on CD, such as DiskWarrior (for Macs) or Norton Utilities (for PCs). These can help you debug your system if files have become corrupted. Another problem is that Adobe

What if I Need to Fix Something?

Hard drives can become wobbly, batteries slip out of their docks, port connectors become loose, and any number of other mechanical breakdowns can occur. Having a small computer tool-kit—complete with miniature flathead and Phillips screwdrivers, replacement nuts, etc.—will always come in handy.

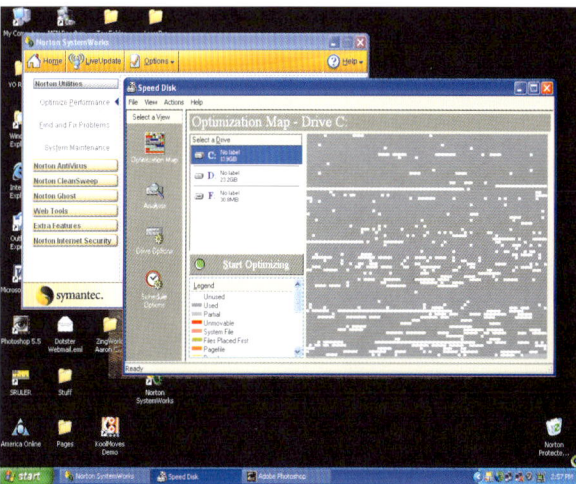

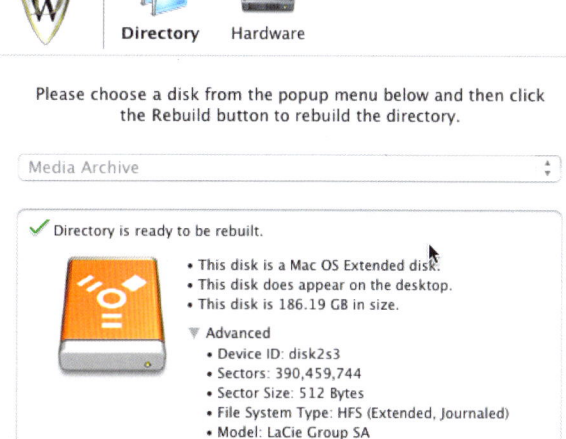

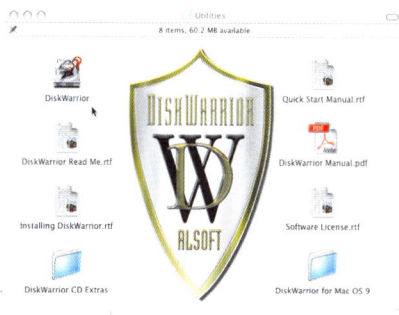

DiskWarrior

The highly regarded DiskWarrior is a Mac OS disk directory repair program, one of a number of similar utilities including Norton (which is cross-platform) that can be used to diagnose and fix damaged hard drives, warn of imminent hard disk failure, and try to recover lost data.

VIRTUAL REALITY

Virtual Reality, Surround Video, 360°s, Full Circle—the names are different, and the technology varies, but the result is the same: a full panoramic image that can be navigated though your Web browser to emulate standing in one place and looking around. 360°s—the term we'll adopt here—would not be possible without digital imagery. Computers have allowed for two things: the seamless stitching of multiple images into a visual continuum, and a means of "playing" or displaying the image in a moving screen controllable by the user.

While many photographers do use film to create their panoramas, the digitization of the image is still crucial to created a "stitched" image, using one or another of the programs created for that purpose. Although the first generation of 360° technology came from Apple's Quick Time team—Quick Time Virtual Reality (QTVR)—many other low-cost, yet effective programs have appeared recently to bring this feature within the reach of most people.

Contrary to expectations, an effective panorama is not the same as a panoramic view, as at a Grand Canyon overlook. Since the camera needs to be oriented on a

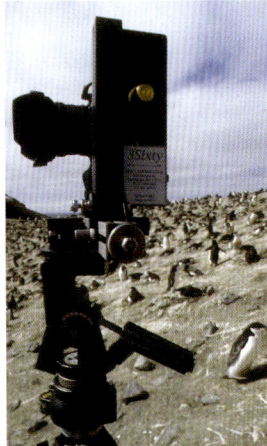

QTVR Tripod Head

Dedicated tripod heads for 360° panoramas include this one from Peace River Studios, which allows for precision rotation of the camera. The camera needs to be set up exactly over the axis of rotation for best results.

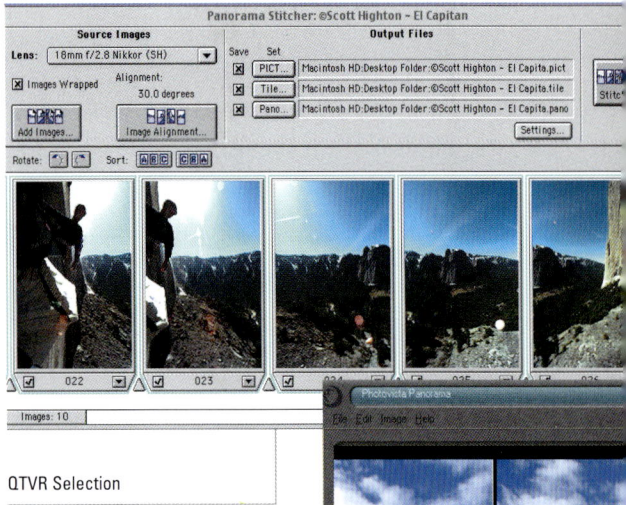

QTVR Selection

The Quick Time Virtual Reality program running on a Mac begins by selecting the image sequence used in building the 360° panorama. Apple's QTVR process was among the first to utilize this interactive Web technology.
© Scott Highton

Flawed Panorama

This panoramic image of Monument Valley in Utah was stitched from 18 separate photographs—each with a dust spot on the image sensor, which appears 18 times in this rough result. Keeping lenses and image sensors clean becomes especially important when doing such photography.
© Christian Kallen

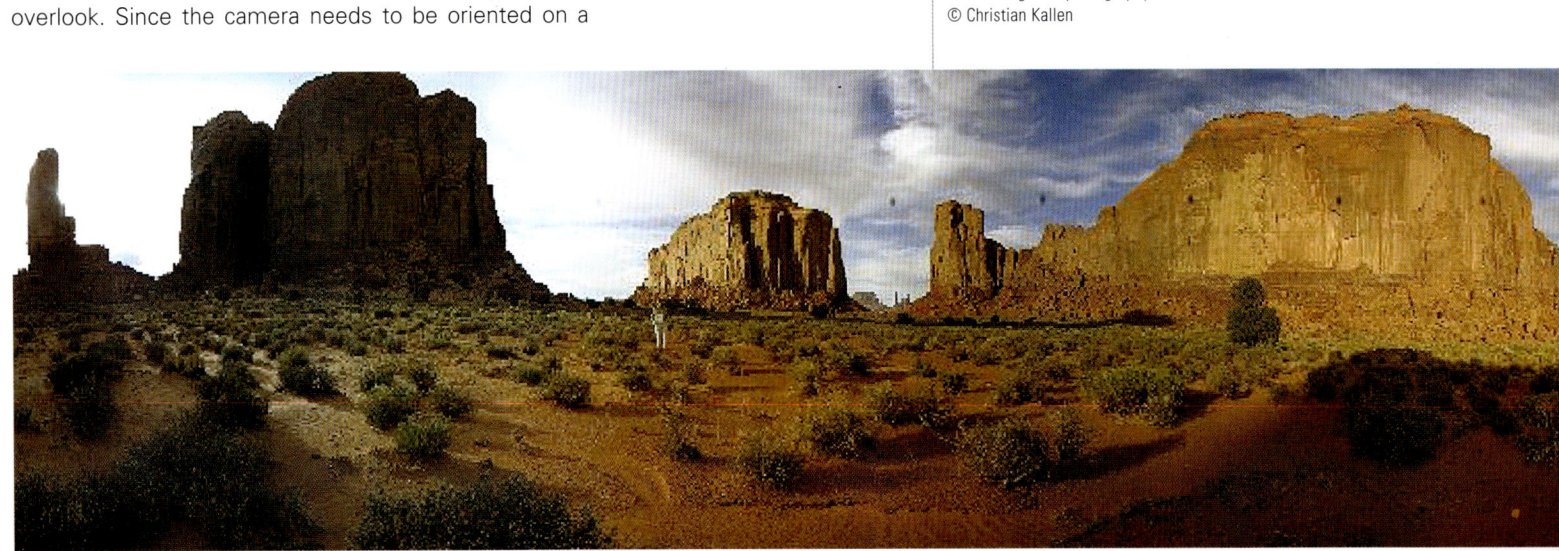

horizontal plane, a "photo op" such as this will show a straight horizon line, with a blue sky above and a jumbled mass of topography below. Far better to place the camera in the midst of varied terrain, where buttes soar and there are near as well as far features in the landscape. Another good location is at a busy street corner or plaza, with plenty of foot traffic or other human activity. On the other hand, you can make a crowded tourist spot appear empty of people, and create an eerie (and unrealistic) moment.

Several tripod mounts are designed for 360° shooting, including the Peace River Studios 3Sixty Camera Mount, and the Kaidan rotator heads, available in different models for different cameras. The camera is attached to the mount, which has geared plates that stop the camera after it rotates a specific number of degrees, ensuring sufficient overlap for the stitching process. The camera should be tripod-mounted, often turned vertically to capture larger Y-axis visuals. The number of images you need for a reliable panorama varies, depending on the field-of-view—a 24mm lens needs about 12 images to work with, while a 35mm needs 18 or even 24.

Great care should be taken to level the camera in all axes, and place the absolute center of the rotation at the lens' field of focus. This helps preserve a constant and picture-perfect point of view throughout the 360° panorama, and avoids distortion.

Interesting 360°s can result from lenses of 17–20mm, shooting 12–14 images in a series, but you may get too much sky or ground in the frame. The 24–35mm range is usually best, with 18 to 24 shots. Anything above 35mm necessitates too many images to create a viable panorama. Remember that zoom lenses easily change length, so turn autofocus off and stay away from anything but the shutter, once the camera is mounted.

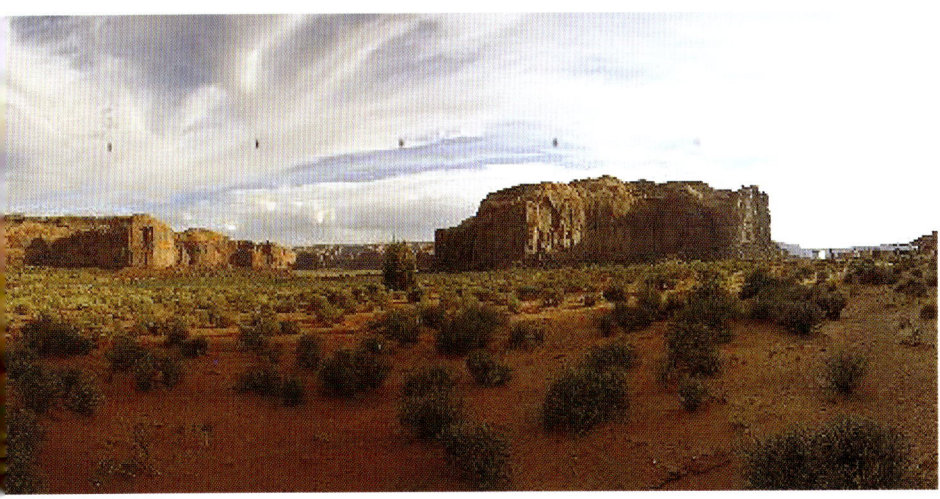

Photovista Selection

The Photovista program is a less-expensive alternative for the PC universe, which allows for similar selection, tweaking, and preview of stitched images in panoramas. Version 3.0 of the program is currently offered by iSee Media. © Christian Kallen

Stitched Result

The result of a Photovista stitching process shows a seamless high-mountain image of the landscape at Big Bend National Park in Texas. Different resolutions of stitched images are selectable, depending on bandwidth and other considerations. © Christian Kallen

DIGITAL VIDEO MULTI-TASKING

In extreme situations it's sometimes necessary to double-task or even multi-task your efforts. For photographers, this can take several forms: field production plus photography, audio capture plus photography, and so on. By far the most common form of multi-tasking is capturing video as well as stills for media use.

Just as digital photography has come into its own for extreme field use in the past few years, so too has digital video. The biggest advantage is that the digital image can be directly imported to a computer via FireWire (also known as iLink or IEEE 1394), enabling loss-free editing and transfer. Today's DV cameras are also affordable, compact, and of near-broadcast quality, but there are caveats. Most consumer-level Mini-DV camcorders utilize a single CCD imaging chip, but for best-quality broadcast, three-chip models (one for each of the primary colors red, green, and blue) are far superior. Then there is price: single-chip Mini-DV cameras start at about $500 on today's market, while professional three-chip cameras begin at around $2,000. As always, you get what you pay for.

A single-chip camera may be adequate for your purposes, and they are smaller, lighter, and cheaper. But converting a single-chip video to streaming media can produce muddy, lifeless video, whereas sharper edges and brighter colors result from the three-chip camcorders. Considering that generating streaming media from extreme adventures is a very common practice, this

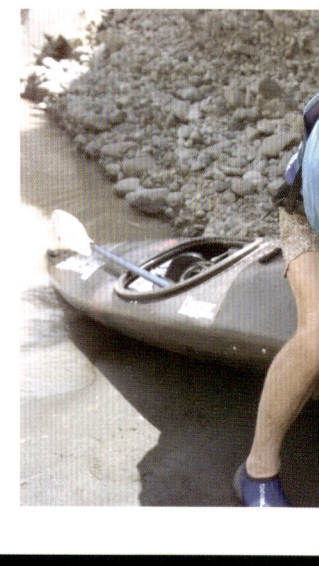

Ambient Light

Video taken in the glow created by lava documents the flow of magma into the ocean, on the south side of Kilauea Volcano, Hawaii. The metadata in the digital image tells us this picture was taken at 05.20 on September 27, 2002 with an Olympus C4040Z, 1 sec, f2.3, ISO 200. © US Geological Survey

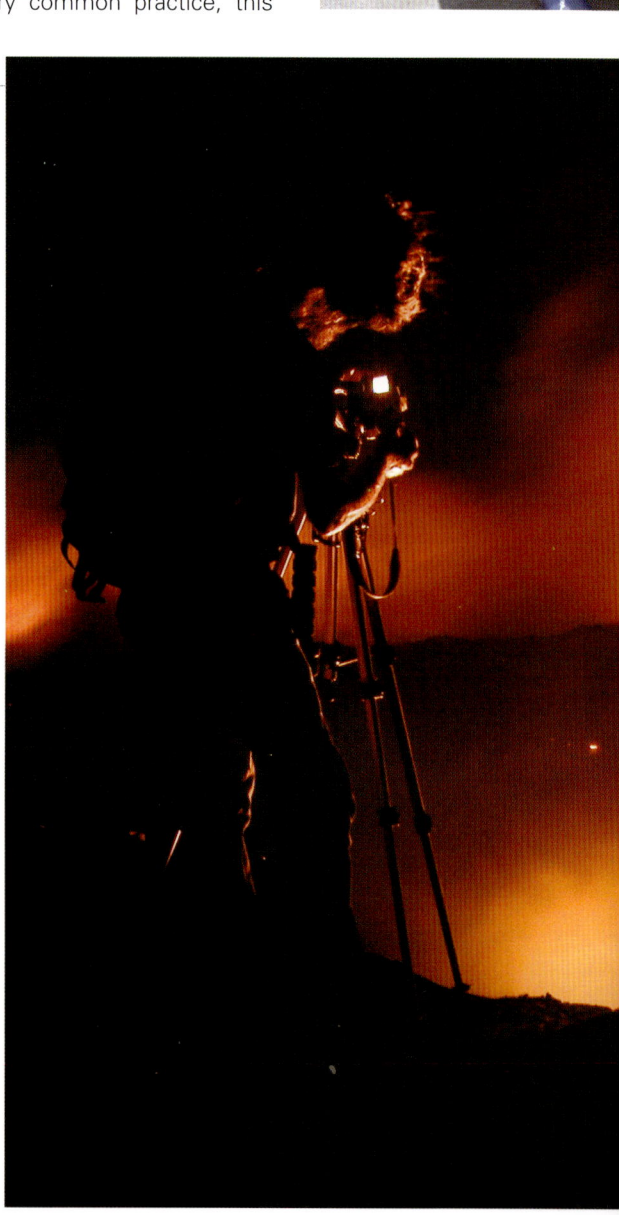

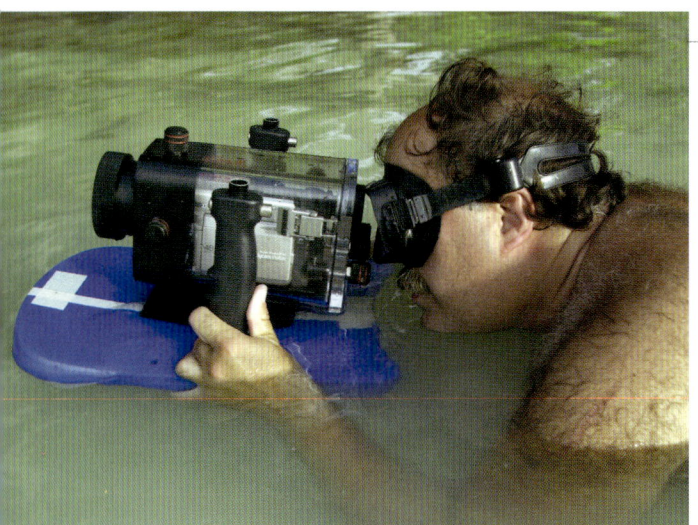

Video Boogie Board

Videographer Franklin Viola maneuvers his camera on a float to capture the action on the surface at Palmyra Atoll for the live Web expedition produced by One World Journeys. Waterproof housing is still advisable in such situations. © Russell Sparkman

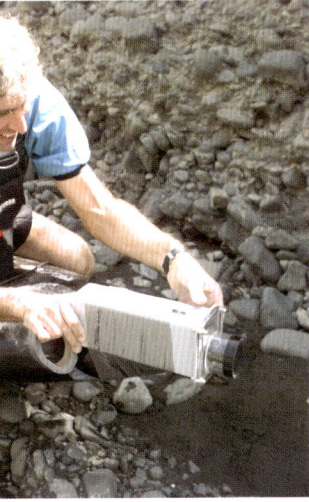

Kayak Cam

Securing a video camera onto the front of a kayak with gaffer tape provides water-level POV for a sequence running the rapids on the first descent of the Tekeze River in Ethiopia.

Shooting the Shooter

Photographer Scott Highton moves in for a close-up of a land iguana on the Galápagos Islands, while he himself is videotaped for a documentary.

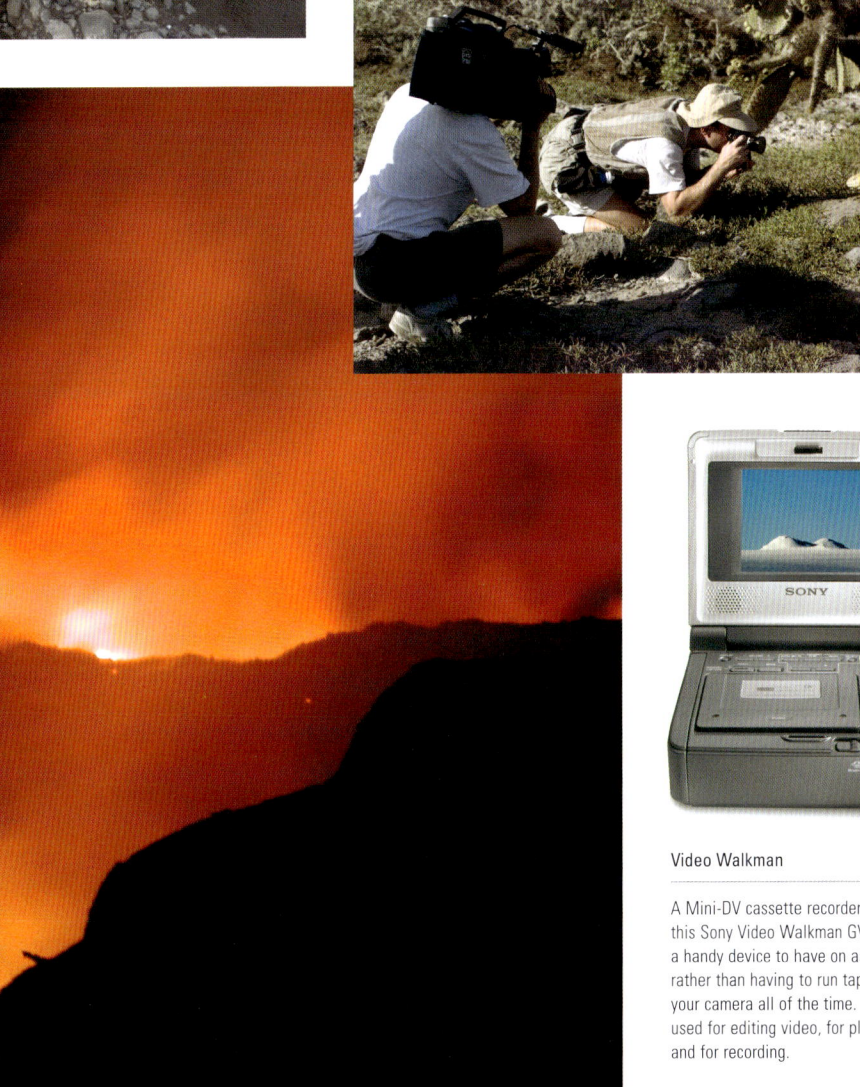

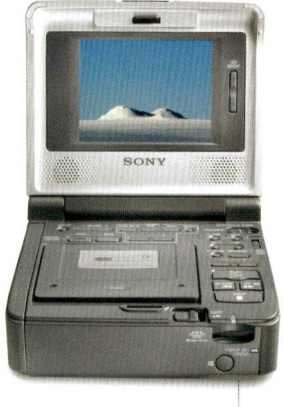

Video Walkman

A Mini-DV cassette recorder such as this Sony Video Walkman GV D1000 is a handy device to have on assignment, rather than having to run tape through your camera all of the time. It can be used for editing video, for playback, and for recording.

difference is not inconsequential. On the other hand, there are times when the extreme nature of the material best conveys the story when it is sub-professional, if not distressed. On a summit push to a remote peak, where the sense of immediacy is paramount, a video from a $500 camcorder—or even a video capture file from a consumer digital camera—may be just what you need.

On the whole, three-chip cameras render color and resolution better. If professional-level video is a requirement, Sony's PD series has long been the industry standard for field use, according to videographer Rob Myers of San Francisco. Their advantages are appealing to the professional—they offer XLR audio jacks (the three-prong connection of professional microphones), and record in the DVCAM format (which records on tape at a different angle from the consumer DV format, writing more information to tape). The current model is the PD-170, which sells for about $3,500. Less expensive are smaller, lighter three-chip models from Sony (the PDX-10, about $2,000), Canon (the GL-2, $2,000), and Panasonic (the DVX-100A, $3,000).

More apt to the multi-tasking photographer is the ability of many of these cameras to take stills as well as video. Many current professional camcorders have the option of switching to "Photo" mode and capturing a progressive-scan still image to its Memory Stick (or other flash media, depending on camera brand). However, the image is often at 72 dpi at 640x480 pixels, adequate for Web use but not for print, though some Mini-DV camcorders (such as the Sony DCR-PC330) promise 3-megapixel images and above. Nonetheless, this is where the field photographer needs to make a choice, between using this feature or simply switching between two cameras, a Mini-DV and a DSLR, for each task.

PHOTO EDITOR—KAREN MULLARKEY

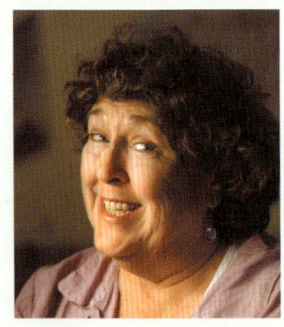

Establishing a healthy relationship with the person who helps select from your images for an assignment is crucial to a successful professional career. Karen Mullarkey has been a photo editor since 1966, when she started at Life *magazine; since then she's worked as director of photography at many major US publications, including* Rolling Stone, Newsweek, New York *magazine, and* Sports Illustrated. *For several years she's also worked with Rick Smolen and David Elliot Cohen on several of their digital projects, including* 24 Hours in Cyberspace *and* America 24-7.

© Don Winslow

Digital photography has done a couple things to the industry, some of which are great. Partly it's enabled photographers right away to see what they've shot, so they know right away if they have it or not. So I tend to get fewer images, which I think is good. The other side is that I find people tend to center-focus everything—they tend to focus on what's in the middle, which I find hugely boring. And it kind of cuts down on the double-truck, because the gutter goes through the center, right? In its own way, digital is sort of the lazy man's way.

There are certainly advantages to digital. For instance, Brian Lanker did a whole series on birds of prey, because he understands that the thing you get with digital is the detail. That can be really spectacular—I can look at the back of a bird he's done, say, and know that I'm seeing something in the feathers that I wouldn't have seen in

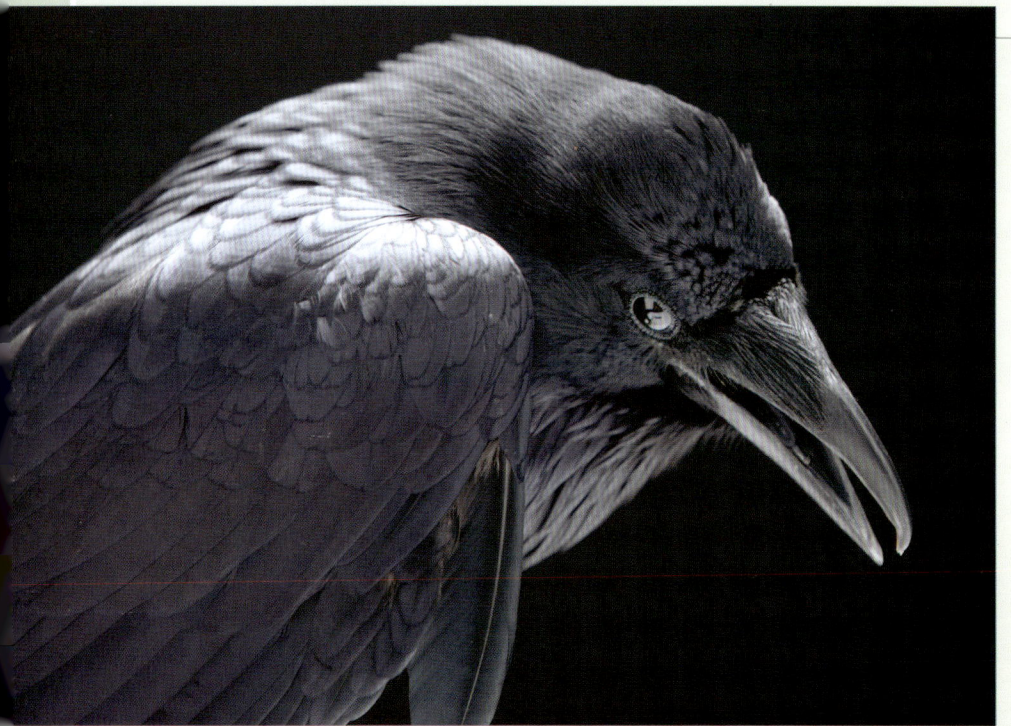

American Crow

This studio shot of a common American crow (*Corvus brachyrhynchos*) shows detail in feathers, down, and bill that communicates a sense of personality. Digital photography of high enough resolution is able to capture such deep detail, and digital print technology can make huge posters of the image.
© Brian Lanker

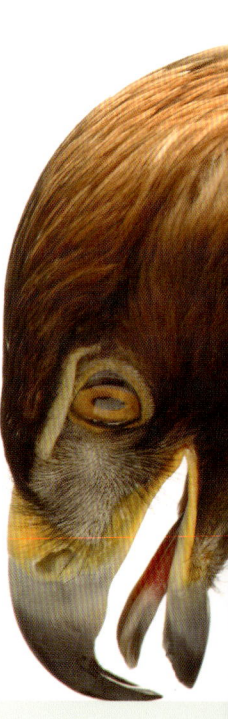

Golden Eagle

Intimate portraits of birds of prey are possible in rehabilitation centers when a portable studio set and backdrop can be utilized. © Brian Lanker

film, unless you'd spent a huge amount of money in the separations. On the other hand, it's still very tough to do a good digital picture in low light, unless you've got a "real camera"—you need a camera that has at least five megapixels or more, because you're just not going to pick up the image unless you're bringing light in to help.

Photographers who come out of the newspaper world know how to work a situation. By "work it," take someone like Bill Luster in Kentucky—he's a great photographer, been with the Louisville paper (*Courier-Journal*) forever... He works the situation four ways, he doesn't just shoot straight on: he goes to the left, he goes to the right, he goes under, he goes over. Shooting multiple points of view, and thinking how the story might evolve to be more interesting. I'm finding that a lot of photographers who are starting out with digital don't work it as much. It breeds a certain visual laziness, because digital is deceptively easy.

I think the greatest drawback with digital is that it makes you think you got the shot before you do. Part of that is that you can preview the image—that's a good thing and a bad thing. I think with people who are just starting out, they'll see the first image and that'll be enough. In the hands of real pros, it drives them to continue. I think that even people who are learning by photographing their kids should shoot a story. That's how they'll wind up getting the best picture.

There are certain relationships that you have to preserve. When you make an assignment, you tell the photographer, "I edit, you shoot." When film first comes in, your loyalty is to the photographer. Once you've picked the best pictures they have to offer, now the loyalty is to the project—it changes, and then it's a question of the best photograph wins. I pick the final photographs without knowing who took them. In the end the responsibility is to the publication.

Ceres—Northern Harrier

This graceful raptor of the open country was injured as a chick when its nest was damaged by a haying machine. Today she serves to help educate visitors to the Cascasdes Raptor Center. © Brian Lanker

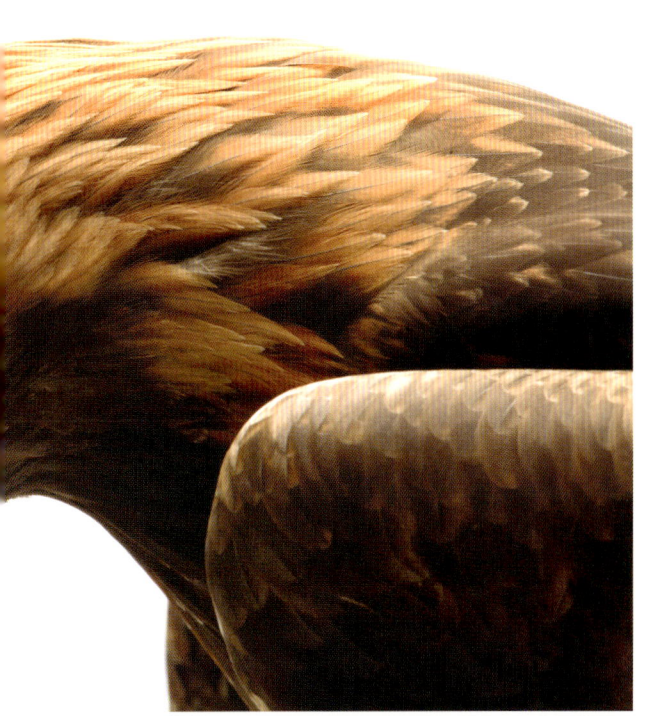

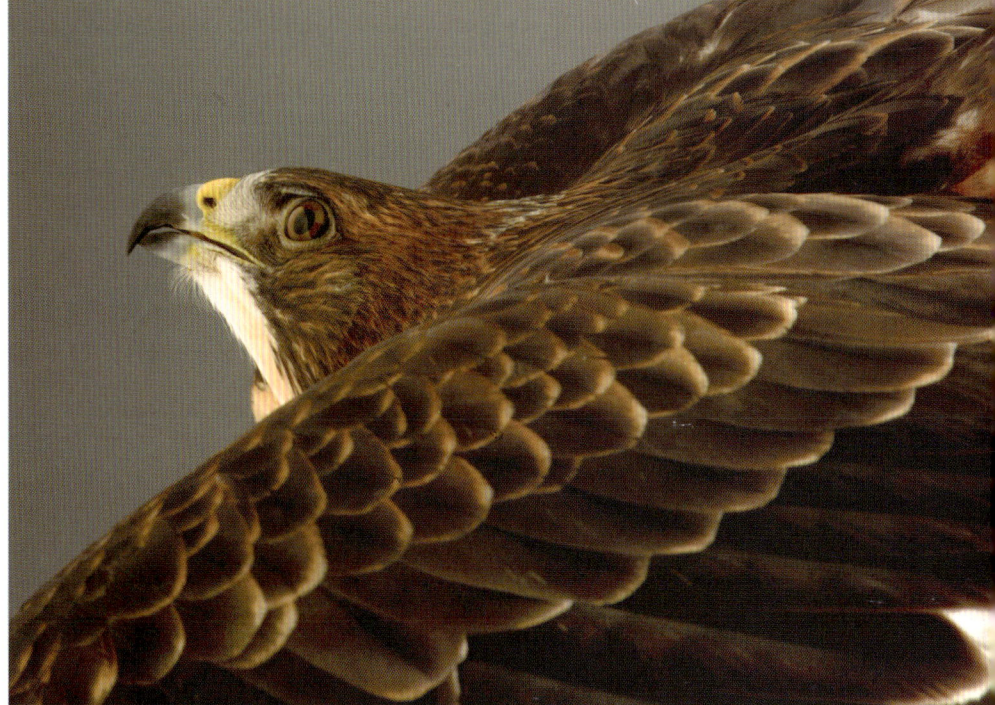

TERRAQUEST AND MUNGO PARK

When the World Wide Web began to grow in importance, one of the first—if not the first—extreme expedition documented was *Virtual Antarctica*. First proposed by Richard Bangs, partner in Mountain Travel-Sobek, it had a small team assembled under the name "TerraQuest" to create a series of so-called virtual expeditions, including this author (Jonathan Chester) as producer, writer, and photographer, Christian Kallen as co-producer and writer, and Brad Johnson as designer.

The initial project was launched in November 1995 with a large website of resource material on the history, geography, and biology of the far south to serve as background. The "live" component of the expedition was the new, compelling feature in 1995, and I was excited by doing daily reporting from this spectacular location.

Since the Antarctic Peninsula is right on the edge of the coverage of the Inmarsat satellite system, the main technical challenge was to transmit the multitude of stories and images back to the Web host for live presentation. This meant that we had to use a cumbersome suitcase-sized Inmarsat B Terminal portable system, which gave us ISDN-speed transmissions.

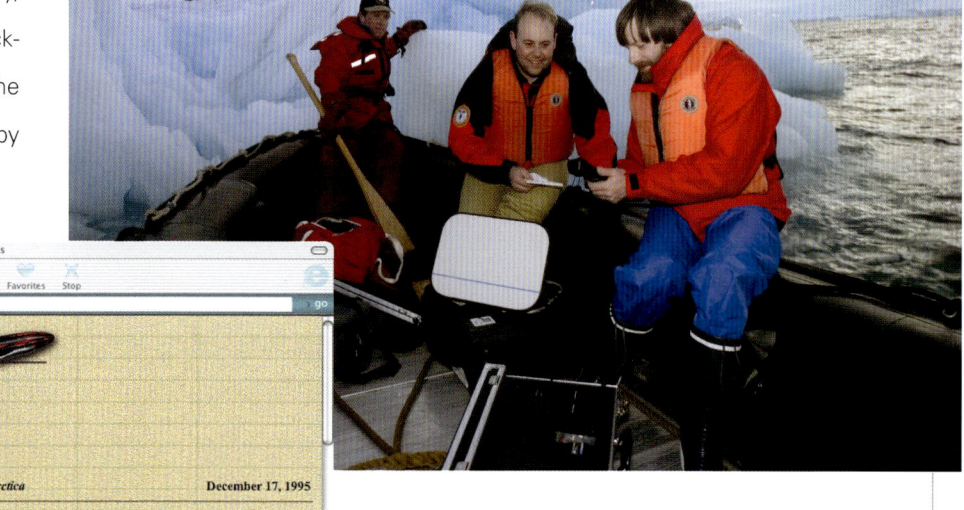

Digital Dispatch

TerraQuest's *Virtual Antarctica* was one of the earliest (1995) "live expeditions" where dispatch text and images were sent back to the Web on a daily basis via satellite. Today, this technology is commonplace. A CD-ROM of the event was also produced.

Floating Upload

Inmarsat communications in Antarctica are at the limit of the technology—the geo-stationary satellites are over the equator, so you have to point the antenna to just above the horizon. On this occasion the TerraQuest field team had to take a Zodiac several miles into the bay to find a place where they could get a signal strong enough to make an M-4 phone call.

Luckily, we had satellite communications specialist Dr. Kevin Twidle, of England's 7E Communications, to install and troubleshoot the system.

Kodak's Digital Science division supplied the DCS 50, 420, and 460 cameras. They were state-of-the-art in 1995, but even the high-end DCS 460 only captured a 2MB file. Shooting for the Web, however, meant that small images were not a big issue; workflow was the real challenge.

Antarctica is a photographer's paradise, so it was easy to find great subject matter to shoot: penguins, whales, seals, and the dramatic mountains that rise out of the sea along the peninsula. We also shot Quick Time Virtual Reality (QTVR) images using a special Peace River tripod head that enabled 16 sequential images to be shot and then stitched together into a 360° panorama.

The *Virtual Antarctica* expedition, still online at www.terra-quest.com, was so highly regarded it is still one of the prime links for people interested in learning about the Antarctic. It was the first winner of the "Best of the Web" InVision Award from *New Media Magazine*.

Much of the same technology, and personnel, was involved in the follow-up *Virtual Galápagos* expedition. This time a boat was chartered to carry technical and journalistic crew through the equatorial islands, and the results were posted live on the Web in May, 1996. Following TerraQuest, Bangs and Kallen were hired by Microsoft to put together a monthly adventure travel magazine online, built around the concept of the virtual expedition. The result was *Mungo Park*, launched in October 1996 with a three-week expedition down Ethiopia's remote Tekeze River. Over the next two years *Mungo Park* evolved to incorporate much of the developing technology and story-telling techniques that have come to define live online coverage, in adventure travel as well as in "real journalism."

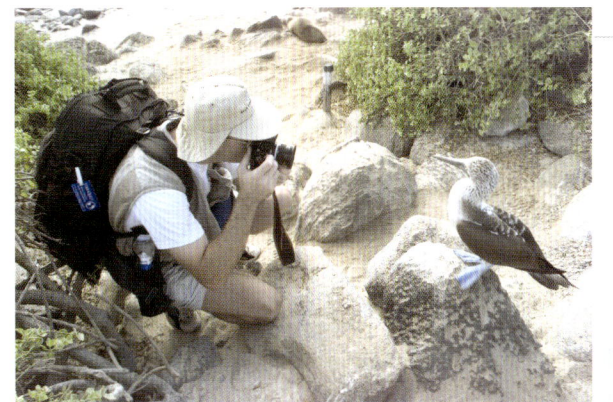

Posing Booby

Scott Highton, one of the photographers on the *Virtual Galápagos* field team, crouches for a portrait of a blue-footed booby, one of three booby species found in the Galápagos. The boobies nest on several islands and are for the most part unafraid of human visitors.

TerraQuest Surfer

The author surfs the *Virtual Galápagos* website as it is updated daily from the ship's work station aboard the *Alta* in the Galápagos. Note the cords securing the computer to the ship's desktop.

Tech Magic

Satellite expert Dr. Kevin Twidle explains the workings of an Inmarsat B terminal to a local on the banks of the Tekeze River. This "high speed" (64KB) terminal was used to beam dispatches each evening back to Microsoft to be posted on Expedia's *Mungo Park* website.

The Bridge

Terraquest's award-winning *Virtual Antarctica* incorporated stylish design elements with in-depth resources covering history, ecology, and wildlife, plus a full guide book and log of the expedition's cruise through the Antarctic Peninsula. A decade after the event the site is still a valuable educational resource for classes and prospective visitors to the far south.

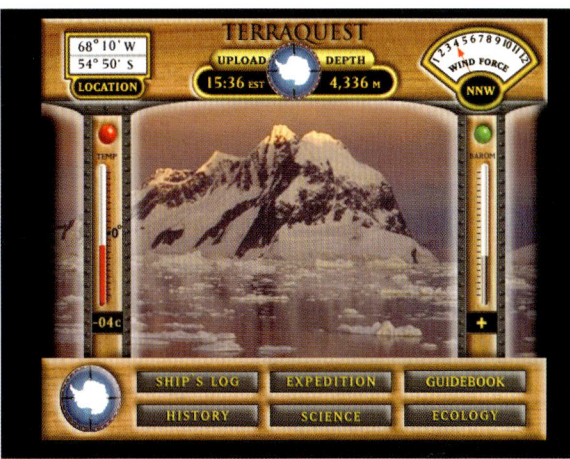

WEB EXPEDITION COVERAGE—QUOKKA

Three of the world's top expedition climbers—the late Alex Lowe, Mark Synnott, and Jared Ogden—were poised on the headwall of the unclimbed face of Great Trango Tower, 6,000 feet (1,800m) above the edge of the Baltoro Glacier in Pakistan. As the American team raced a competing Russian team to the summit, every pitch of their first ascent was documented in daily dispatches from the climbing team by Quokka Sports. The drama was intense, and the coverage global, thanks to the World Wide Web.

A pioneering online sports-content company, Quokka began by covering extreme ocean yacht races. Founders Alan Ramadan and John Bertrand (skipper of the yacht *Australia II* that won the America's Cup in 1983) created a business trying to deliver in near-real time the adventure of many extreme sports. From the Around Alone global circumnavigation yacht race in the heady days of the dot-com boom, they expanded rapidly into other adventure sports, including mountaineering, CART motor car racing, and eventually the Sydney 2000 Olympics. Then in 2001 they went the way of almost all the rest of the Web startups and imploded. Quokka Sports was a great idea looking for a sustainable business model, but creatively and technically it was years ahead of its time.

In its meteoric existence, Quokka produced some of the most ground-breaking coverage of extreme sports, including expeditions to the 26,240-foot (7,950-m) Hidden Peak in China; blind mountaineer Erik Weihenmayer's attempt on Ama Dablam; and an expedition to Everest. But it was the climb on Great Trango Tower in summer 1999 that brought together the North Face's top climbing athletes to challenge an unclimbed alpine big wall, plus a large budget to develop cutting-edge immersive live content.

As producer on this team, I sent out a two-person crew to base camp, including field producer Greg Thomas to handle the digital material that was generated by the climbers. On the wall the climbers themselves carried Sony video cameras and a small Windows CE palmtop. The images and frame grabs were transferred by a memory stick to the palmtop and, once the daily journal had been written, the stories and images were transmitted back to base camp via a 2.4GB wireless modem. The whole arrangement was powered by lithium Expedition Batteries.

At base camp this material, plus additional media generated from the ground, was uploaded to the satellite and so to the production team back in San Francisco. It was our job to massage this into daily journals and image galleries that told the story of the climb.

As the team neared the top of the route, the weather closed in and the climbing got very dicey. It was a heart-stopping final few days. Before this climax we created a feature on the site called "Base Camp Live," where Greg Thomas was able to post directly at will to the site, to keep the world informed of the ascent. He simply sent an e-mail with an attachment to a specific address, where a Perl script parsed the message into a text block and the attachment into a screen image. While this is commonplace today with programs like Contact 3.0, in 1999 the template had to be hand-coded to make it work, and thus the expedition blog was born.

While the images were by necessity only able to be shown at a very low resolution, with many of them starting out as video frame grabs, the strength of the story and the intensive effort, thought, and design that

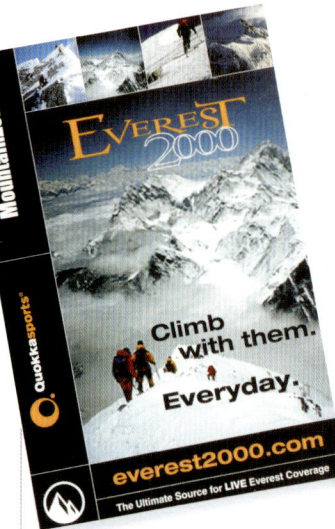

Promo Postcard

Quokka Sports, an innovative but short-lived Web-production company, covered numerous expeditions, including climbs of Mt. Everest, Ama Dablam in Nepal, and Hidden Peak from its China approach. Traditional marketing techniques helped build an audience of fans who, it was hoped, would come back day after day.

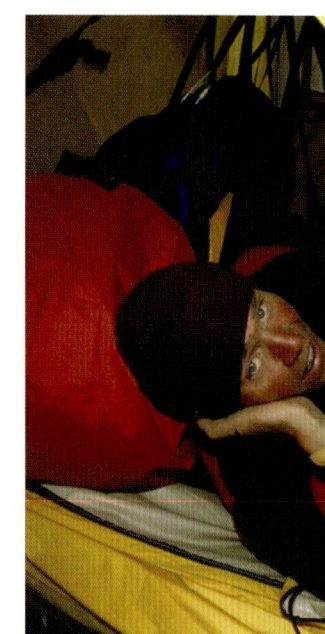

went into their presentation on the website transformed the reports into a compelling story.

With the passing of the many well-funded Web content sites, so went many of the creative efforts. While today's expedition coverage can include bells and whistles, such as interactive maps and Flash introductions, most of the photography and editorial coverage can be rather underwhelming. But there is something to be said for the immediacy of the reports from the ends of the world, and with the availability of low-budget gear (including digital cameras, PDAs, and even satellite phones), no expedition need leave home without its own website.

If you ever dig out the Quokka Great Trango Tower site (which still lurks on the Web, despite Quokka's demise, at http://clients.stamen.com/quokka/trango_tower/frameset_welcome.html), take a few moments to relive Internet and climbing history. This is how expedition reporting used to be, and perhaps will be in the future as well.

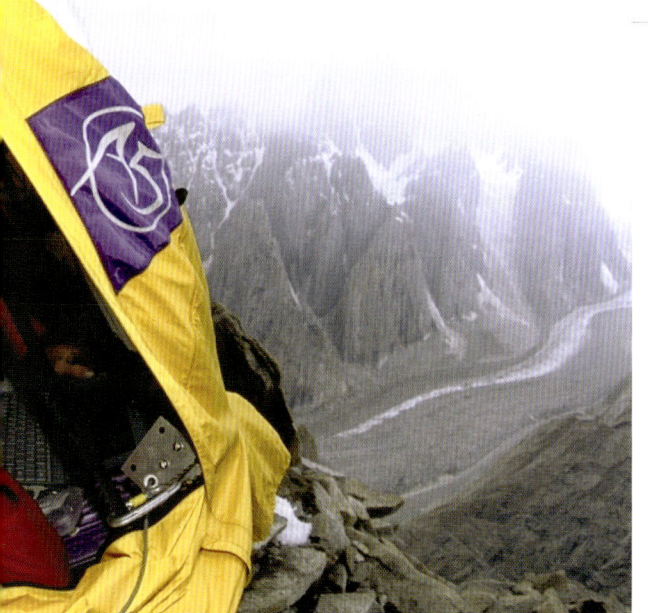

Trango Home

The Great Trango Tower website can still be found online, outliving its development by Quokka Sports. A wealth of media, including audio, video-, and Flash-based modules as well as text and dispatches, illustrate the successful (if problematic) expedition.

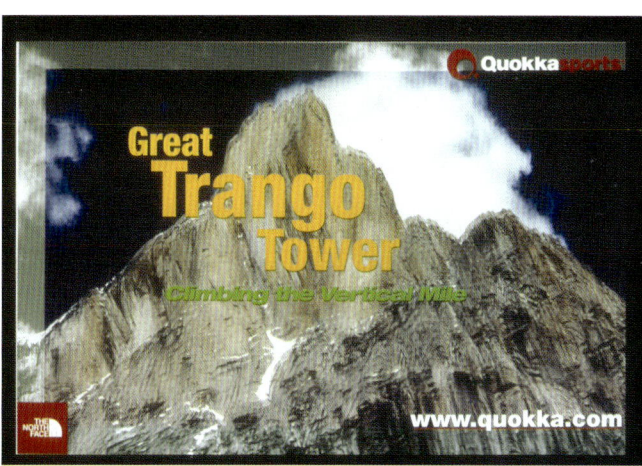

July 31 1999

Climber Alex Lowe hugs Pakistan's liaison officer, Umair Ahmed, as the North Face Climbing Team arrives back at base camp following their successful ascent of Great Trango Tower. © Greg Thomas / Quokka Sports Inc.

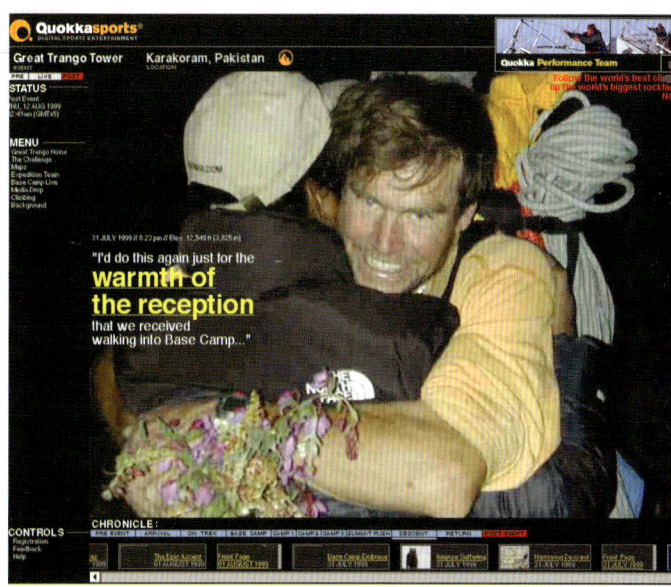

Hanging Habitat

The late Alex Lowe, one of North America's foremost climbers, peers out of the A5 hanging tent on the first ascent of Great Trango Tower in Pakistan's Karakoram Range. The historic ascent by the North Face climbers Mark Synnott, Jared Ogden, and Alex Lowe was covered live by Quokka Sports. © Jared Ogden / Quokka Sports Inc.

Topping Out

Late on the afternoon of July 29, Jared Ogden seen at the West Summit of Great Trango Tower, in a digital image sent shortly thereafter to the website. The success of the team was reported within minutes by the "Base Camp Live" feature on the site, updated by field producer Greg Thomas. A long and dangerous descent lay ahead, keeping the audience in suspense when the team passed out of media contact.

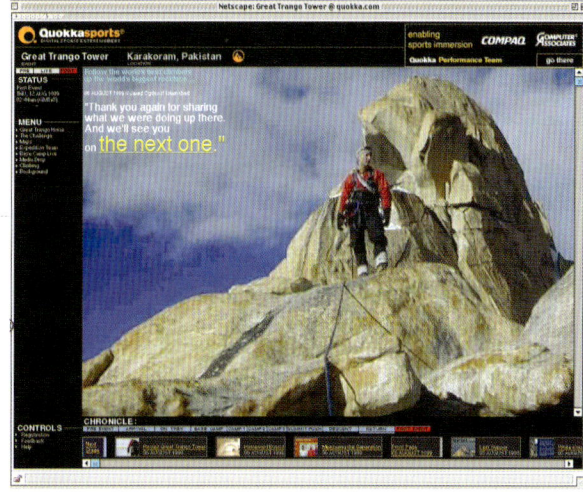

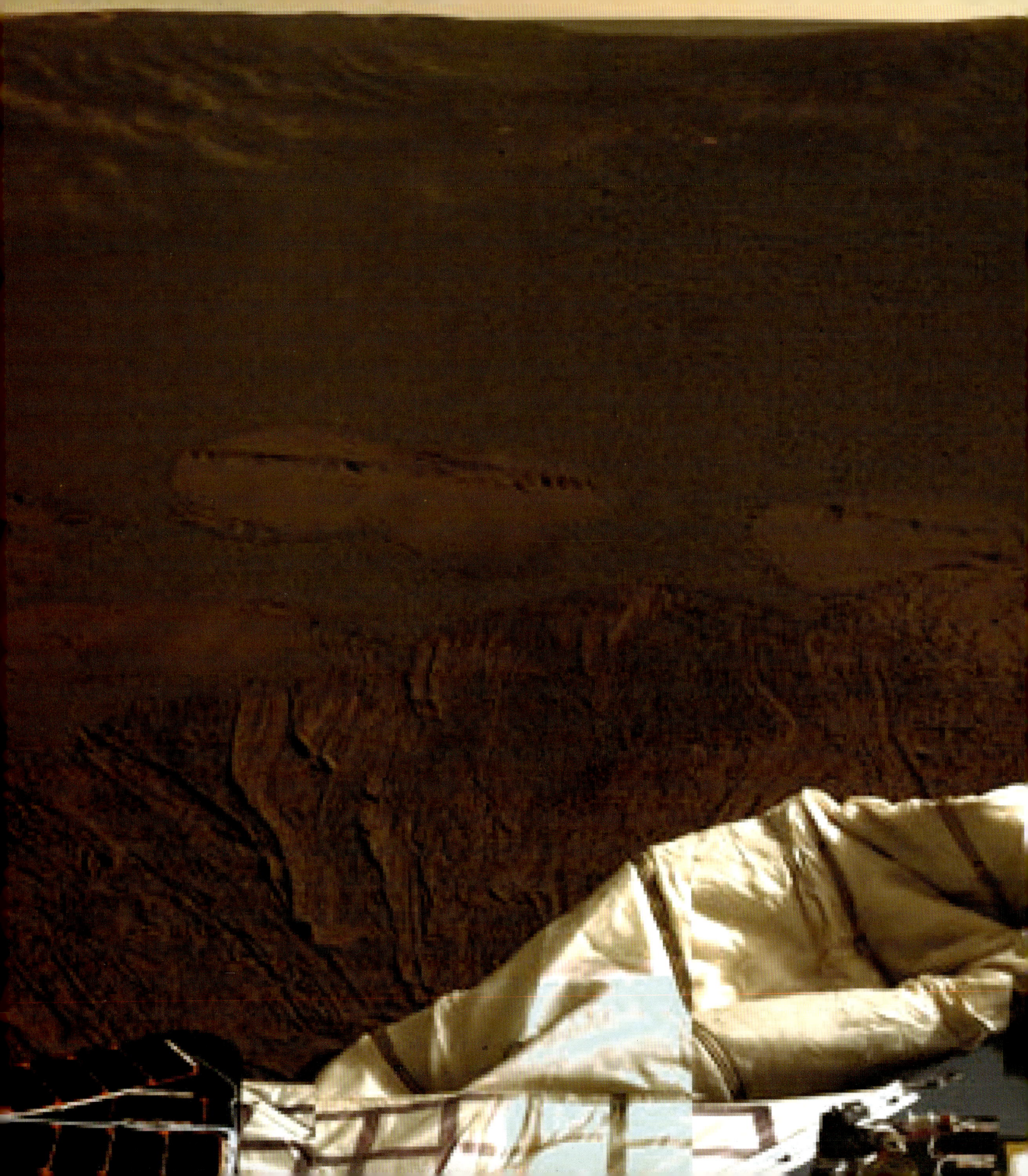

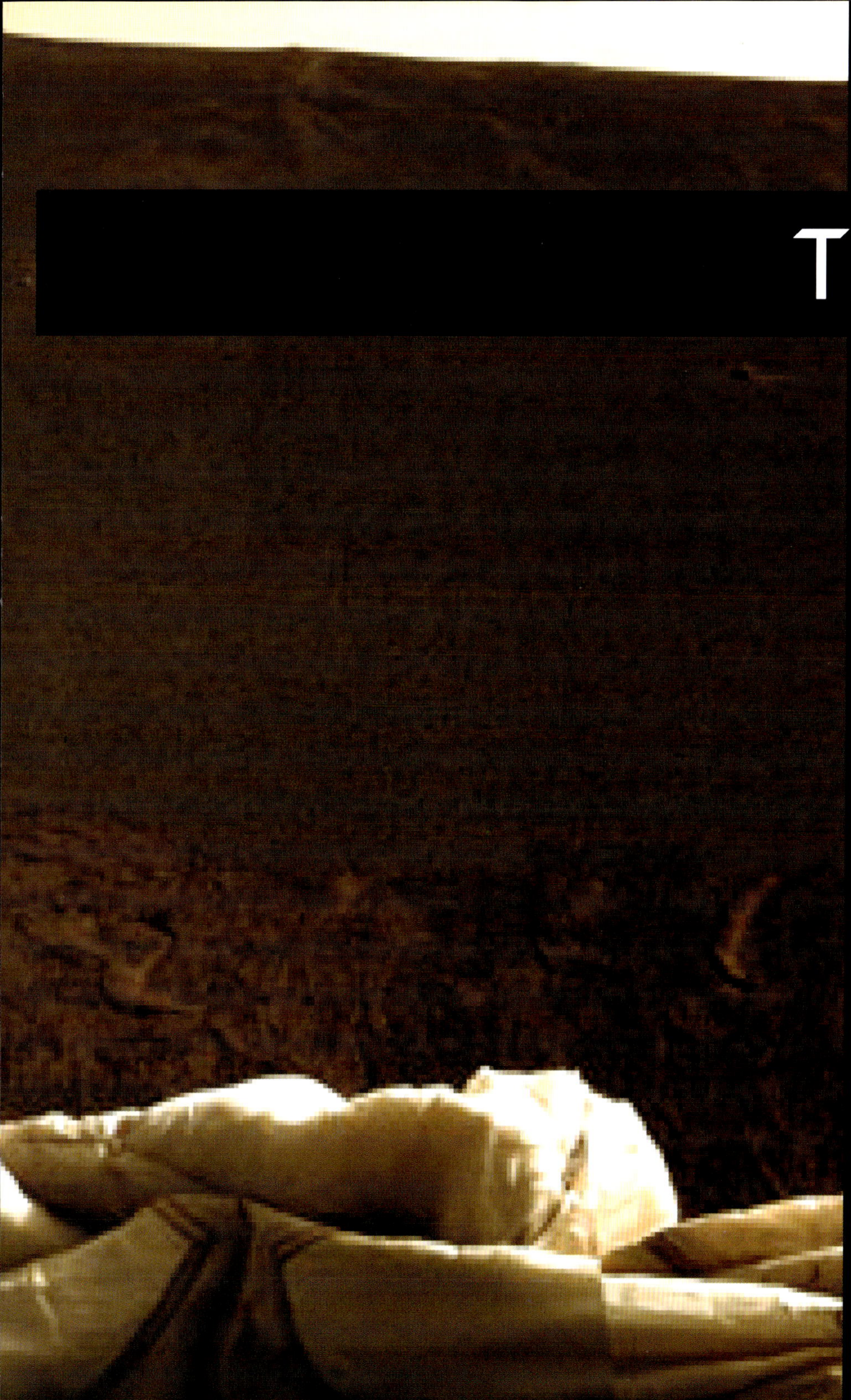

THE FUTURE

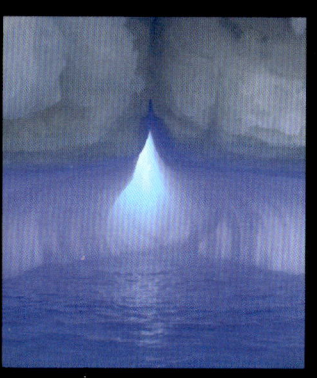

No doubt the explorers of 2015, if there is anything left to explore, will carry pocket wireless telephones, fitted with wireless telescopes.

Thomas Orde-Lees, Shackleton's *Endurance* expedition, 1915

DIGITAL CAPTURE

It's safe to say that five to ten years from now, most of the issues that have limited extreme shooters from going digital will be a thing of the past. Several generations of digital cameras will have been released and, if Moore's Law—the theory that predicts exponential growth by the doubling of the number of transistors on a chip every couple of years—holds true, the result could be significant advances in storage, write speeds, image quality, and other chip-related features.

These technical advances are already felt in the marketplace. Five years ago digital photography was cutting-edge stuff, and consumer sales were cautious. Today it's booming, with the rapid adoption of digital cameras by the consumer pushing camera research, design, and product development. Prices have dropped so dramatically that there is an affordable entry point for consumers and professionals alike.

In many ways the future is also already here. No sooner do most digital photography products hit the market than they are outdated—the next generation is already well into design, if not pre-production. Lots of good ideas, practices, and features are gradually percolating through various brands. For instance, Nikon's D2H has many useful features, including an advanced lithium-ion battery with a detailed battery info memory option, and the optional (802.11b) wireless transmitter enables images to be fed directly back via FTP to a designated laptop or server. These advances and others like them will doubtless be integrated to the next generation of digital cameras, in a rolling tide of innovation.

Another innovation that could open up creative avenues for photographers is Kodak's DCS Photo Desk, which enables IPTC information to be pre-entered into the camera software. Thus, when the images are captured, they are automatically tagged with information such as geographic location, event, or other metadata. The option to have GPS data included in the EXIF data could be an added boon to photographers. Personally, I would like to be able to work on captions using a PDA or a hybrid smart cell phone, and upload this information wirelessly. These developments could reduce or eliminate the need

Sony Cybershot

The notion that modern digital cameras are essentially computers with lenses is borne out in this exploded image of the state-of-the-art, 8-megapixel Sony Cybershot F-828, introduced in August 2003. Despite the high-tech design, the model features a 7x mechanical zoom, replacing the 5x electronically zoomed lens of its predecessors.

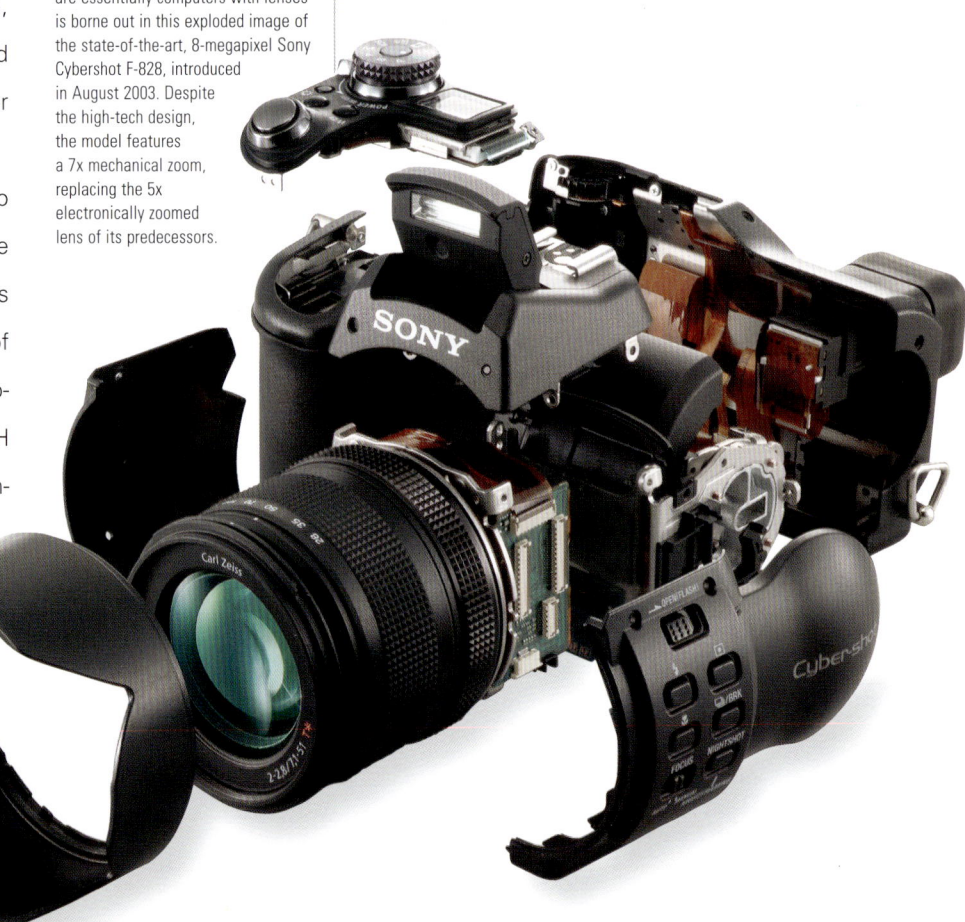

Chip Cleaner

The Olympus E1's dust reduction system features a Supersonic Wave Filter. Located in front of the CCD, between the low pass filter and camera shutter, the filter is activated whenever the camera is switched on. An optical glass filter vibrates more than 20,000 times a second, shaking off any lodged particles, which are then trapped by a sticky surface below.

for a separate card reader, laptop computer, and satellite phone: all functions would be consolidated in one palm-sized unit. This is the trend that Tom and Tina Sjorgen are driving with their Contact software, available through their ExplorersWeb endeavor.

Looking at some of the specific technical trends:

- Chips will have more megapixels. We will see 20-megapixel DSLR cameras in the five- to ten-year window.
- Larger chips with full 35mm dimensions. Full-size chips are already available on some top-of-the-line Kodak and Canon cameras.
- Multiple-card slots. Two-card slots are already available in some consumer cameras, but these are configured as one CF and one XD or SD slot. Having two of the same format would allow writing to two different cards at the same time, creating an in-camera backup, or writing sequentially for long shooting sessions.
- Larger in-camera storage. Something in the range of 10GB, to be used when the flash card runs out of space.
- Bigger and faster buffer. This would enable burst capture of more RAW frames at a professional resolution of 8–12 megapixels. Already the Canon EOS 1D MKII can capture twenty 8-megapixel RAW images at 8.5 frames per second.
- Longer battery life. The development of rechargeable lithium-ion expedition-style battery packs will make lengthy expeditions to truly remote destinations possible.
- Improved image sensing. Digital photography chip technology currently leans towards Bayer sensors. The alternative technology is the X3 chip by Foveon, which uses three layers of photo-sensors to capture more color information. The ability to control color with camera profiles, better white balance, and less sensor noise will also be welcomed.

Foveon® X3 Capture

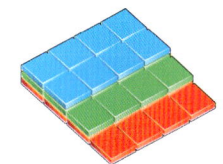 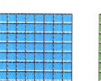

A Foveon X3 image sensor features three separate layers of photodetectors embedded in silicon.

Since silicon absorbs different colors of light at different depths, each layer captures a different color. Stacked together, they create full-color pixels.

As a result, only Foveon X3 image sensors capture red, green and blue light at every pixel location

Mosaic Capture

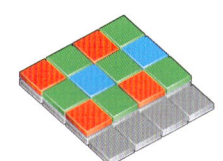 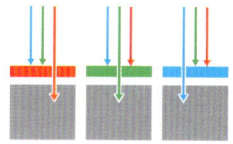

In conventional systems, color filters are applied to a single layer of photodetectors in a tiled mosaic pattern.

The filters let only one wavelength of llight—red, green or blue—pass through to a given pixel, allowing it to record only one color.

As a result, mosaic sensors capture only 25% of the red and blue light, and just 50% of the green

- Better dynamic range. Today digital has about six stops, and the way around this is to combine several exposures (one that correctly exposes the highlights and one that exposes for the shadow detail) in Photoshop. It should be possible to automate this process within the camera. Fuji's Super CCD SR uses two pairs of pixels, low-sensitivity R-Pixels and high-sensitivity S-Pixels, combined together in-camera to give a greater dynamic range.
- Dustproof image sensors. Software techniques offer one solution, like that in Nikon Capture, where shooting a white paper allows you to "remove" sensor dust from a whole batch of images. A hardware solution can be found in Sigma's SD10, which has a filter in front of the sensor to block dust. Electronic cleaning is another technology. The Olympus E1 has a so-called "Supersonic Wave Filter" that vibrates the CCD at a high frequency, causing any dust to drop off onto a sticky material.

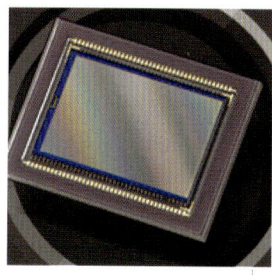

CMOS Sensor

CMOS (Complementary Metal Oxide Semiconductor) sensors are known for delivering high resolution, low noise and low power consumption. Initially used mostly in low-end cameras they are now popular in high end Canon and Kodak DSLR cameras, especially the full frame 35mm versions from both manufacturers.

PROCESSING, STORING, AND ARCHIVING

Laptops and satellite connectivity already mean that the complete digital workflow—capturing, editing, archiving, and sending images—can conceivably be performed in the field on a regular basis. Current software makes Web publishing a drag-and-drop proposition, but it's based on small file sizes, attainable only with either low-market digital cameras or high-resolution cameras that simultaneouly create low-resolution JPEGs.

RAW Processing

RAW files—the unprocessed, uncompressed CCD data files, the digital "negative," if you will—are essential for professional-quality results. They not only provide the greatest dynamic range, but allow such in-camera filters as white balance to be applied after capture, rather than during. The downside is that each camera manufacturer's RAW format is different, based on chip configuration and other factors. Third-party solutions like Capture One and Photoshop CS offer the best place for integration and end-to-end solutions aimed squarely at the professional part of the market. There are other ingesting programs, such as Photo Mechanic, Downloader Pro (PC), and Bibble, to help extract RAW files. Then there is comprehensive photo-management software, such as ACDSee, BreezeBrowser (PC only), iView Media Pro, Foto Station, Portfolio, and Cumulus, and clearly the tools are out there to do almost anything with images captured digitally, from red-eye reduction to DVD archiving. Noise reduction is one of the big areas for development, with Noise Ninja being the leading software contender, as is interpolation (enlarging files for print) that has Genuine Fractals and S-Spline Pro offering comparable solutions.

However, these large programs are more applicable for desktop machines with lots of speed and RAM storage, and not necessarily for field use. The simultaneous dual RAW/JPEG capture technique of some cameras, such as Canon DSLRs, goes a long way toward keeping it simple for the extreme photographer, allowing for low-bandwidth delivery from the field and high-end archiving upon return.

At the top of the digital wish-list for the future is an integrated program that enables serious photographers to work with RAW files and provide not only the same consumer-centric functionality of printing, e-mailing, and creating webpages that is found in the consumer versions, but to add a sophisticated and compact RAW post-processing utility, allowing professionals to do all the correction, management, meta-tag creation, cataloging,

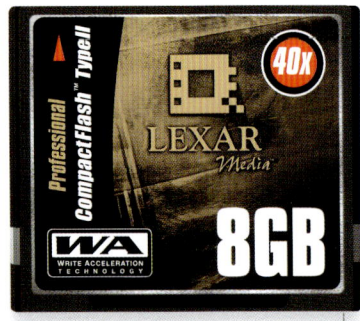

High-Capacity Card

As camera chips capture more and more megapixels, the need for larger cards becomes obvious. This 8GB, 40-speed compact flash card is capable of storing 1,000 or more full-resolution (8-megapixel) images. While expensive (over $4,000 at present), for those extreme shooters going where changing a card can be hazardous or impossible (such as underwater), such a price may seem reasonable.

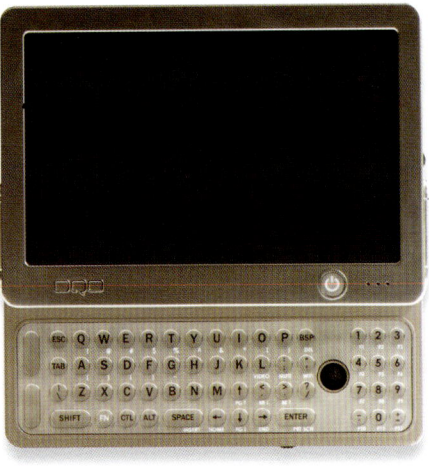

OQO Model 01

This new tiny machine is a fully functional Windows XP computer. The OQO has a 1GHz processor, a 20GB hard drive, 256MB of RAM, a color transflective display, and integrated wireless, as well as FireWire and USB ports. For typing and cursor control it has a complete thumb keyboard with Track Stik and mouse buttons, as well as digital pen and thumbwheel.

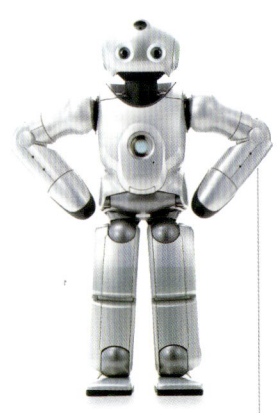

Tomorrow's Photo Assistant

Sony's entertainment robot QRIO can gather information and move around on its own accord. QRIO not only walks on two legs, but can also manage uneven surfaces, dance, recognize faces and voices, and communicate with people based on its own judgments, expressing its feelings through movements, conversation, and its lights. Imagine a photo assistant that never complained of the heat or cold or long hours...

database-driven archiving, and delivery tasks with RAW files. Even better would be "smart software" that remembers or anticipates the photographer's common tasks and then streamlines them for quicker and much more efficient operations.

Storage and Archiving

The foundation of storage is flash memory cards, which will continue to grow ever more capacious and affordable. Laptop computers are also becoming faster, smaller, and cheaper, as are fully functional pocket PC palmtop computers. As more digital shooters take their cameras on the road, there will also be a demand for more robust next-generation Flashtrax-type devices, portable download and archiving tools. With more and more competition in the mobile storage device arena, we should see better features, interfaces, and reduced power demand.

The next step in the digital workflow is to archive images on backup media, currently an area dominated by CDs and large-capacity hard drives. For CDs, the Jobo Apacer Disc Steno has great potential: a battery-powered card reader that automatically burns archive CDs as it downloads the flash card. The logical next step, burning DVDs with their 4.7GB capacity, is bound to become faster and more commonplace, so a similar battery-powered portable DVD writer will doubtless be developed. On the hard-drive front, external desktop FireWire and USB2 hard drives have become the cheapest and most convenient form of storage and now even of archiving. The LaCie Terabyte drive sells for $1,000, which makes this comparable with DVD media costs. Portable HD storage costs will also come down and capacity will increase, conforming to the overall trend.

There are many new optical formats coming to add to the current alphabet soup. There is FVD (Forward Versatile Disc) holding 5.4GB, and EVD (Enhanced Versatile Disc), which holds 9GB. These, like the original DVD, use red lasers to encode and read data. The big next step in optical storage, however, are blue laser drives.

Blue light has a shorter wavelength than red light, which means blue lasers can make smaller infobits, allowing for more storage on the same-size disk. The first version of the new blue-laser format Blu-Ray media disks will hold 23GB, and eventually 27GB-capacity disks will become available. The recorders are already in the marketplace, but they are prohibitively expensive for the independent photographer. As HDTV programming makes its way onto optical media, they will become ubiquitous.

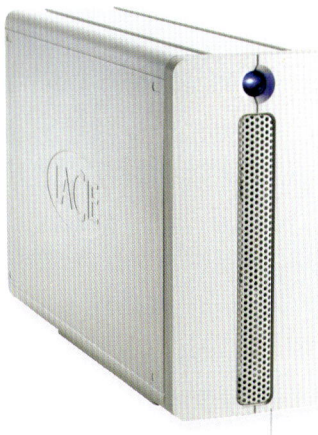

LaCie Bigger Disk

True to its name, this external desktop FireWire 800 or USB 2 hard drive holds a whopping 1 terabyte (1,000GB) of data. Digital photographers who weary of burning CDs or even DVDs to archive their images as their laptop fills to bursting after every assignment will continue to find storage capacity among their greatest needs.

Portable Burner

Portable battery-powered CD burners (like the SnapDisk from PNI Corp.) are an increasingly popular solution for photographers who do not want to carry a laptop around on the road or into the field. There are now several different brands of this type, some of them with the capability of spanning files from large cards (1GB or more) across multiple CDs.

Mini PC

The FlipStart PC is just 4 x 6 inches (10 x 15cm) and weighs 1 pound (484g), but it is a full-fledged PC running Windows XP. If the reality lives up to its pre-release marketing (it's from Vulcan Ventures, Microsoft co-founder Paul Allen's company), then it could be a boon to extreme shooters wanting the smallest possible PC for the field to do video and photo editing—if you can type with your thumbs.

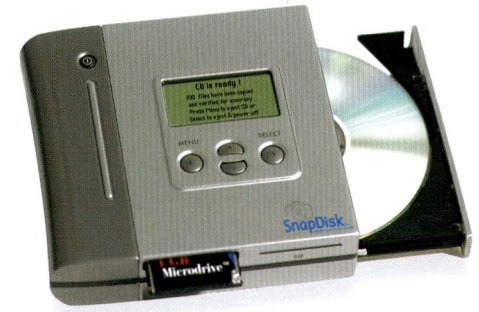

DELIVERY AND MANIPULATION

The obvious next delivery step is the photoblog—the easy and frequent uploading of photographs for public sharing. The world of photoblogging will gain a higher profile as digital cameras become ubiquitous. There are already numerous sites that host visual blogs with easy-to-use software for uploading images (see www.my-expressions.com). A subset of photoblogs called MoBlogs (uploading to the Web from a mobile phone) will gain in popularity with faster upload bandwidth and higher-resolution cell phone cameras.

Just as Napster led to the widespread P2P (peer-to-peer, or computer-to-computer) sharing of music, so will P2P photo sharing become increasingly commonplace. Web-based search engines will, in seconds, provide listings of photos on any subject, making the use of image metatags more prevalent.

Backpackers and travelers, with their cell phone camera, PDA, and photoblog software like Contact 3.0 will send back multimedia stories of their experiences on the road to personal webpages, with photos, streaming video, and text. Every new entry will trigger a SMS (short messaging service) notification to interested friends and family. Cell phones, satellite phones, and cyber cafés, plus WiFi nodes in the most remote corners of the world, will speed these missives on their way.

As better compression tools and higher bandwidth come to many more homes, offices, and cyber cafés, so digital storytelling will become an even richer experience, with possibilities for embedded audio tracks of music and narration, 360° panoramas, mini-movies, and animation yet to be added to the mix.

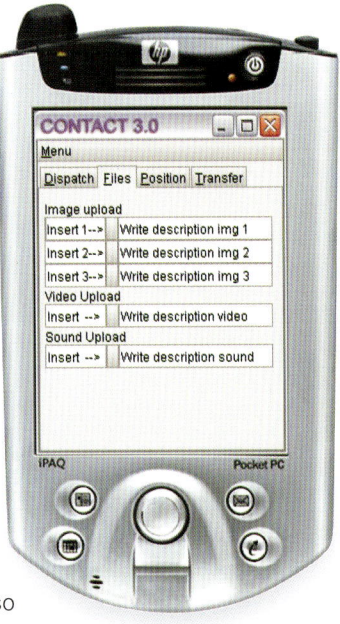

Media Blogger

The concept of Contact software is simple: Tell your story straight from the adventure to the Internet. The new 3.0 version features advanced support for image, sound, and video uploads as well as a supplementary interface to be used from any Internet café around the world. It is built to run on PDAs using Windows Pocket-PC.

Tomorrow's Satphone Today

Thuraya mobile phones have quickly become the favorite of Himalayan expeditions and trekkers. It has a 9.6Kbps data transmit speed and weighs just 7.7 ounces (220g). The satellite system handsets work in GSM or satellite mode, depending on location and need. The footprint is currently restricted to Europe, the Middle East, North and Central Africa, and Asia, but there are plans to extend this to global coverage.

Transmission

More and more high-end DSLR cameras and eventually even consumer cameras will have built-in WiFi capability, as is now found as an option in the Nikon D2H. This will become a way not only of communicating with your computer for downloading images, but for backing up and even printing on the fly, as well as for shipping time-sensitive images across the room, building, or world.

Satellite transmissions of digital images will become easier over the next 10 years as the software becomes more user-friendly and as compression tools and formats (for example, the advanced JPEG 2000 image-coding system based on wavelet technology) become more powerful. We will probably have satellite phones with built-in cameras and Bluetooth communication, in a choice of Iridium, Thuraya, or Orbcom systems. The Inmarsat Bgan high-speed satellite modems, currently

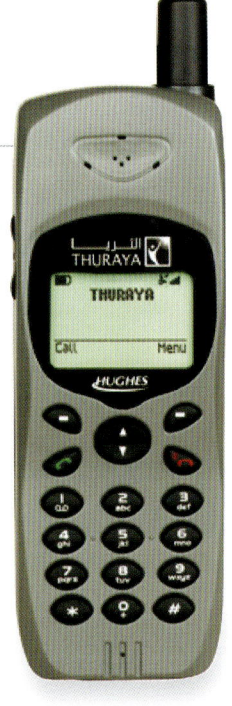

Head Tripping

Tina Sjorgen of ExplorersWeb uses a head-mounted display on a recent attempt to reach both poles in one year (The Poles Wearables Expedition, at www.thepoles.com/indexsp.htm). "Apart from some minor failures, the head-mounted display, wearable computer, and other tech all performed their tasks well. The team had been specifically worried for the liquid crystal displays, which are normally prone to freezing."
© ExplorersWeb.com

DELIVERY AND MANIPULATION

limited to one satellite geo-stationary over the Middle East, will become more compact and will have a global footprint. Through these technologies it will be easier for photographers to share their images and stories from around the world with clients, websites, and archives.

Manipulation

One of the greatest boons of the digital photo revolution is the opportunity to become more creative with image-making. Some professionals welcome the rapidly developing shift to digital, as it enables them to experiment with new and exciting ways to envision or create images that were not possible in the days of film.

Extreme shooters can likewise take risks with how and what they capture, and as the camera and related technologies mature, they can happily communicate all the beauty, action, drama, and energy of extreme locations, subjects, and activities at high-definition resolution. Going to extremes with digital cameras is already possible; in the future it will only get easier, with even better results.

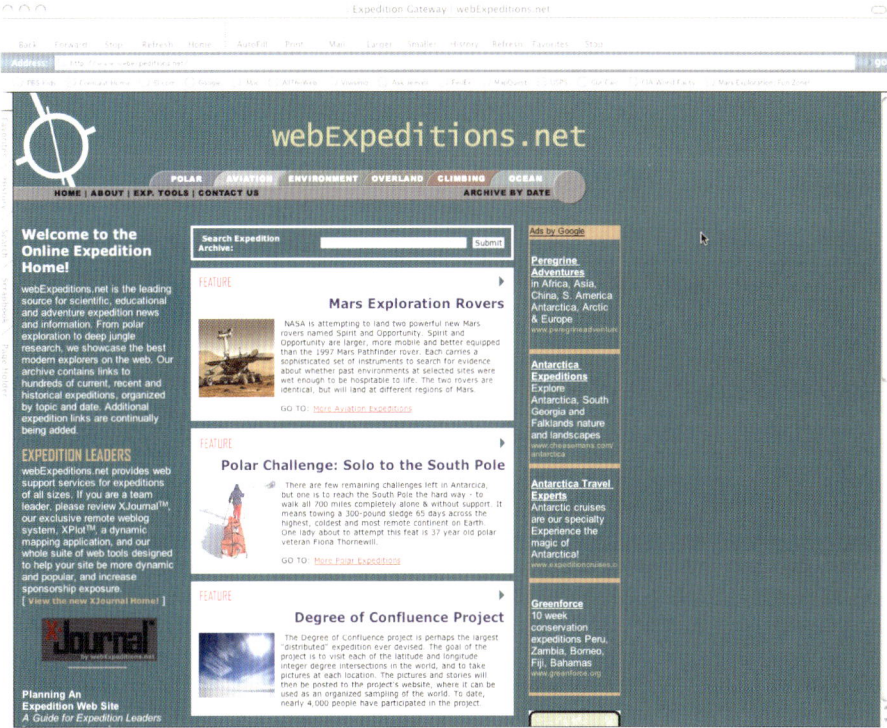

Expedition Communities

There are many sites now that specialize in expedition news and blogs, and several also offer customized software. WebExpeditions.net is one of the better sources for scientific, educational, and adventure expedition news and information.

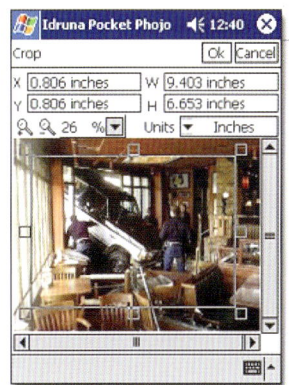

PDA Software

As PDAs and other small devices become more prevalent, so they become more useful. Pocket Phojo by Idruna Software is widely used by photojournalists for filing photos from the field. Designed for Pocket PCs, this application can browse, edit, and tag images on a storage card inserted into the PDA, then transmit them via FTP using companion software.

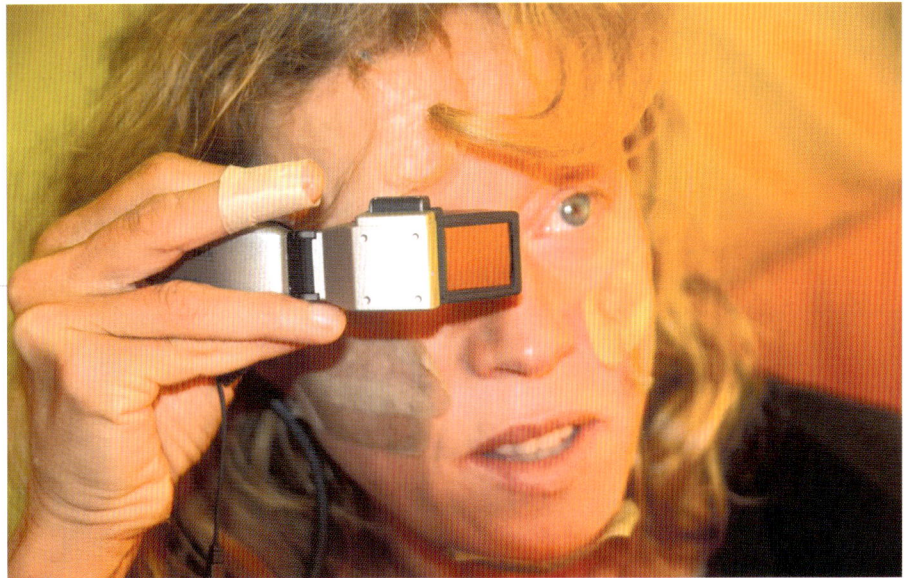

Photo Player

The Lexar Digital Photo Player is another in a long line of "plug-and-play" devices that let you view images directly from flash cards on a TV screen. It accepts multiple card formats, and includes a remote and video cables.

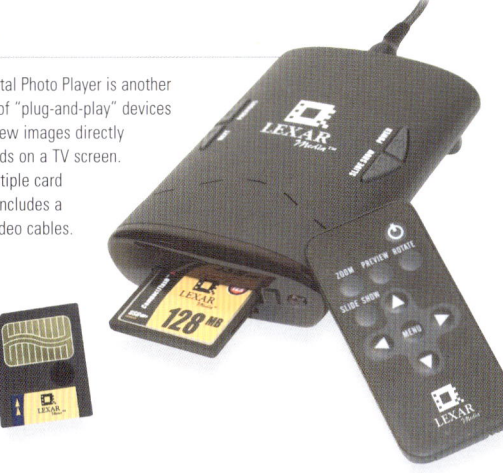

CONTRIBUTING PHOTOGRAPHERS AND EXPERTS

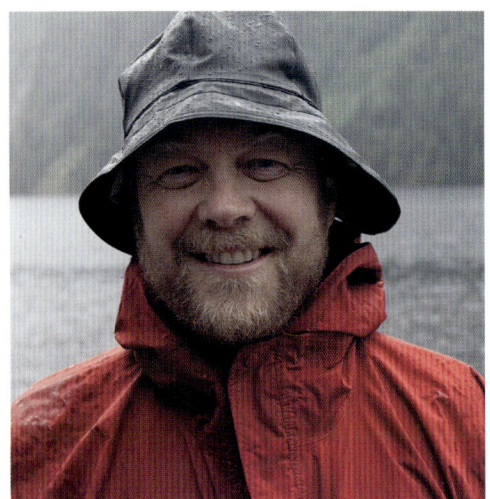

Ralph Lee Hopkins

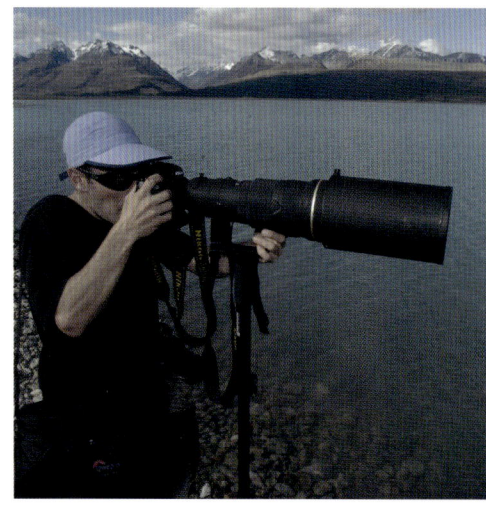

Corey Rich

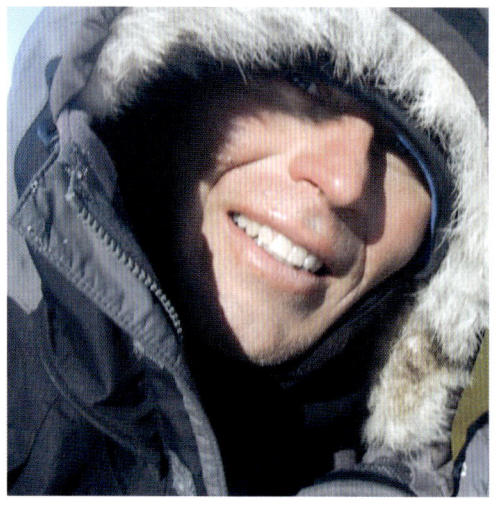

Tom Sjorgen

Morton Beebe became involved in extreme photography as Public Information Officer in Antarctica during *Operation Deep Freeze* in 1957–58, and has since done projects on San Francisco, Russia, France, and submersible sea craft. www.mortonbeebe.com

Michael Brown has climbed Mt. Everest three times, making films for NBC, the Outdoor Life Network, and ABC. He took the first HDTV footage from the summit of Everest for his Emmy-nominated *Farther than the Eye Can See*. www.seracfilms.com

Michael Cardwell, based in the California desert, specializes in photos of venomous and dangerous animals, reptiles, spiders, scorpions, and other arachnids. His motto is, "If people think a creature's dangerous, disgusting, or just plain strange, I probably have photos of it!" www.michaelcardwell.com

Aric Crabbe lives in the Bay Area, and is an avid surf photographer in the region between Santa Cruz and San Francisco. He is a contributing photographer to *Surfing* magazine and on the staff at ANG Newspapers in San Francisco. www.crabbphotography.com

Robert Eplett is a photographer with the California Governor's Office of Emergency Services, who has covered first-response to earthquakes and other urgent situations for years. He can be reached at Robert_Eplett@oes.ca.gov

Kyle Gerstner grew up among the lightning storms, tornadoes, and other meteorological wonders of the Midwest. A native Kansan, he also specializes in landscapes, wildlife, and macro images. www.lightshooter.com

Peter Gill is a whale researcher based in Melbourne, Australia, at Deakin University. Along with **Margie Morrice**, he studies the blue whale population feeding on krill in the Bonney Upwelling, north of Tasmania, using yacht-based and aerial methods. He can be reached at pcgill@ozemail.com.au.

Alan High lives in Stony Plain, in central Alberta, Canada, where he can keep an eye on the Northern Lights that make up much of his portfolio. He is also a firefighter and paramedic. www.willowcreekphoto.com

Scott Highton is a pioneer in 360° photography, both in panoramic and object move formats. He is the creator of the *Virtual Reality Slatebook* and author of the upcoming *Virtual Reality Photography* (Focal Press). www.vrphotography.com

Thom Hogan describes his résumé as "reading like a random walk, albeit an interesting one." He has been a developer of portable computers, object-oriented operating systems, and digital cameras. He prognosticates on gadgets, cameras, and travel on his website at www.bythom.com.

Ralph Lee Hopkins travels regularly as a photographer and expedition leader with a natural history travel company to the world's wild places. He is a geologist by training and specialist in the landscape and wildlife of Baja California and the Colorado Plateau. He can be reached at photo@wilderlandimages.com.

Steve Jarrett has been working on mobile and wireless computing devices since 1993. Now, through his business Steve Jarrett Moblie Computing, he continues to assist major corportions (from Apple to Kodak and Nokia) in the rapidly developing area of cell-phone cameras and wireless technlogies. www.stevejarrett.com

Didrik Johnck of Portland, Oregon, is a professional photographer who has traveled to the farthest corners of the Earth documenting modern-day adventures. He has climbed Everest and Mt. Elbrus with blind mountaineer Erik Weihenmayer, among other accomplishments. www.johnck.com

Kim Johnson Morris is currently a producer and documentary filmmaker based in Boulder, Colorado. She has worked on digital media projects at Quokka Sports, on Everest with Erik Weihenmayer, and in South America on the trail of the condor. She can be reached at kimjohnson100@hotmail.com

Joe Johnston is a staff photographer with the *Union Tribune*, based in San Lusi Obispo on California's Central Coast. jjohnston@thetribunenews.com

Contributing Photographers and Experts

Kurt Jones is a "surf shooter" who lives (and surfs) in Southern California, where his famous shot of a surfer with dolphin at Malibu sparked a global controversy. (It's a dolphin, not a shark.) **www.surfshooter.com**

Christian Kallen is a well-traveled Web producer, writer, and digital photographer, who has worked on *TerraQuest*, *Quokka Sports*, and Microsoft's *Mungo Park* among others. His photography has also appeared online at MSNBC and Slate.com. **www.ckallen.com**

Abner Kingman specializes in photographing sailboat racing and other water sports, from his home base in Tiburon, California. He has a Masters from UC Berkeley's School of Journalism, and a background in marine biology. **www.kingmanphotography.com**

Mark Langley has worked as an engineer, analyst, consultant, and entrepreneur so that he (and his camera) can explore nature at its finest. Mark has recently explored Greenland and the Galápagos by sea kayak. **mark@mlpi.net**

Brian Lanker is a Pulitzer Prize-winning photojournalist whose work for *Life* Magazine and *Sports Illustrated* has received numerous international awards. He was twice named National Newspaper Photographer of the Year. **www.brianlanker.com**

Jessica Brandi Lifland is an SF Bay Area freelance photographer represented by Polaris Images. Her photography has appeared in publications including *Newsweek*, *Time*, *The New York Times*, *USA Today*, *The Chicago Tribune* and *The Philadelphia Inquirer*. Recent projects include the *America 24/7* photographic book project and a photographic essay on family and community life in Kosovo. **www.jessicalifland.com/**

Charley Mace is one of the US's strongest high-altitude mountaineers, having climbed both Mt. Everest and K2. His day job as CFO of Trango, a climbing gear manufacturer, keeps Charley in touch with his passion for all things outdoors. **charleymace@hotmail.com**

Jean-François Maion is a self-described "nomad" whose work focuses on evocative landscape and travel photography that conveys the atmosphere of wild, inhospitable, or remote places. **www.maion.com**

Rory McGuiness is an award-winning natural history filmmaker based in Australia. **rorymcguinness@ozemail.com.au**

Jayson Mellom is staff photographer for the *Union Tribune* based in San Louis Obispo on California's Central Coast. **jmellom@thetribunenews.com**

Peter Menzel has been at the cutting edge of technology during his 30 years as a photojournalist. His books include *Material World*, *Man Eating Bugs*, and *Robo Sapiens*; he was recently a freelancer in Iraq, covering the war as an "unembedded" journalist. He lives in Napa, California. **www.menzelphoto.com**

Marjorie Morrice joined Peter Gill's blue whale research study in 2001. (See **Peter Gill**). **mmorr@deakin.edu.au**

Karen Mullarkey has been a photography editor since the 1960s at *Life*, *Newsweek*, *Rolling Stone*, and many other premier publications. She has also worked on several "Day in the Life" projects, including the recent *America 24-7*. She can be reached at **kmulla@aol.com**.

Rob Myers has shot for broadcast and interactive television, film, video, broadband, and Web productions, and has always shown a keen interest in new and emerging technologies. **www.robmyersproducer.com**

Craig O'Brien flies through the air with the greatest of ease as one of the leading skydiving and sky-surfing photographers. He is also a contract cameraman for commercial films featuring aerial stunts. **www.teamfirestarter.com**

Polaris Images represents photographers and distributes photographs to media industries worldwide. Founded by J.P. Pappis in New York. **www.polarisimages.com**

Corey Rich is a climber, adventurer, and photojournalist who has photographed rock climbing in Mexico, surfing in Panama, ultra-marathon racing in the Sahara Desert of Morocco, and snowboarding in Papua New Guinea. **www.coreyography.com**

Denise Rocco-Zilber is an early adapter to digital photography, having used it for more than 10 years in places from San Francisco to Timbuktu, Fiji to Burma. She lives in Marin County and is at work on a multi-media project about women and adornment. She can be reached at **denise@roccophotography.com**.

Rob Rosen runs Remote Satellite Systems, a vendor of communications solutions for business travelers, corporate clients, and adventure clients based in Santa Rosa, California. **www.remotesatellite.com**

Pasquale Scaturro is a mountaineer, river runner, and resource geologist who lives in Colorado when he's at home, which isn't often. He directs Expedition Specialists International on contract adventures. He can be reached at **pvs@pvsnet.com**.

Tom Sjorgen and his wife **Tina** run ExplorersWeb (www.explorersweb.com), a one-stop shop for extreme adventurers interested in Web coverage of their projects. Natives of Sweden, they have both climbed Everest and gone to the South and North Poles, among other endeavors. Tom and Tina live in New York and can be reached at **tt@explorersweb.com**.

Russell Sparkman is co-author of *Essentials of Digital Photography*, one of the first books on the subject, and a former instructor at the Kodak Center for Creative Imaging in Camden, Maine. He is founder and CEO of Fusion Spark Media, producers of Web-based documentaries, including the award-winning *OneWorldJourneys*. He can be contacted at **www.fusionspark.com**.

Martin Sundberg is a photographer of corporate portraits and adventure sports, based in Berkeley, California. **www.martinsundberg.com**

Don Swanson is a volcanologist at the Hawaiian Volcano Observatory, who enjoys observing and photographing lava for its beauty and sense of wonder. **donswan@usgs.gov**

David Vaskevitch is a digital photography enthusiast who specializes in wildlife and macro. In his day job he is Chief Technology Officer at Microsoft, in Redmond, Washington. He may be reached at **davidv@microsoft.com**.

Jay Wade is an underwater photographer and adventure traveler with a fascination for the Deep Flight Aviator, which he has photographed on a number of occasions. **www.jaywade.com**

James Watt has been diving underwater since 1965, and doing photography for almost 20 years. He now lives in Hawaii, running the Ocean Stock agency for his own and other marine imagery. **www.wattstock.com**

Tim Wimborne is a former chef and freelance photojournalist for Reuters, the *Washington Post*, *National Geographic*, and *Discovery*. Tim now shoots digital on the staff for Reuters, based in Sydney, Australia. **www.timshoots.com**

BOOKS

The Complete Guide to Digital Photography
by Michael Freeman
Lark Photography, 2003
Thames & Hudson, London, 2003

The Digital Photographer's A –Z
by Peter Cope
Thames & Hudson, London, 2002

The Photoshop CS Book for Digital Photographers
by Scott Kelby
New Riders, Indianapolis, 2004

Realworld Digital Photography
by Karin Eisman, Sean Duggan, and Tim Grey
Peachpit Press, Berkeley, 2003

Real World Photoshop CS
by David Blatner and Bruce Fraser
Peachpit Press, Berkeley, 2003

Shooting Digital
by Mikkel Aarland
Sybex, San Francisco, 2003

MAGAZINES

Digital PhotoPro
Werner Publishing Corporation
12121 Wilshire Boulevard, 12th Floor
Los Angeles, CA 90025
www.digitalphotopro.com

Outdoor Photographer
Werner Publishing Corporation
12121 Wilshire Boulevard, 12th Floor,
Los Angeles, CA 90025
www.outdoorphotographer.com

Outside Magazine
400 Market Street
Santa Fe, New Mexico, 87501
http://outside.away.com/

Photo District News
770 Broadway, 7th Floor
New York, NY 10003
www.pdn-pix.com

WEBSITES

PHOTOGRAPHY ASSOCIATIONS AND ORGANIZATIONS

ASMP, American Society of Media Photographers
150 North Second Street
Philadelphia, PA 19106
Phone: 215-451-2767
http://www.asmp.org

EP, Editorial Photographers
www.editorialphoto.com

NANPA, North American Nature Photography Association
10200 West 44th Avenue, Suite 304
Wheat Ridge, CO 80033-2840
Phone: 303-422-8527
www.nanpa.org

NPPA, National Press Photographers Association
3200 Croasdaile Dr, Suite 306
Durham, NC 27705
Phone: 919-383-7246
www.nppa.org

DIGITAL PHOTOGRAPHY WEBSITES

The Digital Journalist (Online digital photojournalism magazine)
www.digitaljournalist.org

Digital Outback Photo (Digital workflow)
www.outbackphoto.com

Digital Photography Review (Digital camera reviews)
www.dpreview.com

Extreme Digital Photography Digital Links Resources
www.extremedigitalphotography.com

Fred Miranda (Software filters forums advice)
www.fredmiranda.com

Imaging Resources (Digital camera and photography reviews)
www.imaging-resource.com

Nature Photographers (Online nature photo portal)
www.naturephotographers.net

Nikon Digital (for Nikon and Canon)
www.nikondigital.org

Robert Farber Interactive Photography Workshop
www.photoworkshop.com

Rob Galbraith Digital Photography (Insights, forums resources, reviews)
www.robgalbraith.com

Russell Brown (Photoshop tips and instruction)
www.russellbrown.com/body.html

SportsShooter.com (Sports photography portal)
www.sportsshooter.com

Steve's Digicams (Consumer digital camera reviews)
www.steves-digicams.com

Wet Pixel (Underwater digital portal)
www.wetpixel.com

DIGITAL CAMERAS

Canon
www.canon.com
www.canoneos.com

Fuji
www.fujifilm.com

Kodak
www.kodak.com

Nikon
www.nikonusa.com

Olympus
www.olympus-global.com

Pentax
www.pentax.com

Sigma
www.sigmaphoto.com

Sony
www.sony.com

EQUIPMENT MANUFACTURERS AND RETAILERS

Aquatech.com (Underwater housings and rain shields)
www.aquatech.com.au

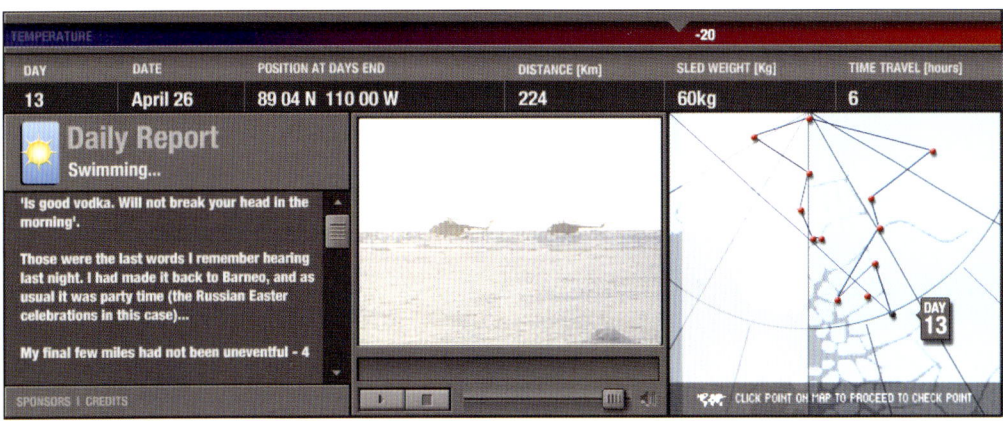
© Ben Saunders

Automated Media Systems (Lithium Expedition Batteries)
www.automatedmedia.com

B&H (Professional camera and video equipment)
www.bhphotovideo.com

Backscatter (Underwater camera housings and cameras)
www.backscatter.com

Calumet Photo (All professional camera and video equipment)
www.calumetphoto.com

Cascade Seal Line (Dry bags)
www.seallinegear.com

Digital Camera Battery (Batteries)
www.digitalcamerabattery.com

Gitzo (Tripods)
www.gitzo.com

Kirk (Tripod head and accessories)
www.kirkphoto.com

Lowepro (Soft cases/bags)
www.lowepro.com

MyDigitalDiscount.com (Digital memory and accessories retailer)
www.mydigitaldiscount.com

Pelican Products (Waterproof hard cases)
www.pelican.com

Photographic Solutions (Cleaning solutions and devices)
www.photosol.com

Really Right Stuff (Tripod heads and camera mounts)
www.reallyrightstuff.com

Singh-Ray (Filters)
www.singh-ray.com

Tamrac (Soft cases/bags)
www.tamrac.com

Underwater Photo-Tech (Underwater camera housings and cameras)
www.uwphoto.com

COMPUTERS, MEMORY, AND ACCESSORIES

Apple
www.apple.com

Dell
www.dell.com

HP iPAQ Pocket PC
www.hp.com

Jobo Apacer Disc Steno (Portable CD writer)
www.jobodigital.com

Kingston Technology
www.kingston.com

LaCie (Hard disk drives)
www.lacie.com

Lexar Media (Flash memory storage/accessories)
www.lexarmedia.com

Panasonic Toughbooks
www.panasonic.com/computer/toughbook

SanDisc (Flash memory storage cards)
www.sandisk.com

SmartDisk Flashtrax
www.smartdisk.com

Sony Vaio Laptops
www.vaio.net

SOFTWARE

ACDSee (Picture viewer)
www.acdsystems.com

Adobe, Photoshop CS, Photoshop Elements
www.adobe.com

Bibble Labs (RAW ingesting software)
www.bibblelabs.com

Breeze Systems BreezeBrowser Downloader Pro
www.breezesys.com

Camera Bits (Photo Mechanic RAW ingesting software)
www.camerabits.com

Canto Cumulus (Digital asset management)
www.canto.com

C1 Capture One (RAW workflow)
www2.phaseone.com

Expressions (Photoblog software)
www.my-expressions.com/index.shtml

Extensis (Digital asset management)
www.extensis.com

Foto Station (Digital asset management)
www.fotostation.com

Indruna Software Pocket Phojo (Pocket PC photo software)
www.idruna.com/pocketphojo.html

iView Media (Digital asset management)
www.iview-multimedia.com

Photomechanic (RAW ingesting software)
www.camerabits.com

Picture Code (Noise Ninja)
www.picturecode.com

Roxio Toast (DVD CD-R burning software)
www.roxio.com

COMMUNICATIONS

7E Communications (Satellite phone equipment)
www.7E.com

Human Edge Tech (Software and expedition communications equipment)
www.humanedgetech.com

Inmarsat (Satellite modems, satellite phones)
www.inmarsat.org

Inmarsat Regional Bgan Technology
http://regionalbgan.inmarsat.com

Iridium (Satellite phones)
www.iridium.com

Remote Satellite Systems International (Satellite phone equipment)
www.remotesatellite.com

Thuraya (GSM / satellite phone)
www.thuraya.com

PANORAMAS / 360°S / VIRTUAL REALITY

Full Screen QTVR
www.fullscreenqtvr.com

International QuickTime VR Association
www.iqtvra.org

iPIX
http://infomedia.ipix.com

Kaidan (VR heads)
www.kaidan.com

Peace River Studios (VR heads)
www.peaceriverstudios.com

PhotoVista
www.iseemedia.com/panorama/productinfo.html

Virtual Reality Photography
www.VRPhotography.com

TRAVEL, EXPEDITIONS, AND ACTIVITIES

Adventure Network International (Antarctic logistics and expeditions)
www.adventure-network.com

The Alpine Club
www.alpine-club.org.uk

American Alpine Club AAC
www.americanalpineclub.org

Antarctic Connection
www.antarcticconnection.com

CDC Travelers' Health
www.cdc.gov/travel

Explorers' Club
www.explorers.org

The Mountaineers
www.mountaineers.org

Photo Safaris
www.photosafaris.com

Polar Magazine
www.70south.com

Quark Expeditions Arctic & Antarctic cruises
www.quarkexpeditions.com

Space Environment Center (Aurora, space weather)
www.sec.noaa.gov

Volcanoes
www.volcano.si.edu/gvp/usgs

EXPEDITION RESOURCES, NEWS, AND JOURNALS

ExplorersWeb—Online expedition portal
www.explorersweb.com

Mountain Zone Online Portal
www.mountainzone.com

National Geographic Online
www.nationalgeographic.com

One World Journeys (Archive photo expeditions)
www.OneWorldJourneys.com

Quokka's Great Trango Tower
http://clients.stamen.com/quokka/trango_tower/frameset.html

Terraquest (Archive virtual expedition site)
www.terra-quest.com

Web Expeditions
www.webexpeditions.net

PHOTOJOURNALISM AND PHOTOBLOGS

Blueeyes Magazine (Online documentary photography)
www.blueeyesmagazine.com

MSNBC Picture Stories
www.msnbc.msn.com/id/3251645

Musarium (Online storytelling)
www.musarium.com

Photo Blogs (Portal)
www.photoblogs.org/top

Washington Post Camera Works (Photojournalism portal)
www.washingtonpost.com/wp-dyn/photo

World Press Photo
www.worldpressphoto.nl

CONSUMER PHOTO SHARING PORTALS

LifeScapes Picasa (Peer-to-peer photo sharing)
www.lifescapeinc.com/picasa

Ofoto
www.ofoto.com

OurPictures (Peer-to-peer photo sharing)
www.ourpictures.com

photo.net. (Online photo portal)
www.photo.net

Picture Trail
www.picturetrail.com

Sony Imagestation
www.imagestation.com

Webshots
www.webshots.com

GLOSSARY

Adobe RGB 1998: The largest "color space" for using the RGB (red, green, blue) color set, formulated by Adobe Systems in 1998. Adobe RGB 1998 is suitable for print production with a broad range of colors. If working only on the Web, the more limited sRGB color space is adequate. Some cameras require setting color space to enable RAW capture.

Algorithm: A step-by-step problem-solving procedure, used in computer terminology to build a palette based on the colors in the image and the number of colors specified in the optimization setting, especially in GIF images.

Archive: The process of organizing and saving digital images (or other files) for ready retrieval and research. Most photographers archive their source files, either as RAW or the largest available JPEG or other format, depending on capture.

Bandwidth: The total flow of information over a given time, usually measured in megabits per second. "High-bandwidth" usually means transmission speeds over ISDN speeds, as in cable modems or DSL connects for home computer users, or T1 or T3 Internet lines for corporate networks. "Low bandwidth" has come to mean dial-up phone modem speeds.

Baud Rate: A measure of the number of characters transmitted per unit of time. Each symbol will normally consist of a number of bits, so the baud rate will be the same as the bit rate when there is one bit per symbol. This is now a largely archaic term, replaced by bit rate.

Bit Depth: This refers to the color or gray scale of an individual pixel. A pixel with 8 bits per color gives a 24-bit image; the more bit depth, the more colors can be digitally represented. Common bit depth includes: 24-bit color resolution (16.7 million colors); 16-bit color (32,000 colors); 8-bit color (256 colors); and 8-bit gray scale (256 shades of gray).

Bit Rate: The rate at which binary digits (bits) are transmitted. The bit rate is measured in bits per second (bps). (*See also* **Byte**.)

Browser: The Internet turned into the World Wide Web with the invention of the browser, an interface that converted HTML code into layout, text, and images. Mosaic was an early browser, and the basis for Netscape and later Internet Explorer. Other common browsers include Opera (for Windows) and Safari (for Macs).

Buffer: The random access memory (RAM) storage inside a digital camera, which temporarily queues images before they're transferred to the storage card. The larger the buffer, the faster the camera is able to take more images. (*See also* **Burst**.)

Burst: Also known as continuous mode, burst refers to the ability of a digital camera to take a rapid series of images; akin to a power winder in film cameras. As a general rule, the larger the buffer, the faster the burst rate. Burst rate is usually measured in frames per second, as 3 fps for the Canon D10.

Byte: A group of 8 bits; a basic unit of digital information.

CCD (Charge-Coupled Device): One of the three basic light-sensitive imaging chips used in digital cameras. The CCD converts light intensity into an electrical signal, which is then converted to digital information. CCDs are natively analog gray-scale devices, but to reproduce color a color mask or "color filter array" is laid down on the sensor pixels. (*See also* **CMOS** and **Foveon**.)

CDMA (Code Division Multiple Access): A cellular technology that competes with GSM technology for dominance in the cellular world.

CD-R: Compact disks that can be recorded only once are called CD-Rs, or more accurately CD-WORM ((Write Once, Read Multiple). These are useful for archiving as their information once written (or "burned") cannot be erased.

CD-RW: Compact disks that can be erased and rewritten are called CD-RW, or read/write. These are more desirable for temporarily transferring large files or folders from one computer to another or for temporary storage. CDs can hold over 700MB of information. CD-RW format, however, is not readable by all CD devices.

CF (Compact Flash) Card: One of several types of "flash memory" cards that are used in digital cameras, and perhaps the most common due to its rugged construction.

Chimping: A playful term referring to admiring your own digital photograph on the preview (or review) monitor on the back of your camera. If used judiciously, this can improve your photography by providing instant feedback to your efforts. On the other hand, excessive chimping drains batteries.

CMOS: One of the three major types of imaging chips in a digital camera. Complementary Metal Oxide Semiconductor chips use the same manufacturing platform as most microprocessors and memory chips, so they are more cost-effective than CCDs' image sensors. They are also smaller and draw less power than CCDs, so CMOS digital cameras run longer on batteries. CMOS chips are used in many high-end digital cameras, such as the Canon 10D, and the Foveon chip is based on CMOS technology.

CMYK: Cyan, Magenta, Yellow, Black are the ink colors used to create color prints. Also known as a reflective color, since it is printed on paper. But converting from RGB (used in digital imagery) to CMYK creates color shift, and color management problems for computers.

Compact Camera: Broadly, a digital point-and-shoot built for minimum size. Such cameras can have high megapixel sizes, but user controls are often minimal.

Compression: The series of algorithms applied to a digital image to reduce its file size without sacrificing quality, at least to a point. JPEG images are compressed, whereas TIFF is a "raw" format.

CRT: The Cathode Ray Tube upon which the television's display is based is the original computer-monitor technology as well. It uses interlaced imaging.

DPI: The measurement of Dots Per Inch (both vertical and horizontal) determines the resolution at which a printer can print, or the number of pixels displayed on a computer screen. The common Windows display uses 72dpi, Apple displays default to 96dpi, and most quality printers output at a minimum of 300dpi.

Drum Scan: The professional technology of scanning prints or transparencies for maximum quality. Drum scanners use Photo Multiplier Tubes (PMTs), which produce better detail in shadow and finer grain, due to less electronic noise than CCD-based scanners.

DSLR (Digital Single-Lens

Reflex): The current high-end consumer and professional standard for photography, combining the convenience of digital capture with the flexibility of user controls and swappable lenses. Nikon and Canon have led the way in entry-level DSLRs; Kodak produced the first, the DCS 460, in 1993.

DV (Digital Video): The motion equivalent of digital photography, capturing video images on a digital-readable medium. Mini-DV is a common format for this media, a compact cassette of digital tape.

DVD Formats: There are many formats of digital video direct, or DVD, media. These include DVD+RW and DVD-RW, DVD-RAM, DVD-ROM, and DVD-R. In broad terms, DVD-ROMs (the kind you get your movies on) are physically the same size as the CD-ROM, or Compact Disk, but can store information at much higher capacity. DVD-Rs are one-time recordable disks, while DVD-RAM is rewritable many times. DVD-RW, DVD+R, and DVD+RW are different technologies of DVD-RAM, with different capacities, and some limited compatibility with DVD players and computers.

EXIF (Exchangeable Image File Format): A standard for storing interchange information in image files, especially those using JPEG compression. EXIF information includes the camera settings that were used when the image was taken, such as pixel dimensions and color space.

Expedition Batteries®: A compact, lightweight lithium-based power system for operating video and film equipment in harsh, remote conditions. Trade name of Automated Media Systems, developed by Stewart Cody.

Export: The act of sending a file out through a specialized mini-application, to print, compress, or to a specialized file format.

Fill Flash: The use of a camera flash in daylight to fill in shadows.

FireWire (also known as i.Link or IEEE 1394): FireWire is an Apple-branded name for the high-speed cable interface based on the IEEE 1394 standard; i.Link is the term used by Sony devices. FireWire is used for transferring images to computers, usually for digital video, at rates faster than USB. IEEE stands for the Institute of Electrical and Electronic Engineers.

Firmware: Computer instructions that are stored in a read-only memory unit rather than being implemented through software. Digital cameras usually have onboard firmware, which in some cases can be upgraded by the manufacturer, using the flash memory card to upload instructions to the firmware.

Focal Length Multiplier: Nearly all digital cameras have image chips smaller than 35mm film, meaning the effective lens size is reduced as if the captured image is cropped. If an image chip is half the size of a 35mm frame—as is roughly the case with the Canon CMOS chips in their EOS cameras—the multiplier is one-and-a-half times, or more precisely in Canon's case 1.6. For wide-angle lenses, this means a 28mm lens captures a field of view that's closer to 45mm (28 x 1.6 = 44.8), which is a distinct disadvantage. In telephoto lenses however, the result is an effective magnification of the image—a 200mm lens becomes a 320mm one.

Foveon: The Foveon chip is a type of CMOS imaging chip that stacks three sensor layers (for Red, Green, Blue sensors) to capture accurate color information with each exposure. Costs and technical constraints (they are limited in low-light situations) have prevented their wide usage thus far (Sigma SD9 and SD10 are the exceptions), but they are acknowledged to have great promise.

Frame Grab: The technique of acquiring a still "frame" from a video stream. Since video is usually interlaced technology, the frame is only approximate, half of an image, which must be "de-interlaced" using smoothing techniques in Photoshop or other image-editing programs.

FTP (File Transfer Protocol): An extremely simple and useful way of transferring large files from one computer to another. A connection is made via FTP software from one computer directly to another, bypassing as much as possible the time-consuming hand-off and server regulations that can limit e-mail transfer.

Gamma: The midpoint between black and white in a tonal range.

GIF (Graphics Interchange Format): Based on 256 colors, this format is designed to produce small, optimized images for Web display. GIF images are best for solid color areas, and often used for graphic images rather than photographs.

GPS (Global Positioning Service): A technology for identifying the exact location of a receiver (usually a handheld or on-board unit, but increasingly

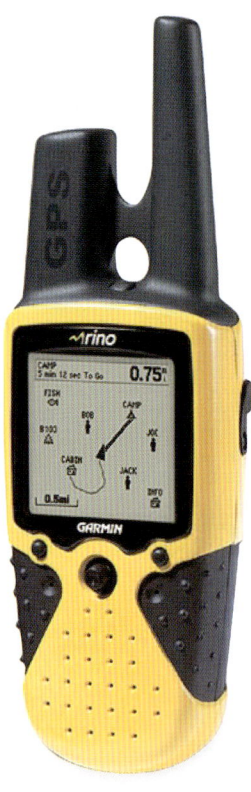

Global Positioning Satellite (GPS) receiver

found in high-end digital cameras) using a network of Earth-orbiting satellites. GPS locations are communicated in latitude/longitude, commercially accurate to within 33 feet (10m).

Gray Card: A neutral gray card is used to set white balance in different lighting conditions. Generally an exposure is made of the card while the camera is in a "set white balance" mode, and appropriate color values are applied to the subsequent set of images. (See **White Balance**)

GSM: The European system of mobile-phone communications, devised by the Groupe Spécial Mobile in 1982. GSM is the standard in much of the world, except the United States.

Histogram: The histogram is a graph showing the distribution of tones in an image. It's often available on a DSLR's review screen for an individual image, and is useful for gauging the optimum accuracy of exposure.

ICC Color Profile: The International Color Consortium defines color profiles to help get correct color reproduction across devices, as from a digital camera to a computer monitor, or a monitor to a print.

IEEE 1394: (See **FireWire**.)

i.Link: (See **FireWire**.)

Import: To bring a digital file into an application. For instance, you can import a RAW file into Photoshop and then work with it as an image, eventually saving it as a JPEG for Web use.

Ingest: Usually, the act of bringing images from a flash card into a computer or other storage device.

Inkjet: A type of printer often used for consumer-level photos. Simply put, the printer squirts minute droplets of ink at the paper from a set of ink cartridges (black, red, green, and blue are the most common) to build up an image.

INMARSAT (International Maritime Satellite Network): An established and reliable network of five communications satellites in geo-stationary Earth orbit. Their overlapping "footprints" allow for near-global satellite communication for subscribers, unfortunately excepting the polar regions.

Interlacing: This is the video technique of drawing alternate bands of information 60 times a second to render 30 frame-per-second resolution. It's based on CRT technology, and while it produces smooth-appearing

CRT technology, and while it produces smooth-appearing video, it can cause problems when converting to still images.

Interpolation: The mathematical formulae that allow for compression and image sharpness by calculating likely values, estimating unknown values that fall between known values. Thus, if a large image has been resized or otherwise changed, interpolation is needed to reproduce the original shapes, tones, and colors of the image as accurately as possible despite of the loss of data.

iPIX: A hardware and software company whose image technology includes panoramic, 360° and hemispheric renderings.

IPTC: Like EXIF, a set of information about digital images written into the metadata of a file. The only category of editable metadata, IPTC lets you add title, caption, photographer credit, and copyright information to each image. The categories were established by the International Press Telecommunications Council (IPTC).

IS (Image Stabilizer): Canon's technology for gyroscopically stabilized lenses. Using long lenses (over 300mm) without a tripod is very difficult, especially in DSLRs because of the focal-length multiplier value between image chip and 35mm film standard. As Canon explains it, "Electronic signals emitted by vibration-detecting gyro sensors are used to move the image-stabilizing lens group in parallel along the optical axis, providing clear picture quality at all times. Actual shooting tests result in improvement equivalent to using a shutter speed that is two steps faster."

ISDN: A data transmission speed of approximately 64 kilobites per second. Many satellite telephones deliver data in ISDN, such as the R-Bgan units. ISDN is an abbreviation of Integrated Services Digital Network.

ISO: Formerly known as ASA, a measure of film's speed or light sensitivity. The higher the ISO, the "faster" the film, and the less light is needed to imprint an image. Most consumer-level digital cameras have an effective ISO of 100, while DSLRs are able to adjust ISOs to 1600 and even higher.

ISP (Internet Service Provider): The company with which an individual or business contracts to provide the gateway to the World Wide Web and Internet.

Java: Java is a scripting language that allows for playable content on the Web.

JPEG or JPG: The now-standard file format for digital images on the Web. JPEG, also known as JFIF, takes areas of 8x8 pixels and compresses the information to its lowest common value. Created by the Joint Photographic Experts Group.

JPEG 2000: A file format with more options and flexibility than the standard JPEG (JPG) file format. JPEG 2000 can produce images with better compression and quality for both Web and print publishing. Unlike traditional JPEG files, the JPEG 2000 format also supports lossless compression.

Keystoning: Keystoning occurs when a projector lens is not perpendicular to the screen, and the distorted image appears as a wedge shape. The term is also used to refer to the distortion occurring when an object is photographed from an angle rather than from a straight-on view.

LCD (Liquid Crystal Display): This technology is commonly used as a lightweight alternative to a CRT display for laptop computers and also in some digital camera review screens, among other uses.

LED (Light Emitting Diodes): These light up when electricity is passed through creating another form of image display, though usually only in large television screens. They are relatively small, and do not burn out, but they use more power than LCDs. On digital cameras and other electronics they are often red in color, and are used to form numbers on digital clocks, transmit information from remote controls, and tell you when your equipment or a specific feature is turned on or off.

Li-ion or Lithium Ion: Lightweight and high-energy, Lithium-ion batteries are popularly used for portable devices, such as computers or video cameras. Though they are more expensive than nickel-cadmium (NiCad) or nickel metal hydroxide (NiMH) batteries, Li-Ion batteries do not use poisonous metals, such as lead, mercury, or cadmium.

Macro: The field of photography that uses a special "macro" (Latin for large) lens for close-up shots, as of flowers, insects, etc. Macro lenses may have relatively normal focal lengths (28mm, 50mm, 100mm), but their construction is optically optimized for close focus.

Mbps: Mbps stands for millions of bits per second, or megabits per second, and is a measure of bandwidth (the total information flow over a given time) on a telecommunications medium. Not to be confused with Megabytes per second (MBps), describing a unit of data transfer to and from a computer storage device.

Megabit: A megabit is a million binary pulses, or 1,000,000 (that is, 10^6) pulses (or "bits").

Megabyte: A megabyte is 2 to the 20th power bytes, or 1,048,576 bytes in decimal notation.

Megapixel: The standard unit of measuring image size in digital cameras. One "megapixel" is one million pixels, or about 1,200 pixels wide by 840 pixels. While this size is adequate for high-quality screen resolution, it's not sufficient for printing digital images. In general, 3-megapixel cameras produce good prints up to 5x7, 4-megapixel is good for 8x10, and 6-megapixel produces good results for larger prints.

Memory Stick (MS): Sony's proprietary flash memory medium, a plastic-encased chip about the size of a stick of gum that fits into card slots on Sony digital still cameras, digital video cameras, computers, and data transfer devices.

Microdrive: The Microdrive is a small hard drive that fits either into Type II PCMCIA card slots or, more recently, Compact Flash media slots. They were the first 1-gigabyte memory card, and they now have capacities of up to 4 gigabytes. These have largely been supplanted by new technology flash cards, which are also reaching above the gigabyte plateau. Microdrives utilize moving parts and are thus more susceptible to failure in extreme conditions.

Moiré: An interference pattern that occurs in print when dot screens are aligned at the wrong angles. The same effect can be produced by mismatched scanner-image resolutions.

Motion Blur: When an object is moving faster than a shutter speed's ability to capture or "freeze" it, the result is motion blur. Photoshop and other image-editing programs sometimes have motion blur filters to simulate this effect, to produce a more active-looking result.

MPEG: A family of digital video compression standards and file formats developed by the Moving Picture Experts Group. MPEG generally produces better-quality video than competing formats, such as Windows Video and QuickTime. MPEG achieves high compression rate, by storing the changes from one

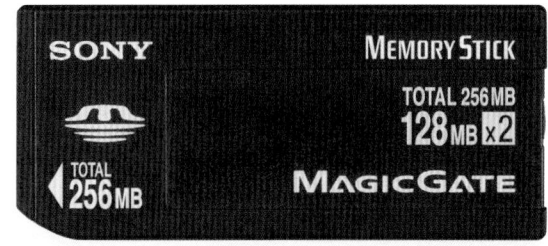

Sony Memory Stick

frame to another, instead of each entire frame. Several generations of MPEG compression are in use, with more in development; MPEG-4 is the current standard.

NEF (Nikon Electronic Format): Nikon's version of Raw. All the other DSLR manufacturers also have their own standards and names for raw capture files.

NiCad (Nickel Cadmium: A common type of rechargeable battery that typically lasts for 700 charge and discharge cycles. If not completely discharged before recharging, the NiCad battery can suffer from memory effect that may reduce the life of the battery. Normally found in AA and AAA sizes.

NiMH (Nickel Metal Hydride): A rechargeable battery that is capable of holding 40 percent more power than a NiCad battery and suffers much less from memory effect. It is also typically more expensive than a NiCad battery and can only be recharged around 500 times.

Noise: The random pattern of small unwanted spots in a digital image that are caused by stray electrical signals. This usually affects the whole image, reducing fine detail and giving an effect similar to film grain. There are a number of software and hardware solutions to reduce noise in digital still cameras and the resulting images. Noise increases with higher ISO settings, longer exposures, and heat.

NTSC (National Telecommunications Standard Committee): Standard broadcast signal received by televisions in the United States. All television broadcasts in the US must meet this standard. If a device is designed for NTSC, it will most likely not work with other television standards such as PAL, which is the standard broadcast signal used in Europe. However, there are certain types of equipment that support both standards.

Online: Being connected to the Internet so as to be able to send and receive e-mails and browse the World Wide Web.

PAL (Phase Alternating Line): A color television system used in Europe, Australia, parts of Africa, and the Middle East. It has 625 horizontal scan lines and 25 frames per second.

PDA (Personal Digital Assistant): Also referred to as palmtop computer, handheld computer, and electronic organizer. It is essentially a device that is designed to be small enough to fit in your shirt pocket, but which has a lot of the functionality most commonly found on a PC. This can include keeping your address book, diary, calculator, e-mail, Word documents, Internet access, and so on.

Photoshop: A powerful professional software program from Adobe Systems used to manipulate images. Pictures can be dramatically changed using Photoshop: colors can be altered, images sharpened, parts of the picture removed or moved. Photoshop Elements is a consumer version of the software with fewer features, but is still very useful for manipulating images. Photoshop has also become a generic term for any digital manipulation of photographic images.

Photosite: The small area on the surface of a photodiode in a CCD or CMOS image sensor that captures a light level for a pixel in the image.

PIM (Print Image Matching): technology enables printing to be achieved easily through the combination of a digital camera loaded with the PIM function and a printer that supports such matching. Print commands are attached to photo data during digital camera photography, and the printer adheres to these commands to print photos with the color match that optimally fulfills the objectives of the digitally composed shots.

Pixel: Derived from the term "Picture Element," the smallest unit of a digitized image. Each square dot that makes up a bitmapped image carries a specific tone and color value.

Pixel Depth: Also known as PPI, or Pixels Per inch—a measure of the resolution of a bitmapped image. (*See also* **DPI** and **Bit Depth**.)

Progressive Scan: The means by which the picture tubes of computer monitors and newer televisions display images. The process uses a progressive scanning tube to send information to each pixel on a screen sequentially—left to right, top to bottom—to create the image. The 720p (progressive) high-definition standard is a progressive-scanning standard. Progressive scan offers higher-quality pictures than does interlaced scan.

Prosumer: A marketing term used to describe the intermediate market for camera equipment, between the consumer market and the professional market.

QTVR (Quick Time Virtual Reality): An Apple operating system extension or format (and software program for stitching together a series of images) producing 360° panoramas or 3D object movies that are navigable on the computer using arrow keys or a mouse.

RAID (Redundant Array of Independent Disks): A multiple set of hard disk drives mounted in a single enclosure, where data is simultaneously written to multiple disks to improve performance and reduce the risk of massive data loss if any single disk fails.

RAM (Random Access Memory): The working memory of a computer, to which the CPU or central processing unit of the computer has direct access.

RAW: A file format created by most high-end (DSLR) cameras, containing all the pixel information with no compression. Each camera manufacturer has its own version of RAW. For Nikon, it is the Nikon Electron Format NEF.

Resolution: The amount of detail shown in an image, whether on screen or printed.

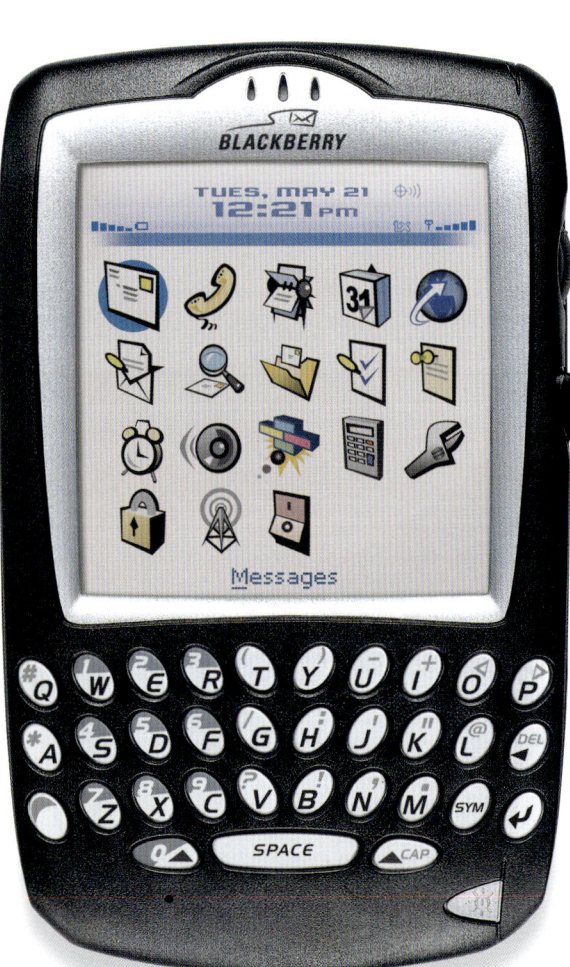

Blackberry 7750 PDA

1024 x 768 pixels for a 17-inch monitor). For printers and scanners, resolution is measured in dots per inch (dpi); the number of drops of ink or toner that can be printed in a square inch.

RGB (Red, Green, Blue): The three primary colors of light, and the system used by computer monitors to display images.

ROM (Read Only Memory): Any memory disk or media that can only be read, not written to. ROM retains its contents without power. Most CDs once burned with data or images, become read-only (i.e. CD-ROM).

SD (Secure Digital) Card: A postage-stamp-sized flash memory card that has a locking switch that can prevent accidental erasure of data once engaged.

Shutter Lag: The time elapsed between the moment when the shutter is depressed and when the image is captured, which can range from irritating to imperceptible in digital cameras.

SIM Card: A "Subscriber Identity Module" card containing a small printed circuit board that is inserted into a GSM/TDMA or GSM-only handset, containing subscriber-related data. SIM cards are also used for some satellite telephones to manage billing details and telephone-number records.

sRGB: The Standardized Red, Green, and Blue color space that was designed by a partnership of Hewlett Packard and Microsoft to be an Internet standard. sRGB is based on the characteristics of an "average" PC monitor.

Streaming: A method of transferring data continuously, often used in media files such as audio or video. Streaming allows you to display the media on your browser before the entire file is transmitted.

SVGA: Short for Super VGA, this is a set of graphics standards designed to offer greater resolution than VGA. SVGA initially supported 800x 600 resolution, or 480,000 pixels, but has since been expanded to include 1024x768 (and higher) pixel displays.

ThreeG, 3G: A new wireless standard promising increased capacity and high-speed data applications up to two megabits. Third Generation wireless employs wideband frequency carriers and a CDMA air interface.

Thumbnail: A miniature representation of a larger image file for onscreen viewing or printed contact sheets.

TIFF (Tagged Image File Format): A cross-platform image file format for bitmapped images that has become a standard for high-resolution digital photographic images which are going to be printed. Some RAW formats are essentially TIFFs.

Tri-mode: Phones that work on three modes: GSM, TDMA (Time Division Multiple Access), analog.

UDF (Universal Disc Format): A universal file system defined by the Optical Technology Storage Association (OTSA), for optical media, designed for data interchange and portability. UDF allows an operating system to read, write, and modify data stored on optical media that was created by another operating system. DVDs are based on the UDF format and CD-R and CD-

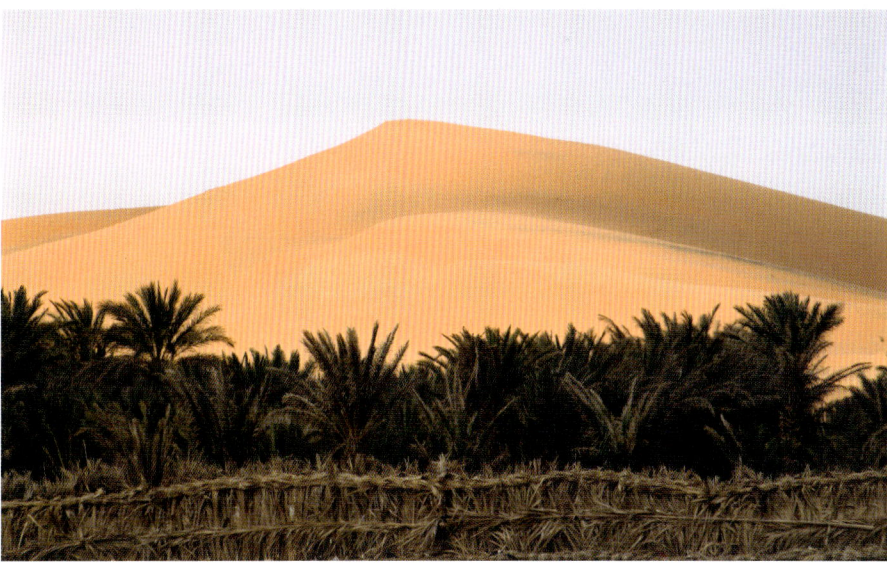

RGB image © Jean-Francois Maion

RW disks use UDF as an optional second standard.

USB, USB 2.0 (Universal Serial Bus): A standard port on most modern computers for the connection of external devices from keyboards to hard drives, card readers, etc. USB supports transfer speeds of up to 12 Mbps. USB 2 can transfer data at up to 480 Mbs. These replace serial and parallel ports and can be plugged in and removed with the computer running.

USM (Unsharp Mask): A sharpening technique achieved by combining a slightly blurred negative version of an image with its original positive.

VGA (Video Graphics Array): A graphics display system for PCs developed by IBM. VGA is one of the *de facto* standards, and the lowest common denominator for PCs. In text mode, VGA systems provide a resolution of 640x480 (with 16 colors). (*See also* **SVGA** *and* **XGA**.)

Virus: A computer program that is deliberately written and distributed to disrupt the operation of any computer that gets infected either via a disk or the Web through e-mail attachments. These can be self-propagating and may render a computer useless or malicious.

VR (Vibration Reduction Lens): Nikon's technology for reducing motion blur, which results from using low shutter speeds when handholding longer lenses. See also *IS (Image Stabilizer)*.

White Balance: A digital still or video camera control used to balance exposure and color settings to correct any color cast that may not be visible to the human eye. In DSLR cameras there are typically an auto white balance setting and presets to cope with cloudy, sunny, overcast, tungsten, and fluorescent lighting. There is also usually a manual white balance setting that is used with a white or gray card.

WiFi: From "Wireless fidelity," used generically when referring to any type of 802.11 network, whether 802.11b, 802.11a, dual-band, and so on. These wireless networks enable notebook computers to share an Internet connection without having to use cables.

XGA: For Extended Graphics Array, an IBM graphic standard based on 1024x768 at 256 colors (and 640x480 at 65K colors) with non-interlaced monitors.

Zip: A method for compressing files on a computer for storing and transmitting them at a reduced size. Many files are stored on servers in a compressed format, making them take up less disk space, and reducing the time it takes for you to download them. You must "unzip" or decompress these files to make them usable by your computer. WINZIP and PKZIP are popular free software programs for the PC that will compress and uncompress files. Aladdin has equivalent programs for the Mac, notably Stuffit.

INDEX

A

AC chargers 44
AC outlets 41
access 38–9
accessories 36–7
acclimatization 22
ACDSee 174
ACeS (Asia Cellular Satellite) 48
acquisition quality 32
ACR 49
Adams, Ansel 6, 60
adapter plugs 44
Adobe 32, 45, 148, 159
Adventure Beacon 49
adventure racing 108–9
aerials 72–3
Africa 8, 24, 48, 84, 142
airlines 38
Alaska 54, 78
alpenglow 68
Alps 16
altitude 8, 16, 22–4
    activities 110, 112, 128
    assignments 141–2, 146, 159
    locations 55, 68, 70
    preparation 41, 46
American Alpine Club 142
American Civil War 96
America's Cup 168
Andes 112
ANI (Adventure Network International) 81
Antarctica 6, 8, 11–13
    activities 122, 126, 132–3
    assignments 166–7
    environment 16, 20, 24
    locations 52–5
    preparation 48–9
    wildlife 80–1
antennae 48
antistatic brushes 66, 158
ANWR (Arctic National Wildlife Refuge) 78
AOL (America Online) 149
Apacer 44, 112, 175
aperture 82, 103
Appalachians 108
Apple 42, 91, 160
aqualungs 58
AquaPix 31, 58
Aquatech 52, 57, 116, 120, 125
Arca 37

archiving 8, 28, 52, 146, 148, 154–5, 157, 174–5
Arctic 8, 24, 48, 54–5, 78–9, 140, 148
Argentina 8, 16, 24, 108
Argos TAT 49
Around Alone 168
artifacts 82
ash 104
Asia 14, 43–4, 47–8, 142
aspect ratio 30
assignments 134–69
assistants 136, 138–9
atmosphere 24, 49
atmospheric pressure 38, 159
audio 46
Aurora Australis 92
Aurora Borealis 54, 82–3, 92
Australia 6, 8, 52, 88, 104
autofocus 68
Automated Media Systems 41, 110
AW (All Weather) 39

B

backlighting 42
backpacking 110–12, 130, 176
backpacks 38–9, 41, 60, 62, 68, 140
backups 28, 31, 41–2
    activities 110, 114
    assignments 151, 157, 159
    desert 66
    drives 43
    future 173, 175–6
    locations 70
    oceans 56
baggage inspectors 38
bags 38–9
Bahamas 90, 122
ball heads 37
balloons 73
Bangs, Richard 51, 166–7
Barton, Otis 122
base-camp communications 40–1, 46–8, 146–7
Bass Strait 88
batteries 28, 36, 40
    activities 110, 114, 126, 130
    assignments 148, 150, 152, 154–5
    future 172–3

locations 57, 64, 67, 70–1
preparation 44, 48–9
subjects 82, 85, 97–8
beacons 49
Beebe, Morton 122–3
Beebe, William 122
Belkin 155
Bertrand, John 168
Bgan system 47–8, 97, 176
Bibble 174
blogs 43, 45, 126, 130–1, 168, 176
blower brushes 36
Blu-Ray media disks 175
blue laser drives 175
Bluetooth 43, 47, 97, 176
boats 90–1, 116–17, 119–21, 124–5, 130, 167
Bogen 37, 84
Bonney Upwelling 88
Bowman, W.E. 27
Brady, Mathew 96
breakdowns 159
Breashers, David 22
breathing apparatus 20
British Mountaineering Council 142
Brooks, Kate 97
Brown, Michael 126–7, 130
Brown, Nicholas 126
Brown, Roger 126
Brunton Solar Roll 110
buffers 29, 72, 80, 101, 125, 173
bulk 38
burning 44–5, 112, 157, 159, 175
burst rates 29, 101, 125, 173

C

cable release 37, 93, 103, 152
cables 38, 41
Calakmul Biosphere Reserve 64
California 6, 16, 19
Camera Bits 45, 114
camera shake 30
camera types 28–9, 31, 35–6
Camp Borneo 55
Canada 8, 54, 78, 82
canned air 66
canoeing 14, 108
Canon 28–32, 35, 45
    activities 110, 114, 118–19, 121, 124–5, 133

assignments 151, 163
future 173–4
locations 58, 70, 74
subjects 79, 82, 87, 91, 94
Capa, Robert 96
captioning 45, 148, 155–6, 172
Capture One 174
car batteries 40–1
carabiners 116
card cleaning kits 35
card readers 155, 158–9, 173, 175
Cardwell, Mike 86–7
carrying cases 38–9
Carstenz Pyramid 24, 130
cataloging 45
CCD (Charge Coupled Device) 29, 31, 36, 66, 82, 115, 158, 162, 173–4
CDs 31, 42–4, 68, 112, 136, 157, 159, 175
cell phones 32–3, 43, 46, 127, 172, 176
cerebral edema 22
CF (Compact Flash) cards 29, 34–5, 42, 68, 70, 110, 173
chamois 41, 65
chargers 85
charters 72
Cherrapunji, India 14
Cherry-Garrard, Apsley 24
Chinook 16
circuit breakers 41
cleaning 36, 52, 58, 66–7, 154, 158, 173
climbing 6, 11, 114–15, 132, 146, 168–9
close-up lenses 30
clothing 52, 64, 67, 87, 104, 125, 140–1
cloud 14, 65, 68, 153
CMOS imaging chip 36, 66, 158
Cody, Stuart 41, 71, 126
Cohen, David E. 164
cold 8, 16–17, 40, 52, 65, 70, 78, 82, 86, 114, 128, 131
COM One 46
Commonwealth Bay 6, 16
communications 46–9
compact cameras 31, 39, 70, 93
Compaq 127
compressed air 158

compression 45, 93, 133, 176
computers 11, 19–20
    activities 128, 133
    assignments 145–6, 148–9, 154–5, 157–60
    future 175
    locations 57, 71, 74
    preparation 40, 42–5, 47
    subjects 84, 88
connectors 35
conserving power 40
Contact 127, 131–2, 168, 173, 176
contrast 36
corrosion 19, 38, 60
cost 28, 47
Costa Rica 64–5
Cousteau, Jacques 58
coverage 33
crime rates 16
Croatia 97
Cross, Will 48
cyber cafés 43, 176

D

Dalton Highway 55
dangerous subjects 86–7
data processing 42
data-rescue systems 35
DC outlets 40–1
deadlines 138, 155
Deakin University 88
Death Valley 19
death zone 68–70
Deep Flight Aviator 122
deforestation 20
dehydration 22, 67, 104, 140
delivery 176–7
Denaly 24
dental checkups 142
depth-of-field 75, 84, 87
desert 18–19, 66–7, 87, 99
diopters 90
dirt roads 20
Disc Steno 44, 68, 112
DiscSteno 175
disease 19, 142
DiskWarrior 43, 159
distribution boards 41
Domke 39
dot-com boom 168
dpi (dots per inch) 156

INDEX

Drake's Passage 80
drying systems 65, 67, 116, 118–19
DSLR (digital single lens reflex) cameras
    activities 118–19, 125
    assignments 151, 159
    future 173–4, 176
    locations 52, 58–9
    preparation 28–32, 36–8, 45
    subjects 80, 87–8, 93, 98, 101, 103
duffel bags 38
dust 18, 20–1, 34, 36
    activities 108, 115, 128
    assignments 146, 151, 153–4, 158
    future 173
    locations 66, 87
    planning 38
    subjects 87, 103–4
DVDs 44, 136, 146, 157, 174–5
Dykinga, Jack 66

E

7E Communication 167
e-mail 28, 43, 46–9, 133, 149, 168, 174
earthquakes 98–9
Earth's axis 24
Ecuador 62
editing 8, 45, 70, 91, 95, 133, 148–9, 154–5, 159, 162, 174
electrical contacts 36
Elements 45
Elsemere Island 55
emergencies 33, 49, 142
emergency services 99
EMT (emergency medical technician) 142
England 97, 167
EPIRB (Emergency Position Indicating Radio Beacon) 49
equator 24, 46, 167
equipment 28–30, 39, 47, 60, 66–67, 72, 114, 141–2, 145, 148
Ethernet 47, 97
ethics 98
Europe 16, 33, 44, 47–8, 97, 144
EVD (Enhanced Versatile Disc) 175
Everest Base Camp 11
Ewa-Marine 31, 39, 57–8, 60, 116
Expedition Batteries 41, 71, 126, 168
expeditions 130–1
ExplorersWeb 41, 45, 49, 107, 126, 131–2, 173
exposure 59–61, 70–1, 82–3, 92, 103, 128
extension cords 41
external battery packs 40
external hard drives 44–5, 68, 157, 175

F

fault lines 99
feedback 79, 118
field-of-view 161
file formats 82
file size 30, 82, 130, 174
file transfer 6–8
film 28–9, 34, 58–9
    activities 110, 114–15, 121, 126, 128, 130
    assignments 165
    future 177
    locations 61, 66, 70–1, 74
    subjects 79, 82, 84–6, 88, 91–4
filters 36, 71, 79, 173
Final Cut Pro 32
fire 16, 20, 98–9, 104–5
fire shelters 104
FireWire 44, 114, 162, 175
fish-eye lenses 30, 57, 60, 82, 90
fjords 55
flagpole holders 52
Flaherty, Robert 126
flash 36, 59, 70, 85, 93, 103, 148, 152–3
flash cards 8, 32, 34
    activities 110, 112, 121
    assignments 150–3, 158–9
    future 173, 175
    locations 71
    preparation 42, 44
    subjects 104
flash mounts 58
Flashtrax 110, 112, 157, 175
floods 98–9
floppy disks 43
focal length 28, 30, 68, 73
fog 60
Föhn 16
food chain 18
Forbes 94
Foveon 29, 173
frame grabs 32, 100, 168
Friday Films 122
FRS (Family Radio Service) 48–9
FTP (File Transfer Protocol) 47, 97, 148–9, 156, 172
fuel 41
Fuji 29, 31, 34, 173
Fujitsu 42
Fuller, R. Buckminster 146
Furious Fifties 24
future trends 170–7
FVD (Forward Versatile Disc) 175

G

Galápagos 8, 62–3
Garmin 49
gear 28–30, 52, 56, 64
    activities 110, 122
    assignments 136, 140–2, 154
    locations 71–2
    subjects 79
generators 40–1, 126, 146, 154
GEO 94
Gill, Peter 88–9
gimbal 37
Gitzo 37
global warming 52, 55, 78
Globestar 48
gloves 42, 52, 140
GoBook 42
goggles 104
Gore-Tex 140–1
Gossen 36
governments 47, 49
GPS (Global Positioning System) 24, 49, 136, 172
gravity 16, 104
gray cards 36, 153
Great Trango Tower 168–9
Greenland 54, 78
ground blizzards 20
GSM (Global System Mobile) 33, 46, 48
guano 52
guerrilla travel 33
guidebooks 136
guides 136, 138–9
GyPSI Personal Locator Beacon 49

H

handing off 48
Handspring 33
hard-drive failure 159
Harmattan 16
Haul Road 55
Hawaii 90
Hawkes, Graham 122
HD (High Definition) 87
head torches 146
health 142–3, 145
heat 17–19, 66–7, 104, 122
helicopters 72, 81, 124, 142
Hewlett-Packard 33, 43, 131
HF (High Frequency) 49
High, Alan 82–3, 104
highlight warning 83
Himalayas 8, 11, 24, 48, 112–13
histograms 83, 153
Hitachi 35
HMS Endurance 6, 171
Honda 40
Hopkins, Ralph Lee 79
hot packs 40
hotshoe mounts 36, 153
housings 31, 39, 57–9, 90, 118, 120, 124–5, 148
Hubble space telescope 88
Human Edge Technology 110
humidity 14, 19, 64–5, 87, 92, 122, 148
Hurley, Frank 6
hurricanes 16, 100–1
hypoxia 22

I

IBM 35, 42, 94, 153
iBook 42, 115
ice dust 20
Iceland 54, 78
icescapes 53
Ikelite 90
iLink 162
imaging chips 30
iMovie 32
India 14, 97
Indonesia 91
infrared 29
Inmarsat (International Maritime Satellite) 46–8, 97, 146, 166, 176
insects 19, 146
insurance 28, 39, 56, 138, 143, 148
inventories 39, 142, 145, 148
inverters 41, 85
InVision Award 167
Iraq War 42, 47, 94, 96
Irian Jaya 24, 130
Iridium 46–8, 132, 142, 176
IS (Image Stabilization) 30, 37, 121
ISDN speed 46
ISP (Internet Service Providers) 149
Itronix 42
iView Media Pro 91

J

Japan 32
Johnck, Didrik 70–1, 128
JPEG files 29, 45, 68, 93, 95, 104, 114, 156–7, 174, 176
Jumar 141
jungle 8, 17–19, 64–5, 130

K

Kaidan 37
Kallen, Christian 166–7
katabatic winds 16
kayaking 39, 55, 60, 108, 118–19
Kelley, Tim 122
Kenyon Gyro Stabilizer 72
keystoning 30
Kilimanjaro 24
Kingman, Abner 120–1, 125
kite boarding 124–5
kites 73
Koch, Stephen 130
Kodak 8, 29–31, 35, 45, 118, 167, 172–3
Kokin system 71
Korean War 96
Kuwait 96, 152

L

LaCie 175
lakes 60–1
Lanker, Brian 164
Lanting, Frans 18
laptops 38, 42, 44, 47
    activities 112, 114–15, 126, 130
    assignments 136, 146, 155
    future 173–5
    locations 52, 68
    subjects 79, 91, 94, 97
large-format printing 28
latency 48
latitude 16, 24–5, 54, 141, 146
LCD (Liquid Crystal Display) screens 40, 44, 57, 59, 65–6, 68, 71, 94, 110, 122, 146
lens flare 118, 128
lenses 28–30, 36, 52
    activities 108, 114–16, 118–20, 122, 124

assignments 148, 151, 153
hoods 118, 128
locations 56–60, 62, 64–8, 72–3, 75
pouches 38
subjects 78, 80, 82, 84, 87–8, 90, 98, 104
LEO (Low Earth Orbit) 46, 48
leveling heads 37
Life 94, 164
LifeBooks 42
lighting 31, 36, 59, 92–4, 122, 124, 128, 146, 153, 165
lightning 102–3
Lindblad Expeditions 79
Linhof 37
lists 148
lithium batteries 40, 110, 172–3
long-term storage 44
longitude 24
Longyearbyn 55
lost-luggage offices 39, 148
low light 92–3
Lowe, Alex 168
Lowepro 35, 38–9, 60
LPG (liquid propane gas) 146
Luster, Bill 165

M

M4/GAN (Global Area Network) system 46
McCurry, Steve 14
McGuiness, Rory 86
macro lenses 30, 36, 59, 84, 87, 90, 108, 148
Macs 32, 42–3, 45–6, 94, 155, 159
mains power 40
maintenance 36, 66, 154–5
Manfrotto 37
manipulation 45, 176–7
maps 136
Mars 8
masks 20
Mawson, Douglas 6, 17
medical checkups 142
megapixels 29, 31–3, 35, 44, 70, 122, 151, 156, 163, 165, 173
memory cards 8, 32, 34, 42, 44, 68, 98, 150–1, 155, 175
Memory Sticks 29, 32–4
Menzel, Peter 66, 94–6, 148
mesh matting 57
metering 103, 128
Mexico 64

microdrives 35, 91, 153
microfiber cleaning cloths 36
Microsoft 8, 33, 43, 45, 84, 167
Microtek 155
Middle East 48, 177
mini-M phones 46
mist 68
model aircraft 73
modems 47, 94, 97, 176
moisture 34, 38, 52, 57, 122, 140, 151, 153
mold 19
monopods 37, 52, 60
monsoon 14
Monteverde Cloud Forest 65
Moore's Law 172
Morocco 115
Morrice, Margie 88–9
Morris, Chris 96–7
Moss, Standford 13
motion blur 93
Motorola 48
mountains 68–9, 132
Movie Maker 32
MPEG files 133
MS (Memory Stick) 42, 110, 127, 155, 163, 168
MSU (Mobile Satcom Units) 46
Mt. Elbrus 70–1, 126
Mt. Everest 11, 22–3, 40, 68–70, 126, 132, 138, 146, 152, 168
Mt. McKinley 24
Mt. St. Helens 104
Mullarkey, Karen 164–5
multi-tasking 162–3
multiplier effect 30
Mungo Park 8, 64, 166–7
Myers, Rob 163

N

Nachtwey, James 77, 97
National Geographic 126
nautical charts 136
navigation 24
ND (neutral-density) filters 36, 71, 79, 103
neck straps 30
neoprene 38
Nepal 47, 68, 142
Nera World Communicator 46
networking 45
New Media Magazine 167
New Zealand 24, 108
news 94–5

NiCads 41
night photography 65
night vision 29
Nikkor 29
Nikon 28–31, 34–6, 40,
activities 108, 110, 125
assignments 151
future 172–3, 176
locations 58, 64–5
planning 45
subjects 82, 84, 88, 90
noise 61, 82, 92–3, 103, 120, 173–4
Nomax suits 104
Norazza 35
North Pole 24, 54–5, 132
North Star 27
Northern Lights 54, 82–3
Norton Utilities 43, 159

O

O rings 58
O'Brien, Craig 74–5
O'Brien, Tanya 74
Ocean Stock 90
oceans 56–7, 132
octopus straps 57
Ogden, Jared 168
Olympus 29, 90, 118, 173
One World Journeys 64
Orbcom 132, 176
Orde-Lees, Thomas 171
oxygen 22

P

pagers 48
Pakistan 47, 168
Palm 33
pan tilt 37
Panasonic 42, 112, 126, 163
panoramas 37, 158, 160–1, 167, 176
paperwork 39
parachutes 74
Paris Match 94
passports 39, 144
Patagonia 14
pay plans 47
PCMCIA ports 42, 155, 158
PCs 32, 42–3, 45–6, 94, 97, 155, 159, 174–5
PDAs 33, 43, 127, 131, 133, 169, 172
Peace River Studios 37, 161, 167

Pelican 38, 52, 60, 67, 116, 125, 146
Pentax 29, 31, 52, 118
performance ratings 34
permits 47, 145
petrol 41
Photo Mechanic 114, 157, 174
photographic clubs 138
photojournalism 94–5
Photoshop 8, 11, 36, 45, 67, 79, 82, 91, 148, 156, 158–9, 173–4
photovoltaic solar electric systems 41
planes 38, 72, 74, 89, 144
planning 26–49, 144, 148–9
PLB (Personal Locator Beacon) 49
plug-in cameras 33
Pocket Wizard 93
point-and-shoot cameras 31, 52, 59, 90, 118–19, 151
polar regions 16, 24, 46, 49, 132–3
polarizers 36, 71, 79
Polaroids 31, 94–5
police 39
Ponting, Herbert 6
pop-up flash 36
portraits 36, 84
post-processing 8, 71, 128, 138, 174
power adapters 44
power spikes 41
power supplies 28, 40
activities 110, 112, 126, 130–1, 133
assignments 146, 148, 150, 153–4
locations 62, 68, 71
planning 41, 44
PowerBook 42
Premiere 32
preparation 26–49, 56, 136–7
previews 40, 66, 71, 118, 153, 155, 165
processing 174–5
professional associations 138
professional cameras 29, 34, 87, 114
prosumer cameras 32, 45
protection 35, 38–9, 56
Provia 89
Pulitzer Prize 66
Puncak Jaya 24
Purcell 142

Q

QTVR (Quick Time Virtual Reality) 37, 160, 167
quality 28
Quantum Turbo 40
Quark Expeditions 81
quick-release buckles 30
Quokka Sports 114, 126, 168–9

R

radios 48–9
rafting 14, 116–17
rain 52, 60, 65
raincovers 60
rainforests 14, 19, 64–5, 87
RAM (Random Access Memory) 42, 159, 174
Ramadan, Alan 168
RAW files 31, 45, 68, 70, 79, 91, 95, 104, 121–2, 157, 173–5
Really Right Stuff 37
recharging 40, 48, 110, 154, 173
reciprocity failure 82, 92
redundancy 28, 42, 112, 151, 159
reflectors 36
remote hard drives 42
remote triggers 37, 93, 103
repairs 66
rescue 49, 143
research 136–7
resolution 32–3, 47–8, 68, 87, 110, 133, 151, 158, 163, 168, 174
reviews 40, 68, 79, 90, 103, 110, 148, 152–3, 158
Rich, Corey 114–15, 128, 130
Richter scale 98
rivers 60–1
Roaring Forties 24
Rocco-Zilber, Denise 64–5
Rocky Mountains 16
Rowell, Galen 6, 68, 135
Russia 54
rust 121–2

S

safari vehicles 84–5
Sagebrush Dry Goods 118
Sahara 16
sailing 6, 14, 120–1
salt 52, 56–8, 60, 120
sand 66–7, 115
SanDisk 34–5
Santa Anna 16
satellite phones

INDEX

activities 126–7, 130–1
assignments 142, 145, 149, 169
future 173, 176
preparation 33, 43, 47
satellite systems 8
  activities 133
  assignments 146, 166–7
  future 174, 176–7
  planning 46, 48
  preparation 28
  subjects 94, 97
scale 68
Scandinavia 54
scientific research 88–9, 100
Screaming Sixties 24
scuba diving 14, 58, 122
SD (Secure Digital) cards 31, 33–4, 173
Sea & Sea 31, 58, 90
Seahorse 38
search and rescue 49
seasonal range 24
sensor conversion factor 82
sensor swabs 66
serial numbers 39, 143, 145
Shackleton, Ernest 139, 171
shutter speed 73, 80, 119, 125
Siberia 54
Sigma 29, 173
signaling devices 49
silica gel 57, 65
SIM cards 47
Sirocco 16
Sjorgen, Tina 107, 131–3, 173
Sjorgen, Tom 107, 131–3, 173
skiing 128–9, 141
skydiving 11, 74–5
SM (SmartMedia) cards 34, 110
SmartDisk 44, 68, 110
smoke 20–1, 104
Smolen, Rick 64, 164
smorkeling 58
SMS (Short Message Service) 48
snapshots 31
snorkeling 14, 91, 122
snow 52, 68, 71, 117, 128–9, 141
snowboarding 128–30
snowline 24
software 45, 67, 93, 127, 131–2, 148–9, 173–6
solar panels 40–1, 48, 110, 126, 130, 146
Sony 29, 32–4, 42, 122
  activities 126–7, 131, 133

assignments 151, 155, 163, 168
South America 11, 43, 48
South Pole 24, 48, 52, 126, 132
Southern Lights 82–3
space 6, 8, 83, 88
Space Environment Center 83
spares 41, 62, 66, 84–5, 108, 115, 119, 151–2, 158
speciality cameras 31
spindrift 20–1
splashproof cameras 31
sports 30, 39
Sports Illustrated 128, 164
spot-beam technology 46
spots 158
spray 14, 20, 39, 57, 60, 118, 120–1
spume 20
storage 20, 35, 42, 68
  activities 110, 112, 116, 130
  assignments 145, 148, 154–5, 157
  cards 28, 30–2, 34–5, 59, 150, 153
  field 44
  future 173–5
streaming media 162
strobes 59, 65, 90, 93, 125
subjects 76–105
submarines 58, 122–3
submersibles 122–3
summer 24, 52
sunrise 20, 103
sunset 20, 103
super-clamps 84
surfing 124–5
Svalbad 78
SVGA phones 32
Sweden 132
Switzerland 108
Synnott, Mark 168

T

Tamrac 39
telephoto lenses 29–30, 60, 68, 78, 100, 119, 125, 151
Tenba 35, 39
tents 146
Terralogic 42
TerraQuest 8, 64, 166–7
test images 31
testing 148–9
text messages 132
ThinkPads 42, 94

Third World 40
Thomas, Greg 168
Thrane & Thrane Capsat 46
thunderstorms 100–1
Thuraya satellite system 47–8, 176
tidal waves 98
TIFF files 157
Time 70, 94
time lags 31
tool-kits 159
tornadoes 16, 100–1
Tostee, Pierre 124
Toughbook 42–3, 112
Toughnote 42
tourism 54, 78
towels 60, 65
tracking 49
transformers 44
transmission 43, 45, 47, 156, 166, 176–7
transportation 20
Travel Document Systems 145
traveling 38–9
trekking 112–13, 130, 140
Tri-band GSM phones 33
Tri-mode CMDA phones 33
tripods 30, 37, 52, 60
  activities 118, 124
  assignments 161, 167
  locations 62, 64, 66
  subjects 93, 103
tropical islands 62–3
tropical rainforests 14, 19, 64–5
troubleshooting 148, 158–9, 167
Tundra Buggies 78
Twidle, Kevin 167
twisters 16, 100
two-way communications 48–9
typhoons 16

U

Ulead 45
UnderDog 40
underwater 11, 31, 58–9, 62, 90–1, 122–3
United Kingdom 14
United States 8, 11, 14, 33, 48, 52, 54, 99, 144–5
USB 42–4, 46–7, 97, 155, 157–9, 175
USGS (US Geological Survey) 99
Ushuaia 24
utility programs 159
UV (ultraviolet) 36, 141

V

vaccinations 142, 145
Vaio 42, 126, 155
Vaskevitch, David 84–5
Velvia 120
VGA 32–3
VHF (Very High Frequency) 49
video 32, 46, 87, 99–100, 122, 126–7, 131, 133, 138, 162–3, 168
videography 75
viewfinders 75, 104
viewing screens 152–3
Virtual Antarctica 8, 166
Virtual Galápagos 167
visas 144–5
voicemail 48
volcanoes 104–5
voltages 41, 44, 52
Vostok, Antarctica 16
VR (Vibration Reduction) 30, 37, 84, 119

W

war 96–7
water 56–7, 59–60, 71, 104, 118, 120, 124–5, 128, 142
waterfalls 60–1
waterproofing 38–9, 42, 52, 57, 116, 118, 120, 125, 148
Watt, James 90–1
wavelet technology 176
weather 72, 100, 128, 141
Web 28, 33, 45, 47–8
  activities 127, 130, 132
  assignments 138, 156, 160, 166–9
  future 174
  subjects 83, 95
WebExpeditions 45
websites 8, 11
  activities 107, 114, 122, 127, 130–1
  assignments 145, 155–6, 166–9
  directory 176–82
  planning 45, 47
  subjects 83, 94–5, 101
Weddell Sea 81
weight 32, 37–8, 49
  activities 110
  locations 68, 70
  saving 40, 78, 130–3, 141
Weihenmayer, Erik 11, 70, 168
westher 140

wet conditions 14–15
Whale Ecology Group 88
white balance 70, 153, 173
white cards 36
wide-angle lenses
  activities 116, 120, 125
  assignments 151
  locations 57, 59, 68
  preparation 28, 30, 36
  subjects 82, 87
WiFi nodes 176
wildfires 104–5
wildlife 30, 37, 49
  activities 119
  Antarctica 80–1
  Arctic 78–9
  assignments 136
  locations 52–5, 62, 65
  subjects 84–5
Wimborne, Tim 104, 108–9
wind 16–18, 52, 66
  activities 115, 118, 120
  assignments 153
  chill factor 16
  subjects 104
  turbines 41
Windows 32, 42–3, 48, 168
windsurfing 124–5
winter 24, 52, 55
Wolfe, Art 84–5
working 39
World Health Organization 142
World Trade Center 97
World War II 96
WR (Water Resistance) 31, 118
write speeds 34

X

XD cards 31, 173

Y

Yosemite Valley 6
Yucatan 64–5

Z

Zambia 85
Zero Halliburton 38
zip disks 42
Zodiacs 52, 57, 80–1
Zonda 16
zoom lenses 29–30, 68, 73, 100

ACKNOWLEDGMENTS

Extreme Digital Photography grew out of the vision of Ilex Press publisher Alastair Campbell, and his search for ways to explore the rapidly developing world of digital photography, which crossed over with my passion for extremes. I must first thank him for giving me the opportunity to make this journey.

I am equally grateful to contributing editor, Christian Kallen, who has labored alongside me from the outset, greatly adding to the book's readability. Christian also contributed text in areas of his own expertise as a leading digital field producer for the assignment section and facilitated many of the interviews. Jessica Brandi Lifland came aboard and assisted with the photo editing. Her connections resulted in many interesting and important photos finding their way into the book. Thanks on this front to Liz Grady, Pauline Lubens, and Polaris Images and to Karen Mullarkey and Kim Shannon from 24/7. Jean-François Maion and Kim Johnson Morris also dug into their digital archives for me at the 11th hour to help fill some gaps. Bob Eplett came to the rescue with disaster images as a result of input from Marjorie Greene of the Earthquake Engineering Research Institute. Base jumper extraordinaire, Nick Feteris, pointed me in the direction of aerial acrobatic images, and John Blaustein gave advice on river rafting.

My good friend from Explorer's Corner, Olaf Malver, connected me up with Mark Langley, a keen digital photographer and traveler. Many other photographer friends—particularly Abner Kingman, Corey Rich, Didrik Johnck, Rob Myers, Peter Menzel, and Tim Wimborne—were early interviewees. Denise Rocco-Zilber and Michael Zilber, David Vaskevitch, Russell Sparkman, Michael Brown, and Mort Beebe all gave up their time to share their expertise. I also had to cast the net wider to fill in many of the gaps in my own experience and imagery of extreme destinations, activities, and technical know-how, and spoke with Alan High, Ralph Lee Hopkins, Thom Hogan, Stephen Johnson, Mike Cardwell, Jim Watt, Brian Lanker, Scott Highton, Tom Sjorgen, and Craig O'Brien.

Thanks to Mark Bolt of Berkeley's Saber's Cameras for the loan of camera equipment for product shots, and Nikon's Mike Phillips, who also assisted with providing cameras. Martha Blanchfield opened up her address book, Rob Rosen of Remote Satellite Systems opened up his treasure trove of photographs, and Fuji loaned a camera for testing.

Outdoor entrepreneur Richard Bangs, who was responsible for my very first and many subsequent digital assignments for TerraQuest and later *Mungo Park* and MSN, continued to assist with this project. I would like to thank all the expedition companions who over the years have accompanied me or helped me prepare for these adventures to all parts of the globe, especially Pasquale Scaturro, Erik Weihenmayer, Stephen Price, Matthew Sanner, Kevin Twidle, Greg Mortimer, and Greg Thomas.

I would like to thank the Ilex Press editorial team of Alastair Campbell, Jenny Manstead, Sophie Collins, Stephen Luck, Alan Buckingham, Ben Renow-Clarke, and designer Hugh Schermuly.

Lastly I would like to thank my wife Kirsty Melville for helping to set me on my own publishing path (beginning with *Going to Extremes*), and who has continued to support my dreams, and our two young adventurers, Katharine and Cormac, whose enthusiasm for the project was an inspiration.

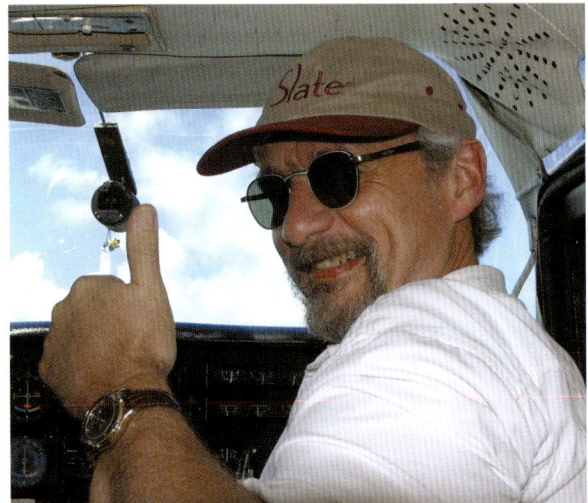

Christian Kallen